STRATEGIC
ENTREPRENEURSHIP

Third edition

STRATEGIC
ENTREPRENEURSHIP

Philip A. Wickham

Prentice Hall
FINANCIAL TIMES

An imprint of **Pearson Education**

Harlow, England • London • New York • Boston • San Francisco • Toronto • Sydney • Singapore • Hong Kong
Tokyo • Seoul • Taipei • New Delhi • Cape Town • Madrid • Mexico City • Amsterdam • Munich • Paris • Milan

To Louise, John and Jill

Pearson Education Limited
Edinburgh Gate
Harlow
Essex CM20 2JE
England

and Associated Companies throughout the world

Visit us on the World Wide Web at
www.pearsoned.co.uk

First published in Great Britain in 1998
Second edition published in 2001
Third edition published in 2004

ISBN 0 273 68226 1

British Library Cataloguing in Publication Data
A CIP catalogue record for this book can be obtained from the British Library

10 9 8 7 6 5 4 3 2
08 07 06 05 04

Typeset in 9.5/13pt Sabon by 35
Printed by Ashford Colour Press Ltd., Gosport
The publisher's policy is to use paper manufactured from sustainable forests.

Contents

**Part 4   Managing the growth and development
            of the venture 473**

This third edition of *Strategic Entrepreneurship* appears at the tenth aniversary of my start in teaching entrepreneurship as a management specialism. When I started, I decided to take a particular approach to the issue of entrepreneurship. First, I argued that entrepreneurship is a universal feature of human experience. This is not to say that local and cultural factors are not important or that differing economic conditions around the world do not impact specifically on entrepreneurial activity, but that they represent a surface veneer on a fundamentally common process. Second, strategic management provides an effective basis for discussing entrepreneurship – not just in the relevance of the concepts it provides, which is true enough, but also in offering an appropriate *language* to talk about entrepreneurship. Thinking about entrepreneurs, and what they do, *strategically* grasps at the complexity of the entrepreneurial process at the right level, in the right way and in the right terms. Third, I rejected the notion of personality as being a fundamental determinant of entrepreneurial inclination or success. Emphatically, this is not a rejection of the notion that psychology has anything new to tell us about entrepreneurship, because clearly it does: it says a lot and often what it says is very important. The rejection is of something more narrow: the claim that 'personality' is a prior, determining and necessary precursor to effective entrepreneurship. This perspective is hardly unique, but it does swim against some strong currents in the field. Ten years on, I still feel it is right and am happy to re-emphasise it in this new edition of *Strategic Entrepreneurship*.

This third edition is still aimed at the more advanced undergraduates and postgraduates on courses in management seeking strategic insights into the way in which entrepreneurs work, the effects they have, how the ventures they create may be described and their success explained, and how new ventures should be planned. It does not presume a prior underpinning of any particular social science or managerial specialism. The emphasis remains on the decisions entrepreneurs must make if they are to design, develop and deliver successful new ventures.

The study of entrepreneurship continues to grow and (to an inevitable degree, fragment) as a field of inquiry. This third edition offers the opportunity to both broaden and deepen the coverage of this field. The text retains at its core the strategic window metaphor as a framework for understanding the way entrepreneurs perceive, explore and exploit opportunities, which has proved to have pedagogic value both at an analytical and a planning level. The coverage is broadened with further discussion of, *inter alia*, issues such as the classification of entrepreneurs, the start-up decision, entrepreneurial resource management, and entrepreneurship and social responsibility.

One addition I do hope will create some debate is consideration of Barbara Minto's *Pyramid Principle* as a way of producing more effective and influential business plans. Some challenges to orthodoxies here are timely. I have been adopting this principle when teaching entrepreneurs business planning for the past three years, with considerable success. I would like to see a lot more empirical work to demonstrate the value of this approach.

In addition, I have introduced some ideas from areas of growing interest in mainstream economics, particularly those relating to the application of ideas in informational asymmetry and game theory. I am concious of the mathematical nature of, and representation of, these ideas and the fact that this can be intimidating. I have endeavoured to relate them in qualitative terms, because I believe even a qualitative understanding can contribute significantly to our understanding of the entrepreneurial process.

In terms of deepening the coverage, this new edition includes three major additions. The first is an extended coverage of economic thinking about the entrepreneur. This is valuable not only because it provides further insights into the economic function of the entrepreneur, but also because it puts thinking about the entrepreneur into a proper historical context. The second concerns the issue of entrepreneurship and personality. While I take the view outlined above, it is not proper to dismiss the link between entrepreneurship and personality lightly, especially as it is one with powerful intuitive appeal and one which many researchers are investigating. My main concern here is not so much to debate the issue to a particular conclusion, but to highlight the problematic nature of the link in terms of theory and methodology and in validating theories linking personality to entrepreneurship. Of particular importance is the recent and quite rapid development in understanding entrepreneurs from a cognitive perspective. These two new chapters develop themes established in the initial 'Nature of Entrepreneurship' chapter in the original editions. I have decided to retain this chapter in an edited form for three reasons. First, it provides a coherent and integrated overview of entrepreneurship that is valuable in its own right. Second, it now signposts ideas explored in more depth in subsequent chapters, and third, its content is sufficient as it stands for many courses in entrepreneurship. Tutors may be inclined (as I am) to use this basic overview for undergraduate courses and use the expanded material for postgraduate courses.

Entrepreneurship remains one of the most active areas of research in the management field. Since the second edition of this text was completed in January 2000, I estimate (and this is probably conservative) that something in the order of 1,000 new peer-reviewed papers and books have been published with significant reference to the entrepreneur or entrepreneurship (that's about one per day!). This figure excludes the enormous number of non-peer-reviewed journalistic articles. Necessarily, I have been selective in the additions made to suggestions for further reading, but I hope the updated readings will provide a way into the latest thinking in this exciting field.

In the third major addition, I have attempted to provide an overview of entrepreneurship as a field of research, its concerns, theoretical approaches and methodologies. I do this not so much because these things are interesting on their own terms (which they are) but for the more practical reason that an increasing number of students wish to undertake research in the entrepreneurship field. This is to be encouraged. Research not only provides new conceptual and practical insights, but it is exciting and a great way to learn as well. To facilitate this interest, I have added some ideas on possible research projects at the end of each chapter (between one and three per chapter). These pick up on themes in the chapter that I feel are worthy of further empirical investigation and exploration. They are aimed primarily at final-year undergraduates and students on taught Masters courses looking for dissertation topics. I have endeavoured to detail projects that are accessible to the management generalist and avoid the need for too specialist a knowledge in economics or any other of the social sciences. I have also recognised the resource limitations for such projects. These are intended to provide inspiration. I only outline a project idea, not define its objectives and methodology fully. They may be considered as starting points for other projects. But this, along with the updated references in the suggestions for furher reading, should provide a good start. Of course, any student interested in a research idea should review it with their supervisory support team before undertaking it. I have chosen areas that I feel would benefit from the research described and would form the basis for an original, valuable dissertation. I would be delighted to be sent the results on any projects undertaken. Conducted with proper rigour, many should provide studies worthy of publication in the peer-review literature. I must beg the forgiveness of colleagues who have published research in these areas, which I have missed (a paper a day is hard to keep up with!). Let me know about them! I hope these developments enhance this text's effectiveness as a teaching tool, both for those who teach and for those who want to learn (and that is all of us!).

I would like to take this chance to thank the team at Pearson Education, who have, once again, made this book possible. Particular thanks for their support to Jacqueline Senior, Liz Tarrant, Matthew Walker and Jane Kerr. I would also like to thank Barbara Minto for her advice. My thanks also to colleagues in the Teesside Business School who have given me the time, space and ideas necessary to develop this text. Deserving of honourable mention are Ted Fuller, David Preece and John Wilson.

The text is supported by resource material including a *Lecturer's Guide* and PowerPoints on the website at **www.booksites.net.wickham**.

Philip A. Wickham
March 2003

Preface to second edition

Over the past ten years, the subject of entrepreneurship has moved from the periphery to the centre of management thinking and education. As we enter the new millennium, an entrepreneurial approach is no longer seen as *an* option but as the *only* option for managers seeking to enhance the performance of their organisations. This is so whether the organisation is a new start-up striving to establish itself in the marketplace, an established business seeking to reinvigorate itself or a governmental or non-profit organisation meeting the opportunity and the challenge of the shifting boundaries between the public and private sectors.

The approach taken by this book is founded on a belief that entrepreneurship should be demystified. It is not, as many of its advocates suggest, a process that is rooted in hidden intuitive processes of a few select individuals and that, in its practice, rises above the restrictive and mundane approach of 'over-formal' strategic management decision making.

The book takes the view that entrepreneurship is a type of management, particularly a form of *strategic management*. It is a very effective form of management to be sure, but one which is transparent in the decisions that entrepreneurs identify, the way they approach making those decisions and the skills that entrepreneurs bring in order to make those decisions happen in real, challenging business environments. This means that entrepreneurship should be regarded as a style of management that can be learnt if managers are dedicated to discovering its secrets and developing its skills. The book aims to contribute to this by providing a logical exploration of the decisions that entrepreneurs face, the development of conceptual models that assist in making these decisions effectively and by offering an agenda for developing the managerial skills necessary to put them into practice.

This second edition provides an opportunity to enhance the book's contribution to this programme. It takes on board the new trends in the world of entrepreneurial activity (particularly those as resulting from the Internet revolution), new ideas on entrepreneurial practice and decision making and from new studies into entrepreneurial behaviour and strategy. These studies have been drawn from the rapidly growing literature into entrepreneurship that, reflecting the traditional eclecticism of the field and its relevance to a wide range of disciplines, is appearing in the management, economic, sociological and psychological journals.

The original framework, the core of which is the 'strategic window' sequence of the entrepreneurial process, is retained. Around this framework there is an extended discussion of the conceptual framework for understanding entrepreneurship, more extensive discussion of the decisions entrepreneurs face and greater coverage of specific issues relating to those decisions. In particular, the book features new material on the definition of entrepreneurship, cognitive aspects of entrepreneurial decision making, entrepreneurial motivation, entrepreneurial innovation and strategy. I have also taken the opportunity to clarify some of the ideas presented in the first edition. These changes reflect the considerable positive feedback the first edition of this book has received and advice offered from users and reviewers. I am very grateful for these comments.

It is hoped that this new edition will improve the utility of the book for academics seeking a grounding in this fast-growing field, students undertaking and tutors delivering courses in entrepreneurship, and managers seeking to develop their entrepreneurial approach. A new series of *Financial Times* articles (with suggested review questions) has been included at the end of each chapter to provide a basis for focused, up-to-date discussion of the issues raised in the text.

I would like to thank all the team at Pearson Education who have not only made the challenging project of producing this text easier to manage but have also made it enjoyable. In particular, I would like to offer special thanks to Liz Johnson, Sadie McClelland, Jane Powell and Penelope Woolf.

Philip A. Wickham
January 2000

Learning outcomes

This book is about entrepreneurship as a *style* of management. It aims to provide an insight into entrepreneurship and entrepreneurial management from a *strategic* perspective. It is suitable for undergraduates, postgraduates and post-experience students on full-time, part-time or distance learning-based courses in entrepreneurship, small business management and strategic management. It provides a useful supplementary source of information about entrepreneurship for specialist courses in areas such as organisational behaviour and organisational change management.

The book also aims to give practising managers, whatever the size, type and sector of their organisation or their position within it, an opportunity to explore the potential for approaching their managerial tasks in a more entrepreneurial style and of undertaking entrepreneurial projects more successfully.

These are challenging aims and obviously no book can 'make' somebody into an entrepreneur on its own. It may inform them; it may highlight the issues that are involved in entrepreneurial success; it may inspire them and give them a sense of direction; but at the end of the day, only the individual can turn themself into an entrepreneur.

However, we must not lose sight of the fact that learning to be entrepreneurial is like learning to do anything else. It is, as we shall see, just a form of *behaviour*, and behaviour is learnt. Being entrepreneurial is certainly a complex and demanding form of behaviour requiring knowledge and skill. Proficiency cannot be acquired overnight, but then few valuable skills can be learnt that quickly.

Learning to be entrepreneurial means learning to *manage* in an *entrepreneurial* way. This means recognising the potential of a situation: the *opportunities* it presents, how *changes* may be made for the better and how *new value* can be created from it. This means being able to spot new possibilities, to recognise the decisions which need to be made and knowing how to follow them through. This book aims to give students and managers who want to understand entrepreneurial possibilities access to those decisions in order to understand how those decisions present themselves and the shape they take. To make this learning effective, this book takes an *active learning* approach.

An active learning strategy

This book, like any management text, can be only a part of the process of discovering and exploring the entrepreneurial option, but it aspires to be a valuable tool in that discovery. It aims to do this in four ways:

1 By being about decisions, not just knowledge

Every entrepreneur has his or her personal store of knowledge. This knowledge is a critical aspect of business venturing. Successful entrepreneurship demands a good knowledge of a particular business, the people who make it up, the industry it is in, the customers it serves and its competitors.

Having knowledge is a *necessary*, but not a *sufficient* condition for entrepreneurial success. What matters is what is *done* with that knowledge, that is how it is used to inform and aid decision making. While every entrepreneur will call upon a different repertoire of knowledge and use it in a wide variety of business situations, all use it to address a remarkably similar set of decisions.

The key learning outcome of the book is an understanding of entrepreneurship not as an abstract subject, but as the pattern of decisions that the entrepreneurial manager must identify, analyse, resolve and follow through. By clarifying these decisions, individual entrepreneurs become aware of the knowledge they have, the knowledge they need and the learning they must undertake, in a way which is specific to the venture they are managing.

2 By presenting frameworks for thinking, not just theories

A framework for thinking is just that: a guide to help us think. It is a conceptual device which highlights certain issues, suggests which factors might be important, draws attention to the way in which they are connected and links together things that might influence one another. A framework for thinking provides a scheme for clarifying the issues that are important in a business situation, helps to indicate the decisions that might be relevant to it and identifies the information needed before a good decision can be made.

A framework for thinking is not intended to reveal fundamental truths. It is intended as an *aide-mémoire* to help decision making, that is as a reminder of what needs to be understood and addressed. This book will develop a number of frameworks for thinking which can be used to aid entrepreneurial decision making. Usually, the best way of presenting a framework for thinking is in a *visual* rather than written format. This makes the elements in the framework explicit and is efficient at depicting their inter-relationships. So, whenever possible, this book will use visual representations.

'Theory' is often met with a great deal of suspicion, especially in the world of business. Some draw a hard line between 'theory' and 'practice'. Surely, it is often suggested, what matters is *practice*: being able to do the job rather than being able to speculate about it. To say that someone 'takes a theoretical view' is a double-edged compliment. It can be downright pejorative and suggest an inability to put ideas into action.

This is unfortunate and arises from a misunderstanding about what theory is and how it works. In fact, we all use theories all the time. A theory is just an expectation that a certain set of circumstances will lead to a particular outcome.

For example, we all subscribe to the 'theory' that if we step off a cliff we will fall; and if we fall we will injure ourselves. This influences our behaviour: we do not step off cliffs. We constantly make theories about the world and test them. If they are useful, that is if their predictions are good, then we will hold on to them. If their predictions turn out to be false, then we will reject them and look for a better theory. We still do this even in situations where our theories must constantly adapt and evolve to make sense of a changing world. This is what the process of learning is all about. In this sense *experience*, including experience in business, is, in part, a matter of having access to a lot of 'good' theories.

3   By taking a strategic, rather than a tactical approach

This book considers that the decisions faced by an entrepreneur must be recognised as *strategic decisions*. The idea of strategy is a very important one in business. In essence, strategy relates to the *actions* that a business takes in order to achieve its *goals*. The idea of something being strategic touches on several things:

- it refers to issues which affect the *whole* organisation, not just some small part of it;

- it concerns the way in which the organisation interacts with its *environment*, not just its internal affairs;

- it concerns not merely what the company does – the business it is 'in' – but also how it *competes*;

- it involves consideration of how the business is performing not only in absolute terms but in *relation* to its competitors.

Tactical issues are still important though. To be successful, an entrepreneurial venture must be effective in its marketing, it must manage its finances competently and it must be proficient in its operations. What a strategic approach means is that entrepreneurs must think of all of these things not as isolated functions but as different facets of the venture as a *whole*. They must be seen to function in unison enabling the venture to deliver value to its customers, to attract investors' money and to grow in the face of competition.

4   By inviting active, not passive, learning

We all learn continually. Formal learning, when we sit down and deliberately acquire new knowledge, is only one, albeit a special, way in which we learn about the world. We learn quite naturally, often without realising we are doing it, particularly when we are motivated and interested in something. (Think about your hobby and consider how much knowledge and skill you bring to it. How much of that was 'deliberately' learnt?) Effective learning occurs when we are called upon not only to retain knowledge but also to *use* it, and then to challenge and *revise* it in the light of experience.

This forms the basis of the *active learning* cycle. The first stage is to set up a framework for thinking, like the ones that will be developed in this book. Once this is in place, the next stage is to use it to *analyse* some situation facing us. The framework for thinking helps make sense of that situation, indicates the factors involved, highlights the important factors and suggests a direction to move forward.

In the third stage we apply the analysis by responding to the situation and taking *action*. A decision is made and followed through. In the fourth stage we examine the *consequences* of that action. We see if the outcomes are the ones we wanted. Did the decision produce the results we wanted? If not, how did they differ from what we wanted? What went right? What went wrong? As a result, we reflect on the framework for thinking that we used, and the actions we took based on it. This leads to a consideration of how useful it was.

We can then revise the framework in the light of our experience, or adjust the actions it suggests to us. This gives us a new framework for thinking which we can use to make new actions. And so we go round the cycle again. Eventually, we will get a framework for thinking that works for us, in our given situation. Then we begin to forget about it! We quickly learn to make decisions without constant reference to this process. At this point we have become experienced. Our knowledge is manifest as an 'unconscious' skill.

Performing as a business decision maker, and putting the resulting decisions into practice through initiative and leadership is a matter of learning. But that learning must be *active* – see Figure A. Active learning of entrepreneurship involves setting up *frameworks* to aid decision making, using them to *guide action* and *revising* them in the light of *experience*.

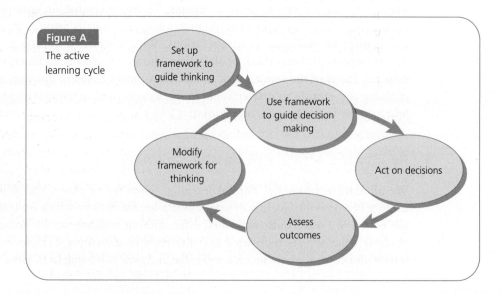

Figure A

The active learning cycle

Set up framework to guide thinking

Use framework to guide decision making

Act on decisions

Assess outcomes

Modify framework for thinking

Layout of the text

The material in this book is arranged so that ideas are presented in a logical order and accessible format. The book is organised into four parts.

Part 1 develops some introductory concepts that will be of use later in the book. The aim of this section is twofold. First, it provides a 'tool-kit' of ideas which will facilitate discussion about the entrepreneur. Second, it aims to put entrepreneurs into their proper *context*. It explores the nature of the entrepreneur and the process by which entrepreneurs create new value. This section is at pains to dispel some common myths about the entrepreneur, in particular, that an entrepreneur is born to be an entrepreneur or that to be a successful entrepreneur one must have a particular type of personality. The emphasis is on the fact that the entrepreneur is just a *manager*, albeit a very effective one.

Part 2 deals with the decisions the entrepreneur faces in giving the venture a direction, that is, deciding what the business will 'be about' and the *strategy* it will adopt. Also considered at this stage is the driving force behind the venture, that is, the *entrepreneurial vision*; what it is, how it might be developed, and how it might be used to give the venture direction and provide a foundation for leadership behaviour.

Part 3 is concerned with the initiation of the venture. This addresses how the entrepreneur can develop a detailed understanding of the opportunity that has presented itself to the business and the ways in which the venture can begin to exploit it. It also deals with the issues of attracting the financial and human investment that is needed to actually start up the business.

Part 4 addresses the issues and decisions that the entrepreneur must consider in successfully managing the growth of the venture and its eventual consolidation. Options for growing the business are explored and the issues that growth creates for the business are highlighted. The book concludes by considering how success may be continued as the venture matures and how the role of the entrepreneur changes.

This follows the process of creating a new venture from planning, through initiation and growth to consolidation. It provides a logical framework for ordering the decisions that the entrepreneur must make and makes them accessible. However, the entrepreneur does not face decisions in a simple order. The entrepreneurial venture constantly faces new possibilities and challenges. It may often have to revisit old decisions. Decisions impact on one another. Making one decision leads to a cascade of others. Managing an entrepreneurial venture is not like planning the journey of a space probe where everything can be calculated in advance. It is more like sailing a yacht, where there is a need for constant tacking of the sails. While planning is an important tool for making sure that the venture stays on course, it does not alleviate the need for continuous assessment of the business's situation or adjustments to respond to the possibilities presented.

A book is constrained by the need to present ideas one after the other in a linear progression. Unfortunately, the world of business does not allow decision making to be linear. Having considered the decisions relating to, say, the initiation of the venture, the entrepreneur cannot then forget about them. There may be a need to go back and reconsider them and their implications. Decisions interrelate and interconnect with one another over time. The shape of one decision will have implications for all the others that must be made.

This indicates that the order in which ideas are presented, although a useful one, is not the *only* one possible. Developing and running an entrepreneurial venture is not like following a recipe. It cannot be reduced to a unique sequence of decisions which must be followed. It is more like painting a picture, where selecting colours from a pallet can form an infinite variety of images. Entrepreneurship is a *creative* process.

This book aims to be self-contained. All the ideas are developed from the ground up and no extensive prior knowledge is assumed. The contents aspire to give a thorough grounding in the strategy of entrepreneurial management. Other than information needed to support the active learning exercises (see below), no reading around the text is required. However, entrepreneurship is a fast growing subject. The suggestions for further reading at the end of each chapter aim to give the student who wishes to explore the discipline further a key starting point from which to do so. The list is not intended to be an exhaustive review of the themes developed in the chapter. Rather, the articles are chosen for their practical style and the scope and accessibility of their approach.

The active learning exercises

As well as presenting frameworks for thinking, this book invites you to apply them and draw them into your own active learning cycle. Two projects are suggested as a way of doing this.

1   Analysing a venture as a role model

The first exercise is an analysis of a practising entrepreneur and the venture they have developed. This will reveal how the frameworks for thinking can be used to make sense of the entrepreneurial process and the decisions that underlie it.

Though you are free to chose any entrepreneur you like, perhaps someone well-known in the public domain or possibly someone less famous whom you know personally, two caveats are advised:

● First, it should be someone who you find inspiring and whose skills you admire. The idea of this exercise is not that you learn the details of the frameworks for thinking, but rather that you gain an understanding of the entrepreneur and a venture to act as a motivating *role model* for you. This does not mean that you must follow their path slavishly, but that you should recognise the decisions that they had to face and understand how they were addressed.

● Second, you must be able to get hold of some information on the particular entrepreneur and their venture. Clearly, information is needed before the analysis can be performed. Such information is not hard to find. The lives and businesses of numerous entrepreneurs are related in biographies. The financial papers regularly report on entrepreneurs and their businesses. Local libraries will have indexes of key articles. Many management textbooks summarise well-known entrepreneurial ventures in the form of case studies. You will not need a great deal of information, or anything which might be considered commercially sensitive to make good use of this exercise. What matters is the *quality* of analysis performed rather than the *quantity* of information gathered.

2   Developing your own venture

The second exercise is to develop an idea for a business venture of your own. It may be one you have already started or with which you are working closely. If you are not in the position of running your own venture, then developing a plan for a new venture is a very good alternative. This plan may be one you have had in mind for some time, or it may be one that has been suggested to you or that you have come up with specially for the exercise. Do not worry if it is not a particularly well-developed idea at this stage. The point of the exercise is that the business idea should be shaped and refined. It will evolve as the exercise progresses. It should, however, be something you consider to be a good idea, something that has possibility and that you feel will be *worth* developing.

It is advised that both these exercises are undertaken as the book progresses. In this way you will get to apply the frameworks for thinking as they are encountered, and it will allow your ideas to evolve. Remember, these exercises are suggested to give you an opportunity to use the frameworks presented as tools to make sense of your own situation.

A positive approach to active learning can, in time, help to make an entrepreneurial style of decision making second nature. If these activities inspire you to start your own venture then so much the better.

Good luck!

Philip A. Wickham
September 1997

Acknowledgements

We are grateful to the Financial Times Limited for permission to reprint the following material:

Case 1.1 from 'The age of enterprise', *Financial Times*, 2 January 2002, © Geoffrey Owen; Case 1.2 'Choppy water', © *Financial Times*, 24 June 2002; Case 2.1 'The capitalist growth machine', © *Financial Times*, 5 June 2002; Case 2.2 'A prestige address can go a long way', from FT.com, © *Financial Times*, 21 November 2002; Case 3.1 'Pay-offs from pursuit of glittering prizes', © *Financial Times*, 12 September 2002; Case 4.1 'New venture from founder of Freeserve', © *Financial Times*, 12 September 2002; Case 4.2 'Heady career of a serial entrepreneur', © *Financial Times*, 7 December 2002; Case 5.1 'Economy: Private enterprise seen as way forward', from FT.com, 12 December 2002; Case 5.2 'Vietnam's change of heart', © *Financial Times*, 28 August 2002; Case 6.1 'Jollibee buzzes on fast food and rapid sales', © *Financial Times*, 15 January 2002; Case 6.2 'Franchising: young and old are targets', © *Financial Times*, 5 June 2002; Case 7.1 'Sticking to what you do best', © *Financial Times*, 30 May 2002; Case 7.2 'O'Brien revels in his paradise islands', from FT.com © *Financial Times*, 10 December 2002; Case 8.1 'Finnish entrepreneur dials the right number', © *Financial Times*, 30 December 2002; Case 8.2 'The value of good connections', © *Financial Times*, 19 December 2002; Case 9.1 'Dial d for disposable', © *Financial Times*, 17 September 2002; Case 9.2 'Myradiobank', © *Financial Times*, 8 October 2002; Case 10.1 'Floods: business keeps its head above water', from FT.com, © *Financial Times*, 21 November 2002; Case 10.2 'Engine of growth hampered by credit shortage', © *Financial Times*, 16 September 2002; Case 11.1 'Brands cross the divide', © *Financial Times*, 10 July 2002; Case 11.2 'When survival lies over the border', from FT.com, © *Financial Times*, 4 June 2002; Case 12.1 'How small entrepreneurs are cutting it at the Fringe', © *Financial Times*, 5 August 2002; Case 13.1 'An entrepreneur of the people', © *Financial Times*, 5 June 2002; Case 13.2 'An entrepreneur's learning curve', © *Financial Times*, 24 January 2002; Case 14.1 'Ministry of Sound looks to flotation', © *Financial Times*, 21 May 2002; Case 14.2 Survey – creative business', © *Financial Times*, 30 July 2002; Case 15.1 'A bridge over the generation gap', © *Financial Times*, 4 November 2002; Case 15.2 'Igabriel links with two investment clubs', © *Financial Times*, 21 August 2002; Case 16.1 from 'A strategy to meet the challenges of entrepreneurship', *Financial Times*, 12 August 2002, © Donald Sull; Case 16.2 'Risk-averse investors fix sights on bullet-proof business models', © *Financial Times*, 16 October 2002; Case 17.1 'If your cup overfloweth, create a new one', © *Financial Times*, 17 June 2003; Case 17.2 'Venture capital firm's new fund will focus on the social sector', © *Financial Times*, 19 November 2002; Case 18.1 from 'Be prepared for when opportunity knocks', from FT.com, 7 August 2002, The Financial Times Limited, © Daniel Muzyka; Case 18.2 'Scotland poor on entrepreneurship', © *Financial Times*, 31 January 2002; Case 19.1 'Fast track to the mass market', © *Financial Times*, 25 July 2002; Case 19.2 'Putting the prime into prime-time TV', © *Financial Times*,

28 May 2002; Case 20.1 'Sending out a strong signal', © *Financial Times*, 30 October 2002; Case 20.2 'Travco: A one-stop shop to the country's many delights', from FT.com, © *Financial Times*, 22 July 2002; Case 21.1 'Rapidly maturing industry needs to set benchmarks', from FT.com, © *Financial Times*, 21 November 2002; Case 21.2 'In search of the right kind of chemistry', from FT.com, © *Financial Times*, 21 November 2002; Case 22.1 'IPOs hint at biotech recovery', from FT.com, © *Financial Times*, 2 May 2002; Case 22.2 'Crown Sports offered £42m for fitness clubs', © *Financial Times*, 3 December 2002; Case 23.1 'Finance: looking for a lending hand', from FT.com, © *Financial Times*, 6 November 2002; Case 23.2 'Fair play and ethnic businesses', © *Financial Times*, 26 September 2002; Case 24.1 'Tapping into UK cashpoints', © *Financial Times*, 10 September 2002; Case 24.2 'Growing pains force China's entrepreneurs to look west', © *Financial Times*, 4 February 2002; Case 25.1 'Pulp friction for Korean entrepreneur', © *Financial Times*, 1 May 2002; Case 25.2 'from John Singleton', *Financial Times*, 22 January 2002, The Financial Times Limited, © Ed Charles; Case 26.1 'Lessons from a grim market', © *Financial Times*, 20 June 2002; Case 26.2 'Angels with their feet on the ground', © *Financial Times*, 24 May 2002; Case 26.3 'Angels growing more cautious', © *Financial Times*, 15 August 2002; Case 27.1 from 'All change in the customised workplace', *Financial Times*, 22 October 2002, adapted from chapter in Chowdhury, S. (ed.) (2000) *Management 21C: New Visions for the New Millennium*, Financial Times Management, © Hamid Bouchikhi and John Kimberly; Case 27.2 'Entrepreneur pays price for nervous energy', © *Financial Times*, 29 May 2002; Case 28.1 'Branson smooth, the softer-textured brand', from FT.com, © *Financial Times*, 30 April 2002; and Case 28.2 'Talking the talk, walking the walk', © *Financial Times*, 4 November 2002 and Case 29.1 from 'The continuity conundrum', from FT.com, *The Financial Times Limited*, 8 November 2002, © Michael Horvath;

In some instances we have been unable to trace the owners of copyright material, and we would appreciate any information that would enable us to do so.

A guided tour

Each chapter begins with a **brief summary** of the ideas and themes to be explored.

Key learning outcome boxes occur regularly through all chapters to **outline the content** of each section.

Chapter 13

Entrepreneurial vision

Chapter overview

The presence of a powerful, motivating personal vision is one of the defining characteristics of entrepreneurial management. This chapter is concerned with exploring the concept of vision and understanding how it can be used by the entrepreneur to give the venture a sense of direction and purpose. It also addresses how vision can be refined, articulated and communicated to make it into an effective managerial tool.

13.1 What is entrepreneurial vision?

> **Key learning outcome**
>
> An appreciation of the power of entrepreneurial vision and of the value it offers for the venture.

Entrepreneurs are managers. They manage more than just an organisation, they manage the creation of a 'new world'. This new world offers the possibility of value being generated and made available to the venture's stakeholders. This value can only be created through change – change in the way things are *done*, change in *organisations* and change in *relationships*. Entrepreneurs rarely stumble on success. It is more usually a reward for directing their actions in an appropriate way towards some opportunity. Effective entrepreneurs know where they are going, and why. They are focused on the achievement of specific goals.

The entrepreneur's vision is a picture of the new world he or she wishes to create. It is a picture into which the entrepreneur fits an understanding of why

267

A **boxed summary** concludes the narrative of each chapter. This links back to the chapter overview and **reinforces the learning outcomes** throughout the chapter.

Highlighting the **academic research** and the debate in entrepreneurship, various themes for project work and further study are suggested.

---

in which the technology is demonstrated to have potential; (2) a prototype stage in which a working form of the technology is developed; (3) a model shop stage in which early production runs are undertaken; and finally, (4) the start-up stage where the product is produced in commercial quantities and delivered to the market. Kazanjian and Drazin (1990) extended this model into the post-start-up phase and considered (1) conception and development; (2) commercialisation; (3) early growth; and (4) stability in market phases. Complementing this, Hansen and Bird (1997) distinguished between ventures that develop and sell before taking on employees and those that take on employees, then develop and sell.

Summary of key ideas

- The supply of entrepreneurs is determined by three sets of factors, namely *pull factors* which promote entrepreneurship as a positive option; *push factors* which drive people out of the established economy; and *inhibitors* which prevent the entrepreneurial option being taken up.

- Managers make the move to entrepreneurship after considering the way the option for an entrepreneurial career can satisfy *economic*, *social* and *self-development* needs.

- The initiation decision has come under continued scrutiny and is being explored from economic, social psychological and cognitive psychological perspectives. A number of models have been proposed.

- The pre-initiation phase is one that demands a number of activities on the part of the entrepreneur. Consistencies in the pattern of these activities across different types of entrepreneur are the subject of a growing number of studies. The extent of activity does seem to be correlated with the level of initial investment the venture requires.

Research theme

Entrepreneurs' motivations for starting a new venture

The model developed in this chapter suggests that individuals are motivated to start a venture because of the utility they see in that option compared to alternatives. This utility is determined over the options' differential abilities to satisfy economic, social and self-development needs. Even if this balance is favourable to moving to entrepreneurship, knowledge, possibility, risk and valence can act as inhibitors or encouragements to the move. An empirical test of this model might take the following form. Develop a questionnaire inquiring into what

---

the entrepreneur sees (saw) as the positive and negative factors encouraging or discouraging the entrepreneurial option. Think of these questions as lying in the following grid:

Choice made (or planned)	Reasons for choice of option	
	Positives (encouragements)	Negatives (discouragements)
Entrepreneurial option		
Alternative option(s)		

Encourage the entrepreneur to put in at least five reasons for each option. Have the entrepreneur rank these in order of importance so that valence can be tested. The survey sample might include a range of entrepreneur types, from nascent, through novice to more experienced singular, serial and portfolio entrepreneurs. Code the responses into the ability of the option to satisfy a particular level of need or its role in the knowledge, possibility, risk and valence factors. By way of analysis, compare the coded responses to the model outlined. Does it provide a good framework for describing entrepreneurial motivation? How does it compare across different sorts of entrepreneur? Are nascent entrepreneurs more naive about what entrepreneurship can offer than practising entrepreneurs? Is Maslow's (1943) prediction that the prioritisation of needs is in the order economic, social and self-development borne out?

Suggestions for further reading

Ahwireng-Obeng, F. and Piaray, D. (1999) 'Institutional obstacles to South African entrepreneurship', *South African Journal of Business Management*, Vol. 30, No. 3, pp. 78–85.

Alsos, G.A. and Kolvereid, L. (1998) 'The business gestation process of novice, serial and parallel business founders', *Entrepreneurship Theory and Practice*, Summer, pp. 101–14.

Amundson, N.E. (1995) 'An interactive model of career decision-making', *Journal of Employment Counselling*, Vol. 32, No. 1, pp. 11–21.

Benacek, V. (1995) 'Small business and private entrepreneurship during transition: the case of the Czech Republic', *Eastern European Economics*, Vol. 33, No. 2, pp. 38–73.

Campbell, C.A. (1992) 'A decision theory model for entrepreneurial acts', *Entrepreneurship Theory and Practice*, Fall, pp. 21–7.

Carter, N., Gartner, W.B. and Reynolds, P.D. (1996) 'Exploring start-up event sequences', *Journal of Business Venturing*, Vol. 11, No. 3, pp. 151–66.

Dandridge, T.C. and Dziedziczak, I. (1992) 'New private enterprise in the new Poland: heritage of the past and challenges for the future', *Journal of Small Business Management*, April, pp. 104–9.

Danis, W.M. and Shipilov, A.V. (2002) 'A comparison of entrepreneurship development in two post-communist countries: the cases of Hungary and Ukraine', *Journal of Developmental Entrepreneurship*, Vol. 7, No. 1, pp. 67–94.

Summary of key ideas

- A wide variety of people can become entrepreneurs. Common backgrounds include inventors with new business ideas; managers unfulfilled by working in established organisations; displaced managers; and people excluded from the established economy.

- Whatever their background, successful entrepreneurs are characterised by being hard working and self-starting; setting high personal goals; having resilience and confidence in their abilities; being receptive to new ideas and being assertive in presenting them; being attuned to new opportunities, receptive to change and eager to learn; and being confident with power and demonstrating a commitment to others.

- Effective entrepreneurs use a variety of formal management skills combined with industry knowledge and personal motivation.

- The way entrepreneurs actually manage their ventures is dependent on the culture in which they operate. Effective entrepreneurs are sensitive to cultural values.

Research themes

Cognitive scripts and incubation

Mitchell *et al.* (2000) describe the use of 'cognitive scripts' to establish entrepreneurs' willingness to establish a new venture, their perceptions of their ability to drive those ventures and the availability of critical resources. Identify entrepreneurs (nascent and/or practising) for whom incubation with an organisation or business sector (both formal and informal) has been important and entrepreneurs for whom it has been less important (i.e. entrepreneurs entering a sector in which they have prior managerial experience or not). Following Mitchell *et al.*'s methodology, establish the cognitive scripts for the entrepreneurs prior to start-up or in the early stages of the venture. How important is incubation experience a factor in the scripts revealed? What are the implications for the development of formal incubation systems?

Entrepreneurial businesses and Hofstede's criteria

Hofstede's original study aimed to compare managerial styles across national cultures. However, it has implications for the way in which entrepreneurial businesses work (and succeed) within a particular country. Is entrepreneurial leadership characterised by a high or low power distance, masculinity, collectivity and (particularly) uncertainty avoidance? Refer to Hofstede's original study and develop

the methodology to survey a sample of entrepreneurial businesses within your own nation. How do the entrepreneurs fare? Are they typical of the generalised national characteristics Hofstede found in the original study or are they quite different? Speculate on how the Hofstede criteria might encourage or discourage entrepreneurial behaviour and the success of entrepreneurial businesses.

Suggestions for further reading

Blanchflower, D.G. and Oswald, A.J. (1998) 'What makes an entrepreneur?', *Journal of Labour Economics*, Vol. 16, No. 1, pp. 26–60.

Busenitz, L.W. and Lau, C.M. (1996) 'A cross-cultural cognitive model of new venture creation', *Entrepreneurship Theory and Practice*, Vol. 20, No. 4, pp. 25–39.

Casson, M. (1994) 'Enterprise culture and institutional change in eastern Europe', in Buckley, P.J. and Ghauri, P.N. (eds) *The Economics of Change in East and Central Europe*, London: Academic Press.

Choudary, M.A. (2001) 'Islamic venture capital', *Journal of Economic Studies*, Vol. 28, No. 1, pp. 14–33.

Delmar, F. and Davidsson, P. (2000) 'Where do they come from? Prevalence and characteristics of nascent entrepreneurs', *Entrepreneurship and Regional Development*, Vol. 12, No. 1, pp. 1–23.

Devashis, M. (2000) 'The venture capital industry in India', *Journal of Small Business Management*, Vol. 38, No. 2, pp. 67–79.

Drucker, P.F. (1985) 'The discipline of innovation', *Harvard Business Review*, May-June, pp. 67–72.

George, G. and Zahra, S.A. (2002) 'Culture and its consequences for entrepreneurship', *Entrepreneurship Theory and Practice*, Summer, pp. 5–8.

Green, R., David, J., Dent, M. and Tyshkovsky, A. (1996) 'The Russian entrepreneur: a study of psychological characteristics', *International Journal of Entrepreneurial Behaviour and Research*, Vol. 2, No. 1, pp. 49–58.

Hartenian, L.S. and Gudmundson, D.E. (2000) 'Cultural diversity in small business: implications for firm performance', *Journal of Developmental Entrepreneurship*, Vol. 5, No. 3, pp. 209–19.

Hayton, J.C., George, G. and Zahra, S. (2002) 'National Culture and Entrepreneurship: A review of behavioural research', *Entrepreneurship Theory and Practice*, Summer, pp. 33–52.

Hisrich, R.D. and Brush, C. (1986) 'Characteristics of the minority entrepreneur', *Journal of Small Business Management*, Oct, pp. 1–8.

Hofstede, G. (1980a) *Culture's Consequences: International Differences in Work-Related Values*, London: Sage Publications.

Hofstede, G. (1980b) 'Motivation, leadership and organisation: do American theories apply abroad?' *Organisational Dynamics*, Summer, pp. 42–63.

Jones-Evans, D. (1996) 'Technical entrepreneurship, strategy and experience', *International Small Business Journal*, Vol. 14, No. 3, pp. 15–39.

Kuznetsov, A., McDonald, F. and Kuznetsov, O. (2000) 'Entrepreneurial qualities: a case from Russia', *Journal of Small Business Management*, Vol. 38, No. 1, pp. 101–7.

McClelland, D.C. (1987) 'Characteristics of successful entrepreneurs', *Journal of Creative Behaviour*, Vol. 21, No. 3, pp. 219–33.

McClelland, D.C. and Burnham, D.H. (1976) 'Power is the great motivator', *Harvard Business Review*, Mar-Apr, pp. 100–10.

Miner, J.B. (1997) 'The expanded horizon for achieving entrepreneurial success', *Organizational Dynamics*, Winter, pp. 54–67.

Mitchell, R.K., Smith, B., Seawright, K.W. and Morse, E.A. (2000) 'Cross-cultural cognitions and the venture creation decision', *Academy of Management Journal*, Vol. 43, No. 5, pp. 974–93.

Mitchell, R.K., Smith, J.B., Morse, E.A., Seawright, K.W., Peredo, A.M. and McKenzie, B. (2002) 'Are entrepreneurial cognitions universal? Assessing entrepreneurial cognitions across cultures', *Entrepreneurship Theory and Practice*, Summer, pp. 9–32.

An extensive list of **further reading** is provided at the end of each chapter.

Each chapter concludes with two or three **selected cases**, all of which are taken from recent Financial Times articles. These are accompanied by points for discussion which encourage **critical reflection**.

Case 27.2

Entrepreneur pays price for nervous energy

29 May 2002

By Sheila McNulty in Houston

Seventeen years ago, when Chuck Watson began building what would become Dynegy, he made a commitment to do what was in the best interests of the US energy company. That is why, Mr Watson told his 6,000 employees, he resigned yesterday as chairman and chief executive.

'Stepping down was not an easy decision,' Mr Watson said in an e-mail. 'It was the right one.'

The collapse of Enron, the US's biggest energy trader, in December had shaken the sector to its very foundations.

Investors and analysts had grown increasingly nervous about companies, such as Dynegy, that were engaged in the murky world of energy trading.

That Dynegy had withdrawn, at the last minute, from a bid for Enron had drawn it into a $10bn lawsuit.

It was not long before the rating agencies began closely reviewing Dynegy's books for a possible downgrade of its debt to below investment grade.

So when Dynegy revealed several weeks ago that the Securities and Exchange Commission was investigating one of its transactions, it marked the beginning of the end for Mr Watson.

It put Dynegy's main shareholder, ChevronTexaco, under intense pressure to stabilise its 26.5 per cent investment in Dynegy. That, in turn, led the US oil and gas company's vice-chairman, Glenn Tilton, to be appointed interim chairman of Dynegy.

'Chuck Watson is the epitome of an entrepreneur,' Mr Tilton told a conference call with analysts following Mr Watson's resignation. It was meant as praise for the man who had built the company. But such a characterisation of Mr Watson also underscored why he had to leave Dynegy and, at only 52, 'retire from corporate life'.

The market wants stability, not corporate life.

'Chuck wanted a freer hand to shape Dynegy and jump on opportunities,' said John Olson, vice-president of research at Sanders Morris Harris, a Houston-based investment banking and securities firm.

'I don't think the board was willing to go that far any more.'

ChevronTexaco insists it did not oust Mr Watson but that the board's independent directors had asked Mr Tilton to take over. Yet it clearly supported Mr Tilton taking time away from his duties at San Francisco-based ChevronTexaco to restore Dynegy's investor stability, build on the company's strong assets and solidify its trading business.

Analysts said Mr Tilton was a strong addition to Dynegy's management team, as is Dan Dienstbier, president of the Northern Natural Gas pipeline company, who will serve as interim chief executive.

Steve Bergstrom, Mr Watson's right-hand man, will continue as president and chief operating officer.

Mr Bergstrom said there would be no change in company focus but that management would meet the board in the next week to 10 days to outline its immediate plans before making them public. 'These are consistent with where Chuck and I were going all along,' he said.

Such statements – that Dynegy would remain the same, even without Mr Watson – were aimed at easing investor fears about how Mr Watson's surprise departure might affect the company and its shares. And they seemed to help, with Dynegy trading up 7.5 per cent at $10 in midday trading.

Mr Tilton said Mr Bergstrom, whom analysts have come to know and respect over the years, was a contender for the top job, should he choose to go for it. Mr Bergstrom indicated he would do so.

'We are going through a transformation in this industry that will change it forever,' Mr Bergstrom said. 'I'm going to bring this [company] out of this thing for Chuck and the whole team.'

Source: Financial Times, 29 May 2002.

Discussion points

1. What issues does the Bouchikhi and Kimberly article raise for the leadership style adopted by entrepreneurs? Does it indicate any ways in which entrepreneurs can (advantageously) distinguish their leadership from that of 'ordinary' managers?

2. What are the leadership challenges to a new leader of Dynegy after the exit of its founding entrepreneur?

Part 1

Introductory themes

Entrepreneurship in the modern world

Of all those who feature in the management of the modern world economy, it is entrepreneurs who most attract our attention. We all have some view of them. We may see entrepreneurs as heroes: as self-starting individuals who take great personal risk in order to bring the benefits of new products to wider world markets. We may express concern at the pace of economic and social change entrepreneurs bring and of the uncertainty they create. We may admire their talents, or we may question the rewards they get for their efforts. Whatever our instinctive reaction to them, we cannot ignore the impact entrepreneurs have on our world and our personal experience of it.

The modern world is characterised by *change*. Every day we hear of shifts in political orders, developments in economic relationships and new technological advancements. These changes feed off each other and they are global. Developments in information technology allow capital to seek new business investment opportunities ever more efficiently. Success is sought out more quickly; failure punished more ruthlessly. Customers expect continuous improvement in the products and services they consume. Some have argued that the rate of change in the modern world is no different to what it has been in the past. This is probably true. But we do seem to be more acutely aware of change and consider it to be an *issue* more than past generations.

One of the key changes in the modern world is that businesses are having to become more responsive. In order to keep their place in their markets, they are having to innovate more quickly. In order to compete, they are having to become more agile. This is not just an issue for profit-making organisations but for all corporate bodies. The boundary between the world of the 'market' and the public domain is being pushed back and blurred.

Consequently, the world is demanding both more entrepreneurs and more *of* entrepreneurs. In the mature economies of the Western world they provide economic dynamism. The fast-growing businesses they create are now the main source of new job opportunities. The post-War growth economies of the Pacific Rim (albeit with a recent stall) are driven by the successes of thousands of new ventures. It is individual entrepreneurs who must restructure the post-communist countries of eastern and central Europe and provide them with vibrant market economies (Benacek, 1995; Luthens *et al.*, 2000; Fogel, 2001; Peng, 2001; Puffer *et al.*, 2001; McMillan and Woodruff, 2002). Looking back over the 12 years since the collapse of communism, it seems this is proving to be a difficult challenge. In the developing world entrepreneurs are increasingly meeting the challenge of creating new wealth and making its distribution more equitable (Ahwireng-Obeng and Piaray, 1999; Zapalska and Edwards, 2001; Trulsson, 2002).

Change presents both opportunities and problems. The opportunities come in the shape of new possibilities, and the chance for a better future. The problems lie in managing the uncertainty these possibilities create. By way of a response to this challenge, entrepreneurs must aim to take advantage of the opportunities while controlling and responding to the uncertainties. This response must be reflected in the way organisations are managed. As we will see, this is the fundamental responsibility of entrepreneurs. To make sense of this responsibility, and how it is managed, we must understand *entrepreneurship* in all its aspects.

This book aims to provide an insight into entrepreneurship that will be valuable to both practising managers, to students of management (who will become the entrepreneurial managers of the future) and to those who research and investigate entrepreneurship. It is for those who want not only to be more informed about entrepreneuriship, but who also want to be more entrepreneurial. It does this by taking a particular perspective on entrepreneurship. This perspective is readily summarised as follows:

- entrepreneurship is a *style* of management;
- entrepreneurial management aims at pursuing *opportunity* and driving *change*;
- entrepreneurial management is *strategic* management: that is, management of the whole organisation; and that, critically:
- entrepreneurism is an approach to management that can be *learnt*.

As we will discover, it is not easy to define, exactly, what an entrepreneur is, or is not.

This book takes a straightforward view. It contends that entrepreneurs are just *managers* who make *entrepreneurial decisions*. This book explores these decisions, what they are, what they involve, and the actions necessary to see them through.

Understanding is as much about recognising our misconceptions as it is about gaining knowledge. There are many myths which surround the entrepreneur. If we are to get to grips with entrepreneurship and recognise the potential to be entrepreneurial these myths must be dispelled. For example, this book rejects the notion that the entrepreneur is someone who is 'born' to achieve greatness. It also dismisses (with some important qualifications) the idea that they are behaviourally 'determined' by psychological forces beyond their control, or that the entrepreneur must have a particular type of personality to be successful. Rather we will regard the entrepreneur simply as a manager who knows how to make entrepreneurial decisions and how to follow them through.

Discussion will not be limited to the issues of owning businesses or starting new ones. These issues may be an important part of entrepreneurship but they are not its entirety. Nor are they an essential component of entrepreneurship: what makes someone an entrepreneur is not their historical or legal relationship to an organisation but the *changes* they create both with it and within it. In addition to exploring entrepreneurial management, this book also intends to 'demystify' the entrepreneur. This is not an attempt to devalue them or the work they do. In fact, the opposite is intended. It recognises entrepreneurial success as the result of personal application, hard work and learning, not as some innate imperative. What this book does aim to do, above all else, is make entrepreneurship *accessible* by demonstrating that good entrepreneurship is based on management skill, and that the entrepreneurial path can be opened by managers who wish to follow it, and recognise that success follows from personal effort, knowledge and practice, rather than a pre-ordained destiny.

Suggestions for further reading

Ahwireng-Obeng, F. and Piaray, D. (1999) 'Institutional obstacles to South African entrepreneurship', *South African Journal of Business Management*, Vol. 30, No. 3, pp. 78–85.

Benacek, V. (1995) 'Small business and private entrepreneurship during transition: the case of the Czech Republic', *Eastern European Economics*, Vol. 33, No. 2, pp. 38–73.

Bettis, R.A. and Hitt, M.A. (1995) 'The new competitive landscape', *Strategic Management Journal*, Vol. 16, pp. 7–19.

Carroll, G.R. (1994) 'Organizations . . . the smaller they get', *California Management Review*, Vol. 37, No. 1, pp. 28–41.

Fogel, G. (2001) 'An analysis of entrepreneurial environment and enterprise devevelopment in Hungary', *Journal of Small Business Management*, Vol. 39, No. 1, pp. 102–9.

Luthens, F., Stajkovic, A.D. and Ibrayeva, E. (2000) 'Environmental and psychological challenges facing entrepreneurial development in transitional economies', *Journal of World Business*, Vol. 35, No. 1, pp. 95–110.

McMillan, J. and Woodruff, C. (2002) 'The central role of entrepreneurs in transition economies', *Journal of Economic Perspectives*, Vol. 16, No. 3, pp. 153–70.

Moore, J.F. (1993) 'Predators and pray: a new ecology of competition', *Harvard Business Review*, May–June, pp. 75–86.

Peng, M.W. (2001) 'How entrepreneurs create wealth in transition economies', *Academy of Management Executive*, Vol. 15, No. 1, pp. 95–110.

Puffer, S.M., McCarthy, D.J. and Peterson, O.C. (2001) 'Navigating the hostile maze: a framework for Russian entrepreneurship', *Academy of Management Executive*, Vol. 15, No. 4, pp. 24–36.

Sandberg, W.R. (1992) 'Strategic management's potential contributions to a theory of entrepreneurship', *Entrepreneurship Theory and Practice*, Spring, pp. 73–90.

Thompson, J.L. (1999) 'A strategic perspective of entrepreneurship', *International Journal of Entrepreneurial Behaviour and Research*, Vol. 5, No. 6, pp. 279–96.

Trulsson, P. (2002) 'Constraints on growth-orientated enterprises in the southern and eastern African region', *Journal of Developmental Entrepreneurship*, Vol. 7, No. 3, pp. 331–9.

Zapalska, A.M. and Edwards, W. (2001) 'Chinese entrepreneurship in a cultural and economic perspective', *Journal of Small Business Management*, Vol. 39, No. 3, pp. 286–92.

Chapter 1

The nature of entrepreneurship

Chapter overview

This chapter is concerned with developing an overarching and integrated perspective of the entrepreneur and entrepreneurship. It reviews the great variety of approaches that have been taken to characterise the entrepreneur, highlighting the lack of agreement on a fundamental definition. Three broad approaches are considered. The first defines the entrepreneur as a manager undertaking particular tasks. The second regards the entrepreneur in economic terms and concentrates on the function they have in facilitating economic processes. The third regards the entrepreneur in psychological terms as an individual with a particular personality.

The conclusion of the chapter is that the entrepreneur is best regarded as a manager and that entrepreneurship is a style of management.

1.1 What is entrepreneurship?

Key learning outcome

An understanding of the main approaches to understanding the nature of entrepreneurship. In particular, the distinction between the entrepreneur as a performer of *managerial tasks*, as an *agent of economic change* and as a *personality*.

The word 'entrepreneur' is widely used, both in everyday conversation and as a technical term in management and economics. Its origin lies in seventeenth-century France, where an 'entrepreneur' was an individual commissioned to undertake a particular commercial project by someone with money to invest. In its earliest stages this usually meant an overseas trading project. Such projects were risky, both for the investor (who could lose money) and for the navigator-entrepreneur (who could lose a lot more!). The intertwining of the notions of entrepreneur, investor and risk is evident from the start. A number of concepts have been derived from the idea of the entrepreneur such as *entrepreneurial, entrepreneurship* and *entrepreneurial process*. The idea that the entrepreneur is someone who undertakes certain projects offers an opening to developing an understanding of the nature of entrepreneurship. Undertaking particular projects demands that particular tasks be engaged in with the objective of achieving specific outcomes and that an individual take charge of the project. *Entrepreneurship* is then what the entrepreneur *does*. *Entrepreneurial* is an adjective describing *how* the entrepreneur undertakes what he or she does. The fact that we use the adjective suggests that there is a particular *style* to what entrepreneurs do. The *entrepreneurial process* in which the entrepreneur engages is the means through which new value is created as a result of the project: the *entrepreneurial venture*.

But this is very general. Offering a specific and unambiguous definition of the entrepreneur presents a challenge. This is not because definitions are not available, but because there are so many: the management and economics literature is well served with suggested definitions for the term 'entrepreneur'. The problem arises because these definitions rarely agree with each other on the essential characteristics of the entrepreneur. Economists have long recognised the importance of the entrepreneur. But even in this discipline, known for its rigour, the entrepreneur remains an illusive beast. The difficulty lies not so much in giving entrepreneurs a role, but in giving them a role that is distinct from that of 'conventional' employed managers. Clearly, this is a distinction that is important but the difficulty is a long-standing one. Reviews of the issue by Arthur Cole, William Baumol, Harvey Leibenstein and James Soltow (all 1968) are still pertinent today and highlight issues still not fully resolved.

William Gartner (1990) undertook a detailed investigation of this matter. He surveyed academics, business leaders and politicians, asking what they felt was a good definition of entrepreneurship. From the responses he summarised 90 different attributes associated with the entrepreneur. These were not just variations on a theme. Many pairs of definitions shared no common attributes at all!

This suggested that the quest for a universal definition had not moved on since 1971 when Peter Kilby noted that the entrepreneur had a lot in common with the 'Heffalump', a character in A.A. Milne's *Winnie-the-Pooh*, described as:

  66 . . . a rather large and important animal. He has been hunted by many individuals using various trapping devices, but no one so far has succeeded in capturing him. All who claim to have caught sight of him report that that he is enormous, but disagree on his particulars. 99

Gartner (1985) is led to conclude that 'Differences among entrepreneurs and among their ventures are as great as the variations between entrepreneurs and non-entrepreneurs and between new and established firms'.

While many definitions of the entrepreneur, or entrepreneurship, might be offered, any one definition is likely to result, in some cases at least, in a mismatch with our expectations. Intuitively, we know, or feel we know, who is, or is not, an entrepreneur. A particular definition will sometimes exclude those we feel from our experience are entrepreneurs or it will include those we do not think are entrepreneurs. This will be illustrated if we consider some of the attributes associated with the entrepreneur.

For example, the notion of *risk* is one that is often associated with the entrepreneur. But this fails to distinguish between entrepreneurs who progress ventures and the *investors* who accept *financial* risk in backing those ventures. Actually founding a new business has been suggested as a defining characteristic (by Gartner himself). However, many well-known entrepreneurs have revitalised an existing organisation rather than building a new one from scratch. Some definitions emphasise the importance of entrepreneurship in providing the economic efficiency that maximises investors' returns. Rewarding investors is important, but it is not the only objective that entrepreneurs pursue. Effective entrepreneurs work to reward all the stakeholders in their ventures, not just investors. Some actively seek profit limiting social responsibilities. Innovation has also been suggested as a critical characteristic. However, innovation is an important factor in the success of all business ventures, not just the entrepreneurial. These points will be expanded upon in the discussion that follows.

We should not be disheartened by this apparent failure. Entrepreneurship is a rich and complex phenomenon. We should not expect, or even desire, that it be pinned down by a single, universal definition. Its variety presents endless possibilities and offers meaning to specific ventures. It is this that makes it so useful and inviting an idea. In any case, being able to define something is not the same as *understanding* it. This book will not offer a definitive definition of entrepreneurship as a starting point. A better approach is to develop a broad picture of the entrepreneur, to characterise entrepreneurs and explore the process they engage in and then move on to create an understanding of how entrepreneurship provides a route to new wealth creation.

As well as a managerial phenomenon, entrepreneurship has economic and social dimensions. The entrepreneur is an individual who lives and functions within a social setting. Entrepreneurs are not characterised by every action they take, but by a particular set of actions aimed at the creation of new wealth with their ventures. Wealth creation is a general managerial activity. Entrepreneurship is characterised by a particular approach to wealth creation. Recognising this gives us three directions from which we can develop an understanding. The entrepreneur can be considered as:

- a **manager** undertaking an activity – i.e. in terms of the particular **tasks** they perform and the way they undertake them;

- an **agent of economic change** – i.e. in terms of the **effects** they have on economic systems and the changes they drive; and as

- an **individual** – i.e. in terms of their **psychology**, personality and personal characteristics.

Each of these three aspects is reflected in the variety of definitions offered for entrepreneurship. The function of each perspective is not merely to characterise entrepreneurs but also to distinguish them from other types of people involved in the generation of wealth such as investors and 'ordinary' managers. The next three sections will explore each of these perspectives in more detail.

1.2 The entrepreneur's tasks

> **Key learning outcome**
>
> An understanding of the tasks that are undertaken by, and which characterise the work of, the entrepreneur.

We recognise entrepreneurs, in the first instant, by what they actually *do* – by the *tasks* they undertake. This aspect provides one avenue for approaching entrepreneurs and the way in which they are different from other types of manager. A number of tasks have been associated with the entrepreneur. Some of the more important are discussed below.

Owning organisations

Most people would be able to give an example of an entrepreneur and would probably claim to be able to recognise an entrepreneur 'if they saw one'. A key element in this common perception is *ownership* of the organisation.

While many entrepreneurs do indeed own their own organisations, using ownership as a defining feature of entrepreneurship can be very restricting. Modern market economies are characterised by a differentiation between the ownership and the running of organisations. Ownership lies with those who invest in the business and own its stock – the *principals* – while the actual running is delegated to professional managers or *agents*. These two roles are quite distinct. Therefore if an entrepreneur actually owns the business then he or she is in fact undertaking two roles at the same time: that of an investor and that of a manager. This is a distinction noticed as far back as 1803 by the classical French economist J.B. Say (Say, 1964 reprint).

So, we recognise many people as entrepreneurs even if they do not own the venture they are managing. In developed economies, sophisticated markets exist to give investors access to new ventures and most entrepreneurs are active in taking advantage of these to attract investors. For example, when Frederick Smith started the distribution company Federal Express he only put in around ten per cent of the initial capital. Institutional investors provided the rest. Do we think less of him as an entrepreneur because he diluted his ownership in this way? In fact, most would regard the ability to present the venture and to attract the support of investors as an important entrepreneurial skill.

It should also be noted that 'ordinary' managers (whatever that means!) are increasingly being given a means of owning part of their companies through share option schemes which are often linked to the company's performance. While this may encourage them to be more entrepreneurial it does not, in itself, make them into entrepreneurs.

Founding new organisations

The idea that the entrepreneur is someone who has established a new business organisation is one which would fit in with most people's notion of an entrepreneur. The entrepreneur is recognised as the person who undertakes the task of bringing together the different elements of the organisation (people, property, productive resources, etc.) and giving them a separate legal identity. Many thinkers regard this as an essential characteristic for the entrepreneur (e.g. Bygrave and Hofer, 1991). The Indian academic R.A. Sharma (1980) sees it as particularly important for entrepreneurship in developing economies. However, such a basis for defining the entrepreneur is sensitive to what we mean by 'organisation' and what we would consider to constitute a 'new' organisation.

Many people we recognise as entrepreneurs 'buy into' organisations that have already been founded and then extend them (as Ray Kroc did with McDonald's), develop them (as George and Liz Davis did with Hepworth's, converting it into Next) or absorb them into existing organisations (as Alan Sugar did with Sinclair Scientific). Increasingly, management buy-outs of parts of existing organisations are providing a vehicle for ordinary managers to exhibit their entrepreneurial talent.

A more meaningful, though less precise, idea is that entrepreneurs *make major changes in their organisational world*. Making a major change is a broad notion. It is too ill-defined and subjective to be the basis for a rigorous definition. But it does go beyond merely founding the organisation, and it differentiates the entrepreneur from the manager who manages within existing organisational structures or makes only minor or incremental changes to them.

Bringing innovations to market

Innovation is a crucial part of the entrepreneurial process. The Austrian School economist (so called because he was one of a number of radical economists working in Vienna in the first half of the twentieth century) J.A. Schumpeter saw innovation as fundamental to the entrepreneurial process of wealth creation. A concise summary of his ideas can be found in a paper he wrote for the *Economic Journal* in 1928. Schumpeter saw entrepreneurs not so much as the lubricant that oiled the wheels of an economy, but as self-interested individuals who sought short-term monopolies based on some new innovation. Once an entrepreneurial monopoly was established, a new generation of entrepreneurs came along with new innovations that aimed to supersede that monopoly in a process Schumpeter called 'creative destruction'. Peter Drucker proposed that innovation is the central task for the entrepreneur-manager in his seminal book *Innovation and Entrepreneurship* (1985). Entrepreneurs must do something new or there would be no point in their entering a market. However, we must be careful here with the idea of innovation. Innovation, in a business sense, can mean a lot more than merely developing a new product or technology. The idea of innovation encompasses any new way of doing something so that value is created. Innovation *can* mean a new product or service, but it can also include a new way of delivering an existing product or service (so that it is cheaper or more convenient for the user, for example), new methods of informing the consumer about a product and promoting it to them, new ways of organising the company, or even new approaches to managing relationships with other organisations. These are all sources of innovation which have been success-fully exploited by entrepreneurs. In short, innovation is simply doing something in a way which is new, different and better.

The entrepreneur's task goes beyond simply *inventing* something new. It also includes bringing that innovation to the marketplace and using it to deliver value to consumers. The innovated product or service must be produced profitably, in addition to being distributed, marketed and defended from the attentions of competitors by a well-run and well-led organisation.

No matter how important innovation might be to the entrepreneurial process, it is not *unique* to it. Most managers are encouraged to be innovative in some way or other. Being successful at developing and launching new products and services is not something that is only witnessed in entrepreneurial organisations. The dif-ference between entrepreneurial innovation and 'ordinary innovation' is, at best, one of degree, not substance.

Identification of market opportunity

An opportunity is a gap in a market where the potential exists to do something better and create value. New opportunities exist all the time, but they do not necessarily present themselves. If they are to be exploited, they must be *actively* sought out. The identification of new opportunities is one of the key tasks of entrepreneurs. They must constantly scan the business landscape watching for the gaps left by existing players (including themselves!) in the marketplace. Opportunity is the 'other side of the coin' as far as innovation is concerned. An innovation (a new way of doing something) is only an innovation if it meets with an opportunity (a demand for a new way of doing something).

As with innovation, no matter how important identifying opportunity is to the entrepreneurial process, it cannot be all that there is to it, nor can it characterise it uniquely. The entrepreneur cannot stop at simply identifying opportunities. Having identified them, the entrepreneur must pursue them with a suitable innovation. An opportunity is simply the 'mould' against which the market tests new ideas. In fact, actually spotting the opportunity may be delegated to specialist market researchers. The real value is created when that opportunity is exploited by something new which fills the market gap.

All organisations are active, to some degree or other, in spotting opportunities. They may call upon specialist managers to do this, or they may encourage everyone in the organisation to be on the look-out for new possibilities. Like innovation, entre-preneurial opportunity scanning differs from that of ordinary managers in degree, not substance.

Application of expertise

It has been suggested that entrepreneurs are characterised by the way that they bring some sort of expertise to their jobs. As discussed above, this expertise may be thought to lie in their ability to innovate or spot new opportunities. A slightly more technical notion is that they have a special ability in deciding how to *allocate scarce resources* in situations where *information is limited*. It is their expertise in doing this that makes entrepreneurs valuable to investors.

While investors will certainly look for evidence of an ability to make proper business decisions and judge entrepreneurs on their record in doing so, the idea that the entrepreneur is an 'expert' in this respect raises a question, namely whether the entrepreneur has a skill *as an entrepreneur* rather than just as a particularly skilful and effective manager in their own particular area. Does, for example, Rupert Murdoch have a knowledge of how to make investment decisions which is *distinct* from his intimate and detailed knowledge of the media industry, backed up by good management and attributes such as confidence, decisiveness and leadership? Is it meaningful to imagine someone developing a skill in (rather than just knowing the principles of) 'resource allocation decision making' other than it being demonstrated in relation to some specific area of business activity?

It is not clear whether such a disembodied skill exists separately from conventional management skills. In any case, such a skill could not be unique to the entrepreneur. Many managers, most of whom would not be called entrepreneurial, make decisions about resource allocation every day.

Provision of leadership

One special skill that entrepreneurs would seem to contribute to their ventures is leadership. Leadership is increasingly recognised as a critical part of managerial success. Entrepreneurs can rarely drive their innovation to market on their own. They need the support of other people, both from within their organisations and from people outside such as investors, customers and suppliers.

If all these people are to pull in the same direction, to be focused on the task in hand and to be motivated, then they must be supported and directed. This is a task that falls squarely on the shoulders of the entrepreneur. If it is to be performed effectively, then the entrepreneur must show leadership. In an important sense, performing this task well *is* leadership.

Leadership is an important factor in entrepreneurial success and it is often a skill that is exhibited particularly well by the entrepreneur, but it is a *general* management skill rather than one which is specific to the entrepreneur. That said, an entrepreneurial path may give the manager a particularly rich opportunity to develop and express leadership skills.

The entrepreneur as manager

What can we make of all this? It would seem that the entrepreneur takes on no task that is not fundamentally different (though it may be different in degree) from the tasks performed by ordinary managers at some time or other. We should not be surprised by this. At the end of the day, the entrepreneur is a *manager*. We may wish to draw a distinction between an entrepreneur and an 'ordinary' manager but if we do so it must be in terms of *what* the entrepreneur manages, *how* they manage, their *effectiveness* and the *effect* they have as a manager, not the particular tasks they undertake.

1.3 The role of the entrepreneur

> **Key learning outcome**
>
> An understanding of the economic effects of entrepreneurial activity.

Entrepreneurs are significant because they have an important effect on world economies. They play a critical role in maintaining and developing the economic order we live under. We have already noted that entrepreneurs create new value. Understanding *how* they do this is of central importance if we are to draw general conclusions about entrepreneurship. This section is a preamble that outlines some key effects of entrepreneurial activity that are drawn into definitions of the entrepreneur. This is self-contained, but Chapter 2 will consider the role of the entrepreneur in more depth from the perspective of different schools of economic thinking.

Combination of economic factors

Economists generally recognise three primary *economic factors*: the *raw materials* nature offers up, the physical and mental *labour* people provide and *capital* (money). All the products (and services) bought and sold in an economy are a mix of these three things. Value is created by combining these three things together in a way which satisfies human needs.

Factors do not combine themselves, however. They have to be brought together by individuals working together and undertaking different tasks. The co-ordination of these tasks takes place within *organisations*. Some economists regard entrepreneurship as a kind of fourth factor which acts on the other three to combine them in productive ways. In this view, *innovation* is simply finding new combinations of economic factors.

Other economists object to this view, arguing that it does not distinguish entrepreneurship sufficiently from any other form of economic activity. While entrepreneurs do affect the combination of productive factors, so does everyone who is active in an economy. It is not clear in this view why entrepreneurship is a *special* form of economic activity.

Providing market efficiency

Economic theory suggests that the most efficient economic system is one in which unimpeded markets determine the price at which goods are bought and sold. Here, *efficient* means that resources are distributed in an *optimal* way, that is the satisfaction that people can (collectively) gain from them is *maximised*.

An economic system can only reach this state if there is *competition* between different suppliers. Entrepreneurs provide that efficiency. A supplier that is not facing competition will tend to demand profits in excess of what the market would allow and so reduce the overall efficiency of the system. Entrepreneurs, so the theory goes, are on the look-out for such excess profits. Being willing to accept a lower profit themselves (one nearer the true market rate), they will enter the market and offer the goods at a lower price. By so doing entrepreneurs ensure that markets are efficient and that prices are kept down to their lowest possible level.

Classical economics provides a good starting point for understanding the effects that entrepreneurs have on an economic system. However, business life is generally much more complex than this simple picture gives it credit for. Firms compete on more than price, for example. Chapter 2 will consider the way different schools of economic thought view the role of the entrepreneur. And, as we will discover, when the strategies entrepreneurs adopt are considered (Chapter 15), the most successful entrepreneurs are often those that avoid competition (at least *direct* competition) with established suppliers.

Accepting risk

We do not know exactly what the future will bring. This lack of knowledge we call *uncertainty*. No matter how well we plan, there is always the possibility that some chance event will result in outcomes we neither expected nor wanted. If we know the *likelihood* (probability) of various possibilities then uncertainty becomes *risk*. Some economists have suggested that the primary function of the entrepreneur is to accept risk on behalf of other people. There is, in this view, a *market* for risk. Risk is something that people, generally, want to avoid (individuals are risk averse) so they are willing to pay to have it taken away. Entrepreneurs provide a service by taking this risk off people's hands. They are willing to *buy* it.

An example should make this clear. We may all appreciate the benefits a new technology, for example the digital recording of television images, can bring. However, there is a risk in developing this new technology. Financial investment in its development is very high. There is also a great deal of uncertainty. Competition between different suppliers' formats is intense. There is no guarantee that the investment will be returned. We now enjoy the benefits of digital technology and yet we, as consumers, have not, personally, had to face the risks inherent in creating it. In effect, we have delegated that risk to the entrepreneurs who *were* active in developing it. Of course, entrepreneurs expect that in return for taking the risk they will be rewarded. This reward, the profit stream from their ventures, is the *price* that customers have 'agreed' to pay (not explicitly, but by being willing to pay an addition cost for the goods provided) so that they can have the benefits of the product and yet not face the risk of developing it.

The idea that entrepreneurs are risk-takers is one which reflects their popular image. The idea of accepting risk was important to the conception of entrepreneurship developed by the classical English economist John Stuart Mill in 1848. However, we must be very careful to distinguish between *personal* risk and *economic* risk. We may face personal risk by exposing ourselves to dangerous situations, climbing mountains for example, but this is not risk as an economist understands it. To an economist, risk results from making an *investment*. Risk is the possibility that the return from an investment may be *less* than expected. Or, to be exact, might be less (or more) than could have been obtained from an alternative investment that was available. As was pointed out in Section 1.2, the roles of the entrepreneur who manages the venture and the investor who puts their money into it are quite distinct.

So, acceptance of risk is something that *investors* do, not *entrepreneurs* as such. However, the popular impression that the entrepreneur is a risk-taker is not completely inappropriate. It recognises that entrepreneurs are good at managing in situations where risk is high; that is, when faced with a situation of high uncertainty they are able to keep their heads, to continue to communicate effectively and to carry on making effective decisions. In this sense entrepreneurs do not accept risk as such, they convert uncertainty into risk (by quantifying it) on behalf of investors. The relationship between entrepreneurs and risk is quite subtle and will be explored further in Section 9.7.

Maximising investors' returns

Some commentators have suggested that the primary role of an entrepreneur is one of maximising the returns that shareholders get from their investments. In effect, the suggestion is that they create and run organisations which generate long-term profits on behalf of the investors that are higher than would otherwise have been the case. This is another aspect of the entrepreneur's role in generating overall economic efficiency.

Investors will certainly look around for entrepreneurs who create successful and profitable ventures although the view that entrepreneurs in the real world act simply to maximise shareholders' returns is questionable. Entrepreneurship, like all management activity, takes into account the interests of a wide variety of stakeholder groups, not just those of investors. Nor is it evident that investors demand that a firm maximise their returns whatever the social cost might be. Whereas Lord Hanson openly placed maximising shareholder returns at the top of his agenda, Anita Roddick would argue for a much broader range of concerns for The Body Shop.

Processing of market information

Classical economics makes the assumption that all the relevant information about a market is available to and is used by producers and consumers. However, human beings are not perfect information processors. In practice, markets work without all possible information being made available or being used (this is a theme that will be developed in Section 2.3). One view of entrepreneurs is that they keep an eye out for information that is not being exploited. By taking advantage of this information, they make markets more efficient and are rewarded out of the revenues generated. This information is information about *opportunities*. The idea that entrepreneurs are information processors is in essence a sophisticated version of the idea that entrepreneurs pursue opportunities and provide competitive efficiency.

One of the ways in which smaller organisations may be more successful than larger competitors is that they may be more adept at spotting and taking advantage of unexploited information (an issue to be considered further in Section 17.1).

In summary, entrepreneurs clearly play an important economic function. It is difficult, though, to reduce this to a single economic process in which the entrepreneur's role is different from that of other economic actors.

1.4 The entrepreneur as a person

> **Key learning outcome**
>
> An understanding of how different views of the nature of individual personality have been introduced into definitions of and understanding of the entrepreneur.

We are all different, not only in the way we look, but in the way we *act* and the way we *react* to different situations. We talk of people having consistent *personalities*. Psychologists have long had an interest in personality and have developed a number of conceptual schemes and exploratory devices to investigate it. Some of these, and how they influence thinking about entrepreneurs, will be discussed in more depth in Chapter 3. This section sets the scene by considering six broad approaches to defining the entrepreneur as a person.

The 'great person'

An immediate reaction when faced with an entrepreneur, or indeed anyone with influence and social prominence such as a leading statesman, an important scientist or a successful artist, is to regard them simply as being special: as a 'great person' who is destined by virtue of his or her 'nature' to rise above the crowd. Such people are born to be great and will achieve greatness, one way or another. The 'great person' view can often be found in biographies (and not a few autobiographies!) of entrepreneurs. It is a nice narrative and an inviting 'angle' biographically or journalistically.

Entrepreneurs can certainly be inspiring, and may provide motivating role models. Generally though, the 'great person' view, however passionate, is not particularly useful. For a start it is self-justifying. If an entrepreneur achieves success, it is because they are great; if they fail then they are not. It is logically tautological. Further, it is not predictive. It can only tell us who will become an entrepreneur after they have done so (and achieved success). There is no test for greatness other than its expression. Furthermore, it assumes entrepreneurship is entirely inate. It sees no role for the wider world in influencing the initiation or progression of the entrepreneur's path. Most damaging, however, is the way it denies the possibility of entrepreneurial success to those who are not (or are not seen or do not feel themselves to be) born to be great persons.

Social misfit

Another view which forms a marked contrast to the great person view but which also has a great deal of currency is the idea that entrepreneurs are *social misfits* at heart. In this view someone is an entrepreneur for an essentially negative reason: they are unable to fit into existing social situations. As a result the entrepreneur is driven to create his or her own situation. It is this that provides the motivation to innovate and build new organisations.

Advocates of this view look towards both anecdotal and psychological evidence for support. Many entrepreneurs achieve success after comparatively unhappy and lacklustre careers working as professional managers. Often they relate their inability to fit into the established firm as a factor in driving them to start their own venture.

Some researchers who have studied the childhood and family backgrounds of entrepreneurs have noted that they are often characterised by privation and hardship which left the person with a lack of self-esteem, a feeling of insecurity and a repressed desire for control. This leads to rebellious and 'deviant' behaviour which limits the person's ability to fit into established organisations. Entrepreneurial activity, it is concluded, is a way of coming to terms with this. It provides not only a means of economic survival but also an activity which enables a reaction against anxiety left by psychological scars. If, as Schumpeter suggests, entrepreneurship is *creative destruction*, then the social misfit view certainly emphasises the entrepreneur as a creative destroyer.

While the idea of the social misfit may provide insights into the motivations of *some* entrepreneurs, any generalisation of this sort is dangerous. For every entrepreneur whose childhood was unhappy and involved privation, another can be found who was quite comfortable and happy. Many successful entrepreneurs recall being dissatisfied when working within established organisations. However, this is not necessarily because they are misfits in a negative sense. Rather it may be because the organisation did not provide sufficient scope for their abilities and ambitions. This in itself may be demotivating and therefore managerial performance in an established firm is not necessarily a good indicator of how someone will perform later as an entrepreneur.

Personality type

The conceptual basis for the personality type view of entrepreneurship is that the way people act in a given situation can be categorised into one of a relatively limited number of responses. As a result, individuals can be grouped into a small number of categories based on this response. For example, we may classify people as *extrovert* or *introvert*, *aggressive* or *passive*, *spontaneous* or *reserved*, *internally* or *externally orientated*, etc. Each of these types represents a fixed category (there is more on such categorisation in Section 3.3).

There is a common impression that entrepreneurs tend to be flamboyant extroverts who are spontaneous in their approach and rely on instinct rather than calculation. Certainly, they are often depicted this way in literature and on film. Detailed studies, however, have shown that all types of personality perform equally well as entrepreneurs. Personality type, as measured by personality tests (more on this in Section 3.2) does not correlate strongly with entrepreneurial performance and success. For example, introverts are just as likely to be entrepreneurs as are extroverts.

Personality trait

The idea of personality *trait* is different from that of personality *type*. While a personality may be *of* a particular type, it *has* a trait. Whereas types are distinct categories, traits occur in continuously variable dimensions.

In a very influential study in the early 1960s, David McClelland identified a 'need for achievement' (along with various other characteristics) as the fundamental driving trait in the personality of successful entrepreneurs. Other factors which have also been viewed as important include the need for autonomy, the need to be in control of a situation, a desire to face risk, creativity, a need for independence and the desire to show leadership qualities.

While conceptually very powerful, the trait approach to the entrepreneurial personality raises a number of questions. To what extent are traits innate? Are they fixed features of personality or might they actually be learnt? To what extent are traits driven by external factors? How does a trait as measured in a personality test relate to behaviour in the real world? Is the same trait expressed in the same way in all situations? Does possession of certain traits lead to entrepreneurship or does pursuing an entrepreneurial career merely provide an opportunity to develop and express them? Do entrepreneurs simply act out the traits they feel are expected of them?

The idea of traits in the personality of entrepreneurs provides a very important paradigm for the study of entrepreneurial motivation. However, the available evidence suggests it is unwise to advocate, or to advise against, an entrepreneurial path for a particular manager based on the perception of traits they might, or might not, possess. This is a theme that will be returned to when the issue of personality testing and entrepreneurship is considered in Section 3.2.

Social development

Both personality type and trait are seen as innate. They are determined by a person's genetic complement (nature) or by early life experiences (nurture) or by some combination of both. (The relative importance of these two things and how they might interact is a highly controversial issue in social theory.) Personality type and trait are also seen as being 'locked into' a person's mental apparatus, and therefore relatively fixed. They can change only slowly, or under special conditions.

The social development view regards personality as a more complex issue. In this view entrepreneurship is an output which results from the interaction of internal psychological and external social factors. The view is that personality develops continuously as a result of social interaction and is *expressed* in a social setting rather than being innate to the individual. The way people behave is not predetermined, but is contingent on their experiences and the possibilities open to them.

In this view, entrepreneurs are not born, they are *made*. While their predisposition may be important it does not have any meaning in isolation from their experiences. A person is not, once and for all, entrepreneurial. He or she may, for example, decide to become an entrepreneur only at one particular stage in his or her life. Equally, he or she may decide to give up being an entrepreneur at another.

A number of factors are seen as significant to the social development of entrepreneurs. In general, they fall into one of three broad categories:

1. *Innate* – factors such as intelligence, creativity, personality, motivation, personal ambition, etc.

2. *Acquired* – learning, training, experience in 'incubator' organisations, mentoring, existence of motivating role models, etc.

3. *Social* – birth order, experiences in family life, socio-economic group and parental occupation, society and culture, economic conditions, etc.

The social development model provides a more plausible picture of entrepreneurial behaviour than those that assume entrepreneurial inclination is somehow innate. Entrepreneurship is a social phenomenon. It is not inherent within a person, rather it exists in the interactions *between* people and with social situations. While entrepreneurs may actively grasp opportunities, they do so within a cultural framework. The social development approach is sophisticated in that it recognises that entrepreneurial behaviour is the result of a large number of factors, some internal to the entrepreneur, and others which are features of the environment within which entrepreneurs express themselves. However, this is also a weakness. While it identifies the factors which might influence entrepreneurship, it usually cannot say *why* they influence it. While social development models are good at indicating what factors might be involved in entrepreneurial behaviour, they often suggest so many factors might be involved that their predictive power is very limited. It can be very hard to test social development models empirically.

The role of personality in entrepreneurial inclination and success is a controversial area. In part this is because there is no general consensus of what the concept of personality actually means or refers to. As Chapter 3 reviews, there are several approaches to the notion of personality within different schools of psychology. Combine this with the lack of agreement on what (or who) constitutes an entrepreneur and the scope for debate will be evident.

Cognitive approaches

Cognitive psychology is a relatively new but increasingly important \
psychological explanation and research. Cognitive psychology deals with t\
which humans (and sometimes other animals as well) obtain, store, process
information about the world. So it is interested in attention and perception, th
processing of raw sensual experiences, storage of information in memory systems and
the way in which information is manipulated by mental routines to drive decision
making. Cognitive psychology is very much an experimental science, with its findings based on repeatable experiments and the testing of hypotheses. Cognitive
psychologists often develop systems models of information processing. There is no
claim that these systems have an anatomical or even neurological representation in
the human brains; rather they are accounts of the way in which the brain works as
a system. Some cognitive psychologists talk of specific cognitive styles and strategies
that reflect generalised ways in which humans process information. For example,
when faced with a new problem some people call to mind methods they are already
familiar with; others will seek out original and new solution methods; some people
seek risky situations, others avoid them; some people are willing to make decisions
with only a limited amount of information, others hold back until they are well
informed. These are only examples. But these examples give a hint that entrepreneurs might be distinguished not so much by their personality, but by the
cognitive strategies and styles they adopt (which may be related to personality but
is not the same thing). This is an issue which is coming under increased research
scrutiny and is a theme that will be developed further in Section 3.3.

1.5 Entrepreneurship: a style of management

> **Key learning outcome**
>
> A recognition that entrepreneurship
> is a style of management aimed at
> pursuing opportunity and driving
> change.

The discussion so far has emphasised
what the entrepreneur is *not*, as much
as what they *are* because it is important
to dispel certain myths about the entrepreneur. In particular, it is important
to discount the theories that the entrepreneur is someone with a particular type
of personality or that certain people are
somehow born to be entrepreneurs. We must also recognise that the entrepreneur
does not have a clear-cut economic role. However, we must now consider what
the entrepreneur actually *is* by developing a perspective that will illuminate the
way entrepreneurs go about their tasks *as* entrepreneurs rather than providing a
potentially restrictive *definition* of the entrepreneur.

What we can say with confidence is that an entrepreneur is a *manager*. Specifically, he or she is someone who manages in an *entrepreneurial way*. More often than
not they will be managing a specific *entrepreneurial venture*, either a new organisation or an attempt to rejuvenate an existing one. The entrepreneurial venture

represents a particular management challenge. The nature of the entrepreneurial venture characterises and defines the management that is needed to drive it forward successfully. Drawing together the themes that have been explored in this chapter, it is evident that entrepreneurial management is characterised by three features: a focus on change, a focus on opportunity and organisation-wide management.

A focus on change

Entrepreneurs are managers of *change*. An entrepreneur does not leave the world in the same state as they found it. They bring people, money, ideas and resources together to build new organisations and to change existing ones. Entrepreneurs are not important as much for the *results* of their activities as for the *difference* they make.

Entrepreneurs are different from managers whose main interest is in maintaining the status quo by sustaining the established organisation, protecting it and maintaining its market positions. This is not to deprecate a desire for equilibrium as an objective: it can be very important and is an essential ingredient in the effective running of a wide variety of organisations, but it is not about driving change.

A focus on opportunity

Entrepreneurs are attuned to opportunity. They constantly seek the possibility of doing something differently and better. They innovate in order to create new value. Entrepreneurs are more interested in pursuing opportunity than they are in *conserving resources*.

This is not to suggest that entrepreneurs are not interested in resources. They are often acutely aware that the resources available to them are limited. Nor does it mean that they are cavalier with them. They may be using their own money and, if not, they will have investors looking over their shoulders to check that they are not wasting funds. What it *does* mean is that entrepreneurs see resources as a means to an end, not as an end in themselves.

Entrepreneurs expose resources to risk but they also make them work by stretching them to their limit in order to offer a good return. This makes them distinct from managers in established businesses who all too often can find themselves more responsible for protecting 'scarce' resources than for using them to pursue the opportunities that are presented to their organisations.

Organisation-wide management

The entrepreneur manages with an eye to the *entire* organisation, not just some aspect of it. They benchmark themselves against organisational objectives, not just the objectives for some particular department. This is not to say that functional disciplines such as marketing, finance, operations management, etc. are unimportant. However, the entrepreneur sees these as functions which play a part in the overall business, rather than as isolated activities.

Entrepreneurial managers as venturers

In short, the entrepreneur is a manager who is willing to *venture*: to create change and to pursue opportunity rather than just to maintain the status quo and conserve resources. Of course, the effective entrepreneur does *all* these things when appropriate. There are times when the status quo is worth sustaining, and times when it is unwise to expose resources. Part of the skill of the effective entrepreneur is knowing when *not* to venture. However, when the time is right, the entrepreneurial manager *is* willing to step forward.

This is a 'soft' definition. There is no hard and fast distinction between the entrepreneur and other types of manager. This does not make the entrepreneur any less special, nor does it make what entrepreneurs do any less important. What it does do is open up the possibility of entrepreneurship. In being 'just' a style of management it is something that can be learnt. Managers can choose to be entrepreneurial.

A very illuminating characterisation of entrepreneurship is offered by Czarniawska-Joerges and Wolff (1991), who use the language of theatrical performance rather than economics to distinguish between *management*, which is:

66the activity of introducing order by coordinating flows of things and people towards collective action;99

and *leadership*, which is:

66symbolic performance, expressing the hope of control over destiny;99

and *entrepreneurship*, which is, quite simply:

66the making of entire new worlds.99

In conclusion, we can say that entrepreneurial management is characterised by its *whole organisation* scope, its objective of creating *change* and a focus on *exploiting opportunity*. These characteristics are shown in Figure 1.1.

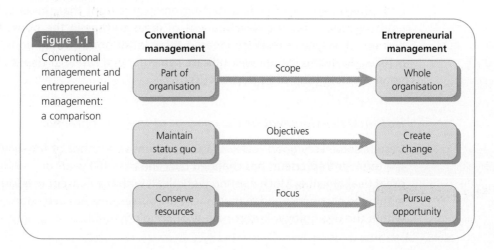

Figure 1.1 Conventional management and entrepreneurial management: a comparison

Conventional management		Entrepreneurial management
Part of organisation	Scope →	Whole organisation
Maintain status quo	Objectives →	Create change
Conserve resources	Focus →	Pursue opportunity

Summary of key ideas

- There is no universally agreed definition of entrepreneurship. The wide variety of definitions in the literature emphasise three aspects:
  - the entrepreneur as a *manager* undertaking particular *tasks*;
  - the entrepreneur as an *economic agent* generating particular *economic effects*; and:
  - the entrepreneur as an *individual* of a particular *personality*.

- The idea that there is an 'entrepreneurial' personality which predisposes people to business success is far from clear and is controversial.

- Some important schools of thought on the entrepreneurial personality include: the great person, the social misfit, the personality type, the personality trait, social development and the cognitive.

- Entrepreneurial management may be distinguished from conventional management by:
  - a focus on change rather than continuity;
  - a focus on new opportunities rather than resource conservation;
  - organisation-wide rather than specific-function management.

Research themes

This chapter has aimed at providing an introduction to the nature of the entrepreneur and the various attempts to define entrepreneurs as a distinct class of economic actors. As a starting point, it is right that this chapter highlights directions for the development of ideas further in the book. I wish to pick up on particular research ideas at these latter points, when understanding is fuller. So at this stage I will indicate some general research themes touching upon the definition of entrepreneurs.

Historical development of the concept of the 'entrepreneur'

Despite some very good reviews, a comprehensive account of the way in which the term 'entrepreneur' has changed over the past 300 years or so would add a great deal of value. Much existing work deals with the concept in a formal sense within the economics and management discourses. Less has been done on its use within the psychology, anthropology or sociology fields. Also of interest might be its use in popular literature. How does the world in general see entrepreneurs? A good starting point for ideas and style would be the edited commentaries of Pollard (2000) on the representation of business in English literature.

Perceptions and associations with the concept of the 'entrepreneur'

Most people have some feelings about entrepreneurs (often quite strong ones!) based on their knowledge and experience of them. I often run brainstorming sessions in which people are invited to suggest the ideas they associate with them. There is an opportunity to undertake this in a more systematic way, using an initial brainstorming to generate associations (e.g. the entrepreneur is dedicated, is ruthless, works hard, and so on), classify those associations as positive or negative (good or bad) and then to quantify the findings in a second stage in which individuals are invited to rate their agreement with the idea (e.g. agree strongly to disagree strongly). Originality would come from classifying respondents in a way that reflects their interaction with entrepreneurs (e.g. only know about them from the news, have worked with one as an employee, have sold things to them, I am one!). Develop your own ideas on how respondents might be classified. Further originality would come from creating a pictorial representation (or mapping) of the results. Relationships between experience of the entrepreneur and attitudes towards them might then be revealed. Any good book on market research will guide details of an appropriate methodology. Gartner's classic 1988 study would be a good starting point.

Philosophical issues in defining the 'entrepreneur'

This is one for the more philosophically minded researcher. Definitions are things we find in dictionaries. But the nature of and the role of the knowledge contained within definitions is a major issue in analytical philosophy (the branch of philosophy that deals with the relationship between knowledge, concepts, language and the world). For example, analytical philosophers distinguish between *ostensive* definitions – those that point to something – and *contextual* definitions – those that set out a list of criteria by which something is recognised. There are other issues, of course. Any good introductory book on analytical philosophy will discuss these issues. My recommendations would be the books by Grayling (1999) and by Hospers (1990). Both are excellent. The project should aim to take approaches to the definition of the entrepreneur and critically evaluate them using the relevant philosophical ideas. Think about answering the following questions: Why do we find it so hard to define entrepreneurs in an exact, and universally agreed way? Is it something to do with our (lack of) knowledge of entrepreneurs (do we need more)? Are entrepreneurs inherently indefinable? Or is our expectation of what a definition of the entrepreneur or entrepreneurship can (or should) do at fault?

Suggestions for further reading

Baumol, W.J. (1968) 'The entrepreneur: introductory remarks', *American Economic Review*, Vol. 58, pp. 60–3.

Barton-Cunningham, J. and Lischeron, J. (1991) 'Defining entrepreneurship', *Journal of Small Business Management*, Jan, pp. 45–61.

Boyett, I. (1977) 'The public sector entrepreneur – a definition', *International Journal of Entrepreneurial Behaviour and Research*, Vol. 3, No. 2, pp. 77–92.

Brockhaus, R.H. (1987) 'Entrepreneurial folklore', *Journal of Small Business Management*, July, pp. 1–6.

Bygrave, W.D. and Hofer, C.W. (1991) 'Theorising about entrepreneurship', *Entrepreneurship Theory and Practice*, Vol. 16, No. 2, pp. 13–22.

Chell, E. (1985) 'The entrepreneurial personality: a few ghosts laid to rest', *International Small Business Journal*, Vol. 3, No. 3, pp. 43–54.

Cole, A.H. (1968) 'Entrepreneurship in economic theory', *American Economic Review*, Vol. 58, pp. 64–71.

Cromie, S. and O'Donaghue, J. (1992) 'Assessing entrepreneurial inclination', *International Small Business Journal*, Vol. 10, No. 2, pp. 66–73.

Czarniawska-Joerges, B. and Wolff, R. (1991) 'Leaders, managers and entrepreneurs on and off the organisational stage', *Organisation Studies*, Vol. 12, No. 4, pp. 529–46.

Deakins, D. and Freel, M. (2003) *Entrepreneurship and Small Firms* (3rd edn), London: McGraw-Hill.

Drucker, P.F. (1985) *Innovation and Entrepreneurship*, London: Heinemann.

Gartner, W. (1985) 'A conceptual framework for describing the phenomenon of new venture creation', *Academy of Management Review*, Vol. 10, No. 4, pp. 696–706.

Gartner, W.B. (1988) '"Who is an entrepreneur" is the wrong question', *American Journal of Small Business*, Spring, pp. 11–32.

Gartner, W.B. (1990) 'What are we talking about when we talk about entrepreneurship?', *Journal of Business Venturing*, Vol. 5, pp. 15–28.

Ginsberg, A. and Buchholtz, A. (1989) 'Are entrepreneurs a breed apart? A look at the evidence', *Journal of General Management*, Vol. 15, No. 2, pp. 32–40.

Grayling, A.C. (ed.) (1999) *Philosophy 1*, Oxford: Oxford University Press.

Green, R., David, J., Dent, M. and Tyshkovsky, A. (1996) 'The Russian entrepreneur: a study of psychological characteristics', *International Journal of Entrepreneurial Behaviour and Research*, Vol. 2, No. 1, pp. 49–58.

Hargreaves Heap, S.P. (1998) 'A note on Buridan's ass: the consequences of failing to see a difference', *Kyklos*, Vol. 51, No. 2, pp. 277–84.

Hisrich, R.D. and Peters, M.P. (2002) *Entrepreneurship* (5th edn), New York: McGraw Hill.

Hitt, M.A., Ireland, R.D., Camp, S.M. and Sexton, D.L. (eds) (2002) *Strategic Entrepreneurship: Creating a New Mindset*, Oxford: Blackwell.

Hornaday, R.W. (1992) 'Thinking about entrepreneurship: a fuzzy set approach', *Journal of Small Business Management*, Oct, pp. 12–23.

Hospers, J. (1990) *An Introduction to Philosophical Analysis* (3rd edn), London: Routledge.

Julien, P.A. (1989) 'The entrepreneur and economic theory', *International Small Business Journal*, Vol. 7, No. 3, pp. 29–38.

Khahlil, E.L. (1997) 'Buridan's ass, risk, uncertainty and self-competition: a theory of entrepreneurship', *Kyklos*, Vol. 50, No. 2, pp. 147–64.

Khahlil, E.L. (1998) 'Buridan's ass, rationality and entrepreneurship: a reply to Hargreaves Heap (1998)', *Kyklos*, Vol. 51, No. 2, pp. 285–8.

Kilby, P. (1971) 'Hunting the Heffalump', in Kilby, P. (ed.), *Entrepreneurship and Economic Development*, New York: Free Press.

Kirby, D.A. (2003) *Entrepreneurship*, London: McGraw-Hill.

Kuratko, D.F. and Hodgetts, R.M. (2001) *Entrepreneurship: A Contemporary Approach* (5th edn), New York: Dryden.

Kuznetsov, A., McDonald, F. and Kuznetsov, O. (2000) 'Entrepreneurial qualities: a case from Russia', *Journal of Small Business Management*, Vol. 38, No. 1, pp. 101–7.

Lambing, P. and Kuehl, C. (1997) *Entrepreneurship*, Upper Saddle River, NJ: Prentice Hall.

Landau, R. (1982) 'The innovative milieu', in Lundstedt, S.B. and Colglazier, E.W., Jr (eds), *Managing Innovation: The Social Dimensions of Creativity, Invention and Technology*, New York: Pergamon Press.

Leibenstein, H. (1968) 'Entrepreneurship and development', *American Economic Review*, Vol. 58, pp. 72–83.

McClelland, D. (1961) *The Achieving Society*, Princeton, NJ: Van Nostrand.

Mill, J.S. (1848) *Principles of Political Economy with Some of their Applications to Social Philosophy*, London: J.W. Parker.

Morris, M.H. (2000) 'Revisiting "who" is the entrepreneur', *Journal of Developmental Entrepreneurship*, Vol. 7, No. 1, pp. v–vii.

Olson, P.D. (1986) 'Entrepreneurs: opportunistic decision makers', *Journal of Small Business Management*, July, pp. 29–35.

Olson, P.D. (1987) 'Entrepreneurship and management', *Journal of Small Business Management*, July, pp. 7–13.

Peterson, R.A., Albaum, G. and Kozmetsky, G. (1986) 'The public's definition of small business', *Journal of Small Business Management*, July, pp. 63–8.

Petrof, J.V. (1980) 'Entrepreneurial profile: a discriminant analysis', *Journal of Small Business Management*, Vol. 18, No. 4, pp. 13–17.

Pollard, A. (ed.) (2000) *The Representation of Business in English Literature*, London: Institute of Economic Affairs.

Say, J.B. (1964) *A Treatise on Political Economy: Or, the Production, Distribution and Consumption of Wealth*, New York: A.M. Kelly (reprint of original 1803 edition).

Scherer, R.F., Adams, J.S. and Wiebe, F.A. (1989) 'Developing entrepreneurial behaviours: a social learning perspective', *Journal of Organisational Change Management*, Vol. 2, No. 3, pp. 16–27.

Schumpeter, J.A. (1928) 'The instability of capitalism', *Economic Journal*, pp. 361–86.

Schumpeter, J.A. (1934) *The Theory of Economic Development* (1961 translation by Redvers Opie), Cambridge, MA: Harvard University Press.

Sharma, R.A. (1980) *Entrepreneurial Change in Indian Industry*, New Delhi: Sterling Publishers.

Soltow, J.H. (1968) 'The entrepreneur in economic history', *American Economic Review*, Vol. 58, pp. 84–92.

Stanworth, J., Stanworth, C., Grainger, B. and Blythe, S. (1989) 'Who becomes an entrepreneur?' *International Small Business Journal*, Vol. 8, No. 1, pp.11–22.

Watson, T.J. (1995) 'Entrepreneurship and professional management: a fatal distinction', *International Small Business Journal*, Vol. 13, No. 2, pp. 34–46.

Webster, F.A. (1977) 'Entrepreneurs and ventures: an attempt at classification and clarification', *Academy of Management Review*, Vol. 2, No. 1, pp. 54–61.

The age of enterprise

FT

2 January 2002

By **Geoffrey Owen**

As a reporter on the FT in the 1960s and 1970s I was constantly being told that this or that industry would, over the next few years, become concentrated in the hands of a few giant companies. Global economies of scale, it was said, would lead inevitably to the extinction of small and medium-sized companies, unless they were highly specialised. How boring the world would have been if this prediction had come true.

Fortunately, what is going on in business today points in the opposite direction. One of the most cheering developments is the deconstruction of the large, bureaucratic corporation and, along with it, the rebirth of the entrepreneur. The dotcom crash notwithstanding, there is every reason to believe that this trend will continue in 2002 and beyond.

What we are seeing is more than the unbundling of overweight conglomerates, a process that began in the 1980s. Whole industries are being reshaped – telecommunications, chemicals and textiles are three obvious examples – under the impact of international competition, stock market pressure and technological change.

Look, for instance, at electronics. Just as International Business Machines' near-monopoly was undermined 20 years ago by the rise of the personal computer, so Intel, one of today's giants, is now under concerted attack from Asian entrepreneurs.

These Asian challengers are doing more than simply imitating what the Americans have done: they are pioneering new ways of designing and making semiconductors. Another case is pharmaceuticals, where the balance of power, at least as far as research is concerned, may be shifting away from the big companies towards the smaller biotechnology groups.

It is true that mega-mergers continue to take place in these industries but more often than not they arise from weakness rather than strength – the proposed Hewlett-Packard/Compaq combination is a notable example – and the hoped-for economies of scale are rarely achieved.

One of the great advantages of globalisation, contrary to the views of protesters, is that it reduces the power of established companies and, by promoting new entry, widens consumer choice. It is a powerful contributor to the gale of creative destruction that is blowing through many industries today.

Allied to this welcome change is the recognition by governments, especially in western Europe, that encouraging entrepreneurs is a better policy than preserving old dinosaurs.

For any British financial journalist, like myself, whose career began at the end of the 1950s, it is still somewhat bewildering to see a Labour chancellor of the exchequer proclaiming the virtues of entrepreneurs and trying hard to ensure that they make as much money as possible. One may criticise Gordon Brown for the methods he has used to reward entrepreneurial success – over-complicating the tax system, for example – but the thrust of his policy can only be applauded and it seems to be producing results.

This new enthusiasm for entrepreneurs is not just a British phenomenon. Germany has often been criticised for its failure to foster new businesses in such fields as electronics and biotechnology but the environment has changed radically in the past few years. The federal and provincial governments have made great efforts to remove institutional obstacles, especially in the financial system, to the creation and growth of high-technology firms. Despite the recent collapse of the Neuer Markt, the 'equity culture' appears to have taken a firm hold, among savers as well as budding entrepreneurs.

All the advanced industrial countries are in the throes of what has been described as a shift from the managed to the entrepreneurial economy*. The argument is that a combination of factors, including the transfer of much commodity-style production to developing countries and the growth of knowledge-based industries in which economies of scale are less important than in, say, steel-making or cars, is enhancing the role of smaller companies. Nimbleness and flexibility are the qualities needed to cope with the turbulence and diver-sity of today's markets and they are not normally found in large corporations.

Of course, this prediction may be no more accurate than the earlier one about the inexorable rise of giant companies. But it is hard to imagine a return to the days of stable markets. Unpredictability is now the norm and that calls for a different industrial structure and a different way of running businesses. All this fluidity makes the task of entrepreneurs and managers more hazardous – but it certainly will not be boring.

Source: *Financial Times*, 2 January 2002,
© Geoffrey Owen.

Case 1.2

Choppy water

FT

24 June 2002

Outrage over corporate executives' excesses has spread to Norway. Minority shareholders are concerned at risks taken by Kjell Inge Rokke, the aggressive Norwegian entrepreneur who heads the Kvaerner engineering group.

Not the risks he takes at work, but in his spare time Knut Traaseth, leader of the Norwegian small shareholders' association, says his telephone did not stop ringing after Rokke flipped his speedboat at over 155 miles per hour during a recent rally off Italy's shores.

Genuine, human concern from the association, which has fought a number of legal battles with the jet-setting billionaire? Alas, no. Callers were worried about the impact on their shareholdings.

Source: *Financial Times*, 24 June 2002.

---

*D.B. Audretsch and A.R. Thurik. What's new about the new economy? *Industrial and Corporate Change*, Vol. 10, No. 1, March 2001.

The author is senior fellow at the Institute of Management, London School of Economics, and a former editor of the FT.

Discussion points

1. Is entrepreneurship in the modern world (post the information technology revolution) radically different from, or just an incremental development of the way entrepreneurs have thought and operated in the past? Do we need a new breed of entrepreneur?

2. Distinguish between 'personal' risk and 'economic' risk. To what extent and in what way do entrepreneurs and investors share these?

Chapter 2

The economic function of the entrepreneur

Chapter overview

Entrepreneurs are, first and foremost, economic actors. The tasks they undertake, their social context and who they are as people are of course important. But we are primarily interested in these aspects because of the economic impact of entrepreneurial activity. This chapter is concerned with providing an overview of economic thinking about, and insights into, the entrepreneur and how it has developed.

The first section will consider the way in which the entrepreneur is recognised and how the effects they have are accounted for in different schools of economic thinking. It might be argued that the inability of the core neo-classical school of economics to address the issue of entrepreneurship is one of the main drivers for the development of alternative schools of thinking within economics generally.

The second section will consider how the economic picture of the entrepreneur is related, in broad terms, to their social and moral role within society.

The final section will consider how new developments in the economics of information can inform our understanding of entrepreneurs and their relation with other stakeholders in the venture. In looking at the broader implications of entrepreneurial activity, we are invited into a series of (often quite specialist) debates within a number of social science fields. A single chapter cannot do full justice to the concerns. By necessity, this chapter will raise more issues than it resolves. The aim is not a comprehensive account; it is to introduce the key issues and a flavour of the debates as reference points for the student of entrepreneurship. Further readings are suggested for the student who wishes to explore these issues in proper depth.

(2.1) The entrepreneur in economic theory

> **Key learning outcome**
>
> An appreciation of a number of different schools of economic thinking and a recognition of the ways in which they see the entrepreneur and the entrepreneur's function, and account for the entrepreneur's economic effects.

Economics is (or at least aspires to be) the most 'scientific' of the social sciences. Yet this does not preclude a wide variety of approaches and differing theoretical perspectives within the field. To some extent, these different schools of economic thinking arise because of concerns with, and a relaxation of, one or more of the fundamental assumptions (inevitably challenged as being unrealistic) of the core neo-classical school of economic thinking. Part of their motivation is to account for the very existence of the entrepreneur as a distinct type of economic actor (an issue first raised in Section 1.4). The schools considered here are not an exhaustive list. Some commentators may divide them up differently. There is debate about how the different schools might be linked or integrated. However, what follows does provide a broad account of different economic perspectives that concern themselves with entrepreneurship and its effects.

The neo-classical school

Economics has a long heritage. Its origins can be traced back to thinking in the fifth century BCE (not just in the Mediterranean, but in China and India as well). Classical economics proper is really a product of the late seventeenth and eighteenth centuries, the industrial revolution and the insights of Enlightenment thinkers. Classical economics introduced concerns still familiar to modern economists: markets, supply and demand, productivity, prices and profits. Economics in its modern form is, however, more recent and can be traced to the mid- to late-nineteenth century and what is referred to as the *marginalist revolution*. The marginalists sought to resolve a long-standing problem in classical economics: that the use value (usefulness) and the exchange value (price) of a good were often unrelated. The resolution came in recognising that exchange value was related to *marginal utility* – the additional benefit a buyer gains when adding goods to his or her existing stock of that good, not the absolute usefulness of the good. The dominance of this insight combined with traditional concerns justifies post-marginalist economics being referred to as *neo-classical economics – new* classical economics. The idea of marginal utility immediately suggested using mathematical functions to model demand and especially the use of calculus as a mathematical technique. This is sometimes referred to as economics' 'mathematical turn' as an extensive use of mathematics is a feature of much modern economic thinking.

Neo-classical economics does not challenge the assumptions made by classical economics. Indeed, it might be argued that it attempts to develop more sophisticated insights from them. These assumptions have been expressed in various ways. The following summary is intended to represent the fount from which many strands of economic thinking emerge. It should be noted that not all these assumptions are *formally* required as some may be derived from others, but it is useful to be explicit here.

Two assumptions are about the way sell–buy transactions work:

1.1   Supply and demand for goods is a function of their price.
1.2   Markets are costless to set up and run: transactions are 'free' and 'frictionless'.

A further four are about the nature of human beings:

2.1   All individuals in an economy are rational and aim to maximise their personal satisfaction (utility) from the goods they might obtain.
2.2   All individuals are perfectly efficient processors of information.
2.3   All individuals know all there is to know, know what others know and know that others know what they know . . . ad infinitum. This is referred to as *common knowledge*.
2.4   Humans demonstrate marginal utility: that is, an individual's demand for a particular good (and hence the price they are willing to pay to gain an extra unit of that good) will decline as his or her possession of that good increases.

Four are about the nature of industries:

3.1   Within an industry all goods are *homogeneous*; that is, the goods from one firm within an industry can be swapped for those of another firm within the same industry without the buyer noticing a difference (the goods have exactly the same utility).
3.2   Within an industry there are an infinite number of firms.
3.3   Between industries all goods are *heterogeneous*; that is, no two goods from different industries can be switched in any way, they do entirely different jobs as far as the buyer is concerned.
3.4   It is costless for the buyer to swap between suppliers within the same industry.

Three assumptions are about the nature of the firm:

4.1   Individual firms are 'atomic': they have no internal structure (of interest). This assumption really claims that all transactions are through the market mechanism. All the firm's resources (including labour) are provided through market exchanges.
4.2   A firm entering an industry does not face any costs in excess of those faced by firms already within the industry.
4.3   A firm leaving an industry can sell the assets it has been using without loss.

Taken together, it can be demonstrated that an economy based on these assumptions will, *inter alia*, have open, efficient markets (supply and demand will be equalised), resources will be used in the most efficient way possible and total wealth will be maximised. Individual firms will take a market-determined price for their product and will increase production until marginal revenues equal marginal costs. These assumptions are clearly unrealistic. They do not paint a convincing picture of the world as we know it and many critiques of neo-classical economics are based on pointing this out. The term *Homo oeconomicus* (economic man) is sometimes used with a hint of sarcasm to suggest that economists are talking about a species different to we *Homo sapiens*. However, the realism of the assumptions is not really at issue. What matters is: do they lead to theories that provide a good description of the way in which the world works? The best answer is: in broad terms, yes. Classical economic theory does lead to a successful generalised picture of human exchange relationships. But there is a lot of detail that cannot be accounted for. There are such things as markets and they do seem to optimise the use of resources (as political experiments in eliminating markets quickly demonstrate). Economies with open and free markets tend to be wealthier and grow faster. However, neo-classical economics cannot explain the existence of entrepreneurs as a distinct class of economic actor. The reason is transparent: entrepreneurs are human beings, and neo-classical theory collects together all human beings under one set of assumptions. So all human beings are the same. It is pointless to talk about *any* distinct set of human beings. We are, if you like, *all* entrepreneurs. It is worthwhile here to reflect back on Section 1.3, where we faced difficulties in attempting to distinguish entrepreneurs from other sorts of economic actor such as managers and investors. Yet we intuitively see entrepreneurs as a distinct class, different from other 'ordinary' managers and, more importantly, we recognise that they have a distinct role to play in making economies work. One motivation for diversions from neo-classical economics is to try to take account of this.

Austrian School economics

Shortly after its inception, a group of economists dissented from the neo-classical school. This School got its name from the fact that many of its leading thinkers, such as Carl Menger (1840–1921), Friedrich von Wieser (1851–1926) and Eugen Bohm-Bawerk (1851–1914) were based in Vienna. Major contributions to the school's thinking include those by von Mises (1949), Hayek (1937, 1940, 1948) and Kirzner (1979, 1982, 1985, 1997). The central critique of classical thinking was not so much about its assumptions, but with the conclusion that economies were in equilibrium and so essentially timeless. A neo-classical economy cannot go anywhere: its equilibrium 'freezes' it into a perfected end-state from which 'it' cannot depart (even if 'it' wanted to, which 'it' would not). Neo-classical economics does not really have any use for the notion of time. In the real world, of course, economies change constantly. New innovations come along. Economies tend to grow in value over time, with many ups and downs along the way. Austrian School economics should really be regarded as a broad church of differing economic ideas rather than as a single approach. However, enough commonality (especially in disagreements with the neo-classical school) justifies the different ideas being united under a single heading. The key idea in Austrian economics is that competition is an ongoing *process* rather than a *force* that sustains an economy at a static equilibrium. Economies, it suggests, are inevitably out of equilibrium. This equilibrium was a perfected end-point towards which the economy might progress over time, but it never got there, because the equilibrium itself was constantly shifting. Conception of human nature was also different. Rather than the perfected, satisfied, information processor, humans are seen as essentially unsatisfied and limited in their intellectual capacity. We are not content, we can imagine better worlds and we do seek changes to achieve them. In an important respect Austrian School economics brings the individual (and individual attitudes) back into economics and it emphasises the exchanges individuals make rather than the equilibrating outcomes of large numbers of impersonal exchanges.

If competition is a process driven by individuals then the role of the entrepreneur becomes clear. Economies are out of equilibrium, leaving some individuals unsatisfied. The entrepreneur emerges because of the opportunity to offer goods and services that satisfy these outstanding needs. In doing so, the entrepreneur moves the economy a little bit closer to equilibrium, increasing its value. It is from this additional value that the entrepreneur gains his or her rewards. Of course, the entrepreneur is not aware of this in a grand sense. Entrepreneurs rarely think at such a level. Rather they are motivated by the possibility of addressing their own needs through the entrepreneurial option. Another way of thinking about this is that entrepreneurs must seek out and exploit information about new opportunities that is not being used (a neo-classical economy uses all possible information). However, this knowledge is not perfect. There is always an element of uncertainty in what to offer, where and when. Entrepreneurs make decisions at a local level, seeking out proximal opportunities in their immediate environment. No one entrepreneur could be aware of all the opportunities an economy might present. This is why there is room for a great number of entrepreneurs. Even acting collectively, though, they can never deliver an unattainable equilibrium. So entrepreneurial activity creates, it does not exclude, possibilities for future entrepreneurs. The Italian economist Attilio da Empoli (1904–1948) made an important, and largely independent, contribution to this line of thinking with his 1926 (translated to English, 1931) work *The Theory of Economic Equilibrium*. Interestingly, Da Empoli's views (as recounted by Wagner, 2001) argue that 'competition' should not be regarded as an adjective (a tag we apply to an organisation denoting its *type*) but as a verb (what the firm *does*).

Heterogeneous demand theory

One of the assumptions in neo-classical economics is that of product homogeneity within industries and product heterogeneity between industries (assumptions 3.1 and 3.3 above). This implies that the products offered by all firms within an industry are perfect replacements for each other and so are effectively identical as far as the buyer is concerned. Products from different industries are totally different and cannot replace each other in any way. Because there are only a finite number of industries, there are a finite number of products. A number of economists have taken issue with these assumptions (Chamberlin, 1933; Robinson, 1933; Smith, 1956; Alderson, 1957, 1965; McCarthy, 1960; Myers, 1996 are of particular note). *Heterogeneous demand theory* points out that firms within a particular industry do not offer homogenous products at a market dictated price. Rather they actively *market* products by distinguishing them to appeal to particular groups of buyers, often with the intention of sustaining a price premium over market norms. So the products supplied by a particular industry may vary greatly. Think about automobiles, travel or beauty products, for example. These are clearly not commodities. From the perspective of a particular buyer, different products within these categories are not perfectly substitutable. The driver of a Porsche may not feel like swapping with the owner of a small family car. A six-month cruise has different appeal to a weekend break. A premium branded beauty lotion makes different claims than an own label product from a discount store. Differentiating products (either by adding features and/or by branding) aims to reduce the product's substitutability with other products – not to the level found between products from different industries, but certainly to the level where buyers will actively choose between them. Ultimately each producer's product is different to that of any competitor, a situation commonly encountered, especially among branded consumer goods. In a sense, each producer seeks a monopoly. This is not as strict a monopoly as found when a single supplier dominates an industry because buyers can ultimately go somewhere else and new producers can move in. It is just that they decide not to. For this reason Chamberlin (1933) labelled such a situation *monopolistic competition*. Similar ideas were developed in the German tradition by von Stackelberg (1933) and in the Italian tradition by da Empoli (1931) (see Keppler, 2001). Smith (1956) suggested that differences between products offered within an industry depended on five things specific to the supplier: *knowledge of markets*, *production process*, the firm's wider *resources*, *product research and development capabilities*, and *quality control standards*.

Differential demand theory suggests that the entrepreneur is fundamentally a *marketer*. He or she looks for what particular groups of buyers want from a product, identifies how existing products fail them and innovates new products that will serve them better. The entrepreneur does not just invent. He or she *positions* products within a market to maximise their difference from competitors and appeal to targeted buyer groups. To sustain this, he or she must innovate within and manage effectively the five factors Smith points out.

Differential advantage theory

Heterogeneous demand theory offers an explanation as to why firms differentiate their products but it leaves us with a rather static picture. Once all firms have differentiated to their (and their buyers') satisfaction, why should they make any changes? It says nothing about the *process* of competition in a *dynamic* sense. Clark (1940) developed heterogeneous demand theory and initiated a strand of economic thinking known as *differential advantage theory*. Clark's notion of *generic competition* has three fundamental aspects. First, buyers and seller do not associate randomly; rather they seek to pair up on a more permanent basis with specific firms seeking to serve the needs of specific buyer groups. Second, firms are limited in their ability to increase prices because, ultimately, buyers can go elsewhere if they feel prices are too high. Third – and this is the aspect that adds dynamism – firms are rivals for buyer's purchases and constantly seek to improve products to make them more attractive than those of competitors. The way in which such rivalry takes place depends on several factors, such as the number of firms relative to the number of buyers, how easy it is to make products different and how much it costs a firm to enter and exit a market. The heterogeneous demand thinkers were, in general, suspicious of differentiated products. It was initially seen as just another attempt to create monopolies. It was even suggested, as monopolies reduce total social welfare, product differentiation should be restricted by law. Clark, on the other hand, asked what exactly does a society *want* from competition, given that the abstract notion of welfare maximisation is not attainable? Clark emphasised the importance of people being able to get the products they wanted, firms surviving and innovating new products, economic growth, job creation and freedom for entrepreneurs to start new ventures. If these were being achieved to a society's satisfaction (a political and moral judgement, not just an economic one), then we should be happy with the competition we have.

Clark also made the point that firms are not profit maximisers in the classical sense. They certainly sought profits and would normally seek to increase them if they could. But not so at any cost. Firms might sacrifice short-term profits for a variety of reasons, including the need to reduce uncertainty, reinvestment for growth or to take on wider community responsibility. Alderson (1957, 1965) developed Clark's ideas with a particular emphasis on growth. What concerned managers most, he suggested, was the survival of the firm rather than profit maximisation. Gaining profits was a way to achieve this, but was not an end in itself. Profits were gained so as to preserve the firm's ability to maintain its differences from competitors, to keep buyers coming back and to grow the business.

The differential advantage approach resonates with the way in which entrepreneurs actually manage their businesses. Entrepreneurs do innovate to make their offerings different to competitors. They are interested in building and maintaining a buying community. Survival is often an explicit objective (especially in the early stages of the venture's life). Entrepreneurs are usually longer-term growth rather than immediate-profit orientated.

Industrial organisational economics

Different firms, and different industries, make different levels of profits. This is something neo-classical economics cannot explain. Industrial organisational economics (IOE) is essentially based on the idea that *excess* profits (those above and beyond those necessary to keep a firm in business) arise due to *market imperfections*. Market imperfections occur when classical assumptions fail to occur. Important instances are when there are only a small number of suppliers, giving rise to monopoly, costs associated with entering and exiting a new market, economies of scale, product differentiation and buyers substituting products from one industry with those of another. IOE represents an approach that is important in management thinking. It has been highly influential in the development of business strategy theory. The school has had three main stages of development. The first stage, initiated largely by Bain (1954, 1956, 1968) suggested that any firm was in a position where its competitive context presented a different mix of market imperfections. This market *structure* presented opportunities for managers to exploit these imperfections. But they could only do this if they built up the right sort of resources and ran the firm in a particular way, so-called managerial *conduct*. If they did so, then the firm's *performance* would be maximised. This *structure–conduct–performance* relationship is specific to each firm.

The second stage is particularly associated with the work of Porter (1980, 1985). Porter inverted Bain's idea. Rather than firms finding themselves in a structural position and then having to adjust their conduct to improve performance, Porter suggested that managers might actively seek out unexploited structures (market positions) that, given current conduct, or conduct that might be developed, would lead to superior performance. Put metaphorically: Bain suggests that if you are feeling cold, put on a coat; Porter suggests moving to somewhere warmer. Porter has been eloquent and effective in communicating his ideas. His books are among the very few economics texts that have mass-market appeal. Part of the attraction is that he talks in ways managers can readily understand and presents issues that they feel empowered to manage. A central suggestion is the idea of 'five forces' that dictate an industry's abilities to make profits: *industry competition*: the way in which firms compete with each other (especially on price); *entry barriers*: the costs faced by new firms when they enter a market in excess of those already present; *power* relative to suppliers and buyers: the ability to dictate terms to suppliers and the inability of buyers to go elsewhere; and availability of *substitutes*: the possibility of the buyer switching to an alternative product from a different industry. Given these factors, a firm will, ideally, seek out a position where competition is not on price, new entrants are restricted, power can be gained over suppliers and buyers, and few substitutes are available. In effect, the firm seeks out a (competitive) monopoly position. Porter's monopoly concept is much richer and more detailed than that provided by the neo-classical school, which limits it to market share dominance.

The third stage in the development of IOE reflects a change in both per-spective and methodology. The change in perspective has been from the (implicit) assumption of the static, 'given' nature of structural market imperfections that surround a firm or sector to a recognition that such imperfections are dynamic and result from interacting decision making by competitors, buyers and suppliers. The shift in methodology has been from studies based on cross-sectional analysis of a number of industries to game-theoretical analysis of *single* industries. This is sometimes referred to as *new* industrial organisational economics to distinguish it from the 'old' organisational industrial economics of Bain and Porter. Ghemawat is a leading thinker in the field and has produced a good account of it (1997). Game theory is quite mathematical. But in essence it concerns itself with situations in which managers make decisions knowing that managers in competing firms will make further decisions in response to their decisions, and so on (see Section 23.4). New industrial organisational economics is particularly powerful when dealing with competition between small numbers of firms in oligopolistic situations.

The role of the entrepreneur is seen slightly differently at each stage of IOE. In the first stage, the entrepreneur is someone who perceives an opportunity to acquire, mould and manage resources in a way that supports the right conduct given the structural imperfections in the markets in which his or her venture is situated. The second stage suggests that entrepreneurs recognise their conduct possibilities and seek out the opportunities presented by available market imperfections. These are, it might be argued, the ends of a spectrum of possibilities. In practice, entrepreneurs might undertake a mix of these options. New industrial organisational economics does not dissent from this. Rather, it adds the idea of the entrepreneur being not just a decision maker, but also a predictor of competitors' (and others') decisions and a refiner of strategic approach given their likely responses.

Resource-based theory

Thus far, relaxing one or more of the core assumptions of the neo-classical model has allowed a far more realistic picture of economic activity in general and competition in particular to be painted. However, all of the schools considered share a feature in common. They do not concern themselves, overtly at least, with what goes on *inside* the firm. Their main emphasis is with the context in which the firm operates. They do not explicitly challenge the notion of firms being atomic. *Resource-based theory* (and the *competence-based* and *resource-advantage* theories below) share an emphasis on internal aspects of the firm as determinants of performance. The central claims of resource-based theory, initiated by the work of Penrose (1959) are that: (a) resources are not inputs to production but collectively provide services that *support* production (resource *bundles*); (b) different firms have different resources available to them (resource *heterogeneity*); and (c) that there is some difficulty in transferring resources between firms (resource *immobility*). Resource heterogeneity suggests that some firms may perform better than competitors if their resources (strictly the services available from those resources) are better able to serve the competed market. Heterogeneity can only be maintained if the better-performing firm retains its resource base *and* competitors cannot imitate it. Imitation may be restricted by a number of mechanisms. A critical resource may be unique (sole access to a critical input, unique managerial talent or exclusive access to a distribution channel). It may be legally bound (a patent or copyright). More subtly, the causal relationship between a complex resource bundle and the resulting performance may not be clear (why, and in what way, does organisational 'culture' enhance performance? Wilcox-King and Zeithaml (2001) explore this issue). Further, resources differ in the ease with which they may be traded. Tangible assets such as production machinery may easily be sold. But organisational learning and a firm's reputation cannot be traded (other than by buying the entire organisation!). A competitor may be able to buy *tradable resources* quickly in the marketplace. But *non-tradable resources* can only be built up (accumulated) over time. And time is all a better-resourced competitor needs to gain, and maintain, a winning edge. Dierickx and Cool (1989) propose that this winning edge can be sustained if non-tradable resources have one or more of five properties. They must be: (a) difficult to build up quickly (a good reputation, for example, cannot be built overnight); (b) easier to add to than to start, so a firm with them can move forward faster than a competitor trying to obtain them (e.g. a firm that already has a strong brand name finds it easier to extend that brand to new products compared to starting a brand from scratch); (c) the resources work better when combined with existing resources (marketing works better for a firm that has good research and development capabilities than one that does not); (d) the resource can be maintained through further investment (e.g. training of staff in good distributors to keep them committed); and (e) why the resource works is ambiguous (why, for example, does an 'entrepreneurial attitude' help a firm?).

The examples here will make it clear that the proponents of the resource-based theory take a broad view of what constitutes a resource. Barney (1991), for example, defines resources as:

B(A)ll assets, capabilities, organizational processes, firm attributes, information, knowledge, etc. controlled by a firm to conceive of and implement strategies that improve its efficiency and effectiveness.c

Managers may recognise all these things as resources and may try to manage them. The problem is that such a broad conceptualisation of resources runs the risk of making resource-based theory self-fulfilling. It predicts that resources lead to performance, but when presented with a firm with unique resources (and all have some unique resources) that is performing well, it is not difficult to retrospectively account for its performance through some description of its resource uniqueness. Comparisons between firms do not help, because each firm is, by assumption, unique. If it falls into this trap, the theory can be no more than rhetoric. This critique aside, resource-based theory does suggest a particular role for the entrepreneur. When faced with an opportunity, he or she must access and acquire relevant resources and then co-ordinate and configure them in a particularly appropriate way so that *collectively* they deliver value in a unique and inimitable manner. And this goes beyond just gaining the right assets and using them efficiently. It includes the management of operational process and 'higher-order processes' such as organisational learning and culture and network relationships (see Section 10.5). Alvarez and Busenitz (2001) and Alvarez and Barney (2002) provide general reviews of resource-based theory in entrepreneurship. Bergmann-Lichenstein and Brush (2001) study how resource bundles develop in an entrepreneurial business over time.

Competence-based theory

Competence-based theory shares many features with the resource-based theory but it has a slightly different emphasis and defines a 'competence' more narrowly than resource-based theory does 'resource'. This approach has developed largely within the field of strategic management. It is nascent in early works within the field (e.g. Selznick, 1957; Andrews, 1971) and has been an undercurrent since. This approach places less emphasis on resource inimitability (which it sees as essentially static) and more on the dynamic replenishment of quickly erodible advantages. Put metaphorically, if resource-based theory sees the winners as those who reach mountain peaks before others, competence-based theory sees them keeping ahead in a (neverending) race that they could fall back in and lose at any time. Prahalad and Hamel (1990) suggest that competitiveness ultimately comes from producing better (more demanded) products more quickly. Such products should be *unanticipated* by competitors. Once competitors see such products are in demand, they will imitate them. But by the time they do, the succeeding firm will have the next round of unanticipated winners in place. To keep ahead, a firm uses its *core competences*. A core competence is anything that: (a) allows access to a wide variety of markets; (b) offers real and perceivable benefits to buyers; (c) is difficult (expensive!) for competitors to imitate; and (d) is extendable to other product/markets in the future. There is a temptation to define core competences in a broad way and, as with resource-based theory, run the risk of making the theory tautological. But given the characteristics of core competences a more limited list of proximal capabilities seems relevant. In particular, core competences deliver an ability to source, process and act on information about opportunities in the marketplace (know what buyers want), innovate new products quickly and effectively, produce those products profitably, and distribute them cost-effectively to a high number of buyers *better than competitors*. Foss (1997) gives a full account of resource- and competence-based thinking within strategic management). Yu (2001) discusses small-firm performance from a capabilities perspective. Jones and Tilley (2003) provide a thorough account of competences and competitive advantage in small businesses.

In a way, competence-based theory offers more hope to the entrepreneur than resource-based theory. Given the characteristics of inimitable resource bundles suggested by resource-based theory, it would seem that advantages would lie with incumbents rather than with entrepreneurs who try to enter a new market. This is because they are better managed in an incremental way than by trying to invent them quickly. While core competences must be managed incrementally, they may, on the other hand be obtained through a radical and unanticipated innovation. The entrepreneur's responsibility, then, is to recognise what core competences are necessary to exploit a particular opportunity, to innovate in their achievement and to sustain them.

Transaction cost economics

The theories considered so far have prioritised the role of the firm's external environment (heterogeneous demand theory, differential advantage theory, industrial organisation economics) or the firm's internal aspects (resource-based theory, competence-based theory) as determinants of performance. However, none addresses (directly at least) a central issue that neo-classical economics could not explain: why do firms exist at all? The problem is this. A firm is an economic organisation within which market mechanisms are inhibited. A firm *is* a firm (an organisation) because it has some permanence. The resources a firm has are not traded within it (attempts to introduce internal markets within firms (see, for example, Cowen and Parker, 1997) do so to generate information, not real trading opportunities). The members of the firm agree to long-term contracts (though what constitutes 'long' varies enormously) that will not be buffeted by market forces. After all, a contract of employment has some duration. The members of the firm do not offer their services in a spot market every day. Why should such institutional arrangements exist at all? This is an issue: because markets generate price information they are the best mechanism for allocating resources to where they can best be used (a neo-classical notion, but none of the theories we have considered so far seriously challenges this). Internally, firms lack this information. This is why one of the main tasks of strategic management theory is to develop guides (portfolio methods) that tell managers how resources should be shared among the numerous projects available to the firm in the absence of clear price guidance. So why do firms exist when they should be less effective than the market nexus?

Transaction cost economics addresses this issue directly. Its origins can be traced back to Coase (1937), but its full fruition in organisation studies has come largely from the work of Williamson (1996 gives a good summary of his numerous contributions). The fundamental idea of transaction cost economics is that market transactions have a cost associated with them that is additional to the value of the good exchanged. Prosaically, when we pay a price for a good, that price must include the cost of the transaction, not just the final value of the good. Markets are not 'free' and 'frictionless' (assumption 1.2 in the neo-classical model). This additional cost arises from the need to search out suppliers and then negotiate, maintain and enforce contracts with them. Williamson (1994) defines it fully thus:

> (The) *ex ante* costs of drafting, negotiating and *safeguarding* an agreement [to transact] and more especially the *ex post* costs of maladaption and adjustment that arise when contract execution is misaligned as a result of gaps, errors, omissions and unanticipated disturbances.

The key point here is that if a contract is not made, or fully specified, then there could be a cost if the transaction does not result in what the buyer expected (either because of genuine misunderstanding or fraudulent behaviour on the part of the supplier). Such contracts could potentially exist wherever there are technologically separable boundaries between inputs. However, if the cost of establishing and sustaining such contracts become too high, then there is a temptation to forgo the market and bring the production of such components 'in house', i.e. within an organisational structure, where the transaction is agreed on a long-term basis and can be fully monitored using organisational mechanisms. Price information is lost, but the cost of this (in reduced decision-making capability) is less than the value gained from reducing contract costs. In the transactional cost view, the entrepreneur is responsible for bringing together a set of transactions within an organisation. He or she will look for transactions where the marginal cost of contracting is greater than the marginal cost of using an organisational lock-in to ensure transaction integrity – in short, make-or-buy and sell-or-add-more-value decisions. What would encourage an entrepreneur to bring an activity into the venture? Transactional cost economics predicts that priority would be given to transactions that: (a) would have a high cost if they went wrong; (b) had a high probability of going wrong; and (c) were difficult or costly to police (using market mechanisms). Entrepreneurs who were more acute in judging these factors and managing the organisational changes necessary to absorb the transactions would be more successful.

Evolutionary economics

'Evolution' is a commonly encountered word. It entered the modern consciousness as a result of the work of Charles Darwin in the nineteenth century, through which he suggested a mechanism – *natural selection* – that led to changes in the form of living organisms over millions of years. Living things are adapted to their environments. Their body forms, biochemistry and behaviour are right for the type of life they live. Natural selection explains this in the following way. First, given any population of the same type of organism (a species), individuals within that species will vary (to some degree) in their ability to gain essential resources (food, water, the chance to reproduce). Given this variation, some individuals within the species will be more successful than others. Second, living organisms reproduce themselves. Genetic mechanisms allow the organism to make (potentially many) copies of itself. Given the chance, the number of individuals (the population) would increase exponentially. However, this copying is not perfect. Reproduction generates further variation. Third, the resources the organism needs are limited (or quickly become so as population increases). Given limited resources, the organisms with variations that allow them to gain resources better will tend to survive and reproduce further. Those without those variations will not, and will not live to see copies of themselves in the next generation. Natural selection not only keeps the population in check, but also ensures that each generation will have individuals slightly different (better adapted) than the previous generation.

This digression into evolutionary theory is necessary because it provides the founding metaphor for evolutionary economics. It uses the natural selection model to explain the variety of, survival of and changes within economic populations. As with the Austrian School, evolutionary economics represents a broad church of ideas rather than a single theory. But what they all have in common is a set of assumptions:

- individual entities within an economy come in particular types, but that there is some variation between individuals within those types;
- the entities reproduce themselves in a sequence of generations;
- variation between entities leads to different abilities to reproduce into the next generation;
- selective forces eliminate those (types or forms) that are less well able to reproduce themselves.

Different strands within evolutionary economics differ in what they see as entities, the nature of the variation they exhibit, the way in which the entities 'reproduce' themselves and the source of selective forces. What constitutes an entity? Is it an individual (e.g. an entrepreneur), a firm, a network of firms, an industry or a whole economic system? How should variation between individuals be described? In terms of personal capabilities, market position, resource endowments or performance? What do we mean by reproduction? Economic entities clearly do not reproduce in the same way living organisms do. Is it just surviving (i.e. still being present in the next generation (time period)? Is it represented by business growth? Is it spawning new products and entering new markets? And what are the selective forces? They must be linked to the (in)ability to gain the resources necessary for survival. But, as seen in the discussion of resource-advantage theory, the meaning of resources is not precise. Does it mean external resources (customers' money, investment capital) or does it mean internal resources (inimitable resources, core competences)? Any combination of these factors could, in principle, lead to a distinct evolutionary theory. They would not necessarily exclude each other. However, any evolutionary view of entrepreneurship faces a decision at this point. How close to the Darwinian metaphor does it wish to stick? Living organisms can change neither themselves nor their environment. They are passive markers of evolutionary change, not active participants within it. Further, Darwinian evolution suggests no overall design or direction of progress. Evolution is blind and acts at instants. Here the metaphor starts to break down. Can the entities in an economic system (individuals or collections of individuals) not make sense of their world and actively participate in it, or even change it? Do they not change themselves in response to new information? Do they not have goals that suggest progress? After all, in Darwinian evolution individuals do not adapt, *succeeding generations* do. Individuals are fixedly adapted from the moment they are born. This can lead to confusion. An example of this is Nelson and Winter (1982) who infer that adaption is 'all regular and predictable behaviour patterns of firms' (p. 14) and that these should be regarded as the equivalent of 'genes' in evolutionary biology. An animal cannot change its genes, but a firm can be unpredictable and change its behaviour patterns. Johnson and Van de Ven (2002) suggest that 'evolutionary' theories of organisations fall into one of four types depending on the extent to which they allow for (a) individual organisations to change themselves – *organisational inertia* and (b) the extent to which the individuals can change their environment – *environment exogenicity*. This scheme is illustrated in Figure 2.1.

Given that each of these approaches uses (some might suggest misuses) the evolutionary metaphor in quite different ways it is worth considering them and their implications for understanding entrepreneurship separately.

Population ecology theory

Ecology is the study of systems of interacting living organisms using the Darwinian paradigm. Because it suggests that economic entities (usually taken as firms) can change neither themselves nor their environment it represents the closest reading of

Figure 2.1			

Johnson and Van de Ven's model of evolutionary theories (with modifications)

	Ability to change firm	
	High	*Low*
Ability to change environment — *High*	Industrial community theory	New institutional economics
Ability to change environment — *Low*	Organisational evolution theory	Population ecology theory

the Darwinian metaphor. Hence, the word 'ecology' in population ecology theory is (analogously) literal. Firms within a sector are homogeneous and are, at best, able to choose which markets to enter and whether to co-operate with each other. But essentially a firm's form, strategy and behaviour are fixed and result from its founding characteristics. The number (and total capacity) of firms within the sector is limited by its *carrying capacity*: the level of (competed for) resources made available, including, critically, the capital customers will provide through purchases. Clearly within this model the role of the entrepreneur is quite limited. Aside from imparting some founding character, the entrepreneur can only select which markets to operate within and whether to co-operate with other firms. The success or failure of businesses is a result of there being sufficient, or too limited, a carrying capacity within the sector. This is not something under the control of the entrepreneur. However, the survival or not of individual firms is not really the concern of the theory; it is the structure of *populations* of firms within industries. A leading early work in this area is that of Hannan and Freeman (1977).

New institutional economics

New institutional theory, like population ecology theory, maintains that firms are limited in the degree to which they are able to modify their internal constitution, but does suggest that firms can modify their environments. Firms are not supposed to modify their environment in any way they wish, of course. Rather, the theory supposes that firms act individually, or collectively, to modify their *legitimacy*. The origins of new institutional economics can be traced back to the work of Hamilton (1932) and Commons (1924). A modern exponent of the view is Hodgson (1993). Within institutional economics, the term 'institution' is meant more widely than that of 'organisation'. According to Hamilton (1932) an institution is:

❝A way of thought or action of some prevalence and permanence which is embedded in a group or the customs of a people . . . (and which fixes) . . . the confines of and imposes form upon the activities of human beings.❞

In these terms an institution is something like what (some) anthropologists regard as a 'culture'. It is a social phenomenon that defines the latitude of what individuals are allowed to do, specifies what they should do and tells them what they cannot do. Although there are several shades of interpretation within this framework, an organisation's resources are regarded as cultural capabilities, not just productive assets. An entrepreneur moving into a new sector (or establishing an entirely new one) will not so much adapt the firm to fit with new opportunities, but seek to build legitimacy with stakeholders such as investors, customers, employees and suppliers and beyond to government and society as a whole. One way of creating legitimacy is for the entrepreneur to present his or herself as an 'outsider' who is challenging (and perhaps being repressed by) an 'old guard' of established businesses that seek to maintain their dominance and hence their ability to exploit their customers, and so is worthy of support. This is certainly a common narrative in press and bio-graphical accounts of entrepreneurs. Ultimately the entrepreneur is not just a creator of firms, but also the architect of a new institutional system of beliefs and values.

Organisational evolution theory

Organisational evolutionary theory regards the unit of evolution as the individual firm, rather than the industry of population ecology. The environment is a given, managers cannot change it in any way. But firms can, and do, change themselves. This is of course consistent with the heterogeneous demand, resource and capability perspectives discussed above. Where it parts company is in the way it views the process of firms achieving the right resources or capabilities. Those outside the evolutionary framework (discussed above) imply (perhaps implicitly) that making an organisation right for the opportunities it exploits is a matter of *design*. The entrepreneur (in particular) constructs the organisation to some sort of strategic 'blueprint'. Organisational evolutionary theories deny the possibility of such a design being available in advance. Rather entrepreneurs learn to structure their organisations and enhance their strategies in a gradual – *incremental* – way as a result of learning that arises from success and failure feedback. Quinn (1978) gives a good account of this manner of strategy formation. In this view entrepreneurs are repositories and facilitators of *organisational learning*. An effective entrepreneur is not one who from the outset is able to plan a particularly effective organisational end form, but one who is able to make an organisation responsive to new informa-tion and reactive towards new opportunities. Different strands of organisational evolution theory allow for and prioritise the evolution of different aspects of the organisation. The most extensive allow for the entrepreneur to modify the organ-isation along a large number of dimensions simultaneously, thus making organisa-tional learning a challenging and complex task. Nelson and Winter's *Evolutionary Theory of Economic Change* (1982) is seminal in this area. Organisational evolution theory removes the need for design in organisational structuring just as Darwin's theory of evolution removed the need for an external designer of living organisms, but, unlike conventional evolutionary theory it makes the individual firm not adapted, but *adaptable*, in a way living organisms are not. Because they can change, selection is between organisations that can learn and those that cannot learn to modify themselves in light of changing environmental (resource providing) conditions.

Industrial community theory

This is the most general evolutionary theory in that it allows for firms to change both themselves and also their environments. This approach gives the 'richest' picture of how entrepreneurs compete, but with some loss of theoretical specificity. Firms are regarded as heterogeneous. Every firm is individual and may vary either in terms of the industry position and/or their internal capabilities. In this respect, the industrial community view is similar to the organisational evolution view. However, the approach shares the perspective of the new institutional view that firms can actively adapt their environments. They do this by forming mutually supporting coalitions or communities of businesses that have an interest in supporting each other. This network of relationships provides conduits along which pass key resources such as productive labour, financing and information. A clear exposition of this perspective is given by Van de Ven and Garud (1989). Within this view, one of the entrepreneur's key roles is to build and maintain this network of relationships, which is critical to resource provision.

Economic sociology

Thus far, all of the perspectives on the role of the entrepreneur have been drawn largely from the economic tradition within the social sciences. Economic sociology casts its net wider to include traditions within sociological thinking as well. This tradition has a long history. The works of pioneering social theorists such as Max Weber (1864–1920), Emile Durkheim (1858–1917) and Karl Polyani (1886–1964) are frequently cited. More recent contributors include Talcot Parsons (1902–1979), N.J. Smelser (1930–) and Granovetter (see 1985). Its more radical strands are influenced by the work of Karl Mark (1818–1883). One of the key claims within the economic sociology view is that economics (both neo-classical and the views derived from it) cannot account for the realities of organisational life because it takes as its starting point the assumption that human beings are (essentially) self-interested and (to a greater or lesser degree) rational. It ignores the role of socialisation and the influence of social structures on human behaviour. In general terms, these are the mechanisms that govern human behaviour and inculcate cultural and moral norms within a society. Some argue these social forces impede pure competitive behaviour and this must be accounted for. Entrepreneurs sometimes seem to hold off on intense competition if they feel such would break social taboos. Others argue that socialisation may actually increase competitive behaviour as some types of socialisation provide legitimacy for aggressive business actions. The society sets harsher rules for the game. All economic sociologists agree though, that sociology (with its theoretical approaches and methodology) brings these forces back into perspective. This view places a lot of emphasis on social relationships, group and organisational cultural values and the role of trust. Within this view, the entrepreneur is not just a manager of a business organisation. He or she is one who is both subject to, and in turn creates, cultural norms through business practice. Examples of study of entrepreneurship within this sociological perspective are those by Mumby-Croft and Hackley (1997) and by Zafirovski (1999).

It might be argued that all of the things these different schools of economic thinking say about the entrepreneur are true, but that each discusses a different aspect of the entrepreneur. Further, integrating the perspective of different schools might provide a more complete picture. There have been many attempts in this direction (see, for example, Cockburn *et al.*, 2000; Makadok, 2001). Of particular interest currently is integration of industrial organisational economic and resource-based perspectives. There are, however, three caveats when considering integration. First, many proponents of the different schools would argue that they have no intention of creating a complete picture; rather they are prioritising the *fundamental* aspect of entrepreneurs' activity. Integration subsumes this issue of priority. Second, integrating different perspectives suggests a more complex role for the entrepreneur and this creates methodological problems in testing the predictions of such integrations. Third, different perspectives are often based on different theoretical assumptions. Theoretically sound integration demands the coherence of such assumptions, which may not always be the case.

(2.2) Entrepreneurship: wealth, utility and welfare

Entrepreneurs, wealth creation and distribution

> **Key learning outcome**
>
> An introduction to some of the broader moral and political issues surrounding entrepreneurship. An appreciation of the economic notions of *wealth maximisation*, *wealth distribution* and *individual utility maximisation*. A recognition of the political and moral stances that are critical of these notions and the distinction between *utility* and *human welfare*. An insight into the debate about whether economic behaviour is determined by our evolutionary heritage or by more immediate social factors, and an introduction to the issue of what determines the morality of an action: *motives* for the act, the act *itself* or the *consequences* of the act.

The world is getting richer. The Western world (Western Europe plus North America) is the global economic power-house (over 70 per cent of total world economic output). Global prosperity has been added to greatly by the growth (albeit with a recent stall) in Southeast Asia, China and to a lesser degree India, and (with some recent economic crises) Latin America. Some growth has occurred in sub-Saharan Africa, especially Southern Africa, though generally economic growth in Africa is a cause for concern. The question of what drives this increase in global wealth is an issue that engenders not just economic, but also political and moral debate. We may attribute this increase in wealth (wholly, or in part) to one or more of three economic institutions: *entrepreneurial activity* (in smaller firms), large, *established corporations* or *government*. While the contribution to wealth creation of private enterprise seems transparent, the role of government is questionable. Most economists would now agree that while government plays an important part in regulating business (setting out the playing field, as it were), managing macroeconomic stability (keeping the playing field level) and redistributing wealth (sharing the rewards for the game), it is not primarily a *generator* of wealth. Rather, government must be regarded as a cost, properly paid for (via taxation) for the services it delivers. The failure of the communist system in central and eastern Europe (and parts of the emerging world), which prioritised government over enterprise, adds weight to this argument. The role of global corporations (of particular concern to the environmental and anti-globalisation lobbies) is important. Undoubtedly, they have a critical function in maintaining wealth levels and driving investment into the developing world. This said, most economists would agree that entrepreneurs create a significant degree of *new* wealth, not least because entrepreneurs challenge the 'old order' by introducing new and innovative products, by driving competition and by challenging monopolies. The answers to these debates lie in economics.

The trend towards an increasingly formal mathematical language for economics has led some economists to regret its emergence from, and particularly its distinction from, its historical form, *political economics*. Political economics was concerned not only with the resource allocation consequences of economic transactions and the arrangement of economic institutions that maximise wealth (the key concerns of modern economics), but also their political implications, ethical justification and moral necessity. Historically, these domains were not seen as essentially distinct. Modern economics, its critics argue, takes for granted the priority of (and without challenge the ethical superiority of) individual wealth maximisation, rather than the distribution of wealth. For example, *Pareto optimality* is a criterion introduced into many mathematical models in economics. Pareto optimality is achieved when an economy is in a state where total wealth is maximised *and* the wealth of any one individual cannot be increased without reducing the wealth of another individual. Pareto optimality is essentially a mathematical formulation about the properties of an economy in equilibrium, when demand equals supply and all markets clear. This criterion does not foreclose the possibility that one individual is very rich, but all others are very poor. Pareto optimality says a lot about the total wealth of an economy, but nothing about how such wealth ought to be distributed within that economy. It can be argued that Pareto optimality is simply a description of the state an economy will finish up with (with certain assumptions allowed). It is not a recommendation that that is how a society *should be*. However, it does imply that any attempt to spread that individual's wealth more evenly (say through government intervention through taxation) will actually reduce the overall wealth of the system and it is hard to disentangle this proposition from political and moral judgements. So be it, critics argue. Better a poorer, but more equitable world! We would prefer to be less well off in a just world, than slightly richer in an unjust world. Such choices take us beyond the formal domain of economics into political and ethical debates. An excellent account of these is provided by Little (2002). These are choices about the kind of world we want.

Socialism has traditionally argued that equality is an end in itself, an end that should have priority over wealth creation. Libertarians (who believe in the right of individuals to make choices (and so create free markets) unencumbered by governmental intervention) would argue that while a more equitable world may be preferable to some, its 'cost' in terms of the restriction of individual liberty is a cost too much. Eco-radicals would claim that conventional economic thinking devalues the natural world because it fails (as they see it) to take account of things for which there are no markets and hence no price. Some feminists criticise conventional economics because it does not account for the value of women who work as home keepers compared to men who sell their labour in a conventional labour market (again, there are no conventional markets within family life). The philosopher John Rawls presented an alternative to the notion of Pareto optimality in his book *A Theory of Justice* (1971). In this work he suggests that an economic system is morally optimal if it fulfils three conditions. First, each individual should have a right to the greatest liberty compatible with a like liberty for all others; second, individuals should, ideally, have equal access to opportunities; and third, this liberty itself should be restricted only if it improves the welfare of the worst off to a level not above that of the second worst off. Government intervention may be necessary to see these three things happen. Hausman and McPherson (1996) provide a general discussion of the moral implications of different avenues of economic analysis.

Entrepreneurs and social welfare

An idea that is fundamental to economics is that of *utility*. Utility can be defined (somewhat redundantly) as being the *usefulness* of a resource or situation or the degree of satisfaction it brings. Modern economics regards utility as the thing rational decision makers *maximise*. The revealed preference school of economics thinks of utility as being revealed through the preferences of decision makers. Many philosophers find this circularity unsatisfactory. Utility, they argue, must be defined in its own terms as the difference it makes to the quality of individual and collective lives. They would argue for a primarily moral as opposed to economic foundation of utility. Some would prefer the term utility were left to economics and let moral philosophers talk about *welfare* instead. Welfare is difficult to define and moral philosophers still debate its exact meaning (for the interested student, Wayne Sumner (1996) provides an accessible account of this debate). Some argue that welfare is a property of the external objects humans consume. Others argue that it is internal to the human mind and is the *effect* that consumption has. But most agree it means more than *just* wealth or possessions. Most would agree that issues such as the quality of life, intellectual and political freedom and opportunity are also important. The economist Amartya Sen recently won the Nobel Prize for his work in this area. His superbly written books make complex ideas in welfare economics understandable and are highly recommended further reading. The responsibility of entrepreneurs to create *welfare*, rather than just *wealth*, is of course a view that one might take a number of different positions on depending not least on one's political and ethical perspective and the resulting belief as to what constitutes welfare. Perspectives range from the idea that entrepreneurs' social responsibilities are prior to and should take priority over economic interest, to the suggestion that entrepreneurs are purely responsible for creating commercially successful business organisations and rewarding investors and have only minimal (if any) wider social responsibility, other than their compliance with legal and basic social norms (the issue of social responsibility will be considered further in Section 12.5). The role of business organisations, not least entrepreneurial organisations, as the harbingers of change, as social entities and in relation to their ethical responsibilities to stakeholders other than investors is an area of growing interest. Some economists suggest we must be wary of the idea of compromise over welfare values. Just because we are aware of our own welfare, it does not mean that the collective welfare of a group of individuals is easy to achieve. A number of so-called 'impossibility theorems' suggest that it is not possible to achieve a collective agreement between democratic individuals (all are equal and no one's welfare is given priority over another's) as to what is the best compromise, the option all will agree is the best (so-called unanimity) in welfare delivery given that small changes in welfare (say because of an individual's inability to decide over minor changes in what he or she wants) are unimportant. Put prosaically, democracy cannot deliver a result that pleases everybody. But, as Winston Churchill would have added, democracy is the worst system of government except for all the rest!

The determinacy of entrepreneurial behaviour

The debate over the moral rectitude of different economic systems is leavened by debate over the extent to which human behaviour is determined by evolutionary imperatives. Social scientists are divided over the contrary views that human behaviour is (largely) consequential on cognitive-psychological patterns established early in our evolutionary history or is much more recent and results from immediate social drivers. This debate will be raised again when evolutionary psychology is noted in Section 3.2. At this stage it is worth noting that the debate is not just one about scientific evidence; it is very much one about the political and moral implications of the beliefs such views (might?) engender. While we may regard entrepreneurial behaviour as being something essentially modern (in evolutionary terms) and motivated by the particular opportunities modern economies present to aspiring individuals, it seems entrepreneurial opportunities may have a deep history. The notion of a 'cave man' (though our ancestors rarely lived in caves) chipping away at a stone tool for his (*sic*) own use, perhaps as part of a small family group, is appealing. However, modern palaeological research suggests that our ancestors were very sophisticated in their social arrangements. Even deep in the Palaeolithic (the old stone age, say half a million years ago, when we should talk about our predecessor species, *Homo erectus*) there is archaeological evidence that tools were not produced by all. Rather, they were the produce of specialists who worked at 'factory sites'. Toolmakers presumably exchanged the tools they produced for food gathered by 'specialist' hunters. The numerous innovations in stone tools that feature as we move to the invention of agriculture some 10,000 years ago can then be properly regarded as entrepreneurial innovations, encouraged as tool producers competed with each other. This suggests that not only are our economic arrangements a consequence of an evolutionarily endowed psychology, but that our psychology is a product of an evolutionary drive for economically motivated social organisation. Ofek (2001) explores this issue at length.

Moral judgements about entrepreneurs

What does all this mean for modern entrepreneurs, the way in which we regard them and the role we see as proper from them? There is no doubt that task differentiation is economically efficient; that specialism creates wealth. It also seems clear that many aspects of our psychology have evolved to maintain economically valuable relationships (this is a point that we will return to when we discuss game theory in Section 23.4). But we should be cautious in concluding that just because a certain mode of behaviour has an evolutionary imperative that we must accept it without question or regard such a mode of behaviour is economically or morally correct. We are not slaves to our behavioural inheritance; our behaviour is flexible and we use it to make our way in the world. Our judgement of the ethical content of what entrepreneurs specifically do (and more generally what *all* ethical agents do) is not confined simply to consideration of the actions they take. Our judgement is also based on the *motivation* agents have when acting and the *consequences* of those acts. Different moral theories are based on differing emphasis on each of these factors. Moral theories that emphasise the motivation of acts are *motivist* theories. We are taking a motivist position, for example, if we judge a business more harshly if it pollutes in an attempt to maximise profits than if it had released exactly the same pollution (and caused exactly the same environmental damage) as a result of an accident it tried to avoid. Ethical theories based purely on the act itself taken are referred to as *deontological* theories. A deontological theory says that some act or other is moral (or otherwise) as a result of the act itself, nothing else. Someone who insists that it is wrong *in any circumstances* to test a new medical product on animals is taking a deontological position. Such a position would insist that no matter what benefits it might bring, testing things on animals is, in itself, inherently and simply wrong. A *consequentialist* position prioritises not the motivation for an act, or even the act itself, but the *consequences* of that act. We may feel it is wrong for a business based in the West to employ (exploit?) 'cheap' labour in a developing country, even if high local wage rates (but low compared to the home country) are paid. If we are swayed by the argument that the employees are better of with the pay on offer than they would be without it, and so the firm is acting ethically, then we are taking a consequentialist position. All of these positions have problems. Motivist theories are based on the belief that we can actually observe (or at least feel the consequences of) someone else's motivation (can we? Why should we judge exactly the same act and consequences (to ourselves) differently if we suddenly find someone's historic motivation to be different to that we believed to be the case?). Deontological theories are inflexible. We tend to ameliorate our judgement in light of the circumstances in which people act (which we do: given any moral rule we can usually find circumstances in which it will not, or should not, hold). Consequentialism assumes that we can predict all the consequences of an act and attribute back to it the future effects it causes (cause and effect is not that simple, nor is predicting the future).

This book is not the place in which to pursue these concerns too far. Rather, the aim of this section is to raise awareness of them as an issue and to recognise the difficulty in making simple (or simplistic) ethical judgements about entrepreneurs and about what moral philosophers refer to as *aretaic* issues: what entrepreneurs *must* do, *could* do and *ought* to do. We will return to the issue of the discretionary responsibilities of entrepreneurs in Section 12.5, where our concerns will be more limited, and address the personal motivations of the entrepreneur and the tactical adoption of different ethical values.

(2.3) Entrepreneurship and information

Key learning outcome

A recognition of the basic ideas of *information economics*, a qualitative understanding of the concept of *informational asymmetry* and *principle–agent contracts* under conditions of *moral hazard*, *adverse selection* and *signalling*, and an appreciation of the way these insights contribute to an understanding of entrepreneurship and the entrepreneurial process, particularly entrepreneur–investor relationships.

In Section 2.1 the fundamental assumptions of neo-classical economics were discussed. These include the belief that individuals are rational and utility maximising, that individuals are perfectly efficient in processing information and that information is freely available. By 'freely available' it is meant that gaining information has no cost, that all individuals know all that there is to be known and all individuals know what every other individual knows. Formally, economists refer to these four features as information being *frictionless*, *perfect*, *symmetric* and *common*. Clearly, these assumptions are unrealistic. Information does have a cost, no individual can possibly know all that there is to be known and different individuals know different things. We rarely know, exactly, what others know. Nascent entrepreneurs all too quickly become aware of the cost of (even basic) market research. If all that was to be known were know, there would be nothing for entrepreneurs to innovate about, and if entrepreneurs knew, and only knew, exactly what their competitors know (and vice versa) there would be no point in the entrepreneur competing at all!

So what happens if we drop the assumptions that information is frictionless, perfect and symmetric? What happens is perhaps the most important revolution in economics of the twentieth century: a field known as *information economics*. The impact of this discipline on economic thinking and discovery cannot be overstated. The interested student is referred to the review by Stiglitz (2000) for a good, accessible account of how this subject has developed and how it has led to an entirely new series of economic perspectives. Relaxing assumptions about perfect informa-tion allows economics to develop a much more realistic picture of the world. This has had considerable importance for economic considerations of entrepreneurship. Like much of modern economics, information economics is highly mathematical. It was born at a time when economics was well into its mathematical turn. Although its understanding only requires a knowledge of (albeit at times quite advanced) algebra it is impenetrable to the mathematically uninitiated. This is unfortunate, because it offers a lot to the understanding of entrepreneurship. This section develops a non-mathematical overview of the main ideas in information economics and the entrepreneurial situations in which it might be applied. The more mathematically confident student who wishes to explore the subject in depth might try a standard work in the field. *An Introduction to the Economics of Information* by Ines Macho-Stadler and J. David Perez-Castrillo is excellent. Informational economics has a number of connections to another revolutionary twentieth-century development in economics: *game theory*. Some aspects of game theory and its significance to entrepreneurship will be discussed in Section 23.4.

Types of informational asymmetry

Information economics takes as its starting point a simple model of the interaction between two economic actors: the *principal*, the individual (or organisation) who wants a project undertaking and contracts an *agent*, an individual (or organisation) who undertakes that project on behalf of the principal; that is, *accepts* the contract. In our context, this represents the investor and the entrepreneur accepting invest-ment to progress the venture. Both of these parties anticipate the way the world will turn out due to events outside either's control in the expectation that both will gain some benefit (utility) from working together. Both face risk or uncertainty. Neither can fully anticipate the events that will occur (their information is not perfect) though they might or might not know the probability with which certain things will happen. This is actually equivalent to saying that not all information is available. We will assume that both are *utility maximising*, that is, both wish to maximise what they gain from the arrangement. After the contract is fulfilled and the events have occurred, both the principal and the agent gain separate outcomes that have a value (or loss) to them. This basic model is depicted in Figure 2.2. This model may appear quite simple compared to real-world economic arrangements, but most real-world situations can be reduced (with some assumptions) to a set of such interactions.

Now we can introduce the idea that information is not only not *perfect*, but is also *asymmetric*. That is, the principal and the agent know *different* things – they do not share *common* knowledge of issues relevant to the project. This is particu-larly significant when the agent knows something the principal does not. There are four basic variations on this theme. In the first, when the agent undertakes some project, the principal is not actually able to observe what the agent does. The agent can put in a level of effort that only he can observe. (It is traditional in information economics to refer to the principal as 'she' and the agent 'he'.) In the second, the

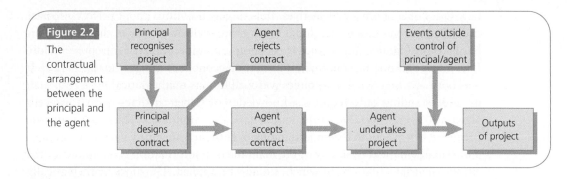

Figure 2.2 The contractual arrangement between the principal and the agent

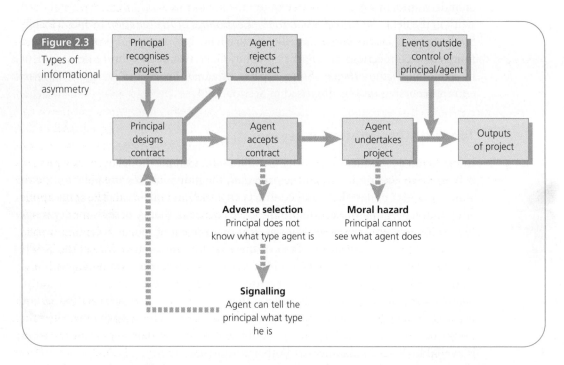

Figure 2.3 Types of informational asymmetry

agent discovers something of relevance to the project that the principal does not know *after* the contract is completed, but before the project (venture) is started. Both of these situations are referred to as *moral hazard*. They may look different but in fact they are variations on a theme. Their mathematical treatment is the same. In the third, the agent knows something that the principal does not know, but this time *before* the contract is agreed. This problem is known as *adverse selection*. In adverse selection, we are usually concerned with the agent (but not the principal) having information on his abilities, or the type of agent he is, that is not shared with the principal. In the fourth, like the third, the agent knows something that the principal does not know but this time decides to inform the principal what he knows. This is known as *signalling*. Note here that signalling is not the agent simply telling the principal what he knows as this would just reduce the problem to a classical one of symmetrical information. These four variations are depicted in Figure 2.3.

In each of these situations, the problem is one of how the principal designs an agreement – a *contract* – that will maximise her outcomes given that the contract must be attractive to the agent (given that he can find other projects to dedicate his effort to). Solving this contracting problem under various conditions of informational asymmetry is the central concern of information economics, and its relevance to entrepreneurship will be immediately evident. Remember the original meaning of the word entrepreneur – an individual who takes on a contract on behalf of an investor. In practice, an entrepreneur may play the role of either principal or agent depending on the situation. A venture capitalist offering money as an investment in a venture is acting as a principal to the agent entrepreneur. A customer accepting a supply contract from an entrepreneur is in a similar position. An entrepreneur acts as a principal if she contracts the efforts of employees or services from a supplier.

Moral hazard is now recognised as an important feature of venture capitalist–entrepreneur relationships. The venture capitalist must trust the entrepreneur to put in the highest amount of effort on behalf of the venture. Although the venture capitalist may put into play monitoring procedures to keep an eye on what the entrepreneur is doing (so reducing the moral hazard) monitoring is expensive and complete monitoring is impossible. At the end of the day the venture capitalist must let the entrepreneur get on with it! The entrepreneur who contracts in services from an individual or firm faces the problem of adverse selection. She can check a person's CV and experience and obtain references, but that individual's real ability to do the job demanded can only be tested on the job, after he is taken on. The same applies to a supplier: no matter how good the sales pitch, the quality of the supplier is only tested if a contract is agreed. The same applies in reverse of course to the entrepreneur as a supplier. An application of this idea is Cressy (2002) and de Meza (2002), who consider the role informational asymmetry plays in driving the 'funding gap' that many entrepreneurs experience when attempting to raise investment.

The use of signalling is of growing interest in management theory, finance and beyond. Put simply, signalling occurs when an agent tells a principal that he is of a particular type (say, an entrepreneur telling an investor 'I am a good entrepreneur and my business will be successful'). Signalling must go beyond simply stating 'I am of this particular type', of course. Anyone can say this. Why should he be believed? Anyone can say, 'I am a going to be a successful entrepreneur'. No matter how heartfelt, there is no guarantee that it is true. To be effective, a signal must be unambiguous (no point if the principal misreads it) and if it is to be believed it must be the case that only an agent of the type that sends the signal 'I am of this type' can send it. One way to ensure this is to make the signal costly to the agent in some way.

A good example of signalling that should clarify this comes not from management theory, but from animal behaviour. Alcock (1993), an ethologist (a biologist who studies animal behaviour), noticed something apparently odd about the behaviour of gazelles being hunted by lions on the Serengeti plains of Africa. Lions hunt, kill and eat gazelles that graze in herds. When a lion approaches a herd of gazelles we would expect them to run away. And indeed they often do. But before they do so, some of the gazelles jump up and down vigorously – behaviour known as 'stotting'. This is odd, because the animal is wasting energy and time that would be better dedicated to making its escape. Why they do this only becomes clear when we appreciate the 'cost–benefit' analysis both gazelles and lions undertake (they do not do this consciously, of course, it is an evolved behaviour due to natural selection). The lion needs to eat in order to survive, but the more they must chase a gazelle in order to make a kill, the more energy they waste (and so must hunt more to replenish it). The frequency of lion kills is quite low. A lion may have to make several chases before succeeding. The gazelle is also interesting in conserving energy. Running away from a lion consumes a lot of energy that must be replaced by more grazing. So the lion will prefer to hunt the weaker and sicker animals in the herd, as they are easier to catch. Hence the healthy gazelle can gain (not be hunted) by signalling to the lion 'don't hunt me – I am healthy and fit. Try another member of the herd'. Of course a gazelle cannot say this directly to a lion, and even if one could, why should the lion believe it? It is in the interest of weak animals to lie. But by stotting, the gazelle is, in effect, saying 'Look: I am fit and healthy – *and I can prove it* – I am so confident that I can outrun you, I am prepared to waste time and energy now, and still beat you. So pick on someone else'. A weaker animal of course, cannot take this risk. So the lion 'decides' it is better to hunt a gazelle that does not stott, exactly the effect the healthy gazelle wanted. Healthy gazelles are often so confident that their signal has been seen and properly read, they do not bother to run even when the lion charges at the herd. The parallels to entrepreneurship will soon become clear.

Contracts under informational asymmetry

We will assume that the contract offered by the principal is one that is rational to her (she maximises her utility) and is just attractive enough to attract a rational (also utility maximising) agent. That is, it is just valuable enough to attract him from the alternatives he has available. To understand the agent's behaviour we must also assume that his effort presents a cost (a disutility) to him that reduces his reward. So he will maximise his returns based not only on what he might gain, but also in terms of how much effort it will cost him to gain it. This disutility of effort is not a suggestion that people are inherently lazy, rather that even a very hard-working person will try to spread his effort in an attempt to maximise his income – less effort on this project might mean that another (with additional rewards) can be taken on as well. Under conditions of symmetric information it is relatively straightforward for the principal to design such a contract. It is simply a fixed sum, just large enough to attract the agent from taking up any alternative project on offer. As the principal knows what type of agent the agent is, can observe (and so police) the effort he puts in, and know what will result from that effort, this maximises the principal's return given that the project goes ahead. Under conditions of moral hazard, adverse selection and signalling, however, contract design is not nearly so straightforward. We will avoid the mathematics of the contract design, save to say that the optimisation problems they present are technically difficult to solve, and further simplifying assumptions are often necessary in order for them to be resolved.

If moral hazard is present, the contract offered must be one in which the pay-off to the agent is dependent on his effort. If it is not, then he will simply put in the lowest amount of effort possible. His effort will make no difference to what he gains as a reward and the less effort he puts in, the less that effort costs. So he must be rewarded for putting in a higher effort. This cannot, of course, be based on the principal *seeing* what he does, because the terms of the moral hazard problem are that she cannot see (monitor) what he does. So they must be based on the outcomes of the project, the value it creates. However, the project's outcomes are not just based on the agent's efforts, they are also based on (unpredictable) events outside the control of the agent or principal (this is a very realistic assumption). Both parties face a *risk*. Making the reward to the agent dependent on the outcome of the project is then a way for the principal to offset risk – to 'sell' some of it – to the agent. So technically, the contract does not reward the agent for his *effort*, but the *probability* that his effort will produce a good result. This result fits with the observed nature of contracts between investors and entrepreneurs. Contracts through which the investor agrees to put a fixed sum of capital into the venture and allows the entrepreneur to take a fixed amount as personal income whatever the business performance would be exceptional. Indeed, it would negate the agent as an entrepreneur. He would simply be an employee. Entrepreneurs must accept some of the risk and be rewarded based on performance. Of course, an entrepreneur might put in minimal effort and still be lucky with the success of the venture. But success here is less probable than success achieved with high effort. The entrepreneur must assume that higher effort brings (more likely) rewards.

Adverse selection (where an agent may be one of several types and the principal cannot find out which in advance) presents a different contracting problem. The solution here is for the principal to offer not one but a *menu* of contracts each offering a different reward based on the type of agent to which it is targeted. Of course, only the agent knows what type he is. The trick is for the principal to arrange incentives so that the agent will take the contract that is best for his type. The principal is inclined to offer the 'better' (to her eyes) agent the most rewarding contract and a less attractive contract to an agent who is not of the best type. To prevent all agents (whatever their type) simply taking the best contract, she must introduce incentives for an agent who takes on a contract that fits his type and penalties for an agent that takes on a contract that does not fit his type (something only he knows). The contracts must be *self-selecting*. Such contract types are common in insurance.

For example, an insurance company offering cover does not know the type of customer being sold to: whether the person buying the cover is a 'good' customer (one who will make an effort to protect himself from the risks present), and is less likely to make a claim, or is a 'poor' customer (one who thinks 'I have insurance so I may as well take a few risks'), who is more likely to make a claim. A solution offered by many insurance companies is to offer a reducing rate of insurance charge – a 'no-claims bonus' – for customers who do not make a claim for an increasing period. So at any one time, a customer has a choice between two contracts: making a claim and losing a no-claims bonus, and not making a claim so as to retain it. Such menus of contracts can apply in sophisticated financing deals for entrepreneurial ventures where the risk is offset (in effect insured against) through a variety of complex financial deals involving mixtures of investment (equity) and loan financing.

Entrepreneurs and venture capitalists find themselves in an exactly parallel situation as gazelles and lions when it comes to signalling. (Like all good analogies this should not be pushed too far, though some entrepreneurs may nod sagely at it!) Venture capitalists want to invest in the best entrepreneurs. Entrepreneurs want to tell venture capitalists 'I am the best – invest in me'. So entrepreneurs must signal this to venture capitalists but in a way that they *could only do* if indeed they are the best. The signal must have a cost. There are many ways in which entrepreneurs can send such costly signals. They may offer the investor a higher than market normal return (this is important in market flotations). The entrepreneur may spend a lot of money calling in consultants and market researchers to back up the claims in the business plan. Certo *et al.* (2001) consider how board structure at initial public offerings may signal confidence in future performance. The most usual way, though, is for the entrepreneur to put his or her own money into the deal. Prasad *et al.* (2000) develop a formal model of the entrepreneur's own contribution as a decision signal. The investor may demand this more as a *signal* than as a substantive contribution. The cost (both in terms of opportunity and risk) to the entrepreneur is then transparent. I once put the question 'Given a particular total level of investment, what percentage do you expect to be contributed by the entrepreneur personally?' to a venture capitalist. She thought deeply and then replied: 'I don't think about percentages. I want just enough so it *hurts*!' Lee (2001) considers the change of a business name to include 'dot-com' as a signal to investors. She finds that investors reward the firm with an increased stock price, especially if the name change is accompanied with announcements on changes in strategic direction (though this was before the burst of the dot-com bubble; I suspect a similar study might have different findings now).

Summary of key ideas

- The entrepreneur is, first and foremost, an agent of economic activity.

- The neo-classical school of economics has little room or use for the idea of entrepreneurs as a distinct class of economic agent.

- Alternative schools of economic thinking do see entrepreneurs as distinct. Important schools include the:
  - Austrian School
  - heterogeneous demand theory
  - differential advantage theory
  - industrial organisational economics
  - resource-based perspective

- competence-based perspective
- transaction cost economics
- evolutionary theories
- economic sociology.

● These schools often highlight particular (and sometimes complementary) aspects of entrepreneurial activity.

● Economics makes assumptions about the nature of man and his social responsibilities. Many find these assumptions not only wrong, but also even offensive if they are taken as recommendations about how people should behave (a libertarian position). Socialist, eco-radical and feminist ideologies are particularly critical of this view.

● Whether (or to what extent) the behaviour of entrepreneurs is 'hard wired' and determined by evolutionary forces or is learnt within a social and cultural setting is controversial.

● Ethical judgements about entrepreneurs are sensitive to whether we are taking a *motivist*, a *deontological* or a *consequentialist* position on moral value.

● Classical economics assumes that all parties to a contract have the same knowledge. This assumption is not sustainable with real entrepreneur–investor (agent–principal) agreements.

● Informational economics has revolutionised thinking about contracts when one party knows something the other does not – *information asymmetry*.

● Information asymmetry leads to one of three situations: *moral hazard*, *adverse selection* and *signalling*.

● Theory suggests that each of these situations is best resolved by different types of contract that share risk between the investor and the entrepreneur. Such contract types are observed in the real world.

Research themes

This chapter has raised a number of issues that cut across a wide range of social science disciplines. Debate on these issues is increasingly technical. However, there are a number of interesting research projects the specialist (or generalist?) in entrepreneurship might tackle.

Entrepreneur's folk-economics

Most economics is theory led. These theories are then tested by empirical observation. The term 'folk-economics' refers not to economists' views of economics, but to 'ordinary' peoples' (i.e. those with no formal training in economics) beliefs and attitudes. Entrepreneurs are usually such. The project might devise a survey to test entrepreneurs' own beliefs about what their economic functions, effects and responsibilities are. Relevant propositions might be devised by considering the different schools of economic thinking and distilling out some key ideas. These can then be put to practising entrepreneurs (or people who hope to become entrepreneurs) and their agreement with the proposition tested (agree strongly to disagree strongly). A surveying technique such as Delphi analysis would be useful here. By way of analysis, the way agreement corresponds to the different schools of economic thinking could be established. Do entrepreneurs' folk-economic beliefs match strongly with any one school? Do they cut across schools? Do all entrepreneurs think their economic role to be the same?

Entrepreneurs and moral judgements about them

The study of corporate responsibility (and its impact on financial performance) is a fast growing area of research. But it has, traditionally, concerned itself with a largely *deontological* view of moral value: it looks at the *acts* entrepreneurs take (such as expression of belief in social responsibility; the employment of minorities and provision of child-care facilities). This rather ignores the motivist and consequentialist aspects of moral judgement. An interesting project would be to take some descriptions of entrepreneurial ventures that raise moral issues and contain information on the entrepreneur's motives, what he or she actually did and the consequences of what they did (*Financial Times* articles are a good source; you may want to construct short case studies yourself so you are sure all the issues are covered). Select a small group (say, 10–20) of people, let them read the article/cases and then lead a brainstorming session on the issues, with subjects indicating their views about the ethical issues in the situation and why they hold those beliefs (be careful not to bias the debate!). Afterwards analyse the results, coding statements as making moral judgements on a motivist, deontological or consequentialist basis. Are judgements usually based on a single basis or on more than one? Which (if any) dominates? A good conclusion would be to highlight the implications in terms of what moral criteria future studies of corporate responsibility and performance should include.

Entrepreneur–investor contracts under informational asymmetry

Informational economics is a (mathematically) technical area. The more mathematically confident student may wish to look into this (Macho-Stadler and Perez-Castrillo, 2001 is a good start). However, there are still some useful contributions that only depend on qualitative descriptions of contract types and do not require a high degree of mathematical understanding or analysis. Get some good descriptions of entrepreneur–investor deals (venture capital deals are particularly useful). These may be obtained from *Financial Times* articles and published case studies. Gompers and Lerner (2002) give a good account of some deals; follow their references through. By way of analysis, ascertain the nature of the informational asymmetry between the entrepreneur (agent) and the investor (principal) (e.g. are they moral hazard or adverse selection?) and see what sort of contract would be predicted. Does the deal reflect this type of contract? How are risks being shared? How are details like monitoring and compensation used to resolve the asymmetry? Did the entrepreneur resort to signalling? If so, how did this signal reassure the investor and why was it expensive to the entrepreneur? A solid methodological justification for such case-based studies is offered by Ghemawat (1997).

Suggestions for further reading

Alchian, A.A. (1950) 'Uncertainty, evolution and economics', *Journal of Political Economy*, Vol. 58, pp. 211–21.

Alcock, J. (1993) *Animal Behavior: An Evolutionary Approach*, Sunderland, MA: Sinauer.

Alderson, W. (1957) *Marketing Behaviour and Executive Action*, Homewood, IL: Irwin.

Alderson, W. (1965) *Dynamic Marketing Behaviour*, Homewood, IL: Irwin.

Alvarez, S.A. and Barney, J.B. (2002) 'Resource-based theory and the entrepreneurial firm', in Hitt, M.A., Ireland, R.D., Camp, S.M. and Sexton, D.L. (eds) *Strategic Entrepreneurship: Creating a New Mindset*, Oxford: Blackwell.

Alvarez, S.A. and Busenitz, L.W. (2001) 'The entrepreneurship of resource-based theory', *Journal of Management*, Vol. 27, pp. 755–75.

Andrews, K.R. (1971) *The Concept of Corporate Strategy*, Homewood, IL: Irwin.

Badcock, C. (2000) *Evolutionary Psychology*, Cambridge: Polity Press.

Bain, J.S. (1954) 'Conditions of entry and the emergence of monopoly', in Chamberlin, E. (ed.) *Monopoly and Competition and their Regulation*, London: Macmillan, pp. 215–44.

Bain, J.S. (1956) *Barriers to New Competition*, Cambridge, MA: Harvard University Press.

Bain, J.S. (1968) *Industrial Organisation* (2nd edn), New York: Wiley.

Barkow, J.H., Cosmides, L. and Tooby, J. (eds) (1992) *The Adapted Mind: Evolutionary Psychology and the Generation of Culture*, Oxford: Oxford University Press.

Barney, J. (1991) 'Firm resources and sustainable competitive advantage', *Journal of Management*, Vol. 17, No. 1, pp. 99–120.

Ben-Nur, A. and Putterman, L. (1998) *Economics, Values and Organization*, Cambridge: Cambridge University Press.

Bergmann-Lichenstein, B.M. and Brush, C.G. (2001) 'How do "resource bundles" develop and change in new ventures? A dynamic model and longitudinal exploration', *Entrepreneurship Theory and Practice*, Vol. 25, No. 3, pp. 37–58.

Bromwich, M. (1992) *Financial Reporting, Information and Capital Markets*, London: Pitman.

Certo, S.T., Daily, C.M. and Dalton, D.R. (2001) 'Signalling firm value through board structure: an investigation of initial public offerings', *Entrepreneurship Theory and Practice*, Winter, pp. 33–50.

Chamberlin, E. (1933) *The Theory of Monopolistic Competition*, Cambridge, MA: Harvard University Press.

Clark, J.M. (1940) 'Towards a concept of workable competition', *American Economic Review*, Vol. 30, pp. 241–56.

Coase, R.H. (1937) 'The nature of the firm', *Economica*, Vol. 4, pp. 368–405.

Cockburn, I.M., Henderson, R.M. and Stern, S. (2000) 'Untangling the origins of competitive advantage', *Strategic Management Journal*, Vol. 21, pp. 1123–45.

Commons, J.R. (1924) *Legal Foundations of Capitalism*, New York: Macmillan.

Cooper, A.C. (2002) 'Networks, alliances and entrepreneurship', in Hitt, M.A., Ireland, R.D., Camp, S.M. and Sexton, D.L. (eds) *Strategic Entrepreneurship: Creating a New Mindset*, Oxford: Blackwell.

Cowen, T. and Parker, D. (1997) *Markets in the Firm: A Market-Process Approach to Management*, Institute of Economic Affairs Hobart Paper No. 134.

Coyle, D. (2001) *Paradoxes of Prosperity*, London: Texere.

Cressy, R. (2002) 'Funding gaps: a symposium', *Economic Journal*, Vol. 112, pp. F1–F16.

Da Empoli, A. (1931) *Theory of Economic Equilibrium: A Study in Marginal and Ultramarginal Phenomena*, Chicago, IL: Christiano and Catenacci.

de Meza, D. (2002) 'Overlending', *Economic Journal*, Vol. 112, pp. F17–F31.

Dierickx, I. and Cool, K. (1989) 'Asset stock accumulation and the sustainability of competitive advantage', *Management Science*, Vol. 35, pp. 1504–11.

Foss, N.J. (ed.) (1997) *Resources, Firms and Strategies: A Reader in the Resource-Based Perspective*, Oxford: Oxford University Press.

Ferguson, P.R. and Ferguson, G.J. (1998) *Industrial Economics: Issues and Perspectives* (2nd edn), Basingstoke: Palgrave.

Ghemawat, P. (1997) *Games Businesses Play: Cases and Models*, Cambridge, MA: MIT Press.

Granovetter, M. (1985) 'Economic action and social structure: the problem of embeddedness', *American Journal of Sociology*, Vol. 91, No. 3, pp. 481–510.

Gompers, P. and Lerner, J. (2002) *The Venture Capital Cycle*, Cambridge, MA: MIT Press.

Hagedoorn, J. (2002) 'Small entrepreneurial firms and large corporations in inter-firm R&D networks – the international biotechnology industry', in Hitt, M.A., Ireland, R.D., Camp, S.M. and Sexton, D.L. (eds) *Strategic Entrepreneurship: Creating a New Mindset*, Oxford: Blackwell.

Hamilton, W.H. (1932) 'Institution', in Seligman, E.R.A. and Johnson, A. (eds) *Encyclopaedia of the Social Sciences*, vol. 8, Guildford, CT: Dushkin.

Hannan, M.T. and Freeman, J. (1977) 'The population ecology of organisations', *American Journal of Sociology*, Vol. 82, No. 5, pp. 929–64.

Hausman, D.M. and McPherson, M.S. (1996) *Economic Analysis and Moral Philosophy*, Cambridge: Cambridge University Press.

Hayek, F.A. (1937) 'Economics and knowledge', *Econonomica*, Vol. 4, pp. 33–54.

Hayek, F.A. (1940) 'The competitive solution', *Economica*, Vol. 7, pp. 125–49.

Hayek, F.A. (1948) *Individualism and Economic Order*, Chicago, IL: University of Chicago Press.

Hodgson, G.M. (1993) *Economics and Evolution*, Ann Arbor, MI: University of Michigan Press.

Hunt, S.D. (2000) *A General Theory of Competition*, Thousand Oaks, CA: Sage.

Johnson, S. and Van de Ven, A.H. (2002) 'A framework for entrepreneurial strategy', in Hitt, M.A., Ireland, R.D., Camp, S.M. and Sexton, D.L. (eds) *Strategic Entrepreneurship: Creating a New Mindset*, Oxford: Blackwell.

Jones, O. and Tilley, F. (2003) *Competitive Advantage in SMEs*, London: Wiley.

Keppler, J.H. (2001) 'Attilio da Empoli's contribution to monopolistic competition theory', *Journal of Economic Studies*, Vol. 28, No. 4/5, pp. 305–23.

Kirzner, I.M. (1973) *Competition and Entrepreneurship*, Chicago, IL: University of Chicago Press.

Kirzner, I.M. (1979) *Perception, Opportunity, and Profit: Studies in the Theory of Entrepreneurship*, Chicago, IL: University of Chicago Press.

Kirzner, I.M. (1982) 'Uncertainty, discovery and human action', in Kirzner, I.M. (ed.) *Method, Process and Austrian Economics: Essays in Honor of Ludwig von Mises*, Lexington, MA: Lexington Books.

Kirzner, I.M. (1985) *Discovery and the Capitalist Process*, Chicago, IL: University of Chicago Press.

Kirzner, I.M. (1997) *How Markets Work: Disequilibrium, Entrepreneurship and Discovery*, Institute of Economic Affairs Hobart Paper No. 133.

Lee, P.M. (2001) 'What's in a name? The effects of '.com' name changes on stock prices and trading activity', *Strategic Management Journal*, Vol. 22, pp. 793–804.

Lensky, G., Lenski, J. and Nolan, P. (1991) *Human Societies: An Introduction to Macrosociology*, New York: McGraw-Hill.

Little, I.M. (2002) *Ethics, Economics and Politics*, Oxford: Oxford University Press.

Lydall, H. (1998) *A Critique of Orthodox Economics: An Alternative Model*, London: Macmillan.

Macho-Stadler, I. and Perez-Castrillo, J.D. (2001) *An Introduction to the Economics of Information: Incentives and Contracts* (2nd edn), Oxford: Oxford University Press.

Makadok, R. (2001) 'Towards a synthesis of the resource-based and dynamic capability views of rent creation', *Strategic Management Journal*, Vol. 22, pp. 387–401.

McCarthy, E.J. (1960) *Basic Marketing: A Managerial Approach*, Homewood, IL: Irwin.

Minniti, M. and Bygrave, W. (1999) 'The microfoundations of entrepreneurship', *Entrepreneurship Theory and Practice*, Vol. 23, No. 4, pp. 41–52.

Mumby-Croft, R. and Hackley, C.E. (1997) 'The social construction of market entrepreneurship: a case analysis in the UK fishing industry', *Marketing Education Review*, Vol. 7, No. 3, pp. 87–94.

Myers, J.H. (1996) *Segmentation and Positioning Strategies for Marketing Decisions*, Chicago, IL: American Marketing Association.

Nelson, R.R. and Winter, S.G. (1982) *An Evolutionary Theory of Economic Change*, Cambridge, MA: Belknap Press.

Nozick, R. (1993) *The Nature of Rationality*, Princeton, NJ: Princeton University Press.

Ofek, H. (2001) *Second Nature: Economic Origins of Human Evolution*, Cambridge: Cambridge University Press.

Penrose, E.T. (1959) *The Theory of the Growth of the Firm*, London: Basil Blackburn and Mott.

Porter, M.E. (1980) *Competitive Advantage*, New York: Free Press.

Porter, M.E. (1985) *Competitive Strategy*, New York: Free Press.

Powell, T.C. (2001) 'Competitive advantage: logical and philosophical considerations', *Strategic Management Journal*, Vol. 22, pp. 875–88.

Prahalad, C.K. and Hamel, G. (1990) 'The core competencies of the corporation', *Harvard Business Review*, May–June, pp. 79–91.

Prasad, D., Bruton, G.D. and Vozikis, G. (2000) 'Signalling value to business angels: the proportion of the entrepreneur's net wealth invested in a new venture as a decision signal', *Venture Capital*, Vol. 2, No. 3, pp. 167–82.

Quinn, J.B. (1978) 'Strategic change: Logical Incrementalism', *Sloan Management Review*, Fall, pp. 1–21.

Rawls, J. (1971) *A Theory of Justice*, Cambridge, MA: Belknap Press.

Robinson, J. (1933) *The Economics of Imperfect Competition*, London: Macmillan.

Rosen, S. (1997) 'Austrian and neo-classical economics: any gains from trade?', *Journal of Economic Perspectives*, Vol. 11, No. 4, pp. 139–52.

Sandler, T. (2001) *Economic Concepts for the Social Sciences*, Cambridge: Cambridge University Press.

Searl, J.R. (2001) *Rationality in Action*, Cambridge, MA: MIT Press.

Selznick, P. (1957) *Leadership in Administration*, New York: Harper & Row.

Sen, A. (1999) *Development as Freedom*, Oxford: Oxford University Press.

Sen, A. (2002) *Rationality and Freedom*, Cambridge, MA: Harvard University Press.

Smith, C.C. (1956) 'Product differentiation and market segmentation as alternative marketing strategies', *Journal of Marketing*, Vol. 21, pp. 3–8.

Stiglitz, J.E. (2000) 'The contribution of the economics of information to twentieth century economics', *Quarterly Journal of Economics*, November, pp. 1441–78.

Sumner, L.W. (1996) *Welfare, Happiness and Ethics*, Oxford: Oxford University Press.

Van de Ven, A.H. and Garud, R. (1989) 'A framework for understanding the emergence of new industries', *Research on Technological Innovation, Management and Policy*, Vol. 4, pp. 195–225.

Von Mises, L. (1949) *Human Action: A Treatise on Economics*, New Haven, CT: Yale University Press.

Von Stackelberg, H. (1933) *Marktform und Gleichgewicht*, Wien: Julius Springer.

Wagner, R.E. (2001) 'Competition as a rivalrous process: Attilio da Empoli and the years of high theory that might have been', *Journal of Economic Studies*, Vol. 28, No. 4/5, pp. 337–45.

Wilcox-King, A. and Zeithaml, C.P. (2001) 'Competencies and firm performance: examining the causal ambiguity paradox', *Strategic Management Journal*, Vol. 22, pp. 75–99.

Williamson, O.E. (1994) 'Transaction cost economics and organization theory', in Smelser, N.J. and Swedberg, R. (eds) *The Handbook of Economic Sociology*, Princeton, NJ: Princeton Univerity Press, pp. 77–107.

Williamson, O.E. (1996) *The Mechanisms of Governance*, Oxford: Oxford University Press.

Yu, A.F. (2001) 'Towards a capabilities perspective of the small firm', *International Journal of Management Reviews*, Vol. 3, No. 3, pp. 185–97.

Zafirovski, M. (1999) 'Probing into the social layers of entrepreneurship: outlines of the sociology of enterprise', *Entrepreneurship and Regional Development*, Vol. 11, No. 4, pp. 351–71.

Selected case material **Case 2.1**

The capitalist growth machine

5 June 2002

By **Martin Wolf**

Sustained economic growth and its uneven spread across the globe are the most important features of the contemporary world. They explain the changing relative power of countries, the combination of unprecedented wealth with continued poverty, the nature of modern war, the rise of democracy and the frustration felt in much of the Islamic world.

Over the past two centuries, measured average real incomes per head have risen at least 20-fold in the world's richest countries. In truth, they have probably risen by far more. This growth was faster in the 20th century than the 19th and faster in the second half of the 20th century than in any previous period.

Yet economists have been unsuccessful in explaining this world-transforming revolution. This at last is changing. A brilliant book* by William Baumol, an emeritus professor at

Princeton University, sheds bright light on the sources of growth. He builds on the insights of Joseph Schumpeter, the Austrian economist, to expose the machine that drives capitalism. In so doing, he explains why, in the past century, the market economy buried socialism – the reverse of what Nikita Khrushchev, the Soviet leader, said would happen.

If we still possessed only the technologies of 1800, little of the past two centuries of growth could have occurred. Yet, contrary to the assumptions of virtually all economic models, this flood of innovations has not been manna from heaven. Prof Baumol argues, instead, that innovation rather than price competition is the central feature of the market process. Competition forces companies to invest in innovation. Otherwise they risk falling behind and, ultimately, being driven out of their markets.

---

* *The Free-Market Innovation Machine: Analyzing the Growth Miracle of Capitalism*, Princeton University Press, 2002.

In Schumpeter's model of the capitalist economy, the engine of innovation was the extraordinary profits offered to the lone entrepreneur. Such profits still entice inventors and innovators. Yet, as Prof Baumol makes clear, the bulk of the innovation that drives economies occurs within existing companies. It is a routine aspect of their behaviour. Overall, such innovative activity will not be particularly profitable: some companies will be lucky; others will not. But the motivation is no longer the hope of exceptional profit. It is the certainty of failure if one is not in the race.

Even heroic innovators do not emerge from outside the market. Thomas Edison was an exceptional inventor and innovator. But he was also a businessman. One of his legacies was research and development itself, which has made the activity of innovation routine. In a more recent market-driven development, the venture capital industry is doing for individual entrepreneurs and innovators what large companies have long done for teams of researchers.

Innovation, then, is hard-wired into capitalism. Vast benefits are poured on everybody. Individual innovators obtain at most a fifth of the economic benefits they generate, argues Prof Baumol.

Why did the innovation machine come so late in history? The answer is that entrepreneurial energy used to be channelled into 'rent-seeking'. In his least harmful form, the rent-seeker is a parasite. At his most harmful, he is a bandit or an invader. In ancient Rome and classical China, commerce was the most disgraceful way to become rich. Behind the anti-capitalists of today can be discerned the same preference for the bureaucrat, priest or warrior over the 'money-grubbing' merchant and his culture of rational calculation or 'greed'.

The necessary condition for the emergence of a market economy that rewards entrepreneurs who introduce productive innovations is simply the rule of law. As Prof Baumol notes: 'There is no occupation whose total economic product is greater than that of the lawyers', though there is also 'none whose marginal contribution is smaller'. In the US at least, it must be negative.

One long-standing concern among economists about innovation has been that it creates monopolies. The possibility of creating a legally protected monopoly provides the incentive to innovate. But it would be better if innovations were as widely diffused as possible throughout the economy. Thus, paradoxically, the market's greatest achievement makes it less efficient.

Prof Baumol argues that such worries are exaggerated. A study of 46 important product innovations suggests that the time taken for competitors to enter the market has fallen from an average of 33 years to three years since the 1880s. Yet the incentive to innovate does not seem to have been undermined: US private research and development has risen sevenfold, in real terms, since the 1950s.

The explanation, suggests Prof Baumol, is that the market has itself found ways to combine innovation with diffusion. Two such methods are licensing and technology-exchange consortia. If the price is right, it pays to offer technology to other companies. The result will be swift diffusion of technology throughout the economy but no loss in the incentive to create it.

This entire way of thinking about the economy sheds light on two important contemporary debates. First, it suggests that open world markets are even more important than supposed, because they ratchet up the competitive pressure on innovating companies.

Second, provided an economy offers an environment in which companies can function, the debate over the details of corporate governance may not be that important. All companies must generate revenue that covers the cost of inputs, or perish. Thus competition among innovative companies should, over time, eliminate failing corporate models. But there may not be one winner. The insider-dominated companies of Japan and Germany could continue to do better in some markets, while the shareholder-dominated companies of the US or UK performed better in others.

What makes capitalism uniquely successful is the built-in pressure to generate new products and processes. Provided companies are forced to compete, the market will find a way to generate and diffuse an unending stream of innovations. The result may not be perfect but it is – and has been – enormously more fruitful than any conceivable alternative.

Source: *Financial Times*, 5 June 2002.

Case 2.2

Biosciences: a prestige address can go a long way

FT

21 November 2002

By **Fiona Maharg-Bravo**

When John McQuillian first based his company, Cambridge Molecular, in a commercial area of Cambridge, he noticed would-be investors were slightly uncomfortable with the surroundings.

'On one side, we had a furniture company, and on the other – believe it or not – there was a condom company,' he says.

'We soon found that the environment made investors uneasy – they were looking for more sophisticated surroundings,' he adds.

He moved the company to Granta Science Park, where it matured and was eventually bought by a larger company in 1999.

For a start-up biotechnology company, location is key. The high risk, high reward and high capital cost nature of the industry means support at the early stages is a crucial element if a project is to be successful. And a prestige address can go a long way.

But biotech incubators and science parks housing early-stage companies offer more than just a piece of credible real estate; they reduce the barriers to entry into a tough industry and help academics make the transition from researcher to entrepreneur.

David Hardman, chief executive of Babraham Bioincubator, says it is very difficult for incipient companies to survive outside the confines of an incubator, particularly given the high capital costs of research equipment.

Incubators are often attached to universities, allowing companies to hire their equipment by the hour.

'With biotech companies, there is a very early burn rate. You simply cannot survive on your own,' he says.

The Cambridge-based incubator, which opened in 1998 and houses 17 start-ups, offers more than 32,000 sq ft of combined laboratory and office accommodation. The Babraham Institute is about to launch another incubator – Bioconcept, which will guide the start-ups in the very first phase – testing the commercial potential of an idea.

It usually takes about 12 months or more to develop a concept sufficiently before the first round of funding – either from a bank or venture capitalist – is put in place. At this point, most companies are ready to enter an incubator.

Finding enough funding is their biggest problem. Most fledgling companies complain that the venture capital market has toughened considerably in recent months as companies recover from poor investment choices at the height of the dotcom bubble.

Gordon Smith Baxter, chief executive of Biowisdom and tenant of the Babraham Institute, says he found it 'massively difficult' to secure financing in the current environment.

'Venture capital companies these days want near-term returns, real businesses and a top management team. The low valuations mean you are practically selling your soul these days for £1m or £2m,' he says.

Incubators can add the most value at the development stage, after the idea itself has attracted some financial backing. They help reduce funding needs substantially by offering tenants free advice, access to facilities and in some cases, free rent.

'When you move into the development phase, you need to multi-task, develop a business plan and secure more funding. The incubator facilitates that process,' says Mr McQuillian, who now runs MerseyBio, a Liverpool-based biosciences incubator.

He says the sector lends itself to big, collective development spaces which nurture a strong community feel. Thinking and operating as a commercial entity is particularly difficult for academics, who may often lack the commercial sense to package the concept correctly.

'The transfer from science lab to the world of business takes a lot of passion and drive. Most scientists just want to see if their ideas "have legs", but lose interest in the commercial aspect,' says Mr Smith Baxter.

Jon Brotchie, a former senior lecturer in Anatomy at Manchester University's School of Biological Sciences, moved from the classroom to the Manchester Incubator building next door to run Motac, a company dedicated to treatments for Parkinson's disease.

He describes the transition as 'rough', but says the proximity to the university made it possible to participate in both the academic and business worlds without compromising either.

After three to five years in the supportive environment, biotech companies are expected to 'graduate' from incubators and go on to bigger and better things. Some of them will be snapped up by larger pharmaceutical companies.

Smaller companies don't compete with the bigger operators directly. Essentially, large

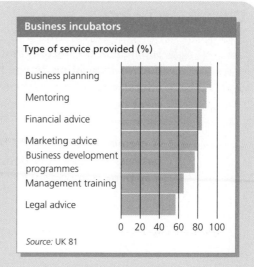

Business incubators

Type of service provided (%)

Business planning

Mentoring

Financial advice

Marketing advice
Business development programmes
Management training

Legal advice

0 20 40 60 80 100

Source: UK 81

companies outsource the high risk to small start-ups.

'Big pharmaceutical companies are hungry for new products, and these small companies provide their pipeline,' says Marie Smith, director of Manchester Innovation.

Aston Molecules is a case in point. After several years at Aston Science Park, it was acquired by US-based OSI Pharmaceuticals in 1996. The company remained on the park until April of this year when it was forced to move out due to space limitations.

John Slack, co-founder and now based in Oxford, says the support he received at the park was key to the company's success, providing contacts and access to Aston University.

Others, such as Motac, will continue to grow organically. The company will soon be moving out of the Manchester Incubator building. 'Moving out is a sign that Motac can stand on its own two feet, independently. It's like moving into your first house,' says Mr Brotchie.

Source: Financial Times, 21 November 2002.

Discussion points

1. Summarise the factors that encourage entrepreneurs to undertake productive innovation rather than exploitative rent seeking. What are the ethical implications of the two forms of entrepreneurship? Should government be empowered to manage the factors or can they be safely left to the market?

2. A premier address might be thought to be a relatively minor factor in business success. How does the idea of signalling explain why investors may think it important?

Chapter 3

The entrepreneurial personality

Chapter overview

This chapter builds on the initial discussion (Section 1.4) of the role of personality factors in entrepreneurial inclination, motivation and performance. The difficulties in relating personality to entrepreneurship are explored, particularly in terms of instrumentalising these fundamental concepts. Different psychological theories of personality are introduced. An introductory account of the increasingly important role cognitive psychology is playing in entrepreneurship studies is offered. The role of personality testing in predicting entrepreneurial behaviour is considered and some difficulties with it explored. The chapter concludes with an introduction to the study of human decision making, focusing on the distinction between normative, descriptive and prescriptive accounts of decision making, the adoption of non-rational heuristics to guide intuitive judgement and their significance to the decision making of the entrepreneur.

3.1 Personality and entrepreneurship: some theoretical issues

The idea that an entrepreneur is, in some way, a special sort of person is commonly held. Surveys I conduct with undergraduates and postgraduates at the start of courses in entrepreneurship suggest that typically 85% of students hold the belief that there is something unique about the personality of entrepreneurs. This belief is persistent. At the end of the course, in which the idea of the entrepreneurial

personality is challenged, 65 per cent
still retain this belief. The arguments
put forward are accepted, but there is
insistence that, intuitively, the idea still
'feels right'. Section 1.4 considered
some general schools of thinking about
the entrepreneurial personality and
some issues with them. This chapter
will expand upon these preliminary
ideas. The primary objective of this chapter is not to offer a resolution, but to
explore the theoretical and methodological difficulties in settling the issue.

The claim that entrepreneurs have a special, or distinctive, personality is, ultimately empirical. It is something that can be examined and demonstrated to be right
or wrong. The methodology for doing this has four aspects: the *instrumentalisation
of entrepreneurship* and *personality*, the *ontology* of personality and theoretical
pragmatics. It is useful to consider these in detail before moving on to consider
different schools of thinking about personality.

Instrumentalisation of the concept of entrepreneurship

Instrumentalisation refers to the methodological approach taken to defining,
characterising and measuring a variable that plays a part in some theoretical
explanation. If the personality of entrepreneurs is to be compared with that of
non-entrepreneurs then a strict specification of who is an entrepreneur is necessary.
As was made evident in Chapter 1, this is not an easy question to answer. The
specification must be in terms of economic function or managerial characteristics.
It cannot be in psychological terms because this would make the theory self-
fulfilling. The claim is that certain tasks, or economic causality, attract (or perhaps
lead to the development of) particular personality types. We cannot use a method
in which individuals judge who, from a sample of individuals, are entrepreneurial
or not, unless we are sure that the judges are not using (explicitly or implicitly)
presumptive personality criteria. A common criterion is simply that a person must
have started his or her own business. An example here is the study by Blanchflower and Oswald (1998). This is useful, because it is quite specific and easy
to observe and confirm. However, it is very broad as it includes small business
managers as well as entrepreneurs who start and develop large ventures. It also
excludes intrapreneurs. The context of, experience of and motivations for starting
a business are highly variable. It would be surprising if all business starters were
unified within a single personality type. More fruitful might be to use the way in
which entrepreneurs are recognised by different schools of economic thinking (see
Section 2.1). However, here, we noted the difficulty in distinguishing entrepreneurs
from other managers. It is a matter of degree. Issues such as identifying significant new opportunities (Austrian School), or being responsible for evaluating and
responding to customer demand (heterogeneous demand school), or significantly

moulding an organisation's resource base (resource-based view), or positioning a business in a particular sector (industrial organisational economic school) might be used as scales. A weighted average approach to assigning a numeric degree of entrepreneurship to individuals might then be adopted.

Instrumentalisation of personality

If entrepreneurial behaviour and effect are to be correlated with personality, then not only entrepreneurship but also *personality* must be a strictly defined concept. There is not, though, a universal agreement on what, exactly, personality is, what its theoretical underpinning should be or how it should be measured (even if it can be measured!). The ways in which different schools of psychology see the personality concept is discussed in more detail below. Whichever conceptualisation is adopted, personality must be something that can be determined *independently* of the individual's specific domain of entrepreneurial activity. Otherwise there is the danger that the domain of activity pre-determines personality allocations, once again making the theory self-fulfilling. For example, we may judge an 'eagerness to take risks' as a personality trait. However, entrepreneurs are in jobs where taking risks is (or is seen to be) a major part of their activity. Individuals in other jobs may not get the chance to take risks. This does not mean that, given the right circumstances, they would not be eager to take risks. If so, then risk taking *is* an aspect of that person's personality, he or she just has not had a chance to reveal it. If risk taking is regarded as (potentially) significant, then there must be a test for risk propensity independent of individuals' task contexts.

Ontology of personality

The way in which theories of personality are approached and constructed is sensitive to assumptions about the *ontology* of personality. Ontology is the branch of analytical philosophy that is concerned with the *existence* of concepts. Broadly, there are three positions. *Realism* is the view that a concept has an actual existence in the world independent of our understanding of it. It is there to be discovered through inquiry. *Positivism* proposes that only that which can be observed is real and that we should be suspicious of things we cannot observe. *Instrumentalism* is the view that concepts exist only in the sense that they provide accounts of the world that lead to useful and correct predictions. A realist view of personality would claim that personality is something individuals actually have and it is the responsibility of research programmes to describe it. A positivist position might be more suspicious. Can we actually observe personality? If so, in what way? Do we need a concept of personality in addition to the notion of 'behaviour'? Personality might be regarded as a way of summarising consistencies and patterns in behaviour, but it is no more than a summary, not something directly observable. An instrumentalist position might claim that personality is a useful concept in that it allows us to account for and predict behaviour and we should accept its existence on this basis.

Theoretical pragmatics

The final aspect of a theory linking personality to entrepreneurship is its *pragmatics*. Broadly, what do we want the theory for and what do we want it to do? There are three sorts of theory with respect to this. A *descriptive* theory is based on independent observations of an individual's personality and their entrepreneurial inclination, behaviour and performance. It then describes correlations between the two. A descriptive theory is simply an account of the way in which the world works. A *normative* theory, on the other hand, goes further. It makes a claim that certain aspects of personality are *necessary* for effective entrepreneurial behaviour. A normative theory can be based on empirical observation within a descriptive theory but usually has an element of theoretical presumption that precedes empirical observation (e.g. that entrepreneurs *must* be individuals who respond positively to change, whether or not this is actually observed). Normative theories direct descriptive theories in a particular direction, suggesting which factors are important and should be the basis of empirical study. Finally, *prescriptive* theories suggest that if one wants to be a successful entrepreneur then one should have (or adopt or develop) a particular personality type. Prescriptive theories are usually based on the edicts of normative theories or findings of descriptive theories. Each of these different types of theory has a different role. Descriptive theories are concerned with how the world is. They regard the personality–entrepreneurship link as a phenomenon that can be discovered and is meaningful in its own terms. Normative theories aspire to make predictions. Given a personality type, then the success or otherwise of that type in an entrepreneurial career can be predicted (to some degree). Personality testing of nascent entrepreneurs makes practical use of normative theories (see below). Prescriptive theories suggest pathways of development to entrepreneurs in that they suggest the personality characteristics entrepreneurs should aim to acquire if they are to be successful. They are important in programmes for education of entrepreneurs. These different types of theories differ in the way they instrumentalise the personality concept and the ontology they ascribe to personality. Descriptive theories require that personality be something observable, measurable and independent of entrepreneurial activity. They may be comfortable with a positivistic or instrumental ontology. Normative theories are not so dependent on observable counterparts of personality. A normative theory may claim personality to be something that cannot be revealed in a positivistic or even instrumental sense, though this would reduce the validity of the theory to many researchers in the field. Prescriptive theories must limit themselves to aspects of personality that can be developed through conscious action, whether they can be independently measured or not.

The way in which the concept of the entrepreneur may be instrumentalised has been discussed in Chapters 1 and 2. The way in which different schools of psychology describe and instrumentalise the personality concept will now be considered.

(3.2) Schools of thinking on personality

> **Key learning outcome**
>
> An introductory understanding of the ways different schools of psychology approach the concept of personality and its implications for thinking about the personality of the entrepreneur.

Psychology, like economics, is a subject that is characterised by numerous different schools that agree on some particulars and disagree on others. Each school has its own theoretical underpinning and methodological approach. Critically, each sees the concept of personality in a different light. Before reviewing the leading schools it is worthwhile to consider what they agree upon. This will reveal the core of beliefs about what 'personality' is. Carver and Scheier (2000, p. 5) develop a definition of personality that covers areas of general agreement across the different schools. They suggest personality is:

- *Organised* – it has a coherent unity and is not fragmented;

- *Active* – personality is maintained by and revealed through dynamic processes;

- *Physical* – personality is a psychological concept, but it is derived from physical (anatomical, neurophysiological) processes, particularly, but not exclusively, in the brain;

- *Causal* – personality determines how an individual will act and react in particular circumstances;

- *Regular* – the personality of an individual is consistent over periods of time, and leads to consistent patterns of behaviour;

- *Manifest* – it shows up in many different ways, including physical states, affective moods, personal feelings, decisions and actions.

Around this core, different psychological schools develop different interpretations of the personality concept. The more important will now be briefly reviewed. Accounts of these different perspectives can be found in any good textbook on the psychology of personality. Carver and Scheier (2000) and Mischel (1999) are recommended. A very accessible introductory account can be found in Jarvis (2000).

Psychodynamic approaches

Psychodynamic approaches to personality see it as the result of a series of internal psychological processes that may work in harmony or in discord. The most famous exemplifier of the psychodynamic approach was the Viennese therapist Sigmund Freud (1856–1939). Freud suggested that such forces psychologically *determined* human behaviour. These were not always under conscious control. The unconscious mind played an important role and these forces were often manifest beyond awareness. Freud suggested three primary processes in the anatomy of the mind: the *Id*, which lies in the unconscious, relates to basic biological urges and impulses. It includes biologically determined instincts that demand immediate gratification. The Id is impulsive and irrational. The *Superego*, on the other hand, manages social behaviour and graces. The Superego, which lies in both the conscious and unconscious, maintains an individual's moral beliefs and is imparted by parents and socialisation processes. The *Ego*, which lies in the conscious mind, mediates between the Id and Superego. It helps the Superego keep the Id in check while making sure that the Superego is informed of the person's deeper wants and needs within the Id. The Ego is rational, calculating and plans ahead. Freud developed his theory based on the presumption that these three processes should work in harmony in a balanced, dynamic way and that if they were out of step then some form of mental strife or even illness would result. These took the form of three anxieties: *neurotic* anxiety, the belief that one's base instincts would take control (and so one would lose control of one's behaviour), and *moral* anxiety about actions one has taken (guilt, regret, embarrassment, etc.). These are derived from *reality* anxiety, justified (at least to self) beliefs that one is in some sort of danger. Motivation arises from the transformation of instincts within the Id. If these are not socially acceptable, then they must be transformed into actions that are. A number of psychologists have added to, and developed, Freud's thinking.

Freud divides psychologists. Some are intensely loyal to his ideas. Others dismiss his work as speculative, unscientific and not testable in any real sense. If the claim is made that entrepreneurs are so, because running one's own venture is a way of managing these anxieties (the 'misfit' school might have some sympathy with this idea) and that motivation arises from motive transformation then these claims are not such that can be empirically validated through objective inquiry. It should be recognised that this is not of immediate concern to researchers who are adopting a subjective methodological approach (such methodologies are explored further in Chapter 5).

Dispositional approaches

A disposition is a tendency to act in a particular way in a particular situation. We may say of a person, he or she is outgoing, or alternatively, introspective. Some people are predictable, others less so. Some people look towards internalised values to judge their acts, others look outside themselves to others' reactions to judge their acts. And so on. Features like this are referred to as *traits*. Traits are dimensions. An individual may have more or less of a trait and be located somewhere along a spectrum. Eysenck (1975) suggested that two key traits were the introvert–extrovert dimension and the emotionally stable–unstable dimension. Combining these two independently gave rise to four basic personality types: stable introverts were *phlegmatic*, unstable introverts were *melancholic*, stable extroverts were *sanguine* and unstable extroverts were *choleric*. A number of workers have developed a five-factor model of traits (see Carver and Scheier, 2000, p. 69). The five factors relate to the individual's characterisation in their approach to *power*, *love*, *work*, *affect* (emotionality) and *intellect*. The idea of traits is linked to some ideas in cognitive psychology (see below). Research has been conducted to see if entrepreneurs are drawn disproportionately from one particular trait group. The findings are generally negative; all trait groups are represented in entrepreneurs as they are in the wider population. However, there are issues of methodology and definition, and research continues.

Biological approaches

This term covers a range of approaches and might include the evolutionary approaches discussed below. Central, though, is the idea that personality is, fundamentally, a biological process. A specific idea is that personality is dictated by genes. If so, personality can be explained through genetics. At face value, this is quite convincing. After all, our genes dictate our bodies, so why not our minds as well? Environmental factors also play a part. We know that personality must, in part, be physically located, because personality can be changed by physical processes (alcohol, narcotics and brain lesions, for example). The central question is, to what extent is behaviour determined by genetics or environment? Some evidence supporting the genetic claim has been obtained from twin studies. Identical twins share their genetic complement, while non-identical twins share just half (the same as any siblings). By assessing the personalities of twin-pairs separated at birth through adoption, any closer match between the personalities of identical twins over that of non-identical must be due to genetic factors. This area of research is highly controversial. Not least in this is the notion that it negates the role of society and personal experience in moulding personality. The study of individual genetic endowments has been transformed by modern DNA technology and the Human Genome Project. To my knowledge, no twin studies have been conducted on entrepreneurs, nor have the genetics of entrepreneurs been explored. Such studies will be an interesting, but frightening, prospect. Can we really imagine venture capitalists giving up reading business plans and talking to entrepreneurs and instead sending them off for DNA testing?

Evolutionary psychological approaches

Evolutionary psychology is based on the premise that modern human cognitive skills are the result of evolution through selective forces. Human beings were essentially 'completed' evolutionarily forces by about 100,000 years ago. Since then we have not changed significantly in terms of physical characteristics and mental architecture. So we cannot look to the modern world to explain our current repertoire of cognitive skills; rather we must look to that period in the late Palaeolithic when we became what we are. An important aspect of our situation then was the growing complexity of social interactions, motivated not least by the possibility of increasing welfare through the exchange of goods. One of the more controversial claims made by evolutionary psychology is that our cognition is modularised. We do not have a single, integrated mental system. The human mind is composed of a series of systems that have evolved to deal with different decision situations. There is debate as to the extent to which these systems are integrated at a higher level. Accessible accounts of this idea, and the debate it has engendered, are given by Badcock (2000), Barrett *et al.* (2002), Carruthers and Chamberlain (2000), Cartwright (2000), Corballis and Lea (1999), Oyama (2000) and Wright (2000). Ham Ofek gives an account of the economic basis of human evolution in his book *Second Nature: Economic Origins of Human Behaviour*. By its nature, though, evolutionary psychology is talking about the psychology of human beings as a *species*, not at an individual level. Its concern is with our *common* psychological inheritance. So while it may offer an explanation of entrepreneurial behaviour in general, it is less well placed (at this time) to explain why one person decides to take on the role of entrepreneur and another does not.

Phenomenological approaches

The schools of thinking so far discussed share a belief in the commonality of personality. Individuals may fall into different categories, but within those categories, individuals 'share' a personality. The phenomenological approach takes issue with this. It emphasises the uniqueness of each individual and the irreproducibility of his or her historical and introspective experiences. It prioritises subjective experience over objective classification. Usually associated with the approach are two beliefs about human beings. The first is that humans are endowed with free will, the possibility of making choices for themselves. In practice, these choices may be restricted by both external and internal factors. In principle, though, these restrictions can be removed, freeing the individual to make free choices. Second, it regards humans as self-perfecting, drawn towards the 'good', in terms of health, welfare and personal maturity. The phenomenological approach is, to a greater or lesser degree, anti-positivistic (see Chapter 5). It does not concern itself with generalisations. It prefers to regard accounts of psychology as essentially personal narratives. There are some good phenomenological accounts of the psychological experiences of individual entrepreneurs. But necessarily, they cannot be extended to the experience of others. Phenomenological approaches cannot explain why some people become entrepreneurs and others do not, simply because it does not set out to.

Behavioural approaches

The animal psychologist B.F. Skinner, who in the late 1940s studied behavioural conditioning in pigeons, founded behavioural psychology. He moved on to extend his ideas to humans. The basic postulates of behaviourism are that psychology must become a 'proper' science and so should only concern itself with what is observable (behaviour) and forget about the unobservable (introspection). In this respect, behaviourism is super-objective and at the opposite end of the scale to phenomenological approaches. Skinner's methodology was to connect human action directly to externally imposed stimuli without calling on the notion of mind as an intervening factor. As might be imagined, Skinner's ideas were, and still are, highly controversial. Skinner's rather brutal behaviourism quickly lost favour when its limitations in explaining some human actions were demonstrated (the most important area is in language development and performance). Some attempts were made to salvage the ideas, but behaviourism has largely been superseded by cognitive psychology (see below), which still connects actions to inputs, but calls upon personal cognitive processes as an intervening mechanism. Most studies into entrepreneurial psychology came at a time after behaviourism was in descent. Despite this, behaviourist ideas are still influential, often at a metaphoric level. Do we not say entrepreneurs are stimulated by new opportunities? Or that making more capital available will encourage more people to become entrepreneurs? Or that certain social, cultural and economic conditions facilitate entrepreneurship? Unadorned with concern over what is actually happening in the individual mind to connect these stimuli to the response of becoming entrepreneurial, these are essentially behaviourist linkages.

Social-cognitive learning approaches

This school moves the debate from concern with personality as something, essentially at least, pre-determined and 'in the head' of the individual to something that results from social experience and interaction. It places emphasis on personality as something that is, to a greater or lesser extent, imparted to the individual by others. Social-cognitive learning approaches are very diverse and this school is not unified by a single methodology or even theoretical outlook. However, there is agreement on the importance of learning in a social context. The role of mentors and leadership are brought into play, as are personal learning styles and strategies. Life experiences such as exposure to incubating organisations are drawn in, along with antecedent (inherent, given) personality factors. This school is influential in the study of entrepreneurship particularly because of its flexibility in dealing with these issues, which are widely seen as relevant. A number of workers have developed social-cognitive learning models of entrepreneurship. An important example includes Cooper (1981), who suggested a model that included three sets of factors influencing entrepreneurial start-up: antecedent influences (those things inherent to the entrepreneur such as genetic endowment, education and life experiences), incubator organisation experience, and environmental experiences (including the availability of opportunities and resources).

The flexibility of the approach, while a strength, is also a weakness. In being able to call upon a wide range of factors, it loses specificity. It can fail to make clear predictions, and the move to entrepreneurship can always be accounted for given the range of explanatory factors available. This is not to say it has not offered a number of important insights, especially when handled by researchers careful to control its methodology.

Attribution-based approaches

All of the ideas explored so far have assumed (implicitly at least) that personality is something we, as individuals, possess. Different schools disagree on how it is located and what its psychological underpinning is, but where it is located is not at issue. Attribution theories take a more radical approach and suggest that personality is not so much something an individual has, but is something awarded to individuals by others. Personality is in the eye of the beholder, not the beholden. Attribution theory was largely founded by H.H. Kelley (1973), who asked why individuals tended to assign objects to particular categories and specific events to certain causes. He concluded that individual decision makers were 'intuitive scientists' in that they used an intuitive analysis of variance to make assignments. In particular they looked at three factors: *consistency*, *distinctiveness* and *consensus*. The suggestion in attribution theory is that when allocating an individual of whom we have experience to a particular personality type (either a formal typing from psychological theory, or our personal intuitive categories) we decide across three factors, here applied to the label of 'entrepreneur':

- *Consistency* in the way in which an individual reacts: for example, we always expect entrepreneurs to react positively and embrace new opportunities.

- *Distinctiveness* in that the individual reacts in a way different to those stimuli we regard as proper entrepreneurial stimuli, to those we do not regard as such: for example, we may expect an entrepreneur to be a tough negotiator in a business setting, but not so in his or her family life.

- *Consensus* in that the entrepreneur acts differently from those we do not regard as entrepreneurs. If *all* people react in a certain way, then there is no point in looking towards that action as a way of distinguishing entrepreneurs from others.

If we see that an individual is consistent in reacting positively to entrepreneurial stimuli, is distinctive in his or her response to specifically entrepreneurial stimuli and is of low consensus in that he or she reacts differently to most others, then we will label that person as an entrepreneur. The important point to note is that it is *we* who are assigning that label, not the 'entrepreneur' him or herself. Kelley's attribution theory has been very influential in the social sciences (Figure 3.1).

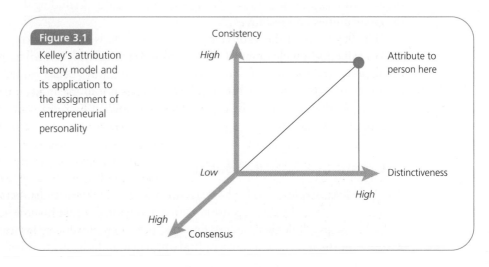

Figure 3.1

Kelley's attribution theory model and its application to the assignment of entrepreneurial personality

Within ten years of its publication, over 1000 papers in the social sciences were published citing it (see Kelley and Michela's review of 1980 for an account of early application and developments of the theory). Important avenues of application are in investigating the way dispositions are attributed to an actor (e.g. Ajzen, 1971), the way in which individuals attribute success and failure to themselves or to external factors beyond their control (e.g. Bernstein and Stephan, 1979) and differences in attribution of causal effect between individuals involved in an event (actors) and those looking in on the event (observers) (e.g. Arkin and Duval, 1975). Despite the number of studies, however, I know of no research that utilises attribution theory to specifically explore how people assign the label entrepreneur to other people. There is a clear research opportunity here.

The limitations of personality models

Personality is a concept of central importance in psychology. It plays a crucial role in aiding our understanding of the social interaction between people and it has both illuminated our understanding of, and enriched our appreciation of, the entrepreneur. However, it is important that we do not let an inappropriate idea of personality distort our view. There is no real evidence to suggest that there is a single 'entrepreneurial personality'. People of all personality types, attitudes and dispositions not only become entrepreneurs but become *successful* entrepreneurs. A consequence of this is that personality testing does not provide a good indicator of who will, or will not, be a successful entrepreneur. To be a successful entrepreneur takes many things: ambition, drive, hard work, effort in learning to understand a business and practice as a manager. But it does not demand a particular personality. Experience shows that a reserved introvert who carefully calculates their next move can look forward to as much entrepreneurial success as their more 'theatrical', and instinctive, counterpart. No one with entrepreneurial ambitions should ever dismiss the option of an entrepreneurial career because they do not feel they are the 'right type' of person. To do so reveals more about their misconceptions of entrepreneurship than it does about their potential.

3.3 Cognitive aspects of entrepreneurship

Key learning outcome

An appreciation of the cognitive approach to understanding entrepreneurial behaviour and the significance of individual cognitive style and strategy in entrepreneurial decision making.

Cognitive psychology (first introduced in Section 1.4) is the branch of the psychological sciences that is concerned with how human beings acquire, store and process information about the world. It attempts to understand how we make decisions, act and react in different situations. Interest has grown in the cognitive aspects of management in general and entrepreneurship in particular.

Cognitive psychology has made great strides in enhancing our understanding of human thinking. It is now recognised that we all have our own cognitive styles that we use to process information and that we adopt particular cognitive strategies when called upon to use that information in order to solve problems. Many of these strategies and styles resonate with our experiences of how other people approach challenges. We may, for example, note that some people are 'big-picture' – that is, they only like to take the essential, important facts into account when they first meet a new problem. Others are 'small-picture'. They like detailed and extensive information before attempting a solution. At other times we may recognise that some people prefer tried and trusted solutions; others are willing, eager even, to find new ways of doing things. At a deeper level, some people compartmentalise new information into a pre-existing set of categories and see new things in established terms. We may regard such people as relatively fixed in their thinking. Other people prefer to set up new categories and so see things in new ways. We may regard these as more open in their thinking. These general observations about how people work, however useful as rules of thumb, cannot be accepted at face value, though. Cognitive psychology is a science. It is concerned with establishing the well-defined and experimentally reproducible processes that are revealed through the actions taken in response to specific cognitive challenges. Cognitive processes are sometimes split into three types:

- *perception processes* – these are concerned with how we see the world and gather information about it. Examples are *complexity–simplicity*, the number of dimensions that are used to categorise the world, *levelling–sharpening*, the use of existing or the creation of new categories to incorporate new information, and *verbalising–visualising*, the use of verbal or, alternatively, visual imagery to develop understanding.

- *problem solving processes* – these govern how information is used when an individual is called upon to make a decision. Examples include *scanning–focusing*, how much information is called in order to solve a problem, *serialism–holism*, referring to whether problems are approached in a linear, reducing way, or are dealt with as an integrated whole, and *adaptation–innovation*, the preference for established solutions or new solutions.

- *task processes* – these are concerned with determining the way in which we approach particular jobs. Themes here include *constricted–flexible*, the preference for new types of task over established ones, *impulsive–reflective*, the tendency to act in a decisive or considered way, and *uncertainty accepting–cautious*, the willingness to take on tasks with an element of risk in them.

Stubbart (1989) and Hayes and Allinson (1994) provide full reviews of cognitive styles and their relevance to management. Cognitive styles and strategies may be linked to, and provide a basis for, what we consider to be personality. They are, however, distinct from it. Individuals may rely on well-honed cognitive approaches, but they are not necessarily invariant over time. Our cognitive approaches are subject to learning and may be modified, either intentionally or unintentionally, in the light of experience. Cognitive psychology is increasingly offering insights that can potentially account for and explain a number of aspects of the individual entrepreneur's inclination towards the entrepreneurial option and their engagement in the entrepreneurial process. Particularly important areas are:

- the influence of cognition on motivation and the entrepreneur's perceptions and valuation of the entrepreneurial option compared to conventional employment alternatives (e.g. Campbell, 1992; Katz, 1992; Amundson, 1995; Eisenhauer, 1995; Robichaud and Egbert, 2001; Uusitalo, 2001);

- the impact of cognition on the individual's ability to spot new business opportunities (e.g. Minniti and Bygrave, 1999; McCline *et al.*, 2000; Key *et al.*, 2002);

- the analytical skills of the individual and his or her ability to evaluate and make proper judgements about the value of that opportunity (see Section 3.4);

- creativity in developing new innovation to capitalise on those opportunities;

- cognitive abilities in terms of considering competitive environments and dynamics (e.g. Giminez *et al.*, 2000; Luthans *et al.*, 2000; Frese *et al.*, 2002; Kreiser *et al.*, 2002a, b; Kristiansen, 2002; Weaver *et al.*, 2002);

- abilities in relation to 'strategic foresight', the potential to imagine future worlds and consider the outcomes of current decisions in relation to them (see Section 13.4);

- judgement over what parts of the world are under personal control and which are not (do entrepreneurs overestimate their ability to control the world as compared to non-entrepreneurs?) (e.g. Neck *et al.*, 1999; Markman *et al.*, 2002; Shepherd and Krueger, 2002);

- the ability to judge risk (either realistically, or perhaps more positively than others, e.g. Stancill, 1981; Chaterjee *et al.*, 2003);

- skills in creating appropriate strategic approaches and plans (e.g. Escher *et al.*, 2002);

- abilities in relation to communicating with and persuading key stakeholders (e.g. Kamm and Nurick, 1992);

- social relationship skills in sustaining and maintaining the organisation (e.g. Katz, 1992);

- the ability to develop personal learning strategies in light of experience (e.g. Minniti and Bygrave, 2001).

The question of whether or not entrepreneurs (as a group) have a cognition (cognitive skills or strategy) that is different from non-entrepreneurs has been the subject of a number of recent studies. Buchanan and Di Pierro (1980) provide a historical and conceptual introduction to this issue. Mitchell *et al.* (2002) lay out the foundations for, and emphasise the potential of, a cognitive approach to understanding entre-preneurial behaviour and performance. Forbes (1999) reviews studies of the role of management cognition (particularly decision heuristics and cognitive schemas) in entrepreneurship. Neck *et al.* (1999) develops the notion that 'thought self leadership', the process of self-influence through the cognitive strategies of self-dialogue and mental imagery, plays a role in entrepreneurial management, and Keh *et al.* (2002) examine the effect of cognitive processes on assessment of opportunities under risky conditions. The theme of cognition and its influence on entrepreneurship will be revisited in Sections 7.4 and 8.3, where cognitive insights into entrepreneurship and culture and the start-up decision, respectively, will be considered.

It is probably premature to insist that entrepreneurs, as a group, share any particular set of cognitive approach. The 'best' cognitive approach in any situation is dependent on a particular situation. Entrepreneurial situations are as varied as any other type of situation. However, it is true that entrepreneurs do tend to be innovative, are receptive to new ideas and do set out to find new ways of doing things. How this general observation can be rationalised in terms of specific, well-defined cognitive strategies is a subject of much interest in cognitive research.

3.4 Entrepreneurship and psychometric testing

> **Key learning outcome**
>
> Introductory understanding of the principles of personality testing, the challenges to developing effective personality tests and their role in entrepreneurship research and investors' selection of entrepreneurs.

Personality testing is part of a more general class of psychological tests generally known as *psychometric* tests. Psychometric tests aim to discover something about an individual's mental architecture by having him or her answer a specific series of questions. These may be on the basis of written answers ('pencil-and-paper' tests) or an interview, or a combination of the two.

In addition to personality tests, psychometric testing includes general intelligence testing (such as the IQ test), tests for particular mental aptitudes and a series of techniques for examining psychological abnormalities. The most famous test here is the *Rorschach test*, in which subjects reveal what they see in a random pattern of ink blots (though few psychologists now take this particular test seriously). Tests that aim to reveal an individual's personality (or personal outlook) face a number of challenges. First, the questions posed must be meaningful and relevant in revealing specific aspects of personality. As will be appreciated from the dis-cussion of schools of thinking about personality above, the relevance of particular questions will be sensitive to theoretical assumptions being made about what, exactly, personality is. Second, the responses must be correlated to particular personality factors with regard for proper statistical methods. Third, the subject must give honest answers to the questions. Their response should not be influenced by what they feel the investigator wants them to say, nor should they answer on behalf of the person they *want* to be, rather than actually *are*. Fourth, if the test is to have any value as a predictive tool, it must be demonstrated that the way in which the subject responds to the test matches up with the way they actually behave in the real world. Fifth, those aspects of personality revealed must be stable over time. All of these issues present significant methodological challenges and much of the research in the psychometrics field is aimed at resolving them (the interested student is referred to a standard work in the field such as Kaplan and Saccuzzo (1997) for details on methodology and research). They are particularly acute when it comes to testing the personality of entrepreneurs. Two groups have a particular interest in this area: researchers who are exploring the links between personality and entrepreneurial inclination, and investors who want to be able to predict the likely performance of an individual seeking financial support. Clearly, there is much sympathy between these two groups and they often work in collaboration. A number of tests have been developed for testing entrepreneurs. The most popular are the proactive personality disposition (PPD) and the entrepreneurial-orientation (EO) scale. Proactivity is defined as the extent to which individuals take action to control their environments. This proactivity is measured by asking subjects how they would react in a variety of situations. The assumption is that the more proactive a person, the more likely he or she is to is to seek out and pursue an entrepreneurial career. Crant (1996) tested individuals' proactivity measures and then correlated them (along with variables such as gender, education and parental entrepreneurship) with intentions to start a business. The study found that pro-activity correlated positively with intention. Becherer and Maurer (1999) tested the proactivity of 215 small business presidents and found that the president's proactivity correlated with the firm's overall entrepreneurial posture (as judged independently), but could not be correlated with the president's leadership style. The EO scale probes the entrepreneur's strategic outlook, rather than personality directly and it can be applied to firms as well as individuals. However, it is a psy-chometric test methodology. The test has eight items that ask, for example, whether the entrepreneur/entrepreneur's firm looks towards introducing new products, or prefers to rely on existing products, whether they tend to initiate actions that competitors react to, or vice versa and whether the entrepreneur prefers bold, far-reaching acts to cautious incremental acts, and so on. Kreiser *et al.* report studies on the regularity of these orientations on an international basis (2002a) and explore how they are affected by environmental uncertainty (2002b). These authors give full details of the test. Weaver *et al.* (2002) also explore the effect of environmental uncertainty on entrepreneurial orientation.

The findings of studies using instruments such as the PPD and EO scale have produced mixed results. As noted above and in Chapter 1, it is fair to say that, at present, no real consensus has emerged as to the link between personality and entre-preneurial behaviour. No test has consistently and robustly demonstrated any clear, significant connection. (The research picture is a bit distorted because researchers, and journal editors, tend to prefer studies with positive results rather than negative. This is an issue in all walks of academic inquiry, not just entrepreneurship. The negative findings of the Blanchflower and Oswald study are a notable exception;

see Section 7.1.) However, research continues and new methodological advances in the future may make the picture clearer (my belief is that cognitive approaches have most potential and are likely to be the most valuable in the future). However, many venture capitalists do insist on prospective entrepreneurs undergoing personality tests before they are awarded investment funds. A number of agencies have started up offering this service to venture capitalists. If they are not going to reveal anything of value, why should they be willing to pay for them? The answer lies (and what follows is very much a personal view) not in personality tests, as such, but in the wider nature of human decision making. We are impelled to make sense of the world. We like regularity and patterns (which is why we see faces and other objects in random ink blots). We like to connect events to clear, unambiguous causes, because then we can make decisions influencing them (or at least feel we can). Unfortunately many aspects of the real world are not connected through simple cause and effect chains; they are causally ambiguous. So we seek, and grasp at, simple explanations that give accounts of why contingencies happen. After all, no matter how often it is demonstrated that astrology, tarot card reading and handwriting analysis is sheer nonsense, with no predictive or explanatory power whatsoever, many people simply refuse to give up their belief in them, because they lose their ability to explain how the world works, something they value greatly. The decision by a venture capitalist to invest or not in a particular one is a major one. It is fundamentally a matter of judgement and that judgement is hard to explain (even good venture capitalists find it hard to explain *why* they are good). A lot of money and risk is involved. That risk is not just financial. The venture capitalist's reputation and career prospects are on the line as well. Anything that can externalise and objectify an investment decision will be valued. So some venture capitalists' belief in the value of personality testing is based not so much on the fact that it highlights the best investment opportunities, but if the final decision is the wrong one, the investor can point to something public and explicit that is outside his or her own judgement to explain why. In short, it is a self-defence mechanism. But such self-defence may be rational if the investor can safeguard his or her reputation using it.

(3.5) Entrepreneurship and human decision making

> ### Key learning outcome
>
> An appreciation of the distinction between normative, descriptive and prescriptive accounts of human decision making, the types of bias that influence decision making and the dangers they present to the intuitive decision maker, and the use of prescriptive methods to improve decision making.

The making of decisions is a fundamental part of the human experience. We can imagine different outcomes and possibilities; we can judge that which we can act to influence and that which we must accept, and we have preferences for some outcomes over others. The study of human decision making is a rapidly growing field of inquiry, both in terms of fundamental decisional processes in cognition and in specific areas of professional decision making, particularly in management, medicine and law. There are three types of theory that aim to explain and predict decision making. The first are *normative* theories. Normative theories identify what is the best (optimal) decision in a particular situation and the process for making it. Such theories are based on sound logical and statistical methodologies. They are often based on an assumption that human beings are rational (they make best use of information) and are utility maximising (they want the best possible outcomes for themselves). The second type of theory is *descriptive*. Descriptive theories provide accounts of the decisions people actually make. Their concern is with what people *really* do, rather than what they *should* do. The final type of theory is *prescriptive*. Prescriptive theories suggest ways individuals can improve their decision-making practice. If human beings were, in fact, perfectly rational and utility maximising then there would be no difference between descriptions of human decision making and normative recommendations. However, descriptive investigations reveal that human decision making usually fails to meet normative standards. A deviation between actual decision-making outcomes and theoretically optimal ones is referred to as a *bias*. A bias is not simply an error caused by not understanding the normative method, or laziness in applying it (after all, normative methods may be difficult to use). Errors would lead to decision outcomes being randomly dispersed around the normative mean. Biases are *consistent* – the bias is usually in one particular direction away from the normative, *prevalent* – they occur in a wide variety of decision contexts, and persistent – they are difficult to *eliminate*, even if the decision maker is informed of the normative method and is rewarded for using it. Important examples of biases include the *anchoring bias* – using an irrelevant and spurious number to make a numerical judgement, the *availability bias* – using prominent instances that are in memory as the basis for making a judgement, the *representativeness bias* – judging low-probability eventualities as of higher probability if they are associated with a highly credible statement, and the *base-rate neglect bias* – ignoring background information in making judgements. Other biases include *framing effects* – judgement changing on the basis of how information is contextualised – and a series of biases associated with judging correlation and causation and the valuation of risk options. Cognitive psychologists have suggested that these biases arise because individuals use deep-seated *heuristics* or practical 'rules of thumb' to make judgements rather than normative methods. These findings have been used to challenge the notion that humans are rational in the sense in which economic theory has traditionally assumed we are – that is, we always seek to maximise our utility, adopting normative methods to do so – and to argue that economics should take a more behavioural approach and take this into account.

There is not space here to explore these issues further (the interested student is referred to the books by Baron (2000), Gilhooly (1996), Hastie and Dawes (2001) and Plous (1993), which offer good introductions to the issues, and the more advanced contributions to Kahneman *et al.* (1982) and Kahneman and Tversky (2000) are also recommended. The key point is that such biases can impact on the quality of decision making both for entrepreneurs and for those supporting them (especially investors). The advantages and dangers of relying on intuitive (heuristic-based) decision making are explored by Myers (2002). Gigerenzer (2002) suggests practical methods for improving decision making.

Summary of key ideas

- The notion that entrepreneurs, as a group, share some aspects of personality that makes them different to non-entrepreneurs is intuitively appealing.

- However, establishing if this is so is problematic.

- Any theory linking entrepreneurship to personality must be clear on what the terms mean and how they can be (independently) measured (instrumentalised).

- This is a challenge with both concepts. It is particularly so with personality.

- Different schools of psychological thinking define, characterise and measure personality in different ways. Important schools include:
  - psychodynamic
  - dispositional
  - biological
  - evolutionary
  - phenomenological
  - behavioural
  - social-cognitive learning
  - attributional.

- Personality testing has been used as both a practical and research tool for evaluating and studying entrepreneurs. However, it is premature to suggest that such testing is unambiguously able to distinguish entrepreneurs from non-entrepreneurs.

- Cognitive approaches consider how humans acquire, store and process information in order to make decisions. Whether entrepreneurs (as a group) are distinct from non-entrepreneurs in their cognitive style and strategy is not yet clear, but it is the subject of extensive research.

- Entrepreneurs are decision makers. The experimental study of human decision making is a fast growing area that promises to illuminate the way in which entrepreneurs think.

Research themes

Presumptions about entrepreneurial personality

As noted at the beginning of this chapter, many people feel, intuitively, that entrepreneurs have a particular sort of personality. This may be researched further using a Delphi technique. The first stage would be to identify a group of individuals (say 30–50) who might be expected to have developed such a belief – for example, practising entrepreneurs, people who work with entrepreneurs, management consultants, academics in the business field, supporting agencies, local and national politicians, etc. Contact them asking four open-ended questions. First, what do they think is and how would they define 'personality'? Second, how would they define the term 'entrepreneur'? Third, what personality characteristics would they associate with the entrepreneur and how are these different from the population as a whole? Fourth, what is the role of these personality characteristics in entrepreneurial success? Once the responses have been collected, go through them coding the points raised. Different people say the same or similar things in different ways. Try to find the core issues in the responses to each question and summarise them as single words or propositions. Next set up a survey based on these propositions. Submit it to each of the original respondents, asking for the degree to which they agree or disagree with the propositions (a Likert scale may be used). Once the findings have been summarised (perhaps graphically), resubmit them to the respondents, getting their final view on the overall findings. You may ask if they would change their original opinion given the aggregated findings. As a final analysis, conclude the nature of people's presumption about the link between personality and entrepreneurial activity. Is this consistent or do people hold widely different views? Is there a core of assumptions? How might these presumptions affect the way in which entrepreneurs see themselves, the personality they aspire to and how those around them see them?

A literature review

There is an extensive literature on the relationship between personality and entrepreneurial inclination and behaviour. References to some of the key studies are given in the suggested reading. A search by an academic search engine will find many more. Consider these studies chronologically. Review each, asking how the concepts of entrepreneur and personality are instrumentalised, make evident the assumptions about the ontology of personality and expose the underlying pragmatics using the scheme discussed above. Are these aspects discussed explicitly in the study or are they implicit? How are the notions of 'entrepreneur' and 'personality' defined? What issues might there be with the instrumentalisations selected? How do they support the methodology used? Do the findings support the notion of an entrepreneurial personality or not? What is the current stage of knowledge and what issues remain to be investigated?

Summarise by discussing the trends in these issues and map out directions for future studies.

Correlating entrepreneurial activity with personality

Identify a pool of individuals who you (based on some explicit criteria that do not involve personality, e.g. managerial history or business type) consider to be entrepreneurs and a complementary set of individuals who are not. Ideally these should be matched for age, sex and sector they are working in. Construct a survey that asks those selected how they would react in certain (briefly described) situations. For example, how they would react if presented with a new business opportunity, or how they would deal with a leadership challenge, or would approach a particular negotiation (the EO scale may be adopted). The aim here is to have the subject reveal something about their personality. It is, of course, being assumed here that the subjects' approach to the situation is an indicator of personality (i.e. a rather behavioural definition of personality). Aim for around twenty or so situations. You may wish to limit subjects' responses to one of a few (4–6) options for each situation. These options may be found by coding responses from an open-ended preliminary study. Once the responses have been collected the next stage would be to have an independent group of judges (perhaps other students) assess the responses and categorise the individuals as entrepreneurial or not. How well does the categorisation judgement match up with the actuality of whether a subject is an entrepreneur or not (based on your initial definition)? Does personality (as revealed by the subjects' responses) provide a good lead indicator of who is, or is not, an entrepreneur? Might a better correlation be obtained if the entrepreneur is defined in a different way? In the summary, consider the limitations of this methodological approach and how it might be improved.

Suggestions for further reading

Ajzen, I. (1971) 'Attributions of dispositions to an actor: effects of perceived decision freedom and behavioural utilities', *Journal of Personality and Social Psychology*, Vol. 18, No. 2, pp. 144–56.

Amundson, N.E. (1995) 'An interactive model of career decision-making', *Journal of Employment Counselling*, Vol. 32, No. 1, pp. 11–21.

Arkin, R.M. and Duval, S. (1975) 'Focus of attention and causal attribution of actors and observers', *Journal of Experimental Social Psychology*, Vol. 11, pp. 427–38.

Badcock, C. (2000) *Evolutionary Psychology*, Cambridge: Polity Press.

Barkow, J.H., Cosmides, L. and Tooby, J. (eds) (1992) *The Adapted Mind: Evolutionary Psychology and the Generation of Culture*, Oxford: Oxford University Press.

Baron, J. (2000) *Thinking and Deciding* (3rd edn), Cambridge: Cambridge University Press.

Barrett, L., Dunbar, R. and Lycett, J. (2002) *Human Evolutionary Psychology*, London: Palgrave.

Becherer, R.C. and Maurer, J.G. (1999) 'The proactive personality disposition and entrepreneurial behavior among small company presidents', *Journal of Small Business Management*, Vol. 37, No. 1, pp. 28–36.

Bernstein, W.M. and Stephan, W.G. (1979) 'Explaining attributions for achievement: a path analytical approach', *Journal of Personality and Social Psychology*, Vol. 37, No. 10, pp. 1810–21.

Blanchflower, D.G. and Oswald, A.J. (1998) 'What makes an entrepreneur?', *Journal of Labour Economics*, Vol. 16, No. 1, pp. 26–60.

Buchanan, J.M. and Di Pierro, A. (1980) 'Cognition, choice, and entrepreneurship', *Southern Economic Journal*, Vol. 46, No. 3, pp. 693–701.

Campbell, C.A. (1992) 'A decision theory model for entrepreneurial acts', *Entrepreneurship Theory and Practice*, Fall, pp. 21–7.

Carruthers, P. and Chamberlain, A. (eds) (2000) *Evolution and the Human Mind: Modularity, Language and Meta-cognition*, Cambridge: Cambridge University Press.

Cartwright, J. (2000) *Evolution and Human Behaviour*, London: Macmillan.

Carver, C.S. and Scheier, M. (2000) *Perspectives on Personality* (4th edn), Boston, MA: Allyn and Bacon.

Chatterjee, S., Wiseman, R.M., Fieqenbaum, A. and Devers, C.E. (2003) 'Integrating behavioural and economic concepts of risk into strategic management: the twain shall meet', *Long Range Planning*, Vol. 36, pp. 61–79.

Cooper, A.C. (1981) 'Strategic management, new ventures and small business', *Long Range Planning*, Vol. 14, No. 5.

Corballis, M.C. and Lea, S.E.G. (eds) (1999) *The Descent of Mind: Psychological Perspectives on Hominid Evolution*, Oxford: Oxford University Press.

Crant, J.M. (1996) The Proactive Personality Scale as a predictor of entrepreneurial intentions. *Journal of Small Business Management*, Vol. 34, No. 3, pp. 42–9.

Eisen, S.V. (1979) 'Actor-observer differences in information inference and causal attribution', *Journal of Personality and Social Psychology*, Vol. 37, No. 2, pp. 261–72.

Eisenhauer, J.G. (1995) 'The entrepreneurial decision: economic theory and empirical evidence', *Entrepreneurship Theory and Practice*, Summer, pp. 67–79.

Escher, S., Grabarkiewicz, R., Frese, M., van Steekelenburg, G., Lauw, M. and Freidrich, C. (2002) 'The moderator effect of cognitive ability on the relationship between planning strategies and business success of small scale business owners in South Africa: a longitudinal study', *Journal of Developmental Entrepreneurship*, Vol. 7, No. 5, pp. 305–18.

Eysenck, H.J. (1975) *The Inequality of Man*, San Diego, CA: EdITS.

Forbes, D.P. (1999) 'Cognitive approaches to new venture creation', *International Journal of Management Reviews*, Vol. 1, No. 4, pp. 415–39.

Frese, M., Brantjes, A. and Hoorn, R. (2002) 'Psychological success factors of small scale businesses in Namibia: the role of strategy process, entrepreneurial orientation and the environment', *Journal of Developmental Entrepreneurship*, Vol. 7, No. 3, pp. 259–82.

Gigerenzer, G. (2002) *Reckoning with Risk: Learning to Live with Uncertainty*, London: Allen Lane.

Gilhooly, K.J. (1996) *Thinking: Directed, Undirected and Creative* (3rd edn), London: Academic Press.

Gimenez, F., Pelisson, C., Kruger, E.G.S. and Hayashi, P. (2000) 'Small firms' owner-managers construction of competition', *Journal of Enterprising Culture*, Vol. 8, No. 4, pp. 361–79.

Hastie, R. and Dawes, R.M. (2001) *Rational Choice in an Uncertain World: The Psychology of Judgement and Decision Making*, Thousand Oaks, CA: Sage.

Hayes, J. and Allinson, C.W. (1994) 'Cognitive style and its relevance for management practice', *British Journal of Management*, Vol. 5, pp. 53–71.

Jarvis, M. (2000) *Theoretical Approaches in Psychology*, London: Routledge.

Kahneman, D. and Tversky, A. (2000) *Choices, Values and Frames*, Cambridge: Cambridge University Press.

Kahneman, D., Slovic, P. and Tversky, A. (1982) *Judgement under Uncertainty: Heuristics and Biases*, Cambridge: Cambridge University Press.

Kamm, J.B. and Nurick, A.J. (1992) 'The stages in team venture formation: a decision-making model', *Entrepreneurship Theory and Practice*, Winter, pp. 17–27.

Kaplan, R.M. and Saccuzzo, D.P. (1997) *Psychological Testing: Principles, Applications, and Issues* (4th edn), Pacific Grove, CA: Brooks/Cole.

Katz, J.K. (1992) 'The dynamics of organizational emergence: a contemporary group formation perspective', *Entrepreneurship Theory and Practice*, Winter, pp. 97–101.

Katz, J.K. (1992) 'A psychosocial cognitive model of employment status choice', *Entrepreneurship Theory and Practice*, Fall, pp. 29–37.

Keh, H.T., Foo, M.D. and Lim, B.C. (2002) 'Opportunity evaluation under risky conditions: the cognitive process of entrepreneurs', *Entrepreneurship Theory and Practice*, Vol. 27, No. 2, pp. 125–48.

Kelley, H.H. (1973) 'The process of causal attribution', *American Psychologist*, February, pp. 107–28.

Kelley, H.H. and Michela, J.L. (1980) 'Attribution theory and research', *Annual Review of Psychology*, Vol. 31, pp. 457–1.

Kikul, J. and Gundry, L.K. (2002) 'Prospecting for strategic advantage: the proactive entrepreneurial personality and small firm innovation', *Journal of Small Business Management*, Vol. 40, No. 2, pp. 85–97.

Kreiser, P.M., Marino, L.D. and Weaver, K.M. (2002a) 'Reassessing the environment-EO link: the impact of environmental hostility on the dimensions of entrepreneurial orientation', *Academy of Management Best Papers Proceedings*.

Kreiser, P.M., Marino, L.D. and Weaver, K.M. (2002b) 'Assessing the psychometric properties of the entrepreneurial orientation scale: a multi-country analysis', *Entrepreneurship Theory and Practice*, Vol. 26, No. 4, pp. 71–94.

Kristiansen, S. (2002) 'Individual perception of business contexts: the case of small-scale entrepreneurs in Tanzania', *Journal of Developmental Entrepreneurship*, Vol. 7, No. 3, pp. 283–304.

Luthans, F., Stajkovic, A.D. and Ibrayeva, E. (2000) 'Environmental and psychological challenges facing entrepreneurial development in transition economies', *Journal of World Business*, Vol. 35, No. 1, pp. 95–110.

Markman, G.D., Balkin, D.B. and Baron, R.A. (2002) 'Inventors and new venture formation: the effects of general self-efficacy and regretful thinking', *Entrepreneurship Theory and Practice*, Winter, pp. 149–65.

McCline, R.L., Bhat, S. and Baj, P. (2000) 'Opportunity recognition: an exploratory investigation of a component in the entrepreneurial process in the context of the health care industry', *Entrepreneurship Theory and Practice*, Vol. 25, No. 2, pp. 81–94.

Minniti, M. and Bygrave, W. (1999) 'The microfoundations of entrepreneurship', *Entrepreneurship Theory and Practice*, Vol. 23, No. 4, pp. 41–53.

Minniti, M. and Bygrave, W. (2001) 'A dynamic model of entrepreneurial learning', *Entrepreneurship Theory and Practice*, Vol. 25, No. 3, pp. 5–16.

Mischel, W. (1999) *Introduction to Personality*, New York: Harcourt Brace.

Mitchell, R.K., Smith, B., Seawright, K.W. and Morse, E.A. (2000) 'Cross-cultural cognitions and the venture creation design', *Academy of Management Journal*, Vol. 43, No. 5, pp. 974–93.

Mitchell, R.K., Busenitz, L., Lant, T., McDougall, P.P., Morse, E.A. and Brock-Smith, J. (2002) 'Towards a theory of entrepreneurial cognition: rethinking the people side of entrepreneurship research', *Entrepreneurship Theory and Practice*, Winter, pp. 93–104.

Myers, D.G. (2002) *Intuition: Its Powers and Perils*, New Haven, CT: Yale University Press.

Neck, C.P., Neck, H.M., Manz, C.C. and Godwin, J. (1999) 'I think I can; I think I can: a self-leadership perspective towards enhancing the entrepreneur through thought patterns, self-efficacy and performance', *Journal of Managerial Psychology*, Vol. 14, No. 7/8, pp. 477–501.

Ofek, H. (2001) *Second Nature: Economic Origins of Human Evolution*, Cambridge: Cambridge University Press.

Oyama, S. (2000) *Evolution's Eye: A Systems View of the Biology–Culture Divide*, London: Duke University Press.

Plous, S. (1993) *The Psychology of Judgement and Decision Making*, New York: McGraw Hill.

Robichaud, Y. and Egbert, R.A. (2001) 'Towards the development of a measuring instrument for entrepreneurial motivation', *Journal of Developmental Entrepreneurship*, Vol. 6, No. 2, pp. 189–201.

Shepherd, D.A. and Krueger, N.F. (2002) 'An intentions-based model of entrepreneurial teams' social cognition', *Entrepreneurship Theory and Practice*, Winter, pp. 167–85.

Stancill, J.M. (1981) 'Realistic criteria for judging new ventures', *Harvard Business Review*, November–December, pp. 60–71.

Stubbart, C.I. (1989) 'Managerial cognition: a missing link in strategic management', *Journal of Management Studies*, Vol. 26, No. 4, pp. 325–47.

Uusitalo, R. (2001) '*Homo entreprenaurus*', *Applied Economics*, Vol. 33, pp. 1631–8.

Weaver, K.M., Dickson, P.H., Gibson, B. and Turner, A. (2002) 'Being uncertain: the relationship between entrepreneurial orientation and environmental uncertainty', *Journal of Enterprising Culture*, Vol. 10, No. 2, pp. 87–106.

Wright, R. (2000) *Nonzero: History, Evolution and Human Cooperation*, London: Abacus.

Yves, R., McGraw, E. and Roger, A. (2001) 'Towards the development of a measuring instrument for entrepreneurial motivation', *Journal of Developmental Entrepreneurship*, Vol. 6, No. 2, pp. 189–201.

Selected case material Case 3.1

Pay-offs from pursuit of glittering prizes

12 September 2002

By **Fergal Byrne**

A hush settles over the audience. Rustlings are stilled, whispers fade to nothing. A figure at the front unfolds a piece of paper. Many in the audience are hoping their name will be read out. Most will, of course, be disappointed. 'And the winner is . . .'

It is not as if entrepreneurs have lots of spare time to take part in business competitions. Yet many do compete for awards, ranging from the nationwide Entrepreneur of the Year contest run by Ernst & Young to more focused events – aimed at African-Caribbean entrepreneurs for example.

While seasoned competitors can cite the many benefits of participating in business competitions, would-be entrants should weigh up the time and energy required against the potential benefits of publicity and – possibly – prizes.

Aftab and Afzaal Ahmed, co-founders of Fixits, which specialises in the design, manufacture and marketing of innovative jigsaws, are keen on business competitions. In their original business plan, competitions featured as a means of supporting the business. Although Fixits is less than a year old, it has entered three competitions.

'We have won over £11,000 cash in competitions, as well as other prizes,' says Aftab Ahmed, including £10,000 as winners of this year's Shell LiveWire young entrepreneur competition. 'That is a lot of money for a small business and it has enabled us to bring forward expansion plans, to introduce new Fixits titles and build a new website for the company. We have effectively been able to put the company to the next stage of its development.'

While prize money – or its equivalent in services and products – is attractive, particularly for early-stage businesses, competitors point to other benefits in terms of support, expert advice, coaching and publicity, which can often be more important.

Bhikhu Patel, co-founder of Waymade Healthcare, a supplier of prescription medicines to retail pharmacies, was awarded – with his brother Vijay – the overall E&Y entrepreneur of the year prize in 2001. For Mr Patel, competing brought a vital outside perspective. 'At each stage the judges challenged our assumptions [and] our business model and tested our ideas – it was very thought-provoking,' he says. 'The endorsement from winning was great for staff morale and very helpful to draw attention to potential partners and suppliers.'

For Kevin Shakesheff, who co-founded Nottingham-based Critical Pharmaceuticals and won the Joint Research Councils' business plan competition in 2002, the support and mentoring during the competition was hugely valuable.

'I know it is easy to say when you have won – but winning was not as important as going through the process,' says Mr Shakesheff, a professor at Nottingham University's Pharmacy School. 'The mentoring network was particularly invaluable. We were each assigned a coach and were put in contact with people who would help us with different parts of the business plan – specialists who knew how to structure licence deals with pharmacy companies, for example. It was an instant network that would have taken years to build up by ourselves.'

Competitors often point to the opportunity to network with other entrepreneurs. 'Being an entrepreneur can be very lonely – it's an amazing experience to meet people who have had to deal with the same challenges, have gone through the same process,' says Dawn Lockett, co-founder of multi-media production company Katapult, which won regional heats to reach the national finals of Shell LiveWire's competition. 'Although we did not win, just participating was really inspiring and the publicity led directly to £30,000 of new business.'

John Devitt, director of Shell LiveWire, puts a value of £5m on the press and publicity associated with the competition and says some 85 per cent of competitors have seen an increase in turnover as a result of taking part.

There are many kinds of competition: some are aimed at start-ups, others focus on business plans or e-commerce. There are awards restricted to young entrepreneurs, awards for technology and exports, and sector-specific awards. Some charge a fee.

Would-be entrants must make sure they understand the goals of the competition and what exactly the judges are looking for. While the competition websites may provide information, an e-mail or call to previous competitors or winners, as well as organisers, can also be helpful. Seasoned competitors recommend paying particular attention to any information about the judges and mentors, as they provide a lot of the value in the competition. For instance, Aftab Ahmed says: 'The judges encouraged us to look at the bigger picture, raising important issues of business development, which we would not otherwise have considered at this stage in our business. For example, what is stopping you from increasing your product range to 50? This really stimulated us and we have indeed started to develop our product range.'

The importance of business plans as a foundation for any enterprise has led to a proliferation of business plan competitions in the UK that support entrepreneurs through the demanding process of drawing up a plan. While many are linked to academic institutions, there are a number of open competitions such as Venturefest, which has tailored itself to reflect the priorities of ordinary investors.

Alison Louden, a Scottish business angel who has served as a business plan judge, says there is a great need in general for better plans presented for funding. 'The core issues that should be addressed in a business plan are customers and marketing. Product marketing is essential, yet 90 per cent of plans one comes across don't really get to grips with it.'

The Small Firms Enterprise Development Initiative biennial awards scheme celebrates individuals who have embraced Sfedi standards to improve the quality of training, advice and development programmes for owner-managers. 'There is now a lot of research to show that if you do take advice from good advisers and trainers, you have a much better chance of surviving those first three years,' says Tony Robinson, Sfedi chairman.

In recognition of the importance of networking, the Cambridge Enterprise Conference's 'launch pad' competition is designed to help its young – less than two-years-old – high-technology entrants to network. 'The launch pad [competition] is designed to help entrepreneurs make good contacts with useful networks. The idea is to formalise a process that has enabled many other Cambridge companies to become successful,' says John Snyder, this year's conference chairman.

Competition sponsors – including banks, law firms, local businesses and national business support networks and agencies – provide funding and credibility to an event. They also benefit in return.

Anthony McGurk, corporate partner in the Cambridge office of law firm Eversheds, sees its sponsorship of the Cambridge Enterprise Conference as an important way of promoting the firm. 'Eversheds wants to help entrepreneurs get a head start and supporting the launch pad

competition will help raise Eversheds' profile among the start-up and spin-out market, which is particularly important to our Cambridge office,' he says.

Judges in competitions usually include entrepreneurs, investors and members of business support organisations. The judging process typically involves submitting a business plan, followed by meetings or presentations, and, in some cases, workshops: although this can be a valuable part of the process, it is also the most time-consuming. And no one wants last year's award to be the only remnant of your business venture.

'I had no idea how much work and time would be involved in taking part in [an] entrepreneur of the year competition,' says Andrew Owens, chairman of Greenergy, a supplier of low-emission energy. 'I could not afford to mobilise my company around a competition, as some others did – although, in retrospect, I wish I had made more of a commitment, given the benefits from winning.'

Source: *Financial Times*, 12 September 2002.

Case 3.2

Unpalatable facts about thinkers outside the box

21 February 2002

By **Richard Donkin**

A report from the UK's Royal Society for the Arts has attempted to shed some light on the dynamics of entrepreneurship. How do entrepreneurs operate? Where do they get their ideas and how do they succeed in such a harsh business world?

Entrepreneurship has been given a bad name by the downturn in dotcom businesses, many of which frittered away millions of

pounds of investors' money in an attempt to grab market share, with business models that were ill-prepared or too derivative, following market innovators in a greedy gold rush.

At the height of the dotcom scramble, business schools and publishers were jumping on the bandwagon, searching for some common elixir of entrepreneurship that could be outlined on paper or in the classroom.

Gerard Darby, the author of the RSA report*, is ploughing a similar furrow but he has concentrated on young entrepreneurs in the belief that their experience has more relevance to anyone planning to start their own business today.

One finding highlighted in the report is that entrepreneurs are not much liked. A Mori survey found that fewer than a third of adults in the UK and only just over a fifth of teenagers admired those who started their own businesses. This seems at odds with the US experience, where succeeding in business is part of the American dream.

Maybe this distrust is sown in the family or at school. According to another survey featured in the report, teachers were prominent in influencing children about their future careers. But what do teachers know about business?

David Darling, co-founder of Codemasters, a computer games software manufacturer, and the 2001 Ernst & Young UK Entrepreneur of the Year, still smarts when he remembers the disparaging attitudes of teachers towards his interests.

'They seemed to be against children being enterprising,' he says in the report. He recalls how he was given a bad mark for writing about a computer game in his computer science coursework. 'The teacher said computer games were a waste of time and not proper business.'

Codemasters today employs 350 people and in the 14 months to June 1999 had profits of GBP25m ($35.8m). The education system, says Mr Darby, is failing to equip children with enterprise skills, which are needed in many walks of life besides running a business.

Many of the entrepreneurs in the study were equally dismissive of business education. Only five of the 44 interviewed in the study had been to business school.

'Business schools tend to train managers rather than entrepreneurs,' says Rouzbeh Pirouz, co-founder of Mondus, an online business-to-business service for small and medium-sized companies.

A persistent image of entrepreneurs is that their driving motive is making money – but this was not reflected in the research. While many of those interviewed were running some kind of business in their teens, their motivation arose either from their enthusiasm for a particular kind of work or from their frustrations with an existing product or service that they believed could be improved.

Adam Twiss, co-founder of Zeus Technology, a business that creates web server infrastructure, says in the report: 'There was no motivation to make money. There was no motivation to change the world. We just thought we could do better, so we tried to.'

The report pointed to some of the characteristics of entrepreneurism. Many of those questioned had parents who had run their own businesses. The father of Demis Hassabis, founder of Elixir Studios, a computer game company, had built up an educational toy company. 'I've never been worried about taking risks,' says Mr Hassabis. 'I guess my parents have been doing it all their lives.'

Some of the entrepreneurs had a history of dyslexia and indifferent results at school but all were prepared to work long hours when building their businesses.

Justin Cooke, founder of Fortune Cookie, a business that has developed innovating ways of using the internet, said he often slept in the office in the first two years of the business.

'I would work until two in the morning, get my sleeping bag out of the cupboard and lie under my desk with the hum of the servers sending me to sleep,' he told Mr Darby.

Mr Cooke said he did not write a business plan until he was two years into the business. This approach mirrors the advice of Mike Southon and Chris West in their forthcoming book, *The Beermat Entrepreneur***. The book, based on Mr Southon's experience as an

---

The Young Entrepreneurs by Gerard Darby is available at www.rsa.org.uk.
** *The Beermat Entrepreneur*, by Mike Southon and Chris West is published by Financial Times/Prentice Hall.

entrepreneur and adviser to new business ventures, looks beyond individual entrepreneurs to the kind of teams they need around them.

Business ideas, says Mr Southon, can be worked out on the back of a coaster, hence the book's title. A more complex plan is less important, he believes, than the people supporting an entrepreneur. Typically, he says, these would consist of a finance specialist, a sales person and a technical innovator working closely with a 'delivery specialist', someone who understood processes.

In the long run, he says, these core specialists, once they have put together a larger team and built the business beyond a workforce of about 20 people, will need to think hard about the future. If they go for growth, members of the original team, even the original entrepreneur, may need to be replaced.

In a phase the authors describe as 'killing the king', they suggest that businesses should prepare to remove the original entrepreneur from operational responsibility when the company has reached a certain size, particularly if the founder begins to react erratically or to build a 'praetorian guard'.

This may begin to explain the public reaction to entrepreneurs. They do not tend to be easygoing people. They are confident, ambitious and obsessed with work but they can also be arrogant, impatient, competitive, manipulative and poor at completing things, say the authors. It may explain why entrepreneurs do not fit easily within big companies. But they usually know how to attract other talented people, who can be equally difficult.

As David Sproxton, co-founder of Aardman Animation puts it: 'Fundamentally, really creative people are almost by definition un-manageable.'

Source: Financial Times, 21 February 2002,
© Richard Donkin.

Discussion points

1. If you were to set up a prize for a successful entrepreneur, what criteria would you use to select the winner? How would you balance individual and personality characteristics against the way the business operates and its success?

2. Why are people suspicious of entrepreneurs? Is it because of who they are or what they do?

Chapter 4

Types of entrepreneur

Chapter overview

Classification often complements definition. It can sort items so that defining characteristics become evident. Definition then enables allocation of particular items to specific categories. However, classification can often be undertaken even if there is no clear definition available. This is so with the concept of the entrepreneur. As Chapters 1 and 2 make clear, there is no single, unambiguous, universally agreed definition as to what an entrepreneur is. This chapter is concerned with outlining a variety of approaches taken to classifying entrepreneurs.

4.1 Classifying entrepreneurs

Key learning outcome

An understanding of how different types of entrepreneur might be distinguished.

Classification of entrepreneurs into different types provides a starting point for gaining an insight into how different types of entrepreneurial ventures work and the disparate factors underlying their success. This provides important insights to researchers of entrepreneurship, investors wishing to judge the opportunity to invest in new ventures, governments developing policy to support entrepreneurs and entrepreneurs themselves when creating strategies for their ventures. After all, we should not expect there to be a single formula for success. Some success factors may be more important for some entrepreneurs than others. What is important to sucess will depend on the type of venture the entrepreneur is undertaking, his or her motivations and the strategic approach taken. There are a number of potential classification schemes. This section aims to give a flavour of the approaches taken rather than a comprehensive review of all the schemes. There are two main approaches: either to classify the entrepreneurs *themselves* or to classify their *ventures*.

The most common types of entrepreneur encountered are either those planning to start up an initial venture, so called *nascent* entrepreneurs, or those running a single business – *singular* entrepreneurs. Singular entrepreneurs at an early stage of venture development when they are still actively learning are referred to as *novice* entrepreneurs. An early move to classify singular entrepreneurs was to differentiate between *opportunist* entrepreneurs, who were interested in maximising their returns from short-term deals, and *craftsmen*, who attempted to make a living by privately selling their trade or the products they produced. Craftsmen were less interested in profits as such, but in being able to earn a stable living from their specialist skills. The idea of the 'opportunist' entrepreneur is quite vague, and a later development was to replace it with two more definite types: the *growth-orientated* entrepreneur, who pursued opportunities to maximise the potential of their ventures, and the *independence-orientated* entrepreneur, whose main ambition was to work for themselves. These latter kinds of entrepreneurs preferred stability to growth and so were willing to limit the scope of their ventures. Craft entrepreneurs can be subdivided into those whose main aim is to secure a steady income and are referred to as *income orientated*, and those who took the risk of expanding the business and faced the challenge of changing their role from being craft operators to being managers of craft operators. Such entrepreneurs are called *expansion orientated*. The term 'craft' is historical. In modern usage it refers not just to artisans, but to any entrepreneur who uses a particular knowledge or skill, in addition to general management skills, that can deliver market value. So it would include independent management consultants as much as producers of arts and crafts. In line with this, a further distinction might be made between craftsmen entrepreneurs whose expertise is based on *traditional skills*, those whose expertise is scientific or *technological* and those whose skills are of a *professional* nature.

The American entrepreneurship academic Frederick Webster (1977) considers classification schemes for both the individual entrepreneur and for their ventures. Four types of individual entrepreneur are recognised within his scheme. The *Cantillon* entrepreneur (named after the eighteenth-century French economist Richard Cantillon) brings people, money and materials together to create an entirely new organisation. This is the 'classic' type of entrepreneur, who identifies an unexploited opportunity and then innovates in order to pursue it. The *industry maker* goes beyond merely creating a new firm. Their innovation is of such importance that a whole industry is created on the back of it. They develop not only new products, but also a whole technology to produce them. Examples include Henry Ford and the mass production of motor vehicles, Thomas Edison and domestic electrical products, and Bill Gates with software operating systems. The *administrative entrepreneur* is a manager who operates within an established firm but does so in an entrepreneurial fashion. Usually occupying the chief executive or a senior managerial role, they are called upon to be innovative and to provide dynamism and leadership to the organisation, particularly when it is facing a period of change. An example here is Lee Iacocca's rejuvenation of the Chrysler Motor Company or Jan Carlzon's turnaround of the Scandinavian Airlines System (SAS). Nowadays administrative entrepreneurs are often referred to as *intrapreneurs*. The *small business owner* is an entrepreneur who takes responsibility for owning and running their own venture. The business may be small because it is in an early stage of growth or they may actually wish to limit the size of their business, because they are satisfied that it gives them a reasonably secure income and control over their lives.

Webster further classifies entrepreneurial ventures by the ratio of the amount that is expected to be received as a result of the venture's success (the *perceived payoff*) and the number of investors involved (the *principals*). Three types of venture are identified:

1 *large payoff: many participants* – i.e. a major venture with the risk spread widely over a large number of investors;

2 *small payoff: few participants* – i.e. a limited venture with the risk taken on by a few key investors only;

3 *large payoff: few participants* – i.e. a major venture with the risk taken on by a few key investors.

The remaining possibility – that is, a small expected payoff with a large number of investors – is not considered to be a likely scenario.

Landau (1982) has proposed that the characteristics of innovation and risk taking discussed earlier might provide a basis for classifying entrepreneurs. He suggests that both factors are independent of each other and may be defined as high or low. This gives the quadrant illustrated in Figure 4.1.

The *gambler* is the entrepreneur (or better, his or her venture) characterised by a low degree of innovation and a high level of risk. The gamble, of course, arises from the fact that without a significant innovation, the entrepreneur is taking a big chance in being more able to deliver value better than existing players in the market. The *consolidator* is the entrepreneur who develops a venture based on low

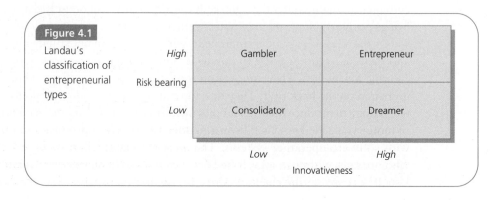

Figure 4.1

Landau's classification of entrepreneurial types

levels of both innovation and risk. This consolidates in that it is really, at best, a marginal improvement on what existing players are doing. Though risks are low, so too must be expected returns. The *dreamer* is the entrepreneur who attempts to combine a high level of innovativeness with low risk. All entrepreneurs would, of course, love to operate here. Many attempt to do so. However, Landau suggests the 'dream' cannot be realised. All innovation, by its nature, introduces risk. The more significant (and hence potentially valuable) the innovation, the greater the risk of the unknown. The final quadrant combines high innovativeness with high risk. This is where true entrepreneurs operate. They (or their investors) must accept risk, but by understanding their innovation and why it appeals to the market they minimise and manage the risks.

Technology-based entrepreneurs are especially important in modern business as it is they who are taking advantage of new scientific developments, especially in the areas of information technology, biotechnology and engineering science, and offering their benefits to the wider world. Investors are attracted by the high growth potential of their ventures. Jones-Evans (1995) offers a fourfold categorisation of such technology-based entrepreneurs based on their technical and commercial experience prior to making the move to entrepreneurship:

- The **'research' technical entrepreneur** – those whose incubation has been in a research environment. Two sub-types are suggested: *'pure research'* entrepreneurs, who have been based in academic research environments and who have not had significant commercial experience, and *'research-producer'* entrepreneurs, who while working in an academic or industrial research environment have had exposure to commercial decision making.

- The **'producer' technical entrepreneur** – those whose incubation has included an exposure to decision making in a commercial setting along with experience in technological development.

- The **'user' technical entrepreneur** – an individual whose main experience has been commercially based but has involved contact with, and the development of knowledge about, a technical development. This may be because they have been employed in its marketing or sales, or perhaps in procuring that technology for a business.

- The **'opportunist' technical entrepreneur** – one who has no previous exposure to a technology but has seen a commercial opportunity in relation to it and has pursued that with a new venture. Opportunist technical entrepreneurs may call upon a general technical knowledge base and are keen to develop an understanding of the new technology and what it offers. Eisenhardt and Forbes (1984) develop an international perspective of technical entrepreneurship.

This approach to classifying technical entrepreneurs is useful for two key reasons. First, it indicates the type of support the entrepreneur will need in order to drive his or her venture forward successfully. The research and producer technical entrepreneur, while in command of the technical aspects of what they are doing, may need support with the commercial management of their ventures. User and opportunist entrepreneurs may call upon dedicated technical experts to underpin their commercial moves. Second, it enables investors to judge the managerial balance of the ventures to which they are called upon to commit themselves. An investor seeks not only a good idea, but also one that has a clear market potential and is backed by a managerial team that can not only invent but also deliver that invention to the customer profitably.

Wai-Sum Siu (1996) has examined the types of new entrepreneur who operate in China and he gives a fascinating snapshot of the people behind this fast-growing economy. Basing his assessment on *employment, managerial, financial, technical* and *strategic* criteria, he identifies five types of entrepreneur. The *senior citizen* undertakes a venture to keep occupied during his or her retirement. The business is small and based on personal expertise. It is privately funded and has no long-term strategic ambitions. *Workaholics* are also retired but show more ambition for their ventures than do senior citizens. They often possess administrative experience and their businesses are bigger, drawing on a wider range of technical skills. Strategic goals may be explicit and employees may be invited to make a personal investment in the future of the venture. *Swingers* are younger entrepreneurs who aim to make a living from making deals. They may have only limited industrial and technical experience and rely on networks of personal contacts. Their ventures may be moderately large, but they tend not to have long-term strategic goals. The main aim is to maximise short-term profits. Funding is provided through retained earnings, family contributions and personal loans. *Idealists* are also younger entrepreneurs who run moderate-sized ventures. However, their motivation is based less on short-term profit than the sense of achievement and independence that running their own venture gives them. They serve a variety of end-markets and their ventures may be based on high-technology products. Financing is through retained profits, family contributions and private investment. *High-flyers* are motivated in much the same way as idealists. However, their ventures are much larger, reflecting success in the marketplace. Again, a variety of products are offered. Corporate goals and strategy tend to be much more explicit than in the idealist's venture, and investment is drawn from a wider variety of sources, including institutional and international agencies.

(4.2) Serial and portfolio entrepreneurship

Key learning outcome

An understanding of the types of serial and portfolio entrepreneurs, the motivation of the entrepreneur to lead a series of ventures and the strategy they adopt to do so.

The motivations of entrepreneurs are many and varied. As will be discussed in more detail later, entrepreneurs are driven by a desire for autonomy, prestige and a sense of achievement as much as, if not more than, the desire to make money. This is most evident in that group of entrepreneurs who, having led one business success, move on to start another. Such entrepreneurs, called *serial entrepreneurs*, (sometimes referred to as *habitual* entrepreneurs) gain their rewards from the establishment and building of businesses, not their long-term management. It is notable that some commentators, for example William Gartner (1985), argue that once the building stage of the venture ends, then so does true entrepreneurship.

Serial entrepreneurs, as well as being particularly interested in the start-up and early growth phase of the venture, may also have particular decision-making expertise in these areas of business development, and therefore gain their personal competitive advantage in relation to managing this stage. Such skills might be reflected in an ability to spot new opportunities, to evaluate markets and in dealing with financial backers. An entrepreneur who can point to a record of success will also be a more attractive proposition to an investor than one who cannot. Further, the capital generated from an initial venture (retained profits or money made through its sale) may provide a source of funds to start up a further venture. The establishment of additional ventures may also reflect the strategic concerns of the entrepreneur. It may be that the competitive advantage gained in the initial business can be successfully transferred to a subsequent one. Further, several businesses may be a way of diluting risk. These strategic advantages must, of course, be measured against the risk inherent in the entrepreneur spreading his or her attention over a broader area. Management buy-outs and buy-ins are a fruitful area for serial entrepreneurs. According to Wright *et al.* (1997a) as many as a quarter of managers involved in buy-ins have previously held a significant equity holding as well as managerial responsibility in another venture. Westhead and Wright (1998) explore a range of factors that might encourage serial entrepreneurship, including geographic setting, managerial experience and financing, and find significant effects for a sample of US ventures. Rosa and Scott (1999) studied multiple start-up, cross-ownership and cross-managerial involvement in a sample of Scottish small businesses. They found these to be quite common and an important factor in high-growth businesses.

Serial entrepreneurs may be sub-divided into two types: those who start new businesses in sequence, only running one at any time, and those who run several businesses simultaneously. The former are referred to as **sequential entrepreneurs**; the latter as **portfolio entrepreneurs**. James Dyson, who started the ball-wheelbarrow business before moving on to the cyclone vacuum cleaner business, is a good example of a sequential entrepreneur. Richard Branson, who has diversified his Virgin group into a number of different areas, is a portfolio entrepreneur. Wright *et al.* (1997b) have suggested that serial entrepreneurs might be classified in the following way:

- **Defensive serial entrepreneurs** are those who undertake subsequent ventures because of a forced exit from an earlier one. This need not be because it failed. It could be because the venture was sold, or floated on the stock market to pay off venture capital investment.

- **Opportunist serial entrepreneurs** are those who undertake subsequent ventures because they perceive the opportunity for financial gain, perhaps on a short-term entry–exit basis.

● **Group-creating serial entrepreneurs** are those who undertake serial entrepreneurship because creating a number of businesses is fundamental to the
strategy they are pursuing. Two sub-types of group-creating serial entrepreneurs
are suggested. **Deal-making serials** use acquisition as a major part of gaining
the new businesses. **Organic serials** start new businesses from scratch and grow
them. This adds up to quite a comprehensive classification scheme, which is
summarised in Figure 4.2.

We should not be overly determined to shoehorn individual entrepreneurs into one
particular category. The classification of a particular entrepreneur may change over
time. At some point all entrepreneurs are nascent and then novice. Most start with a
single business. Serial entrepreneurs start of as singular entrepreneurs. A sequential
entrepreneur may decide to retain a business before acquiring the next and so then
become a portfolio entrepreneur. At any one time, an individual entrepreneur may
fall into more than one category. A portfolio entrepreneur may adopt a mixture
of acquisition and organic growth to expand the portfolio. Strategic and financial
objectives may be seen in parallel, or not be clearly delineated at all. The point of
classification is to guide thinking, not regiment it!

Whatever the approach of the serial entrepreneurs, their desire to succeed with
more than one business demonstrates the excitement the entrepreneurial career offers.

(4.3) Entrepreneurship and small business management: a distinction

> **Key learning outcome**
>
> An appreciation of why the
> entrepreneurial venture is distinct
> from the small business.

Both small business management and entrepreneurship are of critical importance to the
performance of the economy. However, it
is useful to draw a distinction between them
since small businesses and entrepreneurial
ventures serve different economic functions.
They pursue and create new opportunities
differently; they fulfil the ambitions of their founders and managers in different ways.
Supporting them presents different challenges to economic policy makers. Drawing
this distinction is an issue of classification. There are two possible approaches,
namely to make a distinction between the characteristics of *entrepreneurs* and *small
business managers* or between *entrepreneurial ventures* and *small businesses*.

The former is problematic. As discussed in Section 1.4, the entrepreneur is not
distinguished by a distinct personality type and there is no independent test that can
be performed to identify an entrepreneur. The question is consequently a matter of
personal opinion. Some people may regard themselves as true entrepreneurs while
others may judge themselves to be 'just' small business managers. This can be an
emotive issue and it is not clear what benefits are to be gained by forcing people
into different conceptual bags in this way. Rather than trying to draw a distinction
between managers, it is more valuable to differentiate what they manage, that is,

Figure 4.2 A classification scheme for entrepreneurial ventures

Nascent
Planning to start a new venture. Venture not yet initiated.

Singular	Opportunist	Growth orientated	
Running a single venture	Look for profitable deals	Grow business by increasing range of deals	
(Novice in early stages)		**Independence orientated** Seek merely to retain independence	
	Craft Utilise personal skill or knowledge	**Expansion orientated** Grow business by expanding craft production capacity	
		Income orientated Seek merely to provide steady income for self and family	

Serial (or habitual)	Sequential	Defensive	Deal
Involved in running more than one business	Only running one business at any one time. Leave one business before starting next	Start new business after (forced) exit from initial business	New business obtained through acquisition of extant business
			Organic New business initiated and grown from scratch
		Opportunistic Leave initial business and start new business because of perceived better opportunity	**Deal** New business obtained through acquisition of extant business
			Organic New business initiated and grown from scratch
	Portfolio Run more than one business at one time	**Opportunistic** Add on new business because of perceived financial opportunity. No real strategic consideration	**Deal** New business obtained through acquisition of extant business
			Organic New business initiated and grown from scratch
		Group Add on new business because of perceived strategic opportunity. Long-term synergy between existing and new business	**Deal** New business obtained through acquisition of extant business
			Organic New business initiated and grown from scratch

between the *small business* and the *entrepreneurial venture*. There are three essential characteristics which distinguish the entrepreneurial venture from the small business.

Innovation

The successful entrepreneurial venture is usually based on a significant *innovation*. This might be a technological innovation, for example a new product or a new way of producing it; it might be an innovation in offering a new service; an innovation in the way something is marketed or distributed; or possibly an innovation in the way the organisation is structured and managed, or in the way relationships are maintained between organisations. The small business, on the other hand, is usually involved in delivering an established product or service. This does not mean that a small business is not doing something new. They may be delivering an innovation to people who would not otherwise have access to it, perhaps at a lower cost or with a higher level of service. However, the small firm's output is likely to be established and produced in an established way. So while a small business may be new to a locality, it is not doing anything essentially new in a *global* sense, whereas an entrepreneurial venture is usually based on a *significantly new* way of doing something.

Potential for growth

The size of a business is a poor guide as to whether it is entrepreneurial or not. The actual definition of what constitutes a small business is a matter of judgement depending on the industry sector: for example, a firm with one hundred employees would be a very small shipbuilder, but a very large firm of solicitors. However, an entrepreneurial venture usually has a great deal more *potential* for growth than does a small business. This results from the fact that it is usually based on a significant innovation. The market potential for that innovation will be more than enough to support a small firm. It may even be more than enough to support a large firm and signal the start of an entire new industry. The small business, on the other hand, operates within an established industry and is unique only in terms of its locality. Therefore, it is limited in its growth potential by competitors in adjacent localities. A small business operates *within* a given market; the entrepreneurial venture is in a position to *create* its own market.

A word of caution is necessary here, since having the potential to grow is not the same as having a *right* to grow! If it is to enjoy growth, it is still necessary that the entrepreneurial venture be managed proficiently and that it compete effectively, even if it is creating an entirely new market rather than competing within an existing one.

Strategic objectives

Objectives are a common feature of managerial life. They take a variety of forms; for example, they may be formal or informal, and they may be directed towards individuals or apply to the venture as a whole. Most businesses have at least some objectives. Even the smallest firm should have sales targets if not more detailed financial objectives. Objectives may be set for the benefit of external investors as well as for consumption by the internal management.

The entrepreneurial venture will usually go beyond the small business in the objectives it sets itself in that it will have *strategic* objectives. Strategic objectives relate to such things as:

- *growth targets* – year-on-year increases in sales, profits and other financial targets;
- *market development* – activities actually to create and stimulate the growth and shaping of the firm's market (for example, through advertising and promotion);
- *market share* – the proportion of the market the business serves; and
- *market position* – maintaining the firm's position in its market relative to competitors.

These strategic objectives may be quantified in a variety of ways. They may also be supplemented by a formal mission statement for the venture. This is an idea that will be discussed more fully in Chapter 10.

The distinction between a small business and an entrepreneurial venture is not clearcut. Generally we can say that the entrepreneurial venture is distinguished from the small business by its *innovation*, *growth potential* and *strategic objectives*. However, not all entrepreneurial ventures will necessarily show an obvious innovation, clear growth potential or formally articulated strategic objectives, and some small businesses may demonstrate one or two of these characteristics. However, in combination they do add up to distinguish the key character of an entrepreneurial venture, that is, a business that makes significant changes to the world (Figure 4.3).

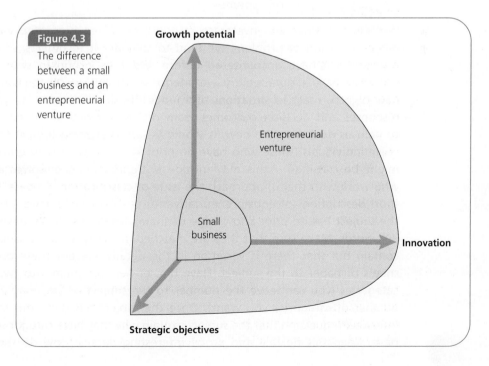

Figure 4.3

The difference between a small business and an entrepreneurial venture

Growth potential

Entrepreneurial venture

Small business

Innovation

Strategic objectives

Summary of key ideas

- Classification of entrepreneurs is important for a number of reasons, including research, government policy and investor analysis.

- An important approach classifies entrepreneurs on the basis of whether they are:
  - craft or opportunity based
  - singular, sequential or portfolio
  - income or growth motivated, and on
  - the strategy they use to expand the business.

- Entrepreneurial ventures may be distinguished from small businesses on the basis of:
  - the presence of a significant innovation on which the venture is founded
  - the articulation of strategic objectives
  - growth potential.

Research themes

Intuitive classification schemes

We human beings are inveterate categorisers. When presented with a new object, situation or problem, we tend to compare it to objects, situations or problems we have encountered before. We then group in with the most similar we have in our memory: we categorise. This influences the way we value new objects, react to situations and judge decisions, because we use values, responses and decision outcomes from our experience of stored categories to help us deal with the new. It would be an interesting project to see how naive individuals (those who have no prior knowledge of how entrepreneurs might be classified – this may include entrepreneurs themselves and those who work with them!) approach the issue of classification. Prepare a series of short descriptions of entrepreneurial ventures (real or imagined – better that the subject has no prior knowledge of them). These should be of about 200–300 words. Make sure that they are matched in the types of information they contain but that there is variation in the details. Present these on separate sheets of paper to the subject. Have him or her sort them into two or more categories (you can leave the number to the subject or you may dictate the number of categories you want). Once the subject has done this conduct an interview requesting that the subject explain why they have categorised as they have. Keep this flexible and probe interesting details. How do such natural classification schemes match with the more formal schemes described in this chapter? Do different individuals agree on the final classification or is it highly variable? Do individuals use the same criteria or not? How does the way in which different subjects weight or prioritise particular features differ? Summarise by exploring what the findings say about the way in which individuals recognise and judge entrepreneurship.

The effect of classification on judgement

For reasons related to those discussed above, we tend to judge things we know (or are told) are in the same category as more similar than things we know to be (or are told to be) in different categories. So if we provide descriptions of two categories and then present a description of an object, situation or decision problem, individuals' judgement will tend to vary if we suggest it is one category or the other *even if the descriptions remain the same*. For example, up to the year 2000 many businesses eagerly sought to classify themselves as 'dot-coms' because they felt they would be favoured by investors. After the dot-com crash when Internet stocks tumbled, most businesses were eager to shake off the label and emphasised the traditionality of their offerings. To a large extent, this reflects a change in investors' assessment of the dot-com category *as a whole*, not the prospects of *individual* businesses. This raises an issue with the classification of entrepreneurs. Collecting entrepreneurs into one category will encourage decision makers to associate them and so bias their judgement. The study might progress as follows. Using the categorisation schemes discussed above, obtain or create short (500 word?) accounts of different types of entrepreneur, their ventures and their performance. Collect these into two categories: one high performing, the other low performing (call these the high- and low-context cases). Next obtain or create an account of a proposed new venture that might be classified with either the high- or low-performing groups (call this the probe case). Take two groups of subjects (at least 25 in each, ideally matched for age, gender and experience) and present each group with all the cases. For one group associate (based on the classification scheme) the probe case with the high performers; for the other group associate the probe with the low performers. So both groups have access to the same information; only the association of the probe case changes. Ask the two groups to judge the likely performance of the new venture. In principle, having access to the same information, they should, on average agree. But does the categorisation affect judgement of the venture's potential? Conclude by considering the implications of the findings for the way in which information about new ventures should be presented.

Cluster analysis of entrepreneurial ventures

Cluster analysis represents a variety of techniques for classifying items based on their descriptive characteristics. The methodology is somewhat mathematical but its principles only require basic algebra (a good introductory account of methods is provided by Aldenderer and Blashfield, 1984). The technique involves taking a collection (the more the better) of entrepreneurial ventures described in some detail (these may be from the same sector, or different ones). As a first stage, have a small group brainstorm on what the different characteristics of each venture are. Given this set of descriptive characteristics, then quantify them. Some characteristics (e.g. rate of growth, age of venture, number of businesses in portfolio, etc.) are directly numerical; others, such as degree of innovation, might require a judgement using a Likert scale (e.g. highly innovative, moderately innovative, etc.). Once each venture is quantified along each characteristic, apply an appropriate clustering technique and see what categories emerge (a number of software packages are available to do this). How does the categorisation change if the weighting of descriptive characteristics is modified? How do these 'empirical' categories match up with the 'prescriptive' ones described above? Is there a general case to be made for the classification scheme you have devised? How might the scheme be used to develop policy for the ventures in each category (e.g. governmental support; investment issues)?

Suggestions for further reading

Aldenderer, M.S. and Blashfield, R.K. (1984) *Cluster Analysis*, Sage University Paper, Series: Quantitative Applications in the Social Sciences, No. 44. Newbury Park, CA: Sage.

Carland, J.W., Hoy, F., Boulton, W.R. and Carland, J.C. (1984) 'Differentiating entrepreneurs from small business owners: a conceptualisation', *Academy of Management Review*, Vol. 9, No. 2, pp. 345–59.

Dunkelberg, W.C. and Cooper, A.C. (1982) 'Entrepreneurial typologies: an empirical study', in Vesper, K.H. (ed.) *Frontiers of Entrepreneurial Research*, Wellesley, MA: Babson College Centre for Entrepreneurial Studies, pp. 1–15.

Eisenhardt, K.M. and Forbes, N. (1984) 'Technical entrepreneurship: an international perspective', *Columbia Journal of World Business*, Winter, pp. 31–7.

Gartner, W. (1985) 'A conceptual framework for describing the phenomenon of new venture creation', *Academy of Management Review*, Vol. 10, No. 4, pp. 696–706.

Gartner, W.B., Bird, B.J. and Starr, J.A. (1992) 'Acting as if: differentiating entrepreneurial from organisational behaviour', *Entrepreneurship Theory and Practice*, Spring, pp. 13–31.

Jones-Evans, D. (1995) 'A typology of technology-based entrepreneurs', *International Journal of Entrepreneurial Research and Behaviour*, Vol. 1, No. 1, pp. 26–47.

Landau, R. (1982) 'The innovative milieu', in Lundstedt, S.B. and Colglazier, E.W., Jr (eds) *Managing Innovation: The Social Dimensions of Creativity, Invention, and Technology*, New York: Pergamon Press.

Parker, S.C. (2002) 'On the dimensionality and composition of entrepreneurship', Durham Business School Working Paper.

Rosa, P. (1998) 'Entrepreneurial process of business cluster formation and growth by habitual entrepreneurs', *Entrepreneurship Theory and Practice*, Vol. 22, No, 4, pp. 43–61.

Rosa, P. and Scott, M. (1999) 'The prevalence of multiple owners and directors in the SME sector: implications for our understanding of start-up and growth', *Entrepreneurship and Regional Development*, Vol. 11, pp. 21–37.

Siu, Wai-Sum (1996) 'Entrepreneurial typology: the case of owner managers in China', *International Small Business Journal*, Vol. 14, No. 1, pp. 53–64.

Webster, F.A. (1977) 'Entrepreneurs and ventures: an attempt at classification and clarification', *Academy of Management Review*, Vol. 2, No. 1, pp. 54–61.

Westhead, P. and Wright, M. (1998) 'Novice, portfolio and serial founders in rural and urban areas (habitual entrepreneurs and angel investors)', *Entrepreneurship Theory and Practice*, Vol. 22, No, 4, pp. 63–100.

Wright, M., Robbie, K. and Ennew, C. (1997a) 'Venture capitalists and serial entrepreneurs', *Journal of Business Venturing*, Vol. 12, pp. 227–49.

Wright, M., Robbie, K. and Ennew, C. (1997b) 'Serial entrepreneurs', *British Journal of Management*, Vol. 8, pp. 251–68.

Wright, M., Westhead, P. and Sohl, J. (1998) 'Editors' introduction: habitual entrepreneurs and angel investors', *Entrepreneurship Theory and Practice*, Vol. 22, No, 4, pp. 5–21.

Selected case material Case 4.1

New venture from founder of Freeserve

12 September 2002

By **Astrid Wendlandt**

Peter Wilkinson, the entrepreneur behind the internet services provider Planet Online and co-founder of rival Freeserve, has ended the secrecy surrounding his latest venture.

He is becoming chairman of an interactive television services provider that aims to compete head-on with Rupert Murdoch's NDS.

Mr Wilkinson, who owns 40 per cent of the start-up called Digital Interactive Television Group (DITG), said he believed interactive television had great potential for growth but was poorly understood by investors, media companies and regulators.

'I think interactive TV is everything people wanted the internet to be. You can have moving pictures and people can find you easily. It is at a fairly embryonic stage and there is no one in the market place.'

Consumer confidence in the future of digital TV suffered a blow recently with the demise of ITV Digital and the precarious finances of cable operators such as Telewest and NTL.

Technical glitches and a lack of a compelling offering have also held back the growth of interactive television. Interactive betting, however, and voting on programmes such as Big Brother on Channel 4, have proved popular.

DITG supplies interactive software and technology to broadcasters including Discovery Channel, Flextech and Disney TV. Its income is derived from licence fees and transaction revenues.

Mr Wilkinson and a small group of friends founded DITG a year ago with £10m. It is expected to break even by end of its current financial year to March on sales of £20m and make profits the year after.

DITG shareholders also own one of its customers Avago, a channel offering games similar to bingo on BSkyB, which has turnover of £200,000 a week. Avago broke even this week after its launch two months ago.

Mr Wilkinson is in talks with retailers to launch dedicated services for them.

He argues that shopping channels offer a cheaper and more efficient platform for retailers to reach out to customers than high street shops. For example, interactive channels on BSkyB reach some 7m households.

Source: Financial Times, 12 September 2002.

Case 4.2

Heady career of a serial entrepreneur

FT

27 December 2002

By **David Blackwell**

The last time anyone served up a Tom Hunter Surprise was at the recent launch in Glasgow of a women's clothing range known as Soviet.

Three burly barmen dressed in black kilts, Soviet tops and Russian hats strolled down the catwalk at the end of the fashion show and launched into a spiel on fancy cocktails.

The Tom Hunter cocktail – an unlikely blend of vodka, schnapps, rum and fruit juices – was invented in honour of the man who surprised House of Fraser shareholders with a bid to take the store chain private yesterday.

Mr Hunter, who made a fortune from the Sports Division retail chain, is winning a reputation for driving a revolution in Scottish attitudes to money and success, prompting the emergence of new businesses. One such is Liquid Assets, the cocktail company started this year by Paul Torrens, a graduate of the Hunter Centre for Entrepreneurship at Strathclyde University.

'Tom Hunter is doing phenomenal things for Scotland,' said Mr Torrens, who believes the help of the Hunter Centre significantly reduced the time necessary to set up his company. 'He is changing the culture.'

Such praise has not always been forthcoming for Mr Hunter, who was almost a textbook case of 'the prophet not without honour, save in his own country' after the sale of Sports Division to JJB Sports in 1998 for £290m. The deal cost 550 jobs and Mr Hunter was vilified by the Scottish media for selling out.

'That did hurt at the time,' said Mr Hunter yesterday. 'But I knew I was not going to run away.' Instead, he began investing in small, fast-growing businesses, then switched to larger investments in retailing and property when he established West Coast Capital, a £200m private equity fund, earlier this year with Jim McMahon, a fellow Scot. The pair take a hands-on approach to their investments, which include Kensington Arcade in London and a large stake in The Gadget Shop.

Mr Hunter, 41, also embarked on his personal mission to foster enterprise in Scotland. Among other things he raised money and contributed £1.5m for an initiative to give primary school pupils a taste of business, and endowed the centre for entrepreneurship at Strathclyde University with £5m.

The university's website describes him as 'a serial entrepreneur, business angel and philanthropist'. No mention is made of his other career as the drummer in CFK, a pop group that raises money for a children's charity. Yesterday he was bashing out the beat to a cover version of Angels, by Robbie Williams, and the group has made a single of the song for release later this month.

Mr Hunter – who does all his deals with the same tightly-knit group of associates – grew up in the mining village of New Cumnock in Ayrshire, helping in his father's grocery store from an early age.

But he still attributes a large part of the success of Sports Division to luck. He started the business by bluffing his way into supplying trainers to a retailer that subsequently went bust.

The feeling that fortune has smiled on him has driven him to try to emulate his hero

Andrew Carnegie, the early 20th century Scottish philanthropist who said: 'He who dies with great wealth, dies in disgrace. Making the wealth is only half of the equation.'

Nevertheless, he has a healthy Scottish respect for thrift, and walked away this year from an attempt to take over Grantchester, the retail warehouse specialist. 'We won't overpay,' he said.

Philip Green, the entrepreneur who owns BHS, has worked closely with Mr Hunter and described him as 'a shrewd investor'. He would do his homework and research on House of Fraser, and whatever he offered would be 'a serious offer – but it won't be win at all costs'.

Source: *Financial Times*, 27 December 2002.

Discussion point

In what ways are serial entrepreneurs different to singular entrepreneurs? Does the existence of serial entrepreneurs add weight to the idea that (at least some) entrepreneurs are driven by internal motivations rather than external forces?

Chapter 5

Researching entrepreneurship

Chapter overview

Entrepreneurship is an active field of research. Like all other disciplines, entrepreneurship has six aspects: phenomena of concern, knowledge, theory, methodology, philosophical concerns and an institutional system. The study of entrepreneurship is a new field and it is very much an 'adolescent' discipline. This chapter considers the field in terms of its core scope, concerns and approach. It concludes with an overview of research paradigms and methodology in entrepreneurship.

5.1 Entrepreneurship: an adolescent discipline

Key learning outcome

An understanding of what constitutes an academic discipline, a recognition of the study of entrepreneurship as a distinct discipline and an appreciation of its connections to other disciplines in the social sciences.

Entrepreneurship is now widely regarded as an independent subject within the social sciences. It is a relatively new subject. It fully blossomed within the field of management about 25 years ago (albeit with important antecedents before that) and has only started to really become distinct from other management studies in the past 15 years or so. As an independent field of study it is much younger than subjects like sociology and anthropology and very much younger than 'traditional' subjects in the natural sciences or the humanities. Murray Low (2001) has called entrepreneurship 'an adolescent discipline'.

What do we mean when we talk about a discipline (subject, or field of inquiry)? Essentially six interconnected, but distinct, things.

First of all a subject has a particular *range of phenomena* that are its concern. This range of phenomena is the list of objects, causes and effects in the world that the subject sets out to investigate. Biology is concerned with living organisms, history with man's past, mathematics with the patterns in nature, and so on. Clearly, entrepreneurship is concerned with the economic effects of, and the management practice of *entrepreneurs*. However, not all subjects have clear boundaries defining where their phenomena of interest begin and end. For example, there is debate as to how distinct the areas of concern of sociology and social anthropology are. The list of things that entrepreneurship is concerned with will depend on the way in which entrepreneurs and entrepreneurship is defined. There is no neat 'bag' that contains what entrepreneurship (and only entrepreneurship) should be concerned with. There is considerable latitude in where entrepreneurship ends and other management disciplines, economics and the broader social sciences begin.

The second aspect of a subject is a collection of statements or propositions about the world. This collection of propositions is what constitutes the *knowledge* that the discipline has accumulated about the range of phenomena it sets out to explore, such as might be found in a textbook. Most philosophers of science doubt that such propositions are straightforward, neutral, statements about the world. How do we know that the knowledge is true knowledge? Philosophers disagree about what the notion of truth actually means. A major issue for some philosophers of science is that discoveries are *theory laden*. This view, known as *constructivism*, implies that the propositions only make sense in light of some theory, or set of theories, about the world and so their truth depends on the assumption that the theory is true in the first place. The set of *theories* used to account for the phenomena constitutes the third aspect of a subject. A theory is a framework that both accounts for and predicts how causes are linked to effects. Not all social scientists would agree that physical scientists' concern with causes and effect is appropriate to the study of human behaviour. While what happens in the outside world are cause–effect *events*, humans engage in premeditated *actions*. An effect has no choice over whether it will occur or not given a particular cause, but a human being can (apparently) chose whether to act or not. So a deterministic causality is replaced with a motivation-action concern: what 'leads' people to do what they do, rather than the causes that 'determine' their actions. In some disciplines a set of incompatible and perhaps competing theories are present. Following the work of the philosopher Thomas Kuhn, such theories are referred to as *paradigms*. These paradigms not only guide the making of particular propositions (and the rejection of others), but also the way in which different propositions are related to each other. Some subjects, the natural sciences come to mind, are dominated by a single, widely accepted paradigm. There is general acceptance as to the theoretical frame within which inquiry should be made. Other subjects, though, are multi-paradigm. There is no dominant theoretical frame. Many social sciences are like this. Psychology is an example (as was seen in Section 3.1 where the entrepreneurial personality was discussed). There is a tendency for younger subjects in general, and the social sciences in particular, to be richer in paradigms. There has been less time for the subject to 'settle down' to a single accepted paradigm. Some thinkers may appreciate paradigm diversity for its own sake and so seek to retain it; others may regard it as a failure of the subject to develop proper understanding of the world and as a distraction. As an adolescent discipline entrepreneurship is paradigm rich.

Theories are constructed on the back of some sort of inquiry into the world. But inquiry must follow certain rules if it is to be accepted as a legitimate form of truth generating inquiry. This fourth aspect of a subject is called its *methodology*. A methodology is a set of rules about how investigations are to take place. Within a subject, claims to new knowledge discoveries will only be accepted if that knowledge has been obtained through the application of a proper methodology. Different paradigms often have their own methodology. So within multi-paradigm disciplines there will often be debate about methodology as well as theory. In the following sections, the concerns of entrepreneurship (its domain), research paradigms, methodologies and a selection of specific research themes will be considered.

In addition, a subject may be associated with some *philosophical perspective* and even a *social agenda*. Knowledge, and the theories it is embedded in, suggests (to the human imagination at least) that the world is a certain way. The physical and biological sciences, for example, suggest that the world is essentially *material* (made up of physical substances and physical substances only) and that all effects have a specific cause; that is, it is *deterministic*. History, on the other hand, traces historical situations to actions that individuals might or might not have taken. History suggests the world is quite *contingent*. Entrepreneurship bridges these concerns. In that it seeks *inter alia* the general causes that lead to business success (an effect) it is presuming determinism. On the other hand, each entrepreneurial venture has its own, unique characteristics and history and so is contingent. The discipline of entrepreneurship deals with a complex phenomenon. These two things might not conflict if we were to confine deterministic and contingent propositions about entrepreneurship to particular aspects of the phenomena: to recognise contingency in individual ventures, but to seek generalisations by comparing many ventures. The pictures of the world (philosophical perspectives) that a subject engenders can also have moral and political implications. Classical economics, in attempting to be a dispassionate and scientifically neutral account of the way in which humans interact, suggests that unconstrained markets in which individuals make free and personal wealth maximising decisions is optimal, or Pareto efficient. As noted in Section 2.2, while this may, strictly, be *only* a formal statement about the mathematical properties of such a system, it is very easy to make the move to suggesting that such a system is *morally* or *politically* optimal as well. Many social scientists are concerned that a reductive account of human behaviour in terms of our genetic complement suggests that actively manipulating the genetic character of future generations (eugenics) is morally acceptable and that this alone is sufficient reason for resisting such reductionist accounts. While entrepreneurship borrows heavily (and quite properly) from economic thinking, economics is not the only disciple that informs debate within the subject. Many (I think most) researchers in entrepreneurship study it in a belief that entrepreneurship is not only morally acceptable, but also morally *desirable*. They study the subject not only with the intent of discovering things about the world that entrepreneurs have created (important enough) but also with an intent of contributing to their future development of it. Entrepreneurship is an applied as well as an academic discipline. However, there are a number of researchers who have made important contributions who are critical (sometimes radically) of entrepreneurship and its effects.

The final aspect of a subject is its *institutional system*. The discovery of new knowledge is a human activity. It is structured. One of the distinctive features about our current age is the way in which research activity is organised. Not that long ago, only a few hundred years or so, it was possible for one person to know pretty much all of what the sciences, history and the humanities had to say. The encyclopaedists were scholars who attempted to summarise all of what was known into a single or few volumes. Inquiry into the world was undertaken pretty much as a hobby. Things changed with the Enlightenment in the eighteenth century. Rapid discoveries based on new and rational modes of enquiry led to an exponential growth in human understanding – far more than any one person could hope to master. This led directly to the fragmentation in different disciplines. Inquiry became professionalised. In the modern age, scholars not only restrict themselves to a single discipline but increasingly a sub-discipline or even a sub-sub-discipline. Along with this fragmentation, new disciplines arose to study newly discovered phenomena in new ways. As well as this fragmentation, there was also integration. Some new disciplines studied specific phenomena using ideas from a range of other more established disciplines. The social sciences are notable here. And within the social sciences, entrepreneurship is very much a case in point. The study of entrepreneurship calls upon economics, psychology, management science, sociology, anthropology, technology studies, systems theory and political science, among others, to provide both theoretical insights and methodological guidance. Individuals will often take up the study of entrepreneurship from a base in one of these subject areas.

The institutional aspect of a subject includes the set of individual teachers and researchers who contribute to the subject, their organisational context such as university departments or consulting firms, and their communication system, including dedicated journals and 'the conference circuit'. These institutions are now global. Applied subjects (and this is particularly the case with entrepreneurship) also have institutional links outside the university system to government and commerce. A (loosely knit) group of philosophers sometimes known as the new sociologists of knowledge place emphasis on this institutional aspect of a subject and (in their most radical manifestation) claim that knowledge within the discipline is entirely the result of the institutional system and that there is no such thing as truth independent of socially mediated agreements. As might be imagined, such views are highly controversial and are not widely accepted but they have been influential. By way of a summary, these six aspects of entrepreneurship as a discipline are detailed in Table 5.1.

Table 5.1	The six aspects of entrepreneurship as an academic discipline	
Aspect of the discipline	**Generally concerned with**	**Specifics of entrepreneurship research**
Range of phenomena	Objects, causes and events (or motivations and actions) the discipline attempts to explain	Creation of new wealth and new organisations by entrepreneurs
Knowledge	The corpus of propositions about the world the discipline (or at least general agreement within it) regards as true (or otherwise)	Propositions ('truths' and 'falsehoods') about entrepreneurship in academic textbooks, journal articles, etc. held by entrepreneurs and those who interact with them
Theoretical systems	Frameworks of explanation that connect causes to events (or motivations to actions)	Drawn from economic, strategic, psychological, sociological and anthropological theory
Methodology	The (generally accepted) 'rules' that govern proper (truth guaranteeing) investigations leading to new knowledge within the discipline	Positivistic *versus* Anti-positivistic
Philosophical perspective	The general 'world view' that underpins the discipline and governs any ethical and moral assertions it makes	Entrepreneurship brings benefits and should be encouraged *versus* Entrepreneurship reduces human (overall) welfare and should be controlled, discouraged or inhibited
Institutional system	The human organisation within a social and economic system that coordinates the discovery of new knowledge within the discipline.	Knowledge creation, co-ordination and transfer through teaching and research in universities and consulting firms and through network links to practising entrepreneurs and their supporters

Adolescence is at once the most wonderful and most troubling time of our lives. Every new discovery is fresh and exciting. The future is full of new potential. We are confident in ourselves and in our ability to make a real difference. No challenge seems too great. But we may be inexperienced, naive even. We make mistakes. We may be awkward and lack confidence compared to our elders. All of these things apply to entrepreneurship as an adolescent discipline. And they all, both positive and negative, add to its excitement.

5.2 Entrepreneurship: the research field

Key learning outcome

Recognition of the main themes in entrepreneurship research and how they are categorised.

What is the range of phenomena with which entrepreneurship should concern itself? There is, of course, no hard and fast answer to this question. If we look at the entrepreneurship literature, however, we do see a central 'core' of concerns with a number of other, more peripheral, issues occurring with varying degrees of frequency. This central core has been defined (Bygrave and Hofer, 1991) as '(A)ll functions, activities and actions associated with the perception of opportunities and creation of organisations to pursue them'. As will be evident from this definition, even this central core is very large. Although it suggests a broad range of research agendas, it does not commend any specifically. Within this core there are a number of distinct sub-fields that are more focused on specific research programmes. In 1988, Low and MacMillan suggested in a very influential paper that there are three essential sub-fields within entrepreneurship. These are as follows.

Process

Process refers to the series of actions taken by, and elicited by, the entrepreneur in the identification of and pursuit of new opportunities. Process includes both the explicit and public aspects of opportunity identification by entrepreneurs and at a cognitive level the innate psychological and decision-making facets of the entrepreneur.

Context

Context refers to the situation within which entrepreneurs work. Context includes the organisational, regional, national and international setting for the entrepreneur's activities with reference to the economic, social and cultural conditions, the availability of resources, the competitive environment and the opportunities and challenges they present.

Outcomes

Outcomes refer to the performance of the entrepreneur in financial, organisational and human terms. A single point-in-time 'snap-shot' of outcomes may be significant, but outcomes only have real meaning in a comparative sense. Two sorts of study compare outcomes. *Longitudinal* studies follow a single or small group of businesses over time to observe how their performance develops. Being a defining characteristic of the entrepreneurial firm, growth of the business is a significant variable here.

Cross-sectional studies, on the other hand, compare a large group of businesses in a single or small group of sectors over a relatively short time period. The competitiveness of entrepreneurial businesses relative to their established counterparts is important here. Performance may mean more than just financial performance. 'Softer' organisational benefits such as employee satisfaction and wider ethical or social performance may also be of interest.

Ucbasaran *et al.* (2001) have suggested that the core of entrepreneurship research might be better described as having five sub-fields. These they describe as follows.

Theoretical antecedents

Theoretical antecedents are those aspects of entrepreneurship research that concentrate on important theoretical departures. As entrepreneurship is influenced by a number of social sciences, these theoretical insights are usually developed from a base in one of the social sciences. Economics, finance and psychology are important. Sociology and anthropology are also influential. Theoretical studies may be quite conceptual in nature. They may be concerned with proposing new theoretical perspectives or gathering empirical evidence to support or disprove existing theoretical ideas.

Types of entrepreneur

A number of studies are concerned with defining and classifying different types of entrepreneur (see Chapter 4). This is important because different types of entrepreneur may need different theoretical antecedents. For example, are all entrepreneurs motivated in the same way? How do the entrepreneurial processes they initiate and are guided by differ? Do they create similar or dissimilar organisations? Do they produce the same type of outcomes? In a more practical sense, do they all respond to the same type of support and encouragement from, say, government? Do they need different systems to provide financial support? And so on. Again, insights can be developed from economic, finance, psychological and sociological perspectives. An important level of distinction is between nascent (prospective entrepreneurs, not yet having started a business), novice (entrepreneurs who have started a business recently), serial (entrepreneurs who have created a series of businesses, one after the other) and portfolio (entrepreneurs who are managing a collection of businesses) entrepreneurs.

The entrepreneurial process

This is parallel to Low and MacMillan's process sub-field. Process studies are usually centred on the process of opportunity recognition, evaluation and exploitation both from an external to the entrepreneur (social, economic, cultural) and internal to the entrepreneur (cognitive, psychological) perspective.

Types of entrepreneurial organisation

What makes an organisation entrepreneurial? What differences do individual entrepreneurs make to the organisations they manage and come into contact with? Organisations can be defined and categorised in a number of ways. Of particular interest in entrepreneurship studies is categorisation by type of innovation (e.g. high-tech, low-tech), rate of organisational growth (e.g. fast growing, slow growing), stage in life cycle (e.g. start-up, early growth, maturity, exit) and origins of the business (e.g. new start-up, franchising, management buy-out, inheritance).

Entrepreneurial outcomes

This is in a similar vein to Low and MacMillan's outcomes. Studies are concerned with growth and performance trends over time and in comparison to competitors.

Ucbasaran *et al.* (2001) suggest a complementary approach. They go on to categorise entrepreneurial research in a hierarchical manner: research dealing with the *individual entrepreneur*, the *entrepreneur's firm*, the *sector* and *industry* the firm is in. Paralleling this is the geographical regional, and the national and international context of the firm. A development of this scheme is illustrated in Figure 5.1.

In 1999, Meyer and colleagues worked as part of a task force entitled *Doctoral Level Education in Entrepreneurship*. This task force concluded that entrepreneurship is, essentially about *creation*. As such, they recommended that the domain of entrepreneurial research should be centred on four issues:

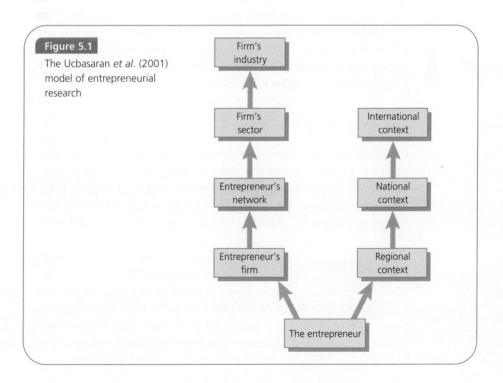

Figure 5.1

The Ucbasaran *et al.* (2001) model of entrepreneurial research

		Small and medium firms	Large corporations
Figure 5.2	Entrepreneurship	Entrepreneurial creation	Intrapreneurial creation
Meyer *et al.*'s (2002) classification of the domain of entrepreneurship	Strategic management	SME performance	Corporate performance

- the creation of new ventures and organisations;

- the creation of new combinations of goods and services, methods of production, markets and supply chains;

- creative recognition of new and existing opportunities; and

- cognitive processes, behaviours and modes of action (especially those that might be regarded as creative) to exploit new and existing opportunities.

As a development of this, Meyer *et al.* (2002) suggested that it was fruitful to consider the intersection of entrepreneurship studies with strategic management. Entrepreneurship is about *creation*, whereas strategic management is about *performance*. Entrepreneurship relates to how opportunities to create new goods and services come into being and are exploited. Strategic management relates to how decisions and actions bring about competitiveness and above-average returns. These issues crossed with the concern for new, smaller businesses and large corporations gives a four-fold classification. With some modifications, this scheme is presented in Figure 5.2.

Entrepreneurial creation

Entrepreneurial creation is concerned with all aspects of the entrepreneur and entrepreneurship that address the issue of how entrepreneurs devise and implement new, innovative products, ideas and ways of doing things. It includes studies into the cognitive make-up of individual entrepreneurs, the discovery and exploitation of new opportunities, and the creation of new organisational forms.

SME performance

SME performance is that aspect that examines how small and medium-sized businesses (especially those that have the potential to be entrepreneurial ventures) perform in both financial and wider terms over time and in comparison to other business organisations. In this respect it has parallels to entrepreneurial outcomes of Low and MacMillan's (1988) and Ucbasaran *et al.*'s (2001) classification schemes.

Intrapreneurial creation

Intrapreneurs are managers who work in an entrepreneurial way as employed managers within larger, established organisations. For obvious reasons, the combination of the entrepreneur's creativity and drive with the financial and market power of the large organisation is something of a Holy Grail in management. This aspect of the discipline looks at the possibility of such a combination, the opportunities it presents and the impediments to achieving it.

Corporate performance

This aspect is concerned with examining the performance of large, established organisations that are not normally regarded as entrepreneurial (in the conventional sense of the word). Again, such studies might be purely financial, or take on wider concerns and be cross-sectional or longitudinal in nature. For those with a more exclusive interest in entrepreneurship such studies provide important reference points and comparisons for evaluation of, and explanation of, entrepreneurial performance.

Combing these four primary categories suggests particular research programmes. Entrepreneurial creation–SME performance suggests *inter alia* studies into how SMEs compete against and win against larger competitors through first-mover advantages. The entrepreneurial creation–intrapreneurial creation intersection suggests studies looking at how the decision making and practice of entrepreneurs can be imitated to advantage by large corporations trying to overcome the inhibitions of bureaucracy, and, through the intrapreneurial creation–corporate performance intersection, looks at the impact this has. Is, for example, entrepreneurial management always better than conventional management, even for the large firm? Finally, the SME performance–corporate performance intersection suggests studies into how business performance is, in general, measured – whether purely financial measures suffice, or a broader balance card taking account of other stakeholder issues may also be needed (a point discussed further in Section 12.5). Also suggested is the specific issue of whether performance measures designed for large corporations are appropriate for SMEs (where the entrepreneur's personal goals are significant) and vice versa.

It should be recognised that all these categorisations represent *elements* of individual studies, not their entirety. Many studies adopt two or more categories. For example, a study might look at how different types of entrepreneur manage the entrepreneurial process differently. Or look at how context influences outcomes. Theoretical antecedents might be developed to explain outcomes, and so on. When designing a new research programme, it is very fruitful to consider the questions that are raised by the intersection between different categorisations of the sub-domains of the discipline, as well as the inter-relationship of the discipline with other areas of the social sciences. In an immediate sense, entrepreneurship draws from other areas of management studies. For example, Brophy and Shulman (1992) and Hills and LaForge (1992) reflect on what finance and marketing, respectively, have to offer the field.

(5.3) Research paradigms and methodology in entrepreneurship

> **Key learning outcome**
>
> An understanding of the notion of a research *paradigm*, the different paradigms adopted in entrepreneurship research and the issue of their *commensurability*.

The concept of a *paradigm* – a collection of theories with a dominant metatheory connecting them that guides inquiry within a discipline – introduced above – was proposed by Thomas Kuhn as a way of explaining the way in which physics had developed. While the concept of a paradigm had little impact in the natural sciences, social scientists took to it with enthusiasm. Kuhn originally intended the concept to explain how one theory gave way to another over time, but social scientists saw it as a way of accounting for the wide variety of approaches within the social sciences at any one time. A seminal study of paradigm variety in organisational science was undertaken by Gibson Burrell and Gareth Morgan (1979). They suggested that the different paradigms could be related in terms of two dimensions. The first is the *objective–subjective* dimension. *Objective* inquiry was concerned with external, verifiable facts about the world that are assumed to be independent of human experience while *subjective* inquiry was concerned with the interpretation of individual human experience. These may only be 'verifiable' in terms of internalised experience and not be repeatable in a traditional scientific way. Burrell and Morgan suggest that there are four aspects to this objective–subjective distinction:

● *Ontology* refers to the nature of the phenomena under inquiry. Are they *realist* – external to the individual that impinge on experience from outside – or *nominalist* – an internal, personal reality constructed by individual consciousness?

● *Epistemology* refers to the nature of knowledge about those phenomena. Positivism regards proper knowledge as being true, timelessly and independently of any one individual and verifiable by independent observation. Anti-positivism is a collection of beliefs that knowledge is, fundamentally, true only in a personal sense, to one individual at one time and that such truth cannot (always, ever?) be established through traditional 'scientific' methods. Rather it is revealed by introspection and interaction with experiencing subjects.

● *Belief about human nature* concerns whether human beings are seen as 'just' another object in the universe with behaviour that is causally determined in the same way all other events in the universe are, or, alternatively, if humans are to be regarded as a special phenomenon in which free will negates deterministic causality: humans *choose* to act, they are not *dictated* to act by external natural forces (though their actions may be guided by social forces). This distinction is often brought into debates about the relationship between man and society.

● *Methodology* is the means of inquiring into the world, whether it is believed that the social world can be inquired into in the same way the physical world is, through repeated experiments in which causal variables are manipulated to test hypothesis – a *nomothetic* methodology – or if it requires a distinct – *ideographic* – methodology in which individual human experience is placed centre stage and the issue is one of revealing that experience rather than testing pre-claimed hypotheses.

The second dimension distinguishes between the different philosophical concerns or social agendas for the paradigms. Some – referred to as *sociologies of regulation* – are largely uncritical of existing society or only claim a need for marginal changes. Their application is in explaining society as it is and how it can be managed better. Other paradigms – referred to as *sociologies of radical change* – are critical of existing society and see the need for it to be modified or reconstructed in a dramatic way if human life is to be improved.

These two dimensions are independent and can be combined into four basic types of paradigm.

● *Functionalism*: the objective-regulation paradigm. This is perhaps the dominating paradigm in entrepreneurship studies and certainly accounts for the majority of studies. It regards entrepreneurship as something that is amenable to scientific (positivistic) investigation and believes that the findings may be used to improve entrepreneurial management. It is represented by all studies that use mainstream economic thinking, cognitive psychology and the more scientific aspects of the other social sciences.

● *Radical structuralism*: the objective-radical paradigm. This paradigm is motivated by a belief in the necessity of radical change in society but believes that the best way to achieve this is through a better scientific understanding of society. The works of Karl Marx (who was critical of the effects of entrepreneurship, but not actually of entrepreneurs themselves) and other socialist economists are influential in this paradigm. At the other end of the political spectrum, it is reflected in the views of some libertarians influenced by the Austrian School view of entrepreneurs who argue that all economic knowledge is fundamentally held by individuals at a local level and that a 'higher-level' knowledge of economic systems does not have substantive meaning.

● *Interpretism*: the subjective-regulation paradigm. This paradigm does not demand a radical change in society works, but does suggest that there are other (perhaps better) ways to understand society in general, including entrepreneurship, than through adherence to scientific method. Concern is often expressed with 'science's' inability to get to grips with personal human experience. Studies within this paradigm often resort to *ethnomethodological*, *phenomenological* and *symbolic interactionist* methodologies.

● *Radical humanism*: the subjective-radical paradigm. A rejection of scientific method also characterises this paradigm. Given the radical dimension, though, often associated with this paradigm is a rejection of 'science' not just because of its methodological limitations but also because it is a 'power structure' used to 'create knowledge' that can be used for purposes of 'domination and exploitation'. Some approaches within radical feminist and anti-capitalist criticism of business practice are located within this paradigm.

The existence of, and value of, these alternative paradigms is an issue of extensive (and often ill-tempered!) debate within the organisational sciences. This debate centres on whether the paradigms are all necessary and whether they may, or may not, be integrated into broader paradigms that can share their methodology, differing concerns and insights. This is an issue referred to as *paradigm commensurability*. Three positions have emerged. The first is that only one paradigm constitutes a proper form of inquiry and that the others are a distraction, leading at best to irrelevant and meaningless findings. This position is often taken by the objective-regulation school, who insist that normal levels of scientific rigour should be applied to the study of entrepreneurship (a position clearly exemplified by Donaldson (1985) and Pfeffer (1993), who both regard paradigm proliferation as something that hinders the development or organisational science), and at times by proponents of both the subjective paradigms, who believe that scientific method is inappropriate to discovery in the *human* sciences. The radicals might add that conventional science is a power structure used to maintain (inequitable and exploitative) social relationships. The claim of incommensurability implies that while all paradigms may be of value, they are so fundamentally different that they cannot be integrated into a single, overarching paradigm. Some of this position (notably Jackson and Carter (1991) and Cannella and Paetzold (1994)) argue that paradigm incommensurability is an insurance against the domination of a positivist 'elite' in organisational science intending to gain an 'imperialistic' hold over all forms of inquiry into it. The final position takes the view that the paradigms are commensurable and that integrating them can lead to new knowledge. Examples here are Hassard (1988, 1991), Willmott (1993), Weaver and Giola (1994) and Mir and Watson (2000, 2001; see also Kwan and Tsang, 2001). A good flavour of the overall debate is provided by Hickson (1988). Gorton (2000) argues that the structure-agency divide between functional and behavioural factors in entrepreneurship research is unhelpful and should be overcome in future projects.

Research methodology is a broad and often technical subject. Given this, that it is usually dealt with in specialist courses within business education programmes and is the subject of a number of excellent texts in its own right, I will confine the discussion here to generalities. The Burrell–Morgan distinction between objective and subjective paradigms is, partly, based on researchers' confidence in different methodological approaches. Objective inquiry is *nomothetic* and is based on prior and external theoretical frames. It can be both qualitative and quantitative (often in combination). Qualitative studies are usually based on categorical descriptions whereas quantitative studies are based on numerical data. The data may be derived from case studies of the development of a single or small group of ventures, longitudinal studies of the development of a single venture over time or cross-sectional studies of a large number of businesses at any one time. Subjective studies use different – *ideographic* – methodologies. *Ethnomethodological* approaches prioritise the 'methodology' individual subjects adopt to make sense of, and make their way in, the world. Inquiry should be focused on revealing these personal methods, not on substantiating preconceived and externally imposed theories. *Phenomenological* approaches share this emphasis, but add that the way in which individuals negotiate their realities through social interaction and within broader social systems is more important than isolated individual experience.

Summary of key ideas

- The study of entrepreneurship has six aspects:
  - the range of phenomena it sets out to explain;
  - the knowledge it has accumulated;
  - the theories it adopts;
  - the methodologies it uses to guide inquiry;
  - its social and political agenda revealed through assumptions and practical applications; and
  - the institutional system set up to co-ordinate new discovery.

- Entrepreneurship is a relatively new – an adolescent – discipline.

- A number of theorists have proposed the core of phenomena that entrepreneurship studies should explain. This includes:
  - the process of entrepreneurial opportunity identification and exploitation;
  - types of entrepreneur and entrepreneurial venture;
  - the outcomes of entrepreneurial activity.

- Entrepreneurship study is characterised by a range of paradigms, including:
  - functionalism;
  - radical structuralism;
  - interpretism; and:
  - radical humanism.

- Each of these paradigms has its own methodological concerns and approaches. All have something to offer towards enhancing understanding of entrepreneurship.

(**Research themes**)

Trends in entrepreneurship research

Given its fragmented, multi-disciplinary and multi-paradigmatic nature, entrepreneurship is a diverse field of study. The claim has been made that the functionalist paradigm dominates. I am confident this is true, but to what extent is not clear. A useful research project would take a collection of journals that deal with entrepreneurship, either specifically or as part of a broader concern with management studies, or beyond into the social sciences generally, and evaluate the trends in entrepreneurship research. From the selected set of journals review the articles over a time period (the publication of Burrell and Morgan's book in 1979 would be a good starting point, though this means a lot of articles so don't be too ambitious in the range of journals considered). Assess what proportion of articles address entrepreneurship directly (if just journals dedicated to entrepreneurship are chosen, this would clearly be all) and the paradigmatic approach they take (using the Burrell and Morgan scheme above to make a judgement). What proportion adopts which paradigm? How many articles express explicitly their paradigmatic assumptions, or, alternatively, leave these implicit? How many attempt to integrate different paradigms? How often are views about paradigm commensurability expressed? If so, which views? What are the overall trends? Conclude by making projections (and recommendations) for the future of entrepreneurship research.

Entrepreneurs' views on research priorities

Entrepreneurship is very much an applied science. The idea that research into entrepreneurship can lead to improved performance for entrepreneurial ventures dominates. But this is a presupposition. How do practising entrepreneurs feel about (formal, academic) research into what they do? Do they feel it has value? If it does, how do researchers help? What should researchers be looking at? What kind of research findings might be valuable? These are important questions. A survey of a sample, either general or of a specific group of entrepreneurs (either from a specific sector, or of a particular type – refer back to Chapter 4) could provide answers. A Delphi analysis approach would be effective. Conclude by making recommendations for future directions in entrepreneurship research given practising entrepreneurs' priorities.

Suggestions for further reading

Aldrich, H.E. and Martinez, M.A. (2001) 'Many are called, but few are chose: an evolutionary perspective for the study of entrepreneurship', *Entrepreneurship Theory and Practice*, Summer, pp. 41–56.

Amit, R., Glosten, L. and Muller, E. (1993) 'Challenges to theory development in entrepreneurship', *Journal of Management Studies*, Vol. 30, pp. 815–34.

Brophy, D.J. and Shulman, J.M. (1992) 'A finance perspective on entrepreneurship research', *Entrepreneurship Theory and Practice*, Spring, pp. 61–71.

Burrell, G. and Morgan, G. (1979) *Sociological Analysis and Organisational Paradigms*, Aldershot: Arena.

Bygrave, W.D. and Hofer, C.W. (1991) 'Theorizing about entrepreneurship', *Entrepreneurship Theory and Practice*, Summer, pp. 13–22.

Cannella, A.A. and Paetzold, R.L. (1994) 'Pfeffer's barriers to the advance of organizational science: a rejoinder', *Academy of Management Review*, Vol. 19, No. 2, pp. 331–41.

Chandler, G.N. and Lyon, D.W. (2001) 'Issues of research design and construct measurement in entrepreneurship research: the past decade', *Entrepreneurship Theory and Practice*, Summer, pp. 101–13.

Davidson, P. and Wilkund, J. (2001) 'Levels of analysis in entrepreneurship: current research practice and suggestions for the future', *Entrepreneurship Theory and Practice*, Summer, pp. 81–99.

Dess, G.D. (1999) 'Linking corporate entrepreneurship to strategy, structure and process: suggested research directions', *Entrepreneurship Theory and Practice*, Spring, pp. 85–103.

Dodd, S.D. (2002) 'Metaphors and meaning: a grounded cultural model of US entrepreneurship', *Journal of Business Venturing*, Vol. 17, No. 5, pp. 519–37.

Donaldson, L. (1985) *In Defence of Organization Theory: A Reply to the Critics*, Cambridge: Cambridge University Press.

Fadahunsi, A. (2000) 'Researching informal entrepreneurship in sub-Saharan Africa: a note on field methodology', *Journal of Developmental Entrepreneurship*, Vol. 5, No. 3, pp. 249–60.

Fay, B. (1996) *Contemporary Philosophy of Social Science*, Oxford: Blackwell.

Gorton, M. (2000) 'Overcoming the structure–agency divide in small business research', *International Journal of Entrepreneurial Behaviour and Research*, Vol. 6, No. 5, pp. 276–92.

Guzmán Cuevas, J. (1994) 'Towards a taxonomy of entrepreneurial theories', *International Small Business Journal*, Vol. 12, No. 4, pp. 77–88.

Harrison, D.E. and Krauss, S.I. (2002) 'Interviewer cheating: implications for research on entrepreneurship in Africa', *Journal of Developmental Entrepreneurship*, Vol. 7, No. 3, pp. 319–30.

Hassard, J. (1988) 'Overcoming hermeticism in organizational theory: an alternative to paradigm incommensurability', *Human Relations*, Vol. 41, No. 3, pp. 247–59.

Hassard, J. (1991) 'Multiple paradigms and organizational analysis: a case study', *Organization Studies*, Vol. 12, No. 2, pp. 275–99.

Hickson, D. (1988) 'Offence and defence: a symposium with Hinings, Clegg, Child, Aldrich, Karpick and Donaldon', *Organization Studies*, Vol. 9, No. 1, pp. 1–31.

Hill, J. and McGowan, P. (1999) 'Small business and enterprise: questions about research methodology', *International Journal of Entrepreneurial Behaviour and Research*, Vol. 5, No. 1, pp. 5–18.

Hills, G.E. and LaForge, R.W. (1992) 'Research at the marketing interface to advance entrepreneurship theory', *Entrepreneurship Theory and Practice*, Spring, pp. 33–58.

Hofer, C.W. and Bygrave, W.D. (1992) 'Researching entrepreneurship', *Entrepreneurship Theory and Practice*, Spring, pp. 91–100.

Hollis, M. (1994) *The Philosophy of Social Science*, Cambridge: Cambridge University Press.

Jackson, N. and Carter, P. (1991) 'In defence of paradigm incommensurability', *Organization Studies*, Vol. 12, No. 1, pp. 109–27.

Jobber, D. and Lucas, G.J. (2000) 'The modified Tichy TPC framework for pattern matching and hypothesis development in historical case study research', *Strategic Management Journal*, Vol. 21, pp. 865–74.

Kiggundu, M.N. (2002) 'Entrepreneurs and entrepreneurship in Africa: what is known and what needs to be done?' *Journal of Developmental Economics*, Vol. 7, No. 3, pp. 239–58.

Kwan, K.M. and Tsang, W.K. (2001) 'Realism and constructivism in strategy research: a critical realist response to Mir and Watson', *Strategic Management Journal*, Vol. 22, pp. 1163–8.

Low, M.B. (2001) 'The adolescence of entrepreneurship research: specification and purpose', *Entrepreneurship Theory and Practice*, Summer, pp. 17–25.

Low, M.B. and MacMillan, I.C. (1988) 'Entrepreneurship: past research and future challenges', *Journal of Management*, Vol. 14, No. 2, pp. 139–61.

Lyon, D.W., Lumpkin, G.T. and Dess, G.G. (2000) 'Enhancing entrepreneurial orientation research: operationalizing and measuring a key strategic decision-making process', *Journal of Management*, Vol. 26, No. 5, pp. 1055–85.

May, T. (1993) *Social Research: Issues, Methods and Process*, Buckingham: Open University Press.

Meyer, G.D., Venkataraman, S. and Gartner, W. (1999) *Task Force on Doctoral Education in Entrepreneurship*. Entrepreneurship Division of the Academy of Management.

Meyer, G.D., Neck, H.M. and Meeks, M.D. (2002) 'The entrepreneurship–strategic management interface', in Hitt, M.A., Ireland, R.D., Camp, S.M. and Sexton, D.L. (eds) (2002) *Strategic Entrepreneurship: Creating a New Mindset*, Oxford: Blackwell.

Mir, R. and Watson, A. (2000) 'Strategic management and the philosophy of science: the case for a constructivist methodology', *Strategic Management Journal*, Vol. 21, No. 9, pp. 941–53.

Mir, R. and Watson, A. (2001) 'Critical realism and constructivism in strategy research: toward a synthesis', *Strategic Management Journal*, Vol. 22, pp. 1169–73.

Morris, M.H. (2000) 'New directions and streams of research', *Journal of Developmental Entrepreneurship*, Vol. 5, No. 1, pp. v–vi.

Pfeffer, J. (1993) 'Barriers to the advancement of organisational science: paradigm development as a dependent variable', *Academy of Management Review*, Vol. 18, No. 4, pp. 599–620.

Schwartz, R.G. and Teach, R.D. (2000) 'Entrepreneurship research: an empirical perspective', *Entrepreneurship Theory and Practice*, Spring, pp. 77–81.

Ucbasaran, D., Westhead, P. and Wright, M. (2001) 'The focus of entrepreneurial research: contextual and process issues', *Entrepreneurship Theory and Practice*, Summer, pp. 57–80.

Weaver, G.R. and Giola, D.A. (1994) 'Paradigms lost: incommensurability vs. structurationist inquiry', *Organization Studies*, Vol. 15, No. 4, pp. 565–90.

Willmott, H. (1993) 'Breaking the paradigm mentality', *Organization Studies*, Vol. 14, No. 5, pp. 681–719.

Private enterprise seen as way forward

FT

12 December 2002

By **John Thornhill**

The decision by the Chinese Communist party to accept private entrepreneurs as party members is the most symbolic recognition imaginable of the importance of the non-state sector in the country's economy.

The one-time vanguard party of the proletariat has now ditched much of its ideological dogma and blind support for state-owned enterprises (SOE) and hitched its future to the success of China's capitalist entrepreneurs.

A study of the country's economic statistics makes this switch readily understandable.

Although China's headline economic growth rate has remained fairly constant at between 7 and 8 per cent for the past few years, this figure conceals the sharply changing composition of the country's gross domestic product.

According to a study by the International Finance Corporation, the value of private sector output expanded 71 per cent a year between 1991–97.

By 1998, the private sector accounted for 33 per cent of China's GDP – rising to 51 per cent if the contribution from the mainly private agricultural sector is included. By the end of last year, there were more than 2m private companies in China employing 22m people.

The advantages of private enterprise over state-directed development are explained by Pu Jianguo, the vice-general manager of the Fuli Textile company, located in the eastern Chinese city of Hangzhou.

This former state-owned enterprise collapsed into bankruptcy in 1996 and was subsequently bought by a private entrepreneur, who has invested heavily in new cotton processing equipment; the company is now trading profitably.

Mr Pu says the old state-owned company was burdened by too much historic baggage.

It was weighed down with debts, responsible for all the welfare and pension obligations of its employees, and faced with constant interference from local government, who vetted all senior management appointments.

'SOEs and private companies are not on the same starting lines in many respects,' says Mr Pu.

He argues, though, that the biggest change is one of mentality. Private entrepreneurs have to take responsibility for their own decisions and are disciplined by success or failure in the marketplace. A SOE, on the other hand is a 'big rice bowl'.

Mr Pu adds: 'In a state-owned company, if you do a good job then the credit goes to your bosses. But if you do a bad job it is all your fault. The system of incentives and punishment is totally bad.'

The challenge now for the government is to continue to shrink these inefficient parts of the state-owned sector without sparking social turmoil, while encouraging the private and foreign-invested sectors to expand and to absorb redundant workers.

This monumental and convulsive task is now proceeding at different speeds and with different degrees of success across the whole of China.

However, Cao Siyuan, an independent scholar and director of the Beijing Siyuan Research Centre, says that more can and should be done to clear the unproductive rubble from the economy, allowing viable businesses to flourish.

Although his statistics suggest that the number of bankruptcies in China has risen from 98 in 1989 to 8,939 last year (about 60 per cent of them state-owned enterprises), this is still way too low in his opinion.

By his reckoning, about 0.09 per cent of companies become bankrupt each year. In the US it is close to 1 per cent. 'If we increased the number from 0.09 per cent to 1 per cent, it would make our remaining companies more efficient. It would add a more competitive edge to the economy and allow good companies to grow,' says Mr Cao. 'It would also help counter deflation.'

The obvious flaw with such a policy is that it would lead to a further mass shake-out of workers among China's 150,000 state-owned enterprises, which still employ more than 50m workers.

Already, the state-owned sector has shed 25m workers between 1998–2001. Concerns about the social consequences of company failures have led to the postponement of a new bankruptcy law that was due to be adopted next March.

The government has been trying to soften the pain of this economic transition by enticing foreign companies into China and stepping up its own expenditure programme to maintain high rates of economic growth.

Since 1998, the government has adopted what it calls a 'pro-active fiscal policy', increasing total public expenditure from 12.1 per cent of GDP in 1996 to 20 per cent last year. As a result, the fiscal deficit has risen 0.7 per cent of GDP in 1997 to 2.6 per cent in 2001.

Although the deficit remains relatively low by international standards, economists warn that this pump-priming policy cannot continue indefinitely without additional revenues being raised.

Meanwhile, the government has been working on plans to bolster China's social welfare and pensions system. Song Xiaowu, chief secretary of the Economic Restructuring Office, says the task has been complicated by the current weakness of the country's capital markets and the sheer expense and complexity of the challenge. 'The cost of shifting from a pay-as-you-go to a fully-funded pension system by 2030 is Rmb3,000bn,' he says.

China's rapid build-up of debt, the overcapacity that plagues many industrial sectors, the decrepit financial system and the pressures of price deflation remind some economists of the flaws of the Japanese model of economic development. But Mr Song argues China has identified these potential dangers early and is determined to tackle them. So long as it can continue to restructure its economy and maintain its momentum, it has time to grow its way out of these problems.

'With economic growth of 7 to 8 per cent, it is a different situation from Japan,' he says.

Source: Financial Times, 12 December 2002.

Case 5.2

Vietnam's change of heart

FT

28 August 2002

By **Amy Kazmin**

Tran Le Nguyen is a fully fledged capitalist – and a communist hero. Kinh Do, his fast-growing Vietnamese company, has 2,000 employees and last year made and sold an estimated $20m (£13.1m) worth of snacks, biscuits and cakes. He has built his brand with dazzling neon billboards that rival a Las Vegas casino and he is now diversifying into bottled water and other drinks.

For his business achievements, the 38-year-old Sino-Vietnamese entrepreneur – who also calls himself Dennis Tran – has been awarded a

Red Star, a new honour dreamt up by a regime that once reserved its praise for soldiers and state factory workers. Communist authorities have also published Mr Tran's success story – with tales of other leading entrepreneurs – in an inspirational book. 'Everyone in Vietnam can tell you the story of his background,' says a Kinh Do executive.

Private enterprise has a newfound respectability in Vietnam. Its Communist leaders aim to maintain their tight grip on power by delivering a vibrant economy that offers the youthful 79m population opportunities for material gain. 'The government has realised that if you want to have some chance of jobs to keep people happy and preserve stability, it has got to be the private sector,' said Mario Fischel, a Hanoi-based economist with IFC, the World Bank's private lending arm.

That change of heart may at last allow Vietnam to achieve the economic potential that has tantalised would-be investors since the early 1990s, when other south-east Asian countries grew more rapidly. 'Vietnam is coming,' says John Shrimpton, a director of Dragon Capital, which manages about $70m in assets in Vietnam. 'Since it was written off in the mid-1990s, we've seen – out of the limelight – diligent application and the emergence of a very competitive economy.'

For a decade after Hanoi first started tentatively relaxing its control over the economy in 1989, private business was merely tolerated, rather than actively encouraged. But Vietnam's constitution was recently amended to guarantee equal treatment for state and private companies, a significant shift. The registration of private companies has also been made automatic, allowing the creation of more than 40,000 private companies – and some 750,000 new jobs – in the past two years. The International Monetary Fund estimates that Vietnam's economy will grow 5.3 per cent this year, accelerating to 6.5 per cent next year and then 7 per cent in the following two years.

The new mood is palpable in Ho Chi Minh City, Vietnam's business capital, where restaurants, nightclubs and glitzy shops cater to an increasingly affluent middle class. NFO Vietnam, a market research group, says that about 17 per cent of urban households had monthly incomes of more than $500 last year, up from 9 per cent in 1999.

Hanoi is even allowing party members to engage in commercial activities and top officials have started to liken the quest for private profit to the effort to defeat US forces during the Vietnam war. 'Your success in the marketplace is no less glorious than a victory on the battlefield,' Pham Van Khai, the prime minister, told Vietnamese businessmen earlier this year.

Vietnam's economy is still dominated by bloated state companies, agriculture and informal household businesses, with registered Vietnamese-owned private companies contributing only about 8 per cent of gross domestic product. But the importance of local private business is rising rapidly. The World Bank estimates private industrial output grew about 20 per cent last year – far outpacing the 12.2 per cent growth by state and foreign-owned companies.

Nguyen Quoc Khanh, a 42-year-old entrepreneur who employs 600 people in his home furnishing and interior design business, is upbeat. 'Before, the big concern was how to play with the government,' he says. 'But now, it is how to play with our business, how to survive with all the competitors. I am ready to expand as much as I can.'

For all their exuberance, Vietnam's budding businessmen – and potential foreign investors – still face obstacles such as red tape, pervasive corruption and severe shortages of credit. 'On the surface, you have a good emerging private sector but behind the scenes there are a lot of weaknesses and disadvantages,' says Do Duc Dinh, a senior economist at Hanoi's Institute of World Economy.

Financial reforms are crucial. State-owned banks still remain reluctant to lend to private companies. Bankers sometimes face criminal prosecution if their loans go sour. So entrepreneurs tend to rely on personal savings – and funds from family and friends. 'There's a lot of frustration,' says Don Lam, a corporate finance specialist at PwC (Vietnam). 'These guys are begging for money and nobody's willing to give it to them.' The tax laws also retain a socialist quality. Personal income taxes are high and punitive taxes are imposed if a company's profits exceed a 25 per cent return on capital, a rule that has encouraged many small companies to distort their accounts. 'If the environment requires you not to be just a risk-taker but also a scofflaw to succeed, that is not healthy,' says Frederick Burke of the law firm Baker & McKenzie.

In addition, businesses routinely encounter obstruction from junior officials. 'The central government is very concerned with the needs of business but when you come to lower-level implementation – either intentionally or out of ignorance – things just aren't getting done,' says Henry Lam Van Hung, who left Vietnam in 1977 and now manages a steel company.

Vietnam's new capitalists are not remaining silent about their woes. Senior business leaders have joined together to lobby the government and have been joined by foreign investors. Hanoi appears willing to listen. At an unprecedented party conclave this year, Communist leaders set an ambitious reform agenda. If they can turn their words into action, some of the underlying barriers to private enterprise in Vietnam will be removed. Hanoi's Communists may then secure the country's capitalists as allies in their effort to remain in charge.

Source: *Financial Times*, 28 August 2002.

Discussion point

Entrepreneurship has a long heritage in the economies of the Western world. But it is quite new in the post-communist world. How might research into entrepreneurship be used to support new entrepreneurs in these regions? What specific research issues does post-communism create? What might be the objectives of such research and which methodologies would be appropriate? Does the emergence of the private sector in these countries present any opportunities for testing particular theories about entrepreneurship?

Chapter 6

The entrepreneurial process

Chapter overview

This chapter is concerned with developing a model of the process by which entrepreneurs create new wealth. It suggests that entrepreneurship, in the first instance, is driven by a desire for creating change on the part of the entrepreneur. This desire for change leads the entrepreneur to bring together three contingencies, opportunity, resources and organisation, in an innovative and dynamic way.

The chapter also considers the limits of entrepreneurship and whether it extends beyond the profit-making domain to the management of artistic, social and cultural endeavours.

6.1 Making a difference: entrepreneurship and the drive for change

Key learning outcome

An understanding of the changes that entrepreneurship drives and the differences entrepreneurs make.

Entrepreneurship is about bringing about change and making a *difference*. The world is not the same after the entrepreneur has finished with it. In a narrower sense, entrepreneurship is about exploiting innovation in order to create value, which cannot always be measured in purely financial terms. Innovation in this sense goes beyond just invention. It means doing something in a way that is new, different and better.

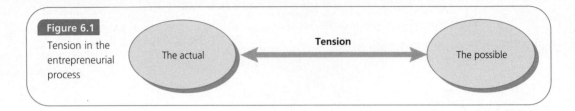

Figure 6.1

Tension in the entrepreneurial process

The actual

Tension

The possible

The entrepreneur is concerned with identifying the *potential* for change for the better. He or she exists in a state of tension between the *actual* and the *possible*, that is, between what *is* and what *might be* (see Figure 6.1). This tension is manifest in three dimensions: the *financial*, the *personal* and the *social*.

The financial dimension: the potential to create new value

Entrepreneurship is an economic activity. It is concerned, first and foremost, with building stable, profitable businesses which must survive in a competitive environment. If they are to thrive and prosper they must add more value and deliver that value to buyers more effectively than their competitors. The new world created by the entrepreneur must be a more valuable one than that which existed previously. The opportunity exploited and the innovation present must create additional value if the venture is to be successful in the long term since it is this additional value that entrepreneurs use to attract and reward the venture's key stakeholders.

A point worth noting here is that in creating *new* value, entrepreneurship is not a 'zero sum game'. Even though business is competitive, it is not inevitable that if an entrepreneur wins then someone somewhere else must lose. Entrepreneurship often presents win–win scenarios. As discussed in Section 2.2, entrepreneurial activity increases the overall value of economies. Entrepreneurs do more than just shift existing wealth around. The new value the entrepreneur creates can be shared in a variety of ways.

The personal dimension: the potential to achieve personal goals

Entrepreneurs are motivated by a number of factors and although making money may motivate some, it is not the only factor, nor necessarily the most important. A sense of achievement, of having created something, or of 'making an entire new world' is often a much more significant driving factor. The entrepreneurial venture can be an entrepreneur's way of leaving his or her mark on the world, reminding it of his or her presence.

Entrepreneurs may also be motivated by the challenge that the competitive environment presents, namely a chance for them to pit their wits against the wider world. Driving their own ventures also gives entrepreneurs a chance to design their own working environment and instils a sense of control. In order to understand entrepreneurial motivation it is essential to recognise that for many entrepreneurs what matters is not the *destination* of the business they finally build up, but the *journey* – the process of creating the business.

The social dimension: the potential for structural change

Entrepreneurs operate within a wider society. In making an 'entire new world' they must, of course, have an impact on that society. They provide the society with new products and access to new services. They provide fellow citizens with jobs. They help make the economic system competitive. This may be good for the economic system as a whole, but not for the less dynamic and efficient competitors they will drive to the wall.

All of this gives the entrepreneur power to drive changes in the structure of a society. The kind of world that an entrepreneur envisages, perhaps the possibility of a better world, can be an important factor in motivating the entrepreneur. It also means that the entrepreneur must (and often eagerly decides to) operate with some degree of social responsibility, sometimes in excess of their incumbent competitors. The kind of world that the entrepreneur would like to see is often a part of their *vision* for their firm and for the future. This vision may be enshrined in the mission that the organisation sets itself.

6.2 The entrepreneurial process: opportunity, organisation and resources

> **Key learning outcome**
>
> An understanding of the factors in the process of entrepreneurial value creation.

Every entrepreneurial venture is different, with its own history. Its successes are the result of it having faced and addressed specific issues in its own way. Nonetheless, it is useful to consider the process of entrepreneurship in a generalised way since this gives us a framework for understanding how entrepreneurship creates new wealth in several terms and for making sense of the detail in particular ventures. It also provides us with a guide for decision making when planning new ventures.

The approach to the entrepreneurial process that will be described here is based on four interacting *contingencies*. The entrepreneur is responsible for bringing these together to create new value. A contingency is simply something which *must* be present in the process but can make an appearance in an endless variety of ways. The four contingencies in the entrepreneurial process are the *entrepreneur*, a market *opportunity*, a business *organisation* and *resources* to be invested (Figure 6.2). Each of these will now be explored in some depth.

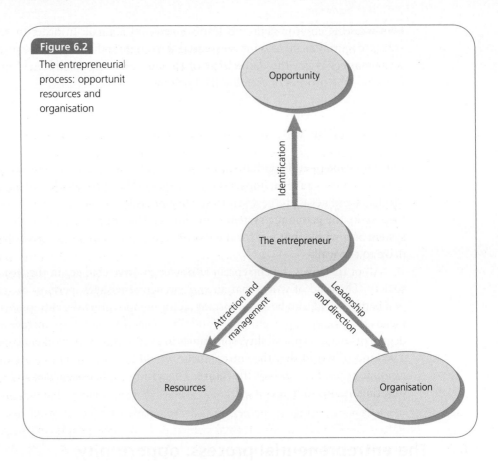

Figure 6.2

The entrepreneurial process: opportunit resources and organisation

The entrepreneur

The entrepreneur is the individual who lies at the heart of the entrepreneurial process, that is, the manager who drives the whole process forward. Entrepreneurs often act singly but in many instances *entrepreneurial teams* are important. Different members of the team may take on different roles and share responsibilities. They may be from the same family, for example the Benetton siblings from Northern Italy who revolutionised the manufacture of textiles, or alternatively, they may be from an existing management team who have joined together to initiate their own venture, perhaps through a management buy-out.

Opportunity

An opportunity is the gap left in a market by those who currently serve it. It represents the potential to serve customers better than they are being served at present. The entrepreneur is responsible for scanning the business landscape for unexploited opportunities or possibilities that something important might be done both *differently* from the way it is done at the moment and, critically, *better* than it is at the moment. The improved way of doing it is the innovation that the entrepreneur presents to the market. If customers agree with the entrepreneur that it is an improvement on what exists already and if the entrepreneur can supply the innovation effectively and profitably then new value can be created.

Organisation

In order to supply the innovation to the market, the activities of a number of different people must be co-ordinated. This is the function of the organisation that the entrepreneur creates. Organisations can take on a variety of forms depending on a number of factors, such as their size, their rate of growth, the industry they operate in, the types of product or service they deliver, the age of the organisation and the culture that it adopts.

Entrepreneurial organisations are characterised by strong, often charismatic, leadership from the entrepreneur. They may have less formal structures and systems than their more bureaucratic, established counterparts. In many respects the entrepreneurial organisation is still learning, but rather than judge this to be a handicap the business turns it into a strength by being receptive to new ideas and responsive to the need for change.

Current thinking on entrepreneurial organisations tends not to draw a hard and fast distinction between those inside the organisation and those who are on the outside. It has been found more productive to think in terms of the organisation in a wider sense as being a *network* of relationships between individuals with the entrepreneur sitting at the centre. This network stretches beyond just the individuals who make up the formal company to include people and organisations outside the venture such as customers, suppliers and investors. The relationships that make up the network are very diverse. Some are defined by contracts, whereas others are defined by open markets; some are formal and some informal; some are based on self-interest, while others are maintained by altruism; some are driven by short-term considerations, and others by long-term interests.

In the network view, the organisation is a fluid thing defined by a *nexus of relationships*. Its boundaries are permeable. The idea of a network provides a powerful insight into how entrepreneurial ventures establish themselves, how they locate themselves competitively, and how they sustain their positions in their markets by adding value to people's lives.

Resources

The final contingency in the entrepreneurial process is resources. This includes the money which is invested in the venture, the people who contribute their efforts, knowledge and skills to it, and *physical assets* such as productive equipment and machinery, buildings and vehicles. Resources also include *intangible assets* such as brand names, company reputation and customer goodwill. All these features can be subject to *investment*. One of the key functions of the entrepreneur is to attract investment to the venture and to use it to build up a set of assets which allow the venture to supply its innovation competitively and profitably.

The entrepreneur plays a critical role in identifying opportunity, building and leading the organisation, and attracting and managing resources. The three external contingencies quickly develop a momentum of their own and become independent of the entrepreneur at the centre. As the organisation grows, it develops processes and systems, and the people within it adopt distinct roles. The entrepreneur must delegate responsibility within the organisation and specialist functions may take over some aspects of the entrepreneur's role. For example, the marketing department may identify opportunities and innovate the firm's offerings to take advantage of them; the finance department may take on the responsibility for attracting investment. In this way, entrepreneurial ventures quickly take on a life of their own. They become quite distinct from the entrepreneur who established them. Consequently, the entrepreneur must constantly address the question of his or her role within the organisation.

6.3 The entrepreneurial process: action and the dynamics of success

> **Key learning outcome**
>
> A recognition that entrepreneurship is a dynamic process in which success fuels success.

The entrepreneurial process results from the *actions* of the entrepreneur. It can only occur if the entrepreneur acts to develop an innovation and promote it to customers. The entrepreneurial process is *dynamic*. Success comes from the contingencies of the entrepreneur, the opportunity, the organisation and resources coming together and supporting each other over time. The entrepreneur must constantly focus the organisation onto the opportunity that has been identified. He or she must mould the resources to hand to give the organisation its shape and to ensure that those resources are appropriate for pursuing the particular opportunity. These interactions are the fundamental elements of the entrepreneurial process and together they constitute the foundations of the *strategy* adopted by the venture.

Opportunity–organisation fit

The nature of the opportunity that is being pursued defines the shape that the organisation must adopt. Every organisation built by an entrepreneur is different. Organisations are complex affairs and there are a variety of ways in which they might be described and understood. The essential features are the *assets* of the organisation, that is, the things which it possesses; its *structure*, namely how it arranges communication links (both formal and informal) within itself; its *processes*: how it *adds value* to its inputs to create its *outputs*; and its *culture*, that is, the attitudes, beliefs and outlooks that influence the way people behave within the organisation (see Table 6.1).

Assets, structure, process and culture are not separate parts of an organisation. They are merely different perspectives we may adopt in describing it. These four

Table 6.1	An outline of organisational *assets*, *structure*, *process* and *culture* for three global entrepreneurial businesses		
Organisation	**McDonald's**	**The Body Shop**	**Microsoft**
Opportunity pursued	Desire for fast, convenient, consistent meals	Desire for toiletries in convenient packaging; a concern for the environment	Desire to process information
Assets	Brand name, outlets, locations, people	Brand name, outlets, locations, people	People, knowledge, patents, brand name
Structure	Series of production/ retail outlets	Series of retail outlets	Project teams based at one location
Process	Production and distribution standardised at outlets. Central financing and marketing	Production centralised. Distribution through outlets. Promotion largely by store presence	Product development, production, distribution and marketing centralised
Culture	Positive attitude, concern for quality, customer focus	Attitude of concern. Emphasis on wider social responsibility for organisation	Innovative and creative 'technophilia'. Emphasis on managerial informality

perspectives on the organisation form a unified whole which must be appropriate for the opportunity that the organisation is pursuing. The organisation must be shaped to *fit* the market gap that defines the opportunity.

Resource–organisation configuration

Resources are the things that are used to pursue opportunity. They include *people*, *money* and *productive assets*. In a sense, an organisation is 'just' a collection of resources, though this does not exhaust possibilities for its description. The *configuration* of the resources is the way in which a particular mix of resources is brought together and blended to form the organisation's assets, structure, process and (through the attitude of the people who make it up) its culture.

Resource–opportunity focus

The entrepreneur must decide what resources will make up the organisation; for example, its mix of capital, how this will be converted into productive assets, and the nature and skills of the people who will make it up are all matters to be decided by the entrepreneur in the first instance. If the organisation is to develop the assets, structure, process and culture that will enable it to fit with its opportunity then the resource mix must be correctly balanced.

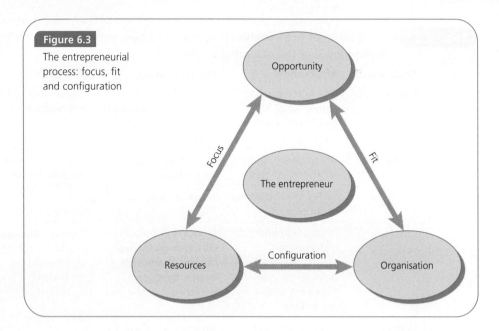

Figure 6.3

The entrepreneurial process: focus, fit and configuration

Entrepreneurs must be active in attracting resources to their venture such as suitably qualified employees, financial backing in the form of investors' money, and the support of customers and suppliers. Even so, they usually find that they do not have access to the same level of resources as established players in a market and because their risks may be higher, they will find the resources to be more expensive. If they are to compete successfully then entrepreneurs must make the resources they can get hold of work much harder perhaps than many established players do. The entrepreneur must be single-minded and *focus* those resources definitely and unambiguously onto the opportunity that has been identified since the performance of the entrepreneurial organisation depends on how well the contingencies of opportunity, organisation and resources are linked together (Figure 6.3).

Learning organisations

These three aspects of the entrepreneurial process – making the organisation *fit* the opportunity it aims to exploit, *configuring* the resources to shape the organisation and *focusing* the resources in pursuit of the opportunity – are not reflected in separate spheres of activity. They merely provide different perspectives on the same underlying management process. However, they do illuminate the essence of the entrepreneur's task and the direction their leadership must take. That leadership must be applied *constantly* since organisations are fluid things and left to themselves they can lose their shape and sense of direction. Furthermore, the entrepreneurial organisation must be a *learning* organisation. That is, it must not only *respond* to opportunities and challenges but must also *reflect* on the outcomes that result from that response and *modify* future responses in the light of experience.

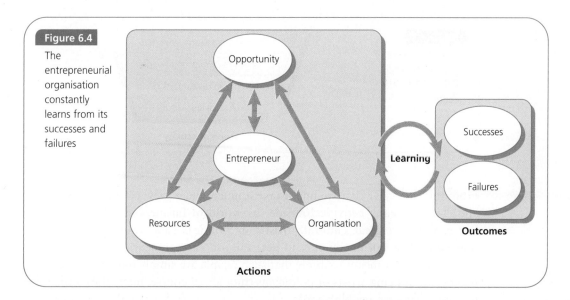

Figure 6.4

The entrepreneurial organisation constantly learns from its successes and failures

The venture cannot afford to acquire assets and set up structures and systems which are incapable of evolving as the organisation develops. Assets and structures must be modified as the organisation grows and changes and, critically, learns from its successes and failures. The entrepreneur must take responsibility for stimulating the firm to change in the light of experience. This learning process is shown in Figure 6.4.

6.4 Beyond profit: entrepreneurship in the social and public domains

Key learning outcome

An appreciation that an understanding of entrepreneurship can help make non-profit-making activities more successful.

Entrepreneurship, as an activity, is intimately associated with the world of business and making profits. However, the picture of entrepreneurship we have developed here has insights that can go beyond purely profit-motivated activity. In particular, we have seen that:

- entrepreneurship is a style of management;

- entrepreneurs are managers who are very effective at pursuing opportunity and creating change;

- entrepreneurship is a social as well as an economic activity; and

- the motivations of the entrepreneur are varied and go beyond a desire to make money; they also involve a desire to create a new and better world.

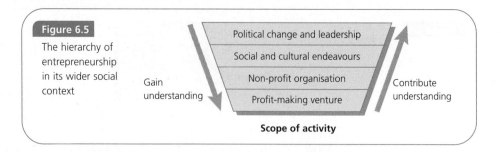

Figure 6.5

The hierarchy of entrepreneurship in its wider social context

From this it is clear that we might take a much wider view of 'entrepreneurship' and consider many activities outside the world of business as 'entrepreneurial'. For example, a great cultural, artistic or political endeavour could be entrepreneurial. It is not uncommon to hear talk of 'entrepreneurial' artists or politicians. This is not meant to imply that such people are simply interested in making money out of being artists or politicians (though, of course, many do!), rather it is to imply that such people approach their careers with drive, ambition and a clear vision of what they want to achieve. In order to fulfil their ambitions they are willing to develop and use entrepreneurial skills such as effective communication and leadership.

A hierarchy of entrepreneurial activities functioning in different social areas can be constructed as shown in Figure 6.5. At the core is what we conventionally understand to be entrepreneurship, namely managing the profit-making venture. At the next level is management of non-profit-making organisations such as charities. Above this we might place endeavours in the social and cultural arena such as sporting and artistic ventures. At the top of the hierarchy there are activities aimed at creating wholesale social change such as political activity. These levels are not completely separate, of course, and there will be some overlap.

Even though we can recognise entrepreneurship in these wider social arenas it is wise to keep management of the profit-making venture as the central concern for entrepreneurship. If we fail to do so the subject could become so wide as to be in danger of losing its coherence as a field of study. Therefore, this book will concentrate on profit-motivated activities. However, this does not mean that insights gained from the management of the profit venture cannot be used to help achieve success in non-profit-making ventures, or, conversely, that an understanding of success outside the business sphere cannot be used to illuminate the ways in which entrepreneurship might be improved within that sector.

In a narrow sense, many non-profit activities may still demand a managerial approach. They often involve managing money. Thus the charity still has to attract financial resources to distribute to its clients; sport may involve financial sponsorship; artists must still sell their creations; political parties must attract money from supporters if they are to function. All these activities can call upon insights from other business areas such as marketing and human resource management. In a broader sense, though, entrepreneurship, perhaps more than many other management disciplines, goes beyond the mere management of money. Money is just a means to an end for the entrepreneur, and the end is the creation of a better world. We may offer a description of entrepreneurship at a fundamental level by claiming that it is about:

❝creating and managing vision and communicating that vision to other people. It is about demonstrating leadership, motivating people and being effective in getting people to accept change.❞

This description reflects entrepreneurship as a management skill practised and perfected in a human setting. As such it can play a crucial part in driving any venture forward whether that venture be in the business, social, cultural or political domain.

Summary of key ideas

- The entrepreneurial process is the creation of *new value* through the entrepreneur identifying new *opportunities*, attracting the *resources* needed to pursue those opportunities and building an *organisation* to manage those resources.

- The process is *dynamic* with the entrepreneur and the entrepreneurial organisation learning through *success* and *failure*.

- As a style of management, entrepreneurship has much to offer to, and also much to learn from, the management of projects in the not-for-profit, artistic and political arenas.

Research themes

Theorising about processes

The entrepreneurial process is one of the core aspects of entrepreneurial research (see Chapter 5). Consider the model of the entrepreneurial process developed in this chapter, in terms of its theoretical and methodological foundations. What paradigm does it represent? What methodologies would be appropriate for validating and developing the model? Could the model be integrated into other paradigmatic approaches? In particular, ask whether it might be used as an interpretive framework for non-positivistic approaches. Could it be used to make sense of cognitive maps of entrepreneurs' perceptions of the issues they face in developing their ventures such as opportunity identification, resource acquisition, organisation creation and competition? Primary information may be gained from interviews with practising entrepreneurs.

Types of entrepreneur and the entrepreneurial process

Chapter 4 discussed various types of entrepreneur. A distinction was made between singular, sequential and portfolio entrepreneurs. Use the contingency model developed in this chapter to propose generic issues in the development of singular, sequential and portfolio ventures, emphasising the contingencies of the entrepreneur, opportunity, resources, organisation, fit, focus and configuration as a guide. Use case studies of each type of venture as a source of information to develop real examples of the issues identified. How do they differ for each type of venture? What are the implications for each type of venture? Are the issues generic across each type of venture? How might these affect the need for external support for different types of venture?

Suggestions for further reading

Batstone, S. and Pheby, J. (1996) 'Entrepreneurship and decision-making: the contribution of G.L.S. Shackle', *International Journal of Entrepreneurial Behaviour and Research*, Vol. 2, No. 2, pp. 34–51.

Bhave, M.P. (1994) 'A process model of entrepreneurial venture creation', *Journal of Business Venturing*, Vol. 9, No. 3, pp. 223–42.

Bouchiki, H. (1993) 'A constructivist framework for understanding entrepreneurial performance', *Organisation Studies*, Vol. 14, No. 4, pp. 549–70.

Gartner, W.B. (1985) 'A conceptual framework for describing the phenomenon of new venture creation', *Academy of Management Review*, Vol. 10, No. 4, pp. 696–706.

Hill, R. (1982) 'The entrepreneur: an artist masquerading as a businessman?', *International Management*, Vol. 37, No. 2, pp. 21–6.

Lessem, R. (1978) 'Towards the interstices of management: developing the social entrepreneur', *Management Education and Development*, Vol. 9, pp. 178–88.

Selected case material **Case 6.1**

Jollibee buzzes on fast food and rapid sales   FT

15 January 2002

By **Roel Landing**

Tony Tan Caktiong, chairman and president of Philippine fast-food chain Jollibee Foods, is rich and successful and quite used to being the centre of attention. But recently he was surprised to be asked for his first autograph.

In the Philippines, people idolise movie stars, sports champions and even military heroes, but very rarely businessmen.

His fan was a franchisee, one of an army of entrepreneurs who built many of the burger outlets that have helped lift revenues and profits for Jollibee even as economic growth has turned sluggish.

The Philippine government expects economic growth to drop from 3.9 per cent last year to 2.8 per cent this year. Yet, Jollibee opened 38 new stores in the first nine months of the year, after adding 31 new outlets last year, bringing its total network to 406 at end-September 2001.

Part of its success comes directly from the slowing economy as executives who have been made redundant have bought franchises, helping boost Jollibee's bottom line. More than half of the fast-food chain's 406 outlets are owned by franchisees who run them in accordance with the strict guidelines set by Jollibee.

'Franchising revolutionised the Philippine food industry,' says Mr Tan Caktiong. It certainly revolutionised Jollibee, turning it from a small ice-cream parlour in the mid-1970s into one of the country's biggest fast-food chains with turnover of 20bn pesos (Dollars 390m) in 2000. It has even outpaced McDonald's, the world's leading hamburger chain. Jollibee, the local copycat, has twice as many domestic outlets as the American original.

Such an achievement by a local hero is made even more impressive as the Philippines is a former colony of the US, where 50 years of direct rule ended in 1946 only to be replaced by another half-century of cultural imperialism, and where the population largely assumes American products are automatically better than local ones. Coca-Cola, for example, has 70 per cent of the soft-drinks market, while a local brand controls just a quarter.

But it is not just the business model that makes Jollibee successful. Its outlets attract thousands of customers with affordable, well-served food suited to the Filipino taste.

Mr Tan Caktiong says Jollibee makes sure its burgers are tastier by marinating the beef patties in special sauces and mixtures before cooking. 'Our food doesn't only taste delicious, it also smells delicious,' he says, adding that, for Asians, it is not bad manners to smell food before eating it.

Its prices, slightly lower than McDonald's, reflect the fact the stores' operators do not have to pay high dollar-denominated royalties and the parent has worked hard to keep costs down.

The company makes its own patties and buns and what it cannot make itself, it buys from suppliers at a good discount. Jollibee has also benefited from the weakening dollar in Australia, where it buys beef.

The trend in the Philippines is also for eating out more. In 1990, Filipinos spent only 7 per cent of their income on food consumed outside the home. Last year, that figure was 10 per cent. Also, households that used to eat in expensive restaurants are going to fast-food restaurants to save money.

And finally, Jollibee has run a clever marketing campaign that portrays the company as a successful Filipino challenger to its big US rival, playing on nationalist feelings.

All these have helped Jollibee buck the trend of a slowing economy.

System-wide retail sales in the first nine months of 2001 went up 20 per cent to 17.6bn pesos, while profit after tax rose 7 per cent to 648m pesos from a year ago.

Last year, sales went up by 12 per cent while net income surged by 41 per cent.

Its success at home is allowing it to start expanding into other types of food and reach out across the world.

It now also runs a pizza and pasta chain, an Oriental fast-food network and coffee-and-pastry shops.

It even operates 23 stores abroad, including eight in California, the home of McDonald's.

Source: Financial Times, 15 February 2002.

Case 6.2

Young and old are targets

FT

5 June 2002

By **Christopher Swann**

Over the past few years the internet has provided most of the hot new concepts in franchising. The internet boom threw up a host of franchise chains, mostly internet service providers. Many have survived the recent decline in technology spending, but it is no surprise that the growth in franchising is coming from elsewhere.

What might best be termed 'social franchises' have been growing strongly, with children and senior citizens becoming the focus of the main growth areas in the US franchise market.

There are two social trends driving this process. Like Europe, the US is an ageing society. The number of senior citizens in the US is expected to double to 70m between now and the end of 2003. The number of people over 85 grew from 3.1m to 4.2m in the 1990s. This has meant that 54m US adults provide domestic and personal care for their elderly relatives.

Meanwhile, problems in the US education system have meant an increasing number of children leaving schools without basic literacy and numeracy skills.

The increasing demand for care for the elderly has led to the meteoric rise of Home Instead, a home help business set up in 1994.

The aim of the chain is to provide cheap non-medical care for the elderly, allowing senior citizens to maintain their independence.

'The average annual cost of a nursing home is $40,000,' says Jim Fowler, vice president for communications of Home Instead. 'But this is partly because they are staffed by medically trained personnel and that level of expertise is not always necessary.'

For those that do not need constant medical attention, Home Instead franchisees provide services such as cooking, cleaning, running errands, shopping and companionship.

'You do not need a certified specialist to make your meals or open letters for you,' says Mr Fowler. Estimates suggest that families with an elderly member buy an average of 22 hours worth of services a week. As a result demand for Home Instead's services is soaring.

In 1997 the chain had total revenue of just $8m. By 2000 this had grown to $74m and revenues are expected to hit $170m this year. Meanwhile, the number of outlets has expanded from 146 in 1999 to 308 this year.

Nor are they alone. Similar chains are also proliferating, including Comfort Keepers, Visiting Angels and Home Helpers.

But as Home Instead observes, its main competitors are also its main clients; family care providers themselves.

The only real brake on growth has been recruitment, concedes Mr Fowler. The average hourly wage for one of its carers is $7.25. With the rewards of the work almost entirely spiritual, the potential work force is limited.

The education market has also been growing at a frantic pace so far this year. At the forefront has been Sylvan Learning, the Baltimore-based education company. The Sylvan Learning Centres in the US seek to plug the gaps left by the state system, providing basic reading, writing and maths skills to children who are falling behind.

With the public school system struggling to attract bright young students into teaching, a perception of the inadequacies of public education has been growing. Sylvan Learning itself highlights a different trend, focusing on the greater willingness of parents to invest in supplementary tutoring.

'It's not just that parents do not want their children to fall behind, they want them to get ahead,' says Steven Drake, vice-president of communications at the company.

Most of the company's franchises are in relatively well-off suburban areas. But the increasing determination of the government to deal with the failures of public education in under-privileged areas is likely to fuel further growth for Sylvan Learning and other education providers.

In January George W. Bush, the US president, signed the so-called 'no child left behind act', which provides federal funds for supplementary tutoring. Under the act, the Federal government will pay for private lessons for under-privileged children – with parents choosing which organisation will provide the services. Although the details have yet to be hammered out, Sylvan Learning is working on the assumption that annual government funding will amount to between $800 and $1,300 per under-privileged child.

'There will clearly be non-profit groups and church organisations offering these kind of services,' said Mr Drake. 'But Sylvan will be in a very strong position to provide tutoring services under the scheme.'

The company is also expanding overseas and recently opened its first outlet in London.

Franchising experts believe that the retreat of the state and the inadequacy of state provisions will create increasing opportunities for franchising. The British Franchise Association has identified care for the elderly in nursing homes as one likely area of expansion.

When governments are seeking to outsource services, it is much easier to deal with a few large providers who can guarantee consistently high services. With each outlet owned by an individual entrepreneur, it is hoped that such care franchises will also be better managed.

As a result, the growth in educational and caring franchises looks likely to be more long lasting than the brief efflorescence of the internet variety.

Source: Financial Times, 5 June 2002.

Discussion point

Consider franchising as a business model. Should it be regarded as a twofold entrepreneurial process: the first stage being initiation of the franchise concept by the entrepreneur, the second expansion through multiplication of outlets? Or is it better thought of as a single process in which the two stages are integrated and should be planned together from the start?

Chapter 7

The entrepreneurial option

Chapter overview

This chapter is concerned with developing a picture of the entrepreneur as an **individual**. It considers the **type** of people who choose an entrepreneurial path, the **characteristics** successful entrepreneurs bring to the job and the **skills** they use. The chapter concludes by emphasising the importance of understanding the entrepreneur in a social setting and the influences exerted by the culture in which they operate.

7.1 Who becomes an entrepreneur?

Key learning outcome

A recognition of the different type of people who take up an entrepreneurial career.

The discussion in Chapter 1 should make it clear that we should be very wary of trying to answer the question 'who becomes an entrepreneur?' by looking for a certain type of personality or trying to identify innate characteristics. In these terms, *anyone* can become an entrepreneur. A more fruitful approach is to look at the broader life experience and events which encourage a person to make a move into entrepreneurship. A number of general life stories or 'biographies' can be identified.

The inventor

The *inventor* is someone who has developed an innovation and who has decided to make a career out of presenting that innovation to the market. It may be a new product or it may be an idea for a new service. It may be high-tech, or it may be based on a traditional technology.

The inventor often draws on technical experience of a particular industry in order to make his or her invention. However, it may be derived from a technology quite unrelated to the industry in which they work. It may be based on technical expertise they have gained as the result of a hobby. Alternatively, the invention may result from a 'grey' research programme carried out unofficially within the inventor's employer organisation or it may be the product of a private 'garden shed' development programme.

It is an unfortunate fact of life that, in general, many such 'inventors' have a poor track record in building successful businesses. This is not because their ideas are not good; their innovations are often quite valuable. More often, it is due to the fact that no new product, regardless of how many benefits it might potentially bring to the customer, will manufacture and promote itself. Successful entrepreneurship calls upon a wide range of management skills, not just an ability to innovate. The entrepreneur must establish a market potential for their innovation and lead an organisation which can deliver it profitably. They must sell the product to customers and sell the venture to investors. Inventors can often be so impressed with the technical side of their innovation (often justifiably) that they neglect the other tasks that must be undertaken. An example of an inventor who combined technical insight with consummate business skills is James Dyson, who built up not one but two highly successful businesses to market innovative products.

The unfulfilled manager

Life as a professional manager in an established organisation brings many rewards. It offers a stable income, intellectual stimulation, status and a degree of security. For many people, though, this is still not enough. The organisation may not offer them a vehicle for all their ambitions: for example, the desire to make a mark on the world, to leave a lasting achievement, to stretch their existing managerial talents to their limit and to develop new ones. It may simply not let them do things *their* way. Such a manager, confident in their abilities and unsatisfied in their ambitions, may decide to embark on an entrepreneurial career.

The question they often face is 'doing what?'. The desire and the ability to perform entrepreneurially means nothing if a suitable opportunity has not been spotted and an innovation to take advantage of it developed. In a sense, the unsatisfied manager faces the opposite problem to the inventor: entrepreneurial ability but nothing to apply it to. If they are to be successful they must put effort into identifying and clarifying a business idea and developing an understanding of its market potential. This can often be resolved by working as part of an entrepreneurial team with an inventor who dreams up the initial idea.

The displaced manager

The increasing pace of technological and economic change means that managers are likely to make an increasing number of career changes during their professional lives. Restructuring trends such as 'downsizing' and 'delayering' mean that unemployment among professional groups is increasing in many parts of the world. This increases the pressure on managers to work for themselves and one possibility is to undertake an entrepreneurial route. The severance package which may be offered by their organisations (often supplemented with training and support) can sometimes facilitate this possibility.

Many managers approach redundancy positively, seeing it as an opportunity to achieve things they could not within the organisation. In effect, they recognise themselves as unfulfilled managers and feel grateful for the push they have been given. Others, however, may not adopt such a positive approach. They may see the uncertainties looming larger than the possibilities. Making entrepreneurship successful is very difficult, if not impossible, unless it is approached with enthusiasm. If a person does not find the prospect of an entrepreneurial career attractive then it is plainly wrong for them. However, one should not underestimate the power of a few early successes to change attitudes and to alter a manager's perception of possibilities.

The young professional

Increasingly, young, highly educated people, often with formal management qualifications, are skipping the experience of working for an established organisation and moving directly to work on establishing their own ventures. Despite some very high-profile success stories, not least with Internet ventures, such entrepreneurs are often met with suspicion. There may be a concern that whatever their 'theoretical' knowledge, they lack experience in the realities of business life. While youthful enthusiasm *may* hide a lack of real acumen, the young entrepreneur should not be dismissed out of hand.

In the mature economies of the Western world, young entrepreneurs have been disproportionally important in leading *new* industries, particularly in high-tech areas such as computing, information technology and business services. The fast-growing emergent economies of the Pacific Rim and the developing world have populations which are generally much younger in profile than those of the West. Entrepreneurs may *have* to be younger if sufficient entrepreneurial talent is to be available to drive the economy's growth. The post-communist world of eastern and central Europe is currently undergoing a radical economic and social restructuring. To a great extent it is young people who are taking the lead and making the adaptations necessary to take advantage of the new possibilities these changes are offering. Delmar and Davidsson (2000) found that some 2 per cent of the Swedish population were considering starting their own business. After exploring a number of social and personal factors they found that gender was the dominant indicator of entrepreneurial intention and age an important secondary factor.

The excluded

Some people turn to an entrepreneurial career because nothing else is open to them. The dynamism and entrepreneurial vigour of displaced communities and ethnic and religious minorities is well documented. This is not because such people are 'inherently' entrepreneurial; rather it is because, for a variety of social, cultural, political and historical reasons, they have not been invited to join the wider economic community. They do not form part of the established network of individuals and organisations. As a result they may form their own internal networks, trading among themselves and, perhaps, with their ancestral countries.

Ethnic entrepreneurship can be very important within a national economy. Small communities often make a contribution to the overall entrepreneurial vigour of a country in a way which is quite disproportionate to their number. Nevertheless, one of the main challenges faced by ethnic entrepreneurs is making the move from running a small business to starting a full-blown entrepreneurial venture. This is because to achieve its growth potential the entrepreneurial venture must spread its network of relationships quite widely in order to achieve its growth potential, and this often involves going beyond the confines of the relatively small community in which it starts. In a sense, this goes against the reason for the business coming into existence in the first place. In making the move, the ethnic entrepreneur may face risks that the non-ethnic entrepreneur does not.

There is growing evidence that after a time, say three or four generations, small business managers from ethnic minorities are increasingly willing to make the move to entrepreneurism. In doing so they add another spur to the wider economy.

In a far-reaching study David Blanchflower and Andrew Oswald (1998) have investigated the factors that lie behind the drive to become an entrepreneur. The basis of their research was information on the *National Child Development Study* (NCDS), a database recording biographical information, psychometric and personality test data on all individuals born in Great Britain between 3 and 9 March 1958. Taking a broad view of entrepreneurship, that is, starting one's own business, the researchers attempted to identify the factors that predisposed individuals to take this career option. They found no correlation between personality factors, important life events and entrepreneurial inclination. This is a finding that reinforces this book's proposition that successful entrepreneurship is not personality dependent. The one thing they did find to be important was receiving a lump sum of money, say, in the form of a legacy, which allowed individuals to make the initial investment in a start-up. The authors then develop an econometric model of entrepreneurial labour economics. This finding confirms the importance of access to initial capital as a key event in the entrepreneurial process.

This is not to say that one cannot become an entrepreneur if one does not receive a legacy. But it does emphasise the importance of building a good relationship with investors. This is an issue that will be explored further in Chapter 23.

Miner (1997) suggests that four primary types of individual become entrepreneurs. These are:

- The *personal achiever* – the individual who is driven to succeed and chooses the entrepreneurial option as the best means of doing this. The personal achiever is characterised by clear objectives, hard work and dedication.

- The *emphatic supersalesperson* – this type is characterised by a well-developed ability to understand customer needs, to empathise with them and to effectively communicate their offerings to them. They are motivated to become entrepreneurs by their ability to deliver sales.

- The *real manager* – the entrepreneur who is motivated by having an organisation large enough to put demands on their managerial abilities. They are motivated to build their own organisations, because of the lack of potential extant organisations present to them.

- The *expert-idea generator* – an individual who is motivated by the entrepreneurial option because it offers them a platform to develop and market an innovation they have created and achieve the satisfaction of seeing it become reality.

Miner considers appropriate routes into entrepreneurship and some of the pitfalls along the way for each type.

7.2 Characteristics of the successful entrepreneur

> **Key learning outcome**
>
> A recognition of the characteristics exhibited by successful entrepreneurs.

Although there does not seem to be a single 'entrepreneurial type' there is a great deal of consistency in the way in which entrepreneurs approach their task. Some of the characteristics which are exhibited by the successful entrepreneur are discussed below. However, we should be careful to draw a distinction between personality 'characteristics' and the character somebody displays when working. The former are regarded as innate, a permanent part of the make-up of their personality. The latter is just the way they approach a particular set of tasks. This is just as much a product of their commitment, interest and motivation to the tasks in hand, as it is a predisposition.

Hard work

Entrepreneurs put a lot of physical and mental effort into developing their ventures. They often work long and antisocial hours. After all, an entrepreneur is their own most valuable asset. That said, balancing the needs of the venture with other life commitments such as family and friends is one of the great challenges which faces the entrepreneur.

Self-starting

Entrepreneurs do not need to be told what to do. They identify tasks for themselves and then follow them through without looking for encouragement or direction from others.

Setting of personal goals

Entrepreneurs tend to set themselves clear, and demanding, goals. They benchmark their achievements against these personal goals. As a result, entrepreneurs tend to work to internal standards rather than look to others for assessment of their performance.

Resilience

Not everything goes right all the time. In fact, failure may be experienced more often than success. Entrepreneurs must not only pick themselves up after things have gone wrong but must learn positively from the experience and use that learning to increase the chances of success the next time around.

Confidence

The entrepreneur must demonstrate that they not only believe in themselves but also in the venture they are pursuing. After all, if they don't, who will?

Receptiveness to new ideas

However, the entrepreneur must not be *overly* confident. They must recognise their own limitations and the possibilities that they have to improve their skills. They must be willing to revise their ideas in the light of new experience. One of the main reasons that banks and venture capitalists give for *not* supporting a business proposal is that the entrepreneur was *too* sure of themselves to be receptive to good advice when it was offered.

Assertiveness

Entrepreneurs are usually clear as to what they want to gain from a situation and are not frightened to express their wishes. Being assertive does not mean being aggressive! Nor does it mean adopting a position and refusing to budge. Assertiveness means a commitment to *outcomes*, not *means*. True assertiveness relies on mutual understanding and is founded on good communication skills.

Information seeking

Entrepreneurs are not, on average, any more intelligent than any other group. They are, however, characterised by *inquisitiveness*. They are never satisfied by the information they have at any one time and constantly seek more. Good entrepreneurs tend to question rather more than they make statements when communicating.

Eager to learn

Good entrepreneurs are always aware that they could do things better. They are aware of both the skills they have and their limitations, and are always receptive to a chance to improve their skills and to develop new ones.

Attuned to opportunity

The good entrepreneur is constantly searching for new opportunities. In effect, this means that he or she is never really satisfied with the way things are at any moment in time. The entrepreneur uses this sense of dissatisfaction to make sure he or she never becomes complacent.

Receptive to change

The entrepreneur is always willing to embrace change in a positive fashion, that is, to actively embrace the possibilities presented by change rather than resist them.

Commitment to others

Good entrepreneurs are not selfish. They cannot afford to be! They recognise the value that other people bring to their ventures and the importance of motivating those people to make the best effort they can on its behalf. This means showing a commitment to them. Motivation demands an investment in understanding how people think. Leadership is not just about giving people jobs to do; it is also about offering them the support they need in order to do those jobs.

Comfort with power

Entrepreneurs can become very powerful figures. They can have a great impact on the lives of other people. Power can be one of the great motivators for the entrepreneur. Effective entrepreneurs are *aware* of the power they possess and recognise it as an asset. They are not afraid to use it and never let themselves be intimidated by it. However, the *true* entrepreneur uses power responsibly, as a means to an end and not as an end in itself.

These are essential characteristics. How they become manifest is, of course, subject to political and economic conditions. They are recognised and judged in a social setting subject to social norms and expectations. How these characteristics are developing in social systems that have undergone major changes (such as the post-communist bloc of central and eastern Europe) is of particular interest. Green *et al.* (1996) and Kuznetsov *et al.* (2000) offer studies of the emergence of entrepreneurial characteristics in Russia.

(7.3) Entrepreneurial skills

> **Key learning outcome**
>
> A recognition of the skills which enhance entrepreneurial performance.

A skill is simply knowledge which is demonstrated by action. It is an ability to perform in a certain way. An entrepreneur is someone who has a good business idea and can turn that idea into reality. To be successful, an entrepreneur must not only identify an opportunity but also understand it in great depth. He or she must be able to spot a gap in the market and recognise what new product or service will fill that gap. He or she must know what features it will have and why they will appeal to the customer. The entrepreneur must also know how to inform the customer about it and how to deliver the new offering. All this calls for an intimate knowledge of a particular sector of industry. Turning an idea into reality calls upon two sorts of skill. General management skills are required to organise the physical and financial resources needed to run the venture and people management skills are needed to obtain the necessary support from others for the venture to succeed.

Some important general management business skills include:

- *strategy skills* – an ability to consider the business as a whole, to understand how it fits within its marketplace, how it can organise itself to deliver value to its customers, and the ways in which it does this better than its competitors.

- *planning skills* – an ability to consider what the future might offer, how it will impact on the business and what needs to be done to prepare for it now.

- *marketing skills* – an ability to see past the firm's offerings and their features, to be able to see *how* they satisfy the customer's needs and *why* the customer finds them attractive.

- *financial skills* – an ability to manage money; to be able to keep track of expenditure and to monitor cash-flow, but also an ability to assess investments in terms of their potential and their risks.

- *project management skills* – an ability to organise projects, to set specific object-ives, to set schedules and to ensure that the necessary resources are in the right place at the right time.

- *time management skills* – an ability to use time productively, to be able to prioritise important jobs and to get things done to schedule.

Businesses are made by people. A business can only be successful if the people who make it up are properly directed and are committed to make an effort on its behalf. An entrepreneurial venture also needs the support of people from outside the organ-isation such as customers, suppliers and investors. To be effective, an entrepreneur needs to demonstrate a wide variety of skills in the way he or she deals with other people. Some of the more important skills we might include under this heading are:

- *leadership skills* – an ability to inspire people to work in a specific way and to undertake the tasks that are necessary for the success of the venture. Leadership is about more than merely directing people; it is also about supporting them and helping them to achieve the goals they have been set.

- *motivation skills* – an ability to enthuse people and get them to give their full commitment to the tasks in hand. Being able to motivate demands an understanding of what drives people and what they expect from their jobs. It should not be forgotten that, for the entrepreneur, an ability to motivate oneself is as important as an ability to motivate others.

- *delegation skills* – an ability to allocate tasks to different people. Effective delegation involves more than instructing. It demands a full understanding of the skills that people possess, how they use them and how they might be developed to fulfil future needs.

- *communication skills* – an ability to use spoken and written language to express ideas and inform others. Good communication is about more than just passing information. It is about using language to influence people's actions.

- *negotiation skills* – an ability to understand what is wanted from a situation, what is motivating others in that situation and recognise the possibilities of maximising the outcomes for all parties. Being a good negotiator is more about being able to identify win–win scenarios and communicate them, than it is about being able to 'bargain hard'.

All these different people skills are inter-related. Good leadership demands being able to motivate. Effective delegation requires an ability to communicate. The skills needed to deal with people are not innate, they must be learnt. Leadership is as much an acquired skill as is an ability to plan effectively. The ability to motivate and to negotiate can be learnt in the same way as project management techniques.

Entrepreneurial performance results from a combination of *industry knowledge*, *general management skills*, *people skills* and *personal motivation* (Figure 7.1). The successful entrepreneur must not only use these skills but learn to use them and learn from using them. Entrepreneurs should constantly audit their abilities in these areas, recognise their strengths and shortcomings, and plan how to develop these skills in the future.

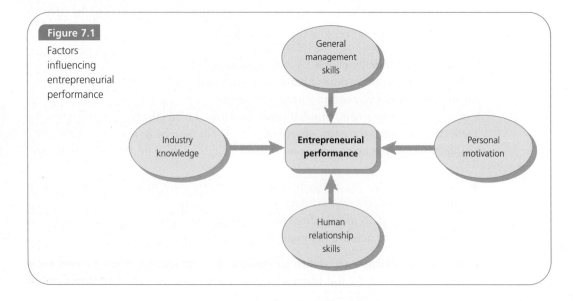

Figure 7.1

Factors influencing entrepreneurial performance

(7.4) Cultural factors in entrepreneurship

Key learning outcome

A recognition that the behaviour of entrepreneurs is influenced by a wide range of cultural and social factors.

Entrepreneurs are not robots blindly fulfilling an economic function. They cannot pursue opportunities or strive for economic efficiency without exhibiting some concern for wider issues. Entrepreneurs are human beings operating within societies which define, and are to an extent defined by, cultures. The analysis of culture falls properly within the domain of anthropology. The insights gained by anthropologists are of increasing interest to those who study business behaviour and performance. One of the driving forces behind this growth in interest has been the impressive economic growth achieved by countries in various parts of the world. Of particular interest at present are the 'tiger' economies of the Pacific Rim. The contribution that a range of structural, social and cultural factors have made to their success is widely debated.

This debate has been rekindled by the recent meltdown in many economies in this region. If cultural factors are called upon to explain long-term success, how might they be called upon to explain short-term collapse? How do 'cultural' and 'economic' fundamentals act together? Many are now suggesting that culture means little in the face of primary economic realities.

An analysis of culture is not a straightforward matter since a culture is not something that can be placed under a microscope. It is something we construct in order to explain the world rather than something we experience directly. There is a gulf between those who think that a culture can be examined as an objective reality and those who think it must be interpreted as something that impresses on our experience at a personal level. There is a debate (often quite heated) within the social sciences community as to the extent to which cultural differences are important. At one extreme there are those who see a much diminished role for culture. It is, at most, the 'icing on the cake' of an underlying psychic unity for mankind. Such an argument is often based on the fact that human beings are all decended from a relatively recent common ancestor and there has been no time for any fundamental evolutionary distinction between different human beings to have taken place. At the other extreme are those who argue that culture is all and that human beings are largely determined by their cultures: human nature is culture specific. Most social scientists take an intermediary position. Clearly, culture plays a role in entrepreneurial behaviour. An American entrepreneur tends to act differently from a Japanese one, who, in turn, behaves differently from a Peruvian one. There are not only great differences *between* these cultures which influence the way entrepreneurs work, there is also a wide variety of ways in which *individual* entrepreneurs work *within* these cultures. Culture is expressed in both the value *judgements* an individual makes and the value *system* of their wider community. What is at debate is the extent to which these differences reflect deep cultural factors or 'mere' social and economic local contingencies. George and Zahra (2002) explore this issue and Busenitz and Lau (1996) develop a cognitive model of the effects of culture on new venture creation. Mitchell *et al.* (2002) examine three questions related to the link between entrepreneurship and national culture using a cognitive approach: Are entrepreneurs different in their cognition? Are these cognitions universal among entrepreneurs? And do they vary across national culture? They conclude that entrepreneurs (as a group) have a cognition distinct from non-entrepreneurs, and that this cognition is largely universal, but that there is some variation in some factors across different national cultures. Mitchell *et al.* (2000) undertook a cross-cultural study of entrepreneurial cognition based on the existence of three types of *cognitive script*. A cognitive script is a knowledge structure that a decision maker has access to. The types of script in this study were specified as:

- **arrangement scripts** relating to knowledge of contacts, relationships, and asset and resource availability;

- **ability scripts** relating to the individual's assessment of their own technical and general managerial abilities;

- **willingness scripts** relating to the individual's commitment to starting or developing the venture and including knowledge of business opportunities, tolerance of ambiguity and confidence in success.

While recognising the study's limitations, the authors conclude that such scripts do account for variations in the start-up decision, that the scripts do vary (to a degree) by culture and that cultural effects moderate the impact of the scripts on the start-up decision. Hartenian and Gudmundson (2000) evaluate the benefits of cultural diversity within small firms and consider whether it should be an explicit objective for the entrepreneur.

There is not scope within this book to consider all these issues in the depth they deserve. We must be content to note that entrepreneurs are necessarily the product of their cultures and that their cultures mould and influence their actions. What follows is meant to give a flavour of the *factors* which are significant to understanding entrepreneurship in a cultural setting and how they might be approached.

Language

The exact number of languages in the world is debated and depends on where the boundary between languages and dialects is drawn. Most experts agree on a figure of around 6,500. These are collected into about ten or so major language families that share vocabulary and grammatical characteristics and that experts assume emerged from a common ancestral language. Different languages within a family are not necessarily mutually understandable (English and German, for example are from the same *sub*-family). Language is a logistical issue in entrepreneurship as language differences limit communication, prevent contracts being drawn up and so inhibit trade. However, the opportunity to trade between different language groups is often strong enough to encourage the formation of 'pidgins' and 'creoles' that provide a basic common language. These were very important in European trade with the Caribbean during the seventeenth century, for example, and have been observed in many parts of the world. The growth of global lingua franca such as English reflects the benefits of a common tongue for entrepreneurs working on a global scale. Such logistical issues are evident. What is more controversial is the suggestion by some social scientists that language creates a human's entire picture of the world (the so-called *Sapir-Whorf* hypothesis) and so is fundamental to explaining cultural experience and differences. Thus, the argument might go, entrepreneurship is facilitated by the presence of words for concepts such as 'risk', 'opportunity', 'investment' and so on. Speakers of languages that do not have such words should not be expected to think about entrepreneurship (if they have such a word!) in the same way as a speaker of English (or other European language that has equivalent words) might do.

Religious beliefs

Religious belief is a very important factor in shaping a culture. It leads to a view of the world which will influence the individual's approach to entrepreneurship. The sociologist Max Weber famously associated the Industrial Revolution in Western Europe and the USA with the attitudes engendered by Protestant religious beliefs known as the 'Protestant work ethic'. Modern commentators speculate on the influence of Confucian 'discipline' to the success of Asian economies. Islamic belief disallows (or at least limits) the setting of interest rates. Such prohibitions on usury were a common part of Christian belief until quite recently. Modern economics sees interest rates not so much as a powerful lender exploiting a weaker borrower, but as something fundamental to setting the price of money and directing it to where it will work hardest. The Islamic banking system has adopted an alternative system of monetary charges to achieve this. Some religious systems set in place quite rigid social stratifications that dictate the class and even job that an individual may take up. Modernisation is providing one means for enterprising individuals to break out of this structure. In India, many entrepreneurs have emerged from the Jain community because their strict vegetarianism and historical refusal to work with animal products excluded them from most conventional occupations, hence they turned to trading. Refer to Devashis (2000) and Choudary (2001) for excellent reviews of venture capital in India and the Islamic world, respectively.

Personal relationships

The type and scope of personal relationships that a culture encourages will be a critical factor in the way entrepreneurial behaviour is expressed. A very important study by the Dutch sociologist of business, Geert Hofstede, analysed human relationships along four dimensions:

1 *Power distance*: the degree of authority people expect between managers and subordinates, and their willingness to accept that power is not distributed equally.

2 *Uncertainty avoidance*: in essence, this is the desire to be in a situation where uncertainty is minimised. Its opposite is a willingness to take risks.

3 *Collectivity*: the need to feel that one is part of a group and that one's actions are sanctioned by that wider group. Its opposite is a desire to exhibit individualistic behaviour.

4 *Masculinity*: the degree to which the culture emphasises 'masculine' values such as the acquisition of money, prioritising the material over the spiritual, a lack of concern versus a caring attitude, etc.

According to Hofstede's study, these four factors give a good account of how attitudes towards personal relationships give rise to different styles of entrepreneurial behaviour over a wide range of national cultures. Hayton *et al.* (2002) provide a review of 21 studies of how entrepreneurial characteristics vary across national cultures using Hofstede's (and other) frameworks. They offer a useful discussion of the methodological difficulties in establishing the link between culture and entrepreneurship and suggest directions for future study.

Attitude towards innovation

Innovation lies at the heart of entrepreneurship, yet to believe in innovation we have to see the world in a certain sort of way. We have to believe in a future that will be *different* from the present. We have to believe that we can act so as to *influence* the world and change it by our actions. Further, if we are to be encouraged to innovate, we must believe that it is appropriate that we are *rewarded* for our efforts in developing innovation.

Many West Europeans will regard these things as 'obvious'. However, they are beliefs which are sensitive to culture. While a West European sees the future as something which brings uncertainties 'towards' them, many cultures, some in west Africa for example, have a different perspective. They draw a distinction between a 'potential time' which is full of things that *must* happen and a 'no-time' of things which might or might not happen. The potential time is *here and now*, a part of the present, whereas no-time is not really a part of time at all. From this perspective, there really is no such thing as the 'future' in the sense that a Western mind sees it.

Even if we believe in a future we may not believe that we can influence it. Physical science has often emphasised that the future is *determined*. Marxism is founded on a belief that the world evolves along a pre-destined path. If an innovation occurs, it occurs because it was meant to occur. Hence, it is not the result of personal inventiveness which might *not* have occurred, and if this is so, why then should we reward the innovator? Hence innovations belong to the world at large, not the individual entrepreneur. Mark Casson (1994) has suggested that such a cultural perspective might be significant to the development of entrepreneurship in the post-communist world.

Networks

A network is the framework of individual and organisational relationships which form the stage upon which entrepreneurial performance is played. It is composed of personal and social contacts as well as economic relationships. A network is shaped by the culture in which it is formed.

The network does not just provide a route for people to sell things to each other. It is a conduit for information. A well-developed network is crucial if entrepreneurial behaviour is to express itself. It defines the terrain in which new business opportunities might be identified and assessed, and it provides a means by which contracts are agreed and risk might be evaluated and shared. It offers an escape route for people who do not think their investments are safe. This occurs not only through formal structures such as stock markets but also through informal confidences and relationships. The structure and functioning of such networks is sensitive to a wide range of cultural factors. The extent to which cultural values strengthen links (so locking individuals together), the scope of linkage they allow (within family group or outside family group), the conditions under which links may be broken (and the penalties for initiating breakage) and the ease with which new links may be formed (new relationships built) are all, to a degree, culturally determined.

It is neither possible nor particularly useful to draw hard and fast rules about managing within a particular culture. However, the idea that a culture provides a perspective within which individuals work might suggest an approach. The entrepreneur must recognise that an individual's response to a particular situation will, to some extent, be shaped by cultural influences. This will affect the way they can be led and motivated. However, the entrepreneur must not forget that individuals are individuals with their own characteristics, and do not necessarily behave with a collective consciousness. Entrepreneurs will also recognise that their own decision making is the product of their cultural experiences. Recognition of these things is becoming increasingly important as the opportunities for entrepreneurial ventures become ever more international. In the global arena, the effective entrepreneur learns to use cultural differences to advantage rather than be impeded by them.

Entrepreneurs who have built global concerns such as Rupert Murdoch (News International) and the late Rowland 'Tiny' Rowland (Lonhro) are renowned for their ability not just to manage people within one culture but to manage across cultures.

Summary of key ideas

- A wide variety of people can become entrepreneurs. Common backgrounds include inventors with new business ideas; managers unfulfilled by working in established organisations; displaced managers; and people excluded from the established economy.

- Whatever their background, successful entrepreneurs are characterised by being hard working and self-starting; setting high personal goals; having resilience and confidence in their abilities; being receptive to new ideas and being assertive in presenting them; being attuned to new opportunities, receptive to change and eager to learn; and being confident with power and demonstrating a commitment to others.

- Effective entrepreneurs use a variety of formal management skills combined with industry knowledge and personal motivation.

- The way entrepreneurs actually manage their ventures is dependent on the culture in which they operate. Effective entrepreneurs are sensitive to cultural values.

Research themes

Cognitive scripts and incubation

Mitchell *et al.* (2000) describe the use of 'cognitive scripts' to establish entrepreneurs' willingness to establish a new venture, their perceptions of their ability to drive those ventures and the availability of critical resources. Identify entrepreneurs (nascent and/or practising) for whom incubation with an organisation or business sector (both formal and informal) has been important and entrepreneurs for whom it has been less important (i.e. entrepreneurs entering a sector in which they have prior managerial experience or not). Following Mitchell *et al.*'s methodology, establish the cognitive scripts for the entrepreneurs prior to start-up or in the early stages of the venture. How important is incubation experience a factor in the scripts revealed? What are the implications for the development of formal incubation systems?

Entrepreneurial businesses and Hofstede's criteria

Hofstede's original study aimed to compare managerial styles across national cultures. However, it has implications for the way in which entrepreneurial businesses work (and succeed) within a particular country. Is entrepreneurial leadership characterised by a high or low power distance, masculinity, collectivity and (particularly) uncertainty avoidance? Refer to Hofstede's original study and develop the methodology to survey a sample of entrepreneurial businesses within your own nation. How do the entrepreneurs fare? Are they typical of the generalised national characteristics Hofstede found in the original study or are they quite different? Speculate on how the Hofstede criteria might encourage or discourage entrepreneurial behaviour and the success of entrepreneurial businesses.

Suggestions for further reading

Blanchflower, D.G. and Oswald, A.J. (1998) 'What makes an entrepreneur?', *Journal of Labour Economics*, Vol. 16, No. 1, pp. 26–60.

Busenitz, L.W. and Lau, C.M. (1996) 'A cross-cultural cognitive model of new venture creation', *Entrepreneurship Theory and Practice*, Vol. 20, No. 4, pp. 25–39.

Casson, M. (1994) 'Enterprise culture and institutional change in eastern Europe', in Buckley, P.J. and Ghauri, P.N. (eds) *The Economics of Change in East and Central Europe*, London: Academic Press.

Choudary, M.A. (2001) 'Islamic venture capital', *Journal of Economic Studies*, Vol. 28, No. 1, pp. 14–33.

Delmar, F. and Davidsson, P. (2000) 'Where do they come from? Prevalence and characteristics of nascent entrepreneurs', *Entrepreneurship and Regional Development*, Vol. 12, No. 1, pp. 1–23.

Devashis, M. (2000) 'The venture capital industry in India', *Journal of Small Business Management*, Vol. 38, No. 2, pp. 67–79.

Drucker, P.F. (1985) 'The discipline of innovation', *Harvard Business Review*, May-June, pp. 67–72.

George, G. and Zahra, S.A. (2002) 'Culture and its consequences for entrepreneurship', *Entrepreneurship Theory and Practice*, Summer, pp. 5–8.

Green, R., David, J., Dent, M. and Tyshkovsky, A. (1996) 'The Russian entrepreneur: a study of psychological characteristics', *International Journal of Entrepreneurial Behaviour and Research*, Vol. 2, No. 1, pp. 49–58.

Hartenian, L.S. and Gudmundson, D.E. (2000) 'Cultural diversity in small business: implications for firm performance', *Journal of Developmental Entrepreneurship*, Vol. 5, No. 3, pp. 209–19.

Hayton, J.C., George, G. and Zahra, S. (2002) 'National Culture and Entrepreneurship: A review of behavioural research', *Entrepreneurship Theory and Practice*, Summer, pp. 33–52.

Hisrich, R.D. and Brush, C. (1986) 'Characteristics of the minority entrepreneur', *Journal of Small Business Management*, Oct, pp. 1–8.

Hofstede, G. (1980a) *Culture's Consequences: International Differences in Work-Related Values*, London: Sage Publications.

Hofstede, G. (1980b) 'Motivation, leadership and organisation: do American theories apply abroad?' *Organisational Dynamics*, Summer, pp. 42–63.

Jones-Evans, D. (1996) 'Technical entrepreneurship, strategy and experience', *International Small Business Journal*, Vol. 14, No. 3, pp. 15–39.

Kuznetsov, A., McDonald, F. and Kuznetsov, O. (2000) 'Entrepreneurial qualities: a case from Russia', *Journal of Small Business Management*, Vol. 38, No. 1, pp. 101–7.

McClelland, D.C. (1987) 'Characteristics of successful entrepreneurs', *Journal of Creative Behaviour*, Vol. 21, No. 3, pp. 219–33.

McClelland, D.C. and Burnham, D.H. (1976) 'Power is the great motivator', *Harvard Business Review*, Mar-Apr, pp. 100–10.

Miner, J.B. (1997) 'The expanded horizon for achieving entrepreneurial success', *Organizational Dynamics*, Winter, pp. 54–67.

Mitchell, R.K., Smith, B., Seawright, K.W. and Morse, E.A. (2000) 'Cross-cultural cognitions and the venture creation decision', *Academy of Management Journal*, Vol. 43, No. 5, pp. 974–93.

Mitchell, R.K., Smith, J.B., Morse, E.A., Seawright, K.W., Peredo, A.M. and McKenzie, B. (2002) 'Are entrepreneurial cognitions universal? Assessing entrepreneurial cognitions across cultures', *Entrepreneurship Theory and Practice*, Summer, pp. 9–32.

Morden, T. (1995) 'International culture and management', *Management Decision*, Vol. 33, No. 2, pp. 16–21.

Olson, S.F. and Currie, H.M. (1992) 'Female entrepreneurs: personal value systems and business strategies in a male dominated industry', *Journal of Small Business Management*, January, pp. 49–57.

Phizacklea, A. and Ram, M. (1995) 'Ethnic entrepreneurship in comparative perspective', *International Journal of Entrepreneurial Behaviour and Research*, Vol. 1, No. 1, pp. 48–58.

Sui, Wai-Sum and Martin, R.G. (1992) 'Successful entrepreneurship in Hong Kong', *Long Range Planning*, Vol. 25, No. 6, pp. 87–93.

Williams, A. (1985) 'Stress and the entrepreneurial role', *International Small Business Journal*, Vol. 3, No. 4, pp. 11–25.

Selected case material Case 7.1

Sticking to what you do best

FT

30 May 2002

By **Jim Pickard**

George Gallagher is proof that cheek can go a long way in business.

A few years ago he was working as a technician for Astra-Zeneca in Alderley Edge, near Chester.

The pharmaceuticals company allowed staff at the site long lunch breaks and every day Mr Gallagher would go into the gym to change out of his blue T-shirt and trousers and slip into a suit.

He would then head for the main office where the group's white-collar management worked. There he contrived to bump into Bob Nolan, licensing director of Astra-Zeneca and now a colleague and mentor.

'I'm an instrument engineer from block 10, where I look after the machines,' the dyslexic 24-year-old told Mr Nolan, before asking him whether the group would be interested in his invention: an intravenous drip monitor that would offer hospitals a cheaper and more reliable alternative to other devices.

No, came the answer.

But Mr Gallagher adds: 'He liked the balls I had, to do what I was doing, and he liked the product.'

The two struck up a friendship and Mr Nolan offered advice and support as Mr Gallagher's business, now called Zi Medical, started up and moved towards seeking a listing on the Alternative Investment Market, which it achieved earlier this month.

That first meeting was not the only time Mr Gallagher has shown his bottle. In the early days of Zimed, as it was then called, he decided the company needed a chairman with a high profile. 'We needed a figurehead for the business. I was this 24-year-old, I had no business history,' he says. 'We needed somebody at the front and looked around at businessmen in our field – and Roger Jones was the top man.'

One phone call later, the two had set up a meeting.

Mr Gallagher and Rhys Owen, a business angel who was taking an active role in the business, drove 150 miles to see Mr Jones at the offices of his company Penn Pharmaceuticals.

Mr Jones agreed on the spot to become company chairman. A year later, he invested £50,000. Now chairman of the Welsh Development Agency, Mr Jones says he was astonished by the simplicity of Mr Gallagher's invention. 'I couldn't believe no one else had done it because it was such an obvious thing to do,' he recalls. He was also impressed by Mr Gallagher's tenacity.

Mr Jones has since stepped down as chairman because of his public role but remains as a non-executive director.

Zi Medical's product is a device that monitors how much liquid is passing through a gravity-based intravenous drip. Without such a monitor, nurses must check a drip every 20 or 40 minutes. It allows hospitals to avoid using pump drips, which are more expensive and can result in 'bolus shots' when excess quantities of a drug are suddenly fired into the body.

The company's float raised £700,000, which will be used to create a sales force and to develop new products such as a device to monitor both the influx and efflux of liquids from a patient. Until now Mr Gallagher – the technical director – has been responsible for sales.

To have reached this stage is a huge relief to the entrepreneur, who sacrificed much to get the company off the ground. Among the many costs were £10,000 for an initial prototype model, £30,000 for patent fees and £54,000 for the final prototype. Although the company won grants – a regional innovation grant of £25,000, a small firms loan of £45,000 and several loan guarantee scheme sums – it was not enough. Mr Gallagher took out six loans from friends, family and banks – 'wherever I could find cash'. He sold his car, motorbike and snowboard. His marriage broke up. 'Last year I got pneumonia twice, and pleurisy, because of the stress,' he says.

When he appeared on the BBC1 *Tomorrow's World* competition 'Inventor of the Year' last year – he won in the 'health innovation' category – he should have been in his sick bed, he says. 'I looked like death.'

Mr Gallagher had always played around with broken engines and other machinery as a child. When he met Rhodri Morgan, the Welsh first minister, at a business function, he told the most powerful man in Wales that 'there needs to be more tangible help for inventors rather than forums, goodwill and bureaucracy'. He scorns the standard advice to focus on a business plan. Instead, entrepreneur-inventors should just get on with what they do best. 'You might as well lick your finger and stick it in the wind – there's too much emphasis on predicting the future at an early stage,' he says.

With sales still low at this stage, Mr Gallagher considers that the business needs an all-out drive to establish itself. The aim is to break even in the second year and achieve sales of £3m.

Mr Jones is confident that his protégé will succeed.

'The Georges of this world are the can-do's. You can bet your life that if you put them in front of a wall they will chip away at it, because they are that determined,' he says.

Source: Financial Times, 30 May 2002.

Case 7.2

O'Brien revels in his paradise islands

10 December 2002

By **John Murray Brown**

Denis O'Brien no longer has to talk up the achievements of his Caribbean mobile phone operation.

The Irish entrepreneur and chairman of Digicel can point to Cable and Wireless's internal report, which openly acknowledges the competitive threat posed by his company to C&W's monopoly in the islands region.

'They admit we've got 65 per cent of the mobile market in Jamaica. If we are fortunate enough to do the same job in all these other places, they'll have a huge problem,' says Mr O'Brien, who says he wants to be the 'Vodafone of the Caribbean'.

Mr O'Brien has invested about $100m of his money in the project – a large slice of the

£240m he pocketed when he sold Esat Telecom, the Irish operator, to BT in 2000.

Indeed it was the same week he finalised the BT deal – at the time Ireland's largest takeover – that he bid for his first mobile licence – in Jamaica. He now has licences in Dominica, St Lucia, Grenada, St Vincent, and is applying in Barbados, Trinidad and Tobago, and in the Cayman and Turks and Caicos islands.

To Mr O'Brien's mind, the Caribbean had many of the characteristics of the Irish market into which he launched Esat. The island states are now liberalising their telecommunications markets.

'It was the only place in the world where there was an opportunity to compete against the incumbent as the second player. You look at China, there are four or five licences. All the countries in Africa have two or three operators,' he says.

Like many monopolies, C&W's infrastructure is outdated – something the company concedes in the report. 'What we're seeing is mobile substitution. People are so fed up waiting to get a phone line they have just started using their mobiles for international calls.'

Given C&W's financial plight, Digicel also believes the UK-based group does not have the cash resources to deliver on its promise to introduce its own GSM service, replacing its older TSMA mobile technology.

In the six months to September, C&W earned £145m from international calls from its regional operations. However in Jamaica, where Digicel has been growing most rapidly, C&W has dropped international prices by two-thirds in advance of liberalisation in March 2003.

Revenues are set to fall similarly.

Mr O'Brien says: 'If we do the same in all the other places it is going to have a real impact.'

Normally, he says, 'you wouldn't even get on an aircraft to Jamaica if you just read the economic statistics'. But, he says, the amount people spend on telephoning is equivalent to European levels.

'People there love to talk,' he says, pointing out that international traffic volumes are fuelled by the West Indian diaspora in Europe and the US.

The market is also ripe for lucrative 'roaming' revenues as tourists on holiday and business travellers in the islands want to use their mobiles to make international calls.

Mr O'Brien had originally set a target of 100,000 subscribers in the first year. In fact, at the end of 2001, Digicel says it had 355,000 subscribers.

By end of 2002, Digicel expects to have about 700,000.

Mr O'Brien now believes C&W is attempting to frustrate Digicel's progress by dragging its feet on an interconnection agreement – the tariff agreement that allows fixed line and mobile customers to talk across different networks.

'We now have the evidence – an internal document. There's no reason to doubt the validity. It shows the strategy for frustrating Digicel.'

Mr O'Brien says he has contacted the chairman and chief executive of C&W to complain, but without any success.

Now he has given warning of an all-out war. 'If you do that to your competitor, he will get vicious. In this circumstance we could get very vicious.'

Source: Financial Times, 10 December 2002.

Discussion points

1. How do the skills of George Gallagher and Bob Nolan complement each other to form an effective entrepreneurial team?

2. Is Denis O'Brien being naive in thinking that just because an entrepreneurial business model has been successful in one country it can be transferred to another?

Chapter 8

Making the move to entrepreneurship

Chapter overview

This chapter is concerned with an exploration of the economic, social and personal factors which encourage or discourage an individual to pursue an entrepreneurial career. The issue of regional and national contingencies is explored. Recent research into the cognitive underpinning of the decision to start a new business is also considered.

8.1 The supply of entrepreneurs

Key learning outcome

An understanding of the forces which encourage and inhibit entrepreneurship.

If we look at any of the world's economies we will see a certain number of entrepreneurs operating within them. The exact number will depend on how we define entrepreneurship, but their importance to the economy within which they operate will be evident. They will be responsible for providing economic efficiency and bringing new innovations to the market. In mature economies, such as Western Europe and North America, they are responsible for most new job creation. In the former communist world, the emergence of an entrepreneurial class is a necessary prelude to establishing a market-driven economic order. The question is, what governs the number of entrepreneurs who will emerge at any given time? The answer to this macroeconomic question lies in an understanding of the factors that lead any one individual to pursue an entrepreneurial career.

If we assume that entrepreneurs are born, or that entrepreneurship is the result of inherent personality characteristics, then the supply of entrepreneurs must be

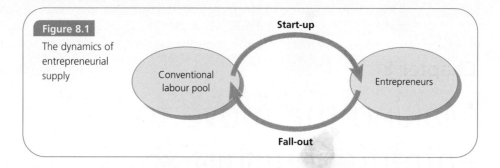

Figure 8.1

The dynamics of entrepreneurial supply

fixed. The number will depend on the number of people who are impelled to pursue the entrepreneurial option by virtue of their inherent characteristics, which are likely to be stable over long periods. This might reflect deep-rooted cultural factors but it will be largely independent of external influences. On the other hand, if we assume that entrepreneurs are managers who have freely decided to become entrepreneurs, then the number of entrepreneurs at any one time will be sensitive to a variety of external factors. A simple approach to explaining this uses a model in which there are two pools of labour: a *conventional* labour pool in which people take up paid employment, and an *entrepreneurial* pool in which people are acting as entrepreneurs. Such a model assumes that there is a clear definition of what constitutes entrepreneurship and that it is distinct from 'ordinary' labour. The assumption that there is a clear dividing line between the entrepreneurial and the non-entrepreneurial, is clearly artificial. However, it does serve to make the model simpler. It can be relaxed and more complex models developed to reflect a finer-grained reality more closely. These more complex models still work on the same basic premise. Managers are assumed to make a choice between the two options: a 'conventional' career versus an 'entrepreneurial' one (Figure 8.1). The process of moving from the conventional labour pool to the entrepreneurial pool is known as *start-up*. The reverse process of moving from the entrepreneurial pool back to the conventional labour pool is *fall-out*. The choice will depend on the relative attractiveness of the two options as perceived by the individual manager.

Two forces are said to work driving the manager from the conventional labour pool to the entrepreneurial: pull factors and push factors. *Pull factors* are those which encourage managers to become entrepreneurs by virtue of the *attractiveness* of the entrepreneurial option. Pull factors might be thought of as the 'come on in, the water is lovely!' aspects of the attractiveness of the entrepreneurial option. Some important pull factors include:

- the financial rewards of entrepreneurship;
- the freedom to work for oneself;
- the sense of achievement to be gained from running one's own venture;
- the freedom to pursue a personal innovation;
- a desire to gain the social standing achieved by entrepreneurs.

Push factors, on the other hand, are those which encourage entrepreneurship by making the conventional option *less attractive*. These might be thought of as the 'get out, the kitchen is too hot!' aspects propelling individuals from conventional employment. Push factors include:

- the limitations of financial rewards from conventional jobs;
- being unemployed in the established economy;
- job insecurity;
- career limitations and setbacks in a conventional job;
- the inability to pursue a personal innovation in a conventional job;
- being a 'misfit' in an established organisation.

The number of entrepreneurs operating at any one time will depend on the strength of the pull and push forces. If they are strong, then a large number of entrepreneurs will emerge. However, the supply of entrepreneurs will still be limited if *inhibitors* are operating. Inhibitors are factors which prevent the potential entrepreneur from following an entrepreneurial route, no matter how attractive an option it might appear. Some important inhibitors include:

- an inability to get hold of start-up capital;
- the high cost of start-up capital;
- the risks presented by the business environment;
- legal restrictions on business activity;
- a lack of training for entrepreneurs;
- a feeling that the role of entrepreneur has a poor image;
- a lack of suitable human resources;
- personal inertia in following through business ideas.

Kouriloff (2000) takes a multi-disciplinary approach to investigating barriers to entrepreneurship, drawing ideas from economics, sociology and psychology, and gives a good account of methodologies for exploring the issue. Politicians and economic policy makers increasingly put the elimination of inhibitors to entrepreneurism at the top of their agenda. This is because they recognise the importance of increasing the number of entrepreneurs within the economy to stimulate growth. Figure 8.2 indicates the type of factors operating on managers considering a move to entrepreneurship.

It will be appreciated that life experiences and situations will have an impact on the decision to make the move into entrepreneurship. A study of business start-ups in Western Australia by Mazzarol *et al.* (1999) revealed that gender, employment by government and redundancy had an impact on an individual's desire to start a

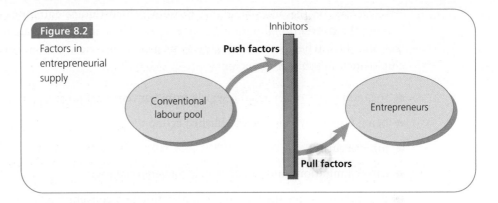

Figure 8.2

Factors in entrepreneurial supply

Inhibitors

Push factors

Conventional labour pool

Entrepreneurs

Pull factors

small business. A host of other factors including age, marital and family status and history of family business were less important. A substantive number of studies have examined factors that support, or hinder, the move to entrepreneurship on a national basis. Nations or regions examined include Australia (Mazzarol *et al.*, 1999; Schaper, 1999), Central Europe (Fitzgerald, 2002), China (Tan, 1996; Zapalska and Edwards, 2001), the Czech Republic (Benacek, 1995), Greece (Maggina, 1992), Korea and the US (Lee and Oysteryoung, 2001), Hungary and the Ukraine (Danis and Shipilov, 2002), Papua New Guinea (Schaper, 2002), Poland (Zapalska, 1997), Russia (Puffer *et al.*, 2001), southern and east Africa (Trulsson, 2002) and South Africa (Ahwireng-Obeng and Piaray, 1999).

Labour economists and psychologists studying the factors that are influential in encouraging entrepreneurship often use models based on sophisticated econometric and statistical methodologies. A full discussion of these is not possible in this book. The student who has an interest in these approaches is referred to the Mazzarol study above, the Blanchflower and Oswald study discussed in Section 7.1 and also a study on business start-up in the UK by Galt and Moenning (1996). Details are given in the 'Suggestions for further reading' at the end of this chapter.

8.2 Influences in the move to entrepreneurship

Key learning outcome

An understanding of the factors involved in making the decision to become an entrepreneur.

Whatever the forces acting on the labour market to encourage entrepreneurship, the decision to become an entrepreneur is an individual and personal one. We need to understand the factors involved in driving and shaping that decision in order to understand entrepreneurs. We are all active in an economy because we seek the rewards it brings. However, an economy is part of a wider pattern of social life and although money is important, we seek more than purely financial rewards from the world in which we live. The decision to pursue an entrepreneurial career reflects a choice about the possibility of achieving satisfaction for a variety of economic and social needs.

We might classify the needs of individuals under three broad headings:

1 *Economic needs.* These include the requirement to earn a particular amount of money and the need for that income to be stable and predictable. The amount desired will reflect the need for economic survival, existing commitments such as the home and family, and the pursuit of personal interests.

2 *Social needs.* These represent the desire a person has to be a part of, and to fit into, a wider group and their desire to be recognised and respected within that group. The satisfaction of social needs is reflected in the creation and maintenance of friendships and other social relationships.

3 *Developmental needs.* These relate to the desire a person has to achieve personal goals and to grow intellectually or spiritually.

A manager seeking to satisfy these needs is faced with a number of possibilities. There may be a choice between two or more conventional career options as well as the possibility of pursuing an entrepreneurial career. The entrepreneurial career itself may present itself in a number of ways. The manager's decision on which path to take will be based on the potential each option has to satisfy the needs they perceive for themselves (Table 8.1). If the entrepreneurial route is seen to offer the best means of satisfying them then this will be chosen. However, making the move between different options will be sensitive to four factors: *knowledge* of entrepreneurial options open, the *possibility* for achieving them, the *risks* they present and *valence* – the way in which the potential entrepreneur is willing to play off different needs against each other. Figure 8.3 represents a model of the factors involved in making the move to entrepreneurship.

Knowledge

The individual must *know* that the entrepreneurial option exists and they must be *aware* of its *potential*. In the case of establishing an entrepreneurial venture, the

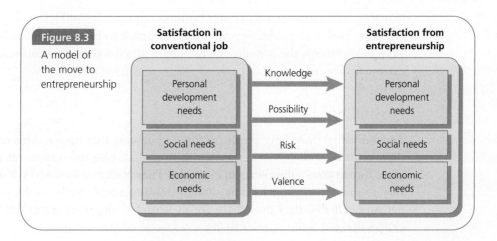

Figure 8.3 A model of the move to entrepreneurship

Table 8.1	A comparison between the potential of entrepreneurial and conventional careers for satisfying economic, social and personal development needs	
	Entrepreneurial career	**Conventional career**
Economic needs	Can offer the possibility of high financial rewards in the long term	Financial rewards typically lower, but secure and predictable
	However, income may be low in early stages and risks are high	Risks are relatively low
Social needs	Entrepreneur creates organisational change	Established organisation usually provides good stage for making social relationships
	A great deal of freedom to create and control network of social relationships	Manager may have only limited scope to control potential of social relationships formed
	Social status of the entrepreneur usually high	Social status of manager variable
Personal development needs	Entrepreneur in control of own destiny	Good potential to pursue personal development
	Possibility of creating an 'entire new world'	However, the direction of personal development may need to be compromised to overall organisational objectives and values
	Venture may be powerful vehicle for personal development and expression of personal values	Career options limited and subject to internal competition
	However, this is dependent on success of venture	

manager must know of a particular business opportunity and have an idea how it might be exploited profitably. After all, the desire to be entrepreneurial must be expressed through the actuality of running a *specific* business venture. It cannot exist in a vacuum.

Possibility

The individual must have the *possibility* of pursuing that option. This means that there must be no legal restrictions on them undertaking the venture (as there was in the former communist bloc, for example). They must also have access to the necessary resources: start-up funding, human resources and access to the established network. Finally, they must have (or at least feel that they have) the necessary experience and skills in order to make a success of the venture.

Risk

The entrepreneur may have a detailed knowledge of a business opportunity and access to the resources necessary to initiate it. However, the entrepreneur will only make the move if the *risks* are seen as being acceptable. The entrepreneur must be comfortable with the level of risk the venture will entail, and he or she must be sure that the potential rewards are such that it is worth taking the risk. It is useful to distinguish between the *actual* level of risk in the venture, and the level of risk that is *perceived* by the entrepreneur. These may be quite different. Entrepreneurs can often be overconfident and under-assess risk. In addition to convincing themselves, entrepreneurs must convince any investors asked to back the venture that the risks are of an acceptable level.

Valence

The conventional career option and the option to start an entrepreneurial venture do not offer separate opportunities to satisfy economic, social and developmental needs; rather they offer a different *mix* of opportunities. The final factor which will influence the option selected is *valence*, that is, the way we are attracted to different options.

Different people are willing to play off different needs against one another in different ways. While many people 'play safe' and give priority to economic needs, by no means everyone does so. Some people prioritise social needs. Thus they may continue to work in an organisation they enjoy, with people they like, even though the option to move to a higher-paid job elsewhere is available to them. The artist starving in a garret or the religious aesthete is pursuing the need for personal development even though it is causing them economic hardship. Similarly, the entrepreneur may be so drawn to the possibilities of personal development offered by the entrepreneurial option, that they will pursue it even though it carries greater economic risks and perhaps, for the foreseeable future, a lower income than a conventional managerial career that is available to them.

An interesting example of valence in action is revealed by Khandwalla in a series of studies of Indian managers and entrepreneurs. Khandwalla (1984, 1985) defines a pioneering-innovative motive which leads individuals to 'make path-breaking achievements through the accomplishment of unique tasks'. This pioneering-innovative drive encourages individuals to pursue an entrepreneurial career even if the financial and personal risks are perceived to be very high.

A decisional model of the motivation to start a business might emphasise the balance of reasoning about the advantages and disadvantages of that move compared to alternatives. Both positive and negative reasons might be articulated for both (Figure 8.4).

The decision requires that a wide range of factors be taken into consideration. Such a decision is termed a *multi-criteria* problem. A lot of experimental work has looked at how individuals compare and integrate the various criteria to arrive at a decision. The findings indicate that decision makers do not usually judge each

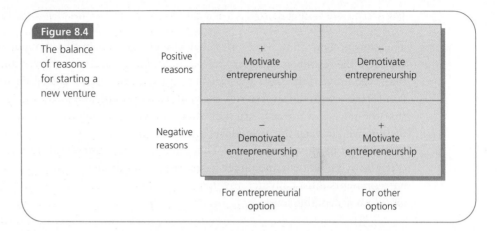

Figure 8.4

The balance of reasons for starting a new venture

reason independently to produce a simple, balanced answer. They often weigh different reasons, giving prominence to some and downplaying others. Different reasons may interact with each other to change the overall priority given to each. So while it is true to say that a nascent entrepreneur will initiate a venture if the positives of doing so outweigh the negatives compared to the positives and negatives of the alternatives, how this judgement takes place may be quite complex. Feldman and Bolino (2000) use Schein's model of 'career anchors' to evaluate the motivations entrepreneurs have. Formal utility-based models of the decision to start a venture are developed by Campbell (1992), Katz (1992), Amundson (1995) and Eisenhauer (1995).

8.3 The initiation decision

> **Key learning outcome**
>
> An understanding of the factors that influence the decision to initiate a venture and how these factors might be modelled.

Starting a new business, working independently and facing the risks this presents – *venture initiation* – is clearly a major decision for individuals pursuing the entrepreneurial option. Economists, social psychologists and cognitive psychologists have started to take a great deal of interest in this particular decision and have explored both the motivations for it and the cognitive processes that underpin it.

Herron and Sapienza (1992) emphasise the primacy of the individual in the initiation. They go on to use ideas drawn from behavioural psychology and organisation theory to develop a model of the initiation decision. The primary inputs to the model are the individual's values, personal traits and socio-economic context along with acquired skills, aptitudes and training. In combination, these lead to the individual having certain levels of aspiration that may or may not be met by their current circumstances. If the aspirations are not met, the individual will be dissatisfied and will start to explore alternatives. If the entrepreneurial option is attractive, then the individual will start to search for business opportunities. Once one or more opportunities have been identified, then the individual will evaluate those opportunities and estimate their value, and make a judgement about the opportunity's *equilibrium* – the balance of rewards (*inducements*) against necessary costs in terms of monetary outlay, opportunities forgone and personal effort (*contributions*). If this equilibrium is satisfactory, then the venture is initiated. Mazzarol *et al.* (1999) develop a model that looks at the interaction of environmental factors (social networks, capital availability, political support, information availability) with personality factors (personal traits, social background, ethnicity and gender) to model the intentionality that is proximal to the initiation decision. Morrison (2000) suggests that the factors usually suggested as being influential in the initiation decision cannot be regarded separately, but must be considered holistically and the 'construct' of entrepreneurial opportunity should be thought of as a symbiotic relationship between entrepreneurial motivation and culture. Shaver *et al.* (2001) suggest a research approach and methodology for inquiring into an individual's reasons for starting a business. Their approach is based on *attribution theory*, a field of social psychology that examines how individuals attribute events to causes and objects to classes.

8.4 The initiation process

> ### Key learning outcome
>
> An appreciation of the tasks involved in initiating a venture and the question of how consistent different entrepreneurs are in their approach.

Actually initiating a business may be the start of the venture's existence, but it is the end of a particular process as far as the entrepreneur is concerned. The nascent entrepreneur must have first engaged in a number of 'pre-launch preparation' tasks such as gathering and processing information, identifying a new opportunity, imagining (and perhaps designing) an innovation to take advantage of it, evaluation and valuation of the opportunity, initial contact with key supporters, acquisition of start-up capital, and legal and contractual arrangements. Some of these tasks are independent of each other and may be conducted at the same time; some may have to wait until other tasks have been completed. A number of studies have examined whether the initiation process is relatively consistent or varies across different ventures (Carter *et al.*, 1996). Alsos and Kolvereid (1998) examined how these tasks were organised by novice, serial and portfolio entrepreneurs, and found significant differences. Van Auken (2000) evaluated the relationship between start-up activity and the size of initial investment in ventures. A positive correlation was observed: the higher the investment, the greater the extent of, and detail in, start-up preparations. Pre-launch preparations in relation to the acquisition of investment capital have been studied by Van Auken (2000) and Kellye and Tullous (2002). Galbraith (1982) suggested a four stage model of the product development phase for hi-tech ventures: (1) a proof-in-principle stage in which the technology is demonstrated to have potential; (2) a prototype stage in which a working form of the technology is developed; (3) a model shop stage in which early production runs are undertaken; and finally, (4) the start-up stage where the product is produced in commercial quantities and delivered to the market. Kazanjian and Drazin (1990) extended this model into the post-start-up phase and considered (1) conception and development; (2) commercialisation; (3) early growth; and (4) stability in market phases. Complementing this, Hansen and Bird (1997) distinguished between ventures that develop and sell before taking on employees and those that take on employees, then develop and sell.

Summary of key ideas

- The supply of entrepreneurs is determined by three sets of factors, namely *pull factors* which promote entrepreneurship as a positive option; *push factors* which drive people out of the established economy; and *inhibitors* which prevent the entrepreneurial option being taken up.

- Managers make the move to entrepreneurship after considering the way the option for an entrepreneurial career can satisfy *economic*, *social* and *self-development* needs.

- The initiation decision has come under continued scrutiny and is being explored from economic, social psychological and cognitive psychological perspectives. A number of models have been proposed.

- The pre-initiation phase is one that demands a number of activities on the part of the entrepreneur. Consistencies in the pattern of these activities across different types of entrepreneur are the subject of a growing number of studies. The extent of activity does seem to be correlated with the level of initial investment the venture requires.

Research theme

Entrepreneurs' motivations for starting a new venture

The model developed in this chapter suggests that individuals are motivated to start a venture because of the utility they see in that option compared to alternatives. This utility is determined over the options' different abilities to satisfy economic, social and self-development needs. Even if this balance is favourable to moving to entrepreneurship, knowledge, possibility, risk and valence can act as inhibitors or encouragements to the move. An empirical test of this model might take the following form. Develop a questionnaire inquiring into what the entrepreneur sees (saw) as the positive and negative factors encouraging or discouraging the entrepreneurial option. Think of these questions as lying in the following grid:

Choice made (or planned)	Reasons for choice of option	
	Positives (encouragements)	Negatives (discouragements)
Entrepreneurial option		
Alternative option(s)		

Encourage the entrepreneur to put in at least five reasons for each option. Have the entrepreneur rank these in order of importance so that valence can be tested. The survey sample might include a range of entrepreneur types, from nascent, through novice to more experienced singular, serial and portfolio entrepreneurs. Code the responses into the ability of the option to satisfy a particular level of need or its role in the knowledge, possibility, risk and valence factors. By way of analysis, compare the coded responses to the model outlined. Does it provide a good framework for describing entrepreneurial motivation? How does it compare across different sorts of entrepreneur? Are nascent entrepreneurs more naive about what entrepreneurship can offer than practising entrepreneurs? Is Maslow's (1943) prediction that the prioritisation of needs is in the order economic, social and self-development borne out?

Suggestions for further reading

Ahwireng-Obeng, F. and Piaray, D. (1999) 'Institutional obstacles to South African entrepreneurship', *South African Journal of Business Management*, Vol. 30, No. 3, pp. 78–85.

Alsos, G.A. and Kolvereid, L. (1998) 'The business gestation process of novice, serial and parallel business founders', *Entrepreneurship Theory and Practice*, Summer, pp. 101–14.

Amundson, N.E. (1995) 'An interactive model of career decision-making', *Journal of Employment Counselling*, Vol. 32, No. 1, pp. 11–21.

Benacek, V. (1995) 'Small business and private entrepreneurship during transition: the case of the Czech Republic', *Eastern European Economics*, Vol. 33, No. 2, pp. 38–73.

Campbell, C.A. (1992) 'A decision theory model for entrepreneurial acts', *Entrepreneurship Theory and Practice*, Fall, pp. 21–7.

Carter, N., Gartner, W.B. and Reynolds, P.D. (1996) 'Exploring start-up event sequences', *Journal of Business Venturing*, Vol. 11, No. 3, pp. 151–66.

Dandridge, T.C. and Dziedziczak, I. (1992) 'New private enterprise in the new Poland: heritage of the past and challenges for the future', *Journal of Small Business Management*, April, pp. 104–9.

Danis, W.M. and Shipilov, A.V. (2002) 'A comparison of entrepreneurship development in two post-communist countries: the cases of Hungary and Ukraine', *Journal of Developmental Entrepreneurship*, Vol. 7, No. 1, pp. 67–94.

Eisenhauer, J.G. (1995) 'The entrepreneurial decision: economic theory and empirical evidence', *Entrepreneurship Theory and Practice*, Summer, pp. 67–79.

El-Namaki, M.S.S. (1988) 'Encouraging entrepreneurs in developing countries', *Long Range Planning*, Vol. 21, No. 4, pp. 98–106.

Feldman, D.C. and Bolino, M.C. (2000) 'Career patterns of the self-employed: career motivations and career outcomes', *Journal of Small Business Management*, July, pp. 53–67.

Fitzgerald, E.M. (2002) 'Identifying variables of entrepreneurship, privatization and competitive skills in central Europe: a survey design', *CR*, Vol. 12, No. 1, pp. 53–65.

Galbraith, J. (1982) 'The stages of growth', *Journal of Business Strategy*, Vol. 3, No. 1, pp. 70–9.

Gallagher, C. and Miller, P. (1991) 'New fast-growing companies create jobs', *Long Range Planning*, Vol. 24, No. 1, pp. 96–101.

Galt, V. and Moenning, C. (1996) 'An analysis of self-employment using UK census of population data', *International Journal of Entrepreneurial Behaviour and Research*, Vol. 2, No. 3, pp. 82–8.

Gilad, B. and Levine, P. (1986) 'A behavioural model of entrepreneurial supply', *Journal of Small Business Management*, Oct, pp. 45–53.

Hansen, E.L. and Bird, B.J. (1997) 'The stages model of high-tech venture founding: tried but true?' *Entrepreneurship Theory and Practice*, Vol. 22, No. 2, pp. 111–22.

Herron, L. and Sapienza, H.J. (1992) 'The entrepreneur and the initiation of new venture launch activities', *Entrepreneurship Theory and Practice*, Fall, pp. 49–55.

Katz, J.K. (1992) 'A psychosocial cognitive model of employment status choice', *Entrepreneurship Theory and Practice*, Fall, pp. 29–37.

Kazanjian, R. and Drazin, R. (1990) 'A stage contingent model of design and growth for technology based new ventures', *Journal of Business Venturing*, Vol. 5, pp. 137–50.

Kellye, J. and Tullous, R. (2002) 'Behaviours of pre-venture entrepreneurs and perceptions of their financial needs', *Journal of Small Business Management*, Vol. 40, No. 3, pp. 233–48.

Khandwalla, P.N. (1984) 'Pioneering-innovative (PI) management', *International Studies of Management and Organisation*, Vol. XIV, Nos 2–3, pp. 99–132.

Khandwalla, P.N. (1985) 'Pioneering-innovative management: a basis for excellence', *Organization Studies*, Vol. 6, No. 2, pp. 161–83.

Kiselev, D. (1990) 'New forms of entrepreneurship in the USSR', *Journal of Small Business Management*, July, pp. 76–80.

Kouriloff, M. (2000) 'Exploring perceptions of *a priori* barriers to entrepreneurship: a multidisciplinary approach', *Entrepreneurship Theory and Practice*, Winter, pp. 59–79.

Lee, S.S. and Oysteryoung, J.S. (2001) 'A comparison of the determinants for business start-up in the US and Korea', *Journal of Small Business Management*, Vol. 39, No. 2, pp. 195–200.

Maggina, A.G. (1992) 'SMEs in Greece: towards 1992 and beyond', *Journal of Small Business Management*, Vol. 30, No. 3, pp. 87–90.

Maslow, A.H. (1943) 'A theory of human motivation', *Psychological Review*, July, pp. 370–96.

Mazzarol, T., Volery, T., Doss, N. and Thien, V. (1999) 'Factors influencing small business start-ups', *International Journal of Entrepreneurial Behaviour and Research*, Vol. 5, No. 2, pp. 48–63.

Morrison, A. (2000) 'Entrepreneurship: what triggers it?', *International Journal of Entrepreneurial Behaviour and Research*, Vol. 6, No. 2, pp. 59–71.

Puffer, S.M., McCarthy, D.J. and Peterson, O.C. (2001) 'Navigating the hostile maze: a framework for Russian entrepreneurship', *Academy of Management Executive*, Vol. 15, No. 4, pp. 24–36.

Schaper, M. (1999) 'Australia's aboriginal entrepreneurs: challenges for the future', *Journal of Small Business Management*, Vol. 37, No. 3, pp. 88–93.

Schaper, M. (2002) 'The future prospects for entrepreneurship in Papua New Guinea', *Journal of Small Business Management*, Vol. 40, No. 1, pp. 78–83.

Shaver, K.G., Gartner, W.B., Crosby, E. Bakalarova, K. and Gatewood, E.J. (2001) 'Attributions about entrepreneurship: a framework and process for analysing reasons for starting a business', *Entrepreneurship Theory and Practice*, Winter, pp. 5–32.

Tan, J. (1996) 'Characteristics of regulatory environment and impact on entrepreneurial strategic orientations: an empirical study of Chinese private entrepreneurs', *Entrepreneurship Theory and Practice*, Vol. 21, No. 1, pp. 31–44.

Trulsson, P. (2002) 'Constraints of growth-orientated enterprises in the southern and eastern African region', *Journal of Developmental Entrepreneurship*, Vol. 7, No. 3, pp. 331–9.

Van Auken, H.E. (2000) 'Pre-launch preparations and the acquisition of start-up capital by small firms', *Journal of Developmental Entrepreneurship*, Vol. 5, No. 2, pp. 169–82.

Zapalska, A. (1997) 'Profiles of Polish entrepreneurship', *Journal of Small Business Management*, April, pp. 111–17.

Zapalska, A.M. and Edwards, W. (2001) 'Chinese entrepreneurship in a cultural and economic perspective', *Journal of Small Business Management*, Vol. 39, No. 3, pp. 286–92.

Selected case material Case 8.1

Finnish entrepreneur dials the right number

FT

30 December 2002

By **Christopher Brown-Humes**

Jyrki Hallikainen is a rare breed of Finnish entrepreneur; a former Nokia employee who left the company to set up his own mobile phone business.

It was a gamble in every sense of the word. Not only did he kiss goodbye to options that would have been highly lucrative by now – he was also trying to set up a business in the shadow of what was soon to be the world's biggest handset maker.

And yet, Mr Hallikainen can have little cause for regret. His company, Microcell, has grown rapidly since it was founded in 1997. Staff numbers have grown from 270 to 670 this year. Turnover soared from €17m ($17.7m) in all of 2001 to €171m in the first nine months of this year. And it has been profitable from day one.

If the progress continues, Microcell will be listed on the stock market in 2004 or 2005. Mr Hallikainen, who owns more than 50 per cent of the group, could even end up richer (at least on paper) than Jorma Ollila, the Nokia chief executive.

That would be quite an achievement for a person who built his company on manpower once cultivated at the regional cellular powerhouses. Many Microcell employees have come from Nokia and others from Ericsson, including Anders Torstensson, chief executive.

But Mr Hallikainen is sensitive about his ten-year stint at Nokia. He won't say what job he did there, only that he was working in R&D. Nor will he say how many people have subsequently left Nokia to join Microcell.

His view of the industry and the reason he founded the company is also very different to Nokia's. 'I felt that telecommunications equipment was a business where companies do not have to make every product themselves,' he says. Nokia, by contrast, is a vertically integrated manufacturer that likes to have control over most aspects of the manufacturing process itself.

As an ODM – an original design manufacturer – Microcell designs, develops and manufactures phones for other handset makers who then distribute and sell them under their own brand, not Microcell's.

Four out of ten of the big handset makers have engaged Microcell to make products for them. Sony Ericsson, for example, has commissioned the group to make its T66 handset. Siemens of Germany and Philips of Holland are also clients. The group made 1m phones between January and May.

Collaborating with ODMs means the big handset makers can get products to the market quicker and cut down on their own research and development, argues Mr Torstensson. But it forces the ODMs to be at the forefront of technical developments in areas such as colour screens and picture messaging.

'The leading brand names will definitely focus more and more on managing their brands and less and less on designing and developing their products. They will want to make sure products live up to the expectation of the brand name. But they don't have to make the product themselves,' he says.

This year ODMs – mostly in Taiwan and South Korea – are likely to produce about 35m phones, according to industry estimates. But the market is growing so rapidly that the figure could rise to as much as 230m (or 40 per cent of the total handset market) by 2006.

Microcell is already Europe's leading ODM and it aims to be the biggest in the world. As part of its expansion this year, it has set up a manufacturing joint venture in China. It has also recently moved its headquarters from Oulu in northern Finland to Zug in Switzerland.

Is Nokia going to be worried by the upstart? It seems unlikely. Given the increasing incursions of a certain US software giant into the mobile telecoms industry, it's probably more concerned by another company whose first five letters are Micro.

Source: Financial Times, 30 December 2002.

Case 8.2

The value of good connections

FT

19 December 2002

By **Jonathon Guthrie**

For four years in the 1970s Don Haddaway, chief executive of Artisiam, a telecommunications consultancy, attended a school in Trinidad where errors were punished with a cane across the knuckles.

It was useful preparation for a career as an entrepreneur, says Mr Haddaway: 'My accuracy went from 0 per cent to 100 per cent very quickly and I am a stickler for accuracy myself now,' he says.

It is just as well. Business does not punish mistakes with gentle reproaches but with the stinging rod of the Trinidadian pedagogue.

'Your failures teach you more than your successes,' says Mr Haddaway, sipping coffee in the foyer of a Northampton hotel. He recalls losing a big assignment after rushing out a sketchy pitch: 'That would have been a very good contract to get – but we did not put in the time and effort,' he admits.

Redundancy turned Mr Haddaway into a consultant, as it has so many executives. For some, it is simply a less embarrassing banner than 'unemployed', under which to prospect for a new job. But Mr Haddaway has stuck with it, creating a tidy little business that employs him, his wife Susan and three others. Last year profits were about £120,000 on sales of just under £300,000. That represents slippage on the first year but Mr Haddaway expects to do better in 2002–03, having won some big new clients.

As global networks head of Thomas Cook, Mr Haddaway ran a call centre division garlanded with industry awards. He achieved a 'world first' by setting up a partnership with Sonera of Finland, allowing customers to order foreign currency by phone. Another innovation was a system that allowed call centre agents to pinpoint travellers in trouble on a computerised map and give them appropriate advice.

None of that cut any ice with Preussag, German owner of the lossmaking travel business. It dispensed with the call centre network in July 2000 and Mr Haddaway went too. 'I was upset but not massively surprised,' he says. 'My feeling was that I should concentrate on the next thing.'

He says he had already called three possible clients to arrange meetings by the time he left the building. Contracting, he felt, would give him the breathing space he needed to reassess his career.

Mr Haddaway's reflections convinced him of one thing: the job security that big employers promise is largely illusory. He says: 'You have a perception of safety but this is because you cannot see everything that is happening. You do not see how close you are to losing your job, time and again.'

When you run your own business, he says, 'you see the risks coming straight at you'. That is preferable, he reasons, because you control the response.

Artisiam – a name contrived to evoke artesian wells drilled into impermeable rock – is based in an annexe of Mr Haddaway's house at Oundle in Northamptonshire. As a knowledge-driven business, it has needed no external finance and Mr Haddaway plans to keep it small and manageable, never directly employing more than 10 or so people.

He is, he says, a 'body-snatcher'. He 'borrows' staff from big companies to work on consultancy projects in the call centre industry. Mr Haddaway gets away with this, he says, because the employers of the 'snatchees' relish an association with Artisiam clients, such as British Sky Broadcasting and Thomson Travel.

Similar audacity impelled Mr Haddaway to hire the Royal Yacht for an evening – 'it was massively expensive' – to present research findings to 40 senior executives from client businesses. He says: 'You have to go beyond what people expect of you.'

It becomes clear that Mr Haddaway believes those expectations are sometimes less flattering than if he were white. He says diplomatically: 'You have to start from the point of view that your work will be critiqued to a higher level.'

His philosophy is that disadvantages are there to be overcome and he is correspondingly low key in complaining about what sounds like prejudice. However, Mr Haddaway reserves a dishonourable mention for an employee at a branch of HSBC, who unthinkingly ticked a box for 'turnover of £5,000 and under' when processing a corporate account application for a certain casually dressed black man. Only a good relationship with the manager of his own branch, in Birmingham, stopped him storming out.

Meanwhile, Mr Haddaway is working with online publisher The Colourful Network to research low levels of uptake for broadband services among disadvantaged communities. He aims to work on a range of issues where ethnicity and technology overlap.

Source: *Financial Times*, 19 December 2002.

Discussion points

1 What is the role of the state in encouraging entrepreneurs?

2 What are the opportunities and challenges to an entrepreneur initiating a new venture in a sector where they have been employed by an incumbent firm?

3 How might a nascent entrepreneur account for, and make use of, his or her success and failure as an employed manager? Consider how the entrepreneur might attribute success to his or her own abilities, the employing organisation or the wider world. What sort of account would make the entrepreneur most comfortable? How convincing would different sorts of account be to the venture's supporters?

Chapter 9

The nature of business opportunity

Chapter overview

This chapter presents an examination of the starting point for the entrepreneurial process, that is, the **business opportunity**. Entrepreneurs are **motivated** by the pursuit of opportunity. An analogy is developed through which a business opportunity can be pictured as a gap in the landscape created by existing business activities. The different types of **innovation** that can fill that gap and so offer a means of **exploiting** opportunity are considered. It is recognised that exploiting opportunities creates new **wealth** which can be **distributed** to the venture's stakeholders.

9.1 The landscape of business opportunity

Key learning outcome

An understanding of what comprises a business opportunity.

All living systems have *needs*. At a minimum, animals need food and oxygen, plants need sunlight and water. Human beings are different from many living organisms in that we are not content simply to survive using the things nature places to hand. We build highly structured societies and within these societies we join together to create *organisations*. Human organisations take on a variety of forms. However, they all exist to co-ordinate *tasks*. This co-ordination allows people to specialise their activities and to collaborate in the production of a wide variety of *goods* (a word taken to mean both physical products and services). Goods have *utility* because they can satisfy human needs. The products produced in the modern world can be used to satisfy a much more sophisticated range of human wants and needs, and to satisfy them more proficiently, than can the raw materials to be found in nature.

An organisation is an arrangement of *relationships* in that it exists in the spaces between people. Organisations exist to address human needs. Their effectiveness in doing this is a function of the form adopted by the organisation and the way it works. As the number of people involved increases, so too do the ways of organising them. In fact, the possibilities quickly become astronomical. This leads to a simple conclusion: whatever the organisational arrangement is at the moment, there is probably a *better* way of doing things! Even if, by chance, we did find the optimum arrangement, it would not stay so for long. The world is not static. Technological progress would quickly change the rules.

Ideas from classical economics suggest that the optimal (that is, the most productive) organisation is one in which individuals work to maximise their own satisfaction from the goods available and freely exchange those goods between themselves. Such behaviour is said to be *economically rational*. While this provides a very powerful framework for thinking about economic relations it is clearly only an approximation. People gain satisfaction from a variety of things, not all are exchanged through markets (how much does a beautiful sunset, or a personal sense of achievement 'cost'?). Nor is it obviously the case that individuals will maximise their own utility without any consideration towards their fellows. We can, and often do, act from altruistic motives.

Even if we *wanted* to act rationally, we probably could not. We simply do not have access to the information we would need to make decisions on purely rational lines. If all the information *were* available, individuals would still be limited in their ability to process and analyse it. In response to this, some economists talk of *satisficing* behaviour. That is, individuals aim to make the best decision available given a desire to address a wider sphere of concerns than purely economic self-satisfaction and taking into account limitations in knowledge.

An opportunity, then, is the possibility to do things both *differently* from and *better* than how they are being done at the moment. In economic terms, *differently* means an innovation has been made. This might take the form of offering a new product or of organising the company in a different way. *Better* means the product offers a *utility* in terms of an ability to satisfy human needs, that existing products do not. The new organisational form must be more *productive*, i.e. more efficient at using resources than existing organisational forms. Yet the decisions as to what is different and whether it is better are not made by economic robots. Both entrepreneurs and the consumers who buy what they offer are social beings who engage in satisficing behaviour. They must also base their decisions on the knowledge they have to hand, and their ability to use it. Furthermore, they make their decisions while following the rules they have laid down for themselves and the rules of the culture that shapes their lives.

We may think of business opportunity as being rather like a *landscape* representing the possibilities open to us. As we look across the landscape we will see open ground, untouched and full of new potential. We may see areas which are built up, leaving few new opportunities to be exploited. We will see other areas which are built up but where the buildings are old and decrepit, waiting to be pulled down, and something new built in their places. Effective entrepreneurs know the landscape in which they are operating. They know where the spaces are and how they fit between the built-up areas. They know which buildings can be pulled down and which are best left standing. Critically, they know where to move in and build themselves.

9.2 Innovation and the exploitation of opportunity

> **Key learning outcome**
>
> An appreciation that innovation is the key to exploiting opportunity.

A business opportunity, therefore, is the *chance* to do something differently and better. An innovation is a *way* of doing something differently and better. Thus an innovation is a *means* of exploiting a business opportunity. Innovation has a definite meaning in economics. All goods (whether physical products or services) are regarded as being made up of three factors: *natural raw materials*, *physical and mental labour* and *capital* (money). An innovation is a new combination of these three things. Entrepreneurs, as innovators, are people who create new combinations of these factors and then present them to the market for assessment by consumers. This is a technical conceptualisation of what innovation is about. It does not give the practising entrepreneur much of a guide to what innovation to make, or how to make it, but it should warn that innovation is a much broader concept than just *inventing* new products. It also involves bringing them to market. Some important areas in which valuable innovations might be made will be discussed below.

New products

One of the most common forms of innovation is the creation of a new product. This may exploit an established technology or it may be the outcome of a whole new technology. The new product may offer a radically new way of doing something or it may simply be an improvement on an existing theme. David Packard built a scientific instrumentation and information processing business empire, Hewlett-Packard, based on advanced scientific developments. Frank Purdue (founder of the major US food business Purdue Chickens), on the other hand, built his business by innovating in an industry whose basic product was centuries, if not millennia, old: the farmed chicken. Whatever the basis of innovation, the new product must offer the customer an *advantage* if it is to be successful: a better way of performing a task, or of solving a problem, or a better quality product.

Products are not simply a physical tool for achieving particular ends. They can also have a role to play in satisfying *emotional* needs. *Branding* is an important aspect of this. A brand name reassures the consumer, draws ready-made associations for them and provides a means of making a personal statement. The possibility of innovations being made through branding should not be overlooked. The British entrepreneur Richard Branson, for example, has been active in using the Virgin brand name on a wide variety of product areas following its initial success in the airline business. To date, it has been used to create a point of difference on, among other things, record labels, soft drinks and personal finance products.

New services

A service is an *act* which is offered to undertake a particular task or solve a particular problem. Services are open to the possibility of new ideas and innovation just as much as physical products. For example, the American entrepreneur Frederick Smith created the multi-million dollar international business Federal Express, by realising a better way of moving parcels between people.

Like physical products, services can be supported by the effective use of branding. In fact, it is beneficial to stop thinking about 'products' and 'services' as distinct types of business and to recognise that *all* offerings have product and service aspects. This is important because it is possible to innovate by adding a 'customer service' component to a physical product to make it more attractive to the user. Similarly, developments in product technology allow new service concepts to be innovated.

New production techniques

Innovation can be made in the way in which a product is manufactured. Again, this might be by developing an existing technology or by adopting a new technological approach. A new production technique provides a sound basis for success if it can be made to offer the end user new benefits. It must either allow them to obtain the product at lower cost, or to be offered a product of higher or more consistent quality, or to be given a better service in the supply of the product. An important example here is Rupert Murdoch's drive for change in the way newspapers were produced in the 1980s. Production is not just about technology. Increasingly new production 'philosophies' such as just-in-time (JIT) supply and total quality management (TQM) are providing platforms for profitable innovation.

New operating practices

Services are delivered by operating practices which are, to some extent, routinised. These routines provide a great deal of potential for entrepreneurial innovation. Ray Kroc, the founder of McDonald's, for example, noted the advantages to be gained in standardising fast-food preparation. As with innovations in the production of physical products, innovation in service delivery must address customer needs and offer them improved benefits, for example easier access to the service, a higher quality service, a more consistent service, a faster or less time-consuming service, a less disruptive service.

New ways of delivering the product or service to the customer

Customers can only use products and services they can access. Consequently, getting distribution right is an essential element in business success. It is also something which offers a great deal of potential for innovation. This may involve the *route* taken (the path the product takes from the producer to the user), or the *means* of managing its journey.

A common innovation is to take a more direct route by cutting out distributors or intermediaries. A number of successful entrepreneurial ventures have been established on the basis of getting goods directly to the customer. This may be an indirect way into high street retailing, for example Richard Thalheimer in the USA with The Sharper Image catalogue or the Littlewoods chain in the UK. Another approach is to focus on the distribution chain and specialise in a particular range of goods. This type of 'category busting' focus has allowed Charles Lazarus to build the toy retail outlet Toys 'R' Us into a worldwide concern.

New means of informing the customer about the product

People will only use a product or service if they *know* about it. Demand will not exist if the offering is not properly promoted to them. Promotion consists of two parts: a *message*, what is said, and a *means*, the route by which that message is delivered. Both the message and the means present latitude for inventiveness in the way they are approached. Communicating with customers can be expensive, and entrepreneurs, especially when their ventures are in an early stage, rarely have the resources to invest in high-profile advertising and public relations campaigns. Therefore, they are encouraged to develop new means of promoting their products.

Many entrepreneurs have proved to be particularly skilful at getting 'free' publicity. Anita and Gordon Roddick, for example, have used very little formal advertising for their toiletries retailer The Body Shop. However, the approach adopted by the organisation, and its stated corporate values, have made sure that The Body Shop has featured prominently in the widespread commentary on corporate responsibility that has regularly appeared in the media. As a result, awareness of their organisation is high and consumer attitudes towards it are positive.

New ways of managing relationships within the organisation

Any organisation has a wide variety of communication channels running through it. The performance of the organisation will depend to a great extent on the effectiveness of its internal communication channels. These communication channels are guided (formally at least) by the organisation's *structure*. The structure of the organisation offers considerable scope for value-creating innovations. Of particular note here is the development of the *franchise* as an organisational form. This structure, which combines the advantages of small business ownership with the power of integrated global organisation, has been a major factor in the growth of many entrepreneurial ventures, including The Body Shop retail chain, the Holiday Inn hotel group and the McDonald's fast food chain.

New ways of managing relationships between organisations

Organisations sit in a complex web of relationships to each other. The way they communicate and relate to each other is very important. Many entrepreneurial organisations have made innovation in the way in which they work with other organisations (particularly customers) into a key part of their strategy. The business services sector has been particularly active in this respect.

The advertising agency Saatchi and Saatchi, founded by the brothers Charles and Maurice in 1970, did not build its success solely on the back of making good advertisements. The brothers also realised that managing the relationship with the client was important. An advertising agency is, in a sense, a supplier of a service like any other, but its 'product' is highly complex and expensive, and its potential to generate business for the client is unpredictable. Thus advertising is a high-risk activity. The brothers realised that if advertising were to be managed properly, the agency had to become an integral part of the management team within the client organisation and not just to create advertisements but to work with them at resolving the issues generated by advertising, as well as helping them to exploit its potential. In effect, they broke down the barrier between their organisation and their customers.

Multiple innovation

An entrepreneurial venture does not have to restrict itself to just one innovation or even one type of innovation. Success can be built on a *combination* of innovations: for example, a new product delivered in a new way with a new message.

9.3 High- and low-innovation entrepreneurship

Key learning outcome

An understanding of the distinction between high- and low-innovation approaches to exploiting business opportunities.

Even though innovation has been defined as a key characteristic of entrepreneurship and has been used as one of the factors that distinguishes the entrepreneurial venture from the small business, particular entrepreneurial ventures differ in terms of the degree of innovation they adopt. Manimala (1999), in a major study of entrepreneurship in India, has drawn a distinction between what he refers to as *high* and *low pioneering-innovativeness*

(PI) entrepreneurship. These two types can be distinguished on the basis of a variety of strategic characteristics, the selection of which reflects the innovation discovered, the business opportunity and resources available and the personal preferences of the entrepreneur. These characteristics are summarised (with modification) in Table 9.1.

Table 9.1	High and low pioneering-innovativeness entrepreneurial strategies	
Strategic characteristics	**Low PI entrepreneurship**	**High PI entrepreneurship**
Idea management	Tend to rely on local contacts and ideas from existing products	Tend to be more inventive and obtain ideas from a wider source, perhaps internationally
	Strategic vision starts limited but may evolve over time	Strategic vision ambitious from the start
	Stick to and repeat earlier successes	Eager for new ideas
Management of autonomy	Prefer to manage autonomy by working with close-knit team	Will appoint individuals with relevant expertise even if personal knowledge of them is limited
	Develop own expertise through experience	Will develop expertise through employment opportunities and formal training
Management of competition	Tend to stick to what is tried and trusted. Avoid competing when experience is limited	Will undertake, new, higher-risk competitive moves
	Tend to build good working relationship with limited number of key customers (say, as sub-contractor)	Greater drive to bring new customers on board. Emphasis on product, quality and service
Growth strategy	Desire for growth but rely on clear and unhindered market opportunity to achieve growth	Desire for growth but more willing to actively compete for market space
	Unlikely to make risky diversification moves	More likely to make risky diversification moves
Human resource management	Tend to rely on known, experienced workers	Experts brought on board as and when needed
	More likely to rely on directions and routines as a means of control	More likely to rely on strategy, culture to exert control
Risk management	Limit risk taking. Tried and trusted route	More likely to manage risk through information, e.g. market researching
	Seeking of institutional and governmental support for expansion moves	Also keen for institutional and governmental support, but more willing to make unsupported risky moves
Network development	Mainly local. Keen to use informal as much as formal networks	Broader base and range of networking. Use local base for further expansion. Also use informal networks, but more adept at managing formal networks

(9.4) Opportunity and entrepreneurial motivation

> **Key learing outcome**
>
> An understanding of how the effective entrepreneur is motivated by business opportunity.

Thus an opportunity is a gap in a market or the possibility of doing something both differently and better; and an innovation presents a means of filling that market gap, that is, a way of pursuing the opportunity. Such definitions, while they capture the *nature* of opportunity and innovation from both an economic and a managerial perspective, do little to relate the *way* in which opportunity figures in the working life of the entrepreneur. Opportunity *motivates* entrepreneurs. Therefore, it is the thing that attracts their attention and draws their actions. But good entrepreneurs are not blindly subject to opportunities; they take control of them. It is important to understand how entrepreneurs should relate to business opportunities and allow themselves to be motivated by them.

Entrepreneurs are attuned to opportunity

Entrepreneurs are always on the look-out for opportunities. They scan the business landscape looking for new ways of creating value. As we have seen, this value can take the form of new wealth, a chance to pursue an agenda of personal development or to create social change. Opportunities are the 'raw material' out of which the entrepreneur creates an 'entire new world'. To be motivated by opportunity entails the recognition that the current situation does not represent the best way of doing things; that the status quo does not exhaust possibilities. While this may be a spur to move forward, it could also create motivational problems. If we are too conscious of *what might be*, do we not become disillusioned with *what is*? Can the entrepreneur ever get to where he or she is going?

There is no simple answer to this question. There are certainly some entrepreneurs who are driven forward because they are not satisfied with the present. However, many, while not losing their motivation for what might be, are still able to enjoy what is. Some gain satisfaction, not from reaching the end-points of their activity, but in the *journey* itself. Others make sure they create space for themselves to take pride in what they have achieved, as well as looking forward to what they might achieve. Entrepreneurs must be aware of their motivation. As well as knowing *what* they want to achieve they must be aware of *why* they want to achieve it and why they will enjoy the *process* of achieving it.

Opportunity must take priority over innovation

It is easy to get excited over a new idea. However, an innovation, no matter how good it is, should be secondary to the market opportunity that it aims to exploit. The best ideas are those which are inspired by a clear need in the marketplace rather than those that result from uninformed invention. Many innovations which have been 'pushed' by new product or service possibilities rather than 'pulled' by unsatisfied customer needs have gone on to be successful. However, without a clear understanding of why customers buy and what they are looking for, this can be a very hit-or-miss process. Mistakes are punished quickly and they can be expensive. Failure is certainly demotivating, but this is not to suggest that new product ideas should necessarily be rejected. It does mean that they provide the inspiration to assess their market potential, not to rush the idea straight into the market.

Identifying real opportunities demands knowledge

One of the misconceptions that many people entertain about entrepreneurs is that they are the 'wanderers' of the business world. The notion that they drift between industries, opportunistically picking off the best ideas missed by less astute and responsive 'residents', is widely held. This idea can be traced back to the view that the entrepreneur is a 'special' type of person. If they are entrepreneurial by character, then they will be entrepreneurs wherever they find themselves. So, they can move at will between different areas of business taking their ability with them. Such an idea is not only wrong, it is dangerous because it fails to recognise the knowledge and experience that entrepreneurs must have if they are to be successful in the industries within which they operate.

Some important elements of this knowledge include knowledge of:

- the technology behind the product or service supplied;
- how the product or service is produced;
- customers' needs and the buying behaviour they adopt;
- distributors and distribution channels;
- the human skills utilised within the industry;
- how the product or service might be promoted to the customer;
- competitors: who they are, the way they act and react.

This knowledge is necessary if good business opportunities are to be identified and properly assessed. Acquisition of this knowledge requires exposure to the relevant industry, an active learning attitude and time. Most entrepreneurs are actually very experienced in a particular industry sector and confine their activities within that sector. Many have acquired this experience by working as a manager in an existing organisation. This 'incubation' period can be very important to the development of entrepreneurial talent.

However, industry-specific knowledge does not produce entrepreneurs on its own. It must be supplemented with general business skills and people skills. If an entrepreneur with these skills were to be transplanted between industries, these skills would still be valuable but they would be unlikely to come into their own until the entrepreneur had learnt enough about the new business area to be confident in making good decisions. It is interesting to note that entrepreneurs who do move between industries demonstrate a skill in drawing out and using the expertise that exists within those different industries. Richard Branson, for example, is renowned for his ability to work effectively with industry specialists.

9.5 The opportunity to create wealth

> **Key learning outcome**
>
> An appreciation of the role of wealth creation in the entrepreneurial process.

Entrepreneurs can often become well-known public figures. They are of public interest because they have been *successful*, and this success has often made them quite wealthy. Their success is of interest in its own right, but their wealth may give them a good deal of social (and perhaps political) power. So while entrepreneurship, and the desire to be an entrepreneur, cannot usually be reduced to a simple desire to make money, it must not be forgotten that making money *is* an important element in the entrepreneurial process.

Business success, and the accumulation of wealth this brings, creates a number of possibilities for the entrepreneur and their ventures to dispose of that wealth.

Reinvestment

If the entrepreneur wishes to grow the business they have initiated then it will demand continued investment. Some of this may be provided by external investors but it will also be expected, and may well be financially advantageous, that the business reinvest some of the profits it has generated.

Rewarding stakeholders

The entrepreneurial venture is made up of more than just the entrepreneur. Entrepreneurs exist in a tight network of relationships with a number of other internal and external stakeholders who are asked to give their support to the venture. They may be asked to take risks on its behalf. In return, they will expect to be properly rewarded. Financial success offers the potential for the entrepreneur to reward them, not just financially, but in other ways as well.

Investment in other ventures

If reinvestment within the venture has taken place, and the stakeholders have been rewarded for their contributions, and there are still funds left over then alternative investments might be considered. The entrepreneur may start an entirely new venture (an option which can be particularly tempting to serial entrepreneurs when their business has matured and they feel that its initial excitement has gone). Another option is that of providing investment support to another entrepreneur.

Successful, established entrepreneurs will often act as 'business angels' and offer their knowledge and experience, as well as spare capital, to young ventures.

Personal reward

Some of the value created by the entrepreneur and their venture (though by no means *all* of it) can be taken and used for personal consumption. Funding a comfortable lifestyle is part of this. It may be regarded by the entrepreneur as a just reward for taking risks and putting in the effort the success has demanded. Some entrepreneurs may also be quite keen to put their money into altruistic projects, for example they may sponsor the arts or support social programmes. This may reflect their desire to make a mark on the world outside the business sphere, which is part of their desire to leave the world different from the way in which they found it.

Keeping the score

For many entrepreneurs, money is not so important in itself. It is just a way of quantifying what they have achieved; a way of keeping the score on their performance, as it were. The money value of their venture is a measure of how good their insight was, how effective their decision making was, and how well they put their ideas into practice.

   As far as the entrepreneur is concerned, money is more usually a *means* rather than an *end* in itself. That we notice the entrepreneurs who are highly rewarded for their efforts should not blind us to the fact that this reward is more often than not the result of a great deal of hard work and it is a reward that is far from inevitable.

9.6 The opportunity to distribute wealth

> **Key learning outcome**
>
> A recognition of who expects to be rewarded from the entrepreneurial venture.

No entrepreneur works in a vacuum. The venture they create touches the lives of many other people. To drive their venture forward, the entrepreneur calls upon the support of a number of different groups. In return for their support, these groups expect to be rewarded from the success of the venture. People who have a part to play in the entrepreneurial venture generally are called *stakeholders*. The key stakeholder groups are *employees*, *investors*, *suppliers*, *customers*, the local *community* and *government*.

Employees

Employees are the individuals who contribute physical and mental labour to the business. Its success depends on their efforts on its behalf and therefore upon their motivation. Employees usually have some kind of formal contract and are rewarded by being paid a salary. This is usually agreed in advance and is independent of the performance of the venture, although an element may be performance related. Employees may also be offered the possibility of owning a part of the firm through share schemes.

People do not work just for money. The firm they work for provides them with a stage on which to develop social relationships. It also offers them the possibility of personal development. When someone joins an organisation they are making a personal investment in its future and the organisation is investing in their future. Changing jobs is time-consuming and can be expensive. Those who decide to work for an entrepreneurial venture are exposing themselves to the risk of that venture, even if they are being paid a fixed salary.

Investors

Investors are the people who provide the entrepreneur with the necessary money to start the venture and keep it running. There are two main sorts of investor. *Stockholders* are people who buy a part of the firm, its *stock*, and so are entitled to a share of any profits it makes. Stockholders are the true owners of the firm. The entrepreneur managing the venture may, or may not, be a major shareholder in it. *Lenders* are people who offer money to the venture on the basis of it being a *loan*. They do not actually own a part of the firm. All investors expect a return from their investment. The actual amount of expected return will depend on the risk the venture is facing and the other investments that are available at the time. The actual return the stockholder receives will vary depending on how the business performs. Lenders, on the other hand, expect a rate of return which is agreed independently of how the business performs before the investment is made. Lenders usually take priority for payment over stockholders, whose returns are only paid once the business has met its other financial commitments. Lenders consequently face a lower level of risk. However, there is still the possibility that the venture might become insolvent and not be able to pay back its loans.

Suppliers

Suppliers are the individuals and organisations who provide the business with the materials, productive assets and information it needs to produce its outputs. Suppliers are paid for providing these *inputs*. The business may only make contact with a supplier through spot purchases made in an open market, or contact may be more direct and defined by a formal contract, perhaps a long-term supply contract.

Suppliers are in business to sell what they produce and so they have an interest in the performance of their customers. Supplying them may involve an investment in developing a new product or providing back-up support. A new venture may call upon the support of its suppliers, perhaps by asking for special payment terms to ease its cash flow in the early days. Information and advice about end-user markets may be provided. The chance to build a partnership with suppliers should never be overlooked.

Customers

As with suppliers, customers may need to make an investment in using a particular supplier. Changing suppliers may involve *switching costs*. These include the cost of finding a new supplier, taking a risk with goods of unknown quality, and the expenses incurred in changing over to new inputs. When customers decide to use the products offered by a new venture rather than one with an established track record they may be exposing themselves to some risk. (This is something the entrepreneur needs to take into account when devising a selling strategy.) The entrepreneur's business may sell to its customers on an open market but, as with suppliers, the possibility of building a longer-term partnership should always be considered.

The local community

Businesses have physical locations. The way that they operate may affect the people who live and other businesses which operate nearby. A business has a number of responsibilities to this local community, for example in not polluting their shared environment. Some of these responsibilities are defined in national or local laws, others are not defined in a legal or formal sense, but are expected on the basis that the firm will act in an *ethical* way.

Corporate responsibility is a political and cultural as well as an economic issue. If the firm is international and operates across borders then the way it behaves in one region may influence the way it is perceived in another. For example, a number of well-known sports shoes manufacturers were criticised recently for paying Indian workers less than half a US dollar for manufacturing shoes that retailed for over $200 in the USA. Whatever the fair 'market' price of labour in India, the firm's managers had to react to the damage this criticism did to the brand names they were trying to market in the West.

Government

A major part of a government's responsibility is to ensure that businesses can operate in an environment which has political and economic stability, and in which the rule of law operates so contracts can be both made and enforced. The government may also provide central services such as education and health-care which the workforce draws upon. These services cost money to provide and so the government taxes individuals and businesses. In general governments aim to support entrepreneurial businesses because they have an interest in their success. Entrepreneurs bring economic prosperity, provide social stability and generate tax revenue.

Distribution of rewards

All the stakeholders shown in Figure 9.1 expect some reward from the entrepreneurial venture. By working together they can maximise its success. Even so,

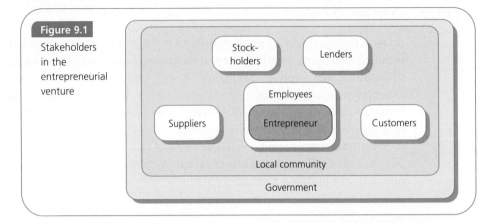

Figure 9.1

Stakeholders in the entrepreneurial venture

the new wealth created by the entrepreneur is finite. It can only be shared so far. The entrepreneur must decide how to distribute the wealth among the various stakeholders. To some extent the entrepreneur's hands are tied since the sharing of the profits is, in part, determined by external markets. Legal requirements and binding contracts also play a part in deciding what goes where.

However, the entrepreneur has *some* freedom to decide who gets what. Customers can be rewarded for their loyalty. Higher payments may be used to motivate employees. Profits can be used to support projects in the local community. Distributing the rewards created by the venture is a great responsibility. Using this latitude for rewarding stakeholders creatively is very important to the future success of the venture. If rewards are distributed in a way which is seen as fair and proper they can motivate all involved in the venture. However, a distribution which is seen as illegitimate is a sure way to cause ill feeling.

9.7 Entrepreneurship: risk, ambiguity and uncertainty

Key learning outcome

An understanding of the role knowledge of business opportunities plays in defining the types of decision an entrepreneur must make.

Entrepreneurs are often characterised as risk takers. Though, as argued in Chapter 1, it is properly investors who take risks, not entrepreneurs, it is certainly true that entrepreneurs *manage* risk and make decisions in relation to it. Strictly speaking, though, decisions made in the face of risk constitute only one type of decision an entrepreneur makes. Modern decision theory clearly distinguishes between decisions made under conditions of risk, uncertainty and ambiguity. All decisions are based on knowledge of three information sets:

- The set of *states of the world*. These are the eventualities that the world may throw up in the future. They are outside the active control of an entrepreneur. An entrepreneur cannot control (or can influence in only a very limited way) factors such as overall demand for a new product, the actions of competitors, government interventions or broader world events. Such states of the world are regarded as discrete: we can distinguish one situation from another. Generally speaking, this is theoretically sound, but in practice it may be difficult to distinguish closely related or fine-grained states such as a competitor launching one product or launching a closely related one.

- The set of *acts*. These are the choices that the entrepreneur can make and has control over. For example, an entrepreneur may decide to launch one product or another, or invest in production machinery rather than advertising and so on. Acts are made in anticipation of the state of the world that will pertain. An act results from a particular decision. As with states of the world, acts are regarded as discrete and distinguishable, at least in principle.

- The set of *outcomes*. Outcomes result from the intersection of an act with a state of the world. They are the payoff expected to happen if the entrepreneur does 'this' and 'that' occurs. So the entrepreneur may invest in developing an export market in the expectation that demand in that market will grow. If it does so, then extra revenue will result. If it does not do so, however, then a lower return will be obtained. The entrepreneur may have invested in developing a new product for the domestic market, but decided not to do so because a launch by a competitor was expected, a launch that would have reduced demand for the new offering. It may turn out that the competitor does not go through with the expected launch, and so the investment in the domestic market would have given a better return than the export drive.

Decisions, then, are made on the basis of knowledge about states, acts and outcomes. Different levels of knowledge about each of these lead to different types of decision:

- Decisions under *certainty*. A decision under certainty is one where the actual state of the world that will occur is known definitely – for example, placing a bet on the sun rising tomorrow. In this case, the decision maker simply selects the act that gives the highest returns. These returns will definitely be obtained. As might be imagined, such decisions under certainty occur very rarely in business life!

- Decisions under *risk*. A decision under risk is one where the states that might occur are known, but it is not known for definite which one will occur. What is known is the *probability* with which each state might occur. Decisions of this type occur in gambling – for example betting that a tossed coin will come up heads or that a thrown die will land with six uppermost. The probability of a head is 1 in 2, that of throwing a six, 1 in 6. A rational decision maker will adjust the bet so that his or her expected payoff is maximised. The probabilities involved in such gambling games is known because the frequency with which the events will occur is known. There may be situations where frequencies are not known, but expert judgement can ascribe a probability – for example, a weather forecaster suggesting that the chance of rain tomorrow is 20 per cent, or a doctor suggesting that a particular treatment has a 90 per cent chance of being successful. Strictly speaking, risk is present only if such probabilities are known.

● Decisions under *uncertainty*. In fact, despite the widespread use of the word risk, decisions under risk are quite rare in business life (they may occur with stock market investments, for example). They are rare because while a manager may have a good knowledge of what might happen, he or she does not usually have detailed knowledge of the actual probabilities of what will happen. For example, a competitor may or may not launch a new product (states of the world). But what is the probability of this? If this is not known at all, the decision is said to be one under *uncertainty*. Under conditions of uncertainty decision makers may adopt a number of guiding rules depending on whether they wish to maximise their minimum return, or minimise the maximum loss they might make.

● Decisions under *ambiguity*. Of course, an experienced manager might suggest that he or she has a 'feel' for whether or not the competitor will launch. This judgement will be based on knowledge of the market and experience with the way the competitor has acted in the past. The manager may resist putting a definite figure on the probability of this, but will be prepared to make a decision based on their intuition that the launch is very likely, moderately likely, unlikely and so on. Decisions under ambiguity lie between those under uncertainty and risk. There is no definite probability for the things that might happen (risk), but the situation is not one of complete uncertainty either. Normative rules for decision making under ambiguity are far from clear and are the subject of research in the decision theory field.

● Decisions under ignorance. Ignorance represents the opposite end of the spectrum to certainty. In this situation, not only are probabilities not known, but even what might happen is not known. Without even this foresight, it is difficult to make any decision at all!

Most managerial, and entrepreneurial, decisions are actually decisions under *ambiguity* rather than risk. With this distinction in mind, it can be argued that what entrepreneurs actually do is not take on risk, but act to convert uncertainty (and ignorance) into risk (via ambiguity) by using their judgement to analyse and clarify the eventualities (states) that might occur, estimate their probabilities and then identify the acts that will maximise payoffs given these eventualities. This is a service that entrepreneurs offer to investors. Investors will take on risk, but they will not take on uncertainty.

Summary of key ideas

- A business opportunity is a *gap* in the market which presents the possibility of *new value* being created.

- Opportunities are pursued with *innovations* – a better way of doing something for a customer.

- Entrepreneurs are attuned to new opportunities and are motivated to pursue them.

- Entrepreneurs decide not only how to create new wealth but also how to distribute it to the venture's *stakeholders*.

- Decisions may be defined in terms of the knowledge available before they are made.

- Entrepreneurs actually turn uncertainty into risk on behalf of investors, rather than take on risk themselves.

Research theme

High and low pioneering-innovativeness (PI) entrepreneurial strategies

Manimala's scheme for distinguishing between high- and low-innovativeness entrepreneurship is described in Section 9.3. This distinguishes between the two types on a categorical and heuristic basis (see also Section 15.6). Using either case study descriptions of a series of entrepreneurial ventures or information obtained from primary surveys (at least 20 ventures in either case), evaluate them in terms of the criteria described. On the basis of these criteria, does Manimala's scheme clearly divide the ventures into high- and low-PI categories? Are there any other factors that discriminate between them? Might more or intermediate categories be needed?

Suggestions for further reading

Donaldson, T. and Preston, L.E. (1995) 'The stakeholder theory of the corporation: concepts, evidence and implications', *Academy of Management Review*, Vol. 20, No. 1, pp. 65–91.

Drucker, P.F. (1985) 'The discipline of innovation', *Harvard Business Review*, May-June, pp. 67–72.

Gray, H.L. (1978) 'The entrepreneurial innovator', *Management Education and Development*, Vol. 9, pp. 85–92.

Katz, J. (1990) 'The creative touch', *Nation's Business*, March, p. 43.

Manimala, M.J. (1999) *Entrepreneurial Policies and Strategies*, New Delhi: Sage.

Dial d for disposable

FT

17 September 2002

By **Alan Cane**

Dial d for disposable Once the yuppies' pride and joy, mobile phones could become as disposable as used tissues. A few years back, US entrepreneur Randice-Lisa Altschul attracted attention by patenting a phone largely constructed of paper. She was plotting a cultural rather than a technical revolution, reasoning that such phones, sold cheaply and programmed for a limited amount of air time, would prove a viable alternative to calling cards, prepaid phones, payphones and conventional mobile contracts. The technology, metallic ink printed on a paper-like substrate to connect the processing chips, was ingenious rather than ground-breaking. In the event, the first disposable phone on the US market has been introduced by Hop-On Communications of Garden Grove, California. At just under $30 (£19) and including 60 minutes of talk time, it's made of plastic rather than paper but the manufacturer has kept the cost down by keeping things simple. For example, voice recognition software substitutes for a keypad. When call time is exhausted, the phone can be sent back for recycling (and a $5 refund) or thrown away. British inventors have been looking at other aspects of the throw-away phone. Stephen Forshaw, a Salford University student, this year won a competition, sponsored by Sony, with a design for a greeting-card phone capable of making a one call only. Dubbed 'PS Call Me', the phone is as thin as a sheet of paper and comes with a tiny earpiece. Forshaw says that as well as sending birthday greetings, it could be used for more prosaic purposes, like registering that a package has arrived safely. But an interesting intellectual property skirmish could be in the offing, as Sheila Harris, an amateur inventor from Chepstow, applied for patents for the same notion two years ago. Her patent agent, Mark Spittle, points out there is nothing too original about the idea of combining a phone and a card. Instead, Harris's application bristles with claims, 43 in all, for original ways in which such a card could be used. The most important, Spittle says, is the concept of a phone that can ring only one number once. 'Lots of people can envisage a phone combined with a greetings card. But the idea of a one shot phone in a greetings card is original.'

As yet, there is no prototype, and Spittle says it is unlikely that Harris plans to market the device. But any manufacturer of a greetings card phone would have to respect her patents if they are granted.

Source: *Financial Times*, 17 September 2002.

Case 9.2

Myradiobank

8 October 2002

By **Alan Cane**

One of the broadcasting world's great mysteries is why so few radio sets with recording capabilities have ever been marketed. Marcus Lovell-Smith, an entrepreneur with water-meter reading and medical-waste disposal enterprises behind him, plans to plug the gap with a device set for launch next year, which he calls 'Myradiobank'.

It's a digital radio tuner capable of recording programmes on to flash memory cards. Lovell-Smith envisages listeners logging on to a website to set up a list of their preferences – it could be individual broadcasts, a specific genre of programme or what he calls bundles: programmes selected by Myradiobank staff dealing with broad topics – such as politics or the environment.

The company has a small amount of radio spectrum which it can use, at dead of night, to transmit recording instructions to the device. The listener retrieves the flash card after recording and listens to his or her chosen selection through a mobile phone, MP3 player, personal digital assistant or any other portable digital device. The recorder can, of course, be plugged directly into a hi-fi system for playback.

The cost of the tuner is likely to be £150–£200. Lovell-Smith argues that it will make it possible to store legally two hours of customised digital music a day, for a fraction of the cost of downloading over a 2.5 or 3G mobile phone network.

Source: Financial Times, 8 October 2002.

Discussion point

If there is 'nothing new under the sun', how can the innovative entrepreneur make sure his or her invention is the one that leads the market?

Chapter 10

Resources in the entrepreneurial venture

Chapter overview

People, money and operational assets are the essential ingredients of the entrepreneurial venture. This chapter explores each of these resource types and the management issues they raise for the entrepreneur. Why investment in such resources leads to risk for the backers of the venture is considered. The concept of resource stretch and leverage is applied to develop an understanding of how entrepreneurs can work their resources harder than established competitors.

10.1 Resources available to the entrepreneur

Key learning outcome

An understanding of the nature and type of resources that the entrepreneur uses to build the venture.

Resources are the things that a business uses to pursue its ends. They are the inputs that the business converts to create the outputs it delivers to its customers. They are the substance out of which the business is made. In broad terms, there are three sorts of resource that entrepreneurs can call upon to build their ventures. These are:

1 *financial resources* – resources which take the form of, or can be readily converted to, cash;

2 *human resources* – people and the efforts, knowledge, skill and insights they contribute to the success of the venture;

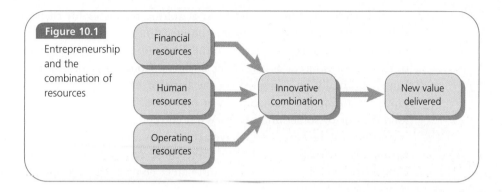

Figure 10.1

Entrepreneurship and the combination of resources

3 *operating resources* – the facilities which allow people to do their jobs: such as buildings, vehicles, office equipment, machinery and raw materials, etc.

The entrepreneurial venture is built from an innovative combination of financial, operating and human resources (Figure 10.1). Thus when Frederick Smith founded the US parcel air carrier Federal Express he needed to bring together people: a board of directors, pilots, operational staff, etc., together with a fully operational airline which was able to give national coverage. This demanded an investment in the order of $100 million.

Regardless of the form they take, all resources have a number of characteristics in common. Resources are *consumed*; they are converted to the products which customers buy and there is competition to get hold of resources. A number of businesses, entrepreneurial and otherwise, will be trying to acquire a particular resource; consequently, managers are willing to pay for resources. Third, resources have a cost.

The cost of a resource is an indication of how it might be used by a business to create new value. Resources are bought and sold by businesses and their cost is determined by the market created for that resource. Resources with the potential to create a lot of new value will be expensive. This cost is not the same as the *value* of the resource to a *particular* business since the value of a resource lies in the way a business will use it, how innovative they will be with it and how hard they will make it work for them.

One type of resource can be converted into another. This process normally involves selling a resource, thereby converting it into cash, and then using this cash to buy something new. However, in some cases resources may be exchanged directly through 'asset swaps'. In places where financial markets are not well developed, such as in parts of the developing world and the former communist bloc, 'bartering' may be important. Not all markets for resources are equally accessible. Some markets are more developed than others. The ease with which a particular resource can be converted back into ready cash is called its liquidity: *liquid* resources are easily converted back, *illiquid* resources are converted back only with difficulty.

Entrepreneurs must be active in acquiring resources for their ventures. The paths through which resources are obtained and exchanged make up the network in which the business is located. In the long run, the entrepreneur only has access to the same resources as any other business. Competitiveness in the marketplace cannot normally be sustained on the basis of having access to unique resource inputs. If an input is valuable, other businesses will eventually find a way to get hold of it or of something like it. What entrepreneurs must do to be competitive is *combine* the resources they have access to in a unique and valuable way – that is, *innovate* with them and then make those resources work harder than their competitors do. It is this which ultimately enables the entrepreneur to deliver new value to the customer.

10.2 Financial resources

> **Key learning outcome**
>
> An appreciation of the financial resources available for use by the entrepreneur.

Financial resources are those which take a monetary form. Cash is the most liquid form of resource because it can be used readily to buy other resources. The following are all financial resources which have a role to play in the entrepreneurial venture:

- *cash in hand* – this is money to which the business has immediate access. It may be spent at very short notice. Cash in hand may be held either as money, i.e. petty cash, or it may be stored in a bank's current account or other direct access account.

- *overdraft facilities* – such facilities represent an agreement with a bank to withdraw more than is actually held in the venture's current account. It is a short-term loan which the business can call upon, although overdrafts are normally quite expensive and so tend to be saved for emergencies.

- *loans* – loans represent money provided by backers, either institutional or private, which the business arranges to pay back in an agreed way over a fixed period of time at an agreed rate of interest. The payback expected is usually independent of the performance of the business. Loans may be secured against physical assets of the business which can be sold off to secure repayment. This reduces the risk of the loan to the backer.

- *outstanding debtors* – this represents cash owed to the business by individuals and firms which have received goods and services from it. Many debtors will expect a period of grace before paying and it may not be easy to call in outstanding debt quickly. Outstanding debtors are one of the main reasons why cash-flow may be negative in the early stages of the venture's life.

- *investment capital* – this is money provided to the business by investors in return for a part-ownership or share in it. Investors are the true owners of the business. They are rewarded from the profits the business generates. The return they receive will be dependent on the performance of the business.

- *investment in other businesses* – many businesses hold investments in other businesses. These investments may be in unrelated businesses but they are more often in suppliers or customers. If more than half a firm is owned, then it becomes a *subsidiary* of the holding firm. Investments can be made through personal or institutional agreements, or via publicly traded shares. A firm does not normally exist solely to make investments in other firms. Individual and institutional investors are quite capable of doing this for themselves. However, strategic investments in customers and suppliers may be an important part of the dynamics of the network in which the business is located. For this reason such investments tend to represent long-term commitments and although they can be sold to generate cash, doing so is not routine.

All financial resources have a cost. This cost takes one of two forms. The *cost of capital* is the cost encountered when obtaining the money: it is the direct charge faced for having an overdraft; the interest on loans; the return expected by investors, etc. In addition to this direct cost, there is an *opportunity cost*. Opportunity cost is the potential return that is lost by not putting the money to some alternative use. For example, cash in hand and outstanding debts lose the interest that might be gained by putting the money into an interest-yielding account.

Financial resources are the most liquid, and thus the most flexible, resources to which the venture has access. However, they are also the least productive. Cash, of itself, does not create new value. Money is only valuable if it is put to work. This means it must be converted to other, less liquid, resources. The entrepreneur must strike a balance. A decision must be made between how liquid the business is to be, how much flexibility it must have to meet short-term and unexpected financial commitments, and the extent to which the firm's financial resources are to be tied up in productive assets.

Such decisions are critical to the success of the venture. If insufficient investment is made then the business will not be in a position to achieve its full potential. If it becomes too illiquid, it may be knocked off-course by short-term financial problems which, in the long run, the business would be more than able to solve. Managing the *cash-flow* of the business is central to maintaining this liquidity balance. The financial resources to which an entrepreneur can gain access will depend on how well developed the economy they are working in is and the type of capital markets available. In the mature economies of Western Europe and the USA, capital is usually provided by explicit and open institutional systems such as banks, venture capital businesses and stock markets. In other parts of the world, provision of financial resources may be through less formal networks. Displaced communities often create financial support networks around the extended family. One of the main challenges to developing entrepreneurism in the former communist bloc is the setting up of supportive and trusted financial institutions.

10.3) Operating resources

> **Key learning outcome**
>
> An appreciation of the operational resources available for use by the entrepreneur.

Operating resources are those which are actually used by the business to deliver its outputs to the marketplace. Key categories of operating resources include:

- *premises* – the buildings in which the business operates. This includes offices, production facilities and the outlets through which services are provided.

- *motor vehicles* – any vehicles which are used by the organisation to undertake its business such as cars for sales representatives and vans and lorries used to transport goods, make deliveries and provide services.

- *production machinery* – machinery which is used to manufacture the products which the business sells.

- *raw materials* – the inputs that are converted into the products that the business sells.

- *storage facilities* – premises and equipment used to store finished goods until they are sold.

- *office equipment* – items used in the administration of the business such as office furniture, word processors, information processing and communication equipment.

Operating resources represent the capacity of the business to offer its innovation to the marketplace. They may be owned by the business, or they may be rented as they are needed. Either way, they represent a commitment. Liquid financial resources are readily converted into operating resources, but operating resources are not easily converted back into money. The markets for second-hand business assets are not always well developed. Even if they are, operating resources depreciate quickly and a loss may be made on selling.

In order to use operating resources effectively it is important that entrepreneurs make themselves fully conversant with any technical aspects relating to the resources; legal issues and implications relating to their use (including health and safety regulations); suppliers and the supply situation; and the applicable costs (both for outright purchase and for leasing). It is in this area that partnerships with suppliers can be rewarding, especially if the operating resources are technical or require ongoing support in their use.

The commitment to investment in operating resource capacity must be made in the light of expected demand for the business's offerings. If capacity is insufficient, then business that might otherwise have been obtained will be lost. If it is in excess of demand, then unnecessary, and unprofitable, expenditure will be undertaken. It is often difficult to alter operating capacity in the light of short-term fluctuations in demand. This results in *fixed costs*, that is, costs which are independent of the amount of outputs the firm offers. Critically, fixed costs must be faced *whatever* the business's sales. Fixed costs can have a debilitating effect on cash-flow. The entrepreneur must make the decision about commitment to operating capacity in the light of an assessment of the sales and operating profits that will be generated by the business's offering, that is, on the basis of an accurate *forecast* of demand. Even good demand forecasting cannot remove all uncertainty and therefore the entrepreneur must be active in offsetting as much fixed cost as possible, especially in the early stages of the venture. This may mean renting rather than buying operating resources. It can also mean that some work is delegated to other established firms. In the early stages of the venture, managing cash-flow and controlling fixed costs may be more important than short-term profitability. It may be better to sub-contract work to other firms rather than to make an irreversible commitment to extra capacity, even if this means short-term profits are lost.

10.4 Human resources

> **Key learning outcome**
>
> An appreciation of the human resources available for use by the entrepreneur.

People are the critical element in the success of a new venture. Financial and operating resources are not unique and they cannot, in themselves, confer an advantage to the business. To do so they must be *used* in a unique and innovative way by the people who make up the venture. The people who take part in the venture offer their labour towards it. This can take a variety of forms:

- *productive labour* – a direct contribution towards generating the outputs of the business, its physical products or the service it offers.

- *technical expertise* – a contribution of knowledge specific to the product or service offered by the business. This may be in support of existing products, or associated with the development of new ones.

- *provision of business services* – a contribution of expertise in general business services, for example in legal affairs or accounting.

- *functional organisational skills* – the provision of decision-making insights and organising skills in functional areas such as production, operations planning, marketing research and sales management.

- *communication skills* – offering skills in communicating with, and gaining the commitment of, external organisations and individuals. This includes marketing and sales directed towards customers, and financial management directed towards investors.

● *strategic and leadership skills* – the contribution of insight and direction for the business as a whole. This involves generating a vision for the business, converting this into an effective strategy and plan for action, communicating this to the organisation and then leading the business in pursuit of the vision.

The entrepreneur represents the starting point of the entrepreneurial venture. He or she is the business's first, and most valuable, human resource. Entrepreneurs, if they are to be successful, must learn to use themselves as a resource, and use themselves effectively. This means analysing what they are good at, and what they are not so good at, and identifying skill gaps. The extent to which the entrepreneur can afford to specialise their contribution to their venture will depend on the size of the venture and the number of people who are working for it. If it is moderately large and has a specialist workforce then the entrepreneur will be able to concentrate on developing vision and a strategy for the venture and providing leadership to it. If it is quite small then the entrepreneur will have to take on functional and administrative tasks as well. Even so, the entrepreneur must be conscious of how the human resource requirements of the business will develop in the future by deciding what skill profile is right for their business and what type of people will be needed to contribute those skills. But employing people with the right skills is not enough; they must be directed to use those skills. They must also be motivated if they are to make a dedicated and effective contribution to the business. This calls for vision and leadership on the part of the entrepreneur.

Human resources represent a source of fixed costs for the business. The possibility of taking on, and letting go of, people in response to short-term demand fluctuations is limited by contractual obligations, social responsibility and the need to invest in training. Further, motivation can only be built on the back of some sense of security. Hence, making a commitment to human resources involves the same type of decisions as making a commitment to operating resources, namely: what will be needed, to what capacity, over what period, must the resource be in-house or can it be hired when needed? However, people are still people even if they are also resources and such decisions must be made with sensitivity.

(10.5) Organisational process and learning as resources

> **Key learning outcome**
>
> Recognition of organisational learning and process as resources critical to the venture's success. Appreciation of the importance of uniqueness, inimitability and non-tradability as characteristics of resources that confer competitive advantage.

The idea that resources are key to the success of a venture was introduced in Section 2.1 with a discussion of the resource- and competence-based views on business performance. It was noted here that what constitutes a resource in these perspectives is quite broad. This section will develop a framework for understanding resources in their wider context and examine further the ideas of resource imitability and tradability as the basis for gaining a sustainable

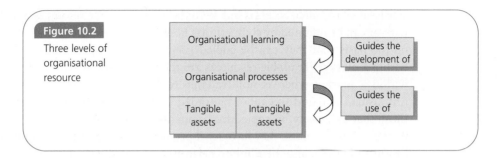

Figure 10.2

Three levels of organisational resource

competitive advantage. The broad definition of resources is at once both an opportunity and a challenge. The opportunity lies in the flexibility of the resource-based perspective to account for a wide spectrum of resource–performance links. The challenge lies in maintaining the theoretical and methodological soundness of the approach given that it can easily become tautological (a circular argument of the form: performance is the result of unique resources, so a high-performing business is such because of its unique resources; and these are freely defined), and the causal link between resources and performance is, in any case, ambiguous. To be rigorous, the approach must be strict in its definition of what constitutes a resource, develop a hypothesis linking that resource causally to performance and then test that hypothesis empirically. An immediate move is to distinguish different types of resource. Clearly, the notion of a resource must be broader than simply physical assets. The resource-based view makes it evident that it is not assets, *per se*, but what the entrepreneur *does* with them that is important. So resources must include the organisational processes that manipulate and utilise assets. But these processes are not static. They must adapt and develop as the venture gets bigger, and its competitive position and situation change. At this level, organisational learning must be counted as a resource. This is depicted in Figure 10.2. The hypothesis is that organisational learning develops organisational processes that then control the use of assets. Assets and processes are (in principle at least) directly observable. Organisational learning is not usually directly observable, but its effect can be gauged by observing changes in the organisational processes. Assets may be divided into three categories. Tangible assets have physical form. Intangible assets do not have physical form, but are nonetheless valuable to the business. Examples here would be patents and brand names. This distinction is made in accounting practice as tangible assets are recorded on the balance sheet but intangible assets are not usually recorded (though some moves have been made in accounting to value such assets). Intellectual assets refer to specific knowledge of technology or products held within the business that directly informs its activities.

What connects the idea of a resource to that of competitive advantage? In short, a resource confers a competitive advantage if it fulfils three criteria:

1. that resource can be used in some way to deliver value to buyers;

2. that resource is unique to the venture;

3. competitors find it hard to imitate or acquire that resource.

The issue of resource access is linked to the idea that some resources may be traded with or can be imitated by competitors. Four types of resource can be distinguished on the basis that they can be copied (imitated) or bought and sold (tradability) within a market. Tradable resources are those that can be 'packaged up' and sold within a market whereas non-tradable resources cannot be detached from the firm using them and so cannot be traded within a market. Imitable resources are those that can easily be copied by competitors. Inimitable resources are not easy to copy, either because they have legal protection, or take time to build up or have causal ambiguity, and their link to performance is not clear. *Commodity* resources are those that are both tradable and can easily be copied. General factory equipment and offices are an example. *Exchangeable* resources are those that cannot be traded, but can easily be copied. An example here might be a unique organisational structure or staff skills and training. *Tradable* resources are those that are not easy to copy, but can be traded freely – patents, copyrights and brand names, for example. Finally, *competitive* resources are those that can neither be traded nor copied. Examples here might include the entrepreneur's visionary leadership, a culture that encourages and rewards the discovery and exploitation of new opportunities or an effective approach to integrating new organisational learning. The most secure competitive advantage is that built on competitive resources. Tradable resources might also be a platform for a time, but being tradable, other entrepreneurs might well set up to establish ventures trading in them, limiting their long-term appeal. Many universities have set up science parks, with the explicit intention of trading in scientific and technological ideas and the patents protecting them. A brand is only valuable if competitors (often larger and better resourced) do not compete with their own brands more strongly.

10.6 Resources, investment and risk

> **Key learning outcome**
>
> An understanding of how and why investing in resources creates risk for the entrepreneurial venture.

In one sense, a business is 'just' the financial, operating and human resources that comprise it. Only when these things are combined can the business generate new value and deliver it to customers. Resources have a value and there is competition to get hold of them. A business is *not* being competitive when it converts input resources into outputs of higher value. It is only being competitive if it is creating more value than its *competitors* can do. Thus resources are used to pursue opportunities and exploiting those opportunities creates new value. The profit created by an entrepreneurial venture is the difference between the cost of the resources that make it up and the value it creates. This is the *return* obtained from investing the resources. Though profits are important for survival and growth, the performance of an entrepreneurial venture cannot be reduced to a simple consideration of the profits it generates. Profits must be considered in relation to two other factors: *opportunity cost* and *risk*.

Resources are bought and sold in markets and so they have a price. This price is not the same as the cost of *using* a resource. The true cost incurred when a resource is used is the value of the opportunity *missed* because the resource is consumed and so cannot be used in an alternative way. This is the *opportunity cost*. If the entrepreneur uses the resources he or she obtains in the most productive way possible then the value created will be higher than that which might have been generated by an alternative investment and so the opportunity cost will be less than the value created. If, on the other hand, the resources are not used in the most productive way possible then some alternative investment could, potentially, give a better return, elsewhere. The opportunity cost will be greater than the value created. Opportunity cost is a fundamental factor in measuring performance. This is because investors are not concerned in the first instance with the *profit* made by a venture but with the *return* they might get if they put their money to an alternative use.

The second factor in considering how well an entrepreneur is using resources is *risk*. We cannot predict the future with absolute accuracy so there is always a degree of uncertainty about what will actually happen. This uncertainty creates risk. No matter what return is anticipated, there is always the possibility that some unforeseen event will lead to that return being lower. Customers may not find the offering as attractive as was expected. Marketing and distribution may prove to be more expensive than was budgeted for. Competitors may be more responsive than was assumed to be the case. Investors make an assessment of the risk that a venture will face. If the risk is high then they will expect to be compensated by a higher rate of return. If they perceive that it is low then they will be happy with a lower return. Consequently there is a payoff between risk and return. The exact way in which expected return is related to risk is quite complex and is a function of the dynamics of the market for capital. The risk–return relationship for investment in an entrepreneurial venture is shown in Figure 10.3. In practice,

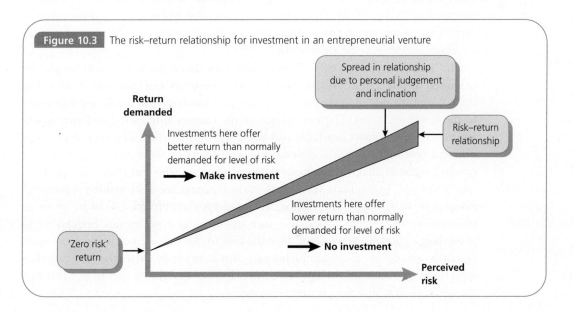

Figure 10.3   The risk–return relationship for investment in an entrepreneurial venture

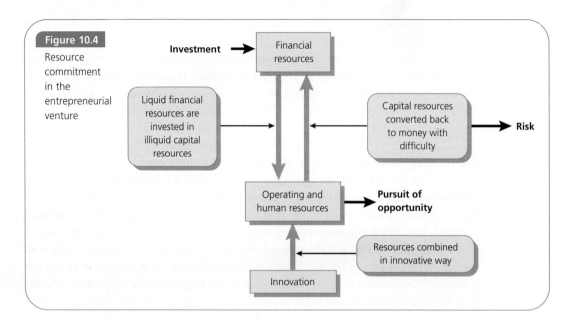

Figure 10.4

Resource commitment in the entrepreneurial venture

institutional investors will aim to hold a *portfolio*, that is, a collection of investments with different levels of risk and return. The objective here is to reduce the overall level of risk for the portfolio.

Risk occurs because resources must be *committed* to a venture. Once money is converted into operating and human resources it is either too difficult or too expensive, or both, to convert it back. Therefore, once resources have been brought together and shaped to pursue a particular opportunity there is no going back if a better opportunity demanding a different shaping of the resources is identified later. In this way, entrepreneurial innovation demands an irreversible commitment of resources (Figure 10.4). The opportunity cost must be faced and it is the investor in the venture who must absorb this cost, not the entrepreneur (although obviously the entrepreneur may be an investor as well).

In summary, if an entrepreneur identifies an opportunity that might be exploited through an innovative way of using resources and then asks investors to back a venture pursuing that opportunity, two fundamental questions will come to the investor's mind. These are: how do the returns anticipated compare to the alternative investments available and what will be the risks? The decision to support the venture or not will depend on the answers to these questions. It should not be forgotten that although investors are people who put *financial* resources into a venture, individuals who work for a business are also making a *personal* investment in it. They expect to be rewarded for their efforts and to be given an opportunity to develop. They also face opportunity costs in not being able to offer their efforts elsewhere, and face the risk of the venture not being successful. Similarly, non-financial commitments may also be made by customers and suppliers who build a relationship with the venture. In this way risk is spread out through the network in which the venture is located.

10.7 Stretch and leverage of entrepreneurial resources

As has been noted earlier, entrepreneurs and their success do appear to be paradoxical. After all, they do not have the same level of resources as established competitors, they lack the internal success factors incumbents have access to (such as costs, established customer relationships) and they do have to pay more for the resources they obtain (paying for the risk premium they present; see Mosakowski (2002) for a recent discussion). The answer to this paradox seems to be that entrepreneurs work their resources harder than do established businesses. The question is, in what way does this working take place? In a very influential paper, Hamel and Prahalad (1993) suggested that ten processes could describe the way that resources were worked. Hamel and Prahalad suggest, 'Competitiveness is born in the gap between a company's resources and its managers' goals'. Their concern in this paper was with business in general, not just entrepreneurship, but it seems entrepreneurs are 'stretchers and leveragers' of resources *par excellence*. The ten processes Hamel and Prahalad discuss are as follows:

- *Convergence* – refers to the creation of a gap between resources and the aspirations of the venture that will act as a driver of competitive advantage. It reflects 'loyalty' to the entrepreneur's vision.

- *Focus* – here refers specifically to a dedication to create and maintain a competitive advantage, and once established, to move on to enhance it and create the next competitive advantage. The entrepreneur must never become complacent with the competitive advantage in place at any one time.

- *Extraction* – new information is coming into the business all the time. Extraction is the process whereby that information is used as the basis of learning about the opportunities available to the venture and how it might enhance its competitive position. That learning must be open and honest, even if it conflicts with long-held and established ideas.

- *Borrowing* – refers to gaining information from all available sources, both inside and outside the business. Effective entrepreneurs use meetings with customers as an opportunity to gain new insights, as well as an opportunity to sell.

- *Blending* – as the venture grows, the people who make it up will tend to specialise in specific areas. This provides the opportunity of improved efficiency. However, individuals can still learn from each other and learn to blend their skills in new and valuable combinations. This is especially important for the entrepreneur, whose role can become detached from the cutting edge of the business as it grows.

- *Balancing* – implies that excellence in one area is not undermined by mediocrity in another. Excellence must be balanced across all areas of the business. The entrepreneur must ensure that examples of excellence in one area provide lessons for, and are shared with, other areas of the business.

● *Recycling* – competitive advantage should be regarded as a resource for the whole organisation, not just some part of it. It should be recycled around the whole venture. This can be particularly important for serial entrepreneurs who wish to transfer competitive advantage in one business to another independent start-up or acquisition.

● *Co-option* – refers to the effectiveness with which the entrepreneur draws other organisations into the venture's network to provide money, skills and information to the venture. It demands an understanding of the structure of the network, what different parties are gaining from the network and the role they play in sustaining the venture.

● *Shielding* – competitive advantage is comparative. It is an advantage *over* competitors. The effective entrepreneur is aware of competitors' (relative) weaknesses, how to use the venture's strengths to attack those weaknesses and how to do so in a way that limits (resource richer) competitors' abilities to counter-attack.

● *Recovery* – relates to the venture's overall agility and its ability to turn information on market opportunities into profitable offerings faster than competitors do. It impacts on every stage in the venture's operations: its ability to obtain information, product development, production, and delivery and distribution.

Necessarily, these ten processes are interlinked. One cannot be managed in the absence of, or without reference to, the others. The entrepreneur will not necessarily see them in these distinct terms, but take them on board in a holistic manner and simply regard them as an integrated aspect of their management practice. However, there is value in considering them separately as a basis for creating strategy out of vision. The stretch and leverage model provides a managerial perspective on a game-theoretical economic model developed by Hirshleifer (2001), who suggests that under certain conditions, the resource weaker competitor may win against the resource richer because it can use its resources to tax the stronger more than the stronger can tax it. This is discussed in more detail in Section 17.1.

Summary of key ideas

● Entrepreneurs must attract resources to their ventures in order to pursue business opportunities.

● Resources occur at three levels: assets, organisational processes and organisational learning.

● Resources are distinguished by the degree to which they can be traded and the ease with which they might be imitated.

● Competitive advantage is most securely based on competitve assets that are difficult to trade and cannot be imitated easily.

- Assets are *valuable* and are traded in *markets*.

- The entrepreneur must *compete* with other businesses to get hold of resources by offering a good return from using them.

- Dedicating resources to a particular venture exposes investors to *risk*, namely the possibility that the return gained will be less than expected.

- Entrepreneurs stretch and leverage their resources to make them work harder in the face of resource richer competitors.

Research themes

Do entrepreneurs stretch and leverage resources?

This study adopts a case-study methodology. Obtain descriptions of a series of entrepreneurial ventures. Case studies are a good source. Ideally they should compare the entrepreneurial firm with a conventional incumbent in the same sector. Otherwise you may find information from a primary research survey. Can you find evidence of the stretch and leverage processes described by Hamel and Prahalad in entrepreneurial businesses? If so, do entrepreneurs recognise these processes in their own management? One way to do this would be to use a survey instrument to outline each process in terms of a short (up to 50 word) scenario and ask entrepreneurs to describe how they would respond to each of these challenges (don't just use the Hamel and Prahalad terms; they will probably not mean much to practising entrepreneurs). For example, a test for co-option might be:

> When you (or one of your people) make a sales call, is your primary objective to:
> (a)   gain a sale
> (b)   obtain information on new opportunities and competitors' activities
> (c)   both of the above

Or for balancing:

> A manager in your business proves to be very effective in dealing with customers. Is your first priority to:
> (a)   keep him/her in the front line with customers
> (b)   promote him/her to lead others working with customers
> (c)   give him/her a wider leadership role and be a champion for the customer within the business

And so on in this style. Code the responses and look for evidence of the Hamel and Prahalad stretch and leverage processes.

Resources and industry structure

The resource-based perspective can be made to make predictions about the performance of individual firms and the structures of the industries in which they are located. Obtain some good descriptions of businesses in a variety of sectors. This may be obtained directly from a survey instrument or published information. Characterise the sectors in terms of the resources they use as discussed in Section 10.2. Attempt to identify sectors that are largely based on commodity resources and those for which competitive resources are more prevalent (other resource types may be included if the sample is large enough). Be prepared to set up strict criteria for judging the inclusion of resources under each type. Categorise them in terms of assets, organisational process and organisational learning. Check if they are tradable and if they are imitable. Best practice is to have someone independently check the categorisation. It can be hypothesised that sectors based on competitive resources will have:

1. higher overall profitability;

2. a greater range of profitabilities (as competitive resources sort the winners from losers); and

3. higher growth performance for winners

when compared to sectors based on commodity resources. Test these predictions using financial data for the sectors. To be statistically robust, at least 25 firms of each resource type should be included.

Suggestions for further reading

Alvarez, S.A. and Barney, J.B. (2002) 'Resource-based theory and the entrepreneurial firm', in Hitt, M.A., Ireland, R.D., Camp, S.M. and Sexton, D.L. (eds) *Strategic Entrepreneurship: Creating a New Mindset*, Oxford: Blackwell.

Alvarez, S.A. and Busenitz, L.W. (2001) 'The entrepreneurship of resource-based theory', *Journal of Management*, Vol. 27, pp. 755–75.

Amit, R. and Schoemaker, P.J.H. (1993) 'Strategic assets and organisational rent', *Strategic Management Journal*, Vol. 14, pp. 33–46.

Bergmann-Lichenstein, B.M. and Brush, C.G. (2001) 'How do "resource bundles" develop and change in new ventures? A dynamic model and longitudinal exploration', *Entrepreneurship Theory and Practice*, Spring, pp. 37–58.

Collis, D.J. (1994) 'How valuable are organisational capabilities?', *Strategic Management Journal*, Vol. 15, pp. 143–52.

Foss, N.J. (ed.) (1997) *Resources, Firms and Strategies: A Reader in the Resource-Based Perspective*, Oxford: Oxford University Press.

Hall, R. (1992) 'The strategic analysis of intangible resources', *Strategic Management Journal*, Vol. 13, pp. 135–44.

Hamel, G. and Prahalad, C.K. (1993) 'Strategy as stretch and leverage', *Harvard Business Review*, March–April, pp. 75–84.

Hirshleifer, J. (2001) 'The paradox of power', in *The Dark Side of the Force: Economic Foundations of Conflict Theory*, Cambridge: Cambridge University Press.

Makadok, R. (2001) 'Towards a synthesis of the resource-based and dynamic capability views of rent creation', *Strategic Management Journal*, Vol. 22, pp. 387–401.

Mosakowski, E. (2002) 'Overcoming resource disadvantages in entrepreneurial firms: when less is more', in Hitt, M.A., Ireland, R.D., Camp, S.M. and Sexton, D.L. (eds) (2002) *Strategic Entrepreneurship: Creating a New Mindset*, Oxford: Blackwell.

Peteraf, M.A. (1993) 'The cornerstones of competitive advantage: a resource based view', *Strategic Management Journal*, Vol. 14, pp. 179–91.

Wernerfelt, B. (1984) 'A resource based view of the firm', *Strategic Management Journal*, Vol. 5, pp. 171–80.

Wernerfelt, B. (1995) 'The resource based view of the firm: ten years after', *Strategic Management Journal*, Vol. 16, pp. 171–4.

Wilcox-King, A. and Zeithaml, C.P. (2001) 'Competencies and firm performance: examining the causal ambiguity paradox', *Strategic Management Journal*, Vol. 22, pp. 75–99.

Yu, A.F. (2001) 'Towards a capabilities perspective of the small firm', *International Journal of Management Reviews*, Vol. 3, No. 3, pp. 185–97.

Selected case material Case 10.1

Floods: Business keeps its head above water

FT

21 November 2002

By **Mark Andress**

For Libor Maly, a Czech internet entrepreneur, the clouds that unleashed a flood of biblical proportions in August have a silver lining.

His company, LMC – which operates the country's largest employment portal, Jobs.cz – was forced to abandon offices in Karlin, Prague's worst-hit business district. It eventually moved into offices 50 per cent bigger than the old at the start of November.

The disruption will reduce this year's revenues by 7 per cent – or several million koruna – none of which Mr Maly will recoup from state compensation or his insurance policy.

That is unfortunate timing for a company investing Kc50m of its own in a powerful programming system that launches in January. But Mr Maly remains hopeful. He reckons today's shrinking job market will expand next year as reconstruction projects kick in.

By the end of 2003 his staff should increase from 35 to 50. 'The floods were the impetus we needed. Without them we'd have stayed in the old office, which we'd grown out of,' he says. 'Our short-term loss will, I hope, turn into long-term gain.'

Mr Maly's strength in adversity, despite his city's worst floods in 500 years, is typically Czech. 'Most businesses that experienced big problems started functioning again very quickly. When the chips are down, Czechs react with courage and solidarity,' says Jaromir Drabek, president of the Economic Chamber of the Czech Republic. 'But it'll take a year before we can say which company was able to continue and who wasn't. In some towns, infrastructure is so badly damaged it'll take several years to put right.'

So far, the government estimates direct flood damage at Kc70bn. The state will pay more than one-third of that as it struggles to keep a ballooning fiscal deficit under control. Finding those funds almost brought the fragile new ruling coalition government down in September when its 'flood package' of tax increases failed to pass through parliament by one vote.

Instead, ministries have freed up to Kc7bn by reprioritising spending, a European Investment Bank loan will provide Kc12bn over three years, and Czech Telecom's planned privatisation will fund about Kc12.5bn of transport infrastructure repairs.

Premier Vladimir Spidla even floated the idea of a flood tax, which could be discussed in mid-December when the cabinet tackles fiscal reform.

In addition, the Czech Republic is set to receive €129m from the European Union's Solidarity Fund, set up to help central Europe's flood-afflicted states. Meanwhile, insurance companies will pay out Kc30.5bn, with the private sector footing the remainder of the bill.

Mr Drabek estimates businesses suffered Kc20bn in direct damage to property and lost production, of which insurers will pay 30 per cent. Secondary damage, such as disruption to supply networks, remains unquantifiable.

State help to flood-afflicted business amounts to providing Kc500m in state guarantees and interest-rate contributions on commercial loans, and a further Kc150m in loans to small enterprises.

By contrast, the state offered cash hand-outs to stricken families, cheap loans for the purchase or construction of homes, and Kc1bn in aid to farmers, who suffered Kc2.5bn in damages to flooded fields.

'State aid to business has hardly been enough, especially compared with how much the state gave its citizens,' complains Petr Kuzel, president of the Prague Chamber of Commerce.

Economically, the floods will have a minor impact on growth. The finance ministry revised its prediction of 2002 gross domestic product (GDP) growth downwards from 3 per cent to 2.7 per cent.

Next year, the economy should bounce back with growth of 3.3 per cent.

Production output is expected to take a hit as damage to several industrial plants, particularly in the chemical sector, results in a shortfall in sales.

Tourism, Prague's lifeblood, took a severe blow as August brought 30 per cent fewer visitors. The industry could suffer a 20 per cent dent in annual takings as misconceptions about the extent of flood damage persist abroad.

Although the waterlogged Prague metro won't resume full service until the spring, the floods' scars remain invisible to the tourist eye, with most attractions reopened long ago.

Construction is set to profit as it puts the country right. Output rose 6.7 per cent in the month after the floods. The industry expects flood-related work to generate Kc5bn next year, 2 per cent of total revenues.

But not everyone is optimistic. Metrostav, the country's third largest construction company, expects turnover to increase 6 per cent instead of the initially projected 10 per cent because it fears customers will cancel or postpone large building projects and focus on reconstruction work instead.

'Small construction companies will profit because there'll be thousands of orders scattered across the country to repair houses, pavements, roads,' says Pavel Pilat, Metrostav's sales director. 'The opportunity for big companies will come when anti-flood barriers and flood basins are built – those are billion koruna orders.'

Source: *Financial Times*, 21 November 2002.

Engine of growth hampered by credit shortage

FT

16 September 2002

By **Stefan Wagstyl**

Otto Tlusty, the Czech owner of MAO, a construction company he founded in 1990, is precisely the sort of entrepreneur that economic policymakers want to encourage.

With 150 workers, he makes a significant contribution to the town of Kladno, near Prague, where he is based. He is not short of ideas, customers or skilled employees, but he cannot secure enough finance to develop his business as he would wish.

Mr Tlusty blames the banks. 'It is very difficult to get credit, even though I have always repaid loans. I have collateral and I often work for municipalities on projects which are partly financed by the European Union,' says the 38-year-old builder. 'It's a numbers game. They only give you loans if you have money already.'

Criticising banks is common among owners of small businesses almost everywhere. But it is particularly frequent in central and eastern Europe because of the region's general shortage of capital.

Small companies are an engine of growth in the ex-communist states, accounting for more than 50 per cent of employment in eastern Europe (excluding the former Soviet Union, except for the Baltic states), according to a European Commission report published this year. These 6m companies are mostly very small, employing fewer than 10 people, often drawn from the owner's family.

These businesses are mostly financed from family funds and from profits. Three years ago a report from Accenture, the management consultancy, found that entrepreneurs were deeply suspicious of banks. 'The overwhelming feeling was that banks were too cautious and that the cost of borrowing was too high,' said the report.

Many entrepreneurs, such as Mr Tlusty, still feel the same. But there is strong evidence that banks are becoming more interested in small and medium-sized businesses and are starting to offer better services at lower costs.

Competition is the driving force. Loans to big companies, especially the subsidiaries of multinationals, attract low margins because these borrowers can afford to shop around. Smaller companies are more likely to stick with one bank for a range of services.

Kurt Geiger, head of financial institutions at the European Bank for Reconstruction and Development (EBRD), says: 'Banks in the region realise more and more that medium-sized companies, if not very small companies, are attractive because larger companies have several ways of raising finance and show less loyalty.'

Recognising the role of small companies in economic development, the EBRD has in the past decade directed €3.5bn, acting mainly through commercial banks. The EU has supported this work through a subsidy for loans to businesses in EU candidate countries in a scheme under which €600m is to be lent via the EBRD.

The EBRD estimates the premium that smaller companies pay for their credit in comparison with big corporations has fallen from 3 to 5 per cent to 2 to 3 per cent, broadly in line with EU rates.

The change is clearest in central Europe, where the banking market – and competition among multinational banks – is most developed. But it is visible even in Bulgaria, where Union Bank, a leading commercial institution, has reduced its premium from 4 to 6 per cent to 3 to 4 per cent, according to the EBRD.

Borrowing costs have declined fastest in Poland, probably because the country has drawn the largest number of multinational banks, creating intense competition for customers.

One foreign banker says that interest charged on loans to medium-sized businesses have actually fallen too far and banks are trying to raise the premium by 0.5 percentage points or so. 'These loans have been violently underpriced,' he says, declining to be identified for fear of giving commercial ammunition to competitors.

But, elsewhere, many bankers remain cautious, notably in the Czech Republic and Slovakia, still recovering from banking crises that involved over-generous lending.

Andrea Varese, a director of Pkosa, Poland's largest privatised bank now owned by Unicredito Italiano, says the higher costs of loans to small companies are justified by the higher costs borne by banks and the higher risks, starting with the fact that the fate of a small business usually depends on a single person – the owner. Mr Varese says: 'If the head of a big corporation dies in an accident, they find a replacement. With a small company they may not find anybody.'

Bank credit officers are gradually learning how to manage such clients. They cannot apply the traditional approach of demanding reams of documents as a small company's true condition can rarely be accurately described on paper. Instead, bankers are being encouraged to visit entrepreneurs at their places of work. One western banker says: 'For some bankers this is revolutionary.'

Banks are also introducing training sessions for entrepreneurs on how to approach banks with credible business plans.

Mr Varese says small companies cannot expect their loans will ever come at the same price as big enterprises. 'The costs are higher whether you are in Poland or in Italy.'

For Mr Tlusty talk of costs is irrelevant. He complains that his bank has in the past granted him a loan only if he signs a blank cheque in the bank's favour.

He does not want to do this again. He will instead try to run the company from its own resources, even if it means taking on less business and employing fewer people.

Source: *Financial Times*, 16 September 2002.

Discussion point

What are the resource issues for entrepreneurs operating in the post-central planning economies of central and eastern Europe and how do these differ from those in mature capitalist economies?

Chapter 11

The entrepreneurial venture and the entrepreneurial organisation

Chapter overview

The fundamental task of the entrepreneur is to create or to change an organisation. This chapter explores what is meant by 'organisation'. The first section explores the way in which entrepreneurs (and other managers) use metaphors (either consciously or unconsciously) to create a picture of the organisations they manage. The second section looks at how entrepreneurs use organisations to control the resources that make up the venture. The third and fourth sections develop a broader view of organisation and consider the entrepreneur operating within a network of resources. The final section considers how this can provide an insight into developing a practical entrepreneurial strategy.

11.1 The concept of organisation

Key learning outcome

An appreciation of how different ideas of 'organisation' aid understanding of the entrepreneurial approach to management.

The notion of 'organisation' is fundamental to management thinking. An organisation is what a manager works for and organising it is what they do. The entrepreneur may create a new organisation or develop an existing one. Whichever of these options they choose, they create a new organisational world. Organising resources is the means to the end of creating new value. If entrepreneurship is to be understood then the nature of organisation needs to be appreciated.

There are a number of ways in which we can approach the concept of organisation. We cannot see any organisation directly, all we can actually observe is individuals taking actions. We call upon the idea of organisation to explain why those actions are co-ordinated and directed towards some common goal. If we wish to understand how an organisation actually co-ordinates those actions we must create a picture of it using *metaphors*. Thus, we can think of the organisation both as an *entity*, an object in its own right, and as a *process*, a way of doing things. The type of metaphor which is used is important because it influences the way in which management challenges are perceived and approached. It underlies the entrepreneur's management style. There are three types of metaphor. *Active* metaphors are created consciously and explicitly as a strategy for developing understanding. An example here is the use of ideas from evolutionary biology to create a model of populations of organisations, which was discussed in Section 2.1. *Dormant* metaphors are those that are clear when we think about them, but we do not often do so. An example here would be the use of the word 'organisation' itself. Its root is clearly related to that of 'organ' and 'organism', suggesting a biological metaphor. Another example is the use of the word 'corporate', which is derived from *corpus*, the Latin word for body (we also talk of a corpus of knowledge). Finally, *extinct* metaphors are those that are so deeply embedded in our thinking that we only very rarely challenge them. Examples here are to 'see' an opportunity (we don't *actually* see it) or for a business to 'feel' its way forward (a business can't actually 'feel' anything). All three types of metaphor are common in business. The student who knows a little geology might recognise the words active, dormant and extinct as referring to different types of volcano. We are using a metaphor to understand metaphors! Gareth Morgan (1986) provides an extensive and critical study of how we understand organisation through metaphor in his book *Images of Organisation*.

Some conceptualisations of organisation which are important to understanding entrepreneurship are as follows.

The organisation as a co-ordinator of actions

People do not work in isolation in an organisation. They get together to co-ordinate and share tasks. Differentiating tasks allows a group of people to achieve complex ends that individuals working on their own could not hope to achieve. An organisation is a framework for co-ordinating tasks. It provides direction, routines and regularities for disparate activities. An organisation has goals which are what the people working together in the organisation aim to achieve as a group. The organisation acts to align and direct the actions of individuals towards the achievement of those goals.

Entrepreneurs are powerful figures within their own organisations. Indeed, the organisation is the vehicle through which they achieve their ambitions, it extends their scope and allows them to do things that they could not do as an individual. The organisation is the tool entrepreneurs use to create their entire new world.

They use their influence and leadership to shape the organisation and direct it towards where they wish to go.

The organisation as an independent agent

An agent is simply something that acts in its own right. Regarding the organisation as an agent means that we give it a character quite separate from that of the people who make it up. The organisation takes actions on its own behalf and has its own distinguishing properties. Thus we can talk about the organisation 'having' a strategy which it uses to pursue 'its' goals. We can talk about the assets 'it' owns and the culture 'it' adopts. This conceptualisation is important from a social and legal perspective. The business organisation is regarded as a legal entity in its own right, quite separate from the identities of its owners and managers. The firm has rights and responsibilities which are distinct from those of its managers. Recognising the organisation as an independent agent is important because it reminds us that the organisations created by entrepreneurs have an existence independent of their creators.

The organisation as a network of contracts

Organisations are made up of people who contribute their labour to the organisation on the basis that they will receive something in return. The organisation is the means people use to pursue their own individual ends. The idea that the organisation is a network of contracts is based on the notion that people work together within a framework of agreements defining the contribution that each individual will make to the organisation as a whole, and what they can expect from the organisation in return. These agreements are referred to as *contracts*.

Organisational contracts take a variety of forms. They may be quite formal and be legally recognised, for example a contract of employment. Frequently, however, a major part of the contract will not be formalised. Many of the commitments and responsibilities that people feel toward their organisation and those they feel it has towards them are unwritten. They are based on ill-defined expectations as to how people should work together and act towards one other. These aspects of the contract may not even be recognised until they are broken by one party. Organisations are built on *trust* and the nature of the contracts that hold the organisation together are a major factor in defining its culture.

The idea of the organisation as a network of contracts is important because it reminds us that individuals do not completely subsume their own interests to those of the organisation, rather the organisation is the means by which they pursue their own goals. They will pursue the organisation's interests only if they align with their own. This concept of the organisation also highlights the fact that the individual's relationship with his or her organisation goes beyond the written legal contract. It is also defined by trust and unspoken expectations. Individuals will only be motivated to contribute to the organisation if those expectations are met, and their trust is not broken.

The organisation as a collection of resources

Organisations are created from resources including capital (money), people and productive assets such as buildings and machinery. The resource-based view of the firm sees it in terms of the collection of resources that make it up. The organisation is built from resources that can be bought and sold through open markets. What makes a particular firm unique is the *combination* of resources that comprise it. Innovation is simply finding *new* combinations of resources.

Having access to appropriate resources and using them both creatively and efficiently is central to entrepreneurial success. It should not be forgotten that people are the key resource since only they can make capital and productive resources work in new and different ways. The idea of the firm as a collection of resources reminds us that the entrepreneur must be an effective manager of resources, which means being a manager of people as much as a manager of assets and processes.

The organisation as a system

A system is a co-ordinated body of things, or elements, arranged in a pattern of permanent or semi-permanent relationships. The notion that the business organisation is a system develops from the idea that a firm takes resource inputs and attempts to convert them into outputs of higher value. The greater the value that is added, the more productive the system. The elements of the organisational system are the people who make it up and the manner in which they are grouped. The actions people take are defined by the pattern of relationships that exist between them. Permanent relationships and consistent actions lead to regular routines and programmes. The systems view of organisation explains the way organisations develop and evolve by drawing on ideas such as feedback loops and control mechanisms.

The idea that the organisation is a system is valuable because it emphasises the dynamic nature of the organisation. It is what the organisation *does* that matters. It also draws attention to the fact that routines take on a life of their own as the system develops its own momentum. Control mechanisms freeze the organisation's way of doing things. This is valuable. They lock in the organisation's source of competitive advantage. However, in order to remain innovative, the entrepreneurial organisation must avoid inertia, which requires a continual assessment of the way it does things and a willingness to challenge existing routines if necessary. Entrepreneurial businesses achieve success by being more flexible and responsive to environmental signals than established firms. New contributions to systems thinking from areas such as chaos theory and non-equilibrium dynamics are providing a valuable new perspective on the way entrepreneurial businesses function and how they succeed.

The organisation as a processor of information

Information is a critical part of business success since information, properly used, leads to knowledge and knowledge can lead to competitive success. The organisation can be thought of as a device for processing information, for example information on what needs the customer has, what products will satisfy those needs, how they can be prepared and delivered efficiently, how their benefits can be communicated to customers and so on. In this view, the performance of the firm is determined by the quality of the information it has and how well it uses it. Further, by co-ordinating the intelligence of the people who constitute it, the organisation as a whole can exhibit intelligence. It not only uses information, but can constantly learn how to use information better.

Innovation is at the heart of entrepreneurship and innovation must be based on knowledge. The idea of the organisation as an information processor highlights the fact that the success of the entrepreneurial organisation does not just lie in its innovation but in the way it *uses* that innovation and learns to go on using it. The entrepreneurial organisation achieves flexibility and responsiveness through its willingness to learn about its customers and itself.

These different perspectives on the organisation are not mutually exclusive; indeed, to some extent they are complementary. None of the perspectives gives a complete picture of what the entrepreneurial firm is about, rather each gives a different set of insights into what the firm is, how it performs its tasks, the relation it has to the people who make it up and what the basis of its success might be. If entrepreneurs are to fully understand their business then they must learn to use all these perspectives to gain a complete view.

(11.2) Organisation and the control of resources

> **Key learning outcome**
>
> An understanding of the way the entrepreneur controls resources in their organisation.

Entrepreneurs use resources to achieve their aims in that they combine resources in a way which is innovative and offers new value to customers. This *is* the pursuit of opportunity. Resources are brought together under the control of an organisation. The power of entrepreneurs to control resources directly is limited because there is only so much that they can do as individuals. Therefore, entrepreneurs must shape the organisation they build and use it to configure the resources to which they have access. As the organisation grows and increases in complexity, tasks must be delegated down the organisational hierarchy. Controlling the resources in the organisation means controlling the actions of the people in the organisation who use them. If entrepreneurs are to be effective in leading and directing their organisation then they must understand how the resources that make it up can be controlled.

Entrepreneurs must make a decision as to what they will control themselves and what control they will pass on to others. The balance of this decision will depend on the size and complexity of the organisation, the type and expertise of the people who make it up, the type of resources with which the organisation is working and the strategy it adopts. This decision must be subject to constant revision as the organisation grows, develops and changes. Even if an entrepreneur has delegated the management of resources to other people within the organisation this does not mean that he or she has given up *all* control over them. A number of control mechanisms are retained (see Figure 11.1).

Directed action

The entrepreneur may retain control by directing that specific tasks are undertaken. The course to be followed will be instructed in detail. The actions are likely to be short term, or repetitive, with well-defined outcomes. By directing specific actions the entrepreneur is using others to undertake tasks he or she would perform themselves but lacks the time to do so.

Routines and procedures

Routines and procedures are used to establish patterns of action to be repeated. No direct control is exercised, but people are expected to follow the course of actions set down. The actions defined by the routine may be specified either in outline or in great detail. The possibility of deviating from the pattern or modifying it will vary depending on the degree of control desired and the need to constrain the outcomes of the actions. When the organisation is too complex to be controlled by directed action, the entrepreneur may concentrate on controlling through procedures.

Organisational strategy

A strategy is a framework for thinking about, and guiding the actions of, individuals within the organisation. The organisation's strategy will be directed towards the achievement of specific goals. It will define the major areas of resource deployment (usually through *budgeting*) and outline the main programmes of activity. The strategy may be imposed by the entrepreneur, or it may be developed through discussion and consensus. People within the organisation might be given a great deal of latitude to develop their own projects of action within the strategy. They will, however, be expected to be guided by the strategy, work towards its goals and operate within its resource constraints. A strategy, even if well defined, offers a greater scope for interpretation than does a routine.

Organisational culture

The concept of organisational culture is a very important one. A culture is the pattern of beliefs, perspectives and attitudes which shape the actions of the people within the organisation. An organisation's culture is largely unwritten. Its existence may not even be recognised until someone acts outside its norms. Culture is very important in creating motivation and setting attitudes. It can be a critical aspect of competitiveness. For example, a positive attitude towards customer service, constantly seeking innovation or greeting change positively are all determined by culture. Things such as these cannot be enforced through rules and procedures so culture is difficult to manage. It is a state of mind, rather than a resource to be manipulated. However, the entrepreneur can help establish a culture in their organisation by leading by example and being clear and consistent about what is expected from people, what behaviour is acceptable to the organisation and what is not. Tom Peters and Robert Waterman (1982), in their highly influential study of US business, *In Search of Excellence*, identified culture as a critical factor in the success of an organisation.

Communicated vision

A vision is a picture of the better world the entrepreneur wishes to create. The vision is the thing that draws the entrepreneur forward and gives them direction. The entrepreneur can, by sharing that vision, communicate the direction in which the organisation must go. If the people who make up the organisation see the vision and accept what it can offer, then the organisation as a whole will gain a sense of direction. However, a vision only specifies an end, not a means. It indicates where the organisation can go, not the path it must take. A vision leaves open the potential for a wide range of possibilities and courses of action. Different courses must be judged in terms of how effective they will be in leading the organisation towards the vision.

The hierarchy of resource control devices

These means of controlling resources form a hierarchy, as shown in Figure 11.1. As it is ascended the entrepreneur becomes less specific in their direction. Their control becomes less direct and immediate. On the other hand, they give the people who work with them more latitude to use their own talent and insights and so make a more substantial contribution to the business. The exact mix of controls used will depend on the size of the organisation, the people who make it up, the tasks in hand and the entrepreneur's personal style. The controls adopted, and the way they are used, will form the basis of the entrepreneur's leadership strategy.

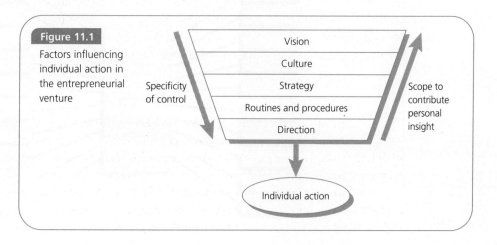

Figure 11.1

Factors influencing individual action in the entrepreneurial venture

Specificity of control

Vision
Culture
Strategy
Routines and procedures
Direction

Scope to contribute personal insight

Individual action

11.3 Markets and hierarchies

Key learning outcome

An appreciation of the distinction between the market and the hierarchy as forms of organisation.

The business world is full of organisations which offer goods and services to each other and to individual consumers. These goods and services are traded in *markets*. Organisations and markets represent different ways in which individuals can arrange exchanges between themselves.

A market consists of a range of sellers offering their goods to a number of buyers. It is characterised by short-term contracts centred on exchanged products, as shown in Figure 11.2. Buyers are free to select the seller they wish to buy from. The seller must offer goods at a price dictated by the market. Classical economics assumes that the goods of one supplier are much the same as the goods of any other, although in practice, sellers may be able to differentiate their products from those of competitors. If this differentiation offers advantages to the buyer, then the seller may be able to sustain a price higher than the market norm. In a market, the relationship between the buyer and seller is centred on the product exchanged between them. The seller has no obligation other than to supply the product specified and the buyer has no obligation other than to pay for it. The relationship is short-term with the buyer being free to go to another supplier in the future.

People do not just use markets as a means of organising exchange, they also form organisations such as business firms. Organisations are sometimes referred to as non-market *hierarchies*, indicating the way in which the individuals who make them assign responsibilities. In a hierarchy individuals still supply a product, their *labour*, to the organisation. Different parts of the hierarchy will supply

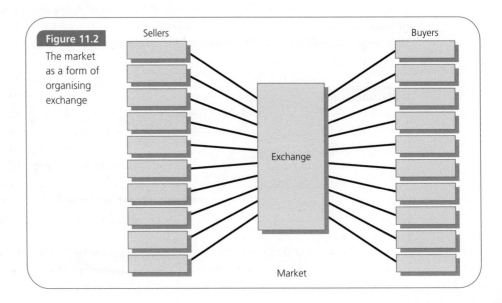

Figure 11.2

The market as a form of organising exchange

Sellers

Buyers

Exchange

Market

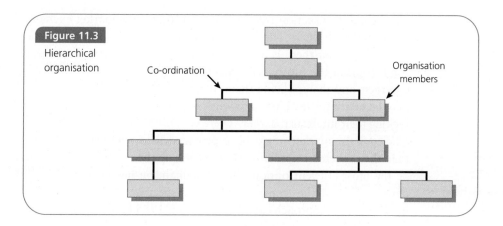

Figure 11.3

Hierarchical organisation

Co-ordination

Organisation members

products and services to other parts and to the organisation as a whole. The factory may pass on its products to the marketing department for example, or the accounts department may supply financial services. In a hierarchy the relationship between individuals goes beyond the mere product or service they agree to supply. It has a long-term character based on both formal and informal criteria. A hierarchical organisation is based on long-term commitments, as depicted in Figure 11.3.

A hierarchy represents a loss of economic freedom. Within an organisation individuals must use each other's services. They cannot shop around in the market for a better deal. Why then do organisations form? The answer is that markets do not come for free. There is a cost associated with assessing what is available. Gathering information may be expensive. If individuals set up long-term contracts then this cost is reduced. Further, if the product is complex and the relationship short term, the seller may be tempted to cheat and supply less than expected. The buyer may face a cost associated with *monitoring* what the seller supplies. The monitoring cost is reduced if the buyer and seller *trust* one other. Trust is best built in a long-term relationship, and most easily built if the buyer and seller are part of the same organisation.

The 'market' and the 'hierarchy' are pure types lying at the opposite ends of a spectrum of organisational types. Organisations in the real world lie somewhere in between. They have some of the characteristics of a hierarchy, with relationships based on long-term agreements and formal contracts, and some of the characteristics of markets in which individuals come and go, offering their labour and services on a competitive basis. This is true not only within organisations, but also between them. Organisations do not just rely on markets, they set up contracts and make long-term commitments to each other. The network provides a more realistic model of how entrepreneurial ventures actually operate than either of the pure types of the market and the hierarchy.

This observation has led to the development of a powerful economic approach to understanding why organisations form and the shape they take. This approach is known as *transaction cost economics* introduced in Chapter 2. The fundamental idea behind transaction cost economics is that some market exchanges have costs associated with them. These costs arise because with some transactions one party may believe that there is a chance that the other party will renege on the deal at some point in the future. This means that they must invest in setting up binding contracts and then policing them. If these contract costs become too high, then it may be better for the parties to work together within an organisational setting, so locking their interests together. There is a cost associated with this move in that the efficiency the market might have provided is lost. However, if this loss is lower than the expected transaction cost, setting up the organisational structure will still be the most efficient option. Oliver Williamson has been at the forefront of the development of the transaction cost perspective, and a full exploration of the insights of this approach can be found in his 1985 book *The Economic Institutions of Capitalism* and his 1991 article.

It is often the case that entrepreneurs prefer to work within an organisational setting rather than 'expose' themselves to market uncertainties. One area of resistance that is often encountered is in entrepreneurs sharing the secrets of their innovation with outsiders, who they feel might 'steal' it. Another is they might doubt the commitment of external investors (particularly banks and venture capitalists) to the broader aims of the venture, asserting that they are 'only out for themselves'. As a result of these concerns, they try to bring as many transactions within their organisation as possible. However real such concerns are, the entrepreneur must be aware of the costs, both direct and in terms of loss of flexibility, in adopting organisation-based rather than market-based solutions.

11.4 Networks

> **Key learning outcome**
>
> An understanding of the concept of the network and its role in the entrepreneurial process.

Individuals use both organisations and markets to facilitate exchanges between themselves. Markets offer a freedom to choose whereas permanent hierarchies emerge when trust is important. Real-life organisations possess some characteristics of both markets and hierarchies. A business organisation has a definite character. It is an agent with legal rights and responsibilities, it has a name. People will know whether they work for it or not. It will have some sort of internal structure.

A business organisation does not exist in isolation. It will be in contact with a whole range of other organisations. Some of these relationships will be established through the market but others may have a longer-term, contractual nature. Businesses set up contracts with suppliers. They may agree to work with a distributor to develop a new market together. An organisation providing investment capital to the venture may be invited to offer advice and support. An entrepreneur may call upon an expert friend to offer advice on marketing. An old business associate may provide an introduction to a new customer. Rather than think about an organisation as closed and sitting in a market, it is better to think of it as being located within a *network* of relationships with other organisations and individuals. In this view the firm does not have a definite boundary. The individuals who make it, and the organisations it comes into contact with, merge into one another. The network is built from relationships which possess both hierarchical and market characteristics. These relationships will be established on the basis of market-led decisions, formal contracts, expectations and trust.

When a new venture is established it must locate itself in a network. This means that it must work to establish a new set of relationships with suppliers, customers, investors and any others who might offer support. The new venture will need to compete with established players. This means that it must break into and modify the network of relationships that *they* have established. A tight network is one in which relationships are established and the parties to them are largely satisfied with these relationships. A loose network is one in which relationships are distant and easily modified. A tight network will be hard to break into, a loose one will be easier. Once a firm is located in a tight network it will find it easier to protect its business from new challengers.

Understanding the nature of the network is important to the success of the entrepreneurial venture. Managing the network will be a crucial part of the strategy for the venture. In particular, the entrepreneur must make decisions in relation to the following questions:

● What is the existing network of relationships into which the new venture must break?

● What is the nature of the relationships that make up the network? Is the network tight or loose? Are the relationships based on formal contracts or on trust?

● How can the new venture actually break into this network of relationships? (Who must be contacted? In what way? What must they be offered?)

● How can the network be used to provide support to the venture?

● What resources (capital, people, productive assets) will the network provide?

● How can risk be shared through the network?

● How can relationships in the network provide a basis for sustaining competitive advantage?

The process of developing answers to these questions will be explored in Part 3 of this book.

In short, a network is a kind of glue which holds a business community together. An entrepreneur initiating a new venture must be active in breaking into a network. Once this has been achieved, the network can be called upon to support them (see Figure 11.4). Thompson (2003) provides a theoretical account of networks and their analysis.

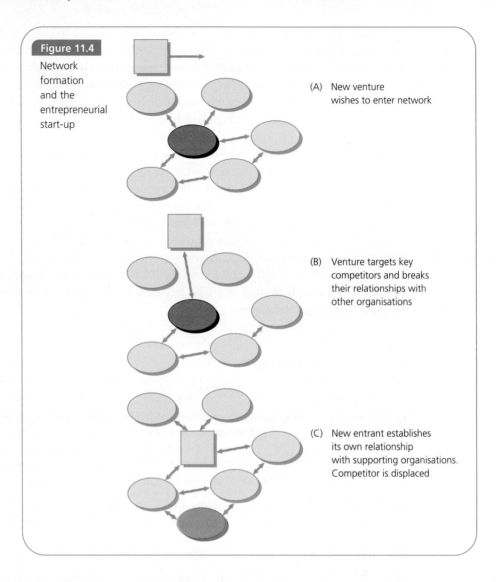

Figure 11.4

Network formation and the entrepreneurial start-up

(A) New venture wishes to enter network

(B) Venture targets key competitors and breaks their relationships with other organisations

(C) New entrant establishes its own relationship with supporting organisations. Competitor is displaced

⟨11.5⟩ The hollow organisation and the extended organisation

> **Key learning outcome**
>
> An understanding of how the network may be used to increase the power of the entrepreneurial organisation.

The idea that an organisation is wider than that part of it which is legally defined as the firm provides the entrepreneur with an opportunity. The network offers entrepreneurs the possibility of moving beyond the limits of their own organisation and achieving a great deal more than it would allow them to achieve in isolation. Two types of organisation in particular use the potential of the network.

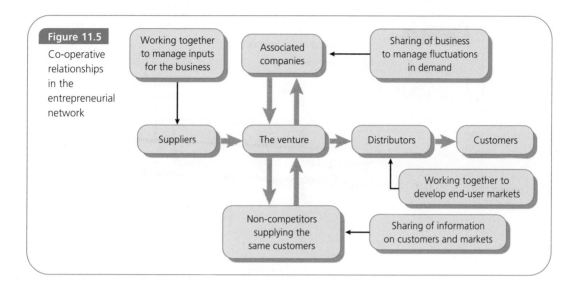

Figure 11.5

Co-operative relationships in the entrepreneurial network

Extended organisations

The extended organisation is one which uses the resources of other organisations in its network to achieve its goals (Figure 11.5). Access to these resources is gained by building long-term, supportive and mutually beneficial relationships. Particularly important are suppliers who provide the venture with the inputs it needs, associated organisations in the same business who can help manage fluctuations in demand, and distributors who can get the firm's goods or services to its customers. Distributors need not be limited to the functions of storing and transporting goods. They can also be active partners in developing a new market and add their support to achieving and sustaining a strong competitive position. The business may also develop a productive relationship with other businesses that supply the same customers with non-competing products. Here information on customers and their needs can be exchanged and market research costs shared. It may also be possible to share selling and distribution costs.

Hollow organisations

The hollow organisation is one which exists not so much to do things itself but to bring other organisations together. In effect it creates value by building a new network or making an existing one more efficient (Figure 11.6). The formal organisation is kept as small as possible, it may only be a single office, and it sticks to its essential or *core* activities. A common example of a hollow organisation is one which simply 'markets' products. It will buy these products from the company which manufactures them. It will use independent distributors to get the product to customers. It may call upon the services of separate market research and advertising agencies. It may even contract-in its sales team. The hollow organisation does not manufacture, distribute or advertise goods or services. It simply exists to bring

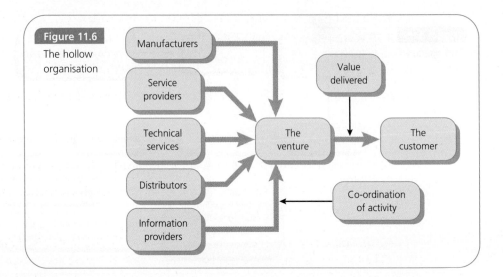

Figure 11.6

The hollow organisation

together the organisations that perform these functions. It is rewarded from the value it creates by co-ordinating their activities.

An excellent example of what can be achieved by adopting a hollow organisational strategy is that of Naxos Records, a venture founded by the Hong Kong-based German entrepreneur Klaus Heymann. This is a business which has established a market-leading position in the low-cost classical CD market. Yet the core organisation does little itself except co-ordinate the production and marketing of the product. Musicians and orchestras (often from eastern Europe) are commissioned as they are needed. Recording facilities are hired in. Production of the CD and packaging of it are outsourced (usually in the Far East). Distribution is via independent retailers.

Factors affecting choice of organisational form

Both the extended organisation and the hollow organisation are attractive options for the entrepreneur. There are a number of reasons for this:

- they are easy to set up;
- the initial investment needed is small and entry costs are low;
- they allow the entrepreneur to concentrate on their core skills;
- they are flexible and can be easily modified;
- fixed costs are minimised;
- they allow the entrepreneur access to the resources of other organisations;
- growth is relatively easy to manage.

Competition to set up hollow and extended organisations can be quite intense because they are both such attractive options for starting new ventures. If they are to be successful entrepreneurs must be quite sure of the strategy they are adopting. In particular they must be confident about:

● where the business will be located in the value-addition chain;

● the value they are adding, i.e. why customers will benefit from what the business has to offer;

● why the product they are offering is different from what is already on offer;

● how they will manage the relationships on which the business will depend;

● how they will sustain those relationships in the face of competitors trying to break the relationships it has established.

These are important ideas which will be developed further in Part 3 of this book.

The Internet has made a great impact on the world of business. New Internet ventures like the book retailer Amazon and the computer supplier Dell have been very high-profile stock market successes. The merger of the media company Time Warner with the online service provider *America On-Line* (AOL) created great interest and initially a considerable mark-up on the stock-market value of the separate companies.

The Internet is primarily a communication system, albeit one of great sophistication and reach. The reason it is creating such high expectations is the way it is enabling information to be stored and accessed by organisations and the facility it offers to pass information between them. Advocates of the potential competitive advantages the Internet are offering to business are keen to draw a distinction between what is referred to as *e-commerce*, the use of the Internet as an adjunct to selling and promotional activities, and *e-business*, the use of the Internet to enhance the performance of the organisation's entire operational stance. E-business goes beyond just selling. It is concerned with managing the business's whole value-addition chain and creating an active, two-way dialogue with the customer, not just sending a message to them.

Strategically, the Internet is encouraging the development of hollow organisations. This is because it is so powerful in co-ordinating the activities of otherwise separate organisations in an efficient and relatively low-cost way. Many new Internet start-ups are concerned not so much with manufacturing or even direct service delivery. They are providing a facility that brings traditional suppliers and potential consumers together. Customers appreciate the power of the Internet in terms not only of making purchase easy but also of its ability to provide information, making the purchase decision more informed. Suppliers recognise the potential to create new business through a relatively low-cost route. However, many also appreciate the tendency of the Internet to make buyer price comparison easier, and so competition keener.

The key question for the Internet-based hollow organisation is not so much gaining entry, which is quite straightforward: it is gaining long-term competitive advantage that presents the challenge. Low entry costs are attractive for entrepreneurs, and investors, because they reduce risk. However, this also means competitors find it easy to follow. Achieving competitive advantage is more difficult. Internet distributors, like any other distributor, cannot significantly alter the final product or service the consumer uses. Internet distributors have lower costs than traditional distributors, but costs can only be reduced so far. In any case, offering the buyer a lower price reduces the venture's profits. Ultimately, successful Internet ventures will be those which build a relationship with customers based on range of offerings, quality of service and reputation supported by a trusted brand. The Internet may be changing the business world, but it is not changing its fundamental rules.

Summary of key ideas

- The entrepreneur must bring the resources they use together in the form of an *organisation*.

- Organisations are best understood through the use of *metaphors*: the things they are 'like'.

- The *open market* and the *closed hierarchy* are pure forms of organisation.

- The entrepreneurial organisation is best thought of as a *network* of relationships defined through markets and formal hierarchies. The network lies somewhere between the two pure forms.

- Entrepreneurs can create new value by building *hollow* or *extended* organisations which co-ordinate the activities of other organisations.

Research theme

The role of networks in intranet ventures

The Internet has provided a number of opportunities for entrepreneurs. As a technology it has particularly facilitated the development of ventures based on networked and hollow organisational forms. Good case studies of many Internet-based ventures are now available. Using such case studies (the more the better), identify networked organisational forms in which the venture itself has only a low resource base, but is active in co-ordinating and focusing the activities of other (established and probably much larger) organisations. What is the structure of network linkages? To what extent does the venture prioritise relationships with these other organisations? How does the venture manage that relationship, and in particular how does it establish and maintain unique access to that organisation and keep competitors out. How does the venture add value as far as customers are concerned? What are the implications for the venture gaining sustainable competitive advantage? (Refer to Chapter 22 for ideas here.) Select case studies of Internet ventures that have been both successful and not. Be prepared to compare the venture with established competitors using a more established organisational form. What does this suggest as to the possibilities, strengths and limitations of the networked organisational form? What are the key success factors for success with the organisational form?

Suggestions for further reading

Anderson, J.C., Håkansson, H. and Johanson, J. (1994) 'Dyadic business relationships within a business network context', *Journal of Marketing*, Vol. 58, pp. 1–15.

Anderson, P. (1992) 'Analysing distribution channel dynamics: loose and tight couplings in distribution networks', *European Journal of Marketing*, Vol. 26, No. 2, pp. 47–68.

Birley, S. (1985) 'The role of networks in the entrepreneurial process', *Journal of Business Venturing*, Vol. 1, pp. 107–17.

Birley, S., Cromie, S. and Myers, A. (1991) 'Entrepreneurial networks: their emergence in Ireland and overseas', *International Small Business Journal*, Vol. 9, No. 4, pp. 56–74.

Boisot, M.H. (1986) 'Markets and hierarchies in a cultural perspective', *Organisation Studies*, Vol. 7, No. 2, pp. 135–58.

Cheung, S.N.S. (1998) 'The transaction cost paradigm', *Economic Inquiry*, Vol. 36, No. 4, pp. 514–21.

Falemo, B. (1989) 'The firm's external persons: entrepreneurs or network actors?' *Entrepreneurship and Regional Development*, Vol. 1, No. 2, pp. 167–77.

Jarillo, J.C. (1988) 'On strategic networks', *Strategic Management Journal*, Vol. 9, pp. 31–41.

Jones, G.R. and Hill, C.W.L. (1988) 'Transaction cost analysis of strategy–structure choice', *Strategic Management Journal*, Vol. 9, pp. 159–72.

Larson, A. (1992) 'Network dyads in entrepreneurial settings: a study of the governance of exchange relationships', *Administrative Science Quarterly*, Vol. 37, pp. 76–104.

Larson, A. (1993) 'A network model of organisation formation', *Entrepreneurship Theory and Practice*, Vol. 12, No. 2, pp. 5–15.

Morgan, G. (1986) *Images of Organisation*, London: Sage Publications.

Perry, M. (1996) 'Network intermediaries and their effectiveness', *International Small Business Journal*, Vol. 14, No. 4, pp. 72–9.

Peters, T. and Waterman Jr, R.H. (1982) *In Search of Excellence*, New York: Harper & Row.

Szarka, J. (1990) 'Networking and small firms', *International Small Business Journal*, Vol. 8, No. 2, pp. 10–22.

Thompson, G.F. (2003) *Between Hierarchies and Markets: The Logic and Limits of Network Forms of Organisation*, Oxford: Oxford University Press.

Tyosvold, D. and Weicker, D. (1993) 'Co-operative and competitive networking by entrepreneurs: a critical indent study', *Journal of Small Business Management*, Jan, pp. 11–21.

Williamson, O. (1985) *The Economic Institutions of Capitalism*, New York: Free Press.

Williamson, O. (1991) 'Comparative economic organization: the analysis of discrete structural alternatives', *Administrative Science Quarterly*, Vol. 36, pp. 269–96.

Brands cross the divide

FT

10 July 2002

By **Bettina Wassener**

For one half of Germany, products such as Nudossi, Halloren and Bautz'ner are household names. The other half of the country is at best dimly aware of their existence.

Such brands – hazelnut spread, chocolates and mustard respectively – are survivors of the post-reunification shake-out of the east German economy. Generations of east Germans have grown up on these brands and believe them to be as good as their western equivalents. Nudossi, according to its fans, is as wonderfully gooey as the western Nutella, Werder Ketchup as nice as Heinz and Fit washing-up liquid as bubbly as Palmolive.

That these brands are finding it almost impossible to gain a foothold in west Germany is a sign of the division that remains in the country, 12 years after reunification. Indeed, the economic discrepancy between west and east Germany will be a key theme of the federal election, which takes place in September.

Yet the west/east divide has also been the basis for the success of OssiVersand, a small mail order company based in the eastern city of Halle. OssiVersand is defying the depression in Germany's retail sector with its business of selling east German goods to *Ossis* (east Germans) who now live in the west.

'Well over 80 per cent of our customers live in western Germany but come from the east,' says Gerhard Franz at OssiVersand. 'They've known these products all their lives but cannot get hold of them, even though in eastern Germany these brands are often market leaders. That's where we come in.'

OssiVersand expects its sales to more than double to €1m (£640,000) this year. While sales in the German retail industry fell 5 per cent year-on-year in the first five months of this year, OssiVersand experienced no collapse in demand after September 11 and saw first-quarter sales triple from a year ago, far exceeding expectations. The company's staff of 10 sent out 16,000 parcels last year and its mailing list has swelled to 50,000 from 4,000 in 2000, mostly through word of mouth.

OssiVersand was the idea of two housewives, one of whom used to bring her friend in the west a dough mix by Kathi, a company whose bakery products are loved and trusted by busy housewives throughout the east. When one day she forgot, the idea was born to offer an order service via the internet.

OssiVersand was founded in July 1999 but the project, meant to be a hobby, was soon overwhelmed by demand and collapsed a year later.

Enter Gerhard Franz, a *Mittelstand* entrepreneur, who was at the time in search of an idea to complement spare management and storage capacities at his business, which produces cellar windows. 'The OssiVersand idea was something promising that fitted well into the gaps we had,' says Mr Franz, who is ironically a *Wessi* from Munich.

Though OssiVersand remains a small niche player, its market is potentially sizeable with more than 2m *Ossis* now living in west Germany. At the same time, there is little prospect that those consumers will be able to get hold of their beloved east German products through conventional distribution.

'If you want to introduce an east German brand in western Germany you face the same hurdles as you would with a completely new product launch,' says Regina Schmidt of Roland Berger, the management consultancy. 'Listing fees and distribution systems cost millions, and advertising costs at least another €10m – anything less has too little impact and is effectively a waste of money.'

Few companies have the necessary funds for this. The eastern brands that are known throughout Germany are mostly those that have massive financial backing, such as Spee washing powder, an eastern brand that was bought by Henkel, the Düsseldorf-based household products giant, in 1990.

Rotkäppchen, the east German maker of Sekt, or sparkling wine, is another exception, and staged the coup of buying western rival Mumm earlier this year.

Rotkäppchen's Gunter Heise explains the company's success by its willingness to invest rapidly in new technology and to bring in the necessary marketing and distribution expertise soon after the fall of the Berlin Wall. By 1994, Rotkäppchen was able to use its 100th anniversary to boost its marketing campaign and start looking west.

Yet Rotkäppchen's sales patterns also illustrate the problems eastern companies face in trying to break into the wallets of the wealthier half of the country. In the east, its market share is well above 50 per cent. In the more fragmented western market, it has a share of only 3.5 per cent.

A massive advertising campaign has increased awareness of its products, so that 87 per cent of people in the west are now familiar with Rotkäppchen (compared with 99 per cent in the east). But that has failed to boost western sales significantly.

More typical is consumer awareness of the Florena brand. In eastern Germany, the 'Nivea of the east' is just as well known as Rotkäppchen but in the west only 24 per cent of the population is familiar with it.

What helps to explain OssiVersand's success is the fact that, on its home territory, many east German products benefit from a high degree of customer loyalty.

'Immediately after the fall of the wall, eastern products were shunned. But this phase did not last long. By late 1992, three-quarters of east German customers said they again preferred east German products,' says Petra Knötzsch of the Market Research Institute in Leipzig. 'What is at play here is not so much nostalgia as a conscious desire to support the local economy and help guarantee jobs.'

At the same time, she says, many eastern brands, produced in efficient and relatively low-wage companies, simply offer good value for money.

Still, says Mr Franz, 'the biggest problem is to create sufficient demand. OssiVersand helps promote these products but a bit of public interest from prominent politicians would do wonders for individual producers, and for the image of east German output as a whole.'

His wish may well be granted. With only 70-odd days of campaigning left, eastern Germany is likely to feature prominently on election itineraries. Expect copious footage of Rotkäppchen-drinking, Nudossi-eating politicians.

Source: Financial Times, 10 July 2002.

Case 11.2

When survival lies over the border

FT

4 June 2002

By **Leyla Boulton**

When Anadolu, Turkey's leading brewer, decided last year to sell its car manufacturing business and to dispose of its bank, it was responding to the country's worst economic crisis since 1945. But even as the company reined in domestically, it made an aggressive push into foreign markets and last year managed to boost its sales of beer and soft drinks to Russia by 50 per cent.

Anadolu's strategy was typical of the Turkish companies that have best survived the 10 per cent reduction in gross national product triggered by the devaluation of the Turkish lira in February 2001. The crisis claimed many corporate victims but many of the survivors are focusing on a narrower range of businesses and accelerating their expansion abroad.

'Ten per cent negative growth means a lot,' says Tuncay Ozilhan, Anadolu's chief executive, who also heads Tusiad, the country's main business federation. 'It needs to be followed by a reforming period.'

Mr Ozilhan, whose family is co-founder and joint owner of Anadolu, has put his money where his mouth is. This year, he sold Anadolu's stake in a carmaking joint venture with Honda to the Japanese group for $37m (ý25m). He also began negotiations to sell a 51 per cent stake in the group's Alternatif Bank to France's Crýdit Agricole Indosuez. 'Ozilhan realised that his previous strategy was wrong. He's very good at beverages but not so good at other things, [such as] banking,' says one western banker.

Apart from operating breweries in Russia, Romania, Kazakhstan, Ukraine and Turkey – where its Efes brand has a market share of 78 per cent – Anadolu is Coca-Cola's partner in Turkey and its franchise-holder in four ex-Soviet republics. It is also still involved in the production of light trucks and buses with Japan's Isuzu and in pencil-manufacturing with Germany's Faber Kastell.

Diversification on this scale defies western textbook recommendations for companies to focus on their core competence. For most Turkish companies, any divestment of a peripheral business is a step in the right direction. Anadolu is likely to face further competitive pressure to specialise – particularly if and when Turkey, a candidate for membership of the European Union, lifts barriers to imports and foreign direct investment.

Bulend Ozaydinli, the recently appointed chief executive of Koc, Turkey's largest industrial conglomerate with interests ranging from tomato paste to logistics, says restructuring is now under way to achieve 'strength in selected sectors'. These areas include car production, white and brown goods, retailing and banking.

'Of course we have to know what's going on in the world [in terms of strategic trends],' says Ahmet Nazif Zorlu, the majority shareholder of Vestel, Turkey's top exporter of consumer electronics. He also produces textiles but is said to be seeking a buyer for his bank, Denizbank. 'Maybe in the future we'll confine ourselves to production and give up services,' he says.

Groups pruning their range of activities are also looking for growth outside Turkey's borders. Vestel, which has had 15 per cent of the EU market for television sets since December, last year derived 80 per cent of its $1.1bn consolidated revenues from exports. Koc aims to increase foreign sales as a share of total turnover from 30 to 50 per cent over the next 15 years.

Koc knows that it cannot rely solely on a volatile domestic market to achieve its long-term goal of becoming one of the world's 200 biggest companies with sales of $40bn, up from $10bn now. This year alone it aims to open two more shopping centres and five supermarkets in Moscow, where its Ramstore joint venture with Enka, the Turkish construction company, is the leading food retailer with 12 stores already.

But Koc sees advantages in a domestic base. 'We see over the next 10 years an opportunity for Turkey to become a production centre for Europe because a lot of [western] European plants will be closed down,' argues Mr Ozaydinli.

There are drawbacks, too, he says. This year Koc bought German and Austrian brands previously owned by France's Brandt group, to get around the perceived disadvantage of a 'made in Turkey' label on its cookers, refrigerators and washing machines. 'We have a handicap as an export-oriented Turkish company,' he says. 'If you have a product manufactured in France or Germany, you get a better retail price even if its quality is worse than the equivalent made in Turkey.'

The trend towards greater assertiveness abroad is not confined to Turkish blue-chip conglomerates such as Koc and Anadolu. Organik, a speciality chemicals producer with sales of $70m, is building a $15m plant in Rotterdam to bring it closer to its customers and raw materials, for which the Dutch port is an important distribution centre.

'To be competitive, we need to face competition on a daily basis and act very quickly. This means investing outside Turkey,' says Aldo Kaslowski, chairman of the privately held group, founded in 1924 by his father, a Polish immigrant. 'We've found the courage to go and compete with the likes of Dow Chemical, BASF and Dupont because they are . . . too big to cater for the specific needs of their customers.'

The Rotterdam plant, to be completed in 18 months' time, will supply Organik's western European customers. Its existing Istanbul factory will serve markets in the Balkans and the Middle East as well as domestic customers in a shrunken market in which, according to Mr Kaslowski, all seven of his local competitors have disappeared over the past year.

But in most cases, analysts observe that while the recent crisis has identified the strong, it has yet to weed out all the weak. 'This crisis showed which conglomerates were well managed and which were not,' says Mr Zorlu, an entrepreneur who left school at 11 and managed his first business at the age of 15. 'We learnt a lot from the crisis and saw the realities.'

The early casualties consisted, on the one hand, of small businesses and, on the other, of those conglomerates whose failing banks were taken over by the state for posing a threat to the banking system.

But some bankers and industrialists say an unspecified number of other medium to large companies are being kept afloat by banks that are reluctant to declare loans to such groups as non-performing.

'The reason we haven't seen too many bankruptcies is because everything's been pushed back,' says Mehmet Sami, executive board member of Ata Invest, an Istanbul brokerage. 'Banks are drip-feeding those corporates that feel they can get out of their present predicament by crying for government help, as in the old days. As the Turkish proverb says: "There's nothing for those who don't cry."'

The coming weeks will clarify how committed the government is to structural reforms promised to the International Monetary Fund, which range from bank restructuring to tax changes.

If, as hoped, the reforms slash inflation and create a healthier macroeconomic environment for sound companies to prosper, they should also have the effect of accelerating corporate restructuring.

A case in point is a three-stage audit of private sector banks to determine which institutions need government funds to meet statutory capital adequacy ratios. The scheme has been billed as the last act in Turkish banking rehabilitation after badly managed banks triggered two financial crises in November 2000 and February 2001. The audit process is expected to be completed in June after missing an earlier deadline of mid-May.

The extent to which Turkey's quasi-independent banking regulators can uncover problem loans will determine the day of reckoning for owners of weak banks and less promising corporate borrowers. This process should also be aided by a framework agreement now being finalised by the banks to co-operate on corporate restructuring with otherwise viable companies that have run out of cash. The World Bank is contributing $500m to encourage banks to take part in a scheme widely referred to as the 'Istanbul approach'.

Wearing his other hat as chief representative of the Turkish business community, Mr Ozilhan expresses sympathy for less successful peers. 'It's like a house of cards . . . everybody is trying to support each other until the good days come back.'

Source: Financial Times, 4 June 2002.

Discussion points

1 What are the barriers stopping former east German companies breaking into the rich markets of the west? Are there still institutional and political barriers or does the fault lie with the organisations?

2 In what respects might the response of Anadolu to depressed local markets be regarded as entrepreneurial?

Chapter 12

The meaning of success

Chapter overview

Entrepreneurship is about success. This chapter is concerned with defining what success really means and the ways in which it can be measured. Business success is considered not only in financial terms but also in a broader social context. The issue of social corporate responsibility is considered. The chapter concludes with an exploration of the converse of success: failure. Failure is not seen as completely negative but rather an experience which is occasionally necessary and which presents an opportunity for the organisation and the entrepreneur to learn.

12.1 Defining success

> **Key learning outcome**
>
> An understanding of what entrepreneurial success actually means.

Entrepreneurs aim to be successful. It is the possibility of success that drives them on and success is the measure of their achievement. Success is, however, quite a difficult concept to define because it is multi-faceted. Both individuals and organisations enjoy success. It may be measured by hard and fast 'numbers' but also by 'softer', qualitative criteria. Success is something which is both visible in public but is also experienced at a personal level.

Success can be best understood in terms of four interacting aspects:

1. the performance of the venture;

2. the people who have expectations from the venture;

3. the nature of those expectations; and

4. actual outcomes relative to expectations.

The performance of the venture is indicated by a variety of quantitative measures. These relate to its financial performance and the presence it creates for itself in the marketplace. The indicators can be absolute and compared to the performance of competitors. Such performance measures relate to the organisation as a whole. However, an organisation is made up of individual people, and success, if it is to be meaningful, must be experienced by those individuals as well as by the organisation. Organisational success is a means to the end of *personal* success. The organisation creates the resources which interested individuals can use to improve their lives. The individuals who have an interest in the performance of the venture are its *stakeholders*. Thus the success of a venture must be considered in relation to the expectations its stakeholders have for it (see Figure 12.1).

The entrepreneurial venture has six groups of stakeholder, each of which has its own interest and expectations from the venture. The *entrepreneur* (and their dependents) expects the venture to be a vehicle for personal ambitions; *employees* expect reward for their efforts and personal development; *suppliers* expect the venture to be a good customer; *customers* expect the venture to be a good supplier; *investors* expect the venture to generate a return on the investment they have made; and the *local community* expects the venture to make a positive contribution to the quality of local life.

The performance of the venture as an organisation provides the means by which individual stakeholders can fulfil their own goals. Personal goals are manifest at three levels:

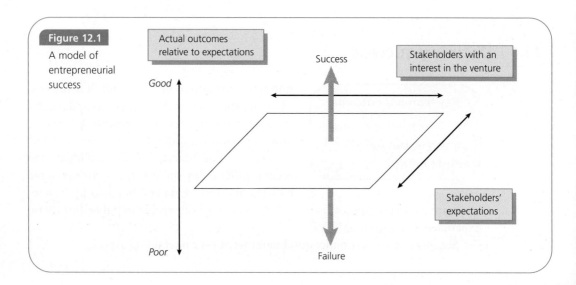

Figure 12.1

A model of entrepreneurial success

Actual outcomes relative to expectations

Success

Stakeholders with an interest in the venture

Good

Stakeholders' expectations

Poor

Failure

- the *economic* – monetary rewards;

- the *social* – fulfilling relationships with other people;

- the *self-developmental* – the achievement of personal intellectual and spiritual satisfaction and growth.

Success experienced at a personal level is not absolute. Success is recognised by comparing actual outcomes to prior *expectations*. At a minimum, success is achieved if outcomes meet expectations and success is ensured if expectations are exceeded. If expectations are not met, however, then a sense of failure will ensue.

Different stakeholders will hold different expectations. They will look to the organisation to fulfil different types of goals. The investor may only be interested in the venture offering financial returns whereas the customers and suppliers will want financial rewards, but they may also hope to build rewarding social relationships with people in the organisation. Employees will expect a salary but this will only be their minimum expectation. They will also expect the venture to provide a route for self-development. The venture will be central to the personal development of the entrepreneur.

Success, then, is not a simple thing. The organisation's financial and strategic performance is only part of the picture. Success is achieved if the organisation uses its performance to meet, or better to *exceed*, the financial, social and personal growth expectations of the people who have an interest in it. The success of a venture depends on how its performance helps stakeholders to achieve their individual goals, and the way different people judge the success of the venture will depend on how well these expectations are met (Figure 12.2). What are the chances that a business will be successful? Nucci (1999) found that for US small

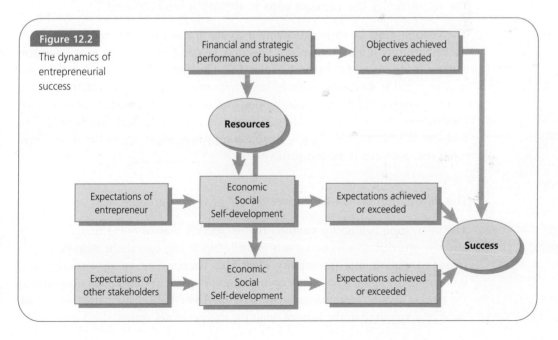

Figure 12.2

The dynamics of entrepreneurial success

businesses, some 20% are terminated by the end of the first year, with 60% gone by the end of the fifth. These do not all represent financial failure. Those actually filing for bancruptcy are quite low. Dennis and Fernald (2001) examine the probability of a new venture's success based on US business statistics. They find that the probability of a venture's success is quite high, but that the probability of a venture providing an entrepreneur with a substantively increased income over conventional alternatives is also quite low.

12.2 Success factors for the new venture

> **Key learning outcome**
>
> An appreciation of some of the main factors involved in the success of a new venture.

A venture is successful if it meets the aspirations of its stakeholders. In order to do this it must survive and prosper in the marketplace. It must attract resources, reward its stakeholders for their contributions and be financially secure. Every venture is different, but a common set of factors lies behind every successful business.

The venture exploits a significant opportunity

The opportunity spotted by the entrepreneur is real and significant. The venture is faced with the possibility of delivering sufficient value to a large enough number of customers to make the business viable in terms of income and profits.

The opportunity the venture aims to exploit is well defined

The venture must be clear as to why it exists. It must understand the nature of the opportunity it aims to exploit. This may be codified in the form of a *mission statement* (discussed further in Chapter 14). The danger is not just that the business may fail to find a sufficiently large opportunity for its innovation but also that in pursuing too many opportunities, and opportunities that are not right for the business, the venture will dilute its resources across too many fronts and fail to focus its efforts on creating a sustainable competitive advantage in the areas where it has real potential to be competitive.

The innovation on which the venture is based is valuable

The innovation behind the venture, that is, its new way of doing things, must be effective and different from the way existing businesses operate. It must be appropriate to exploit the opportunity identified. Recognising an opportunity, and innovating to exploit it, can only occur if the entrepreneur thoroughly understands the market and the customers who make it up. All new ideas, no matter how good, must be scrutinised in the light of what the market *really* wants.

The entrepreneur brings the right skills to the venture

The entrepreneur possesses the right knowledge and skills to build the venture to exploit the opportunity. These include knowledge of the industry sector they are working in, familiarity with its products and markets, general management skills and people skills such as communication and leadership. The entrepreneur must not only have these skills, but also be active in refining and developing them. The effective entrepreneur learns how to learn.

The business has the right people

Entrepreneurs rarely work alone. They draw other people into their ventures to work with them. The business as a whole must have the right people working for it. Entrepreneurs do not need to employ copies of themselves, rather they need people with skills and knowledge to complement their own. The business will need specialists and technical experts as well as people to actually make the product or deliver the service the business offers. It will need general managers and people able to build relationships outside the firm. The people who make up the organisation will be linked in a suitable framework of communication links and responsibilities, both formal and informal. As the business grows, identifying and recruiting the right people to support its growth is a task of primary importance for the entrepreneur.

The organisation has a learning culture and its people a positive attitude

The new venture is in a weak position compared to established players in the marketplace. It is young and relatively inexperienced. It has not had a chance to build up the expertise or relationships that its established counterparts have. It will not have access to their resource levels. The entrepreneurial organisation must turn this on its head and make the disadvantage into an advantage. The entrepreneurial venture must use the fact that it is new to do things in a fresh and innovative way. It must recognise its inexperience as an opportunity to learn a better way of doing things. This can only be achieved if the organisation has a positive culture which seeks ways of developing and which regards change as an opportunity. Adversity must be met as a learning experience. Culture comes down to the attitudes of the people who make up the organisation. They must be motivated to perform on behalf of the venture. The entrepreneur is responsible for establishing a culture in their organisation through leadership and example.

Effective use of the network

Successful entrepreneurs, and the people who work with them, use the network in which the organisation finds itself to good effect. They look towards suppliers and customers, not as competitors for resources, but as partners. They recognise that entrepreneurship is not a zero sum game. If all parties in the network recognise that they can benefit from the success of the venture – and it is down to the entrepreneur to convince them that they can – then the network will make resources and information available to the venture and will be prepared to share some of its risks.

Financial resources are available

The venture can only pursue its opportunity if it has access to the right resources. Financial resources are critical because the business must make essential investments in productive assets, pay its staff and reimburse suppliers. In the early stages, expenditure will be higher than income. The business is very likely to have a negative *cash-flow*. The business must have the resources at hand to cover expenditure in this period. Once the business starts to grow it will need to attract new resources to support that growth. Again, cash-flow may be negative while this is occurring. The entrepreneur must be an effective resource manager. He or she must attract financial resources from investors and then make them work as hard as possible to progress the venture.

The venture has clear goals and its expectations are understood

A venture can only be successful if it is seen to be successful. This means that it must set clear and unambiguous objectives to provide a benchmark against which performance can be measured. Success can only be understood in relation to the expectations that stakeholders have for the venture. These expectations must be explicit. This will be critical in the case of investors, who will be very definite about the return they expect. The business must be sure of exactly what its customers want if it expects them to buy its offerings. Understanding expectations is also important in dealing with employees since it is the starting point for motivating them. The entrepreneur must learn to recognise and manage the expectations of all the venture's stakeholders.

12.3 Measuring success and setting objectives

> **Key learning outcome**
>
> An understanding of the criteria used to set objectives for the entrepreneurial venture and to monitor its performance.

Ultimately, success is personal. The entrepreneurial venture is a vehicle for individual success as much as organisational success. If it is to be an effective vehicle, the venture must be successful as a business. The performance of the venture is subject to a variety of measures including:

- *absolute financial performance* – e.g. sales, profits;

- *financial performance ratios* – e.g. profit margin, return on capital employed;

- *financial liquidity ratios* – e.g. debt cover, interest cover;

- *absolute stock market performance* – e.g. share price, market capitalisation;

- *stock market ratios* – e.g. earnings per share, dividend yield;

- *market presence* – e.g. market share, market position;

- *growth* – e.g. increase in sales, increase in profits;

- *innovation* – e.g. rate of new product introduction;

- *customer assessment* – e.g. customer service level, customer rating.

These performance indicators are quantitative and are relatively easy to measure. They provide definite goals for the venture to attain. They are *strategic* goals in that they relate to the business as a whole and refer to the position it develops in its external market as well as to purely internal criteria. An entrepreneurial venture is distinguished from a small business by the ambition of its strategic goals.

The specifics of the objectives set for the venture will depend on the type of business it is, the market in which it is operating and the stage of its development. They will be used by management to define objectives, evaluate strategic options and benchmark performance. Different businesses will set objectives in different ways: they will vary in specificity; they may be for the organisation as a whole or they may define the responsibilities of particular individuals; they may be based on agreement and consensus or they may be 'imposed' on the organisation by the entrepreneur. The way the entrepreneur defines and sets goals, and uses them to motivate and monitor performance, is an important aspect of leadership strategy.

The objectives of the firm may not be an entirely internal concern. Financial and market performance measures may form part of the agreement made with investors. They provide manageable and explicit proxies for the success of the business and indicate the returns it can hope to generate. They provide a sound and unambiguous basis for monitoring its development. They may also be used in communication with suppliers and customers to indicate the potential of the business and to elicit their support.

12.4) Success and social responsibility

> **Key learning outcome**
>
> An appreciation of how entrepreneurial success impacts on social responsibility.

An entrepreneurial venture touches the lives of many people. All its stakeholders have an interest in its success since this success provides the means by which they can fulfil their personal goals. People have expectations about what an entrepreneurial business can achieve and how it should undertake its business. Some of these expectations are formal, others are informal. Some are explicit, others implicit. Some result from binding contracts, others from trust that has been accumulated. Entrepreneurs perform on a social stage and in creating an entire new world they must take responsibility for its ethical content as well as its new value (this develops a theme established in Section 2.2). The moral dimension of their activity cannot be ignored. The idea of *corporate social responsibility* is one that has come to the fore of business thinking in recent years. The reasons for this interest are many, but important factors include the following. The first is a move from the 'patrician' management of the 1950s and 1960s where managers were relatively free to spend profits as they wished (and often did so to the advantage of non-investor stakeholders) to the more investor-driven management of the 1980s and 1990s, where managers are expected to concentrate on maximising investor returns. Second, concerns with environmental and development issues are growing, with the rise of non-governmental organisations (NGOs) to lobby for them, particularly with government legislators. Third, there is a belief that 'globalisation' is taking power from governments and passing it to (particularly multinational) business. The idea of corporate social responsibility goes beyond simply defining the responsibility of the entrepreneur in terms of stakeholder expectations. After all, a profit maximising firm may still develop rewarding relationships with stakeholders simply as a means to that profit maximisation, in which case (non-investor) stakeholder rewards are an implicit, *means-to-an-end* aspect of strategic objective setting. Advocates of social corporate responsibility generally demand that social and environmental concerns should be an explicit, *end-in-themselves* aspect of strategic objective setting along with an interest in profit creation. This issue is highly controversial. There are, broadly, four positions. At one end, there are those who reject the idea of corporate social responsibility entirely (for example, Friedman, 1962; Henderson, 2001). Rejectors argue that maximising investor return is the only real responsibility businesses have. This position is often caricatured as a mixture of greed and complacency about world issues. This is unfair. What rejectors are claiming is that profit maximisation is the best way to ensure that resources are used in the best possible way, given individuals freedom to choose what they want. At the other end of the spectrum are those who believe that corporate social responsibility (imposed by government if necessary) is a way to limit the power of, and even punish, business (again, especially the large multinational). This belief centres on the idea that 'business has been given too free a rein for too long; it is time it paid back'. The middle ground is occupied by those who do not particularly want to see business punished, but believe that corporate social responsibility improves collective social welfare, even if it does impose some (limited) costs on business (Hutton *et al.*, 1997; De George, 1999) and, finally, those who argue that it is actually good for businesses to adopt corporate social responsibility and that it can improve profitability (a win–win scenario) (Nash, 1995). This latter view has come to dominate among many business academics. A central theme running through these four positions is the relationship between adopting standards of corporate social responsibility and resulting performance. This is an issue that can, in principle, be evaluated empirically, and is explored in the next section. It should not be forgotten that there is no real agreement between different advocates as to what, exactly, corporate social responsibility is. Avishai (1994) develops a historical

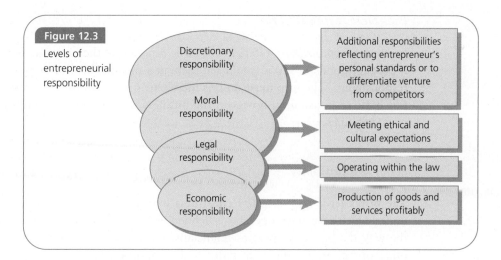

Figure 12.3

Levels of entrepreneurial responsibility

Discretionary responsibility

Moral responsibility

Legal responsibility

Economic responsibility

Additional responsibilities reflecting entrepreneur's personal standards or to differentiate venture from competitors

Meeting ethical and cultural expectations

Operating within the law

Production of goods and services profitably

account of the development of the concept). Joyner *et al.* (2002) summarises definitions of related concepts as follows:

- **Values** are the core set of beliefs and principles deemed to be desirable by a particular group.
- **Ethics** are the conception of which actions are right or wrong, what individuals should seek to do or avoid, with **business ethics** as a specific set of such views relating to business practice.
- **Corporate social responsibility** is the categories of economic, legal, ethical and discretionary activities of a business entity adapted to the values and expectations of wider society.

This section will conclude with an overview of models of corporate social responsibility in strategic objective setting. An early model was developed by Archie Carroll (1979). He suggests a four-dimensional approach to understanding corporate social responsibility, as shown in Figure 12.3.

The first dimension: the *people* to whom the venture has a social responsibility

Potentially, the entrepreneurial venture has a social responsibility towards all those who are affected by its activities, that is, its *stakeholder groups*. Stakeholders may be members of distinct groups but they are also individuals. The venture has responsibilities towards both individuals and organisations or groups.

The second dimension: the *levels* of social responsibility accepted

The business may accept a variety of different types of social responsibility. These may be described as *economic*, *legal*, *moral* and *discretionary*.

Economic responsibility

Economic *responsibility* refers to the basic function of the firm and demands that it produce goods or services and sell them at a profit. This is a minimum level of responsibility. The firm must do this merely to survive within its market. Beyond this basic responsibility, however, the business will recognise a number of other responsibilities.

Legal responsibility

The firm's *legal responsibility* constrains it to operate within the law. The law under which a business operates is defined by the state. Different laws will dictate the way the business operates financially and the way it sets up contracts with other organisations and with individuals. Important examples of laws affecting business are tax and accounting laws and the rules of employment law. A business will be subject to both *criminal* and *civil* law. If the criminal law is broken, the state will act as prosecutor. If a civil law is breached, then it is up to the injured party to bring an action.

Moral responsibilities

A business is a social organisation which operates within a framework of cultural norms. The society within which it exists has ethical standards which it believes must be upheld. These provide rules and norms which create constraints for behaviour. These constitute the firm's *moral responsibilities* and they are difficult to define. They are the unwritten rules about 'what should be done' and 'what should not be done' and they may not be noticed at all until an individual or organisation breaks them. Though a society will not necessarily articulate its ethics and moral standards, they still form an important part of people's expectations and they will react strongly if they are broken.

Discretionary responsibilities

Economic, legal and moral responsibilities comprise the standard constraints operating on the actions of the business. In addition, the entrepreneur may decide to accept *discretionary responsibilities*. Discretionary responsibilities are ones the entrepreneur accepts for their venture even though it is not generally expected that businesses need accept them. They are responsibilities that go above and beyond the norm. Discretionary responsibilities may relate to the way the business treats its employees, the standards it sets for its products or the way it manages the impact of its activities on the environment. They may reflect beliefs and standards which are held dear by the entrepreneur. They may be used to give the business a point of difference from competitors.

The third dimension: the *issues* which form part of the venture's social responsibility

There are a variety of issues which the entrepreneur can accept as part of the venture's social responsibility. Minimum standards in the treatment of employees, occupational health and safety and product liability will usually be subject to legal regulation. Entrepreneurs frequently take a positive attitude towards wider social issues such as the treatment of the environment, relationships with developing nations and ethnic and sexual discrimination. Occasionally, they may also take a stand on much broader issues relating to social trends such as the growth in 'consumerism'.

The fourth dimension: the venture's *approach* to its social responsibility

The business faces a choice in the way in which it approaches its social responsibilities. It may be *defensive*. This means that the business decides that its social responsibilities are a liability and that they hinder its performance. It may then try to avoid them and to minimise their impact. This may boost short-term profits but it can easily lead to a reaction by stakeholders, especially, but not exclusively, its employees and customers. The business must then put its efforts into defending its actions which can lead to a vicious, and expensive, circle. The more the firm seeks to avoid its responsibilities the stronger can be the reaction by stakeholders, so more effort must be put into the defence. This can easily result in a debilitating 'bunker' mentality within the business whereby it feels that its stakeholders are an enemy, rather than partners. Alternatively, the business may decide not to go looking for social responsibilities, but will accept them when confronted by them. In this it is *reactive*. The business does not see social responsibilities either as a source of advantage or as a problem, they are just something else that has to be managed. Accepting social responsibility is probably less expensive than defending against it in the long run, but in being reactive the business is allowing itself to be confronted by uncertainties it would otherwise be able to control. Another option is for the business to be *positive* towards its social responsibilities. It can choose to regard them not as liabilities but as opportunities and use them as a source of competitive advantage. Adopting a positive attitude towards social responsibilities brings them under control. They can be made part of the venture's strategy. They can be used to motivate employees and to build a strong relationship with customers and suppliers, or they can be used to address the wider concerns of investors and so gain their support. A positive approach to its social responsibilities can be made into a success factor for the entrepreneurial business.

Social responsibilities constrain the actions of a business. They often define what it *cannot* do, rather than what it can. This does not mean they are bad for business. They provide a sound, and shared, set of rules within which the business community can operate. They ensure that the benefits of business activity are distributed in a way which is seen to be fair and equitable. This sustains the motivation of all stakeholders in the venture. Businesses are rarely penalised for meeting their social responsibilities positively. On the other hand, they will be punished if they are seen to evade their responsibilities. This ensures that ventures which set high standards are not penalised by being undercut by those that have lower standards.

Taking on discretionary responsibilities and being proactive with them may be a strategic move. If this meets with the approval of customers and other stakeholders, it can provide a means by which the business can make itself different from competitors and gain an advantage in the marketplace. In recognition of this fact, the entrepreneur may specify the business's social responsibilities in its mission statement. Using discretionary responsibilities to give the business an edge need not conflict with the personal values of the entrepreneur. The entrepreneur can only improve the world with those values if the business is successful. The social responsibilities the venture accepts, and how it defines them, are not merely 'add-ons' to the entrepreneur's vision, they lie at its core. They are the character of the new world the entrepreneur seeks to build. Paine (1994) suggest two basic approaches to social responsibility: first, a *legal compliance strategy* in which the firm adheres to the strict letter of the law, thus avoiding costly legal penalties; and, second, an *integrity strategy*, in which the firm aspires to meet the spirit of the law, fulfilling what it sees as the intention of legislators. This framework is applied to a study of ten US ventures by Joyner *et al.* (2002). The study found that entrepreneurs were often willing to go beyond mere legal compliance. Martin (2002) develops a 2×2 matrix model of corporate social responsibility. The vertical axis is split between 'civil foundation' on the bottom and 'frontier' on the top. The civil foundation is instrumental in that it provides a basal level of social responsibility all firms are expected to abide by. Adherence may be by choice guided by social and cultural norms or due to legal imposition. The frontier represents behaviour that is intrinsic in that managers act on their own initiative to adopt particular social responsibility standards above and beyond those expected of the sector as a whole. The horizontal axis is split between 'strategic adherence', in which adopting these higher standards actually increases returns to shareholders (and so is intrinsically motivated) and 'structural adherence', in which case shareholder value is reduced, but society as a whole (arguably) benefits. This last category represents a barrier to social responsibility as adherence may lead to punishment (selling of stock) by shareholders, threatening manager's rewards and, potentially, the independence of the business. Bagley (2003) suggests a decision tree model for choices about social responsibility. The first node asks if the action is legal. If not, it should not be undertaken. If it is, then the next node asks if the action is in line with maximising shareholder value. If it is, then the next node asks if the action is ethical (do other stakeholders, in general benefit?). If so, it should be undertaken. If not, then it should not. If the action does not maximise shareholder value, then the next node asks if it would be ethical *not* to undertake the action (is the imputed cost to stakeholders acceptable given the increased return to investors?). If the answer is yes, then the action should not be undertaken. If the answer is no, then the action should be considered, but investors must be informed of its consequences. A study by Bucar and Hisrich (2001) explores whether entrepreneurs or (non-entrepreneur) business managers in Britain hold (or aspire to) higher ethical standards. He finds no significant difference between the two groups. The contributions to Ben-Ner and Putterman (1998) are recommended for those interested in the debate about how economic priorities establish social norms, and how social norms influence economic behaviour.

(12.5) Social responsibility and business performance

> **Key learning outcome**
>
> An appreciation of the issue of, and the difficulting in dermining if, the adoption of levels of social responsibility in addition to those of the sector as a whole leads to an improvement in, or a detrimental effect on, shareholder value.

Does the adoption of discretionary levels of corporate social responsibility result in an improvement or a reduction in total shareholder (investor) value? Arguments may be offered for both positions. On the one hand, a firm adopting higher levels of corporate social responsibility may develop an enhanced reputation, attracting new customers for whom such values are important. Increased sales lead to increased performance. On the other hand, introducing social and environmental objectives into the business will, at least, complicate managers' tasks and increase the need for co-ordination, thus raising costs. At worst it might limit the most efficient use of resources and force the business to ignore certain new opportunities. Both of these will reduce shareholder value. The total change in shareholder value will reflect the balance of these positive and negative forces. The resulting balance is, in principle, observable. It simply requires that the correlation between adoption of social responsibility and performance be measured. However, this is not as straightforward as it seems. First of all, there needs to be an accepted definition of what corporate social responsibility is. As noted above, there is not. Different commentators prioritise different issues. Second, what do we mean when we say a firm is adopting a particular social responsibility? The bottom line must be how much of its resources are being dedicated to delivering on this responsibility. Conventional accounting does not report on such things, not least because they are difficult to audit. Third, there is the issue of which actions are judged to be 'socially responsible'. Do we regard them as such because they have the right motives, or because they are moral in themselves, or because they have beneficial outcomes? This is an issue explored in Section 2.2, where motivist, deontological and consequentialist approaches to judging moralty were discussed. Different perspectives will change the judgement of the ethical quality of a particular action. Is a firm really being ethical if it adopts corporate social responsibility because it will actually increase its profits? Is protecting the environment, for example, moral in itself, no matter what other costs it incurs? Is a firm that employs low-cost labour in the developing world right to argue that it is in fact acting with social responsibility, because it is providing jobs that otherwise would not be there? Finally we have the issue of what constitutes performance. If this is limited to financial performance (and measuring even this is not unproblematic), then it might be argued that other benefits (and costs) are being ignored. If social and environmental factors are accounted for, how are these to be measured in financial terms when there are not fully formed markets to price them. One group's (personal) estimation of the value created will differ from another's whose (again personal) values and valuations are different. If a 'balanced scorecard' approach is taken, then ipso facto, firms adopting social responsibility will perform better. A number of studies have attempted to address and circumvent these issues, and research in this area is growing rapidly. A review by McWilliams and Siegel (2000) suggests that there are two sorts of study. The first looks at short-run profits after adoption of social responsibility standards, looking at, for example, the effect on share price by specific announcements of new standards (or failures) (an example being Clinebell and Clinebell, 1994). The second looks at long-run profitability by taking a cross-sectional analysis of company accounts and comparing social responsibility adoption with profits over a (relatively) long period (an example being Waddock and Graves, 1997). The findings have been mixed. For example, Aupperle *et al.* (1985) found no relationship between social responsibility and performance. Waddock and Graves (1997) found that profitability correlated positively with financial performance a year later. McGuire *et al.* (1988) found that performance prior to the adoption of social responsibility was important (suggesting that more successful firms were willing to adopt it), but that subsequent performance was not improved. McWilliams and Siegel themselves suggest that earlier studies are at fault because they do not take into account the effect of investment in research and development on corporate performance. Once this is taken into account, they suggest, social responsibility is largely neutral in terms of performance. Of course a mixed picture might be expected. The demand for a general rule: 'does undertaking socially responsible action X lead to an improved (or reduced) performance?' is probably a demand too much. Contingent factors such as the business sector, the expectations of customers, the actions of competitors and the prominence of particular social issues at the time are likely to have a significant impact and be highly variable.

How does this add up as far as the entrepreneur is concerned? Should he or she seek to aspire to a higher level of social responsibility? There is no clear answer. Social responsibilities can constrain the actions of a business. They often define what it *cannot* do, rather than what it can. This does not mean they are bad for business. They provide a sound, and shared, set of rules within which the business community can operate. They ensure that the benefits of business activity are distributed in a way which is seen to be fair and equitable. This sustains the motivation of all stakeholders in the venture. Businesses are rarely penalised for meeting their social responsibilities positively. On the other hand, they will be punished if they are seen to evade their responsibilities. This ensures that ventures which set high standards are not penalised by being undercut by those that have lower standards. Taking on discretionary responsibilities and being proactive with them may a strategic move. If this meets with the approval of customers and other stakeholders, it can provide a means by which the business can make itself different from competitors and gain an advantage in the marketplace (though, for some, this may negate the ethical character of the move). In recognition of this fact, the entrepreneur may specify the business's social responsibilities in its mission statement. Using discretionary responsibilities to give the business an edge need not conflict with the personal values of the entrepreneur. The entrepreneur can only improve the world with those values if the business is successful. The social responsibilities the venture accepts, and how it defines them, are not merely 'add-ons' to the entrepreneur's vision, they lie at its core. They are the character of the new world the entrepreneur seeks to build.

12.6) Understanding failure

Key learning outcome

An understanding of what business 'failure' actually means.

Entrepreneurs are always faced with the possibility of failure. No matter how much they believe that their innovation offers new value to customers and regardless of how confident they are that they can build a business to deliver it, they will ultimately be tested by the market. However many success factors they think are present, they may be found wanting in some respects. Uncertainty and risk are always present. Statistics of business failure are widely reported and they are usually quite frightening. Yet 'failure' is not a simple notion. It implies the absence of success and, like success, it can only be understood in relation to people's goals and expectations. Failure happens when expectations are not met. It is a question of degree and means different things to different stakeholders.

From the perspective of the entrepreneur at least eight degrees of 'failure' can be identified based on the performance of the business and the way the entrepreneur retains control of it. These are listed in an increasing order of severity below.

1   The business continues to exist as a legal entity under the control of the entrepreneur

(a)   *The business performs well financially but does not meet the social and self-development needs of the entrepreneur*

To most outsiders the business may appear to be a success. It may be performing well financially and making an impact on its market. It may be providing for the economic needs of the entrepreneur and his or her dependants but this does not necessarily mean it is meeting higher needs. The work necessary to keep the business running may be disrupting the entrepreneur's social life. The entrepreneur may have had unrealistic expectations about how the venture would satisfy his or her self-development needs. If the entrepreneur feels that he or she has failed in this respect it will be demotivating and can have an impact on their personal performance. The entrepreneur may feel that he or she has failed despite the financial success of their venture.

(b)   The business fails to achieve set strategic objectives

The business may meet the financial targets that have been set for it by the entrepreneur and its investors but even so may fail to meet the strategic targets, such as market share, growth and innovation rate set for it. This may not be of immediate concern if profits are being generated. However, it may warn of challenges ahead and potential problems with the long-term performance of the business. Much will depend on how sensitive to the strategy adopted the performance of the business is and how flexible that strategy is.

(c)   The business fails to perform as well as was planned but is financially secure

The venture may not meet the financial objectives set for it by the entrepreneur and investors but still remain financially secure. The objectives may have been quite ambitious, setting income targets which were very comfortable in relation to necessary expenditure. Though the business may not be in immediate danger investors may feel disappointed in the returns they will receive. Planned investments may have to be forgone. The entrepreneur may be called upon to address the business's strategy and revise its plans to improve performance in the future.

(d)   The business fails to perform as well as was planned, and needs additional financial support

The financial performance of the business may be so weak that income cannot cover necessary expenditure. Cash-flow problems will be encountered and it is likely that the business will not survive without a further injection of cash. This is likely to come from investors but additional support may also be gleaned by agreeing special terms with customers and suppliers. In this instance the entrepreneur is likely to be called upon to address the direction of the business and the way it is being run.

If financial performance falls below a certain level, and the commitments of the business exceed its ability to meet them, then investors and creditors may lose confidence altogether. A change in management may be called for. A number of scenarios are possible.

2   The business continues to exist as an independent entity but the entrepreneur loses control

(a)   The business is taken over as a going concern by new management

The business an entrepreneur creates is separate to them in that it has its own legal and organisational identity. It is possible that the business can continue and prosper even if the entrepreneur is no longer involved in its running. The entrepreneur may leave the business for a variety of reasons. Though successful, the entrepreneur may feel that it doesn't offer them sufficient challenges or they may feel that managing it does not fulfil them (as in 1(a) above). They may sell their interest to a new manager or management team and move on to do something else. If this is what the entrepreneur wants to do then it must be counted as a success. The entrepreneur may, however, be called upon to leave the business against their wishes.

If the business is not performing, its backers may decide that their best interests are served by bringing in new management with different ideas and different ways of doing things. Their ability to oust the resident entrepreneur will depend on how much of the business they own, the ability of the investors to liquidate their investment and the contracts they have with the entrepreneur.

(b) The business is taken over with restructuring

As in scenario 2(a), the entrepreneur is called upon to leave. However, rather than run the business much as it was, the new management team may feel that performance can only be improved if the business undergoes a fundamental restructuring. This can involve changing its employees and making major acquisitions and divestments of assets.

3 The business does not continue to exist as an independent entity

(a) The business is taken over as a going concern and absorbed into another company

One business may be acquired by another through a takeover. It may retain some of its original character, and a modified legal status, by becoming a subsidiary of the parent. It loses its separate identity and all legal character if it is merged with the parent. In this case its employees move to work for the parent and its assets are combined with the parent's assets. A takeover, or merger, may take place at the behest of the entrepreneur who wishes to sell their interest and move on to something else. It may also be instigated by investors who have lost confidence in the entrepreneur and the venture and wish to cut their losses by liquidating their investment. The entrepreneur may, or may not, retain an involvement by becoming a manager for the new parent.

(b) The business is broken up and its assets disposed of

Takeover and mergers take place if there is a belief that the venture has some potential, even if a completely new management approach is called for. If there is no confidence even in this, then the business may be broken up and its assets sold off as separate items. The proceeds are used to reimburse stakeholders.

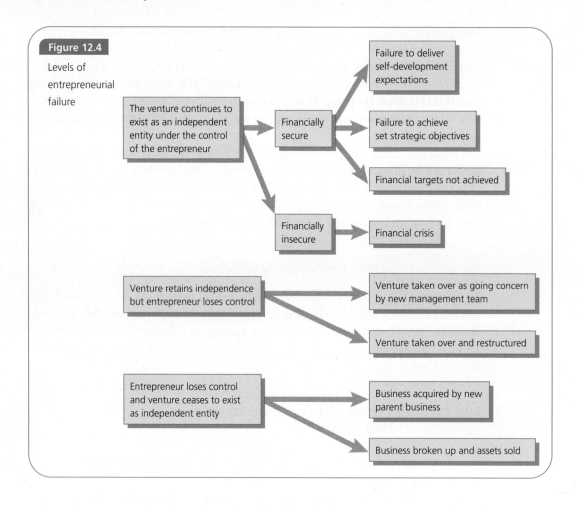

Figure 12.4

Levels of entrepreneurial failure

Creditors and outstanding loans take priority. The investors, i.e. the actual owners of the venture, are only entitled to anything left after all creditors have been paid (Figure 12.4).

Managing failure

Failure is a fact of business life. It is the possibility of failing that makes success meaningful. Failure is not always a disaster and it does not inevitably mean the end of the venture. Failure is part of the learning process. Minor failures can be positive indicators of how things might be done better. Such failures should not be ignored. They must be addressed before they become the seeds of larger failures. Success and failure exist relative to *expectations*. Failure occurs when expectations are not met. Managing success, and managing failure, have a lot to do with managing people's expectations for the venture, keeping them positive, but at the same time keeping them realistic.

Summary of key ideas

● The success of the entrepreneurial venture must be understood through three dimensions – the *stakeholders* who have an interest in the venture; their *expectations* of the venture; and actual *outcomes* relative to those expectations.

● The most effective entrepreneurs define objectives for success in relation to *all* the venture's stakeholders (not just its investors) and operate with a keen sense of social responsibility.

● Many successful entrepreneurs have demanded that their businesses operate with a higher level of social responsibility than other businesses operating in their sectors.

● The issue of corporate social responsibility is complex and of growing interest. There is no clear picture as to whether, in general, accepting higher levels of responsibility increases or decreases shareholder value.

● 'Failure' has many degrees and is an integral part of venturing. Good entrepreneurs learn from failure.

Research theme

Entrepreneurs' perceptions of success

Section 12.1 developed a model of entrepreneurial success based on the venture's ability to satisfy economic, social and developmental needs, the stakeholders involved in the venture and their expectations relative to outcomes. This framework provides a basis for exploring entrepreneurs' belief in and attitudes towards success. Select a poll of entrepreneurs. These may be nascent, novice, singular or portfolio. It would be interesting to correlate beliefs across these different types of entrepreneur. Conduct a survey with the sample group, ascertaining:

● their general thoughts about success;

● who they feel has a role in success, and who has a priority for rewards from the venture's success;

● what needs success aims to satisfy. Have the entrepreneur prioritise economic, social and developmental needs;

● how the entrepreneur sees the role of expectations and how they should be managed (e.g. should the entrepreneur over-promise at the start to get stakeholders on board, or under-promise so that stakeholders will be satisfied with actual outcomes?).

For the analysis, categorise the entrepreneurs in terms of their priorities with regard to the needs their ventures must satisfy (e.g. economic over social and developmental) and their priorities with stakeholders (e.g. investors over employees). Do entrepreneurs fall into neat 'rationalist' (self-priority – economic needs) and 'humanist' (other stakeholder – broader needs) categories, or are they more dispersed? How do the categories identified match with the entrepreneurs' development stage? How do the categories match with the entrepreneurs' management of expectations?

Suggestions for further reading

Atkinson, A.A., Waterhouse, J.H. and Wells, R.B. (1997) 'A stakeholder approach to strategic performance measurement', *Sloan Management Review*, Spring, pp. 25–37.

Aupperle, K., Carroll, A. and Hatfield, J. (1985) 'An empirical examination of the relationship between corporate social responsibility and profitability', *Academy of Management Journal*, Vol. 28, No. 2, pp. 446–63.

Avishai, B. (1994) 'What is business's social compact', *Harvard Business Review*, Vol. 72, No. 1, pp. 38–48.

Bagley, C.E. (2003) 'The ethical leader's decision tree', *Harvard Business Review*, February, pp. 18–19.

Ben-Ner, A. and Putterman, L. (eds) (1998) *Economics, Values, and Organization*, Cambridge: Cambridge University Press.

Bucar, B. and Hisrich, R.D. (2001) 'Ethics of business managers vs entrepreneurs', *Journal of Developmental Entrepreneurship*, Vol. 6, No. 1, pp. 59–72.

Brown, D.M. and Laverick, S. (1994) 'Measuring corporate performance', *Long Range Planning*, Vol. 27, No. 4, pp. 89–98.

Carroll, A.B. (1979) 'A three-dimensional model of corporate performance', *Academy of Management Review*, Vol. 4, No. 4, pp. 497–505.

Clinebell, S.K. and Clinebell, J.M. (1994) 'The effects of advance notice of plant closures on firm value', *Journal of Management*, Vol. 20, pp. 553–64.

Dawson, S., Breen, J. and Satyen, L. (2002) 'The ethical outlook of micro-business operators', *Journal of Small Business Management*, Vol. 40, No. 4, pp. 302–13.

De George, R. (1999) *Business Ethics*, Upper Saddle River, NJ: Prentice Hall.

Dennis, W.J. and Fernald, L.W. (2001) 'The chances of financial success (and loss) from small business ownership', *Entrepreneurship Theory and Practice*, Fall, pp. 75–83.

Dollinger, M.J. (1984) 'Measuring effectiveness in entrepreneurial organisations', *International Small Business Journal*, Vol. 3, No. 1, pp. 10–20.

Douma, S. (1991) 'Success and failure in new ventures', *Long Range Planning*, Vol. 24, No. 2, pp. 54–60.

Friedman, M. (1962) *Capitalism and Freedom*, Chicago, IL: University of Chicago Press.

Griffiths, B., Sirco, R.A., Barry, N. and Field, F. (2001) *Capitalism, Morality and Markets*, London: Institute of Economic Affairs.

Harrison, E.F. and Pelletier, M.A. (1995) 'A paradigm for strategic decision success', *Management Decision*, Vol. 33, No. 7, pp. 53–9.

Harrison, E.F. and Pelletier, M.A. (2000) 'Levels of strategic decision success', *Management Decision*, Vol. 38, No. 2, pp. 107–17.

Henderson, D. (2001) *Misguided Virtue: False Notions of Corporate Social Responsibility*, London: Institute of Economic Affairs.

Hutton, W. (ed.) (1997) *Stakeholding and its Critics*, Choice in Welfare No. 36, London: Institute of Economic Affairs.

Joyner, B.E., Payne, D. and Raiborn, C.A. (2002) 'Building values, business ethics and corporate social responsibility into the developing organisation', *Journal of Developmental Entrepreneurship*, Vol. 7, No. 1, pp. 113–31.

Kaplan, R.S. and Norton, D.P. (1996) 'Linking the balanced scorecard to strategy', *California Management Review*, Vol. 39, No. 1, pp. 53–79.

Longenecker, C.O., Simonetti, J.L. and Sharkey, T.W. (1999) 'Why organizations fail: the view from the front line', *Management Decision*, Vol. 37, No. 6, pp. 503–13.

Martin, R.L. (2002) 'The virtue matrix: calculating the return on corporate social responsibility', *Harvard Business Review*, March, pp. 68–75.

McGuire, J., Sundgren, A. and Schneeweis, T. (1988) 'Corporate social responsibility and firm financial performance', *Academy of Management Journal*, Vol. 31, No. 4, pp. 854–72.

McWilliams, A. and Siegel, D. (2000) 'Corporate social responsibility and financial performance: correlation or misspecification?', *Strategic Management Journal*, Vol. 21, pp. 603–9.

Mole, K. (2000) 'Business advisers impact on SMEs', Middlesex University Discussion Paper Series: Business and Management. Available at: http://mubs.mdx.ac.uk/research/Discussion_Papers/Business_and_Management/dpapmsno_4.pdf.

Nash, L. (1995) 'The real truth about corporate values', *Public Relations Strategist*, Summer.

Nucci, A. (1999) 'The demography of business closings', *Small Business Economics*, Vol. 12, No. 1, pp. 25–9.

Osborne, R.L. (1993) 'Why entrepreneurs fail: how to avoid the traps', *Management Decision*, Vol. 31, No. 1, pp. 18–21.

Osborne, R.L. (1995) 'The essence of entrepreneurial success', *Management Decision*, Vol. 33, No. 7, pp. 4–9.

Paine, L.S. (1994) 'Managing for organisational integrity', *Harvard Business Review*, March/April, pp. 106–17.

Porter, M. and Kramer, M.R. (2002) 'The competitive advantage of corporate philanthropy', *Harvard Business Review*, December, pp. 56–69.

Routamaa, V. and Vesalainen, J. (1987) 'Types of entrepreneur and strategic level goal setting', *International Small Business Journal*, Vol. 5, No. 3, pp. 19–29.

Sacks, J. (ed.) (1998) Morals and markets, *Institute of Economic Affairs Occasional Paper* No. 108. London: Institute of Economic Affairs.

Seglod, E. (1995) 'New ventures: the Swedish experience', *Long Range Planning*, Vol. 28, No. 4, pp. 45–53.

Smallbone, D. (1990) 'Success and failure in new business start-ups', *International Small Business Journal*, Vol. 8, No. 2, pp. 34–47.

Throsby, C.D. (2001) *Economics and Culture*, Cambridge: Cambridge University Press.

Waddock, S. and Graves, S. (1997) 'The corporate social performance–financial performance link', *Strategic Management Journal*, Vol. 18, No. 4, pp. 303–19.

Watson, J. and Everett, J. (1993) 'Defining small business failure', *International Small Business Journal*, Vol. 11, No. 3, pp. 35–48.

Watson, K., Hogarth-Scott, S. and Wilson, N. (1998) 'Small business start-ups: success factors and support implications', *International Journal of Entrepreneurial Behaviour and Research*, Vol. 4, No. 3, pp. 217–38.

How small entrepreneurs are cutting it at the Fringe

FT

5 August 2002

By **Mark Nicholson**, Scotland Correspondent

The Fringe descends this weekend on Edinburgh, the world's biggest festival of comedy, theatre and music. Ed Bartlam and Charles Wood, a 22-year-old English undergraduate and 29-year-old lawyer, have spent the past week, and much money, tarting up the city's underbelly in readiness.

The Smirnoff Underbelly, to be precise, is their quintessential Fringe venue. It's a Gormenghast-like warren of vaults, stair wells and corridors beneath the city's main register office, transformed by the duo at a cost of £39,000 from damp abandonment into three bars and five performance spaces.

The Underbelly is a classic example of Fringe enterprise. Messrs Bartlam and Wood launched the venue two years ago with one performance room, a small bar and five shows. This year the atmospheric venue will host 45 separate acts, stage 55 shows daily and, just possibly, make some money.

'We love doing it, but we're definitely looking for a financial return,' says Mr Wood. Indeed, Mr Bartlam is seriously considering turning this summer hobby into a full-time career. He would not be the first arts professional to launch his career at Fringe.

Paul Gudgin, the festival director, says the Fringe is unique in the UK, perhaps even Europe, in being such a cauldron of artistic enterprise. 'The question is why the Fringe is so good at creating all these micro-businesses and letting them grow. Perhaps the answer is you can start in a small way and if you've got the talent you can go from tiny to the top of the tree in a very short time.'

The Fringe began in the 1950s as a breeding ground for comic, acting and other artistic talent. But less widely appreciated, Mr Gudgin says, is its role as a nursery for the British arts industry, spawning generations of impresarios, venue managers, stage and theatre technicians. 'In artistic terms, it's a showcase. But in business terms, it's a trade fair,' he says.

Over the next four weeks, 691 companies will do 20,342 performances of 1,491 shows in a record 183 venues. Last year box office takings topped a record £6.6m.

'If you want to be an impresario or a technician, this is the place to come,' says Christopher Richardson, himself a classic Fringe entrepreneur, a theatre designer by profession whose first venue beneath a student bar in 1985 mushroomed into the Pleasance, the Fringe's biggest venue, with 188 shows this year and a turnover exceeding £1m. 'A lot of people who are now, for instance, running the BBC – the first time they got to play with these sorts of things was in Edinburgh.'

Moreover, for all its scale and apparently chaotic growth, venue managers suggest the Fringe has become increasingly professionally run – 'considerably better than Railtrack or the NHS', says Mr Richardson.

Edinburgh council and Scottish Enterprise Edinburgh and Lothians, the local development agency, last year identified the Fringe as a local economic opportunity, launching a new training course for venue and event management in concert with the organisers. 'They realised that you have a little group of art entrepreneurs who are making business for the city,' says Mr Gudgin.

For the city, it is big business. The council estimates that all the festivals, including summer's international, book, film, jazz and Fringe festivals and the New Year celebrations, reap £140m.

Source: Financial Times, 5 August 2002.

Breathing life into social responsibility

15 January 2002

By **David Varney**

Business is the dominant institution of the 21st century. Not only is it business that provides national governments with their money, either directly through corporate taxation or indirectly from income tax, but the social and environmental power of business is immense and is being accelerated by globalisation.

Why, then, are we in business so often seen as a cause of global problems when we should be part of the solution? And this after 20 years of dedicated work by Business in the Community, which has encouraged companies to work in society and has publicised the many success stories.

Tomorrow, I take over from Sir Peter Davis as chairman of Business in the Community. He and his board colleagues have done a magnificent job in getting us where we are today.

My vision is to work with the organisation's many members to take corporate social responsibility to the next stage, with a greater emphasis on creativity and innovation. The impact of that on previously intractable social and environmental problems could be immense. The impact on the reputation of business could be equally positive.

Business in the Community has been a success story. The personal involvement of senior executives in social issues is an absolute must if companies are to take this aspect of their role seriously. I can testify how successfully this has been done by the Seeing is Believing programme.

Business in the Community has also worked well to encourage a climate of openness and reporting for business. There are plenty of external pressures promoting this – from the Stock Exchange, from government, from activists. There are also those companies that

have realised that there is little point in a serious engagement with society if you do not measure and report on your social and environmental impact. Doing good by stealth should not be an option: society has the right to know.

So we have a lot of CSR activity by business and a greater awareness of the need to report. This is good – but not enough. We are missing the most obvious trick of all.

Successful businesses are built on innovation, risk-taking, challenging the conventional in favour of the radical. Yet when business-people leave their strategy meetings and walk across the corridor to a CSR discussion, they leave all that behind. Too much CSR is dominated by tired old initiatives that have been brought in a hundred times before – cleaning up this, collecting that – designed to make the company feel good.

What are missing are the strategic thinking and engagement with society that would be routine if we were launching a new product or, in my case, a whole new company. CSR initiatives do not exist in a vacuum. They are part of the wider impact of business on communities and they need to be justified both in business terms and in terms of positive outcomes for society and the environment.

The Seeing is Believing programme will carry on winning new converts to Business in the Community. But my mantra for the future will be 'seeing is doing' – and doing it innovatively and imaginatively.

The business drive behind this is both imperative and real. It is easy to be trapped into marketing goods and services to the affluent white consumer. The business advantage of engagement with CSR is that we can learn to engage with people of different wealth, culture and geography – people who may be vital as skilled employees, suppliers or consumers. No right-minded entrepreneur would neglect those opportunities. All it takes is a little thinking outside the box.

The great advantage of Business in the Community is that it enables companies to share the learning of successful innovation more widely and to create replicable models for others to use.

The suggestion that this is somehow antithetical to the real stuff of commercial life – making money – is false. This is about building a business that is truly sustainable, that delivers long-term shareholder value in a society that expects businesses to be social and environmental players and punishes them if they are not.

Business must also stay in the CSR driving seat if innovation is to be delivered, because innovation and creativity is what we deliver. The contribution that is made to CSR thinking by governments, the voluntary sector, or non-government organisations is immense but it cannot replace the business case. We have to be wary of satisfying the agendas of others without delivering on our own.

My other main task as chairman will be to build a better working relationship with the voluntary sector. That is a two-way street. There are many outstanding examples of partnership between business and charities but if we are to guarantee the success of projects, the voluntary sector must become more businesslike in terms of structure. Otherwise scarce resources will inevitably be diverted from the real task of social improvement, the only raison d'etre for the sector.

In business, such a state of affairs would lead pretty rapidly to rationalisation. There are not the same commercial drivers in the voluntary sector but business organisations can encourage that process – ultimately by focusing their involvement on voluntary sector bodies that are aware of the need for consolidation and coherence in their approach.

CSR is going through a phase of change leading to important opportunities for businesses that get it right. I intend Business in the Community to play a significant role in helping companies to do just that.

The writer is chairman of MMO2, formerly BT Wireless, and takes over tomorrow as chairman of Business in the Community.

Source: Financial Times, 15 January 2002, © David Varney.

Discussion points

1. Using the model of success developed in this chapter, consider if entrepreneurs who generate cultural products (e.g. in arts, media, heritage, entertainment) should regard success in a different light to entrepreneurs who are producing non-cultural products. Do cultural entrepreneurs produce products that are 'inherently' more valuable than non-cultural entrepreneurs? Are they deserving of special support from government? (For a discussion of these issues refer to Throsby, 2001.)

2. Are CSR objectives fundamental to entrepreneurs' responsibilities or are they a distraction from their key responsibility of creating new and demanded products, jobs and investor value?

Part 2

Choosing a direction

Chapter 13

Entrepreneurial vision

Chapter overview

The presence of a powerful, motivating personal vision is one of the defining characteristics of entrepreneurial management. This chapter is concerned with exploring the concept of vision and understanding how it can be used by the entrepreneur to give the venture a sense of direction and purpose. It also addresses how vision can be refined, articulated and communicated to make it into an effective managerial tool.

13.1 What is entrepreneurial vision?

> **Key learning outcome**
>
> An appreciation of the power of entrepreneurial vision and of the value it offers for the venture.

Entrepreneurs are managers. They manage more than just an organisation, they manage the creation of a 'new world'. This new world offers the possibility of value being generated and made available to the venture's stakeholders. This value can only be created through change – change in the way things are *done*, change in *organisations* and change in *relationships*. Entrepreneurs rarely stumble on success. It is more usually a reward for directing their actions in an appropriate way towards some opportunity. Effective entrepreneurs know where they are going, and why. They are focused on the achievement of specific goals.

The entrepreneur's vision is a picture of the new world he or she wishes to create. It is a picture into which the entrepreneur fits an understanding of why people will be better off, the source of the new value that will be created, and the relationships that will exist. This picture is a very positive one and the entrepreneur is drawn towards it. He or she is motivated to make their vision into reality. Vision exists in the tension between what *is* and what *might* be. A vision includes an understanding of the rewards that are to be earned by creating the new world and why people will be attracted to them. Vision specifies a *destination* rather than a route to get there. It is created out of possibilities, not certainties.

Entrepreneurial visions have detail. This detail may be extensive, as if the picture were painted with fine brush strokes. Alternatively, the detail may be limited and the picture drawn from broad strokes. The details may be in sharp focus and thoroughly defined, or they may be quite vague, calling for further clarification. Whatever the shape of the details, the different parts of the vision will fit together to form a coherent whole. To the entrepreneur the vision pulling the venture forward will have an existence of its own, a unity quite separate from its component parts.

A vision is a 'mental' image in that it is something the entrepreneur carries around in their head. This does not mean it is insubstantial, indeed far from it. It is a very powerful tool for the management of the venture. In particular:

- it provides a sense of direction by being the 'light at the end of the tunnel';
- it helps the entrepreneur to define his or her goals;
- it provides the entrepreneur with a sense of 'warmth' and encouragement when the going gets tough;
- it guides the generation of strategy for the venture;
- it gives the venture a moral content and helps define social responsibilities;
- it can be used to communicate what the entrepreneur wishes to achieve to other people;
- it can be used to attract people to the venture and motivate them to support it;
- it plays a crucial role in supporting the entrepreneur's communication and leadership strategy.

Vision is an important tool for the entrepreneur. It defines where the entrepreneur wants to go, illuminates why he or she wants to be there and provides signposts for how they might get there. If it is to be an effective tool, vision must be used actively. However, vision must be properly shaped and nurtured. It must be refined and tested. A vision which is unachievable, or which is based on wrong assumptions, or which points in the wrong direction, will easily lead the venture astray. The entrepreneur must learn to challenge vision. It must be defined and shaped so that it is appropriate, viable and achievable, before it can be put to use.

13.2) Developing and shaping vision

> **Key learning outcome**
>
> An understanding of how entrepreneurial vision can be developed and shaped by the entrepreneur to make it into an effective tool for the management of the venture.

Vision is the starting point for giving shape and direction to the venture. Some sense of vision must exist before strategy development and planning can start. If it is to lead the business in the right direction, vision must be properly examined, refined and evaluated.

Vision develops from the idea that things might be different from, and better than, they are currently. A vision might 'present' itself to the entrepreneur quite suddenly, or alternatively it may emerge slowly, taking shape as the entrepreneur explores an opportunity and recognises its possibilities. No matter how it comes about, vision is something which is constructed personally. It is, first and foremost, a communication with oneself. Communicating with oneself follows similar rules to communicating with anyone else. The objectives behind making the communication should be understood and it must be thought through and properly articulated. If vision is to be used effectively as a force for self-motivation and as a guide to setting goals, developing strategy and attracting support, then the entrepreneur must become aware of his or her vision, isolate it, communicate it to themselves, and refine it.

The vision will be a picture of the new world the entrepreneur seeks to create. It is constructed personally and will vary from entrepreneur to entrepreneur. Whatever form it takes, the entrepreneur must learn to question the vision. At first, the entrepreneur's vision will be ill defined, with its details out of focus. Questioning it helps bring it into focus. Some important questions to ask are:

- What will be the *source* of the value to be created in the new world?

- Who will be *involved* in this new world (i.e. who are the stakeholders)?

- Why will those involved be *better off* in the new world than they are at present?

- In what way will they *gain* (financially, socially, through personal development)?

- What financial reward will be received *personally* for creating the new world?

- What new *relationships* will need to be developed?

- What is the *nature* of the relationships that will be built in the new world?

- Why will this new world fulfil, or offer the potential to fulfil, personal *self-development* goals?

In short, entrepreneurs must understand *why* their vision offers a picture of a more valuable world and how it will reward them and the other stakeholders involved in the venture. To do this they must understand their personal motivation and the motivations of the stakeholders involved. This questioning must be a *continual*

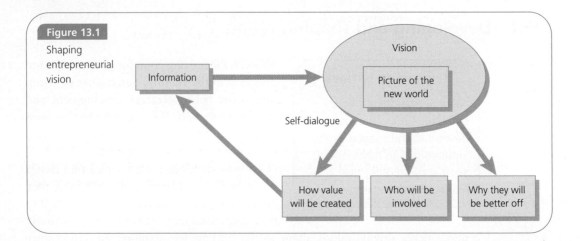

Figure 13.1

Shaping entrepreneurial vision

process. Vision must be constantly refined and kept in focus. While it should provide a consistent and constant sense of direction, it should be kept flexible. Its shape may change as the entrepreneur's understanding of their personal motivations and the motivations of others evolves. To keep it fresh, entrepreneurs should constantly renegotiate their vision with themselves. Vision should always pull entrepreneurs forward. It should never hold them back (Figure 13.1).

13.3 Communicating and sharing vision

Key learning outcome

An appreciation of how entrepreneurial vision can be used to motivate and attract support for the venture.

The entrepreneur's vision gives their venture direction, and motivates them to progress it. Vision is, in the first instance, a personal picture of the new world the entrepreneur seeks to create. If it is to be used to attract other people to the venture this new world must be communicated to them. They must be invited to share in what it can offer. Communication is not just about relating information. It is about eliciting *action* on the part of the receiver. It is not so much about getting people to know things, as about getting them to *do* things. Effective entrepreneurs understand how their vision can be used to motivate others as much as it can be used to motivate themselves.

The first stage must be to understand why other people will find the vision attractive. The entrepreneur must identify what the new world will offer stakeholders, both as individuals and as groups. The questions the entrepreneur must ask in relation to the stakeholders are:

- What benefits will they gain if the new world comes into being?

- How will they be able to address their economic, social and self-development needs better in the new world than they can in the existing one?

- Will they be attracted by the moral and discretionary social responsibility entailed in the vision and the specific issues that it addresses?

- What risks will the new world present to them?

- How credible will they find the possibility of achieving the new world?

- How will they view the journey they must take to get to the new world?

Finding the answers to these questions is part of the process the entrepreneur must go through in shaping and refining their vision. The answers will influence the way they communicate it to others. Some important approaches to communicating vision are as follows.

'I have a dream . . .'

In this approach entrepreneurs are explicit about their vision. They describe the better world just as they see it. The vision is presented as a coherent whole. Its parts fit together to create a unified picture. Entrepreneurs expect other people to find it as attractive as they do and to be drawn towards it.

Talking specific goals

Alternatively, entrepreneurs can break down their vision into a series of specific goals, relating, for example, to economic outcomes, to the value that will be gained, to the relationships that will be created, and to the moral content of the new world. Each of these is communicated separately or in particular combinations. The choice of what is communicated will depend on to whom the vision is being communicated, when it is being communicated in what situation and with what intention.

Talking strategy

Here entrepreneurs do not talk so much about *ends* as about *means*. Strategy relates to the approach that the business will take to achieving its goals and the tasks that must be undertaken in order to create the new world. In this entrepreneurs are reliant on the fact that people will be attracted to the journey as well as the destination.

Story-telling

In using this approach entrepreneurs think of their vision as a 'stage' on which the venture is played out. The stakeholders are actors who play parts on that stage. Entrepreneurs give their vision a dynamic form by describing scenarios and telling stories about what might happen. The communication takes shape by relating future events and the roles that people can play in them. Entrepreneurs aim to motivate people by attracting them to their roles within the story. A study by O'Connor (2002) of high-technology start-ups suggests that entrepreneurs create a range of narratives to draw stakeholders into the venture. O'Connor identifies six basic narrative types in three categories. The themes of these narratives are as follows:

1 *Personal stories*
  A *Founding stories* – autobiographical accounts of why the venture was started.
  B *Vision stories* – stories about innovation and breakthroughs.

2 *Generic stories*
  A *Marketing stories* – stories about the superiority of the venture against competitors.
  B *Strategy stories* – stories about the history of the venture and its future trajectory.

3 *Situational stories*
  A *Historical stories* – stories about the development of the venture's industry.
  B *Conventional stories* – stories about beliefs and attitudes of industry players and customers.

Lounsbury and Glynn (2001) propose a framework for what they refer to as 'cultural' entrepreneurship in which story-telling acts to mediate between the resources the entrepreneur has actually acquired and subsequent resources brought into the venture through its success as a way of creating a new identity for the venture and building legitimacy with key stakeholders.

Why things can be better

The entrepreneur emphasises what is wrong with the world as it is rather than what will be better in the new world. The aim is to push people forward using their sense of dissatisfaction, rather than to pull them forward by using the attractions of new possibilities. While it may shake people out of their complacencies, too much emphasis on this approach runs the risk of simply sounding negative and being demotivating, especially if no positive alternative appears to be offered.

What's in it for you

In this approach entrepreneurs focus on the particular benefits that will be gained by the recipient of the communication. The vision is broken down and 'packaged' for the individual. Tailoring the vision in this way is a good way of ensuring the commitment of a particular person. If over-used, however, the recipient may feel that their commitment is being bought. This approach to communication runs the danger of giving the impression that the entrepreneur regards the recipient as being 'mercenary' and purely motivated by personal gain.

Selecting a communication strategy

These approaches to communicating vision are not mutually exclusive. They are individual strands that can be brought together to make up an overall communication strategy for the entrepreneur's vision. By using a diverse approach to communicating this vision the entrepreneur keeps it relevant, avoids being repetitive and keeps the message fresh to recipients. The particular strategy adopted will depend on a number of factors. Some of the more important include:

- the nature of the vision being shared (how complex is it? how much detail does it have?);

- the entrepreneur's leadership style (is it collaborative, democratic, authoritarian?);

- the stakeholders to whom the vision is being communicated (who are they? how many?);

- the nature of the commitment desired from them;

- the stakeholders' particular needs and motivations (economic, social, self-development);

- the stakeholders' relationship to the entrepreneur;

- the situation of the communication (formal or informal, one-to-one, one-to-many, etc.);

- the medium through which the communication is transmitted (face-to-face, verbal, written, etc.).

An ability to articulate the vision and communicate it effectively to different stakeholders in a way that is appropriate to them and in a way that is right for the situation is the basis on which the entrepreneur builds his or her leadership and power.

13.4 Entrepreneurship and strategic foresight

> **Key learning outcome**
>
> An appreciation of the concept of 'strategic foresight' and recognition of its role in entrepreneurial success.

The notion of entrepreneurial vision suggests that the entrepreneur is anticipating a new, better world. The achievement of that world reflects on both the entrepreneur's ability to engage with and make changes in the world and to anticipate those things the entrepreneur cannot change (the business environment in its wider sense). The entrepreneur must mould the raw stuff of the world. There is potential to shape it into different forms, but the stuff itself does not change. The success of a vision (or success in delivering that vision) is, to a degree, dependent on the entrepreneur having foresight about how the world will be in the future. This aspect of an entrepreneur's abilities is of growing interest in the entrepreneurship research field and is the subject of a new text edited by Tsoukas and Shepherd (2003). Gibb and Scott (1985) define strategic foresight (which they term 'strategic awareness') in terms of it being the ability to assess the total impact of a particular change or decision; to be able to project into the future the effects and consequences of a particular action and think about these in strategic terms. Slaughter (1995) characterises strategic foresight as 'a process that attempts to broaden the boundaries of perception in four ways':

- by assessing the implications of present actions, decisions, etc. (consequent assessment);
- by detecting and avoiding problems before they occur (early warning and guidance);
- by considering the present implications of possible future events (proactive strategy formulation);
- by envisioning aspects of desired futures (normative scenarios).

Strategic foresight is a competence, both for the individual entrepreneur and the organisation as the entrepreneur imparts that foresight into the venture's decision making. Such a competence is a potential source of competitive advantage as it allows the venture to anticipate future opportunities, the means to exploit them and risk issues that will arise in their exploitation in a way that is superior to competitors who lack the foresight. Hamel and Prahalad (1994) refer to a 'highly visible vision of the future', a 'strategic intent' as a source of competitive advantage. A study by Ensley *et al.* (2000) indicates that such entrepreneurial vision does contribute positively to the performance of a venture. Strategic foresight might also be considered to be a part of a broader responsibility of the entrepreneur in turning ambiguity (which cannot be quantified, and so cannot be insured against) into risk (which can). Schoemaker (1997) suggests that strategic vision enables an organisation to differentiate itself through foresight. It is not, however, the remit of the entrepreneur on his or her own, rather it is only effective if organisation members share the vision. He suggests a four-stage process for ensuring that foresight is in fact shared. Kandampully and Duddy (1999) argue for a specific role of strategic foresight in anticipating the value of service delivery to create and maintain lifetime customer loyalty.

Traditional decision theory places restrictions on the knowledge one can have about the future. One may know (or not) what eventualities will occur and be able to refine eventualities with varying degrees of precision. Further, one may have knowledge of the likelihood of particular eventualities taking place. Fuller *et al.* (2003) look beyond conventional decision theory and take a more interpretative approach and regard strategic foresight as a personal competence of the entrepreneur, which is not, necessarily, reducible to conventional decision theoretical concepts. The notion of strategic foresight is an idea that has a long history. As far back as 1934, Schumpeter noted in his characterisation of entrepreneurship as 'creative destruction' that some individuals can see the future in a way which afterwards proves to be true, even if it cannot be established at the moment.

Summary of key ideas

- Entrepreneurs are managers with a *vision*.

- A vision is a picture of the *new and better world* that the entrepreneur wishes to create.

- Vision can be refined and articulated as a *management tool*.

- Vision can be used as the basis of a powerful *leadership strategy*.

- Visionary leadership demands *communication* of the vision in a way which draws stakeholders towards the venture and *motivates* them to work for its success.

- Strategic foresight is a skill in or capability for anticipating the future and predicting the long-term effects of decisions made now. Effective strategic foresight may play a role in entrepreneurial success.

Research theme

Entrepreneurial vision: articulation and communication

As noted, vision can be moulded into an effective managerial and leadership tool. This chapter has developed models of how vision is articulated and communicated. Does this match up with how entrepreneurs articulate and communicate vision in practice? Obtain a series of communications by entrepreneurs that record their communication of vision. Sources might include business plans, case studies, newspaper articles (the FT is a good source), public communications to employees, statements in accounts or media interviews. These sources may be supplemented by primary research asking entrepreneurs to describe their vision for their businesses. How do entrepreneurs develop and shape their vision? How much detail does the vision have? What latitude are they leaving for negotiation about the vision? How are they communicating it? Does the pattern of communication meet with the criteria described in Section 13.3?

Suggestions for further reading

Campbell, A. and Yeung, S. (1991) 'Vision, mission and strategic intent', *Long Range Planning*, Vol. 24, No. 4, pp. 145–7.

Ensley, M.D., Carland, J.W. and Carland, J.C. (2000) 'Investigating the existence of the lead entrepreneur', *Journal of Small Business Management*, October, pp. 59–77.

Filion, L.J. (1991) 'Vision and relations: elements for an entrepreneurial meta-model', *International Small Business Journal*, Vol. 9, No. 1, pp. 15–31.

Fuller, E., Argyle, P. and Moran, P. (2003) 'Entrepreneurial foresight: a case study in reflexivity, experiments, sensitivity and reorganisation', in Tsoukas, H. and Shepherd, J. (eds) *Developing Strategic Foresight in the Knowledge Economy: Probing the Future*, Oxford: Blackwell.

Gibb, A.A. and Scott, M.G. (1985) 'Strategic awareness, personal commitment and the process of planning in the small business', *Journal of Management Studies*, Vol. 22, No. 6, pp. 597–625.

Gratton, L. (1996) 'Implementing a strategic vision – key factors for success', *Long Range Planning*, Vol. 29, No. 3, pp. 290–303.

Hamel, G. and Prahalad, C.K. (1994) *Competing for the Future*, Boston, MA: Harvard Business School Press.

Kandampully, J. and Duddy, R. (1999) 'Competitive advantage through anticipation, innovation and relationships', *Management Decision*, Vol. 37, No. 1, pp. 51–6.

Lipton, M. (1996) 'Demystifying the development of organisational vision', *Sloan Management Review*, Summer, pp. 83–92.

Lounsbury, M. and Glynn, M.A. (2001) 'Cultural entrepreneurship: stories, legitimacy and the acquisition of resources', *Strategic Management Journal*, Vol. 22, pp. 545–64.

O'Connor, E. (2002) 'Storied business: typology, intertextuality and traffic in entrepreneurial narrative', *Journal of Business*, Vol. 39, No. 1, pp. 36–54.

Schoemaker, P.J.H. (1997) 'Disciplined imagination: from scenarios to strategic options (preparing for the future: developing strategic flexibility from a competence-based perspective)', *International Studies in Management and Organisation*, Vol. 27, No. 2, pp. 43–70.

Schumpeter, J.A. (1934) *The Theory of Economic Development: An Inquiry into Profits, Capital, Credit, Interest and the Business Cycle*, Cambridge, MA: Harvard University Press.

Shirley, S. (1989) 'Corporate strategy and entrepreneurial vision', *Long Range Planning*, Vol. 22, No. 6, pp. 107–10.

Slaughter, R.A. (1995) *The Foresight Principle: Cultural Revovery in the 21st Century*, London: Adamantine Press.

Stewart, J.M. (1993) 'Future state visioning – a powerful leadership process', *Long Range Planning*, Vol. 26, No. 6, pp. 89–98.

Tsoukas, H and Shepherd, J. (eds) *Developing Strategic Foresight in the Knowledge Economy: Probing the Future*, Oxford: Blackwell.

Westley, F. and Mintzberg, H. (1989) 'Visionary leadership and strategic management', *Strategic Management Journal*, Vol. 10, pp. 17–32.

An entrepreneur of the people

FT

5 June 2002

By **Khozem Merchant**

He has been called many things but 'chief mentor' clearly ranks among the most satisfying. N.R. Narayana Murthy took on the title after a sideways shift at Infosys Technologies, India's best-known software services company, which he founded and led for two decades. 'As chief mentor, I'll create future leaders of Infosys. Leaders build aspirations. They make people walk on water,' he says.

Alongside India's venal old-guard business leaders, Mr Murthy does appear to walk on water. His promotion of western-style corporate governance, stock options to reward talent and a rigorous professionalism has won admiration.

'He has created a leadership position for himself and his company out of nothing and he's done this to a global rather than a domestic audience. Corporate India needs more like him,' says Phiroz Vandrevala, executive vice-president of Tata Consultancy Services, India's biggest software company.

Mr Murthy, who stepped down as chief executive in March, is still chairman of Infosys, India's second biggest listed exporter of software services. But, at 55, he insists he will be doing more in his new role than conference-hopping abroad. His geekish tendency, his perceived integrity and his espousal of egalitarianism where once there was communism make him a popular ambassador-at-large for India's only globally competitive industry.

'There are plenty of areas where I can add value,' says Mr Murthy, who, with six others, founded Infosys in his bedroom in Poona, near Bombay. Infosys, which became the first Indian company to list on the Nasdaq in 1999, earned net profit of Rs8.08bn (£110m) in the year to March, a rise of 28.5 per cent on the previous year. Its turnover was Rs26bn, up by 37 per cent over the same period. But the company's impact extends beyond a 10-year record of double-digit growth.

Infosys is seen as a benchmark of desirable business practice in India, with its cultivation of young talent, its distribution of stock options to drivers as well as to software engineers and the sale of pizzas and cappuccinos at its new, 55-acre campus in Bangalore.

Much of the credit goes to Mr Murthy and his co-founders, including Nandan Nilekani, chief executive, who pride themselves on creating a company that is less Indian than international. 'We wanted to create a company of the professional, for the professional and run by the professional,' says Mr Murthy. 'It was radical thinking [in India] at the time.'

Mr Murthy has never shied away from radicalism. The son of a south Indian teacher, he grew up in a high-caste Brahmin home full of the socialist spirit of Jawaharlal Nehru, India's first Prime Minister. While in Paris designing software to handle cargo at Charles De Gaulle airport in the 1970s, Mr Murthy canvassed for François Mitterrand, a future French president. 'I saw roads, bridges and personal wealth in Europe. I returned [home] asking myself: "How can I make a difference?"'

But the young Indian left France with his leftwing views softened by market realities. In effect, Mr Murthy returned to India as a social democrat committed to workplace egalitarianism and business entrepreneurism.

Those values, wrapped around a culture of challenging intellectualism, are now embedded at Infosys. It is one reason why Mr Murthy feels comfortable about relinquishing power, though not influence.

At Infosys's leadership centre in Mysore, south India, for example, Mr Murthy will teach leadership skills to bright young employees. A skilled self-publicist, he will demonstrate how self-promotion can turn an individual into a powerful brand-leader, probably citing himself. It is debatable which is the better known name in India: Murthy or Infosys.

Mr Murthy's top colleagues will share the podium at Mysore, where they will evangelise on Infosys's values, such as 'customer delight'; 'fairness' and 'excellence'. The aim is to produce a new generation of leaders cut from the same cloth. They will be in charge as Infosys develops the landscape of skills, from maintenance and implementation to consultancy, to compete with global companies such as Accenture.

Achieving these goals will be difficult. First, Infosys has, by its standards, had a horrid past year as cash-strapped technology companies in the US slashed spending. That has forced Indian information technology to ease its exposure to the US, which for Infosys accounts for 65 per cent of revenues. Second, as India becomes a more expensive business location, IT companies, which for years have prospered from a handsome labour cost advantage, will have to set up base in countries where traditional Indian skills such as process management and the English language can be exploited.

'India will continue to be an important resource [in providing software engineers]. But as the industry climbs the value chain, in certain areas where we need special skills, such as language, we may have to leverage the power of other countries,' he says. China is an example. After a two-year wait, Infosys is to open a software centre in Shanghai, where there is a big potential market for Indian skills.

China could shape the future Infosys; the current Infosys is largely the result of two strategic calls made by Mr Murthy.

In 1996, before the millennium boom showered work on Indian IT, Mr Murthy decided gradually to abandon Infosys's relationship with General Electric, which accounted for 25 per cent of the company's revenues, because he was worried about dependency on a single client. Today Infosys's rivals, such as Wipro, the largest quoted software exporter, have been hit by their huge exposure to single clients that are not just cutting back but also exploiting their privileged position to demand discounts. Infosys has capped its exposure to any single customer at 10 per cent of revenues.

The second call was to defy sceptics and embrace the opportunities given to Indian companies to fix millennium bug problems for IT-deficient companies in the west. This was grunt work. But Mr Murthy argued that code-writing, for example, would ultimately improve margins as higher volumes combined with lower costs; it would help Infosys achieve scale more quickly; and open the door to new, longer-term clients.

All this has made Mr Murthy bigger than Infosys but not beyond criticism. Indian IT is full of New Economy millionaires who find Mr Murthy's 'holier than thou' display of socialist credentials and practised humility tiresome. And in an industry that has learnt to speak with one voice, Mr Murthy has angered many with his willingness to voice the consensus industry view in, say, his dealings with government, only to discredit the position privately or claim it as his own, says a fellow professional. Last, having stepped aside, Mr Murthy, an effective political strategist who has advised the government on IT policy, has disappointed some by deciding to devote more time to the company, rather than the country.

However, he may get another chance – in the field of education, which he regards as central in alleviating poverty.

He sits on the boards of many educational bodies and has spoken on the urgency of raising spending on education to at least 10 per cent of gross domestic product by 2009. Distrustful of official bodies and convinced of private sector execution skills, Mr Murthy wants the management of higher education handed over to big business.

In a speech to technologists, he said: 'Every profitable exporting company should give a mandatory 20 per cent of its PBIDT [profits before interest, depreciation and tax] to a fund managed by eminent people [and] let this group fund higher education services.' Alongside market-driven fees, Mr Murthy suggests generous loans for the needy and heavy use of technology 'to bring the power of distance education and virtual classrooms'.

This vision of a young, technologically literate community could have huge implications for jobs and wealth creation, possibly creating many more like Infosys. Yet, as Mr Murthy told his audience, 'I have always said the only hope for India is to produce 100,000 companies better than Infosys.'

Source: Financial Times, 5 June 2002.

Case 13.2

An entrepreneur's learning curve

FT

24 January 2002

By **Chris Tighe**

So there the business founders were, so eager that they worked in an office in January without electricity, burning £60 worth of Ikea tealights a week as they cut the ill-fitting corners off 20,000 promotional desk calendars.

George Kinghorn, 30-year-old serial entrepreneur, is reminiscing about the rollercoaster ride of setting up Studentmobiles.com in 1999.

Government ministers are fond of urging the UK to embrace an entrepreneurial mindset where failure is seen as a valuable learning experience rather than a source of shame. Less frequently do they stress that learning from painful experience and starting another business requires huge stamina and self-belief.

Mr Kinghorn has both, despite a laconic manner and appearance: 'I'm very goal-oriented. My biggest strength is taking an idea and getting it to fruition.'

He founded Studentmobiles.com, a mobile phone retailer, with Steven Bell while they were on a Durham University Business School course, Gleam (Graduates Learning Entrepreneurship Accelerated through Mentoring).

Both were already running their own businesses and undoubtedly entrepreneurial. Mr Kinghorn's 'graduate' status, though, was more debatable; he had left school, where his main achievement was setting up a toffee-making business turning over £400 a week, with just one GCSE, in business studies. Subsequently he gained a Chartered Institute of Marketing Diploma and his DUBS course gave him a degree-equivalent NVQ level 4 in management.

In one frantic year, Studentmobiles.com catapulted Mr Kinghorn and Mr Bell through the peaks and troughs of entrepreneurial excitement before the business became a subsidiary of Carphone Warehouse, Europe's largest independent mobile phone retailer.

Mr Bell has remained as Studentmobiles' managing director but Mr Kinghorn, who had no wish to become anybody's employee or to leave his native north-east England, is now trying to raise money to expand his latest venture, Touchbase.

Touchbase specialises in multimedia touch-screen systems. Its first big customer has been bakery goods retailer Greggs. Touchbase has created a multimedia touch screen magazine, Touchin', for Greggs' subsidiary Baker's Oven. It is being piloted in its Durham City cafe.

By touching the screen, customers can read articles and advertisements, which can be linked to special offers, with vouchers instantly printed out for redemption in nearby shops.

Customers have been highly enthusiastic, says Baker's Oven managing director Tony Barcroft. He would like to introduce Touchin' to all Baker's Oven's 200 plus stores, but is frustrated at how difficult it has been for Mr Kinghorn to persuade the purveyors of 'risk' capital to take the risk of investing in Touchbase.

'It's unbelievable the lack of vision you see in a lot of people,' says Mr Barcroft. 'It's almost as though it's got to be successful before they will say "of course I would have invested in that".'

Mr Kinghorn has raised £375,000 for Touchbase from private investors; he is optimistic that once he passes the £1m mark, venture capital funding will be easier to access.

Money worries are not new for him. Studentmobiles.com, which toured campuses in 1999 in two eye-catching VW beetles claiming to offer students the best deal on mobile phones, quickly hit cashflow problems.

'It was heartache every day and bedlam, on two hours' sleep,' says Mr Kinghorn. 'The one thing the business school never taught you was how to handle success.'

Compounding their difficulties were website problems. These led to legal action against the designers who, it emerged, had registered Studentmobiles.com in their name. 'I've learned lots of lessons,' says Mr Kinghorn wryly.

He also found that while banks and enterprise agencies can be very risk-averse, lawyers can be entrepreneurial. He still owes money to his solicitors, who helped Studentmobiles.com win back its domain name, but they have continued acting for him as he builds his new business.

As Studentmobiles.com's cashflow problems mounted in late 1999, Carphone Warehouse threw out a £125,000 lifeline in exchange for 70 per cent of the business. After the deal was agreed, dotcom mania broke out. Mr Kinghorn and Mr Bell wished they had struck better terms but it was too late.

Mr Kinghorn is no longer involved in Studentmobiles, having sold his 10 per cent stake to Mr Bell. He received £20,000, plus 10 per cent of Mr Bell's exit value, and the liability of a funky blue VW bought for the business on hire purchase.

He was ready to try again. He set up, briefly, Wasted Youth, an online magazine, then Coffeecomplete, a more successful concept which he sold on.

Touchbase, currently employing 10 people, is a much more substantial venture. Last month it began the roll-out of instore touchscreen promotional units in off-licences owned by the Cellar 5 group. It is also negotiating to provide information points for Seattle Law School in the US.

His Studentmobiles.com experience taught Mr Kinghorn valuable lessons, he says. 'You need a really good team around you, and you need to realise what you don't know a hell of a long time before you need to know it.'

Source: Financial Times, 24 January 2002.

Discussion points

1. In what way is N.R. Narayana Murthy developing, articulating and communicating his vision?

2. Can an entrepreneur's vision accommodate the possibility of failure as well as success? Should it?

Chapter 14

The entrepreneurial mission

Chapter overview

This chapter is concerned with the development of a mission for the entre-preneurial venture. A mission is a formal statement defining the purpose of the venture and what it aims to achieve. It is a powerful communication tool which can both guide internal decision making and relate the venture to external supporters. After establishing how a formal mission can actually help the venture, a prescriptive framework for generating, articulating and communicating the venture's mission is developed.

14.1 Why a well-defined mission can help the venture

> **Key learning outcome**
>
> An appreciation of the value of a formal mission for the venture.

A mission is a formal statement as to the purpose of the venture. It defines the *nature* of the venture, *what* it aims to achieve and *how* it aims to achieve it. It provides entrepreneurs with a way to codify their vision, to be clear about the difference they will make. Recent surveys indicate that some eighty per cent of all major businesses have a mission or value statement of some kind. Developing a formalised mission can be valuable to the entrepreneurial venture for a number of reasons.

It articulates the entrepreneur's vision

Developing a mission offers entrepreneurs a chance to articulate and give form to their vision. This helps them to refine and shape their vision, and it facilitates communication of the vision to the venture's stakeholders.

It encourages analysis of the venture

The process of developing a mission demands that entrepreneurs and those who work with them stand back and think about their venture in some detail. If the mission is to be meaningful, then that analysis must be made in a detached way. Entrepreneurs must be able to subject their own vision to impartial scrutiny and consider how realistic and achievable it is. It will challenge them to consider what they wish to achieve, to audit the resources they have to hand, to identify what additional resources they will need, and to evaluate their own strengths and weaknesses. Developing a mission is a piece of communication with oneself. This process is iterative. Entrepreneurs must negotiate the possibilities of creating new worlds with their ambitions and the actuality of what they can achieve.

It defines the scope of the business

An entrepreneurial venture exists to exploit some opportunity. Opportunities are most successfully exploited if resources are dedicated to them and brought to bear in a focused way. This demands that the opportunity be defined precisely. The business must know which opportunities lie within its grasp and which it must ignore. Often, success depends not only on the venture taking advantage of a big enough opportunity but also on it not being tempted to spread its efforts too wide. The mission helps to distinguish between those opportunities which 'belong' to the venture and those which do not.

It provides a guide for setting objectives

A mission is usually *qualitative*. It does not dictate specific quantitative outcomes. This is the role of *objectives*. The mission provides a starting point for defining specific objectives, for testing their suitability for the venture and for ordering of their priorities.

It clarifies strategic options

A mission defines what the venture aims to achieve. In this it offers guidance on what paths might be taken. The mission provides a starting point for developing *strategic options*, for evaluating their consistency in delivering objectives and for judging their resource demands.

It facilitates communication about the venture to potential investors

Attracting the support of investors is crucial to the success of the new venture. This is not simply a matter of presenting a series of facts to them, rather it demands that the facts be communicated in a way which makes the possibilities of the venture look convincing. One of their first questions will be 'what is the business about?'. This question is posed to entrepreneurs frequently and early in meetings with key (potential) stakeholders. The mission provides the entrepreneur with a clear, succinct and unambiguous answer to this question. First impressions do matter: a well-rehearsed, articulate and confident answer gets the relationship off to a good start. Answering in this way efficiently locates the venture positively in the investors' minds. This facilitates commitment and encourages further inquiry about the opportunity the venture aims to exploit and the rewards it may offer. It also suggests that the entrepreneur has thought about the business in a professional way, that is, has defined its scope and is focused in its goals.

It draws together disparate internal stakeholder groups

The different stakeholders who make up the business may not agree what the business is about. They may disagree on the goals it should have, how it should go about achieving them and how they will benefit if they are achieved. Organisations are frequently *political* and the mission can be used to provide a common point of reference around which to draw internal stakeholders together. It can guide arbitration when conflicts occur. A broad qualitative mission may be more useful than specific objectives in this respect. Often the very detail of objectives reduces flexibility and can provide a focus for discontent and disagreement.

It provides a constant point of reference during periods of change

The organisation driving the entrepreneurial venture will have the potential to achieve growth. Growth is good because it reflects the success of the business and increases its ability to reward stakeholders. It does, however, present the challenge of managing *change*. As the organisation grows and develops, it will be in a state of flux. It will acquire new assets and develop new relationships. Individuals will come and go. New customers will be found, old ones lost. In these turbulent circumstances, the mission can provide the organisation with a fixed point or a recognisable landmark connecting the organisation's past to its future.

It acts as an aide-mémoire for customers and suppliers

The mission statement can be communicated to the other key stakeholders in the venture, namely its customers and suppliers. It locates the business in the minds of customers and reminds them of what it offers and the commitment being made to them. It also gives the venture a presence in the minds of suppliers, reminding them of the opportunity it presents and of the need for their commitment to that opportunity. This encourages them to give the venture priority and service.

Empirical studies correlating business performance with the articulation of mission statements have produced mixed results. A seminal study by Pearce and David (1987) found that for large (Fortune 500) companies performance was positively correlated with the comprensiveness of mission statements. Other studies to find a positive relationship include Falsey (1989), Rarick and Vitton (1995), Germain and Bixby Cooper (1990), Collins and Porras (1991) and Klemm *et al.* (1991). Studies more critical of mission statements include Piercy and Morgan (1994) and Simpson (1994). A replication of the Pearce and Davis study, but looking at small business, undertaken by O'Gorman and Doran (1999) found no correlation between mission comprehensiveness and performance. In studies such as these, care should be taken in attributing (or not) enhanced performance causally to mission articulation. It may be the case, that the mission is helping the business. But it could also be the case that the fact that the business is performing well is giving managers the time, resources or inclination to develop a mission. Equally, developing a mission and performance could both be linked to a third, unidentified factor (overall strategic planning capability, for example). All of these studies examined missions in extant, ongoing businesses. No study (to my knowledge) has examined the role of the mission in attracting start-up funding, something I suggest as the critical role for a mission in entrepreneurial ventures. I will pick up on this in the Research Theme section at the end of the chapter.

Key features of the mission

The mission provides the entrepreneur with a powerful management tool. However, if it is to be effective and to contribute positively to the performance of the venture, it must be right for the business, it should encapsulate useful information and it must be properly developed and articulated.

14.2 What a mission statement should include

> **Key learning outcome**
>
> An understanding of what information should be included in the mission statement for an entrepreneurial venture.

A mission statement may define both *what* the business aims to achieve and the *values* it will uphold while going about its business. It relates both what the business does and why its members are proud of what it does. These two parts are often referred to as the *strategic* and the *philosophical* components of the mission statement, respectively. For example, The Body Shop emphasises corporate values in its mission. It claims to:

❝Make compassion, care, harmony and trust the foundation stones of business. Fall in love with new ideas.❞

The fast-growing Scandinavian furniture retailer Ikea, on the other hand, is much more strategic in its approach to defining products, markets and benefits. The company states its 'business idea' in the following terms:

❝We shall offer a wide range of home furnishing, items of good design and function, at prices so low that the majority of people can afford them.❞

The strategic component of a mission statement can, potentially, include the following elements:

1 *Product/service scope* – this element specifies exactly what the firm will offer to the world. It stipulates the type or range of products or services that the firm will engage in producing and delivering.

2 *Customer groups served* – this element stipulates which customers and distinct customer groups will be addressed by the firm.

Both product/service scope and customer groups need to be specified with three things in mind. First is the *total market* in which the business operates. This is the 'universe' in which the business's offerings are located. Second are the markets that the business *currently* serves since these are the base onto which the business must build its growth. Third are the market sectors, or *niches*, that the business *aspires* to serve. These are where the growth will come from since these niches lie between the current business and the total market. These sectors must stretch the business and make its aspirations demanding, yet they must be realistic given the resources to which the business has access and its capabilities. The sectors must also represent distinct segments of the total market within which the firm's innovation can provide a sustainable competitive advantage.

3 *Benefits offered and customer needs served* – this element specifies the particular needs that the customer groups have and the benefits that the firm's products or services offer to satisfy these needs. Needs (and the benefits that satisfy them) can be defined at a number of levels. Spiritual, social and developmental needs are as important, and often more important than, economic or functional ones.

4 *The innovation on which the business is based and the sources of sustainable competitive advantage* – this element defines the way in which the firm has innovated, how it is using this to exploit the opportunity it faces and how this provides it with a competitive advantage in the marketplace that can be sustained in the face of pressure from competitors.

5 *The aspirations of the business* – this element defines what the business aims to achieve. It indicates how its success will be measured. It may refer to financial performance – for example, to be 'profitable' or to 'offer shareholders an attractive return' – or it may refer to market position – for example, to be a 'market leader' or to be 'a significant player'. Care should be taken that the aspirations are *realistic*, specify an achievement which is *meaningful* and provide a real *benchmark* for measuring achievements.

Pearce and David (1987) summarise these elements slightly differently. Their eight elements are:

1 specification of target customers and markets;

2 identification of principle products and/or services;

3 identification of geographic domain;

4 identification of core technologies;

5 expression of a commitment to growth, prosperity and survival;

6 specification of key elements of company philosophy;

7 identification of the company self concept (including views on key strengths);

8 identification of the firm's desired public image.

In addition to the strategic elements, reference may be made to the discretionary responsibilities taken on by the venture, that is, to the *company values* upheld by the business. The philosophical component of the mission statement illuminates the values and moral standards that the organisation will uphold while pursuing its business. This may refer to the way in which the company aims to treat its employees or customers. It may also specify the discretionary social responsibilities that the business will accept (see Section 12.4). Values may be included in the mission because they reflect the personal principles of the entrepreneur or because the business believes its higher standards will appeal to customers and perhaps investors. These two reasons are not incompatible; indeed, positive values are best upheld by a successful business.

Figure 14.1 shows a schematic representation of the elements in a mission statement for the entrepreneurial venture.

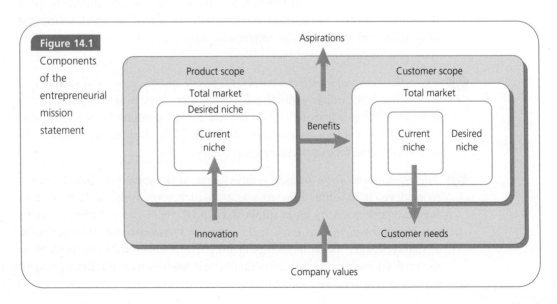

Figure 14.1

Components of the entrepreneurial mission statement

14.3) Developing the mission statement

Key learning outcome

An appreciation of the practical ways in which a mission can be developed for the venture.

If it is to help the venture, the mission must be right for it and it must be appropriate given the opportunity it aims to exploit and the innovation it intends to utilise. Further, if it is to be more than just so many words, then it must inform and influence people's decision making. A mission must be relevant to those who make up the venture and they must take ownership of it. These conditions will only be met if the mission is developed in the right way. The mission should stretch the business but be consistent with its ambitions, be realistic in terms of the opportunity it faces, and be compatible with its capability to exploit that opportunity. The mission must be developed alongside, and be judged in the light of, a strategic audit for the business. An audit of this nature includes:

● consideration of what the entrepreneur wishes to achieve;

● consideration of what other stakeholders aim to achieve and how the venture might help them;

● an assessment of the opportunity the venture aims to exploit;

● an assessment of market conditions;

● an assessment of the challenges and risks that will be encountered in exploiting that opportunity;

● an assessment of the business's capabilities and its competitive advantages;

● an evaluation of the resources the business has access to, future resource requirements and the resource gap this implies;

● an assessment of the structure of, and conditions in, the firm's network.

The entrepreneur must also consider how the mission will be generated. Broadly, there are two approaches.

Through consensus

This approach involves getting the whole, or as many parts as possible, of the organisation to contribute towards the development of the mission. The aim is to gather information, create ideas and gain as many insights as possible for generating and evaluating the mission. Allowing people to be involved in creating the mission also gives them a feeling of ownership and so a commitment towards it. The entrepreneur may go as far as inviting people from outside the formal organisation such as investors, and possibly important suppliers and customers, to make a contribution too. This can be a powerful way of attracting the commitment of these groups and strengthening the network.

Developing the mission in this way may present a logistical challenge, especially if a large number of people are involved. It may be necessary to set up a special forum for the exercise. There is also the question of how the ideas generated will be evaluated and judged and then fed into the final mission. This must be seen to be a rational and fair process, otherwise there is a danger that people may feel their contribution has been ignored or rejected.

By imposition

Alternatively, the entrepreneur may feel that consensus is not the best way to generate the mission. They may decide that it is better for them to develop the mission themselves, or in consultation with a small group, and then to impose it on the organisation as a whole. There may be a number of good reasons for this approach. The entrepreneur may see the mission as an articulation of his or her personal vision which may not be negotiable in the way that a consensus-building approach would demand. The entrepreneur may be the only person who has sufficient knowledge about the business and its situation to develop a meaningful mission. If the organisation is growing rapidly, it may be difficult to keep reassessing the mission as new people come in. It might also be inappropriate; after all, the mission is meant to be a constant in a time of flux. New people as they come on board will be asked to accept the mission as it stands (they may, of course, have been attracted by it in the first place!). The entrepreneur may also feel that it suits his or her leadership strategy to impose the mission on the organisation, that is to be seen to give direction and to 'lead from the front'.

Choice of approach

Both these routes for developing a mission have things to offer. The decision as to which is best will depend on the venture, how complex its business is, the way in which it is developing and the leadership style adopted by the entrepreneur. Developing a mission may in fact be one of the key exercises through which the entrepreneur establishes and demonstrates his or her leadership approach to the venture as a whole.

(14.4) Articulating the mission statement

> **Key learning outcome**
>
> An understanding of how the mission for the venture might be phrased.

Once the mission of the venture has been rationalised in terms of the elements in its strategic component and the values the venture wishes to uphold, then it needs to be *articulated* in the form of a definite statement. This statement then *becomes* the mission for the venture. If it is to be a valuable and an effective tool for the management of the venture it must fulfil several conditions. In particular, it must emphasise what is distinct about the venture; it must be informative; it must be clear and unambiguous; it must have impact; and it must be memorable. A balance between each of these requirements must be achieved. One generic format which includes all the elements described in the previous section is as follows:

  ❝The {*company*} aims to use its {*competitive advantage*} to achieve/maintain {*aspirations*} in providing {*product scope*} which offers {*benefits*} to satisfy the {*needs*} of {*customer scope*}. In doing this the company will at all times strive to uphold {*values*}.❞

The starting point for articulating the mission in this way is to find phrases describing each italicised element. These must be quite short or the mission statement will become too long, therefore it will be difficult to remember and so will lose impact. Single words are best! Not every element need be included, thus if a particular element is obvious, does not really inform or does not distinguish the business from its sector in general then it may be safely dropped. If in doubt, it is probably better to make the mission statement more, rather than less, succinct.

    The business will be faced with numerous opportunities to communicate its mission. It may be posted prominently within the organisation. It may form a starting point for setting objectives. It can be included on promotional material sent to customers. It will feature in the business plan presented to investors. However, not all communication need be so formal. The mission need not always be presented as a formal 'statement', it can easily be slipped informally into conversations. It is, after all, only the answer to the question: 'well, what does your business aim to do?'.

Summary of key ideas

- A *mission* is a positive statement which defines what a particular venture is about and what it aims to achieve.

- A well-defined mission helps the venture by encouraging analysis of its situation and capabilities; drawing together its internal stakeholders; and facilitating communication of the venture to external stakeholders.

- The mission statement can include a definition of the venture's market scope, what it aims to do for its stakeholders, its ambitions and its values.

- Entrepreneurs can use development of the venture's mission as part of their leadership strategy.

Research theme

Entrepreneurs' adoption and valuation of formal missions

A number of studies have been conducted into the adoption of formal missions by large businesses. Much less work has been undertaken on their adoption by smaller and entrepreneurial businesses. A survey methodology may be used to complement work in this area. Select a sample (the larger the better, aim for over 100) of small and entrepreneurial businesses. The sample may be based on discrete subsamples of businesses based on criteria such as sector, rate of business growth, etc. The survey should aim to establish the following:

● Does the business have a formal mission? If so what is it?

● How important does the entrepreneur see the mission as a management tool?

● In what way did (does) it prove valuable (as a focus for analysis; as an internal communication tool; as an external communication tool)?

● What is its primary role in the current running of the business?

● To which stakeholders is it communicated? In what way?

● What decisions has the mission contributed to and supported?

● How valuable has it been in attracting key stakeholders?

In addition, code the elements of the mission statement using the framework described in this chapter. What information does the mission include? By way of analysis, correlate the form of the mission statement and its information content with its perceived value for the different types of venture in the selected sample. Summarise the findings with recommendations for the development and use of formal missions in small and entrepreneurial ventures.

Suggestions for further reading

Baetz, M.C. and Bart, C.K. (1996) 'Developing mission statements which work', *Long Range Planning*, Vol. 29, No. 4, pp. 526–33.

Calfree, D. (1993) 'Get your mission statement working!', *Management Review*, Vol. 82, pp. 54–7.

Campbell, A. (1989) 'Does your organisation need a mission statement?', *Leadership and Organisational Development Journal*, Vol. 10, No. 3, pp. 3–9.

Campbell, A. and Yeung, S. (1991) 'Creating a sense of mission', *Long Range Planning*, Vol. 24, No. 4, pp. 10–20.

Campbell, A., Devine, M. and Young, D. (1990) *A Sense of Mission*, London: Hutchinson.

Collins, J. and Porras, J. (1991) 'Organizational vision and visionary organizations', *California Management Review*, Vol. 34, No. 1, pp. 30–52.

David, F.R. (1989) 'How companies define their mission', *Long Range Planning*, Vol. 22, No. 3, pp. 90–7.

Falsey, T. (1989) *Corporate Philosophy and Mission Statements*, New York: Quorum Books.

Germain, R. and Bixby Cooper, M. (1990) 'How a customer mission statement affects company performance', *Industrial Marketing Management*, Vol. 19, pp. 47–54.

Klemm, M., Sanderson, S. and Luffman, G. (1991) 'Mission statements: selling corporate values to employees', *Long Range Planning*, Vol. 24, No. 3, pp. 73–8.

O'Gorman, C. and Doran, R. (1999) 'Mission statements in small and medium sized enterprises', *Journal of Small Business Management*, Vol. 37, No. 4, pp. 59–66.

Pearce, J. (1982) 'The company mission as a strategic tool', *Sloan Management Review*, Vol. 38, pp. 15–24.

Pearce, J. and David, F. (1987) 'Corporate mission statements: the bottom line.' *Executive*, Vol. 1, pp. 109–16.

Piercy, J. and Morgan, N.A. (1994) 'Mission analysis: an operational approach', *Journal of General Management*, Vol. 19, No. 3, pp. 1–19.

Rarick, C. and Vitton, J. (1995) 'Mission statements make cents', *Journal of Business Strategy*, Vol. 16, pp. 11–12.

Simpson, D. (1994) 'Rethinking vision and mission', *Planning Review*, Vol. 22, p. 911.

Want, J. (1986) 'Corporate mission: the intangible contribution to performance', *Management Review*, August, pp. 40–50.

Wickham, P.A. (1997) 'Developing a mission for an entrepreneurial venture', *Management Decision,* Vol. 35, No. 5, pp. 373–81.

Selected case material   Case 14.1

Ministry of Sound looks to flotation

21 May 2002

By **Sathnam Sanghera** and **Paul Sexton**

Ministry of Sound, the nightclubs-to-music business headed by James Palumbo, the ex-Etonian entrepreneur, is being prepared for a flotation at the end of this year.

The company – in which 3i, the venture capital firm, holds a stake – is pushing ahead with plans for flotation in order to fund acquisitions in publishing, music and radio.

'We are looking to become a public company in the mid-term,' said Mr Palumbo.

'Clearly, markets are tricky and, while we don't need the money, we would like the currency to be able to move more aggressively into various industries.

'It [the float] could be as soon as the end of the year, or more likely next year. The business is totally unleveraged and in good shape to move quickly.'

Mr Palumbo, son of Peter Palumbo, the former Conservative Arts minister, set up Ministry of Sound in 1991 in a rundown warehouse – in Elephant & Castle in south London – which he bought for £250,000. 3i took a 15 per cent stake in the business last year for £24m, valuing the company at about £160m.

Over the past decade the management team behind the group has attempted to build Ministry of Sound into a global brand, moving into CDs, clothing, magazines and bars.

With the UK dance music market experiencing a downturn, the group has now identified radio as a growth area.

'At the moment the radio business is a small fraction of the overall group, but it would be great if it could ultimately be 20, 30, 40 per cent – over three to five years,' said Mr Palumbo.

MoS has an annual turnover of about £100m, an 11 per cent share of the compilations album market and its labels have been behind four number one UK singles in six months including So Solid Crew, DJ Pied Piper and Roger Sanchez.

The company is being advised by Jonathan Goodwin, co-chief executive of Longacre, the boutique investment bank that specialises in media.

Source: Financial Times, 21 May 2002.

Case 14.2

Survey – Creative business: Trevor Rowley

FT

30 July 2002

By **Fiona Harvey**

Interview with Trevor Rowley founder, postoptics.com

So what do you do all day?
I have a brilliant team here, so mostly I run around getting in their way and annoying them. As I'm the business manager, marketing manager, operations manager, whatever you like, I ensure everything is running smoothly, oversee ideas and planning, and generally enjoy life.

You used to be an optician. Now you're an internet entrepreneur. Different?
Totally. I've been really enjoying the change of lifestyle. Before, I used to spend every day testing patients and fitting contact lenses. It was an appointment system, so it was very rigid. Everything was very carefully timed and it was very restricted. You'd have some interesting patients and some boring ones, but apart from that it was all the same. I did that for 17 years. But I don't see any patients at all any more.

Do you miss them?
No.

What sort of things do you do now?
I had a long lunch today with one of the managers here. It was lovely. I would never have been able to do that before.

Isn't it an odd time to be an internet company?
Quite a few of us internet companies have been making money, which I think some people don't realise. We never made a song and dance about the internet, but we've been profitable since the beginning. Lots of people seem to think the internet is wonderful and sexy but it's not. It's just like the phone and fax. It's convenient at certain times.

What's the most popular colour of contact lens you sell?
Today, it's sapphire blue. Followed by violet and then green. It changes all the time, but there's a bit on the website that tells you which is the most popular at any particular time. During the World Cup, far and away the most popular one was the England flag. We sent loads of them to Japan.

Source: Financial Times, 30 July 2002.

Discussion point

Using the framework described in the chapter, develop missions for:
(a) Ministry of Sound
(b) postoptics.com (an Internet retailer of contact lenses)

Chapter 15

The strategy for the venture

Chapter overview

Strategy is a central concept in modern management practice. This chapter looks at business strategy from the entrepreneurial perspective. The value of a well-considered and well-defined strategy to the venture is advocated, and the way in which entrepreneurs can control strategy development is considered. The chapter concludes by exploring the strategies entrepreneurs can use to initiate their ventures.

15.1 What is a business strategy?

Key learning outcome

An understanding of the key elements of the business strategy for the entrepreneurial venture.

The idea that an organisation has a 'strategy' lies at the centre of much management thinking. A strategy can be defined, broadly, as the actions an organisation takes to pursue its business objectives. Strategy drives *performance* and an effective strategy results in a good performance. An organisation's strategy is multi-faceted. It can be viewed from a number of directions depending on which aspects of its actions are of interest. A basic distinction exists between the *content* of a business's strategy, the strategy *process* that the business adopts to maintain that strategy and the environmental *context* within which the strategy must be made to work. The strategy content relates to what the business actually *does* while the strategy process relates to the way the business *decides* what it is going to do. The strategy content has three distinct decision areas: the *products* to be offered, the *markets* to be targeted and the approach taken to *competing*.

Strategy content

Strategy content relates to three things: the final product range, the customers it serves and the advantage it seeks in the marketplace.

The product range

This covers the type and range of products that the firm supplies to its markets (note that the word product here is used in a general sense to include both physical products and services). The decisions the entrepreneur faces here are:

- What type of products should the business offer?
- What should their features be?
- How will they address customer needs? What benefits will they offer?
- What mix of physical and service elements should be offered with the product?
- If the product is to be successful, in what way(s) must the customer find it more attractive then those of competitors?
- What unit cost is acceptable? (How does this relate to price?)
- How wide should be the product range offered? How many product variants will be necessary?

Market scope

The market scope defines the customer groups and market segments that will be addressed by the firm. Key decisions here include:

- How is the total market to be defined?
- What features (e.g. customer types, customer needs, buying behaviour, location) are important for characterising the market and defining its sectors?
- On what group(s) of customers should the business concentrate?
- In what sectors will these customers be?
- Should the firm concentrate its efforts on a narrow group, or spread its efforts more widely?
- Why will the group(s) selected find the firm's offerings more attractive than those of competitors?
- What will be the geographic location and spread of the customers (e.g. local, regional, national, international)?

Clearly, decisions on product range and market scope are interlinked. The decisions made with respect to one influence the decisions that must be made for the others. Therefore, it may be better for the entrepreneur to regard themselves as facing a *single* set of decisions about the combined *product–market domain* of the firm.

Competitive approach

Competitive approach refers to the way in which the firm competes within its product–market domain to sustain and develop its business in the face of competitive pressures. This aspect of strategy content reflects the way in which the firm tries to influence the customer to favour their offerings. Important decisions to be made in relation to this approach include:

- How should the product be priced relative to competitors? (Should a discount or premium be offered?)
- What distribution route will be used to get the product to the customer?
- What financial rewards and incentives will be offered to intermediaries and distributors?
- What support (e.g. exclusivity, preferential selling, display) will be expected from distributors?
- How will the customer's buying decision be influenced?
- What message will be sent to consumers about the product?
- How will the message be delivered? (For example, by advertising, by personal selling, or through distributors?)
- Will customers be encouraged to compare the product to the offerings of competitors? (If so, on what basis: price, quality, features, performance?)
- Or will customers be told that the innovation is so great that there is nothing else like it?

The strategy content which the business aspires to achieve must be consistent with the entrepreneur's vision and the mission they have defined for the venture. Decisions about strategy content must be made in the light of an understanding of 'external' conditions such as characteristics of the market, the competitive situation and the way in which different sectors can be served, and in the light of 'internal' concerns such as the mission and goals of the organisation, the resources it has to hand and its capabilities. The strategy content for the venture is the way in which it competes to sustain and develop its product–market domain (Figure 15.1).

The venture will achieve success if it directs its resources in an appropriate way towards delivering a rewarding and sustainable strategy content. The strategy content dictates the investment of resources that the business must undertake. Investments in financial, operating and human resources will all play a part in supporting the strategy content. Consequently, strategy content decisions must be evaluated in terms of the investments that they entail, the rewards that are likely and the risks involved.

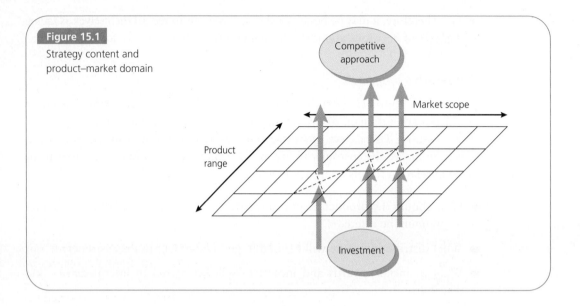

Figure 15.1

Strategy content and product–market domain

15.2 Strategy process in the entrepreneurial business

> **Key learning outcome**
>
> An understanding of the ways in which an entrepreneurial business decides on which strategies to adopt.

The firm's strategy process is the way in which the business makes decisions about the strategy content it wishes to achieve (Figure 15.2). It is reflected in the way the organisation considers its future, how it selects its goals and the way it decides on how to allocate resources in order to achieve them. Strategy process is embedded in the structures, systems and processes that the organisation adopts, as well as its culture and the leadership style of the entrepreneur running it.

One of the most important themes in modern strategic management is the distinction between, and the relative values of, *deliberate* (or *planned*) and *emergent* approaches to strategy creation. A deliberate approach to strategy creation is one in which the entrepreneur sets out to define a strategic policy for the venture in which the future goals and competitive approach of the business are clearly defined and translated into specific objectives. The entrepreneur then sets out to achieve this strategy through an explicit process of implementation in which instructions as to objectives and budgets are passed down the organisation. An emergent approach to strategy creation is one in which future goals and strategic approach are left more ambiguous. Rather, the entrepreneur concentrates on managing the venture's short-term capabilities and exploiting the opportunities that present themselves as the business moves forward. Here, the entrepreneur is not so concerned with where the business is going; he or she just makes sure it goes somewhere interesting.

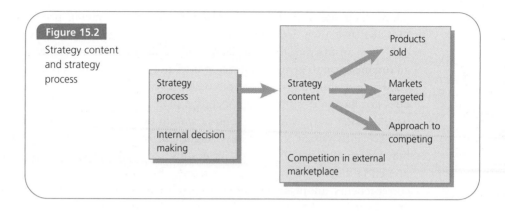

Figure 15.2

Strategy content and strategy process

The traditional approach to strategic management emphasised the deliberate approach. Planning for the future was not just an important responsibility for senior managers; it was their *primary* responsibility. Managers who did not plan were failing in a critical respect. Entrepreneurs who often rejected the strictures of formal planning and advocated action over producing plans were regarded to be particularly at fault.

Of late, though, there has been a reaction against this belief. This is exemplified in Henry Mintzberg's seminal 1994 book *The Rise and Fall of Strategic Planning*. The critique of the planning approach is based on two arguments. The first is that empirical observation of business performance does not show a strong correlation with formal planning activity. Many businesses that do not carry out a lot of planning are as successful as those that invest heavily in it. The second argument is that the planning approach is theoretically flawed. Planning only works if the future can be predicted with some certainty. This is rarely the case, especially for the fast-growing entrepreneurial venture in a dynamic, unpredictable environment. It also assumes that managers can control everything the extended organisation does. Experience of organisations suggests that managers (even entrepreneurs with strong leadership skills) cannot control every detail. As a result, emergent approaches to strategy creation should not be dismissed as wrong. They reflect a perfectly good managerial approach to developing at least some businesses given their capabilities and the opportunities the environment offers them.

As with many debates in which opinions are polarised, the resolution of the planning–emergent debate has, to a great extent, resulted in a broader perspective in which both positions are integrated. Drawing a hard and fast distinction between the stages of creating – *formulating* – and putting into practice – *implementing* – a particular strategy is seen as artificial. 'Implementers' who have played no part in the development of a strategy are unlikely to take ownership of it from the 'formulators' who have. A strategy must be modified between the drawing board and taking to the air.

Entrepreneurs make good strategies happen through leadership, not just planning, and leadership demands listening to people, learning from them and taking their ideas on board. Leadership also means giving people the latitude to make their own decisions and put their own insight into practice. This is the only way an organisation can learn and be flexible. However, leaving room for an organisation to grow and develop does not mean the entrepreneur has no view on where it should go. As we discussed in Chapter 13, even if an entrepreneur does not have a definite, highly detailed plan in mind, he or she should certainly have a vision as to where the venture should be heading. Such a vision may offer a space into which the business might go, rather than a definite destination, but nonetheless it will control its destiny. A cognitive study comparing entrepreneurial intentions with actual outcomes by Jenkins (1997) suggests that many entrepreneurs adopt an emergent approach to strategy creation and are adept at using it.

Colin Eden and Fran Ackermann have suggested an integrated and participative approach to strategy creation in their 1998 book *Making Strategy*. They suggest that good strategies emerge from an interactive process that they refer to as the 'Journey' of strategy, where the word Journey is an acronym for 'Jointly, Understanding, Reflecting and Negotiating'. In this process individuals still have a responsibility for identifying and evaluating strategic options. However, these options are flexible 'opening positions' and can evolve as they are implemented through the 'journey' the strategy takes through the organisation. Making the strategy happen is as important as making it in the first place. In the context of the entrepreneurial venture, this process resonates with the entrepreneur defining, articulating and communicating his or her vision.

The entrepreneurial approach to management is distinct at the level of strategy process, not content. It's not what an entrepreneur *does* (the business they are in) that matters. What makes a manager entrepreneurial is the *way* he or she organises the venture and uses it to innovate and to deliver value to the customer in a way that existing players cannot.

At any point in time the venture will have a strategy content, that is, a product range being sold to a distinct group of customers with a particular approach taken to attracting those customers and competing within the marketplace. The strategy content will evolve as the business grows and develops. New products will be introduced, old ones dropped. The competitive approach may alter as the organisation learns and market conditions change. At any moment in time the entrepreneur and other managers in the organisation will have views and expectations about what the business's strategy content should be in the future. This interest may also extend to other stakeholders such as important customers looking for specific new products and influential investors who offer advice on how the business might develop.

The strategy process adopted by the organisation is defined by the way in which decisions about strategy content are taken. As shown in Figure 15.3, it is reflected in the relationship that exists between the *existing* strategy content, the strategy content *desired* by the business for the future and the strategy content that is actually *achieved*. The results of these decisions influence the investments made by the venture.

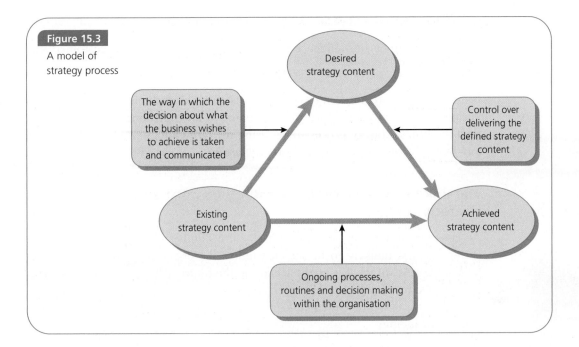

Figure 15.3
A model of
strategy process

The link between existing strategy content and the strategy content achieved in the future

The strategy content of the business will evolve over time. The way in which the business modifies its range of products, changes its customer base and develops its competitive approach will be the result of a series of ongoing decisions and actions taken by the people who make up the organisation. These decisions will occur even if the organisation does not have an explicit strategy to guide them. They may be incremental and the result of short-term pragmatic considerations or they may be made in response to immediate market opportunities. However, this does not mean that these decisions are not controlled. They will be shaped by a wide variety of organisational and environmental factors, including:

● the reporting relationships that define the organisation's structure;

● the mechanisms the organisation adopts to control the allocation of resources;

● the organisation's systems for motivating and rewarding performance;

● the way the organisation manages information and identifies opportunities;

● the organisation's technological competence and any technical developments;

● the organisation's historical performance;

● resource availability within the organisation;

● the organisational culture;

- internal disputes and political infighting within the organisation;

- the expectations and influence of external stakeholders such as customers and investors.

If these features are allowed to control decision making about the evolution of a business's strategy content without reference to an overriding strategic context then the firm's strategy process may, using the terminology of Henry Mintzberg and James Waters (1985), be said to be *emergent*.

The link between existing strategy content and desired strategy content

An emergent strategy may establish itself for a number of reasons. However, an entrepreneur is unlikely to be satisfied unless the organisation operates with at least some sense of what it might achieve in the future. After all, the entrepreneur is motivated by the difference between what *is* and what *might be*. The future state desired by the entrepreneur can take a variety of forms. It will vary in several particulars, including:

- the types of detail it contains;

- how specific those details are;

- the latitude the entrepreneur will accept in its achievement;

- the time period over which it is to be achieved;

- the way in which it is communicated to other stakeholders;

- the extent to which it is negotiable with other stakeholders.

There are a number of ways in which the organisation can become aware of the desired strategy content.

The entrepreneur's communication of their vision

The entrepreneur can articulate and communicate their vision to the rest of the organisation. This may be sufficiently powerful and attractive to motivate the whole organisation. A vision may (deliberately) lack detail but it should highlight the desirability of achieving certain strategy contents in preference to others.

The definition of a mission

The organisation's mission will specify the key elements of a strategy content. The amount of detail it provides will depend on how the strategic component in the mission is specified. The mission will, at a minimum, be able to provide a test as to what strategy contents are desirable and acceptable. The mission may be developed by a process of consensus or it may be imposed on the organisation by the entrepreneur.

The setting of objectives

The desired strategy content may be defined explicitly by the setting of specific objectives. These may be financial or strategic in nature. They may refer to the organisation as a whole, or they may relate to a particular project or they may fall within the responsibility of an individual. Objectives may be subject to negotiation and agreed through consensus, or alternatively, they may be imposed by the entrepreneur without opportunity for debate. The approach taken depends upon the entrepreneur's personal style and leadership strategy. Quantified objectives provide a means of benchmarking the achievement of a desired strategy content.

Through informal discussion

The identification of a desired strategy content may not occur by a formal process. It may become evident through ongoing discussions about the business and the opportunities offered by the market. These discussions may involve a variety of people both within and perhaps from outside the organisation, and they may take place over a period of time.

The link between desired strategy content and achieved strategy content

This link is manifest in the ability of the entrepreneur to actually deliver the strategy content they desire for their organisation. Two things may limit this. The first is the potential to achieve that strategy content in the marketplace. If the strategy content is to be delivered it must be both *achievable* given the market conditions and the competitive forces present, and *feasible* in terms of the resources available to make the necessary investments. The second possible limitation is the control the entrepreneur has over the organisation.

Even though it might be 'their' organisation entrepreneurs are limited in the extent to which they can control the actions of the people who make up their organisation. They cannot enforce their will over it completely. Some of the organisation's strategy will always be 'emergent'. The way in which entrepreneurs control the organisation and ensure that it delivers the strategy content they desire is dependent on a large number of factors. Some of the more critical include:

- their personal leadership style;
- the consensus they build for the desired strategy;
- their ownership of resources;
- the way in which they control resources;
- the control mechanisms and procedures they have established;

- their technical expertise;
- their access to information and their ability to control that information within the organisation;
- the way they set objectives;
- the way in which they reward achievement of objectives;
- their creation of, and the way they are legitimised by, symbolic devices within the organisation;
- their influence over, and control of, organisational politics;
- the relationship they build with external stakeholders;
- the way they manage *attributions*, that is, the way they associate themselves with success and dissociate themselves from failure within the organisation.

The entrepreneur will be motivated by a distinct picture of how the world should be. That is what their vision *is*. Yet they must always match their desire to achieve particular outcomes with their ability to control what the organisation can actually do both internally and in its marketplace. They must also balance their need to control the organisation with giving the people who make up the organisation latitude to make their own decisions and use their insights and intuitions to further its ends.

15.3 Controlling strategy process in the venture

> **Key learning outcome**
>
> A recognition of the decisions the entrepreneur must make to control the strategy process in their venture.

If the entrepreneur is to maintain control of the organisation and focus it on the opportunities that it seeks to exploit then he or she must control its strategy. This demands control of its strategy *process* as well as its strategy *content*. This means controlling the way the organisation identifies options for its future, the way in which these are communicated and shared, the way in which control is maintained over resource investments aimed at achieving the desired outcomes, and the way in which rewards are offered for delivering the outcomes.

The essential decisions that the entrepreneur must make in relation to developing and controlling the strategy process include the following.

Decisions relating to the development of the mission

- By what process will the business mission be developed (through consensus or by imposition)?

- How will it be articulated?

- To whom will it be communicated?

Decisions relating to the development of strategy

- Who in the organisation will be invited to contribute to the development of the desired strategy content?

- How will their ideas be evaluated and judged?

- Where will the information needed to develop the strategy content come from?

- Who in the organisation will collect, store and control that information?

- How will the desired strategy content be communicated to the rest of the organisation?

- How will the strategy content be communicated to external stakeholders?

Decisions relating to the control of resources

- What procedure will control how investment decisions are made?

- Who will have responsibility for what level of investment?

- How will new investments be distinguished from routine payments?

- How will budgets be allocated?

- What budgetary control systems will be put in place?

- How will information on budgetary control be stored, manipulated and shared?

- By whom will information on budgetary control be stored, manipulated and shared?

Decisions relating to the way objectives will be set, monitored and rewarded

- How will objectives be set?

- Who will be responsible for setting them?

- For whom will objectives be set (the organisation, functions, teams, individuals)?

- What will be the nature of the objectives (financial or strategic)?

- Will objectives be negotiable? If so, in what way and by whom?

- What information will be needed to monitor objectives?

- How will this information be collected and stored? Who will have access to it?

- What will be the rewards for achieving set objectives? What will be the response if they are not achieved?

These decisions will be very influential in giving the organisation its form, structure and systems because they will influence the culture it develops. Consequently, they must be subject to constant revision and review as the business grows and develops. Jenkins (1997) used a causal mapping technique (a way of creating a visual representation of the connection of ideas in an individual's cognition) to compare entrepreneurs' intentions (what they plan to do) and outcomes (what actually happened). He found that the causal maps were consistent with intentions, but not outcomes, which he interprets to suggest that entrepreneurial strategies may not be concious and deliberate, but non-deliberate and intended. Rather than plan for a particular future, many entrepreneurs, it would seem, merely respond flexibly to new opportunities as they come along.

15.4 Why a well-defined strategy can help the venture

Key learning outcome

An appreciation of the value in generating an explicit strategy for the venture.

Working under an emergent strategy is a far more common feature of managerial life than many textbooks on business planning would have us believe. Developing, assessing and communicating a strategy content represents an *investment*. It takes time, effort and money to achieve a well-defined strategy. Like any investment, it must be assessed in terms of the returns it will bring in the way it will improve organisational performance. If this return is not forthcoming then the organisation may well benefit from allowing its strategy to be emergent.

There are a variety of conditions under which an organisation's strategy tends to become emergent, for example:

- when its expectations are limited, i.e. when the desired strategic content is not very different from the existing one;

- when it is experienced in pursuing its business, i.e. when knowledge of how to achieve a particular strategic content is well established and not subject to extensive discussion;

- when the competitive environment is stable, i.e. when environmental shocks do not occur;

- when the competitive structure is stable, i.e. when competitors do not tend to infringe on each other's business;

- when the rules of competition are established, i.e. when competitor's reactions are predictable;

- when the industry technology is established, i.e. innovations are few and of limited scope;

- when patterns of investment are routinised, i.e. managers do not seek guidance at a strategic level when making investment decisions;

- when the organisation's leadership is weak, i.e. when power to impose a particular strategy content is limited;

- when the organisation is political, i.e. when agreement on a particular strategy content could not be gained.

These conditions tend to be found in mature, established organisations whose decision making has become routinised and even burcaucratised. They are not the typical conditions to be found in a new, fast-growing venture which is innovating and changing the rules of competition within its marketplace. Thus the entrepreneurial venture would be expected to gain in the following ways from investing in developing a strategy and communicating it to stakeholders.

A strategy encourages the entrepreneur to assess and articulate their vision

A strategy represents the way in which the entrepreneur will achieve their vision. The potential to make a vision into reality will be dependent on the possibility of creating a strategy to deliver it. This possibility will be a function of the *achievability* of the strategy in the competitive marketplace and of the *feasibility* of the strategy in terms of the resources available.

A strategy ensures auditing of the organisation and its environment

A strategy is a call to action. If it is to be successful then it must be based on a sound knowledge of the environment in which the organisation finds itself, the conditions within its marketplace, particularly in terms of the competitive pressures it faces, and of its own internal capabilities and competencies. Developing a strategy demands that the organisation's capabilities and competencies are audited.

A strategy illuminates new possibilities and latitudes

A strategy is developed in response to the dictates of the entrepreneur's vision. However, the process is iterative. Strategy development feeds back to vision. It reinforces the vision's strong parts and asks the entrepreneur to readdress its weaknesses. It clarifies the possibilities the venture faces and the latitude the entrepreneur will accept for the achievement of them.

A strategy provides organisational focus

A strategy provides a central theme around which the members of the organisation can focus their activities. It relates the tasks of the individual to the tasks of the organisation as a whole. A strategy is the stream of actions that make up the organisation. As such it is a unifying principle which gives organisational actions meaning and significance in relation to each other.

A strategy guides the structuring of the organisation

A strategy highlights the tasks necessary for the entrepreneur to achieve his or her goals. Some of these tasks will be short term, others long term; some will be of a 'general' management nature, others will be specialist; some will be concerned with generating and sustaining external relationships, while others will be concerned with internal technical issues. The nature of the tasks that must be undertaken defines the roles that must be filled within the organisation. This in turn guides the entrepreneur in developing a structure for the organisation.

A strategy acts as a guide to decision making

A strategy provides a framework for making decisions. A decision is a response to proffered possibilities. The strategy helps to highlight and evaluate these possibilities. It indicates how significant a particular decision will be, and the impact its outcomes will have. It illuminates the information that will be needed if the decision is to be made confidently. The strategy then enables the various options to be evaluated and the right course of action to be rationalised.

A strategy provides a starting point for the setting of objectives

By specifying the tasks that need to be undertaken in order to achieve desired outcomes, a strategy provides a starting point for defining quantified measurable objectives for both the organisation as a whole, and for the individuals who comprise it.

A strategy acts as a common language for stakeholders

An organisation is characterised by its strategy. The strategy provides the context in which the organisation acts. It is the perspective which enables individuals to make sense of the organisation's actions and their own part in those actions. The organisation's strategy provides a way for its stakeholders to relate to each other: they *interact* through its strategy. Strategy is a common language they can use to talk to each other about the organisation and their relationship to it.

Vision, mission and strategy in the entrepreneurial process

Vision, *mission* and *strategy* are intertwined aspects of a single entrepreneurial perspective (Figure 15.4). Each of these components represents both a different aspect of the world the entrepreneur seeks to create and the means by which they will create it. Together, they turn the entrepreneur's desire to make a difference in the world into an effective management tool for delivering change. This tool works by reconciling the entrepreneur's vision with actual possibilities and capabilities, by articulating that vision so that it may be communicated to others and by defining the actions necessary to progress the venture.

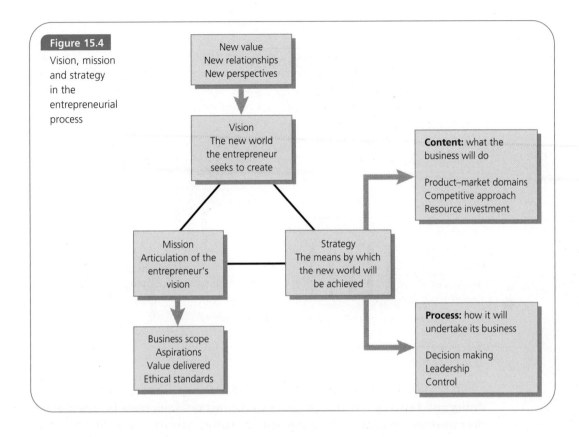

Figure 15.4

Vision, mission and strategy in the entrepreneurial process

New value
New relationships
New perspectives

Vision
The new world the entrepreneur seeks to create

Mission
Articulation of the entrepreneur's vision

Strategy
The means by which the new world will be achieved

Business scope
Aspirations
Value delivered
Ethical standards

Content: what the business will do

Product–market domains
Competitive approach
Resource investment

Process: how it will undertake its business

Decision making
Leadership
Control

15.5 An overview of entrepreneurial entry strategies

> **Key learning outcome**
>
> A recognition of the strategies adopted by entrepreneurs to establish their ventures.

A strategy is the pattern of actions that define an organisation. Every entrepreneurial venture is different, and each has its own strategy. However, there are common and recognisable patterns in the way in which businesses compete with one another. These are called *generic strategies*. Entrepreneurial ventures adopt a number of generic strategies in order to establish themselves in the marketplace. These strategies differ in the way in which the venture offers new value to the marketplace and the market they wish to serve (Figure 15.5).

Product–market domain

The entrepreneur must select the product–market domain in which to establish their venture. This defines the scope of the product they wish to offer to what market segments. The product scope is the range of product categories the firm will provide. Product scope must be understood in terms of the way customers

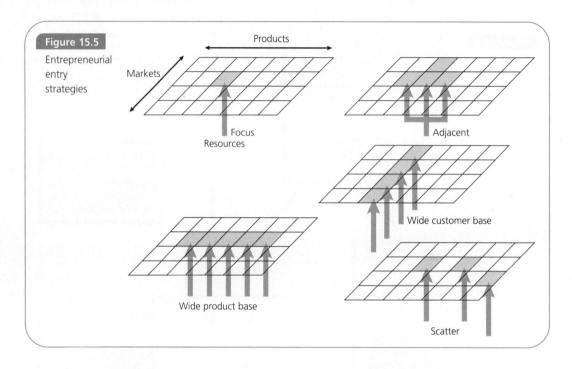

Figure 15.5

Entrepreneurial entry strategies

distinguish between different products in the market. Important factors are product features, product quality, patterns of product usage in terms of place, time and quantity, market positioning, and branding and imagery. The market sectors served are the distinct customer groups addressed by the firm.

Customer groups must be classified in terms of the way their needs both coincide and differ. Important factors for consideration here are demographic and sociographic characteristics, psychographic profile, customer location, buying behaviour and usage patterns. Such analysis is a well-established part of marketing thinking. The entrepreneur has five generic entry strategies in relation to product–market domain. These are:

1. *focused entry* – addressing a single well-defined product–market domain;

2. *product spread* – offering a wide range of products to a single well-defined market;

3. *customer spread* – delivering a single or narrow range of products to a wide base of customers;

4. *adjacency* – offering a wide range of products to a broad customer base. All product–market segments are adjacent in that the characterising features of each segment are continuous or can be related to each other;

5. *scatter* – a variety of different products are offered to a variety of different customers. The segments are not adjacent.

Competitive approach

Competitive approach refers to the way the venture attracts customers by offering them value that existing competitors do not. Generic strategies in relation to this approach include the following.

Offering a new product or service

Delivering the customer an innovative product or service. This must perform a task for the customer, or solve a problem for them, in a way which is both different from, and better than, existing products.

Offering greater value

Offering the customer a product or service which is comparable to those already in existence but at a lower price, so offering them greater value for money.

Creating new relationships

The entrepreneur exists in a network of relationships built on trust. Trust both reduces costs and adds value. The entrepreneur can be competitive by creating new relationships between providers and users, and by managing existing relationships better.

Being more flexible

Customers' needs are not fixed. Even if they are in the same market segment, different customers will present a slightly different set of needs. Further, a particular customer's needs are subject to constant change. However, at any one point in time a group of customers must satisfy their needs with the limited range of products and services on offer. The entrepreneur can create new value for the customer by being flexible in terms of what they offer. This may involve modifying the products and services they provide to make them specific to the requirements of the customer or developing a means by which the product can be continually modified in response to customers' requirements.

Being more responsive

As customer needs change and evolve, existing products serve those needs less effectively. As a result new opportunities emerge and take shape. The entrepreneur can add value in the marketplace by being attuned to those changes, in terms of recognising the new opportunities as they develop and responding quickly to them by modifying their existing offerings and innovating new ones.

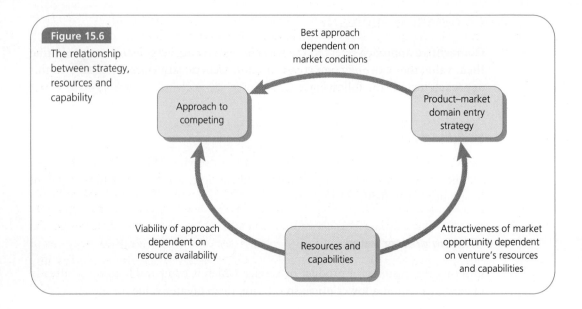

Figure 15.6

The relationship between strategy, resources and capability

Best approach dependent on market conditions

Approach to competing

Product–market domain entry strategy

Viability of approach dependent on resource availability

Resources and capabilities

Attractiveness of market opportunity dependent on venture's resources and capabilities

Choice of entry strategy

These two aspects of generic entry strategy, namely product–market domain and the competitive approach, exist in an iterative relationship to each other. The choice of competitive approach will depend on the particular characteristics of a product–market segment. How that presents itself as an opportunity to the business will depend on the resources it has to hand and its capabilities. Exploiting that opportunity will reward the business with further resources to maintain and expand its presence in its product–market domain. The choice of generic entry strategy depends on the resources and capabilities of the organisation (Figure 15.6).

15.6) Talking strategy: entrepreneurial strategic heuristics

Key learning outcome

A recognition of heuristics as guides to, and indicators of, entrepreneurial decision making.

The discussion of entrepreneurial strategy so far has adopted a formal approach. Entrepreneurial strategy has been described from the 'top-down' perspective, that of an outsider looking in, as much as that of an entrepreneur looking out. This is a legitimate approach. Just as a doctor brings along knowledge and expertise and can diagnose a disease, so the expert in entrepreneurship can recognise strategic approaches individual entrepreneurs may not themselves recognise. Entrepreneurs do not necessarily, or even usually, have formal knowledge of business strategy creation. An expert in strategy may be able to identify the strategic posturing of the venture even if the venture's managers cannot, or do not see any point in articulating it in formal terms. This is not to say that they may be implementing the strategy very effectively!

This distance between the 'professional strategic expert' and the practising entrepreneur must, however, be closed. The expert must be able to resonate with the way in which the entrepreneur actually makes decisions if he or she is to both understand the entrepreneur's venture and be able to effectively articulate support and encouragement. Ronald Mitchell (1997) has advocated attention to entrepreneurs' own 'oral histories' as an approach to understanding entrepreneurship. A very meaningful way of closing the gap has come from recognising the *heuristics* that entrepreneurs use.

A heuristic is a *decision rule* based on insight and experience. It is called into play when an entrepreneur is required to analyse a situation and make a decision in relation to it. Entrepreneurs are often able to articulate, quite succinctly, the heuristics they use. These often take the form of punchy aphorisms. They are rarely specific. Rather they are general statements, 'rules of thumb', that reveal the entrepreneur's attitudes and approaches. These not only provide a practical insight into the approach that the entrepreneur is taking, but they can also be used as analytical devices to describe and analyse entrepreneurs and their ventures (a good example of their use is provided by Manimala, 1999).

Table 15.1 describes a series of entrepreneurial strategic heuristics and their opposites, which might be described as counter-heuristics. As will be appreciated, the terms heuristic and counter-heuristic are interchangeable. A heuristic and its counter both have resonance and reflect an equally valid 'common sense' approach to business. Neither is right or wrong. They must be judged in terms of the entrepreneur's characteristics, the nature of the venture they are pursuing and the success they bring. This list is not exhaustive. It is intended to illustrate the heuristic themes entrepreneurs develop and use.

Table 15.1 Examples of entrepreneurial strategic heuristics

Strategic theme	Heuristic	Counter-heuristic
Innovation	Avoid run-of-the mill products	Stick to what is tried and trusted
	Search out new ideas from many sources	Keep an eye on one or two key areas
Flexibility	Keep an open mind to new approaches	Once you have found a good way of doing things – stick to it
	Success only comes from continual improvement	Keep on using a successful formula
Vision	Develop a vision and never compromise it	Let your vision evolve
	Share a vision – but don't negotiate it	Let others contribute to your vision
Start-up strategy	Start small and build	Go for it big time before someone else does

Table 15.1 *continued*

Strategic theme	Heuristic	Counter-heuristic
Using external support	All businesses benefit from professional help	Professionals are a poor investment. If they know so much, why aren't they rich?
	Build a partnership with investors	Avoid bringing in investors. They are only interested in what's in it for them
Sharing information	(With non-competitors at least) a good way of reducing costs	Never give anything away. Everyone is a competitor!
	Information is power	It's not what we know that matters – it's what we do
Delegation	Leadership is about empowering people to make their own decisions well	It's my job to make all the important decisions
	The only way the business can grow	I don't pass decisions down. Whose business is it anyway!
	We need to push decision making down	I don't delegate. The buck stops here!
Expertise	Developing employee expertise is a priority	The business needs the entrepreneur at the helm
	The most important expert is the entrepreneur	Everyone is an expert in his or her own way
Entry strategy	Limited, confident start followed by expansion	Make yourself known in the market from day one
Expansion	Grow in sure-footed stages	Build quickly on the innovation
	Establish our presence in as many markets as possible, as early as possible	Exploit our established markets before moving on
Competition	Avoid head-to-head conflicts	An entrepreneur must compete. Hit them where it hurts!
Investment	Less risk using own money	Borrow to grow. Use other people's money
Risk	Avoid risk wherever possible	Risk should be managed, but at the end of the day risk is what it is all about
	Entrepreneurs and investors must work together to manage risk and return	Let investors take the risk – I'll have the return!

Summary of key ideas

- A strategy is the means by which the venture will achieve its aims.

- Strategy *content* defines the products the venture will offer, the customer groups to be targeted and the way in which the venture will compete within its markets.

- Strategy *process* defines the way in which the venture will make *decisions* about the strategy content to adopt.

- A well-defined strategy aids the venture by defining the means by which it will achieve its goals in the marketplace.

- A strategy acts as a guide for decision making and provides a common language for the venture's stakeholders.

- Entrepreneurs often express their venture's strategy in the form of *heuristics*.

Research themes

Entrepreneurs' entry strategies

Section 15.5 explored different patterns of entry for entrepreneurs. The entry strategy adopted can easily be accessed by examining the venture's sales literature (a catalogue or price list is ideal, and usually freely available). How does the entry strategy correlate with the initial size of the venture (say in terms of early sales? Get the business's accounts. Most are available on the Internet. Alternatively, a selection of businesses from reports in the *Investors Chronicle* will give financial information and stock market measures such as market capitalisation, which are also appropriate for businesses actively trading shares). Is it the case that businesses with a larger start-up do so on the back of an initial introduction of a range of products or by tacking a range of markets? Or do some businesses become large quite quickly on the basis of a single product–market introduction? Be prepared to set in place strict criteria as to the judgement of the scope of product range and market range. Think about the products and markets strategically. Are the products simply variations on a fundamental product? Are they different products but based on a common technology? Or are they quite diverse products based on different technologies? Are all markets served by the same marketing (sales) effort, or distribution route or do they need different resource bases for their promotion? The paper by Cooper *et al.* (1989) provides a useful methodological template for this type of study.

Entrepreneurs' heuristics

Heuristics are practical decision rules adopted to guide decisions. These are many and varied and, as recounted above, different entrepreneurs may adopt contradictory heuristics. Entrepreneurs may be encouraged to reveal their heuristics. Set up a series of decision situations that entrepreneurs may face. These decisions may relate to resource acquisition, internal management issues, competitive behaviour, business expansion and resource distribution (see above). Outline these using brief descriptions (200–300 words). Identify a pool of nascent and practising entrepreneurs (the more the better – aim for at least 20). Use an interview technique to ascertain what decision the entrepreneur would make in relation to each situation. Then inquire into how the entrepreneur would summarise their decision as a general rule. Code the responses to establish patterns in the heuristics. How consistent are they? Do different entrepreneurs adopt contradictory heuristics? How do the heuristics of nascent and experienced entrepreneurs differ?

Suggestions for further reading

Atkins, M. and Lowe, J. (1994) 'Stakeholders and the strategy formation process in small and medium enterprises', *International Small Business Journal*, Vol. 12, No. 3, pp. 12–24.

Bowman, C. and Ambrosini, V. (1996) 'Tracking patterns of realised strategy', *Journal of General Management*, Vol. 21, No. 3, pp. 59–73.

Calori, R. (1985) 'Effective strategies in emerging industries', *Long Range Planning*, Vol. 18, No. 3, pp. 55–61.

Cooper, A.C., Woo, C.Y. and Dunkelberg, W.C. (1989) 'Entrepreneurship and the initial size of firms', *Journal of Business Venturing*, Vol. 4, No. 5, pp. 317–32.

Eden, C. and Ackermann, F. (1998) *Making Strategy: The Journey of Strategic Management*, London: Sage.

Gallen, T. (1997) 'The cognitive style and strategic decisions of managers', *Management Decision*, Vol. 35, No. 7, pp. 541–51.

Grieve Smith, J. and Fleck, V. (1987) 'Business strategies in small high-technology companies', *Long Range Planning*, Vol. 20, No. 2, pp. 61–8.

Idenburg, P.J. (1993) 'Four styles of strategy development', *Long Range Planning*, Vol. 26, No. 6, pp. 132–7.

Jenkins, M. (1997) 'Entrepreneurial intentions and outcomes: a comparative causal mapping study', *Journal of Management Studies*, Vol. 34, No. 6, pp. 895–920.

Manimala, M.J. (1999) *Entrepreneurial Policies and Strategies: The Innovator's Choice*, New Delhi: Sage.

McDougall, P. and Robinson, R.B. (1990) 'New venture strategies: an empirical identification of eight "archetypes" of competitive strategies for entry', *Strategic Management Journal*, Vol. 11, pp. 447–67.

Miller, D. (1992) 'The generic strategy trap', *Journal of Business Strategy*, Jan/Feb, pp. 37–41.

Mintzberg, H. (1973) 'Strategy making in three modes', *California Management Review*, Vol. XVI, No. 2, pp. 44–53.

Mintzberg, H. (1978) 'Patterns in strategy formation', *Management Science*, Vol. 24, No. 9, pp. 934–48.

Mintzberg, H. (1988) 'Generic strategies: towards a comprehensive framework', *Advances in Strategic Management*, Vol. 5, pp. 1–76.

Mintzberg, H. (1994) *The Rise and Fall of Strategic Planning*, London: Prentice Hall.

Mintzberg, H. and Waters, J.A. (1985) 'Of strategies deliberate and emergent', *Strategic Management Journal*, Vol. 6, pp. 257–72.

Mitchell, R.K. (1997) 'Oral history and expert scripts: demystifying the entrepreneurial experience', *International Journal of Entrepreneurial Behaviour and Research*, Vol. 3, No. 2, pp. 122–39.

Quinn, J.B. (1978) 'Strategic change: logical incrementalism', *Sloan Management Review*, Vol. 20, pp. 7–21.

Selected case material Case 15.1

A bridge over the generation gap

4 November 2002

By **Alan Cane**

Now here's a novelty: a wireless operator in the devastated telecommunications sector whose optimism about the future seems to be justified by its numbers.

Really? The Nasdaq-quoted Nextel is still making a loss and its share price, at just under $9, has fallen from a high point of more than $80 in mid-2000. No operator, however, has been able to evade the market downturn and Tim Donahue, chief executive, feels confident enough to claim: 'We are one of the bright spots in telecoms these days. By every industry metric you can think of, we are ahead of the competition.'

Figures from the brokers Merrill Lynch confirm his contention. While the average US customer is paying his or her telecoms operator $50 (£32) a month, Nextel is raking in $71. Churn, a measure of the number of customers leaving a network for any of a number of reasons, is only 2.1 per cent, compared with the US average of 3 per cent. The lifetime value of a Nextel customer, Mr Donahue claims, is $3,500, compared with an average $2,200 for companies such as Cingular and Verizon.

But, you could well ask: 'What is Nextel?' The company has no presence in Europe and no intention of establishing one. Its operations are pretty well restricted to the US but even there it is hardly a household name, for the simple reason that it has no trade with residential customers.

Its focus is business, utilities and the emergency services; large organisations that can make use of its combination of services: conventional cellular voice telephony, data transmission at speeds in the '2?G' category and a unique capability called 'direct connect'.

2?G is used to describe mobile phone services that come somewhere between today's GSM standard and tomorrow's all-singing, all-dancing multimedia services. The Nextel network operates at between 15,000 and 20,000 bits of information a second, compared with 9,600 bps for GSM. New software is planned that will give apparent rates of 30bps to 50bps.

Direct connect, however, is Nextel's secret weapon, the capability that endears it to customers such as the MGM/Mirage hotel group in Las Vegas and General Motors, and which rivals will find difficult to replicate.

It is a modern take on the old walkie-talkie systems, which have always enjoyed popularity in the US. Nextel handsets, a little bigger than conventional mobile phones, sport a large button on the side. Press the button and you can talk immediately to another Nextel user or to 10,000 or more. @Road, for example, a US transport logistics company, combines Nextel technology with satellite geographic positioning to give its customers better control of their vehicles.

Mr Donahue says: 'Dispatchers know the location of every truck. Regardless of the time of day or day of the week, they can keep better track of their vehicles and send the truckers better information – a new bill of lading, for example, or a change in delivery schedules.

'For that kind of application,' Donahue continues, 'we'll get something like $13–$16 a month per vehicle for fleets of 6,000 to 10,000 long-haul trucks.'

No other US operator can offer a comparable service at present and Mr Donahue believes the cost and complexity will deter new entrants: 'We do not see anybody on the horizon having anything as robust as we have. Some will introduce what they think is direct connect but it will have a problem with latency. When you push the button, there will be a delay of about six seconds before connection. My customers will not put up with that.'

The company has about 10m customers already and expects to add a further 2m this year. Revenues came in at just under $8bn in 2001, with earnings before interest, tax, depreciation and amortisation of $3bn. The company turned earnings positive last quarter and expects to have positive free cash flow in early 2004. 'Or sooner,' Mr Donahue says.

If Nextel continues to fulfil its potential, it will be another feather in the cap of Craig McCaw, the serial entrepreneur and visionary who created the US cellular industry.

He took control of the three-year-old but failing Nextel in 1995, persuaded Motorola, the US telecommunications manufacturer to clean up the company's flaky technology and refocused the group as a supplier of specialist services rather than a competitor for conventional wireless companies.

As O. Casey Corr put it in his biography* of Mr McCaw: 'The base-market opportunity was not existing cellular users or the average housewife but the 17m–18m two-way radio users in mobile work groups [such as] truckers and newspaper photographers.'

Or, as Mr Donahue puts it: 'We look for large business deals. We stay away from consumers who are always looking for a better price, for more minutes of airtime in their bucket.'

Mr Donahue, a long-serving associate of Mr McCaw, was appointed chief executive in 1999. Mr McCaw, with other executives from his Eagle River investment vehicle, retains a seat on the Nextel board. Its chairman is William Conway, managing director of The Carlyle Group, a Washington-based buy-out specialist with strong defence industry connections. William Kennard, formerly US Federal Communications Commission chairman and another Carlyle executive, is also on the board.

In spite of the group's reluctance to become involved in the consumer market, Mr Donahue sees some potential in the youth market for what he describes, by analogy with text messaging, as 'voice instant messaging'. Trials are being carried out in California but, he says cautiously: 'We are very disciplined in our approach. I have to see a return on the business plan.'

Telecoms aficionados will see an instant resemblance between Nextel's technology, called iDEN, and the European equivalent, Tetra. Tetra is being developed for European police and emergency services, but an attempt to create a commercial service, Dolphin, went into administration last year (it has since been acquired by US-owned group Inquam).

Mr Donahue comments: 'The technology is not as good and I don't think the Dolphin folk understood how to go after the business user. They got into the swamp with all the other wireless carriers. It is the kiss of death to compete with those guys without having the public understand you are very different.

'If I were ever interested in Europe, I would test market thoroughly first – in Denmark, perhaps, or France. Europe is different because it does not have the history of two-way radio the US has.'

Source: Financial Times, 4 November 2002.

---

* *Money from Thin Air*, by O. Casey Corr, 2000, Crown Business Publishing.

Case 15.2

Igabriel links with two investment clubs

21 August 2002

By **Astrid Wendlandt**

Igabriel, the technology-focused start-up fund whose members include the pop icon Peter Gabriel and internet guru Esther Dyson, will announce today that it is joining forces with two old economy investment clubs to take advantage of the low valuations placed on many companies.

Venture Capital Report (VCR), a private equity firm, and Private Investors Capital (PI Capital), an investment club, are to merge their activities with Igabriel.

Ms Dyson said: 'The impact the stock market has had on the valuation of private companies has been huge. There are a lot of opportunities for angels and they are very low-priced.'

The combined structure, which will be able to draw on a larger pool of funds, will specialise in early stage investments and development capital in industries such as biotechnology and retail.

PI Capital's 110 members are thought to include Guy Hands, the former managing director of Nomura's Principal Finance group, and Sir Robin Saxby, chairman of ARM, the chip design company that until recently was a FTSE 100 stock.

In exchange for an annual fee of £3,000, members of PI Capital rely on its investment committee and contacts to value and filter business plans and investment proposals they submit to the club. Members are mostly wealthy businessmen and entrepreneurs who wish to invest in opportunities they do not have the time to scrutinise.

'If members see something interesting they have the ability to refer it to the club and the club looks at it carefully,' said David Giampaolo, chief executive of VCR/PI Capital. 'We also know that they can rely on members' expertise and sector experience.' However, VCR's members, who are believed to include Nitin Shah, the entrepreneur who backed Coffee Republic in its early days, do their own due diligence and research on investment propositions.

VCR linked up with PI Capital two months ago. The three entities have invested together about £16m a year over the past three years.

Igabriel was founded in 2000 by Charlie Muirhead, founder of Orchestream, the telecoms software company that is expected to publish its interim results today.

Igabriel, which works in a similar fashion to PI Capital, will own a 15 per cent stake in the latter. Members of the two clubs will be able to invest in VCR. However, VCR's members will not be given such a right. VCR and PI/Igabriel will be regulated separately by the FSA. Deals for PI Capital will range from £750,000 to £2m while VCR will start at £150,000.

Source: *Financial Times*, 21 August 2002.

Discussion points

1. Comment on the strategic approach taken by Tim Donahue and Nextel.
2. Develop a strategy for Igabriel.

Chapter 16

The business plan: an entrepreneurial tool

Chapter overview

A business plan is an essential tool for the entrepreneur. This chapter explores the role of the business plan and the kind of information it should include. It considers the way a business plan can help the venture by guiding analysis, creating a synthesis of new insights, communicating the potential of the venture to interested parties, and promoting management action. The chapter concludes by looking at the ways in which business planning can increase the flexibility and responsiveness of the venture. This chapter also considers ways in which the business plan can be structured to produce an effective and influential communication tool.

16.1 Planning and performance

Key learning outcome

A recognition of the influence of formal planning activity on the performance of the entrepreneurial venture.

Entrepreneurs, like many other managers, are often called upon to prepare formal, written plans. They may do this of their own accord or it may be at the instigation of external investors such as venture capitalists or banks. The picture of entrepreneurs 'locked away' writing formal business plans sits ill at ease with the image of them as dynamic individuals actively pursuing their business interests. Many entrepreneurs object to preparing plans because they feel their time would be better spent pushing the venture forward. They claim that they already know what is in the plan and that no one else will read it!

This objection highlights an important point in that developing a plan demands time, energy and (often) hard cash. It ties up both the entrepreneur and the business's staff. A business plan represents an *investment* in the venture. It must be justified as an investment, that is, in terms of the return it offers the business. The relationship between formal planning and business performance has been the subject of numerous statistical studies; however, no clear picture has emerged. The correlation between *formal* planning and performance is generally weak so it is not possible to say with certainty that formal planning will improve the performance of a particular business. As a result, there has been something of a reaction against formal planning in recent years, especially in relation to smaller businesses. As noted in the previous chapter, Henry Mintzberg has offered a profound criticism of at least a narrow approach to planning in his book *The Rise and Fall of Strategic Planning*. However, a recent study by Perry (2001) indicated a negative correlation between planning and failure rates for US small businesses. Formal planning was not found to be a common activity, but businesses that had planned were less likely to fail than those that had not. Schneider (1998) provides a general defence of planning for the smaller business.

However, the poor statistical correlation should not be taken to mean that performance is unaffected by planning. Statistical studies usually compare 'planning activity' (the definition of this varies between studies) against performance measured in financial or growth terms. Inevitably, these studies must reduce a complex organisational phenomenon to simple variables. Planning is not an easily defined, isolated activity. Rather it is an activity embedded in both the wider strategy process of the organisation and the control strategy of the entrepreneur. Financial performance is important but it is not the only measure of achievement which motivates the entrepreneur. The entrepreneur may compromise financial gains in order to achieve less tangible benefits. They may even *plan* to make this compromise. Intuitively it seems the case that a good plan will lead to an improved performance and, equally, that a bad one will lead the business astray. There is also the problem of distinguishing between the existence of a plan and whether that plan is actually *implemented*.

Statistical studies of planning and performance also face the issue of causation; that is, when two things seem to correlate, how can we be sure which is the cause and which the effect? It may be that the variation in performance observed is not so much due to the mere existence of planning but rather to the *quality* of the planning that takes place. It has even been suggested that planning does not lead to performance, but rather that a good performance allows managers the time and money to indulge in planning!

The planning/performance debate reflects the problems to be encountered in teasing out cause-and-effect relationships in a system as complex and subject to as many variables as an entrepreneurial venture. In short then, it is impossible to give a straight 'yes' or 'no' answer to questions like: 'Should entrepreneurs produce a formal plan?' or 'Should entrepreneurs formalise the way their organisation plans?'. Over-generalisation is unwise. The decision to engage in formal planning, like most other decisions the entrepreneur faces, must be made in the light of what is best for the individual venture, the way it operates and the specific opportunities it faces. Planning, if it is approached in a way which is right for the venture and is aimed at addressing the right issues, would seem to offer a number of benefits. The remainder of this chapter will examine the decision to create a formal plan, explore the ways in which it might benefit the business and suggest ways in which the plan might be structured.

16.2) The role of the business plan

Key learning outcome

An understanding of how the business plan works as a management tool.

The activity of creating a formal business plan consumes both time and resources. If it is to be undertaken, and undertaken well, there must be an appreciation of the way in which the business plan can actually be made to work as a tool for the business. In principle, there are four mechanisms by which a business plan might aid the performance of the venture.

By working as a tool for analysis

A business plan contains information. Some of this information will be that used as the basis for articulating and refining the entrepreneur's vision, for generating the mission statement and for developing a strategy content and strategy process for the venture. The structure of the business plan provides the entrepreneur with an effective checklist of the information they must gather in order to be sure the direction for their venture is both achievable and rewarding (see Schneider (1998) for a development of this point). Creating the plan guides and disciplines the entrepreneur in gathering this information. Hills (1985) emphasises that the level of background market research in entrepreneurs' plans is usually quite low, but investment in market research can have a high payoff, not least in making demand planning more effective. Wyckham and Wedley (1990) demonstrate the value of the plan in distinguishing feasible from unfeasible ventures.

By working as a tool for synthesis

Once data has been gathered and analysed in a formal way then the information generated must be used to provide a direction for the venture. The information must be integrated with, and used to refine, the entrepreneur's vision and used to support the development of a suitable mission and strategy. The planning exercise acts to *synthesise* the entrepreneur's vision with a definite plan of action in a unified way. This synthesis converts the vision into a strategy for the venture, and then into the actions appropriate to pursuing that strategy.

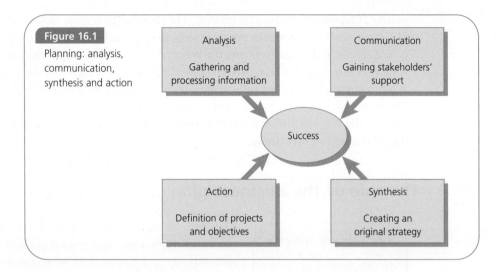

Figure 16.1

Planning: analysis, communication, synthesis and action

By working as a tool for communication

The business plan provides a vehicle for communicating the potential of the venture, the opportunities it faces and the way it intends to exploit them in a way which is concise, efficient and effective. This may be of value in communicating with both internal and external stakeholders. The plan may draw internal people together and give them a focus for their activities. The business plan is particularly important as a tool for communicating with potential investors, gaining their interest and attracting them to the venture.

By working as a call to action

The business plan is a call to action. It provides a detailed list of the activities that must be undertaken, the tasks that must be performed and the outcomes that must be achieved if the entrepreneur is to convert his or her vision into a new world. The plan may also call upon formal project management techniques such as critical path analysis in order to organise, prioritise and arrange tasks in a way which makes the best use of scarce resources.

The four ways in which the planning exercise contributes to the success drive of the venture do not operate in isolation. They underpin and support each other and the performance of the venture (Figure 16.1). Together they define not only the plan that should be developed for the venture, but also the way the venture should engage in planning.

16.3 What a business plan should include

There are no hard and fast rules about what a business plan should include since a business plan must be shaped to reflect the needs and requirements of the venture

Key learning outcome

An appreciation of the type of information to be included in a business plan.

it represents. The entrepreneur and the management team will have their own preferences. The information included will depend on what stage the venture is at: the plan for a new venture may be more exhaustive than the on-going yearly plan for one which is quite well established. Very importantly, the plan will reflect the information required by the audience at whom the plan is directed and the action the entrepreneur desires from them. Financial backers may dictate both the format the business plan must take and the information it should include.

The following list indicates the type and scope of information and themes that might be included in a fairly exhaustive business plan:

- **Mission**
  - *The mission for the venture*: the formal mission statement that defines the business, what it is, what it is aiming to deliver, to whom, why it makes a difference and what it aspires to achieve.

- **Overview of key objectives**
  - *Financial objectives*: the turnover and profit targets for the period of the plan; the growth desired over the previous period.
  - *Strategic objectives*: achievements in the market and gains to be made in market position.

- **The market environment**
  - *Background to the market*: i.e. how the market is defined; the size of the market; major market sectors and niches; overall growth rate; key trends and developments in consumer behaviour and buying habits; and technological developments in the product, service delivery and operations.
  - *Competitors*: key competitors, their strengths and weaknesses; competitors' strategy and likely reaction to the venture's activity.
  - *Competitive conditions*: the basis of competition in the market; the importance of price, product differentiation and branding; the benefits to be gained from positioning.
  - *Competitive advantage of the venture*: the important strengths of the venture relative to competitors; sources of competitive advantage.
  - *Definition of product offerings*: the products/services that the business will offer to the market.
  - *Definition of target markets*: the way in which the market is split up into different sectors; the dimensions of the market important for characterising the sectors; and the market sectors that will be prioritised for targeting by the business.

- **Strategy**
  - *Product strategy*: the way in which the product/service will be differentiated from competitors (e.g. features, quality, price); why this will be attractive to customers.

- *Pricing strategy*: how the product/service will be priced relative to competitors (e.g. offer of a premium, discounting); means of establishing price; promotional pricing and price cutting; pricing policy and margins to be offered to intermediaries.
- *Distribution strategy*: the route by which the product/service will be delivered to the customer; intermediaries (wholesalers, distributors, retailers) who will be partners in distribution; strategy for working with distributors; policy for exporting and international marketing if appropriate.
- *Promotional strategy*: approaches to informing the customer (and intermediaries) about the product/service; advertising message, means and medium; sales activity and approach to selling; sales promotions (including price promotions); public relations activity.
- *Networking*: relationship between the organisation and other organisations in the network; use of the network to create and support competitive advantage.

● **Financial forecasts**
- *Income*: revenues from trading activity; structure of the capital provided by investors.
- *Routine expenditure*: expenditure on salaries, raw materials and consumables; payment of interest on debt.
- *Capital expenditure*: major investment in new assets; how these assets will enhance performance.
- *Cash-flow*: difference between revenues and expenditure by period; cash-flow reflects the liquidity of the business and its ability to fund its activities. If income is more than expenditure then cash-flow is positive. If expenditure is more than income then cash-flow is negative.

● **Activity**
- *Major projects*: the key projects that will drive the venture forward and deliver the objectives; for example, new product developments, sales drives, launches with distributors and advertising campaigns.

● **People**
- *Key players in the venture*: the individuals behind the venture; the skills and experience they will contribute to the business; evidence of their achievements; personal profiles and CVs.

The list above reflects a 'traditional' structure of a business plan that is related in many planning guides. However, a list is just an account of what should be included, not necessarily an instruction on the order in which it is presented. Section 16.6 will consider a more effective way of structuring the plan. The information included in the business plan will depend on how it is intended to use the plan and to whom it will be communicated. The business need not be restricted to a single version of the plan and it may prove advantageous to use different formats for different audiences. A detailed and exhaustive 'master' plan may act as a source for the rapid, and informed, production of such specific plans.

16.4) Business planning: analysis and synthesis

> **Key learning outcome**
>
> An appreciation of how business planning facilitates analysis of the venture's potential and a synthesis of its strategy.

Effective planning requires information. Information is all around us but it rarely comes for free. Information has a cost: this may be relatively low, a trip to the local library perhaps, or it may be very expensive, commissioning a major piece of market research, for example. Even if it has no direct cost, gathering and analysing information takes time. Hence information must be gathered with an eye to how it will be used. The benefits to be gained from having the information must justify its cost.

Information is used to manage uncertainty. Having information means that uncertainty is reduced, which in turn reduces the risk of the venture and improves the prospects of its success. Essentially, the entrepreneur is interested in answering the following questions:

● What are the customer's fundamental needs in relation to the product category? (What benefits does the product offer? What problems do customers solve with the product?)

● How does the market currently serve those needs? (What products are offered? What features do they have?)

● In what way(s) does the market fail to serve those needs? (Why are customers left dissatisfied? How often are they left dissatisfied?)

● How might customer needs be served better? (How might the product on offer be improved?)

Marketing, as a discipline, offers a number of techniques to develop these answers. In addition, the entrepreneur must know:

● How does the better way being advocated add up as a real business opportunity?

● What risks are likely to be present in pursuing such an opportunity?

These final two points are of course critical. Developing an answer to these questions, and understanding the decisions they involve, will be explored fully through the development of the *strategic window* in Part 3 of this book.

Planning certainly supports strategy development but it is not *equivalent* to it. Henry Mintzberg observes that planning is about *analysis*; it is about breaking down information to spot opportunities and possibilities. Strategy, on the other hand, is about *synthesis*; it is about bringing the capabilities of the business to bear on the opportunity in a way which is creative and original. Developing answers to the questions listed above is the analysis part of the equation. Reconciling them into a workable, rewarding strategy is the synthesis part. This synthesis must include both the strategy *content* and the *process* to deliver it.

In order to synthesise an original strategy the entrepreneur must decide:

- How will the venture address the needs of the customer? (i.e. What is the nature of the opportunity that has been identified?)

- Why will the venture's offerings serve those needs better than those of competitors? (What is the *innovation*? Why is it valuable?)

- How will demand be stimulated? (This involves issues of communication, promotion and distribution.)

- Why can the entrepreneur's business deliver this in a way that competitors cannot? (What will be the *competitive advantage* that the business enjoys? What will it be able to do that its competitors cannot do that is valuable for its customers?)

- What is it about the business that enables them to do this? (What are the *competences* and *capabilities* of the business?)

- Why will competitors be unable to imitate them? (In what way(s) is the competitive advantage *sustainable*?)

Planning helps the business by first demanding an analysis of information about the market, customers and competitors. This information provides a sure basis for decision making. Planning goes on to help the business by synthesis, that is, by integrating the information into a strategy. This strategy gives the venture a shape and a direction. It forms the basis for plans and projects which offer definite actions for the people who make up the venture and those who support it to follow. Thus information is valuable because it links the analysis of opportunity with the synthesis of strategy in a planning framework (Figure 16.2).

16.5 Business planning: action and communication

> **Key learning outcome**
>
> An appreciation of how the business plan may be used as a communication tool and as a call to action.

Communication is not just about passing on information. It is an attempt to elicit a particular *response* from someone. In business it is not just what we want people to *know* that matters; it is also what we want them to *do*. The ways the business plan functions both as a piece of communication and as a recipe for action are intimately inter-related.

The business plan is a communication that relates in a succinct way a precise and unambiguous account of the venture *and* what it aims to achieve. It defines the decisions the entrepreneur has made in relation to the opportunity that has been identified; the way the opportunity will be exploited; the value the entrepreneur aims to create as a result of exploiting it; the resources that will be needed in order

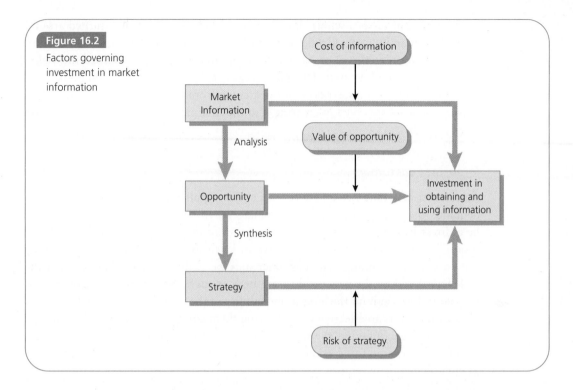

Figure 16.2

Factors governing investment in market information

to progress the venture; the risks those resources will be exposed to; and the projects the entrepreneur will undertake with the resources they receive.

These decisions are communicated with the intention of gaining support for the venture. The entrepreneur will be particularly interested in communicating with and influencing the following groups of people.

Investors

The business plan not only relates the potential of the venture and the rewards it offers to investors but also the risks that it entails. It is also an opportunity for the entrepreneur to convince the investor of the skills they have and make them feel confident that the goods can be delivered. Numerous studies have found that the quality of the business plan and the effectiveness of its communication are critical factors in gaining investors' interest and support. See, for example, the studies by Macmillan *et al.* (1985, 1987), Knight (1994) and Mason and Harrison (1996). This is an issue we will revisit in Chapter 23.

Employees

Employees make their own investment in the business by committing themselves to it. The business plan can give them confidence in the future of the venture. It will also specify the key projects that need to be undertaken, so defining individual objectives and the way in which the role the individual plays fits with the goals of the organisation as a whole. Jan Carlzon, the entrepreneur who turned around the failing Scandinavian Airline Systems (SAS) in the early 1980s, issued each of the organisation's 20,000 or so employees with a plan which outlined the vision and strategy he had devised. This plan became known as the 'little red book'.

Employee commitment does not just come from letting people in on the plan. Letting them get involved in *creating* it in the first place is also a sure way to gain their support.

Important customers

A customer may face a cost in taking on a new supplier. Moving between suppliers demands the time and attention of managers. In some cases there may need to be a direct investment in new equipment so that the products can be used. If the product is new, the customer may have to learn to use it, for example staff may need additional training. The customer may be willing to face these costs if the benefits offered by the new product are high enough. They will resist, however, if they have doubts about the long-term viability of the supplier. Sharing the business plan with them is an effective way of giving them confidence in the entrepreneurial venture and encouraging them to make the necessary commitment. Customers are usually flattered to be asked to become involved with the venture in this way. Therefore, for a new venture, communicating the business plan as well as the product offering can be an important part of the selling strategy.

Major suppliers

Suppliers may also need to make an investment if they wish to supply the venture. This may take the form of dedicated selling and support activity and may even involve developing bespoke products. Although the venture offers the prospect of new business they will, like the venture's customers, resist making the investment if they harbour doubts about the long-term viability of the venture. Again, the business plan may be used to give them the confidence to make an investment of time and resources on behalf of the venture.

In short, the business plan is a communication tool which can be used by the venture to help build the network of relationships which will be critical to its long-term success.

16.6 Structuring and articulating the business plan: the Pyramid Principle

A business plan is not just a repository for facts and statements. It is a business *communication*. And like any form of human communication its impact and influence is determined by *how* things are said as well as *what* is said. The organisation of ideas is as important as the ideas themselves. The structuring of the business plan considered in the previous section places emphasis on the information that must be

Key learning outcome

An appreciation of Barbara Minto's 'Pyramid Principle' technique for structuring and articulating in business communication, and how it can be applied to create an influential business plan.

communicated rather than the case the business plan is attempting to make. The impact of the business plan on key decision makers (particularly, but not exclusively, potential investors) will depend on the way in which information is *delivered* as well as the information itself. Effective business communications work with, rather than against, the cognitive processes human decision makers adopt. The ideas to be explored in this section are based on the work of Barbara Minto, a management consultant who has explored business communication styles and their effectiveness in depth. These ideas are not restricted just to business plans but are effective with any business communication (written or verbal). I am not ashamed to admit I use them for structuring academic papers! Barbara Minto's book *The Pyramid Principle* is highly recommended to those who wish to explore these ideas in more depth. Minto's central idea is based on discoveries in cognitive psychology about the way in which humans store and manage information and then use it to support decision making. It is clear that we human beings are actually quite inefficient information processors. When presented with a lot of information, we inevitably simplify it. We are, at best, able to store between five and nine pieces of information at any one time. From any one communication we only take away one or two key ideas. Further, we do not store information in our brains in a linear way, one idea after another. Rather we build hierarchies of information in which facts are connected together in a network of linkages. Minto suggests that we can use all of these facts to construct communications that will be more effective and influential. First, she suggests, we should consider the *one* key message the recipient will take away, what she refers to as the 'key point'. Given that the recipient is likely to take away only one 'big idea', we should aim to control what that is, rather than let the recipient do it for him or herself. Second, we should order information in a way that builds a hierarchy (a pyramid) of understanding under our control rather than deliver the information linearly and assume that the recipient will order it for him or herself in the way we would wish. In other words, we should take active control of the process of 'translating' both from the idea network to its written (linear) form and translating back again.

Minto's ideas provide useful insights into the preparation of effective business plans. First, the key point or 'big idea'. It is important to recognise what we want the recipients of the plan to *do*, rather than what we would wish them to *know*. Communication transfers information, but this is the means to the end of eliciting action, not an objective in itself. What we wish a recipient of a business plan to do depends on who the recipient is. If an investor, then we hope he or she will provide the investment requested. If a potential employee, then the key point will be 'work for me'; a customer: 'buy from me' and so on. We must then put in place supporting ideas (ideally five to eight) that lay out a case for that big idea. Moving down the pyramid, we should then develop *arguments* that justify the supporting ideas. Finally, at the bottom of the pyramid, we must provide evidence that backs up the

Table 16.1   Pyramid structure of business plan

Key point

Invest in this venture!

Supporting questions

Is there a gap in the market for this product/service?	Does this market have potential?	Why will this innovation fill that gap?	Can this innovation be delivered profitably and at acceptable risk?	Does the venture have a long-term future?	Are the proposers the right people to deliver it?
Arguments					
Individuals have these needs in relation to this product category	Assumptions about market definition	This innovation meets customer needs better than anything currently on offer. It offers unique and attractive benefits	Pricing is sufficient to cover unit production costs	Venture has a sustainable competitive advantage	Managerial experience, capabilities and motivation
Current offerings fail to meet these needs satisfactorily	Demand in this sector is high and is likely to grow	This innovation is new and original	Long-term profits will sustain necessary investment	It is delivering something of value; it is doing so in a unique way; competitors can be fended off	
Recent developments in the product category still leave these needs unmet	Market conditions offer potential to new entrants	Technological and organisational capabilities are in place to effect delivery to market	Distribution route is available	Advantage will be gained in terms of costs, strategic assets, innovation capabilities, reputation and/or organisational architecture	
			Promotional plans have been thought through and costed		
			Risk has been assessed and its management considered	Options for future expansion have been considered	
Evidence					
Primary and secondary customer research	Rationale for market definition	Primary and secondary customer research	Costing data and financial projections	Strategic analysis of venture and competitors	Managers' CVs
Competitor analysis	Market research: market size, growth rate and structure	Product testing and trials	Assumptions about output volumes, prices, costs and demand conditions	Explanation as to why competitive advantage will be gained and sustained	Evidence of relevant experience, qualifications, sector knowledge and previous successes
Product evaluation	Existing supply structure	Evidence of technical and organisational capabilities	Competitor costs and investment benchmarks		Evidence supporting leadership abilities
	PEST analysis		Evaluation of promotional plans and distribution routes		
			Scenario analysis		

Figure 16.3	**Main heading: Introduction**
Organising the Pyramid structure	**Main heading: Supporting question 1** Sub-heading: *Argument 1 – Evidence 1* Sub-heading: *Argument 2 – Evidence 2* Sub-heading: *Argument 3 – Evidence 3* etc. **Main heading: Supporting question 2** Sub-heading: *Argument 1 – Evidence 1* Sub-heading: *Argument 2 – Evidence 2* Sub-heading: *Argument 3 – Evidence 3* etc. **Main heading: Supporting question 3** Sub-heading: *Argument 1 – Evidence 1* Sub-heading: *Argument 2 – Evidence 2* Sub-heading: *Argument 3 – Evidence 3* etc. **Main heading: Summary**

arguments. Table 16.1 illustrates such a structure for a business plan aimed at investors. Six supporting ideas are entered, reflecting the series of questions an investor would wish to see answered. These are the supporting questions I often use, but I would not claim this version is definitive. Other supporting questions may also be appropriate and arguments may be articulated differently.

With this pyramid structure in place, the next step is to construct the business plan around it. The pyramid must be converted into a linear flow of narrative, while still retaining a feel for the underlying pyramid structure. Minto suggests that using headings and sub-headings to indicate different levels of the pyramid is a good way of doing this, and this approach works for a business plan. The headings should be short and to the point and be used to highlight the pyramid structure. They should not be thought of as informative in their own right. Overall the plan has the structure shown in Figure 16.3.

An illustration of the process in action is as follows. The first step is to construct an introduction. The introduction serves two key purposes. First, it is an invitation to the recipient to read the plan, and engage them (don't forget, the majority of business plans sent to venture capitalists are dismissed without being fully read. If attention is not captured in the first few paragraphs, it never will be!). Second, it may be used to lay out the structure of the case to be made for the venture. As a first move, the introduction should put in place the big idea. A good opening would be:

Introduction

This plan proposes a new business venture that offers a major and attractive investment opportunity.

The next step is to relate the supporting arguments in a succinct manner (do not be tempted to over-expand on the ideas at this stage; this will come later):

> It will outline an innovative product (service) that offers unique benefits to customers in a way superior to existing competitors in a market with significant potential. The experienced management team leading the venture are confident that the venture has long-term potential, will be financially sound, and will gain and sustain an advantage over existing competitors.

At this stage, it is important that the recipient is guided in developing a mental image of the business concerned. Too often with business plans, the reader is left to fit together pieces of information about the business from different parts of the plan. This takes effort the reader may not be willing to invest. They may simply reject the plan. Even if they do put in that effort, the picture built is not under the proposer's control. A good way to take control is to relate the venture's mission. Articulating the mission is considered in Chapter 14.

> ### The venture's mission

Following this, the venture's key objectives (financial, market, growth) can be related.

> ### Key objectives

With the introduction in place, the plan can then expand, argue for and evidence the claims made. Each supporting idea is dealt with in turn. For example, the first supporting question is 'Is there a gap in the market for this product?'. Again, following the pyramid principle, the opportunity should be taken to map out the structure of the arguments to follow.

> ### The market gap
>
> There is a significant gap in the market for the new product (service). Customer expectations are high and existing products are not meeting requirements. Recent developments in the product category have not significantly delivered on these expectations.

Now sub-headings can be used to detail each argument in turn and provide evidence for it.

> ### Customer needs and expectations
>
> Customers have high expectations about what this product category should offer. In particular they feel that it should . . .

Now is the opportunity to support these claims with evidence, e.g.:

> This is confirmed by independent market research using focus groups . . .

And then on to the second argument under this supporting question:

> **Customers' attitudes to products already available**
>
> Purchases in this product category are significant [introduce evidence on market size here]. The market is buoyant [introduce evidence on market growth rate here]. While customers do express some satisfaction with current offerings, they have a number of criticisms that add up to a clear opportunity for a new product. Research with focus groups and a telephone survey of a large sample of buyers indicate that the key failings are . . .

And then on to the third argument

> **Recent developments in the product category**
>
> Development of new products in this category is relatively active. X and Y have both launched new products. While these have been relatively successful, they do not address the fundamental failings of the category as seen by customers. Our research indicates . . . [evidence]

Once the first supporting question has been addressed, then the second can be explored in the same way. Then the third. Another example: the venture's long-term potential (supporting question 5):

> **Long-term profitability and growth**
>
> We believe the business will have long-term potential and will be able to hold its position against follower competitors.

Now lay out the arguments:

> As has been illustrated, the venture is offering a product with unique benefits to a large number of buyers. These benefits are unique and are not matched by any existing product [may re-summarise evidence here]. This valuable uniqueness is protectable.

Detail the argument on the last point, depending on particular sources of competitive advantage

---

This will be achieved by:
- access to unique and valuable resources;
- a lower cost structure;
- faster and more effective innovation;
- a better reputation than competitors; and/or:
- performance enhanced through organisational and network architecture.

(Refer to Chapter 22 for a full discussion of these sources of competitive advantage.)

Once this process is completed, a summary can be used to close the plan and encapsulate its ideas in the mind of the recipient. Aim to repeat the key point and the supporting questions once again:

Summary

This plan has highlighted a major investment opportunity. It demonstrates . . . [lay out supporting questions again].

The objective of the summary is to provide a final reinforcement of the key point, 'Invest in me!', not to summarise everything in the plan. Don't be tempted to go through the arguments and evidence again.

This approach gives a business plan a quite different structure to the 'list structure' discussed in Section 16.3. For a start, there is no one section that relates all the market research. Market research is introduced when and where it is needed to back up a claim. So the reader's attention is being drawn to facts that matter, when they matter, rather than as a mass of data, which the reader will not be able to absorb or directly relate to the case for investment being made. Considerations on strategy are integrated with discussion of market opportunity, not separated.

Here are a few points by way of a summary. First, at each stage in the pyramid, summarise the structure below that will follow. Second, it will be recognised that given the number of supporting ideas, arguments and evidence, not much needs to be said at each stage. Do not be tempted to over-expand on points made. If a section is longer than a couple of paragraphs, it is probably better to go back to the pyramid and split the ideas. Third, do not worry too much about repetition. My experience with entrepreneurs introduced to the Pyramid Principle is that they feel they are being repetitive and saying the same thing over and over again. This reflects the fact we valuate originality. However, the value of a business plan is its effectiveness in engendering support, not its literary qualities. In any case, readers do not find the pyramid structure repetitive, just highly informative and impactful.

16.7 Strategy, planning and flexibility

> **Key learning outcome**
>
> An understanding of how planning may be used to make the business responsive, rather than rigid, in the face of opportunity and uncertainty.

Many entrepreneurs are suspicious of formal planning. They may see the written plan as restrictive, and feel that it reduces their room for manoeuvre. They may be concerned that by defining future actions it limits their options. However, these suspicions are ill founded. If approached in the right way, planning increases, rather than restricts, flexibility. The right sort of strategy can make the business more, not less, responsive.

Focus on ends rather than means

Goals should be given priority over plans. It's what the business aims to achieve that matters. It may be that there is more than one way in which the business can reach its objectives. If so, all the possibilities should be explored. Not all are likely to be equally attractive and one route may be given priority. However, a knowledge of the alternatives allows for contingency plans to be made and an alternative course can be followed if some routes become blocked.

Challenge assumptions

What are the assumptions on which the plan is based? For example, what assumptions have been made in measuring the size of markets and the venture's rate of growth, in determining how attractive the innovation is to customers and in gauging the strengths of competitors? How sensitive is the plan to these assumptions? What will happen if they are wrong? How can the plan be 'immunised' against poor assumptions by building in contingencies for when they are wrong?

Model scenarios

What are the likely outcomes if the plan is implemented? How certain are these outcomes? In the face of uncertainty what is likely to be the *best* of all possible worlds and what is likely to be the *worst*? What is the *most likely* outcome? Determine what scenarios will result if an *optimistic*, a *pessimistic* and a *realistic* attitude is taken to the outcomes that are expected (particularly in relation to income and expenditure). How will the business fare in the face of each eventuality? How exposed is the business if the pessimistic scenario comes about? Has it (or can it get) the resources to manage the optimistic? Furthermore, have investors been made party to all scenarios, not just the best?

Create strategic flexibility

At the end of the day, a strategy is just a way of doing things. Strategic flexibility is a way of doing things well when faced with uncertainty. It involves actively responding to outcomes and adjusting activity, not just blindly following set plans.

Strategic flexibility comes from questioning moves. For example, can the product or service be modified in the light of consumer responses to it (*positive* as well as negative)? If one target market is proving hard to break into, can an alternative one be approached? Can costs be managed in response to demand (for example, how exposed is the business to fixed costs?)? If some relationships in the network prove to be less valuable than expected can new relationships be built quickly?

Leave space to learn

The way in which entrepreneurs and their businesses meet opportunities and respond to challenges is dependent on how they see the world, the knowledge that they have and their range of skills. All these factors must evolve through learning. The entrepreneur must constantly question the business. Are the underlying assumptions still valid? Is this still the best way to do things? Success does not speak for itself and it is important to question why a particular outcome is a success. What was done right? In what way might they have been even *more* successful? What were the failings? How might they be avoided next time? Learning is an active process. The good business plan identifies and highlights those areas where learning can take place. In short, a good strategy should be about flexibility, about enabling the business to take advantage of opportunities as they take shape and to manage the unexpected. It is not about setting a rigid course of action.

Summary of key ideas

- There is no simple correlation between investment in planning and business performance, though there is evidence that planning may be important in small business survival.

- A business plan can help the entrepreneurial venture by:
  - ensuring that a full analysis of the situation and the environment has been undertaken;
  - encouraging the synthesis of insights to generate a vision and a strategy;
  - acting as a call to action;
  - being a medium for communication with both internal and external stakeholders.

- Barbara Minto's 'Pyramid Principle' can be adopted to produce impactful and influential business plans.

- A well-defined business plan will actually increase the venture's flexibility, not impair it.

- The level of formality in planning will be influenced by the level of investment in the start-up, the involvement of external stakeholders (especially, but not exclusively, investors), the availability and cost of information, external support and the entrepreneur's personal style.

Research themes

Impact of pyramid structuring

Using the framework in Table 16.1, obtain information for four business plans (aim for 2,000–3,000 word descriptions, a typical length for a business plan). These may be imaginary, based on case studies or based on business plans you have access to. For each of the four data sets, construct two different versions of the plan, the first in which information is delivered in a linear way with the 'big idea' up front and then a supporting idea, its argument and then its evidence, then on to the next supporting idea followed by its argument and evidence and so on, until all supporting ideas have been covered, and then a pyramid version which starts with the 'big idea', then all the supporting ideas, then all the arguments, then all the evidence. Take a sample of decision makers (fellow students would be ideal). Split them into two equal groups and offer each group the four plans, two linearly structured and two pyramid structured. Switch the ordering between the two groups. Have each subject rate the four business plans in terms of their attractiveness as investment opportunities. This could be by ranking, or on a Likert scale (e.g. would definitely invest, may invest, probably would not invest, would definitely not invest, etc.). Compare the ratings across the two different structures. Does pyramid structuring make the plan more attractive?

Information acquisition from business plans

This is a variation on the theme of the project above and might be included with it. Using the described method, create four business plans with linear and pyramid structures. Set up a comprehension test for subjects who have read the plans. This might include questions about the venture's products, its target markets, how it will gain competitive advantage, the capabilities of the management team, etc. Centre these on the supporting questions and arguments within them. I suggest about 10 questions in total. A multi-choice format will make analysis easier. If Barbara Minto's reading of cognitive psychology is correct (and there is a lot of evidence to suggest it is), then individuals should achieve better comprehension from the pyramid structure than the linear. Let the subjects (again, fellow students would be ideal) read the plans (set a time period, say 15 minutes) and then take the plan away so the subject cannot refer back to it. Then present the comprehension test (again, set a time limit). Analysis should concentrate on the comprehension scores and how they correlate with plan structure. Is the prediction borne out?

Suggestions for further reading

Ackelsburg, R. (1985) 'Small businesses do plan and it pays off', *Long Range Planning*, Vol. 18, No. 5, pp. 61–7.

Allaire, Y. and Firsirotu, M. (1990) 'Strategic plans as contracts', *Long Range Planning*, Vol. 23, No. 1, pp. 102–15.

Ames, M.D. (1994) 'Rethinking the business plan paradigm: bridging the gap between plan and plan execution', *Journal of Small Business Strategy*, Vol.5, No. 1, pp. 69–76.

Bhide, A. (1994) 'How entrepreneurs craft strategy', *Harvard Business Review*, Mar–Apr, pp. 150–61.

Bracker, J.S., Keats, B.W. and Person, J.N. (1988) 'Planning and financial performance among small firms in a growth industry', *Strategic Management Journal*, Vol. 9, pp. 591–603.

Chakravarthy, B.S. and Lorange, P. (1991) 'Adapting strategic planning to the changing needs of a business', *Journal of Organisational Change Management*, Vol. 4, No. 2, pp. 6–18.

Cooper, A.C. (1981) 'Strategic management: new ventures and small business', *Long Range Planning*, Vol. 14, No. 5, pp. 39–45.

Grieve Smith, J. and Fleck, V. (1988) 'Strategies of new biotechnology firms', *Long Range Planning*, Vol. 21, No. 3, pp. 51–8.

Hamel, G. and Prahalad, C.K. (1993) 'Strategy as stretch and leverage', *Harvard Business Review*, Mar–Apr, pp. 75–84.

Harari, O. (1994) 'The hypnotic danger of competitive analysis', *Management Review*, Vol. 83, No. 8, pp. 36–8.

Higgins, J.M. (1996) 'Innovate or evaporate: creative techniques for strategists', *Long Range Planning*, Vol. 29, No. 3, pp. 370–80.

Hills, G.E. (1985) 'Market analysis and the business plan: venture capitalists' perceptions', *Journal of Small Business Management*, Vol. 23, pp. 38–46.

Hopkins, W.E. and Hopkins, S.A. (1994) 'Want to succeed? Get with the plan!', *Journal of Retail Banking*, Vol. XVI, No. 3, pp. 26–31.

Kim, W.C. and Mauborgne, R. (2000) 'Knowing a winning business idea when you see one', *Harvard Business Review*, Sept–Oct, pp. 129–38.

Knight, R.M. (1994) 'Criteria used by venture capitalists: a cross cultural analysis', *International Small Business Journal*, Vol. 13, No. 1, pp. 26–37.

Macmillan, I.C., Siegel, R. and Subba Narashima, P.N. (1985) 'Criteria used by venture capitalists to evaluate new venture proposals', *Journal of Business Venturing*, Vol. 1, pp. 119–28.

Macmillan, I.C., Zeeman, L. and Subba Narashima, P.N. (1987) 'Effectiveness of criteria used by venture capitalists in the venture screening process', *Journal of Business Venturing*, Vol. 2, pp. 123–38.

McKiernan, P. and Morris, C. (1994) 'Strategic planning and financial performance in UK SMEs: does formality matter?' *British Journal of Management*, Vol. 5, Special Issue, pp. S31–41.

Mason, C. and Harrison, R. (1996) 'Why "business angels" say no: a case study of opportunities rejected by an informal investor syndicate', *International Small Business Journal*, Vol. 14, No. 2, pp. 35–51.

Minto, B. (1996) *The Pyramid Principle*, London: FT Pitman.

Mintzberg, H. (1994) *The Rise and Fall of Strategic Planning*, London: Prentice Hall.

Perry, S.C. (2001) 'The relationship between written business plans and the failure of small business in the US', *Journal of Small Business Management*, Vol. 39, No. 3, pp. 201–8.

Schneider, T.W. (1998) 'Building a business plan: a good business plan will not ensure success, but the lack of one is a formula for failure', *Journal of Property Management*, Vol. 63, No. 6, pp. 1–2.

Schwenk, C.R. and Shrader, C.B. (1993) 'Effects of formal planning on financial performance in small firms: a meta-analysis', *Entrepreneurial Theory and Practice*, Vol. 17, No. 3, pp. 53–64.

Shuman, J.C., Shaw, J.J. and Sussman, G. (1985) 'Strategic planning in smaller rapid growth companies', *Long Range Planning*, Vol. 18, No. 6, pp. 48–53.

Thurston, P.H. (1983) 'Should smaller companies make formal plans?', *Harvard Business Review*, Sept–Oct, pp. 162–88.

Waalewijn, P. and Segaar, P. (1993) 'Strategic management: the key to profitability in small companies', *Long Range Planning*, Vol. 26, No. 2, pp. 24–30.

Wyckham, R.G. and Wedley, W.C. (1990) 'Factors related to venture feasibility analysis and business plan preparation', *Journal of Small Business Management*, Vol. 28, No. 4, pp. 48–59.

A strategy to meet the challenges of entrepreneurship

FT

12 August 2002

By **Donald Sull**

The Roaring Nineties were boom times for entrepreneurs. The venture capital flowed, the hype was loud and everyone wanted to get in on the act. Then came the hangover, and it was severe. In the aftermath, many people are asking themselves whether the boom was all smoke and mirrors without underlying economic substance. As investors, employees and customers rush back to the security of established enterprises, some even question whether entrepreneurship in general is a scam.

A little perspective is in order. The dotcom boom and bust is only the most recent example of a recurring cycle in economic history. Technical, regulatory or demographic changes periodically allow people to do things in new ways. Hundreds or thousands of entrepreneurs pursue related opportunities. Some succeed, creating tremendous value. Most fail and sink noiselessly into obscurity.

In the first decades of the 20th century, more than 400 entrepreneurs created new companies to manufacture car tyres. By 1920, the industry had produced 122 millionaires in a single city. Then came the shakeout. Within a decade, the five largest producers controlled 80 per cent of the market. This cycle has happened before and it will happen again.

The dotcom boom and bust did remind us, however, of one enduring truth about entrepreneurship – it is a risky business. Entrepreneurship consists of pursuing opportunities by trying something new. The more novel a venture is, the harder it is to predict how things will turn out. They can go very well or they can go very poorly.

In some cases, entrepreneurs can anticipate the risks: Will the technology work? Will the customers buy the product? Entrepreneurs must also contend with things they do not know they do not know. These unknowns – the questions the entrepreneur did not even think to ask – can prove deadly.

The most effective way to deal with risk is to acknowledge it exists, accept it as an unavoidable aspect of entrepreneurship and actively manage it. I use the term 'disciplined entrepreneurship' to describe six mechanisms to manage risk actively.

Screen opportunities. No opportunity is risk-free. However, entrepreneurs can often distinguish between manageable sources of uncertainty and deal-killers by vetting the opportunity before putting their time, money and credibility on the line. An entrepreneur's plan – whether it is an ill-formed notion or a 200-page business plan – resembles a scientist's working hypothesis.

The entrepreneur's hypothesis posits that, if they try something new, they will create value exceeding the cost of the resources they need. Like a scientist, the entrepreneur can identify and analyse underlying assumptions before conducting an expensive experiment in the real world.

Much of this screening takes place informally through discussions with friends and colleagues. There are, however, more structured ways to vet an opportunity. Entrepreneurs can ask themselves a series of simple questions to highlight flaws in their idea (see below).

Entrepreneurs can evaluate their assumptions against their experience, other people's opinions and common sense. Translating a written business plan into a spreadsheet model of pro forma financial projections forces an entrepreneur to make explicit assumptions about the variables that drive cashflow, such as sales growth and customer acquisition costs. Can both these assumptions be true at the same time?

Match money and opportunity. Money can not buy love but cash is the ultimate hedge against an uncertain future. Cash buys time and any other resources needed to respond to unforeseen changes. Remember, though, that all investors are not created equal. Friends and family, business angels, venture capitalists, incubators and corporate investors differ widely in what they bring to the table in addition to money. Investors can bring contacts, expertise in an industry, experience in building a start-up and credibility.

Potential investors also differ in their appetites for risk. Seasoned venture capitalists can live with 70 per cent of their portfolio companies sputtering along or even failing outright, as long as the other 30 per cent succeed. An entrepreneur's brother-in-law may look at failure very differently. Investors also differ in what they expect as a reward for bearing the risk. The venture capitalist looks for rapid growth and an enormous upside, while the brother-in-law may want nothing more than a reasonable return and something to talk about at the country club.

The costs of a mismatch between an opportunity and the investor can be disastrous. One start-up producing all-natural hair products, for example, could have been a nice regional business. Instead, the founders accepted money from a group of investors who wanted big returns and rapid growth. They expanded nationally to get big fast, taxed their limited resources and ultimately went out of business.

Entrepreneurs also need to consider their own preferences. How much control am I willing to give up? Would I rather get rich with my investors or remain king of my own domain? What level of risk can I live with? Could I personally guarantee a loan and still sleep at night? Stage experiments Entrepreneurs stage experiments whenever they try

something on a small scale or reduce a major source of uncertainty before committing resources. Investors often require entrepreneurs to stage experiments. Venture capitalists, for example, generally dole out funding in successively larger rounds of financing while reserving the option to pull the plug if the experiments reveal bad news. Most entrepreneurs run experiments intuitively. They hire employees as consultants before bringing them on full time or they develop crude prototypes before designing a full-blown product.

When entrepreneurs recognise that they are conducting experiments, they can actively design and run them to increase effectiveness. They can, for example, begin with inexpensive tests on important sources of uncertainty. Consider a large building project in which thousands of things can go wrong and right. Experienced developers begin by conducting an environmental assessment. These tests are relatively cheap and, if the land has environmental problems, there is no point in proceeding.

Targeted experiments work well when an entrepreneur understands how to obtain the missing information. But what about situations where an entrepreneur is ignorant of the risks? In these situations, an entrepreneur can run experiments that test the entire plan on a small scale. For example, they might choose to launch in a regional market before rolling out nationally or working with a representative customer to develop a prototype.

Before running experiments, entrepreneurs ask themselves a few questions: Has anyone run this experiment already? What did they learn? Can we run this experiment cheaper? Can we run it faster? Could we convince someone else, say, a customer or an alliance partner, to subsidise this experiment?

Write good contracts. Entrepreneurs enter into contracts all the time. Some are formal documents such as term sheets, employment agreements and leases. Others are informal deals with employees, investors or partners. These 'handshake' deals can be every bit as binding as formal documents, since courts will often enforce implicit contracts. Even if they would not, the cost of a damaged reputation may induce the entrepreneur to honour their word.

Contracts can be a powerful tool for managing risk. The process of negotiating a contract, particularly with experienced counsel, can alert an entrepreneur to things that could go wrong or that had never occurred to them. Even reading a simple document such as a commercial lease can be an eye-opening experience for someone who has never considered the things that can go wrong in renting space.

Before entering into a contract, an entrepreneur should ask a few basic questions. How many of these contracts have I written in the past? How many has the other party written? (If there is a big gap, you need help.) Do I understand everything in this contract? Can I separate the critical clauses from the peripheral ones? If I could change only three terms in this contract, what would they be? The devil is in the details but the trick is figuring out the details that matter.

Assemble a team. People often picture the entrepreneur as a solitary figure, toiling away in the obscurity of a garage. In fact, entrepreneurship is very much a team sport. The most effective entrepreneurs surround themselves with people who complement their strengths and offset their weaknesses. Like investors, team members can provide much more than their labour. Each early recruit is critical: they represent a large percentage of all staff and help define the culture of the venture in the future.

In assembling teams, entrepreneurs should consider all the people they can call on for help, not just those people who directly report to them. Entrepreneurs might visualise themselves as standing at the centre of a series of concentric circles, with their immediate team around them. The next circle consists of formal advisers, including the board of directors, lawyers, accountants and paid consultants. The outermost circle consists of other stakeholders, including investors, customers and suppliers, all of whom can help the entrepreneur manage risk. Before hiring someone, ask: What gaps do they fill in the team? Industry expertise? Start-up experience? Who do they know? Who knows them? Do they share our values?

Forge partnerships. To execute their plan, entrepreneurs must often form partnerships with other companies that control required resources, such as a brand, technology or access to distribution. Collaborating with established companies can be a matter of life or death for start-ups, yet many entrepreneurs struggle to forge and manage these relationships. At one extreme, they try to do everything in-house, spreading limited resources too thin. Or they rush willy-nilly into partnerships with any company that will say yes, without fully evaluating the value of the relationship in business terms.

Entrepreneurs can bring discipline to the partnering process. They should decide on those activities to do in-house and those to outsource. Drawing the value chain of all the activities and resources needed to pursue the opportunity can help focus on what the company should do, identify gaps in the chain and suggest criteria for evaluating partners to fill those gaps.

In structuring partnerships, entrepreneurs can choose from a spectrum of deal forms, from loose licensing agreements to enduring joint ventures. This raises important questions. What are we trying to accomplish? How do we get there? How will we structure the governance? What milestones will we set along the way? And, finally, how do we get out? What do we do if things go well? If things go poorly?

I call this approach to enterprise and risk 'disciplined entrepreneurship'. Of course, there is more to entrepreneurship than discipline. The creativity to invent things, the passion for a vision, the grit to make it happen. Discipline and entrepreneurship are not the same thing. But neither are they incompatible. This is important to bear in mind as we edge towards the next wave of enterprise.

Five questions to ask:

- What is the phrase that pays? The discipline of describing an opportunity in a short phrase forces the entrepreneur to strip away the peripheral aspects and distil an opportunity to its essence.

- Why is the opportunity still here? If it's such a great opportunity, why hasn't someone done it already? Maybe it's too early.

- What has changed to give rise to the opportunity? Entrepreneurs need to point to specific changes in the competitive, technical or regulatory environment to explain the origin of their opportunity. They need more than the simple desire to be an entrepreneur.

- What pain are you solving for the customer? Opportunities to solve a customer's pain are often more robust than those that address less pressing desires.

- How big is the market? It is often difficult to forecast the market for a new product or service with precision. However, back-of-the-envelope calculations can provide a rudimentary estimate of market size and provide a check on overblown ambitions.

Source: *Financial Times*, 12 August 2002, © Donald Sull.

The writer is an assistant professor of business administration at Harvard Business School.

Case 16.2

Risk-averse investors fix sights on bullet-proof business models

FT

16 October 2002

By **Nuala Moran**

Venture capital is supposed to be about risk, but in common with every other category of investor, the current state of the markets is making venture capitalists risk-averse.

This is not only reducing the level of investment in Europe's fledgling IT companies, it is also raising the bar in terms of how advanced start-ups must be to get funding.

According to PricewaterhouseCoopers' 2001 Money for Growth Survey, which questioned 1,400 venture capitalists across Europe, investment in European technology companies fell 35 per cent from €11.5bn in 2000 to €7.4bn in 2001. And the evidence to date is that investment has fallen further during 2002.

'The best advice to give an IT company searching for funding is to make every best effort to fund its first year of operations on its own,' says Patricia McLister of Enterprise Ireland, a government body specialising in advising Irish technology start-ups.

'An IT start-up will find it much easier to raise finance if they can show a working solution that is in the marketplace and generating revenue. No one can raise money off a business plan anymore,' she adds.

Michael Wand of The Carlyle Group, one of the largest private equity investment firms, agrees. 'The dotcom model, "Give me £20m and I will develop a company", no longer applies. Start-ups have to go back to the previous model, where there was a revenue stream from the start.

'I don't think there is less money out there, it's just that less is being invested because people are more cautious.'

As a result, entrepreneurs looking for funds can expect to be asked the following questions: Is the technology established? Is there a technology vision? Is there market 'mind share'? Is there some sort of a customer base?

'If all these things come together, investors will be interested,' says Mr Wand.

However, Carl Allen, a specialist in venture capital at Giga Information Group, the IT market analysts, says it is very difficult for start-ups to build revenues at the moment because IT budgets are down and large companies are not buying new technologies.

'Nothing me-too is going to raise money at the moment. But even if your technology bridges a gap, you need a bullet-proof business model, with partnerships and a defined route to market.'

The change in sentiment among venture capitalists has had huge implications for Brightstar, the incubator set up by British Telecommunications to spin out companies based on technology developed at its Adastral Park R&D laboratories near Ipswich in eastern England.

Harry Berry, Brightstar's chief executive, says: 'Our model was high-tech, taking patents and building a business plan; we then looked for A [first] round funding from the market to turn the R&D into a product.' In 2000, four projects graduated to the incubator, in 2001, ten.

'However the tap turned off completely last year, so anything embryonic couldn't get money. The VCs that are investing are regrouping and putting money into what they've already got.'

Mr Berry's solution was to set up what he calls an 'accelerator', and start executing the business plans of start-ups in the incubator himself, adding the management team and an external chief executive, and putting in the first round of cash.

'We'd got great technologies which were unique. Why suffer in a year when the market was down? Just because the market is down doesn't mean the technology isn't any good.'

However, he adds: 'In this market you have got to be realistic. To get a company off the ground there has got to be an addressable market now. I've got things that will be a raging success two years from now, but that's no good.'

The focus in 2002 has been on expanding the revenues of six companies in the accelerator, and now they have a combined turnover of £35m, with the two largest turning over £20m in total.

'The revenues are going great, and now we have got investors wanting to take a slice of these companies,' says Mr Berry. 'Valuations are still lousy, but if I get companies to break-even I don't need to sell them.'

In order to push the companies in the accelerator, Mr Berry had to stop investing in bringing concepts into the incubator, highlighting the difficulty at present of finding seed money to move from R&D to products. With private sector venture capitalists writing themselves out of this part of the company development cycle, it is falling to public sector bodies to provide seed funding.

Enterprise Ireland, for example, has stepped in to maintain the momentum of company formation during the downturn, making investments of up to €150,000 in start-ups. 'But we won't give 100 per cent even at this stage; we still expect companies to find matching funding,' says Ms McLister.

The agency backed 76 companies in this way in 2001. The number backed this year is similar, but the investments are smaller.

However, there are venture capitalists who argue their attitudes have not shifted and that the market has merely reverted to the *status quo ante*, before it was subverted by the dotcom boom.

'We have not changed our views as to what you need to do to create value in a business,' says Martin McNair of Advent Venture Partners. 'Clearly this is a time to proceed with caution, but nevertheless there are good deals out there.'

Advent is continuing to put money into new companies and has recently invested in start-ups including a telecoms software business, an electronics design automation company and an artificial intelligence specialist.

Mr McNair says it is a 'complete nonsense' for venture capitalists to be demanding a company has revenues, or even profits. 'Venture capital is supposed to be about risk. The longer standing VCs who have been around understand this, and the rules don't change. We are still investing in pre-revenue companies,' he says.

'But we do expect product development to be at the point were it is clear it will work, that the intellectual property is tied up, and that we are comfortable that people will want to buy it.'

Source: *Financial Times*, 16 October 2002.

Discussion points

1. What are the advantages to an entrepreneur who has fully evaluated competitors and their offerings in the business plan?

2. What is the best way for the entrepreneur to communicate the venture's risks in the business plan? (Consider the recipient's expectations and reactions and how these might be managed.)

Part 3

Initiating the new venture

Chapter 17

The strategic window: identifying and analysing the gap for the new business

Chapter overview

Entrepreneurs identify and exploit new opportunities. This chapter considers why there will always be gaps in a market that the entrepreneur can exploit, despite the presence of established businesses. The chapter goes on to develop a picture of opportunity as a strategic 'window' through which the new venture must pass.

17.1 Why existing businesses leave gaps in the market

Key learning outcome

An understanding of why an established business environment will always leave opportunities for the entrepreneur.

In principle, established businesses are in a strong position relative to entrepreneurial entrants. This is because they have gained experience in their markets through serving customers; they have experience in operating their businesses; they have established themselves in a secure network of relationships with customers and suppliers; they face lower risks and so their cost of capital is usually lower; they may enjoy lower costs by having developed experience curve economies; and they have an established output volume which gives them economy of scale cost advantage. Despite these advantages, entrepreneurs do compete effectively against established, even securely entrenched, players. They identify and exploit new opportunities despite the presence of experienced competitors. There is always, it seems, a better way of doing things. There are a variety of reasons why existing businesses leave gaps in the market that the innovative, entrepreneurial venture can exploit.

Established businesses fail to see new opportunities

Opportunities do not present themselves, they have to be actively sought out. A business organisation has not merely a way of *doing* things; it also has a way of *seeing* things. The way in which a business scans the business environment for new opportunities is linked to the systems and processes that make up that organisation. *Organisational inertia*, that is, resistance to change in response to changing circumstances, is a well-documented phenomenon. An established organisation can become complacent. It can look back on its early success and take its market for granted. Its opportunity-scanning systems can become rigid and bureaucratised or caught up in political infighting. It might adopt a particular perspective or 'dominant logic' which leads it to see the world in a certain way. That perspective may not change as the world changes. As a result it may be less attuned to identifying new opportunities in the market than a hungry new entrant. For example, IBM missed the opportunity for software operating systems that would enable Bill Gates's Microsoft to become one of the world's largest companies.

New opportunities are thought to be too small

The value of a new opportunity must be seen as relative to the size of the business which might pursue it. The chance to gain an extra £100,000 of business will mean far more to a business with a turnover of £1 million than to one with a turnover of £100 million. As a result 'small' opportunities may be ignored, or at least not pursued vigorously, by large, established players. The smaller new entrant will, however, find them attractive. They may prove to be just the foot in the door they need!

Technological inertia

Opportunities are pursued by innovation. An innovation is founded on some technological approach. However, a technology is simply a way of doing things. It is a means to address a need. An established organisation may regard its business as based on a particular technology rather than the serving of customer needs. It might prefer to rely on the technological approach 'it's good at'. However, new technological approaches to satisfying needs can develop rapidly. Such technological inertia leaves the field open for new entrants to make technological innovation the basis of their business.

For example, the last mechanical typewriter manufacturer closed recently. The typewriter industry had a great deal of expertise in designing, manufacturing and marketing machines which produced documents. The manufacturers were very good at their business. However, they defined themselves in terms of the mechanical technology used by typewriters. They did not think of themselves as providing customers with a document management service. As a result, they were easy prey for a whole generation of entrepreneurs who moved in with electronic word processing products, which provided a much better way to manage documents.

Cultural inertia

Along with its technology, an established business has its own 'way of doing things'. This way of doing things – its culture – influences the way in which it delivers value to its customers. The best way to deliver value to customers will change as the competitive climate evolves. If the business does not change its way of doing things to meet new challenges then it may not be in a position to exploit new opportunities. Newer entrants may take advantage of this by adopting a culture more appropriate to the altered climate.

Thus the Swedish entrepreneur Jan Carlzon turned Scandinavian Airline Systems (SAS) into a great aviation success story by changing its culture from one where the needs of aircraft and airports were managed to one where the needs of customers were given priority.

Internal politics

Managers in established organisations often engage in political infighting. This occurs when individuals and groups do not feel their interests and goals are aligned with each other or with the organisation as a whole. Organisations pursue new opportunities in order to achieve their objectives. Being focused on a new opportunity demands a commitment to objectives. If this is not present then, at best, there will be disagreement on the value that particular opportunities present. At worst, different factions will work against one other. As a result, opportunities will slip by. This will leave the more focused and less political new entrant free to exploit them.

Anti-trust actions by government

Governments are concerned to ensure that monopolies do not distort the workings of an economy. If a firm is felt to be gaining too much dominance in a market, then the government may be tempted to act against its growth. By definition, this action will work against the dominating players and so will favour the new entrant. An example of this is topical. At the time of writing, a number of entrepreneurs in the information technology sector are eagerly awaiting implementation of the US Supreme Court ruling that the giant Microsoft be split into two. The court's ruling is based on the belief that Microsoft's monolithic market power is restricting entrepreneurial entry into the sector and hindering the development of smaller players who are already present.

Government intervention to support the new entrant

In general, governments are acutely aware of the importance, both economic and political, of small and fast-growing new firms in an economy. They are responsible for providing economic efficiency, for bringing innovations to market and for creating new jobs. As a result governments are tempted to provide support for both the smaller business and the new entrant. This can take the form of tax incentives and more liberal employment laws or it can be more direct and involve cheap loans and credit. Support may also be offered for technical development, education and consulting. Again, this support tips the balance in favour of the new entrant.

Economic perspectives on entrepreneurial gaps

The points made above relate to how businesses function. They are *institutional* effects. In these terms, established businesses leave gaps largely because they lack adeptness in exploiting some opportunities, leaving a space into which entrepreneurs can move. The classical economic perspective suggests that such institutional effects represent a failure of economic efficiency and that the managers of established businesses are not acting fully rationally. If managers of established firms were more effective, then they could devise strategies that would keep out entrepreneurial upstarts.

However, a number of recent mathematical studies are challenging this conventional view. An analysis by Richard Arend (1999) suggests it may not always be the case that incumbents will exploit new opportunities, *even if they are aware of them*. In this study, Arend explores economic interactions in quite a subtle way. The study suggests that under some circumstances established businesses may still leave gaps for new entrepreneurial entrants (who will become competitors) even if they are aware of the entrepreneurial opportunity that is available and act rationally to exploit it. Arend's argument is developed using a game-theoretical perspective. Game theory is a branch of mathematics that is concerned with the way in which a set of agents will act to achieve the outcomes they desire given that the actions of one agent will affect the outcomes of all others (see Section 23.4). Individual agents must judge the actions (the *strategy*) they adopt, given the likely actions of other agents, knowing that other agents will modify their strategies in response to the actions they take. Game theory has proved to be very important to economics, particularly in describing competitive behaviour.

Reflecting the mathematical rigour of game theory, Arend's article is somewhat technical. However, the basic argument can be stated qualitatively. Classical economics suggests that competing firms have only one optimal strategy if they wish to maximise profits. This conclusion is based on two assumptions, though: first, that all competitors have equal access to the technology that is used to create and deliver the industry's products (a condition economists refer to as *exogenous*); second, that this technology is fixed and does not change over time (technology is *stable*). In general terms, we can regard 'technology' as being the chance to exploit a new opportunity.

If we make the (more realistic) assumptions that technology is changing in a way that promises to make firms more efficient (new opportunities are coming along) and that all firms have equal access to this technology then something interesting happens. Under these circumstances firms have not one but two optimal strategies. Even though the technology (opportunity) is offered to the firm by the 'outside' world (firms do not have any research and development costs) they still face a cost in integrating that technology into their operations (that is, investing in exploiting the opportunity). The first strategy a firm can adopt is to ignore the technological advance, not face the cost of integrating it, and so maintain short-term profitability. This is referred to as a *static efficiency strategy*. The second option is to integrate the technology. This increases short-term costs but it offers the promise (with some risks, of course) of increasing long-term profitability. This is referred to as the *dynamic efficiency strategy*. There is no (efficient) middle ground between these strategies. A firm must choose one or the other and both are equally valid attempts to maximise profits.

Using a game-theoretical argument, Arend demonstrates a remarkable result. Under such conditions incumbent players will, in certain circumstances, ignore technological advances and allow new entrants to take advantage of them, *even if the new entrant eventually displaces them*. In doing so they are still acting rationally. This is because, once locked together in a competitive battle, at no point can the incumbent increase its profitability by switching to the new technology. Further, no such move can increase the total profitability of the two firms. Hence, even if managers were willing to make the move, investors with an interest in both firms would not support it.

While this argument may sound arcane, Arend uses it to make predictions about entrepreneurial entry under different situations of competition and technological change. His empirical evidence bears out the model. The conclusion is that the institutional 'inefficiency' of established players in exploiting new opportunities might not be inefficiency at all. Leaving gaps for entrepreneurs may just be an inevitable (and for the wider world a welcome) feature of competitive life. In a similar vein, Ghemawat (2002) uses game-theoretical methods to explain why entrepreneurial new entrants were more inclined to be innovative than monopolistic incumbents in the telecommunications industry (p. 117) and the steel industry (p. 143) when it came to new product and new production process development, respectively. Another formal analysis suggests a reason why new entrants can, despite their weakness relative to powerful incumbents, not only survive, but win the competitive battle. Jack Hirshleifer (see 2001) considers a game-theoretical model of two competitors who can each dedicate their resources either to producing a particular good or service or to directly competing with rivals. Like all mathematical models of business interactions, this is based on simplifying assumptions, but these are not unrealistic if we consider an entrepreneur splitting his or her resources between, say, increasing production capacity or advertising against competitors. This discussion will consider the qualitative implications of the model, not its mathematical detail. Students interested in this detail should follow the reference. Intuitively, we might argue that the more resource-rich (more powerful) player would be in an advantageous position. However, the model suggests that, at least under certain conditions, the weaker (resource-poorer) player can win. Hirshleifer calls this the 'paradox of power'. The model considers the interaction of the two competitors and asks, if they act rationally, how will they split their resources between 'production' and 'competition'. Given some assumptions (which are not particularly unrealistic), and certain conditions (which are likely to occur in some competitive battles) the model finds that the weaker player can gain more from competing than the stronger player. In effect, the weaker player is in a position to 'tax' the stronger player through competition at a higher rate than the stronger can 'tax' the weaker, in which case, the weaker player will win. Hence the 'paradox'. Hirshleifer's model is largely theoretical. But it fits with the intuitive notion that entrepreneurs win against stronger competitors because they 'work' their resources harder and in a more agressive way. Hirshleifer's model is important in that it provides a counter to the notion of resources = power paradigm. It provides a rational explanation of why entrepreneurs, sometimes at least, can win. Being theoretical, it is crying out for empirical validation, a point considered in the research theme at the end of this chapter. A somewhat salutory reminder that the entry of an entrepreneur into a market does not imply that if they win, others lose is provided by Bhide (2000). There are scenarios where harmony, rather than strife may emerge.

A word of warning

The large, established business, despite its inherent advantages, leaves gaps into which the ambitious new entrant can move because they often undervalue new opportunities, are complacent about them and are unresponsive due to internal inertias. While exploiting this, entrepreneurs should never forget that this is a fate that can also await them as their businesses grow!

(17.2) The strategic window: a visual metaphor

> **Key learning outcome**
>
> An appreciation of how the metaphor of the 'strategic window' can be used to give form to the process of identifying and exploiting opportunity.

Metaphors are ever-present in our communication. They represent an attempt to illuminate an idea by drawing attention to something it is like. Understanding is created because we can draw parallels between the two ideas and see how the interconnectedness of themes in one idea might be reflected in the other. Metaphors may be *active*. We can use one deliberately to create effect. For example, we can say that an entrepreneur is like the 'captain of a ship' and the idea of the entrepreneur taking charge and leading a group who share an interest and taking them somewhere new is created. At other times they may be *dormant*. A dormant metaphor is one that is used frequently and we may not recognise it as a metaphor unless we think about it. As noted in Chapter 11, the word 'organisation' shares its roots with the words 'organism' and 'organic'. This dormant metaphor is reflected in much thinking about organisations. An *extinct* metaphor is one that we use so often that we may never recognise that it is a metaphor. Note the visual metaphor implied in the use of the words 'see', 'draw', 'parallel' and 'reflected' in the sentences above. An active metaphor that can be used to help us picture, and remember the details of, the process of identifying, evaluating and exploiting a new business opportunity is that of the *strategic window*.

The first stage in this metaphor is to picture a solid wall. This represents the competitive environment into which the entrepreneur seeks to enter. The wall is solid because of competition from established businesses. They are active in delivering products and services to customers in an effective way. The entrepreneur can do nothing new or better and so new value cannot be created. However, as we discussed in the previous section, established businesses leave gaps. There are areas where entrepreneurs *can* do something new and better. These gaps represent windows of opportunity through which the entrepreneur can move. It is through the window that the entrepreneur can see the 'whole new world' he or she wishes to create. The first task of the entrepreneur is to scan the business environment and find out where the gaps, the windows, are.

Having spotted a window the entrepreneur must measure it. The entrepreneur must be sure that the window – the opportunity – is big enough to justify the investment needed to open it. Opening the window represents the start-up stage of the venture. Moving thorough the window means developing the business and delivering new value to customers. The final stage is closing the window. The window must be closed because if it is not, competitors will be able to move through after the entrepreneur and exploit the opportunity themselves. Closing the window refers to building in competitive advantage, in short, ensuring that the venture's customers keep coming back, so that competitors are locked out.

This metaphor – opportunity as a window, exploiting that opportunity as moving through the window – is a powerful *aide-mémoire* for analysing, and planning, the process of opportunity identification and exploitation. We will now explore each stage in more detail.

Seeing the window: scanning for new opportunities

This involves scanning the solid wall presented by existing players to find the windows and spot the gaps in what they offer to the market. This process demands an active approach to identifying new opportunities and to innovating in response to them.

Locating the window: positioning the new venture

This involves developing an understanding of where the window is *located*. It demands an understanding both of the *positioning* of the new offering in the marketplace relative to existing products and services and of how the venture can position itself in the marketplace relative to existing players to take best advantage of the opportunity presented.

Measuring the window

This involves evaluating the opportunity and recognising the potential it offers to create new value. In short, it means finding out how much the opportunity might be worth. This demands getting to grips with the market for the innovation, measuring its size, understanding its dynamics and trends, evaluating the impact the innovation might make in it and ascertaining how much customers might be willing to spend on it. Measuring the window also demands that the entrepreneur develop an understanding of the risks the venture might face.

Opening the window: gaining commitment

Having identified, located and measured the window, the next stage is to *open* it. Opening the window means turning vision into reality, i.e. actually starting the new business. Critical to this stage is the need to get stakeholders to make a commitment to the venture, to attract investors and employees, to develop a new set of relationships and to establish the venture within its network. Once the window is opened, then the entrepreneur can move through it, metaphorically speaking, by actually starting up the business.

Closing the window: sustaining competitiveness

Once the window has been opened and the entrepreneur has passed through it then the window must be closed again. If it is not, then competitors will follow the entrepreneur through and exploit the opportunity as well. This will reduce the potential of the entrepreneur's business. Closing the window to stop competitors following through means creating a long-term *sustainable competitive advantage* for the business. This provides the basis on which the entrepreneur can build the security and stability of the business and use it to earn long-term rewards.

Each of these stages presents itself to the entrepreneur as a series of *decisions*. Developing the business means addressing those decisions. The following five chapters will explore these decisions in detail.

Summary of key ideas

- A business environment is full of opportunities because existing businesses always leave gaps. There is always the potential to create new value. This may be because of both institutional failings on the part of incumbents and game-theoretical interactions between competitors.

- The *strategic window* is a visual metaphor which allows entrepreneurs to make sense of the opportunities they pursue.

- The six stages of the strategic window are: *spotting, locating, measuring, opening, moving through* and *closing*.

Research theme

Note: Chapter 17 introduces the idea of the strategic window metaphor in general terms and Chapters 18 through to 22 expand on its different stages. Research ideas specific to each stage are given at the end of each chapter, but the interested student may like to consider the integration of projects from different stages into a wider project dealing with the metaphor in its broader context.

Entrepreneurs' narratives of opportunity identification

Entrepreneurs usually love to tell stories, not least about how they got the inspiration for the venture they started. The strategic window metaphor offers a means of structuring such narratives. Select a pool of entrepreneurs (practising entrepreneurs at the novice or later stage should be prioritised). Using an interview, invite them to freely discuss how they identified a new opportunity, innovated to take advantage of it, evaluated the potential for the new innovation, initiated and developed the venture and built in sustainable advantage. This open-ended discussion should be allowed before the entrepreneur is prompted to discuss particular aspects in more detail. How does this narrative fit with the strategic window metaphor? Does the metaphor account for the different stages described for the venture? Is the order of the narrative in line with that of the metaphor? The interview may conclude with the entrepreneur being introduced to the metaphor and being asked if it makes sense of their experience and allows them to describe it better.

Suggestions for further reading

Abel, D.F. (1978) 'Strategic windows', *Journal of Marketing*, July, pp. 21–6.

Arend, R.J. (1999) 'Emergence of entrepreneurs following exogenous technological change', *Strategic Management Journal*, Vol. 20, pp. 31–47.

Bettis, R.A. and Prahalad, C.K. (1995) 'The dominant logic: retrospective and extension', *Strategic Management Journal*, Vol. 16, pp. 5–14.

Bhide, A. (2000) 'David and Goliath, reconsidered', *Harvard Business Review*, Vol. 78, No. 5, pp. 26–7.

Cyert, R.M., Kumar, P. and Williams, J.R. (1993) 'Information, market imperfections and strategy', *Strategic Management Journal*, Vol. 14, pp. 47–58.

Ghemawat, P. (2002) *Games Businesses Play: Cases and Models*, Cambridge, MA: MIT Press.

Hannan, M.T. and Freeman, J. (1984) 'Structural inertia and organisational change', *American Sociological Review*, Vol. 49, pp. 149–64.

Hirshleifer, J. (2001) 'The paradox of power', in *The Dark Side of the Force: Economic Foundations of Conflict Theory*, Cambridge: Cambridge University Press.

Kim, W.C. and Mauborgne, R. (2000) 'Knowing a winning business idea when you see one', *Harvard Business Review*, September–October, pp. 129–38.

Prahalad, C.K. and Bettis, R.A. (1986) 'The dominant logic: a new linkage between diversity and performance', *Strategic Management Journal*, Vol. 7, pp. 485–501.

Yao, D.A. (1988) 'Beyond the reach of the invisible hand: impediments to economic activity, market failures and profitability', *Strategic Management Journal*, Vol. 9, pp. 59–70.

If your cup overfloweth, create a new one

FT

17 June 2002

By **Jonathon Guthrie**

I have been thinking a lot about ladies' underwear recently, though purely in the line of duty. I met a lingerie entrepreneur last week who illustrates how to create a profitable niche business in a market dominated by huge companies, partly by exploiting their natural limitations.

The tale has relevance to all entrepreneurs as a reminder of their classic role: creating wealth by spotting opportunities so obvious no one else had noticed them. The trick, says Professor Martin Binks of Nottingham University Business School, is to think 'market, market, market', before getting hung up on 'product, product, product'.

The original preoccupation of Sarah Tremellen, founder of Bravissimo, a retailer of lingerie and swimwear for large-breasted women, was finding a bra to fit her when pregnancy took her up to a G cup.

In her search she discovered the lingerie departments of big retailers had two weak points: their products and their service. They offered a wide range of bras in cup sizes A to C. Above that, choice was limited and styles were disappointing: imagine garments that could have been stitched from stout canvas in 1940s Rochdale to protect Bomber Command air crews from shrapnel.

The service was equally poor. Bras, like shoes, are uncomfortable unless they fit. Mrs Tremellen was not impressed with the measuring skills she encountered, or the attitudes of the waif-like shop assistants.

'It's not fair when people are treated as freaks and made to feel uncomfortable,' Mrs Tremellen says. 'Logic told me there were lots of other women who needed a specialist retail chain but at the same time I wondered why no one had set one up, because it seemed so obvious.'

Overcoming her doubts, she launched Bravissimo eight years ago. She started modestly with mail order. This year the company is on course to make operating profits of more than £1m on turnover of about £15m. The company employs 140 people at four shops, its warehouse and its head office. Sidelines include low-cut leisure wear with in-built bras tougher for observers to spot than chemical warheads in Iraq.

I think Bravissimo has a good chance of fulfilling Mrs Tremellen's ambition of operating 15 destination stores across the country. Big retailers have increased their supply of larger-sized bras, possibly in response to specialist competition. But it is tough for them to squash upstarts such as Bravissimo, because they are fixated on keeping stock levels low to maximise their return on capital. In contrast, each Bravissimo store stocks 2,000 items and its warehouse promises next-day delivery of 5,000 products. The stores are also unusually highly staffed. Extra service means customers are happy to pay £20 to £30 per bra, compared with £10 to £15 at a mainstream retailer.

Crucially, Bravissimo has created a brand with positive associations for a customer base of more than 500,000 people. This should help protect it from rival specialists.

This ticks an important box for Prof Binks. 'The problem for innovators,' he observes, 'is that unless they have a strong brand or well-patented products, their profit stream will eventually disappear in the vortex of competition.'

Bravissimo's niche brand-building is similar to that practised by Saga, another admirable private business. Saga, which provides products and services, including holidays, insurance and media, to the over-50s, also boasts qualities hard for big competitors to copy. Operating profits have risen an average of 20 per cent a year over five years. The last reported figure was £38.8m on sales of £344m.

Sidney de Haan, a hotelier, set up Saga as a specialist tour operator in the 1950s to help him fill empty rooms in the off season. In 1984, Saga launched its magazine as a tool for selling holidays. By the late 1980s, Saga was using the publication to experiment with financial services, in which the group has since built a healthy business. The company, now run by Roger, Sidney de Haan's son, recently diversified into radio. It operates two regional analogue stations, playing the tunes of smooth crooners to a Hobnob-dunking mass market.

By catering to older people, Saga has created a kind of horizontal niche stretching across several sectors. According to Tim Bull, strategy director, Saga competes in insurance with giants such as Direct Line and Royal Sun Alliance, in travel with Thomson and Kuoni and in radio with any large media group you care to name. However, big rivals are unlikely to challenge Saga as a provider of multiple products and services to 50-plus purchasers. The accepted wisdom is that cross-sectoral diversification destroys focus.

There is, of course, a flip side to success stories such as Bravissimo and Saga. This is the struggle that niche businesses face to maintain margins when they lack strong brands or patented technology. A curry tycoon I know provides an example. A while back, oven-ready Asian meals made by big food groups resembled the curries produced by my old school's canteen. These consisted of left-over meat, with a dash of chilli and a few sultanas to suggest the lost splendours of the Mughal court. My contact knew he could do better and built a thriving business selling unbranded ready meals through big store chains.

Since then, competitors have multiplied and ruthless supermarket buyers have driven down prices and profits. A lucrative niche, our masala magnate has discovered, can prove scarily ephemeral. Find a way to own it and thereby preserve it – as Bravissimo and Saga are seeking to do. Or be prepared to get out quick.

Source: Financial Times, 17 June 2002.

Case 17.2

Venture capital firm's new fund will focus on the social sector

FT

19 November 2002

By **Florian Gimbel**

Catalyst, the London venture capital firm, is teaming up with The Big Issue, publisher of a magazine that aids the homeless, to launch the UK's first socially oriented venture capital fund.

Rodney Schwartz, Catalyst's founder and chief executive, said the firm was hoping to raise £50m ($79m) from institutions to invest in private companies in the education, healthcare and renewable energy sectors.

He insisted that the new venture, The Social Sector Fund, would not be a charity in disguise. 'We are seeking to demonstrate to investors that financial returns – at least matching comparable VC funds – can be realised through investing in the social sector,' he said. 'Social benefits will be created by default.'

The Big Issue, which is to receive an unspecified share of the fund's profits, approached Catalyst a year ago with the idea of a new fund, offering its expertise in spotting entrepreneurial talent in the social sector. In the US, a similar publication, Street News, is sold by the homeless.

Jon Norton, who helped to initiate the project on behalf of The Big Issue, said potential investors could take heart from the success of the magazine, which had sought to achieve a social end through business efficiency.

'The point is that people can get themselves out of homelessness by working for The Big Issue as distributors,' he said. 'All our profits are ploughed back into services for the home-

less. But if we didn't do that, we would be on a par with other successful publishers.'

Mr Schwarz said the new fund was exclusively focused on profit-oriented companies with professional management. This would help it to avoid clashes between investors and a company's idealistic entrepreneur, who may balk at the idea of a trade sale or initial public offering.

'The social sector poses challenges in this regard as there may not be the same hunger for wealth as elsewhere,' said Mr Schwartz. 'Catalyst aims to address this primarily through careful screening of management.' He said the new fund was also meant to encourage other private equity houses to invest in the sector.

Source: Financial Times, 19 November 2002.

Discussion points

1 Evaluate the gaps left in the market, and why, by major players for the niche player Bravissimo. Could these gaps be exploited further to secure the growth of the venture?

2 Is Catalyst working out of a sense of pure altruism or does it see a real market gap in the social sector? Does it really matter?

Chapter 18

Seeing the window: scanning for opportunity

Chapter overview

The first stage in using the strategic window is identifying it. This chapter looks at how new opportunities may be spotted, screened and selected.

18.1 Types of opportunities available

Key learning outcome

An understanding of the types of opportunity that present themselves to the entrepreneur.

An opportunity is the chance to do something in a way which is both different from and better than the way it is done at the moment. It offers the possibility of delivering new value to the customer. In its details, every opportunity is different, but there are some common patterns in the way in which opportunities take shape.

The new product

The new product offers the customer a physical device which provides a new means to satisfy a need or to solve a problem. A new product may be based on existing technology or it might exploit new technological possibilities. It might also represent a chance to add value to an existing product by using an appropriate branding strategy.

The new service

The new service offers the customer an act, or a series of acts, which satisfy a particular need or solve a particular problem. Many new offerings have both 'product' and 'service' dimensions. Robert Worcester, for example, built the enormously successful market research business, MORI, founded not so much on the basis that business and politicians wanted a *product* (market information) as on the recognition that they wanted a *service* that would help them make decisions.

New means of production

A new means of producing an existing product is not an opportunity in itself. It will offer an opportunity if it can be used to deliver *additional* value to the customer. This means the product must be produced at lower cost or in a way which allows greater flexibility in the way it is delivered to the customer. For example, Takami Takahashi, the founder of the diversified Japanese multinational Minebea, grew the business from being a small niche player in the ball-bearing market by exploiting its experience in small component manufacturing to offer low-cost products to the electronics, engineering and precision instruments markets.

New distribution route

A new way of getting the product to the customer means that the customer finds it easier, more convenient, or less time consuming to obtain the product or service. This may involve the venture developing an innovative way of getting the product to the end user or a new way of working with intermediaries.

Improved service

This is an opportunity to enhance the value of a product to the customer by offering an additional service element with it. This service often involves maintaining the product in some way but it can also be based on supporting the customer in using the product or offering them training in its use. Frederick Smith's inspiration for the US parcel service Federal Express was a recognition of the gap in the market for a business that would be dedicated to providing a high-quality parcel delivery service. This gap was left by existing suppliers, chiefly passenger airlines, which offered a parcel service as a side-line to use up excess weight capacity on aircraft but did not consider it to be an important part of their business, and so did not consider the service element to be important to their customers.

Relationship building

Relationships are built on trust, and trust adds value by reducing the cost needed to monitor contracts. Trust can provide a source of competitive advantage. It can be used to build networks which competitors find it hard to enter. A new opportunity presents itself if relationships which will be mutually beneficial to the entrepreneur and the customer can be built. Rowland 'Tiny' Rowland's ability to develop close and trusting relationships with African leaders was an important factor in the success of the Lonhro empire. The Saatchi brothers did not merely provide an advertising service, they also concentrated on building relationships with their clients.

Opportunities do not have to be 'pure'. It is often the case that a particular opportunity comprises a mixture of the above elements. A new product may demand an additional support service if customers are to find it attractive. Getting the product to them may demand that relationships are formed. The entrepreneur must take an open mind and a creative approach to the way in which opportunities may be exploited.

18.2) Methods of spotting opportunities

> **Key learning outcome**
>
> An appreciation of the methods which might be used to identify new opportunities.

It is often assumed that entrepreneurs are graced with some special kind of insight that enables them to see opportunities and the way in which they might be exploited. While creativity is certainly important, the view that entrepreneurs work purely by inspiration undervalues the extent to which they are rewarded for the hard work involved in actively seeking out and evaluating new opportunities. There are a variety of techniques that can be of help in this search. Some are rather rough and ready while others are more formal. Some are so straightforward the entrepreneur may not even realise that he or she is using them. They may be articulated in the form of a heuristic or rule of thumb. Others are complex and may demand the support of market research experts if they are to be used properly. It is useful to be aware of the ways in which a market may be scanned for new opportunities, and of the techniques available to assist in this process.

Heuristics

Entrepreneurial heuristics have been considered earlier in Section 15.6. Heuristics are an integral part of creativity. The heuristics entrepreneurs call upon to generate business ideas can be seen to involve two types. The first are *analysis* heuristics. These are the cognitive strategies entrepreneurs adopt in order to gain and integrate new information about the world, to understand the patterns in this information and to spot market gaps. The second are *synthesis* heuristics. Synthesis involves using a cognitive strategy to bring the ideas developed from analysis back together again in a new and creative way, generating a new perspective on customer needs and how they might be addressed. Analysis is about spotting opportunities; synthesis is about creating innovations that might exploit those opportunities. These two sets of heuristics lie at the centre of a process with information as an input and new business opportunities as an output (Figure 18.1). This process is *iterative*. Each cycle refines the insight into the opportunity and makes it clearer. This process may be made explicit but more often it is simply the

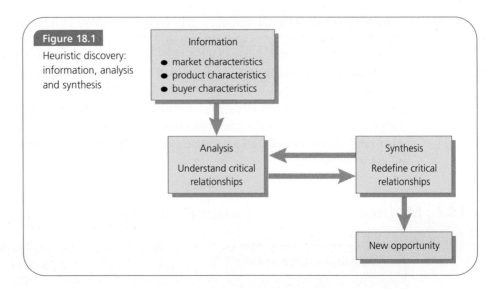

Figure 18.1

Heuristic discovery: information, analysis and synthesis

way in which the entrepreneur has learnt (perhaps even *actively* taught him- or herself) to develop a decision when faced with opportunities and challenges.

Problem analysis

This approach starts by identifying the needs individuals or organisations have and the problems that they face. These needs and problems may be either explicit or implicit. They may or may not be recognised by the subject. The approach begins by asking the question 'what could be better?'. Having identified a problem, the next question is 'how might this be solved?'. An effective, rewarding solution represents the basis of a new opportunity for the entrepreneur. This approach demands a full understanding of customer needs and the technology that might be used to satisfy them.

Customer proposals

A new opportunity may be identified by a customer on the basis of a recognition of their own needs. The customer then offers the opportunity to the entrepreneur. Customer proposals take a variety of forms. At their simplest they are informal suggestions of the 'Wouldn't it be great if . . .' type. Alternatively, they can take the form of a very detailed and formal brief, for example, if the customer is an organisation and a large expenditure is involved. Some organisations are active in 'reverse marketing' their needs to potential suppliers. Whatever the means used, an effective entrepreneur is *always* keen to solicit ideas from customers.

Creative groups

An entrepreneur does not have to rely on his or her own creativity. The best entrepreneurs are active in facilitating and harnessing the creativity of other people too.

A creative group consists of a small number of potential customers or product experts who are encouraged to think about their needs in a particular market area and to consider how those needs might be better served. The customers may be the ultimate consumers of the product or service or they may be industrial buyers.

Creative groups need control and leadership and their comments to be properly analysed if they are to be really informative. Getting people together in the right environment may also present a logistical challenge. Many market research companies offer specialist services in setting up, running and interpreting such creative group sessions.

Market mapping

Market mapping is a formal technique which involves identifying the dimensions defining a product category. These dimensions are based on the features of the product category. The features will differ depending on the type of product, but indicators like price, quality and performance are quite common. The characteristics of *buyers* may also be used to provide a more detailed mapping. A map is created of the market by using the feature–buyer dimensions as *co-ordinates*. Products separate out into distinct groups depending on their location on the map. The map defines the *positioning* of the product. The map may be used to identify gaps in the market and to specify the type of product that might be used to fill them.

A variety of statistical techniques are available for sorting out the information and presenting it in a two-dimensional form. Often, though, just an imaginative sketch will do. The map then provides a powerful visual representation of what is in the market, how different offerings are related to each other and, critically, the gaps that are present in it.

Features stretching

Innovation involves offering something new. This means looking for ways in which changes might be made. Features stretching involves identifying the principal features which define a particular product or service and then seeing what happens if they are changed in some way. The trick is to test each feature with a range of suitable adjectives such as 'bigger', 'stronger', 'faster', 'more often', 'more fun' and so on and see what results from such testing.

Anita Roddick's Body Shop provides a good example. Her initial inspiration was to provide good quality toiletries in packs much *smaller* than those offered by other high street retailers. (Environmentalism came later!)

Product blending

As with features stretching, this technique involves identifying the features which define particular products. Instead of just changing individual features, however, new products are created by blending together features from different products or services. This technique is often used in conjunction with features stretching. Both features stretching and features blending make good team exercises and can prove to be quite good fun. A good example here is Alan Sugar's success with the Amstrad stack hi-fi system which combined the features of CD player, tuner and amplifier in a single unit.

The combined approach

Effective entrepreneurs do not rely on inspiration alone. They actively encourage creativity by thinking methodically about the market areas in which they have expertise. They also encourage other people such as employees, independent technical experts and customers to be creative on their behalf. The techniques listed are not exclusive of each other. They may be used together. Using them in a new way offers the potential to identify new and unexploited opportunities. For example, Richard Branson, the chief executive of the highly diverse Virgin Group, is renowned for his ability to bring out the creative talents in those around him.

18.3 Screening and selecting opportunities

> **Key learning outcome**
>
> An understanding of the decisions to be taken in selecting opportunities.

Not all opportunities are equally valuable. A business with limited resources cannot pursue every opportunity with which it is faced. It must select those opportunities which are going to be the most rewarding. The key decisions in screening and selecting opportunities relate to the size of the opportunity, the investment necessary to exploit it, the rewards that will be gained and the risks likely to be encountered. Specifically, the entrepreneur's decision should be based on the answers to the following questions.

How large is the opportunity?

● How large is the market into which the innovation is to be placed? (What products will it compete with? What is the total value of their sales?)

● What share of the market is likely to be gained? (How competitive will it be against existing products? What percentage of customers can be reached? What fraction will convert to the innovation?)

● What gross margin (revenue minus costs) is likely? (What price can be obtained? What is the unit cost likely to be?)

● Over what period can the opportunity be exploited? (How long will customers be interested? How long before competitors move in?)

What investment will be necessary if it is to be exploited properly?

- What are the immediate capital requirements? (What investments in people, operating assets and communication will be required to start the business?)

- What will be the long-term and ongoing capital requirements? (What future investments will be necessary to continue exploiting the opportunity?)

- Does the business have access to the capital required?

- If the opportunity is as large as expected will the business have sufficient capacity?

- If not, can it be expanded or be (profitably) offset to other organisations?

- What human resources will be needed? Are they available?

What is the likely return?

- What profits will be generated? (What will be the rates? What will costs be like?)

- Over what period?

- Is this attractive given the investment necessary? (How does return on investment compare to other investment options? What is the opportunity cost?)

What are the risks?

- How sound are the assumptions about the size of the opportunity? (How accurate were the data on markets? Have *all* competitor products been considered?)

- What if customers do not find the offering as attractive as expected?

- What if competitors are more responsive than expected? (Have all competitors been considered? How could they react in principle? How might they react in practice?)

- To what extent is success dependent on the support and goodwill of intermediaries and other third parties? (How will this goodwill be gained and maintained?)

- How sensitive will the exploitation be to the marketing strategy (particularly in relation to pricing, selling points against competitors, customers targeted) that has been adopted?

- Can adjustments be made to the strategy in the light of experience? How expensive will this be?

- Can additional resources be made available if necessary? (Will these be from internal sources or from investors?)

- What will be the effect on cash-flow if revenues are lower than expected?

- What will be the effect on cash-flow if costs are higher than expected?

- How should investors be prepared for these eventualities?

- How should future revenues be discounted?

- Under what circumstances might investors wish to make an exit? (Will this be planned or in response to a crisis?)

- If so, how will they do it? (By being paid from profit stream or by selling their holding?)

Opportunities only have meaning in relation to each other. The entrepreneur must select opportunities not in absolute terms but after comparing them with each other. A business (like an investor) will find an opportunity attractive only if it represents the *best* option in which they have to invest for the future. Opportunities must be prioritised. They must compete with each other for the business's valuable resources. What matters is not so much cost but *opportunity* cost, that is, not the cost of actually using resources, but the potential returns lost because they were not used elsewhere.

18.4 Entrepreneurial innovation

> **Key learning outcome**
>
> An appreciation of market, technological and capability knowledge as the basis for entrepreneurial innovation.

Innovation lies at the heart of the entrepreneurial process and is a means to the exploitation of opportunity. Economically, innovation is the combining of resources in a new and original way. Entrepreneurially, it is the discovery of a new and better way of doing things. Innovation goes beyond invention. The new way does not stand on its own merits. It will only create new value if it offers customers an improved way to approach tasks and to solve problems. Innovation is not something that happens at some point in time. It is a process. This process of innovation can be described in terms of Figure 18.2.

The first stage is the identification of a new opportunity, a gap in the market competitors are leaving unfilled in their way of doing things. This opportunity must be evaluated. This evaluation consists of both a *qualitative* aspect (Who are the potential customers? What needs do they have? Why are existing products not meeting these?) and a *quantitative* aspect (How much would exploiting the opportunity be worth? What level of investment is appropriate?). The next stage is designing an innovation that will fulfil customer needs. This may involve invention, the creation of a new product or service, but it goes beyond this. Innovation also includes an understanding of how a new product can be delivered to customers and how it might be promoted to them. The final stage is the actual delivery of the

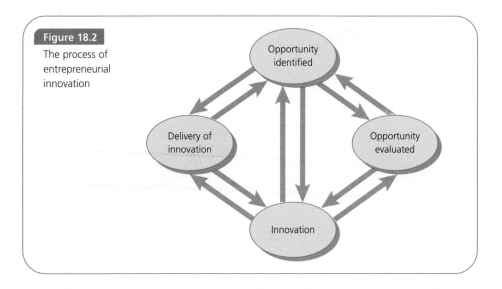

Figure 18.2

The process of entrepreneurial innovation

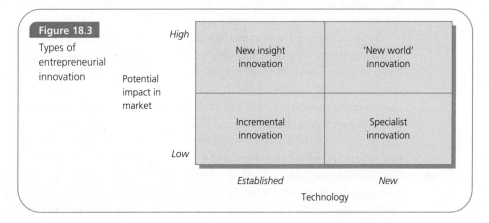

Figure 18.3

Types of entrepreneurial innovation

innovation to customers. Each stage is iterative. Understanding of the opportunity develops as potential innovations are considered. Means of delivery and promotion will be explored as the innovation takes shape. The opportunity and the innovation may be reconsidered in terms of promotional and distribution constraints.

Of course, innovation has many degrees. Any new way of doing things is an innovation. The magnitude may be of any order. One way of understanding the type of innovation an entrepreneurial venture is exploiting is to consider the technological base of the innovation, whether it is established or new, and the venture's ambitions in terms of market impact. Figure 18.3 illustrates the four quadrants these alternatives define.

Incremental innovation is concerned with minor improvements to an existing technology with limited market ambitions. If market ambitions are higher, but still based on modifications to existing technology, and competition will be dependent on a new way of using the technology, then the innovation can be described as *new insight innovation*. If the innovation is based on a new technology, but with

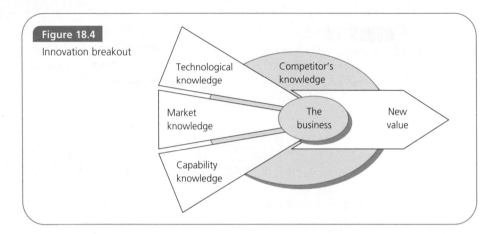

Figure 18.4

Innovation breakout

limited market ambitions, and competition will be based on an appeal to a narrow group of customers, then the innovation can be described as *specialist innovation*. An innovation founded on a new technology with high market impact ambitions can be called a *'new world' innovation*.

Innovation is a knowledge-based process. A new way of doing things must be based on a new way of seeing things. Successful innovation is founded on knowledge in three areas. *Market knowledge* is concerned with customers, their needs, demands, likely demand growth and what competitors are supplying. *Technological knowledge* relates to the effective development and production of the product or service aimed at the customers. These two areas of knowledge must be brought together with a third knowledge area. This is *capability knowledge*, the venture's understanding of what it does and why it does it well. This includes knowledge of the informational, cost, flexibility and human advantages the venture can call upon to compete effectively. If these three knowledge areas are brought together in a new, inventive and valuable way to drive the innovation process then the venture has the potential to break out of the trap that the industry's 'what we do and how we do it' thinking sets and so create new value (Figure 18.4).

Innovation is not, of course, something that is unique to the entrepreneurial venture. All businesses, no matter how mature, must be active innovators if they hope to maintain their position in the market. There are differences between the way entrepreneurs manage innovation and the way it is progressed in the large, mature firm. Entrepreneurial innovation is driven by vision, the desire to create a new world. Corporate innovation tends to be strategy driven. Though managerial vision may be important, the main driver is the recognition by the business that it must move forward if it is not to be left behind. Entrepreneurial innovation is, as far as the venture is concerned, radical. Its success or otherwise will have a major impact on performance. Corporate innovation is more likely to be marginal. Success will add to the business's performance rather than be fundamental to it. Entrepreneurial innovation usually involves the whole business. The venture's structure and processes will be defined around the need for innovation. A large business is more likely to compartmentalise the management of innovation within a particular function or teams. These different approaches are not hard and fast alternatives. They are ends of a spectrum. Entrepreneurs are particularly good at managing the innovation process. This is one of the main reasons why intrapreneurship (entrepreneurship within an established business) is of such interest. This is an issue to be considered in Section 28.3.

Summary of key ideas

- The first stage in the strategic window is *spotting* it.

- Spotting the window means identifying a new opportunity in terms of the possibility of creating new value.

- There are a variety of methods, both formal and informal, by which entrepreneurs can spot new opportunities.

- Entrepreneurs are constantly attuned to new opportunities.

Research theme

The process of opportunity spotting

One of the great mysteries of entrepreneurship is the creative process that leads entrepreneurs to discover new opportunities. This is the subject of much research, especially in the cognitive field. Necessarily, much of this research is based on a technical understanding of cognitive science and the student with this background may wish to follow through some of the references in Section 3.3. However, there are opportunities for research in this area that do not demand a high level of theoretical sophistication. Much remains to be done in simply describing and categorising the processes through which entrepreneurs spot new opportunities. Select a sample of entrepreneurs. These may come from a variety of sectors and stages in the venture's life. Use a survey technique to ascertain issues such as:

1. Was the entrepreneur opportunity or motivation led? (i.e. Did he or she spot a business idea that inspired him or her to become an entrepreneur, or did he or she decide to become an entrepreneur and was then active in identifying a business opportunity to pursue?)

2. To what extent was the opportunity a 'flash of inspiration' or did the entrepreneur positively work at a problem to gain a 'eureka' insight?

3. If the latter, how much effort was put into this process? Was working on the problem separated from the insight by a period of cognitive incubation?

④ To what extent was the entrepreneur already experienced in the product/ technology/business sector of the innovation? Was the innovation from a sector outside the entrepreneur's current experience?

⑤ Was organisational incubation important? (Examine the role of both formal incubators such as business schools and informal incubators such as incumbent employers.)

⑥ What other support did friends, family, external experts and support agencies provide?

⑦ What other support would the entrepreneur have liked?

In evaluating the results of the survey, attempt to develop a general model of opportunity identification, taking into account the possible variations in the factors discussed. The more entrepreneurs investigated, the more valuable this study will be. It may be best to focus on a limited number of sectors at first to build up a coherent initial model before moving on to apply it to a wider range of sectors. It is likely that the opportunity spotting process will be sensitive to sector particulars (e.g. high-tech ventures will be different to retailers).

Suggestions for further reading

Assael, H. and Roscoe Jr, M. (1976) 'Approaches to market segmentation analysis', *Journal of Marketing*, Oct, pp. 67–76.

Hague, P. (1985) 'The significance of market size', *Industrial Marketing Digest*, Vol. 10, No. 2, pp. 139–46.

Haley, R.I. (1968) 'Benefit segmentation: a decision-orientated research tool', *Journal of Marketing*, July, pp. 30–5.

Johnson, R.M. (1971) 'Market segmentation: a strategic management tool', *Journal of Marketing Research*, Feb, pp. 13–18.

Mattson, B.E. (1985) 'Spotting a market gap for a new product', *Long Range Planning*, Vol. 18, No. 1, pp. 87–93.

Selected case material **Case 18.1**

Be prepared for when opportunity knocks – Thur 15

FT

7 August 2002

By **Daniel Muzyka**

Opportunity has taken a front seat in management thinking. The reasons are simple: opportunities no longer last as long or function as predictably. In a world of accelerated technological development, world trade and globalisation, companies need to search for opportunities if they are to renew their product or service lines. Not surprisingly, competition often arises from the least likely quarters and may involve whole new approaches to customer needs.

Several things have been learned about opportunities recently; most interestingly, that they are often more complicated and subtle than first imagined. Furthermore, they are not necessarily embodied in products but in other aspects related to producing the product or service (such as skills required, knowledge and access to customers).

Opportunities don't always present themselves clearly or in an orderly way: sometimes they appear when salespeople meet customers, or when suppliers discuss their product lines with operations managers. In addition, many 'large' opportunities are the result of seemingly small products, services or initial prototypes. One should be careful in judging any opportunity as 'unworthy' or 'too small' if it is associated with other values such as introducing into the organisation skills, broader networks or personnel. Finally, it is often necessary to develop an opportunity with a network of individuals and organisations. Opportunities that one can simply pick up and execute single-handed are few and far between.

Even large, successful multinational corporations must adopt new approaches to identifying and seizing much larger numbers of opportunities to adapt and grow. Companies need not only to provide for new technological and product development, but must also mobilise and reward staff in the identification and pursuit of new opportunity. This is a characteristic that has long distinguished adaptive companies such as 3M.

Managers need to increase their opportunity 'bandwidth' and rely on both investment in new product development by organisational units and the 'random' development of opportunity by individuals and teams throughout the organisation.

If organisations are to witness more opportunity, they must equip a broader group of people to search for, identify and be willing to capture chances. For people to pursue opportunity, there needs to be a shared sense of what it is; in effect, they must possess models of opportunity. Creating such a shared sense is not necessarily something organisations see as a priority.

Some perspectives

The identification, selection and pursuit of opportunity are natural human activities. The first lesson is that there is no 'pool' of available opportunity. There is no 'law of conservation of opportunity'. The identification and pursuit of opportunity is a conscious activity that requires effort. Some opportunities, though technically achievable, are not captured for years.

Dr Daniel F. Muzyka is dean of the Faculty of Commerce and Business Administration at the University of British Columbia (Vancouver) where he is also a professor of management.

Another lesson is that opportunity is not the same for everyone. Louis Pasteur was quoted as saying: 'Chance favours the prepared mind.' Opportunity is much the same. One rarely identifies a good opportunity in an unfamiliar field, both in an individual and a corporate sense. Some companies have looked at the degree to which products and services have been profitable if both the technology and the customers are new.

Results tend to show that the ability to exploit existing knowledge of either the customer or the technology gives a better perspective on opportunities. Asymmetric knowledge and skills, combined with differences in networks, often account for differences in the perception and quality of execution in capturing opportunity.

Related to this last point are two additional lessons in opportunity:

● being first mover is not always most important;

● not every market comes down to 'winner takes all'.

First-mover advantage has been much discussed, particularly when combined with the notion that the first and fastest will take the whole market. Some technologies appear to be natural (near) monopolies because they provide common platforms (such as Microsoft's operating system), but they are not necessarily the first product introduced. Sometimes it is better to be a 'fast follower', building on knowledge provided by the first mover, and a number two in the market that exploits superior knowledge or capabilities.

At a recent lecture at a business school, I sat through presentation after presentation where newly minted MBAs preached that their business concept would succeed given that they invented the concept first. While listening, I was reflecting that most of the early inventors of spreadsheet languages have disappeared. I further reflected that some of the early providers of PCs don't exist any longer or are suffering.

Opportunities either arise from or create real customer need. Understanding customers is essential for successful development of entrepreneurial opportunities. The ability to excite customers about a product or service is a fundamental part of this development. It is not the ability to sift through reports from experts who suggest that 'all you need is 2 per cent' of this 'fast-growing market' that results in the perception of real opportunities. Understanding customer need and how you can create and fill that need is crucial to triggering customer purchase and loyalty.

Understanding customer needs at a fundamental level has distinguished many successful service businesses as they compete with established enterprises. Some examples in the airline business include Virgin Atlantic and Southwest Airlines. They are successful because they understood the unmet customer need first and customer requirements second. They were then were able to combine this with a fundamental understanding of the economics of the business.

There are two observations about opportunity that are not always popular. First, opportunity does not last forever. Customer needs and technological opportunities move on. The mark of successful, long-run growth enterprises is that they are constantly searching for ways to build on existing opportunities as well as working to develop new ones.

The second observation is that many profitable, successful opportunities are both simple and boring. It goes with a phrase heard regularly from contented long-run entrepreneurs: boring is beautiful! Boring businesses attract less attention from analysts and are often last to receive the attention of those attempting to introduce technological improvements. One person became very successful as a producer of hamburger buns in the UK in the 1980s. Even though baking was well established, the segment had not been exploited. This may be very successful but not necessarily terribly exciting as a 'new age' business.

Three initial tests

Though it is hard to generalise, managers should test their favoured opportunity against three conditions: balance, profit and risk.

First, the company should demonstrate a 'balanced desire' to pursue opportunity. Successful opportunities should have a number of characteristics. Opportunity is pursued by individuals and teams who are more likely to be successful at things they feel are useful and interesting, even if this is not rational. Ask people proposing an idea whether they feel it is worth their time and effort. Managers should also assess other factors:

- the value to customers of a new product or service;

- an organisation's ability to produce and deliver a product;

- access to resources (primarily financial) to capture an opportunity.

Selecting the opportunities that are balanced in these respects is important. Venture capitalists, for instance, value the ability to implement an opportunity above all. They will take a B-grade economic opportunity implemented by an A-grade team over an A-grade opportunity implemented by a B-grade team. The presence of the necessary skills and attitudes ranks high on their list. Venture capitalists will assess the leadership potential and track record of the entrepreneur and the management team, as well as their functional capabilities. Larger organisations do the same thing when pursuing opportunities internally.

Second, the presence of a reasonable business and profit model is important. Do you understand where and how you make money? Is profit (not just revenue) realised in reasonable time? It is the discipline of understanding and arguing the business model that is captured in writing a business plan. Many successful business models are profitable due to several factors.

For example, one successful entrepreneurial business developed a chain of stores in small shopping centres outside towns. The stores generated good revenue (though not extraordinary). However, the development of the land just outside town created significant returns as additional stores were built.

Third, have you undertaken a reasonable risk analysis? The meaning of 'reasonable' is important here, because detailed risk analysis is not likely to be effective or efficient: things change too quickly. If you wait for all data to be available, the opportunity is gone. Having said this, it is still reasonable to assume that a full understanding of the 'differential' risks in an opportunity have been thought through.

Differential risks are not generic, that is, not in the category of the 'economy declining' or 'industry weakness'. Often, the key measures of financial risk in ventures are expressed in 'time to break-even' and 'time to payback'. The longer one waits, no matter what the nominal internal rate of return, the higher the risk exposure.

Evaluation

After weighing up the opportunity in these terms, assessment should turn to three dimensions: the scale, the scope and the span of the opportunity. Scale refers to the potential size of the opportunity. Scope refers to its value, both in the short run (for example, gross margins or value added) and in the long run (for example, access to more opportunities in the future). Span refers to how long it is likely to last.

One might think of the value of the opportunity as expressed by the combined value of the three items. An opportunity may have a great deal of potential if it isn't very large in scale, but has high margins that last a long time. Also, if the scale is very large and the value added extensive, the opportunity may be good even if it does not last as long.

The following questions give some indication of the scale presented by an opportunity:

- Is the potential customer group easily identifiable and large?
- Is value to the customer high?
- Are competitive offerings not meeting customers' needs?
- Is the overall industry in growth or being redefined?

Scope may be measured by gross margin and whether the opportunity creates capabilities and follow-on opportunities. The span may be assessed by a variety of measures, including the strength and vindictiveness of competitors; the ability to create post-entry barriers; and the inherent length/position of the technologies in their life cycle.

All of these may determine how long the opportunity may last. For instance, an opportunity that involves the construction of significant barriers (post-entry barriers) or areas of cost, which must be confronted by subsequent entrants, is one that will stand longer. Also, opportunities that exist in a broader market where potential competition is not very aggressive tend to last longer or have a longer span.

Few opportunities are extraordinary on all three measures. A new toy may have extraordinary scale and scope (high margins). It may, however, only last one season. A pollution control service may have extraordinarily high scope (when the problem occurs, someone may pay virtually anything for immediate service), but there may be limited potential (only so many pollution incidents in a given period). The opportunity may, however, last for quite a while.

Finally, many an opportunity has been lost to an organisation because it was not expressed in a context that could be appreciated by others. Given the biases and irrationality that are often present in human relationships,

it remains for the proposer to be aware of the perspectives and needs of potential stakeholders. Be careful to present the idea in a way that is intelligible to the receiving party and that, in its presentation, you are able to express your understanding of their needs and sensitivities with regard to opportunity. Importantly, opportunities are often better accepted if one acknowledges their weaknesses up front.

Warnings to e-business

It is a fallacy to suggest that somehow digital business should not be governed by economics, business strategy and investment finance. While e-business has helped us redefine certain limits in business practice (such as speed and market leverage), it has not obviated the need for a return on investment, the need to manage cash flow and working capital, and the strategic need to create competitive advantage.

Economics@Real.World

As noted earlier, e-business opportunities are not exempt from needing to make a profit. There has unfortunately been a strong focus on revenue models without much consideration of how a profit would be achieved. Entrepreneurs should be concerned about profit.

Giving it away

Many e-businesses, especially those in retail, suffer from a low-price entry strategy. Their plans are predicated on prices that, it is argued, will prove irresistible to consumers. However, entrepreneurs should be careful not to give away their products. This has become particularly evident during the crash of various online retailers. When they were 'forced' to become profitable, they were required to raise their prices. When they did raise their prices, customers disappeared. It is clear there was little value to customers beyond price in several of these cases.

Penetrating new markets

E-business management teams often fail to appreciate that every consumer in a marketplace will not necessarily switch over to the internet for their needs immediately. Winning customer confidence takes time and changing consumption patterns can take even longer. There has been significant 'cash burn' on some e-businesses that have tried to enter markets.

Growth

How many sites are you proposing? What will be the upper limit on web usage in various consumer groups? How many sites will people visit regularly? Is there a danger of further dividing the market by creating yet more speciality websites?

Adding value

Many e-businesses assume that value is added for the consumer simply by e-delivery. The fact that consumers of a similar kind are flocking to another website and that people are becoming increasingly focused on the internet does not necessarily imply that a given consumer looks for given needs on the internet. Be clear about how much value is added beyond that from 'information' or 'access'.

Leveraging everyone else

Look carefully at where money is being generated. Many business opportunities ride on the same underlying revenue model: advertising. In a world where advertising on the web is becoming ubiquitous and advertisers are increasingly concerned about efficacy, how far can one justify another e-commerce business on the strength of other people's value added?

Common errors

There are several common mistakes that limit the success and ultimate potential of opportunities.

Fads

Don't jump into the pool just because everyone else has. Fads are wonderful distractions that are not meant for everyone. Even experienced venture capitalists have fallen victim in large numbers. When everyone gets excited about a particular opportunity, it becomes difficult to justify why you have not complied with the trend and given in by investing in a particular area. In fact, there may be less risk in investing rather than not investing. By not investing, you may be criticised for 'missing the boat', even though the boat might have sunk.

Adaptation

Most successful entrepreneurs will admit that what they end up producing and selling is generally very different from their original concept. It is through the process of development, testing and early introduction that one realises the 'true' opportunity. Always be willing to adapt. This is one reason why inventors (that is, people who produce inventions rather than opportunities) are often not successful entrepreneurs. Simply stated, they are not willing to adapt their original inventions to meet real or evolving customer need.

Miscalculating competition

Another common flaw is not to fully appreciate the nature and degree of competition. While a product or service may be 'first in category', it is often substituting for an old application or service or it competes for time with other consumer activities. Be careful to recognise full competition or other substitutes.

Low price entry

Finally, be clear about the value you are providing and do not fall victim to a low price entry strategy. Offering customers low prices may seem to make sense, but it often sends the wrong signal about the value of a product or service, wakes up competition and can put the business at risk from low cash flow. Furthermore, customers feel resentful when prices are raised right after they adopt a product or service. This is a trap into which many inexperienced entrepreneurs have fallen.

Conclusion

The pursuit of opportunity is fundamental to business. Whether a business will survive in the long run has significantly less to do with the resources it controls and significantly more to do with the opportunity it can create or access.

Realising opportunity requires heightened awareness of the need for opportunity among all people in an organisation and their understanding of what sorts of opportunity make sense. Employees need to develop reasonable models of what constitutes opportunity in their industry. This demands experimentation and education. It also requires shared learning about what does not constitute an opportunity, in other words, what the traps are in identifying opportunity.

Source: *Financial Times*, 7 August 2002, © Daniel Muzyka.

Case 18.2

Scotland poor on entrepreneurship

31 January 2002

By **Harriet Arnold** and **James Buxton**

The dire state of entrepreneurship in Scotland has been emphasised by the latest report from the Global Entrepreneurship Monitor, carried out by the Hunter Centre for Entrepreneurship at Strathclyde university, writes James Buxton.

It gave Scotland a low score for entrepreneurial activity and put it in the bottom category of small developed nations, along with Denmark, Israel and Norway.

The analysis found Scotland's score on 'opportunity entrepreneurship' (businesses started to exploit unique market opportunities) was about half that of the other small states. The proportion of people in Scotland who personally knew an entrepreneur was half that of similar countries. Although Scotland scored well on access to formal sources of finance, the percentage of the population investing in someone else's new business was a quarter of the average.

The report comes as Scottish Enterprise, the development agency for Scotland, is to refocus its business start-up efforts on companies that have potential for high growth. A new high-growth business unit will call on the skills of private sector specialists such as venture capitalists and intellectual property lawyers.

Source: *Financial Times*, 31 January 2002.

Discussion points

1 Do opportunities 'exist in the world', independently of entrepreneurs, or are they something inherent and personal to individual entrepreneurs?

2 Is a region's low level of enterprise a consequence of a lack of entrepreneurial individuals or a lack of entrepreneurial opportunities?

Chapter 19

Locating the window: positioning the new venture

Chapter overview

The second stage in using the strategic window is to locate it. This means relating the opportunity to the business activity of established firms and understanding it as a gap in what they offer to the market. The idea of positioning provides a powerful conceptual framework for doing this.

19.1 The idea of positioning

Key learning outcome

An appreciation of how the concept of positioning may be used as a guide to entrepreneurial decision making.

The idea of positioning provides a very powerful tool to aid entrepreneurial decision making. Positioning provides a framework for *locating* the venture in relation to its competitors. Existing suppliers to a market do not serve its customers as completely as they might. They leave gaps in the market which a new venture can attempt to fill, so gaining a foothold in that market. Identifying the window of opportunity means spotting where these gaps are. A new venture is, at face value, in a weak position relative to established competitors. Even if the established players had not previously spotted the window of opportunity, a new start-up will signal its presence to them. Their greater resources, established network of relationships and lower costs may put them in a much stronger position to exploit the window.

Positioning the venture means locating it in relation to a market gap such that it can exploit that gap in a profitable way. This involves structuring the business so that it can serve the requirements of a particular market niche *better* than existing competitors. An effective positioning means that the business will be able to develop a *competitive advantage* in serving this niche. This makes the niche *defendable* against competitors. It also enables the new venture to move into the market in a way which avoids direct head-on competition with established players. Head-on competition is usually a difficult game for the new venture to play since the playing field is tipped in favour of the established player. At best, head-on competition will prove to be expensive, and at worst, it will result in failure for the new venture.

Positioning relates to a *location*, and location means occupying a *space*. Understanding positioning and using it as a decision-making tool demands an appreciation of the characterisation of the competitive space in which the venture operates. In general, a competitive space is characterised by the ways in which competitors seek to distinguish themselves from each other. Two distinct approaches to positioning provide different and complementary insights. *Strategic positioning* looks at the way in which the business's approach to delivering value to its customers is distinct from that of its competitors. Strategic positioning is concerned with the way in which the business *as a whole* distinguishes itself in a valuable way from competitor businesses. *Market positioning*, on the other hand, looks at the way in which the business's *offerings* to the market are differentiated from those of its competitors. Market positioning is concerned only with the business's products and services. Strategic positioning and market positioning can be used as decision-support tools for the entrepreneurial business.

19.2) Strategic positioning

> **Key learning outcome**
>
> An understanding of the decisions which define the venture's strategic positioning.

Identifying a strategic position is a fundamental element of the strategic planning process. A strategic position is the way the business as a whole is located relative to competitors in the playing field of the market, that is, the *competitive space*. Derek Abell (1980), in his book *Defining the Business*, suggests that this competitive space can be defined along four dimensions.

Stage in value addition

The goods that are bought by consumers, or which are used by those who provide services to them, are usually highly refined. Yet, ultimately, they are all made from raw materials obtained from the earth. However, there may be a lot of businesses that play a role in the process between the extraction of a raw material and the delivery of the final product.

Consider, for example, a home computer that has been purchased from a distributor. That distributor will have purchased the computer from a hardware manufacturer. The manufacturer will have bought a variety of components such as silicon chips, plastic parts and glass screens from component suppliers. Those

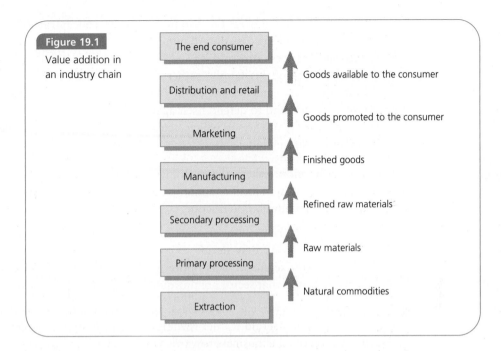

Figure 19.1

Value addition in
an industry chain

The end consumer

Goods available to the consumer

Distribution and retail

Goods promoted to the consumer

Marketing

Finished goods

Manufacturing

Refined raw materials

Secondary processing

Raw materials

Primary processing

Natural commodities

Extraction

component suppliers will have made them from refined raw materials obtained from suppliers of pure silicon, plastics and glass. These suppliers will have refined their products from raw commodities obtained from the businesses that collect sand and extract oil from the earth. This process whereby the outputs of one business provide the inputs for the next business along is called the *value addition chain* (Figure 19.1).

An entrepreneur must decide what stage, or stages, in the value addition process they expect their venture to occupy. This resolves itself into questions about the inputs and the outputs of the business. These questions are:

● Will the business make a particular input (which might be a physical product or a service) for itself or will it buy it in?

● Will the business sell on a particular output to another business for further processing or will it try to add that value itself?

The decisions made in response to these questions must be based on an appreciation of the competences of the business, its resources and its competitive advantage relative to both competitors and the businesses adjacent to it in the value addition chain.

Customer segments addressed

It is rare that a business can serve the needs of an *entire* market. The strengths of a particular business lie in the way it can appeal to certain groups of customers.

When Richard Branson started the Virgin Airline he concentrated on business passengers who wanted to cross the Atlantic. Alan Sugar, when founding his consumer electronics business Amstrad was explicit about the fact that he was targeting the 'lorry driver and his family' rather than the hi-fi aficionado. Selecting a well-defined customer segment enables the business to focus limited resources, to concentrate its efforts and to defend itself against competitors.

There are a variety of ways in which a customer segment can be defined. Some of the more important include:

- *Geographic location*: where the customer is. Many entrepreneurial ventures start out serving a small local community. As they grow they expand to achieve national and even international scope.

- *Industry*: the industrial sector of organisational buyers. In its early stages an entrepreneurial venture may decide to concentrate on selling its product to a particular industry segment. This option may be attractive because the needs and buying habits of that sector are thoroughly understood by the entrepreneur.

- *Demographics of buyer*: e.g. social class, age, personal attitudes or stage in life cycle. For example, Gerald Ratner revitalised the high street jewellery trade in the UK by targeting his business towards young, relatively low-income people.

- *Buying process*: the way the product is bought and the role of influencers and decision makers. Entrepreneurs may concentrate their efforts towards businesses which buy in a certain sort of way. For example, business service firms such as the market research company MORI are adept at negotiating the complex decision-making process that lies behind the buying and use of market research in large organisations.

- *Psychographics*: buyers' attitudes toward the product category. Richard Branson, for example, has moved his Virgin brand into personal financial services on the basis that it offers trust in an area where many buyers have suspicions about the existing products on offer.

Customer needs addressed

Consumers and businesses have many, and complex, needs and wants. No single business could hope to serve them all. An entrepreneur must decide exactly which of the customer's needs his or her venture will exist to serve. Success depends on gaining customer commitment, and the best way to do that is to genuinely serve the needs and to solve the problems they have.

Customers may be aware of their needs or they may not have articulated them to themselves yet these needs can be explicit or implicit. Different needs are not independent of each other, they often interact and must be prioritised. Satisfying one need may mean that others go unsatisfied. The entrepreneur must learn to understand the needs of their customers, to rationalise them and to distinguish them from each other. The entrepreneur must often articulate the needs of customers on their behalf.

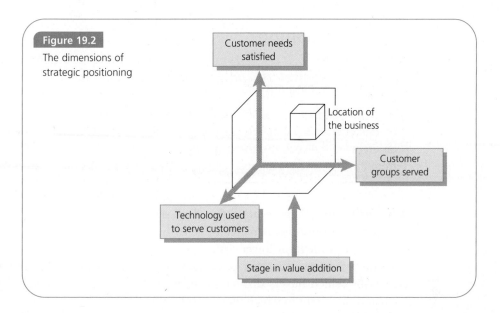

Figure 19.2

The dimensions of strategic positioning

Means of addressing needs

Satisfying a need represents an end and there are a number of means by which that end can be achieved. The need to communicate with someone, for example, can be served by a postage stamp, a telephone, the Internet or by going to visit them. Having decided which particular customer needs they will satisfy, the entrepreneur must decide the means, or *technology*, that they will adopt in order to do so. Alan Sugar recognised people's desire to be entertained by listening to music. He provided them with electronic equipment to replay recorded music. He might, conceivably, have served that desire by building concert halls or by providing a service whereby musicians would come and play to people in their homes. For whatever reasons, these were technological alternatives he avoided.

The industry-building entrepreneur is often the one who has recognised a whole new technological approach for addressing a basic need. Henry Ford recognised that a low-cost motor car was a better way of moving from one place to another than horse and cart. Bill Gates recognised that a computer with the right software could transform the way in which a variety of domestic and office information-processing tasks were performed. Innovation is not just about creating new technology. It is about understanding how a particular technology can be used to address a need in a new and fruitful way.

These four dimensions as shown in Figure 19.2 describe the strategic positioning of a venture or its location in competitive space (see also Day, 1984, p. 21). This is the niche where the new venture sits. It defines who its competitors are and the way in which they are competitors. Of course, merely occupying the niche is not enough. The business must structure itself and adopt operating processes and a culture which allow it to serve that niche effectively.

19.3) Market positioning

Key learning outcome

An understanding of how the idea of market positioning can be used to differentiate the venture's offerings from those of its competitors.

Strategic positioning describes the way the venture is located in a competitive space. *Market positioning* describes the way its outputs, products and services are located in the marketplace relative to those of competitors. Success will only be achieved if the new venture offers customers something which is *different* from and more *attractive* than that offered by existing players. This means it must offer them greater value by being more suited to their needs or the same level of benefits at lower cost.

The first stage in market positioning is to develop an understanding of the criteria by which buyers distinguish between the different products on offer to them and the extent to which they consider them to be substitutable. Some general factors in market positioning are:

- *price* – how the offering is priced relative to competitors;

- *perceived quality* – quality seen as high or low (what matters is perceived value for money, i.e. quality relative to price);

- *demographic imagery* – up-market versus down-market, young versus old; dynamic versus conservative;

- *performance* – high performance or more limited performance;

- *number and type of features* – e.g. advanced versus basic; complex versus simple; hi-tech versus low-tech;

- *branding imagery* – the associations that the branding elicits;

- *service and support* – additional assistance offered in understanding, using and maintaining the product;

- *attitude towards supplier* – positive or negative associations gained from ethical stance of supplier.

Different buyers will prioritise and weight these factors differently.

One way of thinking about positioning is to consider three aspects of the product or service being offered. A product can be positioned using one or more of the three ways in which its consumer relates to it – see Figure 19.3. At the centre is the *functional core*; that is, the features of the product or service which actually deliver its functional benefits. Surrounding this functional core are the aesthetic attractions of the product or service. These include design and branding elements which make the product or service attractive to use. At the outer level are the *emotional*

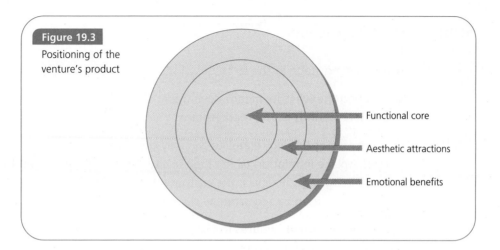

Figure 19.3

Positioning of the venture's product

Functional core

Aesthetic attractions

Emotional benefits

benefits. These are those aspects of the product or service which appeal directly to the consumer's emotional and spiritual needs rather than their purely functional ones. This may be achieved through branding which allows the consumer the chance to say something about themselves by being seen to consume the product. It may also be enshrined in the way the product is sourced, or the values adapted in its production.

The aim of positioning is to reduce the extent to which the customer feels that the product or service is *substitutable* by those of competitors. In effect, this means focusing the offering on the needs of the customer in a unique and effective way. The positioning need not be solely in its functional core. Differentiation can often be achieved very effectively by giving the product or service a unique aspect in its aesthetic attractions and emotional benefits. For example, a £3.99 digital watch may be as good as a Cartier watch for telling the time, but the owner of the Cartier would not think it a good swap! The buyer may see their purchase set into a wider social and moral context. The actual 'physical' products offered by The Body Shop are easily imitated by other high street retailers, but its customers still feel that The Body Shop offers them something more valuable because of its ethical stance. The eponymous chain of jewellers set up by Gerald Ratner revolutionised the UK jewellery retailing sector in the 1980s but did not pretend to be offering products of the highest quality. Nonetheless it was felt to be fun, accessible and unstuffy by its young customers. Charles and Maurice Saatchi of Saatchi and Saatchi reinvented advertising in the 1960s and 1970s by positioning themselves as partners in the management process rather than by just supplying advertisements for clients. The McDonald's chain of fast-food outlets as established by Ray Kroc are not just places to eat; they are an invitation to share the American Dream.

Positioning is a valuable entrepreneurial tool. It guides the entrepreneur in offering the customer something new and valuable and it avoids the need for head-on competition with established (and more powerful) players. Effective positioning is a critical success factor for the new venture.

Summary of key ideas

- The second stage in the strategic window is *locating* it.

- Locating the window means developing a *position* for the new venture and its offerings to the marketplace.

- *Strategic positioning* relates to the way the venture fits in the marketplace in relation to its stage in the value addition chain; the customer groups it serves; the customer needs it addresses; and the technology it adopts to serve its customers.

- *Market positioning* relates to the way the venture's offerings fit in the marketplace in relation to the offerings of competitors.

Research themes

Entrepreneurs' conceptualisation of market positioning

The concepts of strategic and market positioning discussed in this chapter are relatively technical and adopt a language that most entrepreneurs would not be familiar with. This is not to say that entrepreneurs do not have a sensitive and sophisticated intuitive idea of the positioning of their ventures. This may be explored by evoking entrepreneurs' cognitive maps of their competitive environment. An interview technique is best here. The key issues to be ascertained are as follows:

1. What products/services do entrepreneurs see as their competitors? A more detailed picture can be gained by having the entrepreneur detail competitor products as close, near or distant competitors (an 'onion ring' picture of the competitive environment).

2. On what basis are the entrepreneurs including competitors? Possibilities include the competitors being see by virtue of them:

   - being in the same industry (if so, check on how the entrepreneur perceives the industry sector);
   - sharing the same technology;
   - being available through the same distribution channel;
   - being made by the same production process;
   - being alternative purchases by customers.

These factors may be used in combination. Explore the entrepreneur's perceptions and identify the two that the entrepreneur believes dominate. Be careful not to lead the entrepreneur down a particular path; make sure it is the entrepreneur's perceptions that are being revealed.

3 The entrepreneur may then be introduced to the idea of market mapping. Set out a rectangular space with the two dimensions that are most important in the entrepreneur's classification strategy. Have him or her plot the location of his or her own product and those of competitors. Once the entrepreneur is satisfied that this represents his or her picture of the competitive environment, inquire into how the entrepreneur sees their products' competitive edge over the competitors identified. Does the entrepreneur agree that the map makes their ideas on positioning clear?

4 A more sophisticated approach might use more than two dimensions of competitor product discrimination and use a more formal mapping technique (this will take time to analyse and depict, so two interviews are likely to be necessary). A further sophistication would be to have the entrepreneurs connect their view of the performance of their venture's products causally to its (unique, valuable) positioning.

Entrepreneurial entry and innovative positioning

Innovation is intimately associated with entrepreneurship. Consequent from the view that entrepreneurs are innovators is the belief that entrepreneurs enter new markets in an unoccupied niche with a product that is different to those being offered by existing suppliers. But how true is this? The concept of market positioning offers a way of testing the proposition. Obtain details on a number of entrepreneurial start-ups with good, detailed information on the new product (service) the entrepreneur is offering and those already available. Create market maps of the product category using the descriptive criteria described above (additional criteria might be introduced). The more criteria introduced, the more incisive will be the findings. However, if more than two criteria are introduced, more sophisticated mapping techniques will be needed. How distinct is the entrepreneur's offering? Do entrepreneurs introduce into new niches? How does the degree of originality affect later performance. It might be hypothesised that the level of innovation is sector dependent. The study might look in detail at one particular sector or be a cross-sectional evaluation of a number of complementary sectors.

Introduction and expansion of strategic positioning

The model of strategic positioning developed above can be used to describe both the initial positioning of new entrepreneurial ventures and the selection of expansion strategies. Obtain descriptions of a number of entrepreneurial ventures with details on the stage in value addition, customer groups targeted, the particular needs of those customers and the technology adopted to serve those needs. Ideally these should cover both introduction and subsequent expansion. How focused are entrepreneurs in their entry? Do they seek unoccupied strategic positions or are they willing to compete in already occupied positions? What are the preferred modes of expansion (value addition, vertical integration, new needs with existing customers, new customers, new technologies)? Is a single mode of expansion preferred or are several tackled at once? Again, this could well be sector dependent so both detailed studies of a single sector and cross-sectional studies of several would be valuable.

Suggestions for further reading

Aaker, D.A. and Shansby, J.G. (1982) 'Positioning your product', *Business Horizons*, May–June, pp. 56–62.

Abell, D.F. (1980) *Defining the Business: The Starting Point of Strategic Planning*, Englewood Cliffs, NJ: Prentice Hall.

Datta, Y. (1996) 'Market segmentation: an integrated framework', *Long Range Planning*, Vol. 29, No. 6, pp. 797–811.

Day, G.S. (1984) *Strategic Market Planning*, St Paul's, MN: West Publishing, p. 21.

Day, G.S., Shocker, A.D. and Srivastava, R.K. (1978) 'Customer-orientated approaches to identifying product-markets', *Journal of Marketing*, Vol. 43, pp. 8–19.

Garda, R.A. (1981) 'Strategic segmentation: how to carve niches for growth in industrial markets', *Management Review*, August, reproduced in Weitz, B.A. and Weley, R. (eds) (1988) *Readings in Strategic Marketing: Analysis, Planning and Implementation*, New York: Dryden Press.

Selected case material Case 19.1

Fast track to the mass

25 July 2002

By **Jonathon Guthrie**

Does motorsport have a nurturing side? It is difficult to imagine when you see Formula One racer Rubens Barrichello pulling aside on Ferrari team orders to let star driver Michael Schumacher steal first place.

But this ruthless industry has nevertheless yielded Graham Mulholland, a 28-year-old entrepreneur, the opportunity to build a components business now making parts for high-performance road cars. The next step is to enter the volume automotive market.

Promoters of the motorsport industry believe there should be more cross-fertilisation of this kind, in which technology developed for low-volume, high-cost racing applications spills over into bigger, more price-sensitive markets.

Mr Mulholland, whose company EPM Technologies employs 30 people, spoke about taking motorsport technology to road car applications at a conference this month, promoted by the Department of Trade and Industry's Innovation Unit and opened by Sir Jackie Stewart.

EPM employs workers with skills in cutting fabric that are now largely redundant in its Coalville base in Leicestershire, once an important centre for textile manufacturing. Mr Mulholland says: 'We have a huge resource of textile skills here that is very under-utilised'.

At one of EPM's three small factories in Coalville, employees use shears to cut out the raw material for car parts from great bolts of plastic-impregnated glass fibre. These are glued to moulds and cooked while subjected to a vacuum to make the lightweight structures, such as body panels, that EPM specialises in.

Mr Mulholland used to do that job. He started in the garage of his father's home after becoming intrigued by composite technology as an aspirant Olympic canoeist. After a stint at a canoe making company in Derby, Mr Mulholland set up his own enterprise in 1997 targeting motorsport customers, beginning with just 'a telephone, a notebook and a motorsport directory'.

In his first year he made wheel arch liners and fuel tanks for Subaru and Nissan rally cars, generating turnover of £80,000. Other early clients were the Ford rally team and F1's Arrows.

Mr Mulholland recalls cross-country dashes to deliver parts, one of which was interrupted by the flashing blue lights of a patrol car. 'The policeman let me off because I was delivering Damon Hill's dashboard,' Mr Mulholland recalls.

EPM's turnover was £130,000 in 1998, £400,000 in 1999, £500,000 in 2000 and £1m last year. Mr Mulholland anticipates the figure will rise to more than £2m this year, with gross profits at about 40 per cent.

When EPM started, the percentage of sales generated by motorsport was about 80 per cent. 'This was what catapulted us forward into finding new partners,' says Mr Mulholland. Taking on more work for sports carmakers, such as Aston Martin and TVR, has reduced the percentage to about 50 per cent.

EPM's growth is partly the result of developing handling techniques that let it use composite material for new purposes. The fabric it buys from a subsidiary of Saint Gobain, the French glass maker, has a relatively coarse weave. But EPM can make it into smooth exterior parts, such as bumpers and front panels, as well as less cosmetically sensitive components.

The advantage of the material over the plastics that many carmakers favour for bumpers and wheel arches is that it is lighter and stronger, although it is more fiddly, and therefore more expensive, to process.

One problem is that its clever handling techniques cannot easily be patented. 'The only solution is to keep innovating,' Mr Mulholland says. 'Five years from now I think we should have turnover of between £8m and £15m if a couple of planned applications come off. We should also have the best composites business in Britain.' It is revealing that Mr Mulholland, who otherwise appears driven by his commercial ambitions, wants to be the *best* more than the *biggest* composites business.

EPM appears set to grow large enough to pose some interesting new problems for its young owner, both in delegating management duties and scaling up production.

Mr Mulholland sees the trend for much greater variation in vehicle specifications as playing to EPM's strengths. Production runs in the hundreds of thousands annually would be challenging but he expects in a few years to be turning out 'three to four thousand vehicle structures a week'.

Many motorsports specialists, despite exhortations from organisations such as regional development agencies to diversify, have preferred to restrict themselves to the clubbable, low-volume world of racing.

Competition on the track is cut-throat, but for a small business, the mass market can appear an even more frightening place.

EPM is planning to test whether that caution is really justified.

Source: Financial Times, 25 July 2002.

Case 19.2

Putting the prime into prime-time TV

FT

28 May 2002

By **James Lamont**

African public broadcasters traditionally dish up tired fare to their audiences. With little capacity to produce their own programmes or buy contemporary ones, they fill airtime with the cast-offs of European and US networks: martial arts films, talent contests or the test-panel.

In one of the more eccentric cases, Angolan viewers were subjected to the UK television adaptation of Evelyn Waugh's Brideshead Revisited dubbed into Portuguese. The drunken antics of English aristocrats could only have added more confusion to the frayed lives of Luanda's civil war-wearied residents.

Now a Ghanaian entrepreneur hopes to offer African viewers more inspiring viewing. George Twumasi, vice-chairman of the London-based African Broadcasting Network (ABN), is touting a package of largely US-sourced programming to Africa's broadcasters.

Using digital technology, ABN distributes two hours of peak-time programming a day to about 60m people across countries such as Rwanda, Namibia, Ghana, Kenya, Nigeria and Zambia.

The attraction for Africa's impoverished broadcasters is that the service comes for free. ABN merely requires a cut of any ad revenues its programming might attract.

Convincing public broadcasters to sign up is no mean feat, however, as they are resistant to private-sector intervention. But they face stiff competition for their urban, educated viewers who are migrating to subscription satellite services, such as South Africa's MultiChoice.

'Public broadcasters don't want to give away any autonomy to outsiders. It's a cycle of deprivation,' says David Keighley, the corporate affairs director of the Association of International Broadcasters.

Research on African viewing habits is scant. But what is sure is that the continent's audiences are highly aspirational. They want to break their own cycle of deprivation.

Source: Financial Times, 28 May 2002.

Discussion point

Consider the strategic and marketing positioning of:
(a) EPM Technologies in the global motor components sector;
(b) ABN in the global broadcasting sector.
What opportunities for expansion do these positionings offer?

Chapter 20

Measuring the window: analysing the opportunity

Chapter overview

The third stage in using the strategic window is to **measure** it, that is, to **quantify** the opportunity and develop an understanding of how much new value might be created. Obtaining information on the opportunity is seen to be an investment in the business, and must be considered as such. Key issues relating to the analysis of opportunity are considered. Methods of market analysis are considered in overview.

20.1 The need for information

Key learning outcome

An appreciation of the importance of managing and using market information effectively.

Relevant market information is extremely useful to the entrepreneur. Entrepreneurs are decision makers. They are different from other types of manager because they make the decision to *venture*. Venturing means stepping out into the unknown, and information provides a map of how to move forward into this unknown. Information eliminates uncertainty and so reduces *risk*. However, information on its own is not enough: if it is to be valuable, it must be analysed, understood and acted upon.

Information does not come for free, it has a cost. While the entrepreneur will know many things simply as a result of his or her experience within an industry, a lot of additional information may need to be gathered actively. Even if the information has no direct cost (for example, information gathered 'free' from a public library) valuable time is used in collecting it. Some information can have a high direct cost; for example, information obtained through formal market research surveys can appear very expensive to the entrepreneur just starting out. However, information represents an *investment* in the business. It is used to increase the performance of the business. The payoff for that investment needs to be appreciated before the information is gathered.

Information can guide action. However, lack of information should not be an excuse for *inaction*. While it may be sensible to hold back on a move until more information is available and that move can be made with more confidence, there are other times when the entrepreneur must rely on their instincts and 'go for it'. If they wait too long, someone else may make the move first. While information reduces risk, the entrepreneur cannot expect to eliminate *all* risk and sometimes they must make a step into the dark. The entrepreneur must walk a narrow path between making ill-informed and ill-judged decisions and an inertia caused by the venture becoming more interested in gathering and analysing information than in taking direct action. The founders of organisation systems thinking, F.E. Kast and J.E. Rosenzweig, called these two extremes 'extinction by instinct' and 'paralysis by analysis' (also see Langley, 1995).

Strategic management provides a wide variety of tools and conceptual frameworks to aid decision making. A variety of formal methods is available to guide resource allocation and make competitive moves. While the entrepreneur would be foolish to shun the insights that can be gained through such formal analysis of information they should not be solely dependent on it. Often it is the overall *pattern*, not the *detail*, that matters. They must learn to develop their intuition and make judgements based on holistic thinking and their own heuristic approach. The successful entrepreneur learns to see the wood before the trees.

(20.2) Analysing the market and identifying key issues

> **Key learning outcome**
>
> An appreciation of the importance of analysing and understanding market conditions.

If they are to be successful, entrepreneurs must understand the market in which they are operating. This understanding is important because success depends on their ability to serve that market in a way which is better than that of their competitors.

There are a number of issues about which the entrepreneur must be informed if they are to make effective decisions in relation to their venture. These issues fall into four broad categories. These relate to the existing market conditions and the opportunity they present, the way in which the entrepreneur might innovate and offer something of value to the market, the way in which the entrepreneur can get the venture started and the way in which competitors are likely to respond to the venture. Some specific information requirements are:

● *general market conditions* (customers' needs and requirements; the size of potential markets; market growth rate and trends in its development; the structure of customer groups and segments; and customer and consumer buying behaviour);

- *the attractiveness of the innovation* (customers' satisfactions and dissatisfactions with current offerings; customers' reaction to the entrepreneur's new offering; competitor pricing and customers' pricing expectations; and likely volume of demand);

- *the way the new venture can be initiated and positioned in the marketplace* (resource requirements for start-up; resource requirements for the later development of the venture; the structure of the network in which the venture will be located; sources of investment capital; customers and customer groups to be given priority; and means by which the customer might be informed about the new offering);

- *the way in which competitors might react to the new venture* (the nature, type, strengths and weaknesses of competitors; strategies adopted by competitors; and likely actions (strategic and tactical) by way of a response to the entrepreneur's start-up).

Information of this nature is available from a variety of sources. Some of it will be knowledge the entrepreneur already holds about his or her industry. Some may be obtained from existing published sources such as market reports and trade publications, and such sources are referred to as *secondary* sources. Alternatively, primary research involves a bespoke analysis of a market situation using market research techniques in answer to specific questions.

In many instances the entrepreneur may feel quite informed on these issues. In other instances it may be felt that information is lacking and greater certainty is needed. The entrepreneur must never be complacent. The rule must be always to challenge knowledge and assumptions. When deciding upon the degree of precision required for information, two questions must be asked. First, how sensitive will decision making be to the accuracy of the information used as the basis of those decisions? Second, with respect to this, is the cost of gaining the information worth the return it offers?

(20.3) Analysing the opportunity: qualitative methods

> **Key learning outcome**
>
> An appreciation of the methods by which the 'whys' of the opportunity may be understood.

There are two types of question that must be asked if a business opportunity is to be fully appreciated. Both may be answered by appropriate market research and analysis techniques. The first set of questions relate to the nature of the opportunity, its qualities and the approaches that might be taken to exploiting it. These are the 'who?', 'what?' and 'why?' questions. They are best answered using *qualitative* methods. The second set of questions relate to the value of the opportunity and the effort that should be put into exploiting it. These are the 'how much?' and 'how many?' questions. These are best answered using *quantitative* methods.

Qualitative methods might be used to answer questions of the following sort. Who are the customers? How are they defined as a group? How are they differentiated from non-customers? What needs do these customers have in relation to the product category (in terms of functional, social, emotional and developmental needs)? How do they articulate their needs (explicitly or implicitly)? How well do consumers find that current offerings satisfy those needs? In what ways are current offerings unsatisfactory? What are the customers' attitudes towards the product category in general (positive, negative or mixed)? Why do non-customers not use the product category? How might they be attracted to it? If the product is not available, how might other types of product be used as a substitute? How does this define a gap for an innovative offering? How do customers go about buying a product? How are they normally informed about the product category? What is their knowledge of the product category? Who influences their decision when making a purchase? Who influences the consumer when they use the product? How is such influence exercised? How do they greet innovations in the product category: positively or with suspicion?

Many entrepreneurs will feel confident in their ability to answer these questions based purely on their experience in a particular industry sector working with customers and a particular product category. However, if the area is new to them, or they feel the innovation they are offering changes the rules, or they just wish to challenge assumptions then obtaining answers directly from customers and potential users will be a valuable exercise. There are a variety of methods for doing this.

Actively listening to customers

Customers must, ultimately, be the source of all information on a market and the opportunities it presents. After all, it is they who buy the product and reward the entrepreneur. Even an informal conversation with a customer can provide a good deal of information about their concerns, what they find satisfactory, what less so, what might be better, and so on. If this information is picked up on, it can be of enormous value to the acute entrepreneur. Acquiring this information demands *active* listening.

Listening is a communication skill. It does not come naturally. When in conversation, we often use the other person's speaking time as a chance to consider our reply rather than actually listen to what they are saying. It is easy to be distracted, but active listening demands that the conversation be kept on track. The right sort of questions must be asked. The listener should lock onto key phrases and comments and these should be explored if further information might be yielded. Non-verbal communication (facial gestures, body language) should also be noted. What does the conversation reveal about the customer's way of thinking about the product category? Is decision making rational and logical or is it influenced by emotional factors?

Selling situations provide a good opportunity to listen to customers. In fact, it is as important to listen to what they say as it is to present the product to them. Objections to making a purchase should be received positively. After all, if a customer is saying why they will not purchase this time, they are giving a clue as to how they could be persuaded to do so next time.

In-depth interviews

The in-depth interview is really a structured conversation. The objective of the conversation is to gather information and the specific information required is defined in advance. A series of questions to be asked are set out before the interview and these questions are used to prompt the interviewee. The interviewer can introduce additional questions if a particular avenue is opened up and is considered to be worth further exploration.

In-depth interviews are a very effective and flexible way of getting to know the customer and their way of thinking. They are, however, time consuming (for both interviewer and interviewee) and so can prove to be expensive if a large number need to be performed.

Focus groups

A focus group is a gathering of a small group of customers (usually about five to eight) who are questioned about their attitudes and opinions on a particular product category. This reveals not only their thinking as individuals, but also the way they interact with each other when considering the product.

Focus groups can be very revealing and can give substance to vague feelings about gaps in markets. However, they are difficult to run. Controlling them and keeping the discussion on track can be difficult. Interpreting what has been said is also a professional task. Focus groups work best when the right sort of venue is used. Video or sound recording facilities are needed. It can also be difficult to bring even a small group of buyers (especially industrial buyers) together. Consequently focus groups are often most productive when run by trained market researchers.

Usage and awareness studies

A usage and awareness study is based on a written questionnaire which is mailed to users of the product category. The questionnaire aims to explore the users' attitudes and feelings towards the product category, their knowledge of what is on offer, and the way they use products in the category. They provide written answers to the questions or tick prefigured questions and then send their answers back. Such studies can be used to confirm ideas on the types of gap that exist in a market. Usage and awareness studies are an efficient and (relatively) low-cost way of gathering the view of a large number of customers. However, return rates can be low. Care must be taken in the way in which they are designed and interpreted, and appropriate statistical methods must be adopted.

Product trials

A very effective way of obtaining customers' opinions on a new product, and how they view it in relation to alternatives, is to let them use it in the way they would be expected to under normal circumstances and then question them about their experience. Product trials work well when the offering is very innovative, when the customer has limited experience of the category and needs exposure to the product before they can give an opinion on it. Product trials can be very informative. They can be used as part of the development process for a new product. They are particularly good at identifying what the customer finds attractive about the product and so can be used to refine the selling points of that product.

However, product trials do demand that the product is available to be tested. If the product is not in production then expensive working prototypes may be needed.

Many entrepreneurs also feel unsure about revealing their product too early, especially if competitors might imitate it quickly.

20.4 Analysing the opportunity: quantitative methods

> **Key learning outcome**
>
> An appreciation of the methods which can be used to quantify a market opportunity.

Qualitative methods can be used to give shape to the nature of a market opportunity and the ways in which it might be exploited. However, they say little about how much that opportunity is worth and the entrepreneur needs to know whether an opportunity is worth pursuing and, if so, what amount of investment is sensible. To support this type of decision quantitative methods are needed. The kinds of questions answered by quantitative methods include the following. How large is the market (its volume)? How much is it worth (its value)? How fast is it growing? How large are the key segments in the market?

Market value and volume can be resolved into three subsidiary issues. How many customers are there in the market? How often do they buy? How much do they buy when they do so? These three factors together define the overall demand in the market and may be illustrated as in Figure 20.1.

As well as accepting this pattern of demand the entrepreneur may be seeking a strategy that expands overall demand by increasing the number of users, purchase amount or purchase frequency. Such expansion is likely to reduce overall competitive pressures as business can be increased without affecting competitors' sales. Also, distributors will be attracted by such a strategy. In addition, quantitative methods can be called upon to answer questions such as the market shares of competitors supplying the market and the level of investment they make to maintain and develop that share. In broad terms, three approaches can be used to obtain this information.

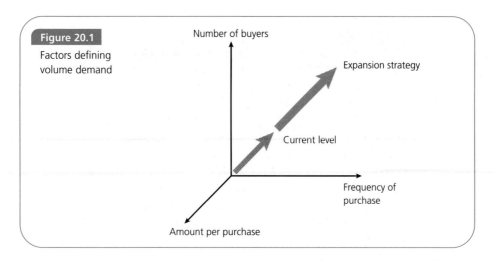

Figure 20.1
Factors defining
volume demand

User audits

User audits involve questioning of a representative sample of users to learn how much they purchase and how often they make purchases in a particular product category and whose products they buy. This may be achieved by mailed questionnaire, telephone interview or face-to-face questioning. By classifying different types of customer, user audits can give information on the market segments that characterise the market and their relative sizes.

Distributor audits

Distributor audits involve monitoring how a particular product type moves through a distribution chain. A representative sample of distributors is asked to provide information on how much of a particular item they buy, how frequently they buy it, how much they keep in stock and how much they sell over a particular period.

Manufacturer's output

The market is assessed by adding together the outputs of all or a representative sample of the manufacturers who contribute products to the market.

All three types of audit can be carried out at regular intervals to give an indication of the extent to which and the ways in which a market is growing.

A reliable quantitative assessment of a market is time consuming and can prove to be expensive. The entrepreneur may undertake the exercise personally but is more likely to call upon the agencies of professional market researchers. Again, the entrepreneur must balance the need for reliable information with the investment he or she feels is proper for obtaining it.

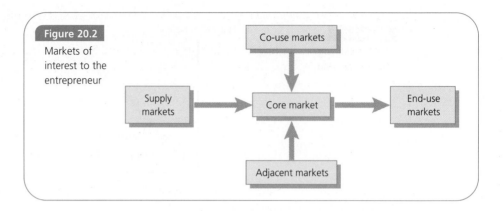

Figure 20.2

Markets of interest to the entrepreneur

A lot of information on various markets is routinely published by a variety of organisations. This information is quite easily accessed. Although such *secondary* information can be very informative, its value is limited. Only rarely will it examine a market from exactly the perspective that the entrepreneur would wish to see it. This is not least because the entrepreneur should be looking at the market in an innovative way and seeking new relationships between markets.

When examining markets, from either a qualitative or quantitative perspective, a little lateral thinking can be valuable. Insights may be gained not only by asking questions about the market itself, but also by asking questions about *related* markets (Figure 20.2). The effective entrepreneur also thinks about *end-use* markets (for example, when Lord Hanson bought the London Brick Company he wasn't thinking about the market for bricks but the growing market for new houses), about *supply* markets (for example, Alan Sugar of Amstrad was aware not only of the market for domestic hi-fi equipment but developments in the market for electronic components) and about the *co-use* market for products used in association with the product in question (thus Bill Gates of Microsoft did not so much concern himself with analysing the market for computer software but with the growth in ownership of computer *hardware* which would need software to operate it).

As always in entrepreneurship, a fresh and innovative approach to asking questions can pay dividends.

20.5 Analysis and planning formality

Key learning outcome

An understanding of the factors that encourage and discourage the preparation of formal plans for new ventures.

Business plans can take a variety of forms and vary greatly in their content and detail. A plan might be just a few ideas on a piece of paper, or be a highly formal and detailed document containing a lot of information. That information may have been gathered by external experts such as market researchers and management consultants. What determines the formality of the plan? It must be recognised that the more formal a plan, the higher its cost. This is not just in terms of the entrepreneur's time and energy, but also in the direct cost of obtaining information. A formal plan represents an investment in the venture and must be justified by the return it can offer. An entrepreneur is wise to keep the formality of the plan in line with its role. Six factors would be expected to determine the level of formality of (and hence the necessary investment in) the plan.

- *The cost of start-up* – the higher the level of initial investment in the venture, the more likely that the plan be formal. This reflects both the inherent risk in higher-cost start-ups and the fact that the proportion of the overall budget spent on planning will decrease.

- *The involvement of external stakeholders* – this is linked to the previous point. If external investors are involved in supporting the venture, they will expect to see a formal, well-evidenced and reassuring plan making a case for the viability of the venture. Other stakeholders, such as key employees and customers, may also need to be convinced with a formal plan.

- *The availability and cost of information* – before the plan can be written, the information to go into it must be obtained. In some instances, information is readily available. This may be because the entrepreneur is in an incubator organisation (formal or informal) that makes access to information easier and less expensive. In other instances information may not be readily available or may only be obtained at high cost. Easily accessed, low-cost information will encourage planning formality.

- *Perceptions of business risk and ambiguity* – decisions are based on information. Risk occurs when the range of things that might happen is known along with the probabilities of the different eventualities. Ambiguity occurs when those probabilities are not known for certain. Formal market research is a way of gauging probabilities more accurately and so turning ambiguity into risk. It can illuminate risky eventualities in a way that allows them to be managed with more certainty, both by entrepreneurs and investors. The higher the level of perceived risk and ambiguity, the more formal research will be encouraged.

- *External support with planning activities* – a number of support agencies assist with business planning. Important examples include business schools that run educational programmes involving developing business plans as a learning device. These are often practically orientated and are undertaken on behalf of practising entrepreneurs and governmental schemes that subsidise professional consultants to prepare plans for entrepreneurs. If external support is available, then planning formality will be encouraged.

- *The entrepreneur's personal style* – formal planning requires knowledge of the principles and methods of business planning. Not all entrepreneurs have this. Further, some entrepreneurs may be suspicious of, and doubt the value of formal planning. Planning may not fit with their personal analytical style.

More formal plans may be produced by those who are comfortable with, and see the value of such plans.

Summary of key ideas

- The third stage in the strategic window is *measuring* it.

- Measuring it means developing an understanding as to the size of the opportunity and what it might be worth.

- A business opportunity is analysed by *qualitative methods* which answer 'what' and 'why' questions and *quantitative methods* which answer 'how much' and 'how many' questions.

- Information can be expensive. Effective entrepreneurs weigh the value of information against the cost of obtaining it. Information is regarded as an *investment* in the business.

Research theme

Factors affecting opportunity analysis formality

This research theme investigates the degree of formality in entrepreneurs' evaluation of the market they are entering (or have entered) and their investment in detailed market research. Some ventures are based on the entrepreneur's extant and intuitive knowledge with no formal research. At the other end of the spectrum, external consultants and market research specialists may be brought in (at considerable cost!) to support the entrepreneur. Some of the factors that might be postulated as important in influencing the decision about how much to invest in formal market research include:

1. The level of initial investment in the venture. Higher levels of investment will tend to make higher levels of expenditure on market research seem more reasonable.

2. The risks in the venture. The higher the risks (more specifically, the ambiguity the venture faces), the more the entrepreneur might be tempted to acquire information that brings that ambiguity under control.

3. The involvement of external stakeholders. The more external stakeholders (particularly, but not exclusively, investors) are involved, the more the entrepreneur might be tempted to invest in independent evidence to bring them on board. This will tend to correlate positively with the initial investment in the venture.

4 The entrepreneur's personal style. Formal research is likely to be more demanded by entrepreneurs who are familiar with the techniques and whose personal decision-making style is sympathetic with explicitly rational (information-based) decision making as opposed to an implicit, intuitive approach.

5 The entrepreneur's current experience of the product technology/market sector (say, as a result of incubation in an incumbent). The lower that experience, the more the entrepreneur might be tempted to invest in additional information.

These five factors are (broadly) quantifiable (at least on a 1–5 Likert scale) and may be discovered through a survey of a pool of entrepreneurs. (Some may feel more comfortable with a tick-box banded answer than giving an exact figure to what initial investment and expenditure on market research was.) Make an attempt to quantify the entrepreneurs' own time commitment to research as well as explicit costs. The direction of the five factors discussed should be expected to correlate positively with the entrepreneur's investment in market research (as a proportion of total initial investment in the venture). Does this hypothesis hold out empirically? Statistical analysis of variance could be used to indicate the relative importance of the five factors.

For the student interested in a good discussion and information about advanced techniques in the mapping of cognitive perceptions about strategic situations, *Mapping Strategic Thought* edited by Anne Sigismund Huff is highly recommended.

Suggestions for further reading

Eisenhardt, K. (1989) 'Making fast strategic decisions in high-velocity environments', *Academy of Management Journal*, Vol. 32, pp. 543–76.

Huff, A.S. (1993) *Mapping Strategic Thought*, London: John Wiley & Sons.

Kast, F.E. and Rosenzweig, J.E. (1970) *Organization and Management: A Systems Approach*, New York: McGraw-Hill.

Langley, A. (1995) 'Between "paralysis by analysis" and "extinction by instinct"', *Sloan Management Review*, Spring, pp. 63–76.

Marlow, H. (1994) 'Intuition and forecasting – a holistic approach', *Long Range Planning*, Vol. 27, No. 6, pp. 58–68.

Selected case material **Case 20.1**

Sending out a strong signal

FT

30 October 2002

By **James Lamont**

Alan Knott-Craig, the chief executive of Vodacom, is discreet about almost everything but his hobby. The head office of South Africa's largest mobile telephone network, north of Johannesburg, does not echo with ring tones but rather the clank of rigging, fluttering flags and rushing water. Its atrium is criss-crossed with steel-strung gangways and aluminium masts, while Mr Knott-Craig's customary blue-and-white-striped polo shirt suggests he has nipped into his office from an ocean cruiser's cockpit.

But Mr Knott-Craig has had to become a little less discreet about the performance of his company. As a private concern, it kept its five-year record of 55 per cent growth in profit before tax well under wraps. Senior executives say Vodacom was shy of talking about its booming profits because it was doing almost too well in a country set on redistributing corporate wealth to the black majority.

But its biggest shareholders – Telkom, South Africa's telecommunications utility, with 50 per cent and the UK's Vodafone with 31.5 per cent – are encouraging more openness.

Telkom is heading for a listing on the New York and Johannesburg stock exchanges by the end of March. Its market valuation has slipped over the past two years as the global telecommunications market has weakened. So the government is anxious to polish its investor appeal to make the best of an untimely flotation.

Vodacom is a flagship asset, which analysts believe is likely to hold greater allure than the traditional fixed-line operation. Its market dominance in South Africa and strong growth potential in Africa lend it considerable investor appeal. Moreover, the softly spoken Mr Knott-Craig, aged 50, has held on to his job since 1996, making him one of the longest-serving telecommunications chief executives in South Africa.

In preparation for Telkom's listing, Vodacom has made public its annual report for the first time. The size of its profits is startling. Over the year to the end of March, Vodacom increased its revenues 22 per cent to R16.2bn (£1.04bn). Net profit rose 72 per cent to R2.34bn, making the eight-year-old company one of the best-performing telecoms companies in the world.

Since its introduction in South Africa in 1994, mobile telephony has far outstripped initial forecasts. Vodacom projected that it would have 250,000 users after five years of operations; in fact, it had almost 2m users. Today, its subscriber base has surged to 6.3m users and is still growing rapidly.

The country's three mobile operators – Vodacom, MTN and late entrant Cell-C – have about 12m users between them. But Mr Knott-Craig believes the market has plenty of room to grow. He is forecasting 15m users by the end of next year and a market saturation point at 19m people. There are, however, some local obstacles to consumer growth. Without HIV/Aids ravaging the country, the total user base could have stretched to 30m among a population of just over 40m people.

'HIV/Aids will result in us not having as good a market as we could have had,' says Mr Knott-Craig. 'But there is no huge dark cloud on the horizon. It's of bigger importance in a labour-intensive business like mining where you might stand to lose half your workforce.'

Mr Knott-Craig's business plan is nothing if not ambitious. His drive is backed by a cold-eyed enthusiasm for personal technology as a tool of development. He believes the mobile telephone is the great South African panacea.

It brings democracy to people who after years of racial division can now talk to one another. In an economy with about 40 per cent unemployment, it also offers the chance of finding work. Billboards by roadsides show small-time entrepreneurs – painters, truck drivers and gardeners – advertising their services with cardboard signs on which a mobile phone number is scrawled. Beneath the advertisement are the words: 'Empower Yourself'.

'Cellphones today are as powerful as personal computers were three years ago. The cellphone will become the PC of Africa,' Mr Knott-Craig says.

His company's goal is to extend mobile telephony to as many people as can afford it, as quickly as possible. Market share is its holy grail. The introduction of pre-paid charge cards has helped expand its customer base market without exposure to debt. About 83 per cent of the customer base is prepaid. The rest are served by more upmarket contracts. But a wave of secondhand handsets making their way to Africa from Europe promises to make access even easier. They are expected to cost as little as R100 each.

Mr Knott-Craig plays down the company's more direct link with Europe: its shareholding by Vodafone. The companies share similar branding and a little of the same corporate unorthodoxy. But Vodacom has a brand of corporate evangelism peculiar to post-apartheid South Africa, rather than showing any sign of being a distant outpost of a UK parent. The benefit Vodafone brings is in benchmarking Vodacom's performance, capital expenditure and network quality against operations in 28 other countries. The comparisons, with the exception of the rand exchange rate, work in Vodacom's favour.

Vodafone's African arm is adding new countries to the group's global reach. As the South African market approaches its limit, Vodacom is tapping new growth in neighbouring countries. It has operations in the Democratic Republic of Congo, Tanzania, Mozambique, Zambia and Lesotho. Angola and Zimbabwe present future opportunities.

Vodacom has 300,000 users outside South Africa – a fraction compared with its cash-generating home market. But the number is likely to grow as it rolls out prepaid telephony in environments where the fixed-line infrastructure is weak or simply does not exist.

Vodacom has taken a more cautious approach to Africa than its rival MTN, which is weighed down by US-dollar-denominated debt used to build a network in Nigeria. It is content to stick closer to home where it can support network expansion from Johannesburg.

'For South African companies, there are better opportunities in southern Africa than elsewhere. When they do try to do things elsewhere [such as in Australia and Europe], they don't do that well,' says Mr Knott-Craig.

'Other people are scared of Africa. For people in America, Europe and Asia, Africa is jungle, lions and more jungle.'

The decision to stay close to home is wise – not just from a logistical point of view but also because of a lack of management experience. Like many South African executives, Mr Knott-Craig has only just discovered what lies to the north of South Africa. They are accustomed to operating in a semi-developed market. African countries were off-limits and unknown to South African executives during their early careers under the apartheid regime.

On a recent visit to Kinshasa, Mr Knott-Craig was stunned by the sheer numbers of people and – a common sight in the developing world – their willingness to travel by clinging on to the outside of trains. But he was also struck by the stylish clothing the city's residents could afford.

So far, the Congolese appear to be showing as much curiosity about Mr Knott-Craig and mobile telephones as he does about them. The same craving for development that sustained the South African expansion is likely to drive growth in its neighbours.

'People come and touch the shop [in Kinshasa] just to be part of the dream,' he says.

Source: *Financial Times*, 30 October 2002.

Case 20.2

Travco: A one-stop shop to the country's many delights

FT

22 July 2002

By **Francesco Guerrera**

If you are a tourist in Egypt, it is difficult to escape Travco's attentions. Whether you are looking for a Nile cruise, a tour of the Pyramids or a week diving on the Red Sea, you are bound to come across one of the 25 companies that make up the Travco travel empire.

A privately-owned tourism mini-conglomerate with operations ranging from souvenir shops to hotel construction, Travco is the largest local travel company in Egypt. According to its own estimates, three out of four tourists used some of the group's services during their stay in Egypt last year.

Founded in 1979 as a small travel agent offering Nile cruises, Travco now has 10 branches in Egypt and offices in Dubai and Japan. Its main business comes from European travellers but it has also a sizeable operation in local travel. The man behind Travco is Hamed El Chiaty, an Egyptian entrepreneur. He and his family own most of Travco Holding but TUI, the German tour operator, is a minority shareholder in Travco Travel, the group's main travel subsidiary.

The scale of Travco's operations is a rarity in Egypt's highly-fragmented tourism sector. With revenues of E£85m ($22m) in 1999 and more than 8,000 employees, the company dwarfs the hundreds of one-hotel companies that have sprung up in the country's tourism hotspots since the market was freed from state control in the 1970s.

Larger groups, such as the publicly-quoted Orascom Hotels and the state-owned Misr Travel, rival Travco in parts of its operations, but neither is a one-stop travel shop on the same scale.

Being one of tourism bellwethers in a country where the industry's fortunes can change overnight due to political or economic instability is not easy, according to Tewfik El Kady, general manager of Travco's main hotel subsidiary, Sol Y Mar.

'Over the past 10 years, we had a lot of hard times, such as the Gulf War and the Luxor incident (in 1997 in which 58 tourists where killed by Islamic militants), but we have been able to bounce back,' he says, in the company's headquarters in central Cairo's Zamalek district.

The current situation is not as dramatic as in the aftermath of the Gulf War's outbreak or Luxor, but there are signs that the industry is unlikely to repeat the boom year of 2000.

After a year during which tourism in Turkey was disrupted by an earthquake, Egypt's main rival for revenues of the sun-seeking Europeans has come back, helped by a sharp devaluation in its currency.

Mr El Kady says that the plunge in the prices of package holidays to Turkey is putting pressure on Egyptian travel groups such as Travco.

The recent incident in which Chechen militants held 120 tourists hostage in an Istanbul hotel could change the situation again.

'The European tour operators are telling us: "Turkey is pushing prices down so you have to do the same".'

Mr El Kady says that a number of smaller Egyptian operators, especially on the Red Sea coast, have slashed hotel rates to remain competitive, but Travco is refusing to offer big discounts for fear of compromising quality and driving tourists away. He says the company is keen to keep its hotel occupancy rates at about 75 per cent all year round – above the Egyptian's market 65 per cent average – but without sacrificing margins and long-term revenues.

'As a rule of thumb, one happy tourist brings 21 additional customers, while one unhappy tourist drives away a potential 100 customers, so you have to be very careful that you don't reduce the quality.'

Travco's answer to the renewed price pressure is to look for new destinations to differentiate its offering from the myriad smaller rivals.

The company has recently opened a luxury resort in Egypt's western desert, an area virtually untouched by tourism, which many experts believe could become an important destination in the next few years.

Mr El Kady says that being one of the first companies in the area enables Travco to achieve high margins by avoiding the price competition of the crowded markets of the Red Sea and Nile cruises.

But in order to succeed in its quest for new locations, Travco needs the government's help. Mr El Kady says President Mubarak's administration has heeded the private sector's call for more infrastructure in new tourist areas but more needs to be done.

'We need roads, hospitals, airports. If you have infrastructure, people will come,' he says.

Source: Financial Times, 22 July 2002.

Discussion point

What level of investment (including entrepreneur's time and expenditure on formal market research) would you regard as appropriate for analysing the opportunity for initiating:

(a) a national mobile phone operator

(b) a travel operator?

Chapter 21

Opening the window: gaining commitment

Chapter overview

The fourth stage in using the strategic window is to **open** it. This means initiating the business and drawing the commitment of stakeholders towards it. This chapter looks at how the venture can enter and establish itself in the business network. The key issues relating to attracting financial and human support are considered along with the specific issue of gaining the commitment of distributors.

21.1) Entering the network

Key learning outcome

An appreciation of the way in which a new venture redefines the network of relationships that exist within a business community.

Having spotted the window, that is, having identified a new opportunity, and having located and measured the window, that is, having defined and quantified the opportunity, the entrepreneur must then *open* that window. This means initiating the business. Initiation demands that a variety of stakeholders be drawn into the venture. The new venture and the entrepreneur driving it must create a new set of relationships with those stakeholders. Yet, in most instances, those stakeholders will already have relationships with a variety of other (possibly competing) organisations. In effect, starting a new venture means *redefining* the relationships that stakeholders have with third parties and with one another. The new venture must enter an existing network of relationships and, in doing so, modify that network of relationships. If the venture is to enjoy long-term success it must do this in a way which *increases* the overall value of the network to those who make it up.

The relationships in this network are both competitive and collaborative. The entrepreneur must decide on the way these two dynamics are to be complemented and balanced as the network is redefined. This balancing act must be considered in relation to each and every stakeholder and stakeholder group.

Relationship with investors

Investors seek out opportunities to invest. They look for the best returns on the capital they provide, consistent with a certain level of risk. Because capital, like any resource, is both valuable and limited, investors are selective in the investments they choose to support. Investors are less interested in the cost of an investment than its *opportunity cost*: the money that will be lost if an investment is not made *elsewhere*.

Entrepreneurs must compete for the attentions of investors. If an entrepreneur offers an investor an investment opportunity, then they are limiting the possibility for investment in other ventures by that investor. One entrepreneur's success in attracting investment capital will be another's, perhaps many others', failure. This is harsh. Yet, in the long run, this competition generates an overall increase in value for *all* entrepreneurs in two ways. First, by defining opportunity costs it provides a strong signal as to which opportunities are worth pursuing and which are not. Second, by offering investors a good return, it generates the capital that can be used to make further investments.

Relationship with suppliers

To a supplier, an entrepreneurial venture is a potential new customer. At face value this is good since a new customer offers the prospect of new business. However, the new venture may also complicate life for a supplier. The venture may be competing with an existing customer of the supplier. While the venture may be offering the potential for additional business it may also be simply threatening to replace one set of business arrangements with another. The supplier may not always see the entrepreneurial venture as new business. They can also see the costs of gaining one new (and untried) customer only to face the risks of losing an established one. Suppliers prefer entrepreneurs who intend to expand a market, rather than just to replace existing producers within it.

If the business is characterised by close and strong relationships between supplier and customer then that relationship may be strained if the supplier is called upon to provide for a customer's competitor. While in many economies a strong legal framework exists to ensure that trading is free and fair and that strong customers do not coerce weaker suppliers, and vice versa this is not always the case. Even if a strong legal framework exists, informal agreements and expectations can still be influential.

In short, when approaching suppliers the entrepreneur must be conscious not only of the new business they are offering them but also of the way the relationship they are proposing to build will affect the existing relationships the supplier enjoys. New business may not always be as attractive as it first appears!

Relationship with employees

Entrepreneurial ventures can only be progressed if the right human skills are in place. They demand productive labour, technical knowledge, business insight and leadership. Human inputs are traded in markets. Some categories of human skill may be in short supply. If this is the case the entrepreneur may have to compete to get hold of them. This competition takes the form of offering potential employees attractive remuneration packages and prospects for development.

If one entrepreneur employs an individual with a skill which is valuable and in short supply then another cannot employ that individual. More critically, perhaps, it is likely that the entrepreneur will attract such a person from an existing business. Most would agree that individuals should have the right to offer their skills and insight to whomsoever they wish. Furthermore, the demand for people with rare talents, reflected by the rewards they are offered, provides an incentive for others to develop those skills.

In practice, however, individuals do not market themselves as commodities within a 'perfect' labour market. They build close relationships with the organisations for which they work. People are motivated by more than just the financial rewards of working. The 'contracts' individuals have with their organisations go beyond the simple terms of the formal written contract of employment. They involve unwritten, often unarticulated, expectations and loyalties on both sides.

As a consequence, while an entrepreneur seeking to attract an employee from a competitor is a proper functioning of the labour market, it can also be seen in negative terms as a kind of illegitimate 'poaching'. This can be traumatic and cause ill-feeling, particularly when the business community is close knit and the employee is felt to be offering not just their general experience, skills and insights but also insider knowledge to a competitor. Some employers use formal contractual devices to restrict the movement of employees in possession of sensitive knowledge to competitors.

While the entrepreneur should never feel ashamed at offering individuals a good reward for the skills and talents they have invested in creating for themselves, the effective entrepreneur must be sensitive to the human dimension of the business they are operating in and its rules when recruiting people. More often than not these rules about what is acceptable and unacceptable in recruitment practice are unwritten.

Relationship with customers

Customers are a key stakeholder group for the entrepreneur. It is their interest in what the venture offers, and their willingness to pay for it, that ultimately provides the money which the entrepreneurial venture will use to reward all its stakeholder groups. The best way to attract the interest of customers is to provide them with goods and services which *genuinely* satisfy their needs, solve their problems and meet their aspirations.

A customer will not usually have a need which is both explicit and completely unsatisfied. Rarely will the entrepreneur be offering the customer something which they need in addition to everything else they consume. It is much more likely that they will be offering something that will *replace* something else they are using. In short, even an innovative entrepreneurial business will be competing with the potential customer's existing suppliers. Suppliers and their customers do not relate solely through the medium of a market. They also interact at a human level via the business network. In some instances this relationship may be trivial. In many, however, the relationship is far-reaching, deeply established and complex. The relationship may not be sustained by economic self-interest alone but also by friendship and trust.

When a new venture approaches a customer, it is asking not only that the customer buy the offering, but also that they stop buying or replace the offering provided by a competitor. The success of the selling approach will depend on more than the way the entrepreneur's offering competes against the one they seek to oust. The wider relationship they seek to end and the new one they offer to replace it will also be important. If the entrepreneur is to be successful in marketing and selling his or her products and services to customers they must consider not just the product or service, but also the nature of the individual and organisational relationships that exist between customer and supplier in the marketplace. The entrepreneur must be prepared to create more rewarding relationships. This point will be developed further in Section 22.1.

When starting their ventures entrepreneurs are not just offering their product or service into a melée of short-term market exchanges. They are breaking and then reforming a pattern of relationships. Those relationships are governed by rules, some formal, some informal, some based on self-interest, and others governed by altruistic motives. Some are articulated openly, while others are not even recognised – until they are lost. Effective entrepreneurs understand those relationships, and the rules that govern them, so that they can successfully manage their position within the network. This is not to say the entrepreneur should not occasionally break the rules, but they should be aware that they *are* breaking the rules and know *why* they are doing it.

21.2 Gaining financial investment: key issues

> **Key learning outcome**
>
> A recognition of the main issues associated with attracting financial investment to the new venture.

An entrepreneur will be interested in obtaining a variety of different resources in order to progress his or her venture. However, it is money that is likely to take first place on the list of priorities. This is understandable. Money is the most liquid of resources. Once it has been obtained it can be used readily to obtain the other things the business needs.

Attracting investment capital is one of the primary functions of the entrepreneur. It is a process that raises a number of critical issues. The entrepreneur must consider these issues carefully and make some fundamental decisions in relation to them. This section will examine the issues in overview. They will be expanded upon in Chapter 23.

What level of investment is required?

Broadly, how much money will be needed to start the venture? This will of course depend on the nature of the venture, the opportunity it is pursuing, the stage in its development and the plans the entrepreneur has for the future. Initial investment levels are sensitive to the strategy the business is pursuing, in terms of the initial scope the business must have and the potential this leaves for growth. Some ventures can start on a small scale and build up over time. Anita Roddick started The Body Shop with a single outlet and a loan of £4,000. The business grew as new outlets were added incrementally over time. On the other hand, when Frederick Smith started the US air freight business Federal Express, he realised that if the business was to work he needed to offer customers a full service from the start. That meant acquiring a fleet of aircraft and a relatively large administrative and support structure. He sought $90 million of start-up financing.

Where is the investment to come from?

While there is an overall 'market for capital', there are a number of sources of investment capital. For example, the entrepreneur's own funds, bank loans, government loans, venture capital, share issues, business angels (experienced manager–investors who offer their expertise to new ventures along with capital), and so on. In other words, the market for capital is a fragmented one. Different capital providers occupy different niches in the market. They are characterised by the way they look for different types of investment opportunity, accept different levels of risk, expect different types of return and assume different levels of involvement in the running of the venture. To be effective in managing the project of attracting funds the entrepreneur must understand these different markets and the way in which they work.

What is the capital structure of the investment to be?

The *capital structure* of the venture is simply the mix of different investment sources that are used. In broad terms it refers to the ratio of 'equity' to 'debt' capital, that is, the mix of investors who expect a return that will be linked to the performance of the venture to those who expect a fixed return based on an agreed interest rate whatever the performance of the business. In addition, loan capital may be unsecured or secured against some assets of the business.

The capital structure of the venture reflects the way in which the entrepreneur is sharing risk with the investors. Clearly a secured loan exposes the investor to a lower level of risk than an equity share. At the same time, capital which exposes the investor to risk is more expensive than capital which does not. So by adjusting the capital structure entrepreneurs can, in effect, 'sell off' the risks inherent in their venture to different degrees.

How will the investors be approached?

Entrepreneurs and investors need to get in touch with each other before they can work together. Usually, the onus is on the entrepreneur to initiate the contact. That contact must be managed. While investors try to make rational decisions about investment opportunities they are not calculating machines. They are still human beings who are influenced by *how* things are said as well as *what* is said, and first impressions are important. The way in which the entrepreneur first approaches the potential investor can have a bearing on the outcome of that contact. In essence, three things must be considered: the *who* of the contact, the *how* of the contact and the *what* of the contact.

First, the entrepreneur must identify suitable sources of investment – that is, *who* to contact. This involves identifying organisations that provide investment capital. However, organisations do not make decisions, *individuals* do and the entrepreneur may find it productive to find out which individual or individuals they should approach within the organisation. They may also consider the decision-making structure within the organisation, i.e. not only who actually takes the investment decisions but who influences them in that decision and the way in which their decisions are policed and judged within the organisation.

Second, the entrepreneur must consider the *how* of the contact. Should it be formal or informal? Does the investor lay down a procedure for making contact? (Most banks and venture capital companies, for example, do.) Does the investor expect a written proposal or a verbal one in the first instance? If it is verbal, do they expect a one-to-one chat or a full-blown presentation? If it is a written one, do they lay down a format for the proposal or do they give the entrepreneur latitude in the way they communicate? Many investors will simply reject a proposal out of hand if they are not approached in the right way.

Third, they must consider *what* to tell the investor. At the first contact stage, attracting the investor's attention and encouraging their interest is likely to be as important as giving them information. This will be particularly so if the investor is receiving a large number of approaches. Is it necessary to relate a detailed picture or will a broad outline be more effective? How much room for manoeuvre is there here if the communication has to comply with a set format?

What proposition is to be made to the investors?

The entrepreneur must consider what, exactly, they are offering the investor. Some of the critical dimensions here are:

- the amount of investment required;
- how that particular investment fits with the overall investment profile for the venture;
- the nature of the investment (e.g. loan or equity, secured or unsecured);
- the level of return anticipated;
- the nature (particularly the *liquidity*) of any security being offered;
- the degree of risk to which the capital will be exposed;
- the way 'in', i.e. how the investment will be made (what amount of money at what time);
- the way 'out', i.e. how the investor will get their return (what amount of money at what time);
- the degree of *control* the investor will be given over (or be expected to contribute to) the way the venture is run.

These things constitute the 'package' that the entrepreneur is offering to the investor. It is on the basis of these factors that investors will make their judgement as to whether the investment opportunity is of the right sort for them. The entrepreneur must never forget that they are *selling* the venture to investors. The entrepreneur must put as much effort into this selling exercise as he or she would do in selling the business's products to customers.

21.3) Gaining human commitment

> **Key learning outcome**
>
> An appreciation of how the commitment of key people to the venture may be gained.

On its own investment capital can achieve nothing. It must be used by *people* to progress the venture. The money obtained by one entrepreneur is exactly the same as the money obtained by another and, indeed, exactly like that held by established businesses. If an entrepreneurial venture is successful then it must be because its people do something *different* and *better* with the money to which they have access.

While it is conventional in management theory to talk of human beings as a 'resource', it should always be remembered that they are a *special* type of resource. There is more to gaining human commitment than simply bringing people into the business. They must certainly be attracted to the venture in the first instance. Once in, their motivation and dedication must be maintained and constantly developed. The entrepreneur does not just *recruit* to their venture, they must also *lead* it.

The entrepreneur faces a number of decisions in relation to developing the commitment other people have towards the venture.

What human skills are required?

Businesses need a variety of different types of human input. Technical skills, communication skills, functional skills and analytical skills are all critically important to the success of a venture. Different ventures need different mixes of these skills in order to progress. The entrepreneur must decide what profile of skills and experience is right for their venture as it stands now, and what profile will be needed as it grows and develops. In light of the fact that human resources are as likely to be scarce as any other, this may mean prioritising some requirements over others.

Where will those skills be obtained from?

Where are the people with those skills? Are they working for other organisations? If so, are they working for competitors or for non-competitors? If they are working for competitors what issues will recruiting them raise?

What will be offered to attract those who have the skills?

In the first instance, this means pay and other aspects of the remuneration package. The entrepreneur must offer a package which is competitive in light of what other employers are offering. But pay is not the entirety of what an organisation offers an employee. Human needs go beyond purely financial concerns. It is critical to ask what the venture offers people as a stage on which to build social relationships. Is it a friendly environment? Will it be fun to work for? Further, what does the venture offer in the way of potential for self-development? How can people progress within it as it expands? What roles will they play? How does the venture represent a theatre for personal growth?

An entrepreneurial venture must compete for people not just with other entrepreneurial ventures but also with established organisations. The venture offers potential employees much the same thing that it presents to financial investors, that is, risk but with the promise of higher returns. The employee is exposed to the chance of the venture failing. However, there may also be the possibility of much higher rewards in the way of personal development, experience and achievement. Of course, financial investors and employees draw upon quite different mechanisms to manage risk and their exposure to it.

The entrepreneur must be aware of why the option of working for a dynamic, fast-changing, fast-growing organisation might be attractive (and why it might be unattractive) to potential employees.

How will potential employees be contacted?

People must be recruited. There are a variety of means for doing this. In the first instance personal contact and word of mouth can be very productive. If this is not possible then a more formal means of recruiting is called for. This may demand advertising (say, in a specialist press). It may even be felt expedient to delegate the task of attracting people to a specialist recruitment agency.

How will potential employees be evaluated?

Having contacted and attracted the interest of potential employees, then some evaluation and selection procedure must be invoked. Taking on a new employee represents a major commitment for both the business and the employee. Any effort expended in ensuring that the person is right for the organisation, and that the organisation is right for the person, at the recruitment stage, is likely to pay dividends. Mistakes can be expensive and painful for both parties. This is not just a process of ensuring that the person has the right technical skills but also that their attitudes and approach will fit with the organisation's approach, values and culture. However, the entrepreneur should be careful: there is strength in diversity!

If the entrepreneur knows a potential employee well, and has experience of the way in which they work, then the recruitment process may be quite informal (often little more than a job offer over a drink). If they are not acquainted with the person (and the contribution they might make) then at least some sort of interview is required. Some would go further and ask for some sort of *psychometric* or *attitudinal* testing. Of course, these tools exist to aid the entrepreneur in making recruitment decisions. They cannot make them on their own!

Should a skill be in-house or should it be hired when necessary?

Resources are scarce in the entrepreneurial venture. The entrepreneur must make the resources they have work hard. One question they should always ask when faced with the need for a particular human skill is whether it is best to bring that skill in-house, i.e. to recruit someone to perform the task, or to use an external agency to provide it. So should the business employ a financial expert or call on the assistance of a firm of accountants? Should it take on research and development staff or delegate a project to a university?

The 'employ or hire' decision is influenced by a variety of factors. How much of a particular skill input is required? Over what timescale will it be required? Will the business have a long-term need for it? How much control does the entrepreneur need over the person contributing that skill? How much will it cost to employ someone versus hiring them?

It may often appear that the hiring option is the more expensive. However, this expense needs to be considered in the light of the costs of recruitment. There are also risks associated with bringing someone new into the business. What contribution will they *really* make? How will they fit? How will existing employees get along with them? Further, hiring someone tends to add to the business's marginal costs whereas employing them adds to fixed costs. Hiring may be more attractive from a cash-flow point of view especially when the venture's output may be variable and unpredictable. In light of this, in general, employment should only be considered when there is a clear, consistent, long-term need for a particular skill or a particular expertise within the business.

The way the business will gain from the additional level of control that comes from having the skill in-house should also be considered. If the business aims to develop a competitive advantage based on knowledge and an ability to use it to deliver value to the customer then it goes without saying that this knowledge should be held by people who are dedicated to the business.

Leadership and motivation strategy

Commitment is not just given, it must be maintained. In this the entrepreneur must be conscious of their own leadership and motivational strategy and the way they use it to bring out the best in their people. Developing and applying this strategy takes practice. The entrepreneur is the venture's key human resource. The skill they provide comes from being able to manage vision and use it to lead the organisation.

21.4 Establishing a presence with distributors

> **Key learning outcome**
>
> An understanding of decision making by distributors and the issues entrepreneurs face in gaining access to distribution channels.

Distributors are often at the neglected end of business thinking. They are sometimes regarded as a necessary evil: a part of the value addition system (productive!) businesses must put up with. Many accounts of entrepreneurship regard them as hurdles that entrepreneurs must overcome if their business is to be successful. To be sure, 'glamorous' distributors such as the major retailers get a lot of attention (albeit often critical), but far less attention is given to smaller distributors. This neglect is unfortunate. Distributors create real economic value. They do so in four ways. First, they provide a logistical efficiency. Buyers can obtain a wide variety of purchases with a single journey. Second, they provide information in that they give buyers the opportunity to compare different producers offerings' alongside each other, thus enhancing competitive efficiency. Third, they can support with the promotion of goods, working as partners with producers. Fourth, and this is perhaps the most important aspect of their value addition, they provide producers with *liquidity*. A manufacturer may wish to produce a quantity of a good at any one time (capitalising on economies of scale). However, if that good is stored in the manufacturer's warehouse, then capital is tied up. By agreeing to buy a quantity in advance of customer demand, then the manufacturer can turn that stock into cash to fund the next phase of production.

In principle, strategic decision making by distributors is relatively straightforward. If the distributor is concerned with maximising profit, then they should only consider three things when deciding which (producers') goods to distribute:

- the *margin* on the good – the difference between the price the good can be purchased for and the price it will be sold for;
- the *rate of sale* of the good – how many units will be sold in a period;
- the *cost of storing* (and displaying) the good for the period before it is sold.

The cost of holding items is an *opportunity cost*, given that other items might be stored and displayed. In effect, the distributor is maximising the relationship:

Profit (on stocked item) per period = (Margin on item × number of items sold in a period) – cost of holding items over that period.

This calculation may be intuitive and based on the distributor's experience, but increasingly distributors (and not just large retailers) are using computer software to do this calculation (often referred to as direct product profitability or DPP). This is not to negate the effect of personal relationships in producer–distributor networks, but these are often (usually) built and maintained on the basis of such prior (implicit or explicit) calculations. It is for this reason that most distributors (be they major retailers or small wholesalers) rarely carry more than about three (usually one or two) competitor products in any one-product category.

What does this mean for the entrepreneur seeking the support of distributors? In short, appropriate distributors will be attracted if, and only if, in light of this calculation, the entrepreneur is offering a better deal than existing suppliers are. Consider the situation from the distributor's perspective. The entrepreneur may claim to be offering an innovative product that is new, different and better than that offered by existing suppliers and that will create new benefits to buyers. But all the distributor will see is that existing sales (from existing suppliers) will be replaced by sales of the entrepreneur's new item – no gain to them, and a lot of additional cost. Why should they replace the extant competitors' products, especially if they have a good relationship with existing suppliers? How might the entrepreneur improve on the deal and encourage the distributor to switch? The calculation suggest how. Either give higher margin, so the distributor gains more from every sale; and/or promise a higher rate of sale (i.e. *faster* overall demand) or propose that storage and display costs will be lower. Each of these options presents a decisional challenge to the entrepreneur. The higher the margin offered the lower (given production costs) the revenues to the entrepreneur. In effect, the entrepreneur is *buying* (with forgone profits) a presence with distributors. A higher rate of sale is only plausible if demand for the entrepreneur's good is absolutely higher than that of competitors (i.e. an expansion of the market) and, in any case, rate of sale will be dependent on the availability of competitor products. This can reduce to a self-fulfilling 'we will sell more, provided you exclude them' scenario. Rate-of-sale may be increased by effective promotion to the end buyer, but this has costs of its own. Storage and display costs are fundamentally about the resources the distributor must apply to maintain that storage and display, but this often reduces to the physical volume of the good (given that the distributor is displaying to capacity), so the entrepreneur must offer to support display with direct financial support (additional to that offered by competitors), something which again introduces additional costs. Of the three options – increasing margin, additional payments to support storage costs and support with promotion – entrepreneurs usually prefer the latter and make it the mainstay of their negotiation with distributors. Margin is likely to be an irredeemable cost of sale as negotiating reduced margins is difficult; promotional support is an investment that might be scaled back in the future.

In summary, distributors create real value. However, their inherent (and quite rational) conservatism does present a barrier to entry for new entrepreneurs. Entrepreneurs will face costs in bringing distributors on board and excluding existing competitors. However, the entrepreneur who has caught the attention (and support) of a distributor has a competitive advantage in that future entrepreneurs will have to go through the same process (undertake the same investment) if they wish to replace them.

Summary of key ideas

- The fourth stage in the strategic window is *opening* it.

- Opening the window means gaining the *commitment* of stakeholders and actually starting the venture.

- Distributors may be key allies, but their decision making must be understood if they are to be used effectively.

- The key commitments are financial support from *investors*; productive support from *employees* and *network contacts*; agreements to provide inputs by *suppliers*; and agreement to purchase outputs by *customers*.

Research themes

Entrepreneurs' management of resource acquisition

What guides an entrepreneur's decision as to whether to bring human and operating resources into the venture on a permanent basis (hold), or, alternatively, to hire them in as and when necessary? It might be hypothesised that the following factors would be important:

- Internal demand for the resource: is this only needed for short period or regularly required?

- How important the resource is to the venture: marginal or critical?

- How easy it is to obtain the resource on a short-term basis (how well developed is the external market for the resource): easy or difficult?

- To what extent *unique* access to the resource is a source of competitive advantage: not significant or significant?

- To what extent the entrepreneur must invest in developing the resource: to a low degree or high?

● The difference in cost between short-term hiring and long-term holding: low hire to hold or high hire to hold ratio?

In each case, the former would be predicted to encourage hiring in, the latter to encourage permanent holding and internal development of the resource. For a particular set of ventures, identify a range of human and operating resources relevant to those ventures that vary across these factors. Use questionaires or interviews with the entrepreneurs leading those ventures and inquire into their hire or hold decisions. Have them rationalise those decisions. Do the rationalisations meet with these hypothesised criteria?

Network modelling and entrepreneurial entry

This study adopts a case-study methodology. To be effective a significant number of cases (say around twenty) need to be considered, but the analysis for each is quite focused. Obtain descriptions of a number of entrepreneurial ventures. Case studies are a good source. A picture may be built up by undertaking secondary research from published sources or by primary research. For each venture, summarise the organisations that form its immediate network. A network model has two parts. The first considers an entrepreneurial venture and its links to other, resource-providing, individuals and organisations such as key employees, distributors, end users, capital providers and suppliers. The second considers the nature of those links. In particular, how significant the resource provided is to the venture, the competition between suppliers of that resource, the nature of the relationship and how tight the link is (e.g. can the venture shift to an alternative provider? How high are switching costs? What are the risks in going elsewhere? How important is trust in the relationship? How high are search, contract establishment and monitoring costs?). The theory of networks suggests that entrepreneurs find it difficult to enter tight networks but are secure once in, and find it easy to enter loose networks, but are susceptible to future entrants once in. Is this borne out in practice? Identify sectors in which linkages are tight, moderate and loose. Then consider the rate of new entry and exit by entrepreneurs into the sector. A useful source of this information is VAT registration and deregistration statistics. Looser networked sectors should have a higher rate of entry and exit compared to tighter networked sectors. Is the prediction of the model realised?

Suggestions for further reading

Cook, W.M. (1992) 'The buddy system', *Entrepreneur*, Nov, p. 52.
Gartner, W.B. (1984) *Problems in Business Start-up: The Relationships among Entrepreneurial Skills and Problem Identification for Different Types of New Venture*, Babson, Wellesley Park, MA: Centre for Entrepreneurial Studies.
Hall, W.K. (1980) 'Survival strategies in a hostile environment', *Harvard Business Review*, July–Aug, pp. 75–85.
Schoch, S. (1984) 'Access to capital', *Venture*, June, p. 106.

Rapidly maturing industry needs to set benchmarks

FT

21 November 2002

By **Sheila Jones**

Twenty years ago the idea of business incubation had barely taken root in Britain. Even by the mid-1990s, only 25 incubation units had been created. But the landscape has changed dramatically in less than a decade.

Encouraged by a flourishing sector in the US and the success of science parks and early incubators in the UK, the idea has taken off.

The government drive in the 1990s was to encourage more of Britain's universities to harness the commercial power of their research and to engage and collaborate with the private sector. It was no longer enough to teach and research – the universities had to be enterprising too.

Gordon Brown, Chancellor of the Exchequer, says he is now placing enterprise and innovation at the heart of his strategy to lift the UK's economic performance and to narrow the wealth gap between regions.

In doing so, he acknowledges the role that new and growing businesses play in injecting dynamism into the economy. Yet while the government has emphasised the importance of business creation to the country's competitive position, the UK still lags behind the US in entrepreneurial activity.

Incubation units designed to nurture ideas and innovation are now seen as central to the aim of tackling regional imbalances in wealth and business creation, as well as improving the country's competitive position globally.

Almost 250 incubators now operate in the UK, supporting an estimated 5,000 fledgling businesses and many more new centres are in the pipeline. As the industry has developed, new business models have evolved alongside. Incubators today offer services to sectors as diverse as pop music, agriculture, computer games, aerospace, digital and medical technologies.

Expectations are high. Yet the sector is young and still defining itself, says Peter Harman, deputy chief executive of UK Business Incubation, the industry body created in 1998. Everybody understands the basic aim of providing a nurturing, supportive and creative environment for entrepreneurs and to harness the development of ideas, he says.

But the industry needs to set benchmarks, without being prescriptive. It is a view shared by the EU's Enterprise Directorate for the 900 business incubators across the EU.

'Some people have a limited understanding of what an incubator is and that is something we need to deal with,' Mr Harman says.

'In the past four years, we have presided over rapid growth in incubation and we have talked about it in a very holistic way. But we do not have a definition. We have reached a level of maturity where we now need to benchmark and measure. We need a national standard of some sort.'

The idea is to examine best practice across the sector and to set parameters, such as optimal levels of work space, public-private funding ratios, types of support services and levels of direct aid such as subsidised space. It also aims to establish the sorts of funding regimes that might suit particular goals such as regeneration or targeted schemes within particular incubators.

At Coventry and Warwick universities, for example, enterprise fellowship schemes with one-year placements and an interest-free loan are offered to free up alumni to develop a business idea. On Merseyside, a new bio-incubator has been able to call on EU funding for regeneration as it is designated as a poor region.

The wider aim of benchmarking is to bring greater focus to the work and funding of incubation in developing enterprises and technologies and their contribution to wealth creation and regeneration.

Regional Development Agencies (RDA) and government departments, for example, need to know that their efforts to promote innovation or regeneration through public funding is going to something that is what it says it is and that the funding will add value rather than simply provide space for a new business.

'There is confusion about what a real incubator is,' Mr Harman says. 'Some may be simply managed work space, and that is not to criticise such provision, but they are light years away from what an incubator is.

'There may be some pain because judgments will be made. It is a moveable feast and there are different needs for different types of incubation. But there is no point saying that incubation is going to improve things unless you have benchmarks and identify what you need.' The benchmarking process, being carried out with the Small Business Service, is expected to be complete by next spring.

Private funding for incubator businesses is a constant struggle. 'It is a risk business,' says Mr Harman. The collapse of the technology and dotcom sector has discouraged investors such as venture capitalists. But incubators say that good ideas will usually find a backer, whether that is a 'business angel' or an individual investor willing to back a risky project. At later stages of development, incubator businesses have to compete with the rest of the world for larger funds from more mainstream investors.

Against this background, the incubator sector welcomes the government's emphasis on promoting early stage businesses through funding schemes and tax incentives, which aim to promote wealth creation and regeneration in the regions.

Pump-priming for specific goals such as regeneration has become an important aspect of incubator development. Some schemes target regional development, such as the Regional Innovation Fund to support local economic strategies, while the government's Phoenix Fund is designed to encourage entrepreneurship in disadvantaged areas. Sectors are also targeted in areas including the internet and biotechnology, while the £75m SBS Business Incubation Fund is designed to encourage new facilities and services.

One criticism of government-backed support and aid schemes is that they are too often one-size-fits-all.

'It is not a sausage machine,' says David Kingham, chief executive of Oxford Innovation, one the UK's first incubator companies and now a network of 12 incubation centres. 'If we are to empower entrepreneurs, we need to be able to offer services rather than packages and say to them: "Here are the services, you choose what you like".'

Mr Kingham would also like to see greater decision-making powers at local level where he believes agencies are better placed to understand local business needs than officials in London or even in regional agencies.

It has long been argued that innovation in the UK is hampered by a risk averse culture. It is cited as one of the reasons Britain lags the US in entrepreneurial activity. But this is probably a misconception, says Nick Smailes, initiative director at the SetSquare incubation scheme that draws together Bristol, Bath, Southampton and Surrey universities with RDA partners in the south-east and south-west.

'We are all going up a learning curve, including the government,' he says. 'The US is more advanced than anybody because they have been doing it for a long time. There is a different culture towards start-ups in the US and considerably more people who are used to investing in equity.

'But on risk, I am not sure we are that different. In this country the problem is that if you start up and fail that often leaves you branded. In the US, failure is seen as a valuable experience and maybe that's the distinction.'

The Centre for Strategy for Evaluation Services, suggests in a recent benchmarking study of EU-based incubators that US and European centres operate in different ways, but that each has strengths, providing scope for the two to learn from each other.

The US, it says, is strong in company financing and in some management functions, while European centres have developed expertise in entrepreneur training, virtual networking and in integrating incubator functions into broader strategies.

It is this particular strength – in integrating incubation with regional economic strategies, or tackling regeneration and deprivation – that the government wants to nurture.

The government is 'going in that right direction' in seeking to promote entrepreneurship, particularly through fiscal incentives, says William Sargent, chairman of the Small Business Council, which advises the government on the needs of smaller businesses.

'There is a political will and a recognition in government of what is needed. All the government can do is facilitate and enable by removing barriers where possible. They cannot create economic activity,' he says.

However, Mr Sargent also argues that while the private sector is allowed to make mistakes and may go on to fail or flourish, the government is over-cautious.

'We need officials to take risks,' he says. 'The issue of accountability is important and there is a strong culture of being careful and of course that is right. But we need risk takers in the public sector as much as in the private sector.'

Politically difficult decisions may have to be made, he says, not just on particular projects, but also on funding. The government cannot please everybody all of the time with a proliferation of funding schemes. 'If you spread your money too thinly, it is difficult to be effective.'

Source: Financial Times, 21 November 2002.

Case 21.2

In search of the right kind of chemistry

21 November 2002

By **Christopher Swann**

Incubators are the point at which two worlds meet. The aim is to bridge the gulf between business and academia.

Those involved in incubators see their function not only to nurture fledgling ventures but to mediate in disputes and misunderstandings between academics and entrepreneurs.

'Britain is full of innovative individuals but entrepreneurs are slightly more thin on the ground,' says David Hardman, head of commercial affairs at the Babraham Institute. 'Academics often lack the acumen necessary to

run a business. We are a halfway house, offering a stepping stone to the commercial world.'

Incubators often serve as a dating agency, pairing academics with the entrepreneurs capable of bringing their ideas to market.

Imperial College Innovations – one of the most successful incubators with 55 business spin-outs – runs an introduction network to pair up eligible academics with eager entrepreneurs.

This network consists of several hundred commercially minded people who have expressed an interest in serving as chief executives, non-executive directors or consultants to technology start-ups.

The key to establishing a business on a sound footing, says Colin Kinner, head of funds management at Imperial College Innovations, is the board of directors which establishes the strategic direction for the company.

'The role of the commercial people who are brought in is not to take over the company but rather to guide it,' he says. 'It is important to get the chemistry right between the academics and the business people.'

A crucial period in the development of a venture comes when the lead professor in a project has to decide what role the commercial people will take in the business.

This can determine the success or failure of a venture, according to David Kingham, chief executive of Oxford Innovation.

He argues that ventures are more likely to be successful when the lead professor decides to delegate managerial responsibilities and take a back seat as research director or even research adviser.

Clashes between a chief executive officer and a founding research director are not infrequent.

'Both the chief executive and the founding professor tend to have quite forceful personalities so differences do sometimes arise,' says Mr Kingham.

One element of the solution is providing separate space. In many cases the scientists can remain in the university laboratories while the business people are housed in office space.

'There is a need for separate worlds,' says Mr Kingham. 'This makes it easier for the academic as well, since it is clearer which hat is being worn at any particular time.'

Despite its impressive record, Imperial College Innovation cannot yet offer subsidised premises to its spin out companies, but it acknowledges the importance of office space for a start-up company. 'It might seem trivial, but it makes a much more positive impression on venture capitalists who are interested in funding a start-up,' says Mr Kinner.

Another potential area of conflict is over valuations.

'Academics can be prone to underestimate the proportion of the value of a company that is represented by successful management,' says Mr Kingham. 'Even if the idea is brilliant, it may take huge resources to bring it to market. As a result, academics are sometimes unrealistic about the value of the company at an early stage.'

Again, Oxford Innovation seeks to bring about a meeting of minds. The organisation runs technology finance panels at which academics can meet patent agents, bankers, accountants and entrepreneurs before presenting their ideas to business angels or venture capitalists.

'Sometimes this leads to a more realistic assessment of the value of an early stage company and other times it just helps improve the sales technique of the academics,' says Mr Kingham.

Universities, too, are often unrealistic about how quickly they can make money out of their intellectual property, according to some incubators. Academics also frequently underestimate the difficulty of securing venture capital funding.

Business angels, private investors who take a punt on early stage companies, are often more forthcoming with funds, says Mr Kingham. As a result, Oxford Innovation runs a network of business angels. 'The aim is to set up more of a market place for this kind of funding,' he says.

Another argument for academics delegating managerial responsibility to more experienced managers, Mr Kinner says, is that it increases the chances of securing funding.

'You want to communicate to investors in a language they will understand and often this is best done by an entrepreneur rather than a lead scientist,' he says. 'When our start-ups are presenting to groups of venture capitalists, a commercial chief executive generally takes the lead.'

In their zeal to prove their commercial credentials, universities can often be tempted to spin out companies with no real future, argues Mr Hardman.

'There is a danger that we will become involved in a numbers game, with universities boasting about how many spin out companies they have produced,' he says. 'But many of these ideas will not be the basis of a profitable company and the university would do better licensing the intellectual property to an existing company.'

Although a large number of Britain's higher education institutions are actively pursuing a more commercial strategy, only 32 make money from intellectual property while 33 have actually lost money. Only three make more than £1m.

Despite the emphasis being placed on technology transfer, the bulk of universities are still making relatively modest sums from their intellectual property.

A substantial rise in these figures will be ultimate evidence that the gulf between universities and business has been bridged.

Source: Financial Times, 21 November 2002.

Discussion points

1. How important are incubation and mentoring to supporting entrepreneurial start-up? Are entrepreneurs inherently self-starting or do they need a push?

2. Should the government set up and support incubator organisations or is it best left to the market? If so, how should entrepreneurs and incubator managers share the rewards of business success?

Chapter 22

Closing the window: sustaining competitiveness

Chapter overview

The final stage in using the strategic window metaphor is to **close** it. This means giving the venture some unique and valuable character so that competitors cannot follow through the window and exploit the opportunity it has identified as well. The concept of **competitive advantage** is introduced; what it is, how it can be established and how it can be maintained are considered.

22.1 Long-term success and sustainable competitive advantage

> **Key learning outcome**
>
> An appreciation of how business success is dependent on creating, developing and sustaining competitive advantage in the marketplace.

Having opened the strategic window by gaining financial and human commitment to the venture, the entrepreneur must ensure that the long-term potential for success is not eroded by competitors moving in. Entrepreneurs must close the strategic window to limit the possibility of competitors following them and exploiting the opportunity as well.

The notion of *sustainable competitive advantage* provides a powerful conceptual approach to recognising the ways in which the strategic window can be closed to help guarantee long-term success in the marketplace. It provides an insight into the decisions that must be made in order to keep the business in a position where it can compete effectively. Competitive advantage is a central pillar of strategic thinking, which has been developed by Professor Michael Porter (1985) in particular.

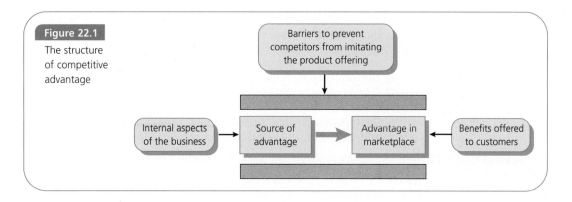

Figure 22.1

The structure of competitive advantage

Barriers to prevent competitors from imitating the product offering

Internal aspects of the business → Source of advantage → Advantage in marketplace ← Benefits offered to customers

It is important to distinguish between a *competitive advantage*, which must be understood in terms of what the business offers to the marketplace, and the *source* of that competitive advantage, which relates to how the business is set up to deliver that offering to the marketplace. Business life is, by definition, competitive. A particular competitive advantage may be imitated, in which case it loses its value. If a business is to enjoy a competitive advantage over the long term it must be one which competitors find difficult, and in business that means *expensive*, to copy. Consequently, a full delivery of competitive advantage demands decisions at three levels (Figure 22.1):

1 what will be offered to the marketplace that is unique and valuable – the *competitive advantage*;

2 how that offering will be maintained by the business – the *source* of the competitive advantage;

3 how that competitive advantage will be protected from imitation by competitors – the way it will be *sustained*.

Competitive advantage

Competitive advantage is located in what is offered to the marketplace. A competitive advantage is present if the business consistently offers the customer something which is *different* from what competitors are offering, and that difference represents something *valuable* for the customer. In short, a competitive advantage is the reason why customers spend their money with one business rather than another.

The entrepreneur must decide what type of competitive advantage they aim to pursue. Some of the more critical include:

● offering the customer a *lower price*, that is, better value for money;

● differentiating the offering through its *features* or *performance*, that is, an offering which satisfies needs or solves problems for its customers better than a competitor's product does;

- differentiating the offering through *service*, that is, addressing needs or solving problems in a more effective way, or supporting the use of the product more effectively;

- differentiating the offering through *branding*, that is, through investment in communicating quality and the business's commitment to the offering;

- differentiating the offering through *brand imagery*, that is, by building in associations which address social and self-developmental needs as well as functional needs;

- differentiating through *access* and *distribution*, that is, by giving the customer easier, more convenient, less disruptive or less time-consuming access to the offering.

The sources of competitive advantage

Being able to *consistently* offer something different and meaningful in the ways described above will only occur if the business is itself different from its competitors in some way. A competitive advantage in the marketplace must be delivered from within the business and be supported by it.

The English academic Professor John Kay has developed a perspective on competitive advantage which sees it as having its source in one of four distinct capabilities:

1. the *architecture* of the business, that is, its internal structure;

2. the *reputation* of the business, that is, the way key stakeholders view it;

3. the way the business *innovates*, that is, its ability to come up with new and valuable ideas;

4. the business's *strategic assets*, that is, valuable assets to which it has access and its competitors do not.

These four distinctive capabilities are quite general and apply to all businesses. They can be related to four specific sources of competitive advantage for the entrepreneurial venture making its presence felt in the marketplace. These are *costs*, *knowledge*, *relationships* and *structure*.

Cost sources

The business may enjoy an advantage due to lower costs. In economic terms this means that the business will be able to *add value* more efficiently. Cost advantages may be gained from four key areas:

- *Lower input costs* – the business may have access to input factors which are cheaper than those available to competitors. This can include raw materials, energy or labour. Lower input costs can be gained by a number of means.

Particularly important are access to unique sources of inputs (say, through special contractual arrangements or from geographic location) and achieving buying power over suppliers.

- *Economies of scale* – a business must dilute its fixed costs (which are independent of output) over revenues (which are dependent on output). Hence, *unit* costs tend to fall as output increases. Fixed costs are those which must be borne regardless of the output achieved. These typically include 'head office' costs and often much of the marketing, sales and development activity. A larger output means that these costs are being used more productively. It may then give a business an overall cost advantage over competitors.

- *Experience curve economies* – experience curve economies are a consequence of the business learning how to generate its outputs. As a business gains experience in adding value, the cost of adding that value is reduced. In short, practice pays! A large number of studies over a variety of different industries has found that a strict mathematical relationship holds between unit cost and output experience. This relationship is exponential. That is, costs fall by a fixed amount every time output is doubled. This means that for a linear output, the cost reductions achieved in a particular time period are seen to fall off as time goes on. This exponential relationship is shown in Figure 22.2.

    Like economies of scale, experience curve economies are related to output. However, the two should not be confused. Whereas economies of scale depend on output in a particular *period*, experience curve economies are a result of *cumulative* output. In general, the firm with the highest cumulative output in a market will be in a position to have developed the lowest unit cost. Most studies of experience curve economies have concentrated on production costs. However, the principle is a general one and applies to any cost of adding value. So experience curve economies may be sought in other parts of the firm's value addition process such as sales, marketing, procurement, etc.

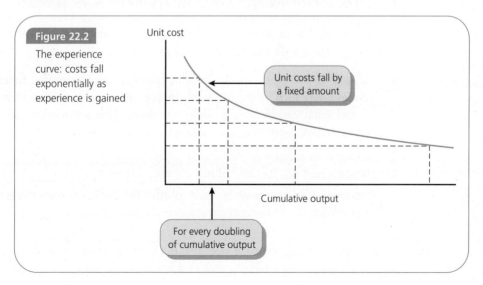

Figure 22.2

The experience curve: costs fall exponentially as experience is gained

Unit cost

Unit costs fall by a fixed amount

Cumulative output

For every doubling of cumulative output

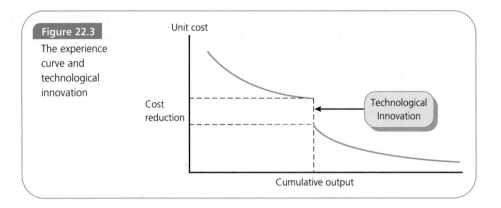

Figure 22.3

The experience curve and technological innovation

- **Technological innovation** – a firm's costs are, technically, the cost of adding a particular amount of value to an input in order to create a saleable output. Costs are related to the technology used by the business to add value. A technological innovation can provide a cost advantage by enabling value to be added more efficiently. In practice a technological innovation can be used to 'reset' the experience curve at a lower level (Figure 22.3). Such innovation often relates to production technology but in principle it can apply to any value-adding activity within the organisation.

Knowledge sources

Knowledge can be valuable. A firm may enjoy a competitive advantage if it knows things that its competitors do not. This knowledge might be in any one of a number of areas:

- *Product knowledge* – a special understanding of the products (or services) that make up the market. Critically, this knowledge must be used to create offerings which are more attractive to buyers. Product knowledge must be used in conjunction with knowledge of the *market*.

- *Market knowledge* – special insights into the way the market functions. This includes areas such as the needs of the consumer, the way in which customers buy and what can be used to influence them. This knowledge can be used to create effective marketing and selling strategies.

- *Technical knowledge* – a special understanding and competence in making and delivering the offering to the marketplace. This knowledge is not valuable on its own. Rather it must be used to offer the customer something different: a better product, a lower cost product or a better service.

Knowledge does not come for free. It is the result of investment. Product and technical knowledge arise from research and development activities. Market knowledge comes from market research and market analysis. It should be remembered that knowledge is not in itself valuable. It only forms the basis of a competitive advantage if it is used to deliver new value to the customer.

Relationship sources

Relationships are not just a 'nice to have' add-on to business activity, they are fundamental to it. A relationship establishes trust and trust adds value by reducing the need for contracts and monitoring. A business may be able to build a competitive advantage on the basis of the special relationships it enjoys with its stakeholders. Building relationships is essential if the business is to locate itself in a secure, and supportive, network.

The idea of entrepreneurial networks has been considered earlier in Section 11.4. The notion of building competitive advantage on the basis of relationships resonates with the idea of locking the venture into a set of secure and rewarding network links that competitors find it hard, or at least expensive, to break. Networks built on trust and confidence are valuable because they minimise transaction costs. Kay (1996) considers the role of trust in developing and maintaining economic relationships.

- *Relationship with customers* – a firm's relationship with its customers is, of course, a critical dimension of its success. The relationship can be built in a number of ways. Much depends on the nature of the products being sold to the customer and the number of customers the firm has to deal with. A business selling a small number of highly valuable products to a few customers is in a different situation from one selling a large number of relatively low-value items to a great number of customers.

  Relationships can be personal, that is, created through individual contact. Account management and sales activities are important in this respect. The sales–buyer interaction is both a one-to-one contact and a conduit through which value can flow from the business to its customers. If a large number of customers are involved, and personal contact is not possible, then contact may be sustained via the media through advertising and public relations.

  Critical to the relationship with customers is *reputation*. A reputation for delivering products which do what they say they will and for delivering them with a high degree of service, and for undertaking business in a fair and equitable way, is invaluable. Reputation can be hard to build up. It is, however, quite easy to lose.

- *Relationship with suppliers* – suppliers are best regarded as partners in the development of an end market. They are integral to the network the business needs to build up around itself. A business can put itself in a stronger position to deliver value to its customers if its suppliers themselves show flexibility and responsiveness. Further, suppliers can be encouraged to innovate on behalf of the business. All of this means that the relationship with suppliers has to go beyond just the concern with negotiating over prices. Though suppliers need to share value with their customers, the game need not be zero sum. A customer working with its suppliers can address the end market better and create more overall value to be shared than one working against its suppliers.

● *Relationship with investors* – of all stakeholders it is, perhaps, investors who have the most transparent relationship with the entrepreneurial venture. In economic terms their concern is the most one-dimensional: they are concerned to maximise their returns. Investors are, however, still human beings. They engage in communication and relationship building with the entrepreneur. They respond not only to actual returns but also if they feel their interests are being properly addressed by the entrepreneur.

The support of investors can be critical to success. Any venture will have its ups and downs, especially in its early stages. When things are not going too well, the support of investors is invaluable. If they insist on liquidating their investment then, at best, problems will be exacerbated; at worst, the business may not survive. The support of investors can be maintained by developing a strategy to communicate actively with them. This will involve managing the investors' expectations, building their confidence in the venture and avoiding 'surprises' which lead investors to make hasty judgements.

● *Relationship with employees* – building a motivating and productive relationship with employees is one of the entrepreneur's most important activities. It is the employees who deliver the actions which convert the entrepreneur's vision into reality. The entrepreneurial venture may not enjoy many of the cost, technical and relationship advantages that established players can call upon. All they have is their people, their interest, motivation and drive on behalf of the business. The entrepreneur must draw this out by understanding their employees' motivations and adopting the right leadership strategies.

Structural sources

The final area in which the entrepreneurial business can aspire to develop a basis for competitive advantage is in its structure. Structural advantages arise as a consequence not so much of *what* the business does but the *way* it goes about doing things. This is a function not only of its formal structure, the pre-defined way in which individuals will relate to each other, but also in its informal structure, the 'unofficial' web of relationships and communication links which actually define it, and its *culture*, which governs how those relationships will function and evolve. Since new entrants are unlikely to enjoy cost advantages in the early stages of the business at least, and because relationship advantages take time to build up and knowledge advantages require investment, the entrepreneurial business is likely to be highly dependent on structure-based advantages.

A business can gain a competitive advantage from its structure if that structure allows it to perform better in the marketplace. Such a structural advantage may arise from having the business co-ordinated by a strong leader who keeps the

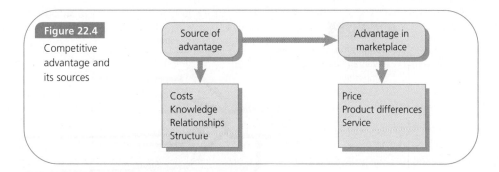

Figure 22.4 Competitive advantage and its sources

Source of advantage → Advantage in marketplace

Costs
Knowledge
Relationships
Structure

Price
Product differences
Service

business on track and focuses it on the opportunities at hand. Such leadership ensures that resources are used effectively. The business may also be better at gaining information from the marketplace and using it to make decisions.

This might allow it to be more responsive to the needs of customers and so be quicker to offer them new products and services.

Another structural advantage can arise if the individuals who make it up emphasise *tasks* (what needs doing) rather than *roles* (what they feel their job descriptions say they should do). Such an attitude enables the business to be flexible, to focus on its customers and keep fixed costs to a minimum.

Competitive advantages in the marketplace can be built on a number of platforms within the organisation (Figure 22.4). Costs, knowledge, relationships and structures may all be used to offer the customer value in a way that competitors cannot. This makes them sources from which a competitive advantage may be developed in the marketplace. They have the potential to bring success to the venture. However, if this success is to be long term, the competitive advantages must be maintained in the face of competitive activity. They must be *sustained*.

22.2 How competitive advantage is established

Key learning outcome

An appreciation of the ways in which competitive advantages may be established but can be lost to competitors.

The business world does not stand still. Competitors are aware of each other to varying degrees. They become *acutely* aware if they lose business, or at least are prevented from gaining it, by the activities of a competitor. They may go on to develop an understanding of *why* that business is performing better than they are. A successful business cannot hide its competitive advantage for long. Competitors will then be tempted to imitate and recreate that competitive advantage for themselves. This may be easier said than done. If competitors find a competitive advantage hard to imitate, then the entrepreneurial firm may go on enjoying the rewards that advantage offers. If the advantage is hard to imitate it is said to be *sustainable*.

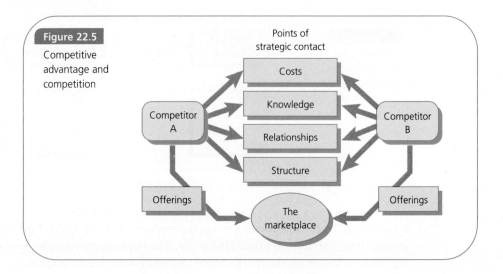

Figure 22.5

Competitive advantage and competition

A reverse perspective is illuminating in this instance. To understand how competitive advantage may be sustained demands an appreciation of how it can be *lost*. Quite simply, a competitive advantage is lost if a competitor *gains* it. In order to offer something that gains an advantage in the marketplace, a business must create for itself the *source* of that advantage. The framework developed in the previous section applies, so competitive advantage is lost to competitors if they achieve lower *costs*, or gain *knowledge* that was exclusive to and valuable to the venture, or build a stronger network of *relationships* than the venture enjoys, or develop *structural* advantages (advantages in the way the business organises itself).

An entrepreneurial venture must constantly strive to prevent competitors gaining a relative advantage in these areas. While the venture actually meets its competitors in the marketplace the basis of competitive advantages provides the points of *strategic contact* between the venture and its competitors. It is these things which give the venture the *power* to compete (Figure 22.5).

The entrepreneur must be on their guard as to the ways in which competitors might gain the upper hand in terms of competitive advantage. They must consider the possible ways in which competitors might gain the advantage, and be aware of these when they are developing their strategy. A sound strategy must be built on a competitive advantage which can be sustained. Knowing this is part of understanding the nature of the market, the players who make it up and competition within it. The decisions which relate to developing a competitive advantage must be made in relation to the considerations on how *costs*, *knowledge*, *relationships* and *structure* deliver advantages in the marketplace.

Considerations in relation to cost advantages

Here the chief considerations relate to how cost advantages may be used in the marketplace to achieve volume gains (in other words, how price sensitive the customer is); how competitors can use factor prices to their advantage; and how volume gains are rewarded with further cost reductions (i.e. to what extent volume and cost are linked in a virtuous circle via economies of scale and experience effects). Also important is how established the cost structure of the industry is. In particular, is a technological innovation that changes the cost rules likely to occur, and if so, how quickly will it spread through the sector?

Some important specific questions are:

1 How important is price to the customer?

2 How important is price to intermediaries and distributors?

3 Can volume be gained if price is reduced (that is, is demand elastic)?

These questions may be answered by the use of appropriate market research techniques. Some key discoveries to be made through market research are:

- Have all the players in the market access to the same inputs?

- Do some players enjoy exclusive access to low-cost inputs?

- Are economies of scale important?

- If so, does one player have a significant *period* volume advantage?

- Are experience economies important?

- If so, has one player a *cumulative* volume advantage?

- Do any players have a *technological advantage* that influences costs?

- Is a technological innovation that will alter costs likely in the future?

- If so, how quickly would such a technological innovation spread through the industry?

- How expensive would it be to adopt any such cost-reducing technological innovations?

These questions may be answered by an analysis of the industry's structure and from knowledge of its technological base. The answers will illuminate the possibility of sustaining a cost-based advantage. In short, it will be sustainable if price is important to the customer and one player can gain a cost advantage from experience or technological sources.

Considerations in relation to knowledge advantages

Here the considerations relate to how exclusive knowledge may be gained, used and protected by the players in a sector.

Some important specific questions are as follows.

- Is the knowledge the industry uses established or is it in a state of rapid development? (This involves consideration of whether the industry is a 'high-tech' one which spends heavily on product research and development or marketing research.)

- Do the businesses in the industry use a common pool of knowledge or do they rely on their own localised knowledge?

- Is knowledge developed 'in house' or are external organisations (for example, business service firms such as market research agencies and consultancies and 'non-profit' organisations such as universities) important?

- How important to the industry are knowledge protection devices such as patents, copyrights and registered designs?

Again, these questions can be answered through an appropriate analysis of the industry, its environment and its technology. Clearly, knowledge which is important to delivering customer value, is localised and is protectable offers a more sustainable basis for competitive advantage than knowledge which is accessible to all.

Considerations in relation to relationship advantages

Relationships are the 'glue' that holds the business network together. If relationships are long term and secure, then the network can be thought of as 'tight'. If relationships are transitory and easily broken, then the network is 'loose'. A new entrant will find a tight network hard to break into. It may be expensive to break old relationships and establish new ones. On the other hand, once a location in that network has been established the business will find it easy to defend its position. Conversely, a loose network, while being easy to enter, will offer little security from competitors. Some important specific questions are:

- What means are used to establish and maintain relationships with customers? (Personal contact (e.g. sales activity) or contact via the media (e.g. advertising).)

- Are relationships with customers long term or short term? (Consider whether purchases are one-off or repeat. Is after-sales support important?)

- What *risks* does the buyer face in buying and using the product? (What sort of investment does it entail? What can go wrong when using it?)

- How can a sense of *trust* between the buyer and seller aid the management of those risks?

- How important is the seller's *reputation* to the buyer?

- On what basis can reputation be built? (Consider issues such as product quality, service, ethical standards, behaviour.)

A particularly effective entrepreneurial strategy is to identify a sector in which the network is loose and to create value through 'tightening it up' by offering a higher level of commitment and service. This also locks out competitors and makes the advantage gained sustainable.

Considerations in relation to structural advantages

As noted in the previous section, structural advantages arise as a consequence not so much of *what* the business does, but the *way* it goes about doing things. A business can gain an advantage over its competitors by having a structure in which roles are more flexible (which can lead to lower costs), by being more focused on the market and so more responsive to signals from customers and competitors, and then by using those signals to make faster and better decisions about how to serve the customer. Some important specific questions are:

● What kind of organisational *structures* do businesses in the sector adopt? (Consider, in particular, how important are functional departments, team working, *ad hoc* structures.)

● How important are *formal* structures? (Consider how the way things *really* happen compares to the way businesses say they *should* happen.)

● What kind of *decision-making processes* are used? (Over what timescale are plans made? Who is involved in decision making? How are particular decisions justified within organisations?)

● How do firms in the sector identify, process and respond to market signals? (Consider whether the market research is formalised. How is pricing policy determined? How is new product development organised?)

● What *cultures* are adopted by businesses in the sector? (Consider customer focus versus internal concerns; entrepreneurial versus bureaucratic attitudes; the importance of tasks versus roles.)

● What leadership styles are adopted? (Consider whether they are authoritarian or consensus based. Is power exercised through the control of resources or the communication of vision? Is there a focus on tasks or a focus on people?)

Rigid structures provide the entrepreneur with a means of focusing and directing their organisation but they are ambivalent as a source of competitive advantage. It may be better to allow people to use their skills and insights by pushing decision making down the organisation – particularly when it is in a turbulent environment.

Understanding the answers to all of these questions gives the entrepreneur an insight into the way they can establish a competitive advantage in the marketplace in a way which has a secure and distinctive base within their business. Further, it indicates the potential which a particular competitive advantage has to be *sustainable* in the face of competitive pressure.

(22.3) Maintaining competitive advantage

> **Key learning outcome**
>
> An understanding of the ways in which competitive advantage may be sustained.

Identifying a competitive advantage, that is, something the customer finds both different and attractive, and securing that on the basis of some aspect of the business, be it *costs*, *knowledge*, *relationships* or *structure*, in a way which both provides a source for that advantage and differentiates the business from competitors is the *starting point* for long-term success. In order to *ensure* that it happens, the business must make sure that the competitive advantage cannot be imitated, and so the profits it promises cannot be eroded, by competitors. The entrepreneur must decide not only what the competitive advantage of the venture they establish will be but also how it will be *sustained*.

Sustaining cost advantages

The key decision here is how will the business keep its costs lower than competitors? There can only be *one* cost leader in a market. If it is to be based on scale and experience curve economies, cost leadership demands *output volume* leadership. This means gaining and maintaining the highest (or at least highest volume) market share. This can prove to be expensive if the market is price sensitive. Competitors will be willing to compete by cutting their prices. The cost leader will have to use their cost advantage to establish a price below that of competitors' costs. This may mean a low, or even zero, profit margin. A cost leadership strategy may mean a long haul with poor profit levels until competitors have been 'seen off'.

The temptation to increase prices to gain short-term profits must be resisted since this will create a 'price umbrella' under which less efficient competitors can shelter. If the entrepreneur is a later entrant to the market and coming in from behind, then they may need to invest heavily in the short term to gain a rapid cumulative volume advantage over competitors. Again, this can prove to be expensive in the short run with substantial returns offered only in the long term. This, of course, introduces a number of risks.

Further, even though experience cost reductions are a function of output volume they do not occur by right. They have to be *managed*. For the cost leader, cost control has to take centre stage, i.e. driving costs down must take priority over all other considerations. This demands that powerful cost control systems be in place. This in turn will influence the leadership and motivation strategies adopted by the entrepreneur and the culture of the organisation they create. Such 'single-minded' organisations are not to everyone's taste, a factor which needs to be considered when recruiting and building the management team.

If the cost leadership is to be established on the basis of a technological innovation then the entrepreneur needs to be sure why they, and they alone, will have access to that technology. It is best to assume that competitors will eventually gain access to the innovation even if it is secured through patents and other intellectual property devices (see below). In respect to this it is best to use the innovation as the *starting point* to gain an initial cost advantage, which can be built on and sustained using scale and experience effects.

Even if all this is achieved, the entrepreneur must be sensitive to the attentions of anti-trust regulators. A strategy which achieves a large market share on the basis of squeezing competitors out on price may be a just reward for doggedly pursuing efficiency. To outsiders, however, it may seem like an unfair monopoly.

In conclusion, there can only be one cost leader in a market. A cost leadership strategy is one which is challenging and, in the short term at least, expensive, to sustain.

Sustaining knowledge advantages

Knowledge advantages are based on understanding of both the product and the market. These two things operate in tandem with one other. An understanding of what is offered must be tempered with an understanding of why the customer wants it. Generally in business, knowledge soon becomes public. Even if knowledge is 'secure' within the business, the process of launching products and promoting them to the customer sends clear signals to competitors.

Knowledge may be 'protected' by means of patents and other intellectual property devices such as copyrights and registered designs. In principle, these prevent competitors from using the knowledge. They grant the holder a monopoly over the innovation arising from the knowledge. In some industries intellectual property is very important, for example in the biotechnology industry. In others, such as engineering, it is less so. However, the use of intellectual property devices as a means of securing a competitive advantage should be approached cautiously. Patents and other devices are not granted for every new idea, rather they must reflect a *significant* technological innovation. Even if the new idea is significant, the registration process is time consuming, demands the aid of experts and can be expensive. Registration may also involve the public posting of the invention prior to any patent being granted. In effect this means presenting the patent to challenge by holders of other patents. This can tip off competitors. Often not just one but a number of variations of the idea will have to be patented in order to ensure that competitors do not get round the patent by presenting minor variations to the market.

Furthermore, the patent registration will have to be obtained in a variety of regions if global cover is desired. If comprehensive cover is not obtained then competitors may get round the patent by producing the product in an area where the patent does not hold. Even if global cover is obtained, some countries are lax (because of weak legal structures or even, in some cases, as a matter of policy) in enforcing intellectual property law. If the law-enforcement mechanisms will act to protect the patent, it is still down to the patent holder to police their property and challenge infringements. Even if all this is done, there are strict time limits on the protection offered.

These drawbacks do not mean that patents are not valuable, just that they should not be relied upon to provide a source of competitive advantage on their own terms. Rather, they should be used *tactically* to provide an initial advantage which can then be used to develop other advantages based on cost and relationships.

Sustaining relationship advantages

Relationships are valuable because they establish *trust* and trust brings down costs for a variety of reasons. First, it reduces the need for a buyer to be constantly scanning the market for offerings. They simply go to a supplier they know. Second, it eliminates the need to establish detailed contracts between buyer and seller. Third, it eliminates the need for a constant *policing* of those contracts. In this context, we may consider *all* stakeholders to be engaged in contract building with the venture, not just customers, though of course a trusting relationship with the customer is particularly important and has immediate payoffs.

If trust is built up it can then form the basis for sustaining competitive advantage. Given that cost and knowledge advantages are most easily accrued by the large (and that usually means the established) business, trust can be a potent ingredient in entrepreneurial success, particularly in the early stages of the venture.

Trust can only be built by establishing and developing relationships which exist on a number of levels. At one level is the experience the parties have of each other through personal contact, say as a result of direct selling activities. The salesperson is not just informing the buyer of a firm's outputs; they are acting as an ambassador for the business as a whole. At the next level is communication through the media using advertising and public relations activity. Product branding and company image are important mediators. At another level is the general *reputation* that a business builds in the mind of the buyer through their wider experience of it. Reputation is established not through absolute outcomes but through outcomes in relation to *expectations*. Quite simply, if expectations are exceeded then a stakeholder will be very satisfied by the outcome; if they are not met then the stakeholder will be disappointed and feel let down.

Thus a strategy for building and maintaining trust must have three interlocking aspects:

1. *The management of expectations.* The entrepreneur must take charge of what the other party (be they a customer, an investor, a supplier or an employee) expects to come out of the relationship. While entrepreneurs are right to strive to deliver on behalf of the stakeholders in their venture they must avoid 'over-promising' as this can easily lead to disappointment, dissatisfaction and a feeling that trust has been broken if what has been promised is not delivered.

2 *The management of outcomes.* Entrepreneurs must take responsibility for what their venture delivers finally to its stakeholders. They must ensure that these outcomes at least meet, or are better than, what the stakeholder expected. If for any reason they are not (and no one, not even the most effective entrepreneur, can control all contingencies) then the entrepreneur is faced with the challenge of addressing the stakeholder's disappointment and managing the process of rebuilding trust. The details of how this must be done will vary depending on the stakeholder, the circumstances and the extent of failure that has occurred. The golden rule, however, is that disappointment should never be ignored!

3 *The management of communication.* Expectations and the delivery of outcomes occur on a stage built by communication. Communications between the entrepreneur (and the venture's staff) and stakeholders can take a variety of forms. They can be formal or informal, personal or impersonal, directed to a specific stakeholder or widely broadcast. They may take place via a variety of media. The entrepreneur must be aware of the communication channels that connect and draw the venture's stakeholders together, learning how to use them and how to reinvigorate them constantly. He or she must also take control of how those channels are used. In particular, the entrepreneur must take clear responsibility for the promises that are being made on behalf of the venture; not just the promises they make themselves, but also those being made by other people on behalf of the venture.

Sustaining structural advantages

Structural advantages arise when a business, by virtue of the way it organises itself, becomes more attuned to signals from the marketplace, more acute in its decision making and more flexible in responding to the needs of customers. Such responsiveness is a product of the organisation's structure, that is, the network of responsibilities and communication links which give the business its form.

As with relationship advantages, the entrepreneurial business is in a strong position to enjoy structural advantages over larger businesses. Established, older businesses may be hampered by internal structures. These structures may serve an important function but once started they tend to develop a momentum of their own. This can mean that they continue to exist after their usefulness has declined. In the entrepreneurial business, on the other hand, internal structures will be in a state of flux and will be forming in response to market demands.

Decision making within the established firm may also be less acute. Key decision makers may be insulated from the realities of the market, the signals it is sending and the opportunities it is presenting. Decision making may also be distorted by internal 'political' concerns which put internal factional interests ahead of those of the customer and the business as a whole. The entrepreneur, however, should be using the venture's organisation to facilitate and focus decision making, rather than to hinder it. In addition, they are in a position to use strong leadership to draw disparate groups together and co-ordinate their actions.

This demands that entrepreneurs keep themselves in touch with their market and that they do not allow themselves to be 'swamped' by their organisations. Communication systems should be designed with the primary objective of feeding information about the market to decision makers. While information on the internal state of the business is important, this should be used to support market-orientated decision making, not be used to compromise it.

Competitive advantage is *dynamic* not static. Once a venture gains a competitive advantage in the marketplace it must use the success this brings to constantly reinvent the advantage. Success offers rewards in excess of market norms. These rewards must be reinvested in the business. This investment should not be aimed at merely reinforcing the existing competitive advantage but at modifying it and, if need be, creating the basis for entirely new ones.

If the venture aims to become a *cost leader* then it must invest in volume leadership and cost control. If it aims to use *exclusive knowledge* then it must invest in developing its understanding of the products and services offered to the market, the way in which they meet the needs of customers and the way in which customers decide to buy. If *relationships* are to be used then investment must take place in developing existing relationships and creating new ones. This means managing expectations, outcomes and communication, and all of these in turn mean investment in the people who communicate to customers on behalf of the business. Maintaining a *structural advantage* demands investment in human and communication systems. The business cannot afford to become stale, that is, to let its structures gain a life and a *raison d'être* independent of their function in serving the market. It also demands investment in *change*. Change is not only a structural phenomenon, it also represents development in individual attitudes and organisational culture. The rewards gained from a competitive advantage must be reinvested to maintain, develop and renew the basis of that advantage within the business (Figure 22.6).

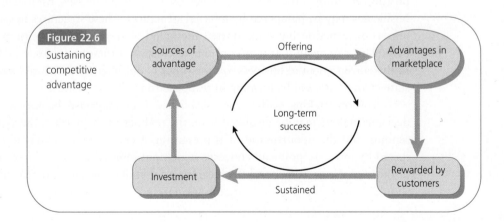

Figure 22.6

Sustaining competitive advantage

Summary of key ideas

- The final stage of the strategic window is *closing* it.

- Closing the window means creating a *competitive advantage* so that the venture can go on exploiting the opportunity in the face of competitive pressures.

- A competitive advantage is something the business can do that is valuable for the customer which competitors find difficult to match.

- A competitive advantage has a source within the business. The key sources are lower *costs*; *knowledge* of the product and market; stronger *relationships* within the network; and a more flexible and responsive organisational *structure*.

- A competitive advantage must be actively maintained if it is to be *sustainable*.

Research theme

Competitive advantage and the success of Internet ventures

The past few years have seen the start-up, success and failure of a large number of Internet-based entrepreneurial ventures. Good case studies have been written describing these ventures in detail. Undertake an analysis of a sample of these (ideally 10 or more), describing ventures that have been successful and some that have not, looking for sources of competitive advantage, the firm's core competences and how these were used to underpin the success of the venture. As a comparitor, also evaluate incumbent non-Internet-based ventures in the same sectors. Use John Kay's framework described in this chapter and Prahalad and Hamel's competence-based approach described in Section 2.1 to guide this evaluation. How does the presence of sources of competitve advantage and core competences correlate with the long-term performance of the venture? What are the implications for planning and developing strategy for new Internet-based ventures?

Suggestions for further reading

Abernathy, W.J. and Wayne, K. (1974) 'Limits of the learning curve', *Harvard Business Review*, Sept–Oct, pp. 109–19.

Bamberger, I. (1989) 'Developing competitive advantage in small and medium-sized firms', *Long Range Planning*, Vol. 22, No. 5, pp. 80–8.

Barnett, W.P., Grieve, H.R. and Park, D.Y. (1994) 'An evolutionary model of organisational performance', *Strategic Management Journal*, Vol. 15, pp. 11–28.

Brock Smith, J. and Barclay, D.W. (1997) 'The effects of organisational differences and trust on the effectiveness of selling partnership relationships', *Journal of Marketing*, Vol. 61, pp. 3–21.

Doney, P.M. and Cannon, J.P. (1997) 'An examination of the nature of trust in buyer–seller relationships', *Journal of Marketing*, Vol. 61, pp. 35–51.

Ghemawat, P. (1985) 'Building strategy on the experience curve', *Harvard Business Review*, Mar–Apr, pp. 143–9.

Kay, J. (1993) *Foundations of Corporate Success*, Oxford: Oxford University Press.

Kay, N.M. (1996) 'The economics of trust', *International Journal of the Economics of Business*, Vol. 3, No. 2, pp. 249–60.

Lieberman, M.B. and Montgommery, D.B. (1988) 'First mover advantages', *Strategic Management Journal*, Vol. 9, pp. 41–58.

Pitt, L.F. and Jeantrout, B. (1994) 'Management of customer expectations in service firms: a study and checklist', *The Service Industries Journal*, Vol. 14, No. 2, pp. 170–89.

Porter, M. (1980) *Competitive Strategy: Techniques for Analysing Industries and Competitors*, New York: Free Press.

Porter, M. (1985) *Competitive Advantage: Creating and Sustaining Superior Performance*, New York: Free Press.

Russell, M. (1984) 'Scales true economies', *Management Today*, May, pp. 82–4.

Snell, R. and Lau, A. (1994) 'Exploring local competencies salient for expanding small businesses', *Journal of Management Development*, Vol. 13, No. 4, pp. 4–15.

Stevens, H.H. (1976) 'Defining corporate strengths and weaknesses', *Sloan Management Review*, Spring, pp. 51–68.

Teas, R.K. (1993) 'Expectations, performance evaluation and consumer's perceptions of quality', *Journal of Marketing*, Vol. 57, pp. 18–34.

Tellis, G.J. and Golder, P.N. (1996) 'First to market, first to fail? Real causes of enduring market leadership', *Sloan Management Review*, Winter, pp. 65–75.

Voss, C. (1992) 'Successful innovation and implementation of new processes', *Business Strategy Review*, Spring, pp. 29–44.

Zahra, S.A., Nash, S. and Bickford, D.J. (1995) 'Transforming technological pioneering into competitive advantage', *Academy of Management Executive*, Vol. 9, No. 1, pp. 17–31.

Zeithaml, V., Berry, V. and Parasuraman, A. (1993) 'The nature and determinants of a customer's expectations of a service', *Journal of the Academy of Marketing Science*, Vol. 21, No. 1, pp. 1–12.

IPOs hint at biotech recovery

FT

2 May 2002

But some analysts say the market is driven by venture capitalists, write **Patrick Jenkins** and **David Firn**

Could Britain's biotechnology bubble be forming again? Following Thursday's flotation announcement from Corin, an orthopaedic device maker, and recent IPO promises from YM Biosciences and Ark Therapeutics, optimists believe 16 months of inactivity is about to give way to a buoyant market for new biotech listings.

Sir Christopher Evans, a biotech entrepreneur and now chairman of Merlin Ventures, a big investor in Ark, is sanguine. 'Ark is a bloody good company. If it can't get away, it doesn't bode well for anyone.'

But pessimists say the hurdles remain high, even for the best candidates. There is a lack of interest in IPOs – with only four main market floats this year – and investor sentiment in biotechs is even more negative.

'The whole sector has been making huge promises,' says Kate Bingham, a partner at Schroder Ventures Life Sciences. 'But they haven't delivered.'

Fingers have been badly burnt – not only by companies that have collapsed, such as Scotia Holdings last year and Bioglan Pharma in February, but also by declining valuations of relatively healthy companies.

Companies that have experienced drug testing setbacks have lost on average 50 per cent of their valuations this year, according to Goldman Sachs data.

That is better than the 1997 rout following collapses at British Biotech and Cortecs, but liquidity has suffered.

The average daily volume of shares traded in any UK listed biotech – bar Celltech, the biggest – is just 89,000. With any stock transaction moving the share price, it is

little wonder investors are spurning such companies.

'Biotech sentiment is always either 100 per cent on or 100 per cent off. Right now, it's 100 per cent off,' says Steve McGarry, analyst at Goldman Sachs. 'Any biotech that floats now is either brave or desperate.'

Desperation, Mr McGarry argues, is exactly the motivation for this first clutch of floats. 'The VC backers want out and are pushing for a float no matter what the state of the market.'

Jeremy Curnock Cook, a former fund manager, agrees: 'The venture guys are beginning to hurt. Having to hang on for a market upturn is ruining their performance figures.'

But the VCs' pain could be the market's gain. Pre-IPO financing has taken companies further down the line to commercial launch and profitability and should reduce the risk profile for investors.

'That is the critical difference this time round,' says Mr Curnock Cook. 'Investors will want products that are close to commercialisation.'

Microscience, the vaccine company, RiboTargets and Strakan, the drug discovery companies, and Inpharmatica and Oxagen, the genomics companies, have each raised more than GBP25m from VCs in the past year or so.

Corin shares will be priced at 100p–110p, valuing the company at GBP39m, and 50 institutions will invest a total GBP32m, GBP10m more than envisaged.

Is the apparent early success of the Corin float a harbinger of better times for the sector? Some bankers say it won't be. Corin, they say, has attracted investors because it makes tangible products and is profitable, while companies such as Ark and YM are founded on biotech's traditional blue-skies research, and investors remain nervous.

The likes of Adprotech, the protein engineering company, and DeNovo, the cell research group, could face a similar attitude. For them and for continental Europeans, the Ark float will be the one to watch. A clutch of European companies – Wilex, Atugen, Micromet, Morphochem and Epigenomics – are ready to go.

The situation is most critical in Germany, where generous support for biotechnology

created more than 300 start-ups in the past decade.

Many of them raised venture capital at the height of the technology boom in 2000. But the crash of the Neuer Markt – Germany's junior exchange – last year has denied them access to public capital.

Andrew Allars, fund manager of Prelude Trust, says: 'The trouble with the market last time was that there was too much rubbish too early. I just hope this recovery will be more gentle and discriminating.'

Source: Financial Times, 2 May 2002.

Case 22.2

Crown Sports offered £42m for fitness clubs

3 December 2002

By **Sophy Buckley**

Steve Lewis, an entrepreneur, has offered £42m for the fitness clubs business of Crown Sports, the health and leisure club operator subject to a hostile takeover bid by its chairman.

Mr Lewis, who sold Axis – the sports club operator he founded – to Crown in 2001 for just under £15m in cash and shares, yesterday said he made his move after seeing the value of his holding fall.

He and other former Axis shareholders own about 3 per cent of Crown.

He said he has yet to receive a formal response but that he planned to sell the poorer performing clubs, tighten management costs and take the company private.

He said: 'The stock market doesn't reflect reality. The share prices reflect sentiment and people's perception of future profit when they have no real idea [of what's going to happen].'

He said sustainable growth was not rewarded, just plans designed to produce fast growth.

'Just look at Cannons. It is probably the best performing company in the business but when it was a public company it was perceived as too conservative,' he said. News of Mr Lewis's offer comes as Jeff Chapman, who has stepped aside as chairman of Crown and who owns a 30 per cent stake, is considering lifting his 5p a share offer, worth £14.5m, possibly to 7p a share.

His original offer, made in October, was rejected as insufficient by the independent directors.

They argued that even after paying back debt, which stands at about £34m, greater shareholder value could be gained from breaking up the company.

Their assessment gained credence last month, when it was revealed that Alan Tait, who used to work for Crown in the golf division, had offered £14.5m, backed by a leading clearing bank, for the eight golf clubs. The independent directors have said they have also received other indicative offers.

Mr Lewis said that his offer, which is subject to due diligence, taken with Mr Tait's offer, was worth more to shareholders than Mr Chapman's, which was made through his vehicle Bennelong.

The independent directors could not be reached yesterday for comment.

The shares closed unchanged at 7p, giving the company a market value of £20.4m.

Source: *Financial Times*, 3 December 2002.

Discussion point

Compare and contrast the ways in which:
(a) a biotech firm
(b) a chain of sports clubs
might viably gain and sustain competitive advantage within their sectors.

Chapter 23

Gaining financial support: issues and approaches

Chapter overview

Attracting financial support for the venture is one of the entrepreneur's most important tasks. This chapter considers the supply of investment capital and how backers actually go about selecting investment opportunities. The chapter concludes by advocating that a major factor in successfully attracting investment is the entrepreneur having an understanding of the questions that investors need to ask and being prepared to answer them.

23.1 Sources and types of financial investment

Key learning outcome

A recognition of the different sources of capital available for investment in the entrepreneurial venture.

Investment capital is a valuable commodity. As with any other commodity, markets develop to ensure that supply meets demand. Though 'capital' is itself an undifferentiated commodity (one five-dollar bill is exactly like any five-dollar bill!) a number of different types of supplier emerge to offer investment capital. These different types of supplier differentiate themselves not in what they supply but in the *way* they supply the capital, the *price* they ask for that capital and the *supplementary services* they offer.

The interaction of supply and demand results in a *price* being set for the capital. This price is the *rate of return* the supplier (the lender or investor) expects from their investment. A number of factors influence the cost of the capital being offered. The critical factors are the *risk* of the investment (that is, the probability that the return will be less than that anticipated) and the *opportunity cost* (that is, the return that has to be forgone because alternative investments cannot be made). This *risk-rate of return line* provides one of the key dimensions along which investors differentiate themselves. In principle this mechanism should ensure that the amount of capital provided should be equal to that demanded by entrepreneurs. However, many entrepreneurs complain about a 'funding gap' – an inability to get hold of capital to support their ventures. Some politicians agree with them and demand that banks serve them better. However, market failure (due to capital providers' monopoly position, say) is only one explanation. It could also be the case that the entrepreneur's assessment of the risks of his or her venture are lower than those of investors so the entrepreneur thinks the capital on offer is coming with too high a price tag. The issue of entrepreneurs' (over)optimism and its impact on investors is explored further in Section 23.4. The funding gap might also arise as a result of informational asymmetry between the entrepreneur and investor (an idea encountered in Section 2.3). Whatever its source, the funding gap presents problems to entrepreneurs, investors and the wider world that benefits from entrepreneurial activity. Harris (1995) investigates organisations that are attempting to address the funding gap.

Like in many markets, suppliers in the market for investment capital differentiate themselves. This differentiation is based on the type and level of capital they provide and the level of risk they are prepared to accept. Key supplies of capital include the following.

Entrepreneur's own capital

This is money that the entrepreneur owns. It may derive from personal savings, or it may be a 'lump sum' resulting from a capital gain or a redundancy package, in which case it might be quite a significant amount. The research by Blanchflower and Oswald quoted in Chapter 7 revealed the importance of inherited money in start-ups. Serial entrepreneurs liquidate their holdings in their ventures once they mature in order to pursue new business ideas. Clearly, the entrepreneur is free to use this capital as he or she wishes.

Informal investors

An entrepreneur may attract investment support on an informal basis from their family and friends. The expectations of what the returns will be, and when they might be gained, are usually set informally or, at most, semi-formally. Harrison and Dibben (1997) study the nature of informal investor decision making and find that in addition to rational evaluation of the business plan, personal trust in the entrepreneur is also important.

Internal capital networks

Many communities, especially those based around a group of people who are displaced and who are, or at least feel, excluded from the wider economic system, show strong entrepreneurial tendencies. This often enlivens and enriches the economy as a whole. Important examples include a variety of Asian groups in Britain, North Africans in France, Chinese expatriates in South-East Asia, and the Lebanese in West Africa. Such groups often encourage investment among themselves. These communities set up *internal capital networks* which direct capital towards new business opportunities within the community. These networks often have an international character. In emerging economies they provide very important conduits for inward investment.

Though often quite informal in a narrow legal sense, these networks are guided by a rich set of cultural rules and expectations. Risk, return and the way in which returns are made are often embedded in complex patterns of ownership and control of ventures.

Retained capital

The profits that a venture generates are, potentially, available to be reinvested in its development. However, such profits belong neither to the venture nor to the entrepreneur; rather they are the property of the *investors* who are backing the venture (this group may, of course, include the entrepreneur). Reinvesting the profits might offer a good investment opportunity, but it is an opportunity which the investor will judge like any other on the basis of risk, return and the possibility of taking the profits and seeking alternative investment opportunities.

Business angels

Business angels are individuals, or small groups of individuals, who offer up their own capital to new ventures. They are usually people who have been successful in business (perhaps as entrepreneurs themselves) and as a result have some money 'to play with'. Investment structure and return expectations vary, but are usually equity-based and codified in formal agreements. Business angels differ from other types of organisational investor in one important respect. They like to get involved in the ventures they are backing, and in addition to capital backing, they offer their skills, insights and experiences. As a result they usually seek investment opportunities in ventures where their knowledge or business skills are appropriate. Business angels are also more likely to select ventures in their own geographical locale. The development of informal venture capital in the UK is considered by Harrison and Mason (1996). Tashiro (1999) presents a good account of business angels in Japan.

Retail banking

Retail or 'high street' banks usually offer investment capital to new start-ups and expanding small firms. Support is almost inevitably in the form of loan capital and returns are subject to strict agreement. The bank will expect the entrepreneur to make a personal commitment and may seek collateral to reduce the risk of the deal.

The decision-making processes within banks that provide small business funds is explored by Berger and Udell (2002). Brau (2002) investigates the extent to which banks price anticipated owner-manager agency costs in their lending.

Corporate banking

To an extent the corporate banking sector picks up where retail banking stops. Corporate banks are interested in bigger investment opportunities and may settle for longer-range returns. Loan capital dominates but some equity may also be offered. Deals may be quite complex and involve conversions between the two forms of investment. Again, a significant commitment by the entrepreneur and asset security may be sought.

Venture capital

Venture capital is a critical source of investment for fast-growing entrepreneurial ventures. Venture capital companies usually seek large investment opportunities which are characterised by the potential for a fast, high rate of return. As such, they tend to take on higher degrees of risk than banks. Venture capital companies will rarely involve themselves with investments of less than half a million dollars and typically seek annual returns in excess of 50 per cent to be harvested over five years or less. Usually the deals are equity-based and they may be complex. However, a clear *exit strategy*, which enables the returns to the venture capital investment to be liquidated quickly, must be in place. A number of studies (e.g. Zacharakis *et al.* (1999) and Riquelme and Watson (2002)) have explored venture capitalists' judgements on the factors that lead to success and failure in entrepreneurial ventures. Devashis (2000) and Choudhury (2001) provide detailed accounts of the operation of venture capital systems in India and the Islamic world, respectively. Cook (2001) considers small business financing in the developing world.

Public flotation

A public flotation is a means of raising capital by offering shares in the venture to a pool of private investors. These shares can then be bought and sold in an open stock market or, in continental Europe, a *bourse*. There are a variety of stock markets through which capital may be raised. All mature economies have national stock markets of which London, New York and Tokyo are among the most important internationally. There are a number of *emerging* stock markets which trade stock from companies in the developing world and in the post-command economies of central and eastern Europe (that is, the economies that were under communist control until the late 1980s).

In addition to the stock markets for established companies, there are special stock markets for smaller businesses and for fast-growing ventures. The most important European small-company stock market is the Alternative Investments

Market (AIM) based in London. This market has some 265 companies listed and a capitalisation of nearly $10 billion. Other European small business markets include the Nouveau Marché in Paris, Easdaq based in Brussels and the Neuer Markt in Frankfurt. It is planned to link all these markets through a network dubbed EURO.NM. Small and fast-growing business investment in the USA is carried out through a market known as Nasdaq.

Government

Very few governments nowadays fail to see that they have an interest in encouraging enterprise. New businesses create jobs, bring innovation to the market and provide competitive efficiency. Across the world, however, governments differ in the extent to which and the way in which they engage in intervention to support the creation and survival of new and fast-growing businesses.

Support is usually given to new start-ups when capital for investment is hardest to obtain and when cash-flow can be at its tightest. Generally direct government investment is in decline. However, there are a number of quasi-governmental agencies which can direct grants towards the entrepreneurial start-up. In addition to capital grants, government may offer support in the form of consulting services and training. Examples of this include the Training and Enterprise Councils (TECs) in the UK and the Small Business Administration (SBA) in the USA. In continental Europe (and increasingly also in central and eastern Europe) local chambers of commerce play an important role in this respect. In addition to overt support, governments often give smaller firms a head-start through tax breaks.

Commercial partnerships

An entrepreneurial venture may look towards existing businesses as a source of investment capital. This will usually occur when the established business has a strategic interest in the success of the venture, for example if it is a supplier of a particularly innovative and valuable input. The support demonstrated by IBM for Microsoft in its early days is a case in point. Commercial partnerships can also occur when the venture is developing a technology which will be important to the established firm. The wide range of investments by established pharmaceutical companies in biotechnology start-ups in the 1980s provides an example of this.

There is a range of arrangements by which the established firm can impose control over its investment in the entrepreneurial venture. At one extreme is complete ownership, and at the other is a simple agreement to use the venture as a favoured supplier. In between there are a variety of forms of *strategic alliance*.

Choice of capital supply

The types and range of investment capital providers operating in an economy depend on the stage of development of that economy and a variety of other political and cultural factors. The choice of capital supplier by the entrepreneur is a decision which must be made in the light of the nature of the venture, its capital requirements, the stage of its development and the risks it faces.

23.2) How backers select investment opportunities

> **Key learning outcome**
>
> An appreciation of the process by which investors select investment opportunities.

Investment is a buying and selling process. The entrepreneur is trying to sell the venture as an investment opportunity, and the investor is looking to buy opportunities which offer a good return. As such, a consideration of the marketing-buying behaviour behind investment deals can provide an insight into how that process might be understood and so be managed to be more effective.

Tyebjee and Bruno (1984) have developed a model of the investment process. Though these workers used the model to understand venture capital investment, it is generic in form and so can be used to understand investment in general. The model is outlined in Figure 23.1.

The model identifies five key stages in the investment process and these are as follows.

Stage I: Deal origination

Deal origination is the process by which the entrepreneur and the investor first become aware of each other. This results from a mix of *searching* activity by the investor and *promotional* activity by the entrepreneur. Few venture capitalists actively search for new opportunities. They wait for the entrepreneur, or often a third

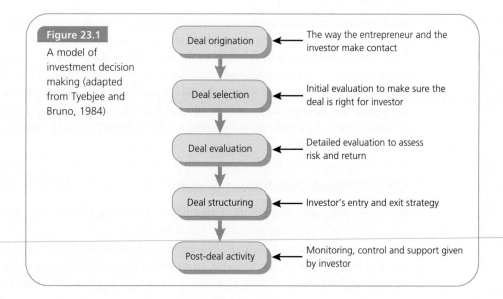

Figure 23.1
A model of investment decision making (adapted from Tyebjee and Bruno, 1984)

- **Deal origination** ← The way the entrepreneur and the investor make contact
- **Deal selection** ← Initial evaluation to make sure the deal is right for investor
- **Deal evaluation** ← Detailed evaluation to assess risk and return
- **Deal structuring** ← Investor's entry and exit strategy
- **Post-deal activity** ← Monitoring, control and support given by investor

party working on behalf of the entrepreneur, to approach them. Similarly, retail and corporate banks place the onus on the entrepreneur to make the first move.

If the business has shares which are available on a market then private and institutional investors will be active in seeking out stock which fits their portfolio and offers them an attractive return. Business angels are often informed about investment opportunities through informal networks of business contacts.

Stage II: Deal screening

Many investors specialise in certain types of investment. Deal screening reflects the initial evaluation of the proposal to see if it fits with the investor's profile of activities. Important criteria include the amount of investment being sought, the type of technology on which the venture is based, the industry sector of the venture and the venture's stage of growth.

Stage III: Deal evaluation

If the proposal fits with the investor's portfolio of activities, then a more detailed evaluation of the proposal may be carried out. The objective of this exercise is to compare the returns offered by the venture to the risk that it faces. The key factors to be considered in this evaluation will be the potential for the venture in terms of the innovation it is offering, the conditions in the market it aims to develop and the competitive pressures it will face. If this potential is good then consideration will also be made of the ability of the management team behind the venture to actually deliver it. The investor will also be interested in any security the entrepreneur can offer, say in the form of readily liquidisable assets.

Stage IV: Deal structuring

Deal structuring concerns the decisions that must be made in relation to how the initial investment will be made and how the investor will see that investment bear fruit. The critical issues in relation to the investment stage will be how much the entrepreneur is seeking and over what period that investment is to be made. Critical to the return stage will be the actual return offered, how long the investor must wait before that return is seen and the form it will take. For example, will it be cash or will it be a share in the company? If it is a stake in the company can it be liquidated readily?

Stage V: Post-investment activity

Investors, especially those with a significant interest in the venture, will usually retain a degree of involvement in it. There are two broad areas of post-investment activity: *monitoring* and *control*. Monitoring relates to the procedures which are put in place to enable the investor to evaluate the performance of the business so they can keep track of their investment. Financial reporting by way of a balance sheet and profit and loss account (see Section 24.2) provides a legally defined means by which the investor can monitor the business. Important investors may demand more frequent and detailed information, perhaps going beyond purely financial data. Steiner and Greenwood (1995) examine deal structuring and post-deal investment activities by venture capitalist. They conclude that breaking into the venture capital network is a significant task for the entrepreneur and that relationships are more important than business plans in securing deals. They also find that in many instances, a deadline imposed by the venture capitalists may be missed by the entrepreneur as a result of delays on the part of the venture capitalists themselves!

Control mechanisms give the investor an active role in the venture and power to influence the entrepreneur's and the venture's management decision making. One common control mechanism is for the investor to be represented on the firm's management team, perhaps as a director. Business angels often offer this not just as a control mechanism but, because of their experience and insights, as a positive contribution to the management of the venture.

This model highlights some of the key areas of information that are needed by the investor before they can make an effective investment decision. Providing that information and answering the investors' questions must form the basis of the entrepreneur's communication strategy towards the investor. This model can be seen in operation in a study by Mason and Harrison (1996) in which they describe the investment process of one particular group of business angels in great depth. The group under study was formed by a retired UK businessman after seeing business angels operate in the USA. Its members, selected on the basis of experience, compatible personalities and commitment, were attracted by an advertisement in the business opportunities column of the *Financial Times* newspaper. Deals were initiated by a variety of means, including newspaper advertisements and by independent business brokers. About half of all deals were initiated by the entrepreneur approaching the group. About one quarter were initiated by the group approaching an entrepreneur and the remaining quarter were the result of introduction by independent agents. All deals were initially offered in the form of a written proposal. Initial screening was undertaken by an individual member of the group. Some 80 per cent of the deals were eliminated at this stage because they did not look financially viable. The remaining 20 per cent were summarised in a standard format and offered to the whole group for comment. If the group felt the deal was worth exploring further (about 10 per cent of all initial proposals) then a project leader was appointed to evaluate the proposal in detail. This was done in conjunction with two other members of the group. This involved background research and a meeting with the investee company. After due consideration, the project team would make a formal presentation and recommendation to the whole group. If, and only if, all members of the group were in favour of the deal, then a formal offer would be made to the investee company. The project team would consider how to structure the deal for entry and exit and would probably offer support in the management of the venture. As in many areas of management, decision making in practice may differ markedly from the decision-making process managers claim to follow. In a study of differences in Australian venture capitalist in-use and espoused decision criteria, Shepherd (1999) found that venture capitalists tended to overstate factors that were relatively unimportant to and understate factors that were in fact important to their decisions. Morris *et al.* (2000) examine venture capitalists' support for portfolio entrepreneurs in South Africa.

23.3 The questions investors need answering

> **Key learning outcome**
>
> A recognition of the kind of information investors need before they can make an investment decision.

In a narrow sense investors are *rational* in that they seek the best possible return from their capital for a given level of risk. However, such rational behaviour is dependent on investors having information from which to make decisions and on their being able to make those decisions efficiently. Neither of these conditions is ever met fully. There is always an *informational asymmetry* between entrepreneur and investor. Clearly, the entrepreneur knows more about his or her venture than does the investor. That is why the investor employs the entrepreneur to run the business! Even if investors have all the information necessary to make an investment decision, they are still human beings who suffer the same cognitive limitations that all human beings face. Though they may be practised in making investment decisions, those decisions are not necessarily optimal in a precise economic sense. Rather, investors, like all human decision makers, exhibit *satisficing* behaviour; that is, they make the best decision given the information available, their abilities and the influence of cultural factors. Studies of business angels, for example, have revealed that they rarely use formal methods to determine the return on the investments they make mathematically, rather they seek investments that 'feel right'. A study by Shepherd (1999) draws a distinction between espoused and in-use decision making by venture capitalists. His findings indicate that the criteria venture capitalists *say* they are using may be different from what they *actually* use in decision-making practice.

Before an investor will make an investment they will need some information about the venture. Thus the entrepreneur will need to answer a series of questions about it. The key questions are as follows.

Is the venture of the right type?

Many, if not most, investors specialise in certain types of business. Private investors and business angels may confine themselves to industry sectors in which they have knowledge and experience. Some venture capitalists focus on investment opportunities in certain technological areas; for example, biotechnology or information technology. Another important dimension of specialisation is the *stage of development* of the business and the nature of the financing it requires. Of late, venture capitalists have shifted their attention away from new start-ups and have moved to investing in lower-risk management buy-outs (MBOs). Banks will support new start-ups through their retail arms, but will deal with expansion financing through their corporate operations.

The investor will need to be assured that the venture is in the right area and at the right stage for them.

How much investment is required?

Investors will be interested in the amount of financing required. This will be judged in relation to the business the investor is in, their expertise and the costs they face in monitoring and controlling their investments. Retail banks will offer loans from a few hundred to tens of thousands of pounds. Venture capitalists, on the other hand, are not interested in investments of less than about £250,000, and are only really interested in investments of several million pounds sterling. A market flotation is usually concerned with raising at least £5 million.

The key question is, is the investor really the right source given the level of investment needed?

What return is likely?

The return on investment is the likely financial outcome of making a specific investment. The investor will want to know on what basis this has been calculated. Further, he or she will ask how reasonable it is given the potential for the venture and its management team. The decision to invest will be based on an assessment of the returns in relation to the risks and how the investment opportunity compares to others available. However, it should be noted that even for quite large investments, this comparison may be made on an intuitive rather than an explicit basis. Certain investors specialise in different levels of risk. Venture capitalists seek more risk than retail banks. Specialist high-growth markets usually reflect higher-risk investments than mainstream ones.

What is the growth stage of the venture?

Critically, this question relates to what the investment capital is required for. Is it to start a new business or is it to fund the expansion of an established business? Is the venture at an early stage in its growth, requiring capital to fund an aggressive growth strategy, or is the business at a mature stage with the capital to be used to fund incremental growth? How does this impact on the risk entailed and return offered? Is this stage of growth right for the investor?

What projects will the capital be used for?

This question relates to how the capital will be used within the venture. Is it to cover cash-flow shortfalls which result from strong growth or is it to be used for a more specific project, such as development of new products, funding a sales drive or marketing campaign or entering export markets? Again, the question is how does this impact on risk, return and specialism from the point of view of the investor?

What is the potential for the venture?

The investors will want to know what the venture can be expected to achieve in the future. This will depend on two sets of factors: first, on its *market potential*: that is, how innovative its offering is, how much value this offers the customer in relation to what is already available, and the possibilities and limitations the venture faces in delivering this innovation to the customer. Second, it depends on the quality of the entrepreneur and the management team: that is, the skills and experience of the venture's key people and their ability to deliver the potential that the venture has. The critical question is, will the investor find the venture's potential attractive and if not, why not?

What are the risks for the venture?

To an investor, the risk of the venture is the probability that it will not deliver the return anticipated. Critical to judging this is an understanding of the assumptions that have been made in estimating the likely return. Some critical areas are assumptions about customer demand, the ability of the business to manage its costs, the ability of the venture to get distributors and other key partners on board, and the reaction of competitors.

The investors' judgement of risk will also depend on their ability to exit the investment by liquidating their holding. An investor will ask exactly how liquid the business is and whether or not the investment can be secured against particular liquidisable assets. How do the risks match up with what the investor will expect?

How does the investor get in?

The investor will wish to know exactly how their investment is to be made. Is it to be a lump sum upfront or will it take the form of a regular series of cash injections? The entrepreneur must ask whether this is the way the investor normally operates.

How does the investor get out?

The investor will want to know how they will see their return. Will it take the form of cash? If so, will it be a single cash payment at some point in the future, or will it be a series of payments over time? Alternatively, will it take the form of a holding of stock in the firm? If so, how can such a holding be liquidated? Loans are usually paid back in cash form whereas an equity holding will mature as a holding in the firm. Venture capitalists with equity holdings will insist on a clear exit strategy which will enable them to convert their equity to cash, either by selling on a market or converting it with the venture.

What post-investment monitoring procedures will be in place?

An investor will want to know the means by which they will be able to keep track of their investment. A business plan will normally be required before an injection of capital is made. The business plan is an excellent way of communicating and of managing the investors' expectations. Regular financial reports will provide key information on the performance of the business and its liquidity (and hence its exposure to risk). The entrepreneur must consider whether the monitoring procedures on offer will be greeted as adequate by the investor.

What control mechanisms will be available?

Monitoring is of little use unless the investor can use the information gained to influence the behaviour of the venture's management. Investors who hold shares can signal their approval or otherwise by buying and selling their stock in the market. This buying and selling changes the value of the company. The ultimate sanction is for the value of the business to fall to a level where a takeover can happen and a new set of managers be brought in.

Large investors will usually take a more direct route to control. This may be by lobbying the venture's management or by having a representative permanently on the firm's board. The question that must be asked is how the control mechanisms on offer will influence the investor's decision.

Communication skills

Entrepreneurs and investors meet through a process of communication. Communication is a human process involving not only the passage of information but also an attempt to influence behaviour. Entrepreneurs communicate with investors not just because they wish to tell them about their ventures, but also because they want the investors to support them.

The process of communication between an entrepreneur and an investor is not just a matter of the *what* of the answers but also the *how*. The entrepreneur can exert a positive influence on investors by understanding the questions they are asking, by ensuring that the answers to those questions have been explored, and, where appropriate, by having hard evidence to back up the answers given.

Venture capitalists reject the vast majority (over 95 per cent) of proposals made to them. Though banks may back a higher proportion of proposals, rejections still greatly outnumber acceptances. Even if the business idea is sound, an investment of time and energy in making sure that proposals and other communications to backers are sympathetic to their information needs, and are well constructed as pieces of communication, will help the investor make their decision and will reflect positively on the professionalism of the entrepreneur. This will ensure that the venture is in the forefront of the race to obtain capital.

In a very entertaining article, Kawasaki (2001) lists the top ten 'lies' of entrepreneurs in their claims to investors. These lies (a strong word, self-delusion may be fairer) are tempting, but examining them reveals why investors will not be impressed. In ranked order, these are as follows.

1. 'Our projections are conservative' – Really? Most entrepreneurs exaggerate.

2. 'A large player estimates our market will be worth (add your own billions here!) by 2005' – So what? Why should I believe them?

3. 'A major buyer will sign a deal next week' – Call me back when you have a signature!

4. 'Key employees are set to join as soon as we get funded' – Well, I'll fund you as soon as they join. People first – then money!

5. 'We have no competition' – So either there is no market – or you haven't looked!

6. 'We want a non-disclosure agreement on our business idea/plans' – Why? If it is so easy to copy, how are you going to maintain a business on the back of it?

7. 'That major competitor is just too slow to present a threat' – Really? How did they get to be big then?

8. 'We are glad the bubble has burst' – So are we, because we are going to charge more for our capital.

9. 'Patents make our business defensible' – No they don't. Patents usually get copied somehow!

10. 'We only need 1% of the market' – Not much ambition, then?

Make sure the business plan does not fall into any of these traps!

23.4) Playing the game: game-theoretical ideas on the entrepreneur–investor relationship

> **Key learning outcome**
>
> To recognise the basic principles of game-theoretical thinking and appreciate the light this can throw on the entrepreneur–investor relationship.

So far our discussion of the entrepreneur–investor relationship has dealt with the practical issues relating to the specifics of that relationship. There is, however, a theoretical perspective on generalised relationships between agents (people or organisations who are free to make decisions) that is of immense power and illuminates the nature of decision making in those relationships greatly. This is called *game theory*. Along with information economics (discussed in Section 2.3), game theory has revolutionised economic thinking in the twentieth century. Games might be regarded as rather trivial affairs, distractions after the hard work of making money is done. And so they were by economists (aside from an interest in gambling, which is of economic significance) until mathematicians in the 1950s and 1960s recognised their economic importance. Of note here are John Von Neumann and Oskar Morgenstern with their groundbreaking book *The Theory of Games and Economic Behaviour*. Also important is John F. Nash, who demonstrated the central significance of games to economic theory with a series of papers. The central idea of game theory is (beautifully!) simple. Unfortunately, the works of Von Neumann, Morgenstern and Nash work are of a highly technical nature and not for the mathematically faint-hearted. But this does not prevent a straightforward and (largely) non-mathematical exposition of the key ideas.

A game is formally an interaction between two or more 'players' (agents or decision makers) who can each play one of two or more different 'strategies' (acts or decisions). However, the 'winnings' (payoffs or outcomes) of the game for each player depend on the acts of all other players, not just the act of that particular player. The simplest game is one in which there are two players each able to select one of two acts. Each player selects his or her act without knowing what the other player has chosen to do and gets his or her winnings without any other decisions being made (we say the game is instantaneous). Game theory assumes that the players are rational. This means more than just sensible in their decision making. It means that the player will *always* take the action that is expected to maximise his or her outcomes (winnings) and that he or she recognises that other players are also rational and will do exactly the same. Although the idea of rationality has come in for criticism by many social scientists, it is not a bad approximation to the realities of economic life. We can represent the game with a 'payoff matrix' as follows.

	Player B	
	Decides to do act 1	Decides to do act 2
Player A — Decides to do act 1	A wins a_{11} B wins b_{11}	A wins a_{12} B wins b_{12}
Player A — Decides to do act 2	A wins a_{21} B wins b_{21}	A wins a_{22} B wins b_{22}

The winnings can take any values of course. But if we set them such that a_{21} is greater than a_{11} which is greater than a_{22} which is greater than a_{12} (don't worry! An example will soon make this ordering clear) then we get a special type of game called a *prisoners' dilemma*. The reason this particular game is so called comes from an example offered by Albert Tucker in the 1950s. This example also illustrates why the game is so important in economic thinking.

Consider two people who have been arrested on suspicion of a crime and have been put on trial. At the trial, the judge offers both defendants a deal, on which they must make an immediate decision. This is put to each defendant in private, so they have no knowledge of what the other has decided to do. The deal put by the judge is this: 'you may confess to the crime, or not confess to it. If you both confess, then I will be sure of your guilt, but I will appreciate you not wasting the court's time, so I will give you three years' each. If neither of you confess, then, though the evidence is against you, I will err on the side of caution and just give you one year each. If, however, you confess, but the other defendant does not, then I will, as a reward for your cooperating with the court, release you with a suspended sentence and imprison your accomplice for five years. I am putting this same deal to the other defendant. Do you wish to confess or not?'. Such courtroom 'plea-bargaining' deals are not common in European courts but do happen in the USA.

The payoff matrix for this situation is as follows:

		Prisoner B	
		Not confess	Confess
Prisoner A	Not confess	Both get 1 year	A gets 5 years, B goes free
	Confess	A goes free, B gets 5 years	Both get 3 years

What is the rational course of action here (given that imprisonment is not enjoyed and a rational subject would wish to minimise his or her period of imprisonment)? Well, a joint refusal to confess presents the minimum *total* period of incarceration, two years. However, consider the position of prisoner A (prisoner B is in exactly the same position). First she considers that B has not confessed. In which case, her best strategy is to confess (she will then go free). Then she considers the alternative, that B *has* confessed. If she does not confess, then she will face five years. She can reduce this to three by confessing. In short, whatever the other prisoner has decided, her best option is to confess. Confessing is a strategy that is said to *strongly dominate* not confessing (it is always better than the alternative, whatever the other agent has done). But B being in the same position will go through the same argument and also decide to confess. The result will be that both prisoners will get three years. Yet, by both not confessing, both could have minimised their sentence to one year each. The prisoner's dilemma actually represents a dilemma in that both prisoners cannot obtain (at least by thinking and acting rationally) the minimum period of imprisonment. Have you ever attended a major sporting event or a rock concert? If so, then you may have personally experienced an example of the prisoners' dilemma. Let's take it that sitting down is preferable to standing at such an event. If everyone sits, then everybody is comfortable. But any one person can gain a better view (an advantage) by standing. But if he does, then those behind must stand to get a better view. Result, everyone stands, even though all would have been more comfortable sitting.

What has all this to do with entrepreneurs and investors? Quite a lot, because entrepreneurs and investors can often find themselves in a prisoners' dilemma situation, and neither is likely to come to the decision that would best benefit both parties. At least, not without some sort of mechanism to help them reach an optimal agreement. But more on this in a little while. Game theory relies (as any form of mathematical modelling must) on simplifying complex social situations so as to describe them and to discover why people make the decisions they do. This is not really a compromise. The point of game theory is to capture the *essence* of the interaction between players (and their decisions), not its peripheral details. We can always increase the complexity of the model to take account of subtleties, but this can cost in terms of the model's clarity. So we will describe the relationship between an entrepreneur and an investor in somewhat simplified terms, though these will be recognised as being realistic. Cable and Shane (1997) provide a comprehensive review of the entrepreneur-venture capitalist relationship in prisoner's dilemma terms.

Entrepreneurs and investors live in a world of competition. Not with each other, we might argue, because by working together they can both win, but with other entrepreneurs and other investors. Entrepreneurs compete with each other for investors' resources. Investors compete with each other for opportunities to invest in good entrepreneurial opportunities. The dynamic of the competition is the rate of return entrepreneurs offer investors and the rate of return investors, in turn, demand. Of course, the cake entrepreneurs create is only so big. If a higher return is offered to an investor, then the return to the entrepreneur must be that much lower and vice versa. When offered an investment opportunity an investor can make one of two decisions: to support that venture or not (there may be subtleties in the agreement, but this is essentially it). This decision will be based on the return the venture is offering relative to the risk that venture presents and the return that can be obtained elsewhere with other investment opportunities (of varying levels of risk). An entrepreneur presenting his or her business plan to an investor wants, of course, to make a good impression. He or she wants the investment to take place. He or she also wants the investor to see the risks in the venture as being as low as possible so that the return the investor demands is as low as possible. A business plan is an anticipation. It is a projection of what might happen in the future. The future is not fully predictable. So a business plan offers a good deal of latitude for interpretation of the 'facts' that go into it. Entrepreneurs are keen to put a 'positive spin' on the plan: how innovative the product is, the attractiveness of the market, the positive interest of potential customers and the weakness of competitors, and so on. This optimism is likely to be reflected in cash-flow and profit projections. And all it takes is unchallenged optimism; there need be no suggestion that the entrepreneur is being consciously dishonest (though of course he or she can be). However, the greater such optimism, the less likely it will be that the entrepreneur can actually deliver what the plan says will be delivered. (It is useful here to reconsider some of the points on managing investor expectations made in Section 12.1). The entrepreneur can get away with this because he or she is the expert on the business being presented, not the investor, and the investor must accept what the entrepreneur is saying.

Investors of course recognise this. This is why they challenge business plans rather than accept them at face value. But at the end of the day, the investor must accept (or not) what is being offered. In *simple* terms this means that the entrepreneur also has two options available to him or her: to present a *realistic* plan (which presents risks as higher, but is deliverable) or to present an overly *optimistic* plan (which minimises present risks, but cannot actually be delivered). So we have two players, each able to take one of two actions where the 'winnings' (return from investment in the venture) for both depend on what both parties do – we have a formal game. This is depicted in the following payoff matrix:

		Investor decides to	
		Invest	Not invest
Entrepreneur decides to	Present a realistic (deliverable) plan	Entrepreneur gets return E Investor gets return I	Entrepreneur gets return E' Investor gets return R
	Present an overly optimistic (undeliverable) plan	Entrepreneur gets return e Investor gets return i	Entrepreneur gets return e' Investor gets return R

Let us consider the winnings in terms of them being returns from investment in the venture. If the investor backs a realistic plan then both parties win, the investor gets a return I and the entrepreneur a return E. If the plan is overly optimistic, however, the entrepreneur gets a return e and the investor a return i. Why does the plan make a difference to the returns? Because of the rate of return the investor will ask for. If he or she backs a plan that understates risks (and he or she believes that risk assessment), they will ask for a rate of return lower than if they fully recognised the risks. What the venture delivers (we may assume) is independent of what the entrepreneur offers, so he or she gains by having an overly optimistic plan accepted. If the investor decides not to invest then his or her return is always R, the return that is obtained from an alternative investment. The entrepreneur goes elsewhere for his or her investment, but presumably gets a worse deal (presumably the investor was the preferred investor). In this case, if the plan is overly optimistic then the entrepreneur gets a return E'; if a realistic plan is presented, then the return is e'.

How do these returns stack up? Well, for the entrepreneur the order is:

e is greater than E is greater than e' is greater than E'

The rationale is that an optimistic plan always costs less in returns demanded by the investor and the preferred investor is offering a better deal than that offered by any other investor. For the investor the returns stack up as:

I is greater than R is greater than i

The rationale here is that a realistic plan will encourage them to ask for a proper rate of return for the risk. If they decide to invest this should be better than the alternative investment available. However, if they have a strict portfolio and are asking a market rate of return then any underestimation of risk will lead to a return that is actually lower than that offered by a (market) alternative. (It is worthwhile to refer back to Section 10.6 for clarification on this point.) Though this sounds rather convoluted, it does represent a scenario that often occurs in practice. The point is that it represents a prisoners' dilemma. To see why, consider the rational choice for the entrepreneur. Whether the investor decides to invest or not (and so the entrepreneur goes elsewhere), a greater personal return is obtained by presenting an overly optimistic plan. Whatever the investor does, the entrepreneur gets a greater return by presenting a more positive (if undeliverable) plan.

But now consider the rational choice for the investor. He or she knows that the entrepreneur (being rational) will present an overly optimistic plan. In which case, the best option is not to invest, because it will lead to a return that can be improved by going elsewhere. So the entrepreneur and investor do not get together. But then both lose. The entrepreneur has to go to an investor they would prefer not to and the investor misses out on an investment opportunity that they would have found attractive (against alternatives). Empirical studies confirm this model. De Meza and Southey (1996) develop the model and apply it to bank lending to small businesses. They find that 'over optimism' by would-be entrepreneurs can explain entrepreneur's reliance on loans (rather than equity), low interest rate margins and credit rationing. However, investors and entrepreneurs do get together. How is the prisoners' dilemma solved for them in practice?

Practical resolution of the dilemma

Human beings are creative, though. In practice, mechanisms have emerged to deal with this dilemma and produce a resolution that allows both parties to make an agreement. We will go on to consider these in detail. Before doing so, it is important to recognise that the word *emerge* is the right one. There is no suggestion that entrepreneurs or investors have consciously designed these mechanisms with the prisoners' dilemma problem in mind. The dilemma wasn't formally recognised until the 1950s, and investors and entrepreneurs have been getting together for many centuries. These mechanisms are the result of trial and error. The interesting thing is that the arrangements that have been found to work in practice can be seen through a game-theoretical perspective as means to ensure that a *rational* decision maker will conclude that co-operation (in our example, presenting a realistic business plan) is the best option. This said, game theory is increasingly being called upon to provide practical guidance in designing contracts for real business deals.

A mechanism for resolving a prisoners' dilemma in a social setting is usually composed of five inter-related elements. These are *repetition* (with *reputation*), *negotiation*, *contracting*, *punishment* and *external intervention*. Most practical social mechanisms involve a combination of these elements. They all play a role in sustaining the relationship between entrepreneurs and investors.

Repetition involves the game being played more than once. This would happen if the entrepreneur and the investor work together on more than one venture or if the one venture needs subsequent investment. If this happens, then an entrepreneur who presents an overly optimistic plan and fails to deliver on it is unlikely to get investment next time. So if the entrepreneur and investor will have a long-term relationship the entrepreneur will be encouraged to present a realistic plan. If players are coming into repeated contact, then the *reputation* of a player becomes important. Investors prefer serial entrepreneurs who have a reputation for delivering to those who have not. But not all entrepreneurs are serial entrepreneurs. Reputation will not be so important to an entrepreneur who is seeking a one-off investment and will not need to call upon that reputation in the future. In which case the other mechanisms become important.

Negotiation is a fundamental part of the entrepreneur–investor relationship. Negotiation involves not just agreeing over how big a slice of the final cake each party will get, it also involves poring over the plan the entrepreneur is presenting. Investors are aware that entrepreneurs put a positive spin on their plans. The investor seeks to challenge their optimism. They demand evidence to back up claims. The more independent that information the better. For really big deals, entrepreneurs may call in independent consultants to write and present plans for them, as Frederick Smith did when seeking $90 million to start Federal Express. Investors may themselves call in consultants to check facts for them. Some may demand personality testing for the entrepreneur to make sure he or she has the potential to deliver the plan (this issue is considered in Section 3.2). In game-theoretical terms, all of this is about eliminating the space for the entrepreneur's unguarded optimist, thus ensuring the investor is making a decision on a realistic plan.

But all of this can be costly. It is worth investing in it for big deals, but it is prohibitively expensive for smaller ones. *Contracting* is a mechanism through which investors can, in effect, insure themselves against the possibility that the entrepreneur is presenting an overly optimistic plan. The contract is structured by the investor on the assumption that the entrepreneur knows things that they do not. This brings in ideas on the economics of asymmetric information discussed in Section 2.3. Formally, the investor's problem is one of *adverse selection*. The contract is so designed that it is in the entrepreneur's interest to present a realistic plan. The investor offers two contracts, one designed on the assumption that the entrepreneur is 'good' and will actually deliver the optimistic plan, the other on the assumption that the entrepreneur is 'poor' and will not deliver. Only the entrepreneur knows whether he or she is 'good' or 'poor'. So the investor must build in an incentive so that the entrepreneur accepts the plan that is designed for his or her type. So there must be a reward for delivering on the plan, encouraging the entrepreneur to present one that is realistic. This reward must be additional to the normal returns of the investment (which the entrepreneur will gain whatever he or she presents), or there will be no incentive. Conversely, there might be a cost if he or she does not deliver. Though this sounds complicated, a contract that actually delivers this is very simple and is almost universal in venture capital and bank investment deals: insist that the entrepreneur puts in some of his or her own money into the venture. This aligns the interests of the investor and the entrepreneur. It makes the entrepreneur an investor as well, an investor who does know whether the entrepreneur is 'good' or 'poor' and has an interest in investing according to the type.

Punishment sounds severe. But all it means is that the entrepreneur is exposed to a cost that reduces the gains they make from presenting an overly optimistic plan to below those they make from presenting a realistic plan. In terms of our game-theoretical model above, this means that there is a cost, c, if the entrepreneur gains E that brings $(E - c)$ down to below e. Rationally, the entrepreneur will then prefer e and so present a realistic plan. Most investment deals include the possibility of some sort of action if the venture is not progressing towards its projected financial targets. This may take the form of a monetary penalty, but the possibilities here are limited. If the venture is not able to pay its promised return, then it is not likely to be able to pay an additional 'fine'. More likely is the possibility of the investor moving in, replacing the entrepreneur with alternative managers, or, in extremis, foreclosing on the deal and having the business broken up with the aim of recovering the investment from the sale of assets. Of course, if the entrepreneur can be shown to be actually fraudulent in what has been presented to the investors, legislative action is a possibility.

External intervention is a mechanism whereby a third party moves in to ensure that the entrepreneur presents a realistic plan. To some extent, independent consultants can play this role. As noted, either the entrepreneur or the investor or both may call them in, especially if the deal is a big one. Of course, the legal system within which the entrepreneur and investor are operating sets standards of honesty in their dealings, with the threat of punitive action if these standards are breached. As indeed do the general cultural rules in which they operate. These may not be legally codified, or may take semi-legal status as guidelines from professional bodies.

As qualified at the beginning of this section, these mechanisms have not been designed as a specific response to the prisoners' dilemma. They are long-standing parts of the warp and weft of business deals. What the game-theoretical perspective adds is a coherent and unified theory of why these mechanisms work in terms of modifying rational behaviour and ensuring that entrepreneurs and investors can avoid *rationally* deciding not to work together and so both lose. Entrepreneurs often complain at the impositions investors make: the need to invest their own money, the right investors claims to intervene in the business and the threat of punitive action if the venture does not perform. The game-theoretical perspective suggests that, however onerous, such mechanisms are necessary to make the entrepreneur–investor relationship happen at all.

Summary of key ideas

- Financial support is a critical factor in the success of the new venture.

- Suppliers of investment capital are differentiated by the *amount* of capital they will supply, the *risks* they will undertake and the way in which they will expect to see their investment *mature*.

- Investors select investment opportunities by *filtering* them for suitability. This filtering process has formal analysis and informal 'intuitive' aspects.

- The vast majority of investment proposals are rejected.

- Effective entrepreneurs approach investors with an understanding of the *questions* for which they will need answers before they decide to support the venture.

- Professional investors are acute to, and dismissive of, extravagent claims in business plans.

- The prisoners' dilemma provides an illuminating game-theoretical model of entrepreneur–investor interactions and can explain why entrepreneurs and investors can sometimes fail to agree to mutually rewarding deals.

Research themes

The entrepreneur–investor relationship is a subject of considerable research. This often involves quite sophisticated finance theory. However, there are a number of valuable projects that might be undertaken that do not demand such technical knowledge.

The nature of the funding gap

Entrepreneurs often complain of a funding gap: their inability to gain investment for start-up or business expansion. It has been proposed that this funding gap is not so much due to market failure, but to a lack of communication between entrepreneurs and investors. The framework described in Section 23.2 suggests the information that entrepreneurs should be offering to potential investors in relation to the questions investors need answering. Conduct a two-stage survey with practising entrepreneurs who have received funding and (ideally) some who have not and with capital providers (ideally different types such as high street banks and venture capitalists). In the first stage, have the investors spontaneously identify the information they require and the entrepreneurs spontaneously indicate the information they feel investors want. How do these compare? Are there any important pieces of information the entrepreneurs do not feel is necessary that the investors value? In the second stage, present a list of information categories based on the framework here described. Have the investors indicate their prioritisation of, and valuation of, those categories. Similarly, have the entrepreneurs indicate their views of the priority and value of that information for investors. Again, is their any mismatch between the priority and value ascribed to the information between the two groups? Have entrepreneurs who have received funding a better understanding than those who have not? Summarise by making recommendations as to how entrepreneurs might be better supported in making funding bids.

Entrepreneurs, investors and the prisoners' dilemma

Game-theoretical studies are mathematically challenging, but the prisoners' dilemma model developed in Section 23.4 does make some qualitative predictions. As with the study above, identify three groups: entrepreneurs who have received funding, entrepreneurs who have not received funding and relevant investors. A prisoners' dilemma will arise if the entrepreneur is overstating the potential of the venture and understating its risks and investors are assuming that they are doing so. Survey the three groups inquiring into their attitudes towards the communication of potential and risks. With the entrepreneurs, present a series of propositions such as 'it is best to be optimistic in presenting potential returns', 'it is best to be pessimistic when presenting potential returns' and 'it is best to understate risks' and so on and have them state their agreement or otherwise with them (use a Likert scale: agree strongly, agree a little, . . . , disagree strongly, and so on). With the investors, present propositions such as 'entrepreneurs always tend to understate risks', 'entrepreneurs are usually over optimistic when predicting returns', and so on. Again, have the investors indicate their agreement with these propositions. Do the entrepreneurs' and investors' attitudes suggest a prisoners' dilemma might occur? Is there any significant difference between the attitudes of the entrepreneurs who were successful in gaining funding and those who were not? If so, summarise by making recommendations as to how the dilemma might be resolved.

Suggestions for further reading

Berger, A.N. and Udell, G.F. (2002) 'Small business credit availability and relationship lending: the importance of bank organisational structure', *Economic Journal*, Vol. 112, pp. F32–F53.

Boocock, G. and Woods, M. (1997) 'The evaluation criteria used by venture capitalists: evidence from a UK venture fund', *International Small Business Journal*, Vol. 16, No. 1, pp. 36–57.

Brau, J.C. (2002) 'Do banks price owner-manager agency costs? An examination of small business borrowing', *Journal of Small Business Management*, Vol. 40, No. 4, pp. 273–86.

Cable, D.M. and Shane, S. (1997) 'A prisoner's dilemma approach to entrepreneur-venture capitalist relationships', *Academy of Management Review*, Vol. 22, No. 1, pp. 142–176.

Camp, S.M. and Sexton, D.L. (1992) 'Trends in venture capital investment: implications for high-technology firms', *Journal of Small Business Management*, July, pp. 11–19.

Choudhury, M.A. (2001) 'Islamic venture capital', *Journal of Economic Studies*, Vol. 28, No. 1, pp. 14–33.

Cook, P. (2001) 'Finance and small and medium-sized enterprise in developing countries', *Journal of Developmental Entrepreneurship*, Vol. 6, No. 1, pp. 17–40.

Devashis, M. (2000) 'The venture capital industry in India', *Journal of Small Business Management*, Vol. 38, No. 2, pp. 67–79.

Fletcher, M. (1995) 'Decision-making by Scottish bank managers', *International Journal of Entrepreneurial Behaviour and Research*, Vol. 1, No. 2, pp. 37–53.

Haar, N.E., Starr, J. and Macmillan, I.C. (1988) 'Informal risk capital investors: investment patterns on the east coast of the USA', *Journal of Business Venturing*, Vol. 3, pp. 11–29.

Hall, J. and Hofer, C.W. (1993) 'Venture capitalists' decision criteria in new venture evaluation', *Journal of Business Venturing*, Vol. 8, pp. 25–42.

Harris, S. (1995) 'Managing organizations to address the finance gap', *International Journal of Entrepreneurial Behaviour and Research*, Vol. 1, No. 3, pp. 63–82.

Harrison, R.T. and Dibben, M.R. (1997) 'The role of trust in the informal investor's investment decision: an exploratory analysis', *Entrepreneurship Theory and Practice*, Summer, pp. 63–81.

Harrison, R.T. and Mason, C. (1996) 'Developments in the promotion of informal venture capital in the UK', *International Journal of Entrepreneurial Behaviour and Research*, Vol. 2, No. 2, pp. 6–33.

Kawasaki, G. (2001) 'The top ten lies of entrepreneurs', *Harvard Business Review*, January, pp. 22–3.

Knight, R.M. (1994) 'Criteria used by venture capitalists: a cross cultural analysis', *International Small Business Journal*, Vol. 13, No. 1, pp. 26–37.

Landström, H. (1993) 'Informal risk capital in Sweden and some international comparisons', *Journal of Business Venturing*, Vol. 8, pp. 525–40.

Macmillan, I.C., Siegel, R. and Subba Narashima, P.N. (1985) 'Criteria used by venture capitalists to evaluate new venture proposals', *Journal of Business Venturing*, Vol. 1, pp. 119–28.

Macmillan, I.C., Zeeman, L. and Subba Narashima, P.N. (1987) 'Effectiveness of criteria used by venture capitalists in the venture screening process', *Journal of Business Venturing*, Vol. 2, pp. 123–38.

Maier, II, J.B. and Walker, D.A. (1987) 'The role of venture capital in financing small business', *Journal of Business Venturing*, Vol. 2, pp. 207–14.

Mason, C. and Harrison, R. (1996) 'Why "business angels" say no: a case study of opportunities rejected by an informal investor syndicate', *International Small Business Journal*, Vol. 14, No. 2, pp. 35–51.

Morris, M.H., Watling, J.W. and Schindehutte, M. (2000) 'Venture capitalist involvement in portfolio companies: insights from South Africa', *Journal of Small Business Management*, July, pp. 68–77.

de Meza, D. and Southey, C. (1996) 'The borrower's curse: optimism, finance and entrepreneurship', *Economic Journal*, Vol. 106, pp. 375–86.

Murnighan, J.K. (1994) 'Game theory and organizational behaviour', *Research in Organisational Behavior*, Vol. 16, pp. 83–123.

Murray, G.C. (1992) 'A challenging marketplace for venture capital', *Long Range Planning*, Vol. 25, No. 6, pp. 79–86.

Norton, E. and Tenenbaum, B.H. (1992) 'Factors affecting the structure of US venture capital deals', *Journal of Small Business Management*, July, pp. 20–9.

Ray, D.M. and Turpin, D.V. (1993) 'Venture capital in Japan', *International Small Business Journal*, Vol. 11, No. 4, pp. 39–56.

Rea, R.H. (1989) 'Factors affecting success and failure of seed capital/start-up negotiations', *Journal of Business Venturing*, Vol. 4, pp. 149–58.

Riquelme, H. and Watson, J. (2002) 'Do venture capitalists' implicit theories on new business success/failure have empirical validity?' *International Small Business Journal*, Vol. 20, No. 4, pp. 395–420.

Roberts, E.B. (1991) 'High stakes for high-tech entrepreneurs: understanding venture capital decision making', *Sloan Management Review*, Winter, pp. 9–20.

Rock, A. (1987) 'Strategy v tactics from a venture capitalist', *Harvard Business Review*, Nov–Dec, pp. 63–7.

Shepherd, D.A. (1999) 'Venture capitalist's introspections: a comparison of "in use" and "espoused" decision policies', *Journal of Small Business Management*, Vol. 37, No. 2, pp. 76–87.

Steiner, L. and Greenwood, R. (1995) 'Venture capitalist relationships in the deal structuring and post-investment stages of new firm creation', *Journal of Management Studies*, Vol. 32, No. 3, pp. 337–57.

Sweeting, R.C. (1991) 'UK venture capital funds and the funding of new technology-based businesses: process and relationships', *Journal of Management Studies*, Vol. 28, No. 6, pp. 601–22.

Tashiro, Y. (1999) 'Business angels in Japan', *Venture Capital*, Vol. 1, No. 3, pp. 259–73.

Tyebjee, T.T. and Bruno, A.V. (1984) 'A model of venture capital investment activity', *Management Science*, Vol. 30, No. 9, pp. 1051–66.

Van Auken, H.E. (2001) 'Financing small technology-based companies: the relationship between familiarity with capital and ability to price and negotiate investment', *Journal of Small Business Management*, Vol. 39, No. 3, pp. 240–58.

Von Neumann, J. and Morgenstern, O. (2001) *Theory of Games and Economic Behavior*, Dusseldorf: Verlag Wirtschaft und Finanzen (first published 1944).

Zacharakis, A.L., Meyer, G.D. and Castro, J. De (1999) 'Differing perceptions of new venture failure: a matched exploratory I study of venture capitalists and entrepreneurs', *Journal of Small Business Management*, Vol. 37, No. 3, pp. 1–14.

Selected case material **Case 23.1**

Finance: looking for a lending hand

FT

6 November 2002

By **Elizabeth Rigby**

Alasdair Flint becomes annoyed when he talks about banks.

He believes his successful opera stage-set company – with an annual turnover of about £1.6m – folded because a bank refused to extend his overdraft.

'We had just lost a contract and it was a bit surprising,' recalls Mr Flint, whose company used to make sets for opera houses from London to Italy. 'We needed something like a week's turnover – about £60,000 – to tide us over until the next job came in. But the bank was not helpful. The closure cost 30 jobs.'

Mr Flint's experience may be extreme, but elements are familiar to inner city companies looking for finance.

The Inner City 100 survey suggests banks – and venture capitalists – have sometimes failed to see the opportunities emerging from unfashionable urban areas.

Companies are almost unanimous in complaining that access to finance – particularly in the shape of bank loans and overdrafts – is a big barrier to business growth.

One-quarter of companies in the index also say credit problems hampered progress in their start-up phase. Financial exclusion became more stark when gender and ethnicity come into play.

Entrepreneurs add that local bank managers are too risk averse. Christopher Neave, founder and chief executive of Ultralase, an eye laser treatment company, was forced to turn to an 'angel investor' – an individual ready privately to back a project – after his business was written off by the bank as being too 'speculative and risky'. He has since completed a £6.5m venture capital backed management buy-out.

It becomes easier once businesses are established. Eighty per cent of the 75 companies seeking growth finance in the index have found it through overdrafts and bank loans.

By this stage, relations between bank managers and entrepreneurs have usually become more cordial, with 80 per cent of the Inner City 100 saying they were satisfied with their bank.

Peter Ibbetson, head of business banking at National Westminster, part of the Royal Bank of Scotland (RBS) group, puts discord in the early stages down to entrepreneurial inexperience and incomplete business plans.

'The starting off bit is often interpreted by the entrepreneur as the banks being difficult. But it is about marrying the passion of the entrepreneur with balance and discipline.

'When we say: "you bring the passion and we'll bring the financial discipline", you can see the dawn break on their faces.'

The RBS group, which provides banking for 40 per cent of the Inner City 100, also insists that these teething problems beset entrepreneurs across the UK, not just those in deprived areas.

Inner city investment is also a big growth area for Barclays, already the second biggest lender to the Inner City 100 with 23 per cent of the market. In 2001, businesses in such areas accounted for 10 per cent of all its new business starts.

Peter Kelly, head of financial exclusion at Barclays, thinks banks are becoming more aware of the potential inner cities can offer. 'It is a particularly interesting market. There is a community focus but there is also a business imperative as well.'

In the longer run, the increasing appetite on the high street to harness growing businesses should work in the entrepreneurs' favour.

As Mr Ibbetson explains: 'We try to be as responsive as we can to support growth. If we don't, the entrepreneurs will go elsewhere.'

Beyond the bank manager, entrepreneurs can also look to venture capitalists or public business finance schemes to raise money, although both methods carry their own difficulties.

Venture capital funding is hard to attain. At the moment, European venture capitalists invest £5.8m in a typical start-up. This reflects their desire to invest only in larger projects and to take big equity stakes. Accordingly, only 5 per cent of the Inner City 100 have used venture capital funding.

But Philip Newborough, managing director at Bridges, a venture capital fund that only invests in inner cities, reckons that providing risk finance for inner city companies – about 60 firms in the US already do this – is a rich seam to tap.

Bridges has raised a £40m fund from a mix of public and private backers. The government contributed £20m, with the remainder coming from institutional investors, including venture capital groups 3i, Apax partners and Doughty Hanson.

Mr Ibbetson argues that banks can play a role in finding equity for businesses since a good bank manager will know about local business angels and other funding opportunities.

He points out that part of the problem in finding equity is an unwillingness on the part of entrepreneurs to give up control: 'In the US they share their success and share their equity.'

Indeed, 40 per cent of the Inner City 100 do not want to lose control of their business, while a further 34 per cent say they do not want to share ownership.

In the long-run, the renewed focus on inner cities by the government, venture capitalists and banks, suggests funding opportunities will improve.

Source: *Financial Times*, 6 November 2002.

Case 23.2

Fair play and ethnic businesses

FT

26 September 2002

By **Jonathon Guthrie**

Kofi Kusitor has the rare distinction of having been refused finance to start an internet business in the late 1990s, when lenders and venture capitalists were throwing money at the sector.

Asked whether his African descent had anything to do with it, Mr Kusitor replies: 'Absolutely.' The white bank manager in Putney spent 'three minutes looking at my business plan before he threw me out of his office', says Mr Kusitor. The Colourful Network, which runs websites for an African Caribbean audience, was instead funded with loans from friends and family. It is now – also unusually for an internet business – making a small profit.

Many African Caribbean business-people tell tales of rejection similar to Mr Kusitor's. But white entrepreneurs complain just as loudly about bank managers blind to the brilliance of their business brainwaves. The difference is they lack the opportunity to impute racism as a motive for refusal.

It is therefore significant that a report from the British Bankers' Association, published today, found the poor performance of African Caribbean entrepreneurs in raising start-up money from banks could not be wholly attributed to their characteristics, or those of their businesses.

The report, which also has the support of the Department of Trade and Industry and the Bank of England, stops short of accusing banks of discrimination. But only just.

Not surprisingly, banks are a little uncomfortable with this. Richard Roberts, head of SME research at Barclays, says the report advances 'no data to suggest there is actual discrimination' against African Caribbeans. He believes the judgment of the report's authors, led by the respected Monder Ram, professor of small business at De Montfort University, has been swayed by anecdotal evidence from case study interviewees.

Survey data in the report shows African Caribbean entrepreneurs are much less likely to access bank finance to start their businesses than Asians or whites. But Mr Roberts believes this partly reflects self-exclusion by black entrepreneurs who assume that banks will automatically turn them down.

Andy Brenan, director of retail banking at the BBA, says whether the discrimination is real or merely perceived is irrelevant. The important thing is for the banks to tackle the problem, by reaching out to the community that believes itself to be disadvantaged.

That gets banks neatly off the hook. But at the same time it would be a shame if recriminations over banks' past failings were to detract from efforts to improve future performance.

Similarly, one controversial finding should not be allowed to skew assessments of a report that has taken two years and thousands of working hours to produce – and comes to many other useful, if less sensational, conclusions.

Prime among these is the finding that, overall, businesses owned by members of ethnic minorities do not suffer any clear disadvantage in dealing with banks. The researchers went to some pains to establish this, conducting a survey of about 1,000 companies set up by entrepreneurs of all races and following up with case study interviews. The aim was to meet a call from the Bank of England in 1999 for detailed research into the relationships between banks and businesses owned by minorities.

However, there are big variations in the success of different groups. Black businesses, which are concentrated in unpromising areas such as hairdressing and the arts, are finding the going toughest, says the report. Their growth is lower, they are more likely to make losses and their success in getting bank loans after starting up is poorer.

In contrast, Asian-owned businesses appear to be doing well. Take those owned by entrepreneurs of Pakistani origin; here there is a good spread sectorally, with 43 per cent of the businesses surveyed active in retail or wholesale and 34 per cent in professional services. About 34 per cent had been able to access bank start-up finance, the same figure as for white-owned businesses. Their success in getting top-up bank loans was similarly high. The proportion reporting profits – 74 per cent – beat that of the white control group.

Chinese-owned businesses also appear to be prospering. More than 70 per cent were making a profit from activities split equally between restaurants, retail or wholesale and professional services. Chinese entrepreneurs had an unusually high propensity for accessing start-up finance from banks and did well in winning extra funds from the same source.

Ethnic groups with high exposure to the restaurant trade, such as those of Chinese and Bangladeshi origin, were the least dependent on their own group for sales. Bangladeshi businesses made up just a quarter of sales to Bangladeshi customers. African Caribbeans were highly reliant on their own group, which provided almost two-thirds of turnover. That is a concern, says the BBA, because a limited market naturally constrains growth prospects.

The report found that while ethnic minority entrepreneurs were mostly happy with their own banking relationships, they believed banks were, broadly, unhelpful to businesses run by non-whites.

To Mr Brenan that is a signal for BBA members to act on practical recommendations in the report, intended to help allay those suspicions. Prof Ram and his colleagues believe banks should work harder to raise their profile among ethnic minorities, recruiting intermediaries such as local accountants, solicitors and community groups to help them.

Banks also need to employ more ethnic minority staff: 'We still have some way to go here,' Mr Brenan admits. Training on cultural differences would help prevent such basic gaffes as inviting Muslims to business lunches during Ramadan.

The report provides a matching wish list for the government's Small Business Service and development agency Scottish Enterprise, calling for greater engagement with minorities and a more vigorous effort to share best practice.

Does it really matter whether the UK's ethnic minority businesses prosper and feel themselves to be part of the commercial mainstream? Mr Brenan's answer is an unequivocal Yes. Current demographic projections suggest whites will become a minority in British cities such as Birmingham and Leicester over the next two decades. Banks that can identify and nurture the best black and Asian entrepreneurs should find the relationship a profitable one.

Vibrant small businesses also fulfil a useful social function in providing employment for local people and positive role models for the young. Successful black entrepreneurs send a strong signal that there are appealing ways to earn money and win respect.

Source: Financial Times, 26 September 2002.

Discussion points

1. Banks are private enterprises with their own shareholders. Where do their responsibilities lie? To shareholders or to wider society? Should banks take more risks (with reduced profits) in order that more entrepreneurs start-up? Should government intervene to ensure this happens. Where does this leave the responsibility of the entrepreneur to produce an attractive, risk-managed proposition to lenders?

2. What should be governmental objectives when regulating the relationship between entrepreneurs and investors?

Part 4

Managing the growth and development of the venture

Chapter 24

The dimensions of
business growth

Chapter overview

The potential for growth is a defining feature of the entrepreneurial venture. This chapter is concerned with an exploration of the process of business growth. A multi-faceted approach is developed and the growth of the entrepreneurial venture is considered from **financial**, **strategic**, **structural** and **organisational** perspectives. The chapter concludes by considering how the growth of the venture creates opportunities for, and impacts on, the lives of its stakeholders.

24.1 The process of growth

Key learning outcome

An appreciation of the general dynamics of business growth.

Business growth is critical to entrepreneurial success. The potential for growth is one of the factors which distinguishes the entrepreneurial venture from the small business. Organisational growth, however, means more than just an increase in size. Growth is a dynamic process. It involves development and change within the organisation, and changes in the way in which the organisation interacts with its environment. Though an organisation grows as a coherent whole, organisational growth itself is best understood in a multi-faceted way. It has as many aspects as there are aspects of organisation itself. The case for a multi-perspective approach to understanding organisational growth and change was made very effectively by Henry Mintzberg in his book *The Structuring of Organisations* (1979).

Given the multi-faceted nature of organisation the entrepreneur must constantly view the growth and development of their venture from a number of different perspectives. Four perspectives in particular are important: the *financial*, the *strategic*, the *structural* and the *organisational*.

1. *Financial growth* relates to the development of the business as a commercial entity. It is concerned with increases in *turnover*, the *costs* and *investment* needed to achieve that turnover, and the resulting *profits*. It is also concerned with increases in what the business owns: its *assets*. Related to this is the increase in the *value* of the business, that is, what a potential buyer might be willing to pay for it. Because financial growth measures the additional value that the organisation is creating which is available to be distributed to its stakeholders, it is an important measure of the *success* of the venture.

2. *Strategic growth* relates to the changes that take place in the way in which the organisation interacts with its environment as a coherent, *strategic*, whole. Primarily, this is concerned with the way the business develops its capabilities to exploit a presence in the marketplace. It is the profile of opportunities which the venture exploits and the assets, both tangible and intangible, it acquires to create *sustainable competitive advantages*.

3. *Structural growth* relates to the changes in the way the business organises its internal systems, in particular, managerial *roles* and *responsibilities*, reporting *relationships*, *communication* links and resource *control systems*.

4. *Organisational growth* relates to the changes in the organisation's *processes*, *culture* and *attitudes* as it grows and develops. It is also concerned with the changes that must take place in the entrepreneur's role and leadership style as the business moves from being a 'small' to a 'large' firm.

The four aspects of growth described are not independent of each other. They are just different facets of the same underlying process. At the heart of that process is the awarding of valuable resources to the venture by external markets because it has demonstrated that it can make better use of them, that is, create more value from them, than can the alternatives on offer. That better use of resources is a consequence of the entrepreneur's decision making.

The *strategic* perspective must take centre stage. It is this which relates the needs of customers to the ability of the business to serve them. *Financial* growth is a measure of the business's performance in serving the needs of its markets, thus it is a measure of the resources the market has allocated to the firm. The firm must convert those resources into assets. These assets are configured by the structure of the organisation. Additional resources means increasing the *assets* the business holds which in turn demands changes to the *structure* in which they are held.

This structure only provides a framework, however (Figure 24.1). The decisions which the individuals who make up the organisation make and the actions that they take in relation to the assets it owns are governed by wider dimensions of

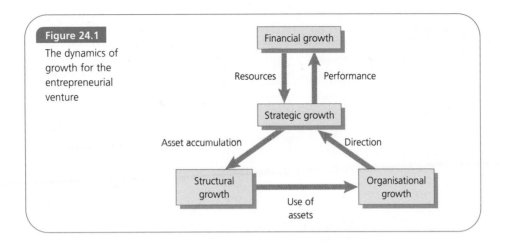

Figure 24.1

The dynamics of growth for the entrepreneurial venture

the organisation such as its culture and attitudes. Strategic growth has a *direction* and that direction results from the vision and leadership the entrepreneur offers.

It must also be added that although growth is a *defining* feature of the entrepreneurial venture, this does not mean that an entrepreneurial business has a *right* to grow. It merely means that, if managed in the right way, it has the *potential* to grow. Growth must be made an objective for the venture. It is an opportunity that must be managed effectively if it is to be capitalised upon. For the entrepreneur, growth is a reward for identifying the right opportunities, understanding how they might be exploited and competing effectively to take advantage of them.

24.2   Financial analysis of growth

Key learning outcome

An understanding of the way in which financial growth is recorded, reported and analysed.

The financial performance of a firm is important to all its stakeholders. A sound financial position brings security for employees, offers customers the prospect of good service and investment in future offerings, and promises suppliers a demand for their outputs. Investors, of course, have an interest in seeing a good return on their capital. They will take particular note of the financial performance of the businesses they have chosen to back.

Investors and businesses communicate in a number of ways. The degree of personal contact will depend on the type of investors, the amount of investment, and the stage of the business's development. The nature of the economic system in which the business is operating is also important. Investment systems in different parts of the world vary in both their formal and informal aspects. One key difference is in the way the investor seeks to influence the management of the business. If the business seeks investment in an open stock market then two main means are available to effect this. If the stock market is 'liquid' (as it tends to be in the UK

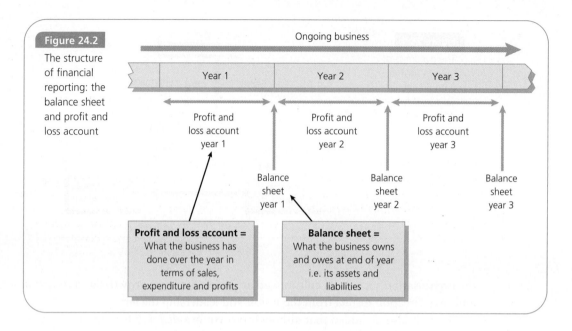

Figure 24.2

The structure of financial reporting: the balance sheet and profit and loss account

and the USA) then investors can signal their assessment of the firm's performance by buying and selling shares. An increasing share price offers the business security for obtaining further investment. A falling share price can make a business susceptible to takeover. Other economies (typically those in continental Europe) tend towards a greater degree of intervention by investors. Institutional shareholders (such as pension funds and banks) may appoint directors to act on their behalf.

If the business has not yet reached the stage where it is ready to offer investment stock to the stock market and is reliant on private and institutional investment such as banks and venture capital instead, then a high degree of both investor scrutiny and involvement is likely.

Whatever the nature and means of the interaction between business and investor, financial reporting provides a common language by which they can communicate with each other. At the centre of this communication are two documents: the *balance sheet* and the *profit and loss account* (Figure 24.2). The balance sheet is a summary of *what the business owns*, that is, its *assets* and *liabilities*. It represents the state of the business at *a point in time*, specifically the date of the report. The profit and loss account is a report on *what the business has done* over the previous period, that is, its trading activity in terms of *sales* (or *turnover*), the *expenditure* involved in achieving those sales and the resulting *profits*. The reporting period is normally one year but can be a shorter interval if investors see the need for more detailed tracking.

The balance sheet

The balance sheet is so called because it is usual to show the assets and liabilities of the firm as being equal (i.e. balancing). The details presented on the balance

Table 24.1   The balance sheet

Assets	**Liabilities**
Tangible assets The value of all buildings and machinery etc. owned by the firm	*Short-term creditors* All creditors (people and organisations to whom the firm owes money) due for payment within one year
+	+
Intangible assets The valuation of the things 'owned' by the firm, which have no physical form but can, potentially, be bought and sold, e.g. brand names and goodwill	*Long-term creditors* All creditors due for payment after one year. Important elements include: ● loan repayment due after one year; ● dividends planned for investors (including the entrepreneur's remuneration); ● long-term repayments agreed with suppliers; ● taxes owed to the government
+	+
Current assets Cash in hand, stock (including finished goods, work in progress and raw materials), creditor and trade debts owed to the firm	*Called-up share capital* The permanent capital of the firm in the form of the face value of issued shares
+	+
Investments Investments held by the firm in other businesses, government stock and other financial instruments	*Capital reserves* The profits held by the firm. Properly, these are the property of the investors in the firm. Some may be distributed to investors in the form of dividends; others may be retained for future investment
=	=
Total assets	**Total liabilities**

sheet vary between different countries; however, some of the key lines are as indicated in Table 24.1.

A number of important relationships can be derived from the balance sheet. Some of the more important are:

1 The fundamental balance sheet identity:

Total assets = Total liabilities

2 Net assets are the assets the business will actually have available over the coming year. Net assets represent the sum of assets and working capital. They can also be defined as:

Net assets = Total assets − Short-term liabilities to outsiders

Because of the balance sheet identity, net assets must be equal to the total of shareholders' funds.

3 Net current assets (also known as *working capital*) are those resources which are *liquid*, that is, they either already exist in the form of cash, or are expected to be turned into cash within twelve months of the report date. The definition is:

Net current assets = Current assets − Short-term liabilities

4 Capital employed is a measure of the total resources available for use by the firm's management. It is defined as:

Capital employed = (Long-term creditors + Called-up share capital
+ Capital reserves)

The profit and loss account

The profit and loss account provides a summary of the revenues obtained as a result of trading activity over the period in question. The key lines are shown in Table 24.2.

Profits for a period represent the difference between income and outgoings. A number of different measures of profit level are important:

1 *Gross profits* – the basic profits generated by the business. This is sometimes referred to as profit before interest payable and tax (PBIT):

Gross profits = Sales − Cost of sales

2 *Profit before tax* – profits left after interest on debts has been paid:

Profit before tax (PBT) = Gross profits − Interest

3 *Profit after tax* – profits left after any tax owing to the government has been paid:

Profit after tax (PAT) = PBT − Tax

4 *Retained profits* – any profit left after tax has been paid is properly the property of the firm's shareholders. Some of it may be distributed to them in the form of dividends. Some may, however, be retained by the firm for future investment. Such profits are called *retained profits*. The retained profit figure on the profit and loss account is equivalent to the *capital reserves* figure on the balance sheet:

Retained profits = PAT − Dividends

Ratio analysis

The performance of the entrepreneurial venture must be measured not only in terms of absolutes – the new value it generates – but also in relative terms, i.e. the

---

Table 24.2 The profit and loss account

Income

Turnover from normal trading activities
The income generated as a result of the firm's normal business activities

Extraordinary income
Additional income which is a result of activities that are not part of the firm's usual profile of business

Income from investments
Income received as a result of investments owned by the firm in other businesses or other investment instruments

---

Outgoing

Cost of sales
The expenditure that was necessary to deliver the sales that were achieved. Important cost elements are:
● raw materials and factors;
● salaries;
● purchase (or rental) of machinery and equipment;
● depreciation charges on machinery and equipment; and
● sales and marketing expenditure

Interest on debt
Payments to cover interest charges on outstanding debts

Extraordinary expenditure
Expenditure that has been made but which is not typical of the expenditure the business normally faces. It is a result of special circumstances or a one-off activity. Critically, it is expenditure the business does not expect to face again

Taxation
Money owed to the government as a result of taxation

Dividends
Money to be paid to investors as a return on their investment. (This may include some of the entrepreneur's remuneration insofar as the entrepreneur is an investor.)

---

new value created given the resources the entrepreneur has to hand. An investor in the venture is interested not so much in 'profits' as in the *returns* the venture will offer for a *given level of investment*.

Ratio analysis can be used to provide a valuable insight into the performance, condition and stability of the venture. As its name suggests, it is based on an evaluation of the ratios between different lines on the balance sheet and profit and loss account.

Three types of ratio are important. *Performance ratios* indicate the way the business is performing, that is, the value it is creating from the resources to hand. *Financial status* ratios provide an indication of the financial security of the venture and how exposed a backer's investment is. If the venture has a stock market listing, then *stock market ratios* can be used to compare the performance of an investment in the venture with alternative investment opportunities. Some of these ratios will now be explored in more detail.

Performance ratios

Profit margin

The profit margin of a business is the ratio (expressed as a percentage) of profits to turnover. It is defined as:

$$\text{Profit margin} = \frac{(\text{Profits} \times 100\%)}{\text{Turnover}}$$

The usual profit level for this ratio is profit before tax, but other profit measure levels may also be used.

Return on investment

Return on investment (ROI) is *the* fundamental measure of a venture's performance. Two different ROIs are used. Return on equity (ROE) is the ratio of profit after interest payments have been made but before tax (and normally before extraordinary items too) to shareholders' funds:

$$\text{Return on equity} = \frac{(\text{Profit before tax} \times 100\%)}{(\text{Called-up share capital} + \text{Capital reserves})}$$

Return on net assets (RONA) is the ratio of gross profit to net assets:

$$\text{Return on net assets} = \frac{(\text{Gross profit} \times 100\%)}{\text{Net assets}}$$

Although these two measures are related, they offer slightly different perspectives on the performance of the venture. ROE gives *investors* (especially ordinary shareholders) an indication of the profits which are (potentially) available to them in relation to the investment they have made in the venture. RONA gives the *venture's management* an indication of the profits they are generating (which can later be distributed to lenders, investors and taxing authorities) in relation to the assets that they have available to them. In more technical terms, RONA is a performance measure which is *independent* of the capital structure of the firm.

Turnover ratios

In general, turnover ratios are those which look at the number of times some measure of the firm's asset ownership generates some measure of the firm's income. Two are particularly important.

Net asset turnover (NAT) indicates the number of times annual sales are generated by the firm's net assets. It is defined by:

$$\text{Net asset turnover} = \frac{\text{Sales}}{\text{Net assets}}$$

In a similar manner, fixed asset turnover (FAT) indicates the number of times annual sales are generated by fixed assets:

$$\text{Fixed asset turnover} = \frac{\text{Sales}}{\text{Fixed assets}}$$

Financial status ratios

An investor is not only interested in the performance of the firm they have invested in but also in the *risk* that that investment entails. A key element of risk for the entrepreneurial venture is its ability to meet the liabilities it accepts given the revenues it generates. *Financial status ratios* can be used to gain an insight into the business's position with regard to its liabilities. Two sorts of financial status ratio are useful. *Solvency ratios* give an indication of the firm's general financial health and its ability to meet its long-term liabilities. *Liquidity ratios* give an indication of the firm's ability to meet its short-term liabilities where it is called upon to do so in a crisis.

Solvency ratios

The debt ratio represents the capital structure of the firm. It is the ratio of debt (that is, money which has been borrowed at a fixed rate of interest) to equity (that is, money obtained from investors whose return will depend on the overall performance of the venture). It is defined as:

$$\text{Debt ratio} = \frac{(\text{Long-term debt} \times 100\%)}{\text{Capital employed}}$$

where

Capital employed = (Long-term debt + Called-up share capital + Retained profits)

A related ratio is called *gearing*:

$$\text{Gearing} = \frac{(\text{Long-term debt} \times 100\%)}{\text{Shareholders' funds}}$$

where

Shareholders' funds = (Called-up share capital + Retained profits)

Clearly, the debt ratio and gearing provide related information. The debt ratio is more frequently used in the UK whereas gearing (also referred to as leverage) tends to be quoted in the USA.

Interest cover is a ratio of profits to interest owed to those who lend money to the venture. It gives an indication of a firm's ability to pay interest on its debts. It is given by:

$$\text{Interest cover} = \frac{\text{Profit before interest and tax (PBIT)}}{\text{Interest on long-term debt}}$$

Liquidity ratios

Liquidity ratios are concerned with *short-term* liabilities. Two ratios are particularly important. The *current ratio* is the ratio of current assets to current liabilities.

$$\text{Current ratio} = \frac{\text{Current assets}}{\text{Current liabilities}}$$

where Current liabilities are those short-term creditors who expect payment within one year.

The *acid test* (or *quick ratio*) is a straight measure of a firm's ability to pay its short-term creditors immediately from its liquid assets. It is defined as:

$$\text{Acid test ratio} = \frac{\text{Liquid assets}}{\text{Current liabilities}}$$

Liquid assets are cash and short-term debtors (and therefore equal to current assets minus stock). An acid test of 1.0 or more indicates that the business is 'safe'. It would, if demanded, be able to pay off its short-term liabilities from the liquid assets it has in hand.

Stock market ratios

If the venture has issued shares and is floated on a stock market, then a number of ratios can be used to evaluate the performance of the business and investments in it. To calculate these ratios, the information given in financial reports must be supplemented with routine reports on share price performance. This information is provided daily by the *Financial Times* and is available via the Internet.

Earnings per share

Earnings per share (EPS) are the profits potentially available for each share that has been issued. Profits are measured after interest and taxation but normally before extraordinary items have been paid.

$$\text{Earnings per share} = \frac{\text{Profit after tax}}{\text{Number of shares issued}}$$

Note that if more than one type of share has been issued then the ratio usually refers to ordinary shares.

Price/earnings ratio

The price/earnings ratio (PE ratio) is the ratio of the price at which a share in the business is trading on the stock market to the earnings per share:

$$\text{Price/earnings ratio} = \frac{\text{Market price of share}}{\text{Earnings per share (EPS)}}$$

$$= \frac{\text{Market price of share} \times \text{Number of shares}}{\text{Profit after tax}}$$

The market price per share multiplied by the number of shares represents the market's valuation of the firm as a whole. It is sometimes referred to as the firm's *market capitalisation*.

The PE ratio is an indication of the market's confidence in the business, both in terms of the risk it represents and its future growth potential. A relatively high price relative to earnings indicates that the market regards the investment as being of relatively low risk or that the value of the investment will increase in the future.

Dividend yield

The dividend yield represents the payment made to investors on each share as a proportion of the market value of the share:

$$\text{Dividend yield} = \frac{\text{Dividend per share}}{\text{Market price of share}}$$

The dividend yield will be dependent both on the total profits generated by the business and on the way in which management offer them back to investors or, alternatively, retain them for future investment. A young, high-growth business may have a relatively low or even zero dividend yield. However, investors will still value their investment and hang on to it if they feel the venture has the potential to offer high rewards in the future.

Dividend cover

Dividend cover is another measure which indicates the division of available profits by management between passing them to shareholders and retaining them within the business for future investment. Dividend cover represents the number of times the management could, potentially, have paid the actual dividend offered out of the profits that were available to shareholders. It is defined by:

$$\text{Dividend cover} = \frac{\text{Earnings per share}}{\text{Dividend per share}}$$

Clearly, stock market ratios are dependent on share price, which is adjusted constantly as new information (both on the business specifically and on the economy in general) reaches the market. This information can be followed in the *Financial Times* or on a variety of Internet sites. The annual financial report is an important factor in providing this information but it is far from its entirety. A share price is just an estimation by an investor of the value of their investment. This valuation responds to the way in which the entrepreneur (and other managers) communicates with, and the message that is sent to, investors.

24.3 Financial growth

> **Key learning outcome**
>
> An understanding of how financial analysis provides a context for understanding the financial growth and development of the venture.

The report of the financial situation, that is, the balance sheet and the profit and loss account and the ratios that can be derived from these items, provides those interested in the venture (the entrepreneur, other managers, investors and taxing authorities) with a wealth of information which provides a basis on which decisions may be made. However, decisions must be made within a broader context which needs to consider both the firm's performance *relative to its particular business sector* and the overall *trends* in the firm's performance.

There are no absolute measures of performance. The profit margin or return on investment (or any other performance measure) to be expected from a venture will depend on the sector in which the business operates. What matters is not so much the performance of the venture but its performance *relative* to key competitors and to market norms. Similarly, the expected financial status ratios will vary between different industry sectors. The factor which determines how investment capital is distributed between sectors offering different levels of return is, of course, *risk*. The way in which risk is anticipated by investors can be gleaned from a close examination of the stock market ratios of players within a particular sector. An entrepreneurial venture is not static. It is undergoing constant growth and development. Investors and other decision makers will colour their decisions not just by reference to the indicators for the business at a single point in time but by evaluating the *trends* in its performance. This will be particularly important for investors who are not expecting immediate returns from the venture but who are willing to accept some risk for the promise of higher returns in the future. Investors' decision making (particularly the key decision of whether to hold or exit from their investment) will be influenced by four main factors.

The underlying performance (return on investment) of the venture

Investors will be interested in the performance of the venture not just in absolute terms but relative to their *expectations* of that performance. Their expectations will be a result of their knowledge of the business and the sector it operates in, and of the promises offered by the entrepreneur driving the venture.

The growth in the value of the venture

The *growth* of the venture can be qualified by a number of financial criteria. Growth in *income* (and by implication, *outgoings*), *assets* and *capital* are equally important. Some of the key indicators to follow include changes in turnover, changes in cash profits, changes in tangible assets, changes in total assets, and changes in shareholders' capital. Growth in these measures can be followed both in absolute terms and as a proportion of absolute values. Proportional changes can be indicated as an index or as a percentage. A *growth index* is calculated as:

$$\text{Growth index} = \frac{\text{Value of measure in year}}{\text{Value of measure in previous year}}$$

Growth as a *percentage* is given by:

$$\text{Growth \%} = \frac{(\text{Value of measure in year} - \text{Value in previous year})}{\text{Value of measure in previous year}} \times 100\%$$

When making a comparison it is often useful to *discount* for general inflation in an economy. This enables the *real* growth of the venture to be measured. To discount for inflation the *nominal* growth calculated for the venture must be divided by the inflation index for the period under consideration:

$$\text{Real growth} = \frac{\text{Nominal growth}}{\text{Inflation index}}$$

Usually, the general retail price index is used but other more specialist inflation measures may be adopted. If inflation is quoted as a percentage it can be converted by the following formula:

$$\text{Inflation index} = \frac{[(\text{Inflation as \%}) + 100]}{100}$$

Growth by the venture is usually received positively. Expansion of the venture drives an increase in the underlying value of a shareholder's investment. Growth also indicates that the venture has a successful formula and so, *in general*, it signals a reduction in risk. Growth does not, however, come for free. It must be *paid for* and a high level of growth may make cash-flow tighter and so lead to less favourable financial status ratios. This may make the venture slightly more risky in the short term, particularly if there is a crisis and short-term liabilities have to be met.

The trend in the risk of the venture

While growth tends to reduce risk overall, the specific level of risk faced by the business is, to a degree, under the control of the entrepreneur and other managers. An important factor is the debt ratio (or, alternatively, gearing) of the venture. Debt, on the whole, is cheaper than equity finance. However, debt must be repaid whatever the performance of the business. Debt repayment must take priority over the repayment of equity or dividends. Therefore a high debt ratio does expose the business (and that means its investors) to more risk.

No generalisation can be made about the optimum level of debt to equity. This is a complex issue and not only are interest rates and industry risk relevant, but taxation effects also have an influence. Comparison to industry norms can provide a rough and ready guide.

Financial status and (if the firm has floated shares) stock market ratios provide an insight into the overall risk status of the venture. In general, as the business grows, matures and stabilises investors will expect risk to be reduced. Having faced risk initially they become ready to enjoy the return they are owed.

The dividends yielded by the venture

At the end of the day, investors will wish to see a capital gain through their investment. This may take the form of them receiving dividend payments on the shares they hold or by selling those shares. These two approaches to liquidating investment differ in timing rather than substance. The buyer of the share does so in the expectation of a future flow of dividends. An independent market values the investment on the basis of the cash-flow it can generate.

Managers in the venture will make a decision about how much of the profits generated is to be passed on to the shareholders and how much is to be retained within the business for future investment. Shareholders will either agree to this split or will not. They will show their approval (or otherwise) either by direct interference in the firm or, if their investment is liquid, by buying or selling their shares thus raising or depressing the share price. In general, while investors may be willing to see managers recycle profits back into a young, fast-growing venture they will at some point expect to see a real cash reward for their investment. As the firm matures, it is likely that investors will expect a greater proportion of profits to be given back to them.

A general scheme for analysing the financial growth of an entrepreneurial venture is indicated in Figure 24.3.

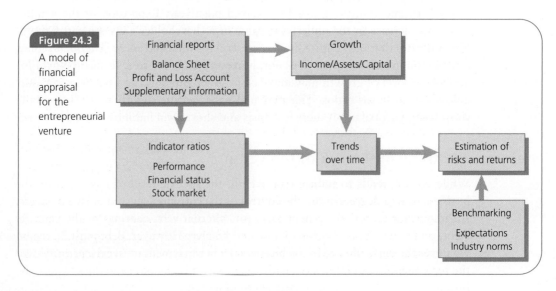

Figure 24.3 A model of financial appraisal for the entrepreneurial venture

(24.4) Strategic growth

Key learning outcome

An understanding of the ways in which competitive advantage can be developed as the venture grows.

The strategic approach to organisational management regards the organisation as a single *coherent* entity which must be managed in its entirety. It locates the organisation conceptually in an *environment* from which it must draw resources and *add value* to them. The organisation must then distribute the new value created to its stakeholders. The strategic approach also recognises that the organisation is in *competition* with other organisations which also seek to attract and utilise those resources.

From a strategic perspective, the organisation is able to compete for resources by virtue of the *competitive advantages* it develops and maintains. Growth represents the business's success in drawing in resources from its environment. It is a sign that the business has been effective in competing in the marketplace. This suggests that the business has built up a competitive advantage and has managed to sustain it in the face of competitive pressure. However, a competitive advantage is not static. Sustaining an advantage simultaneously develops and enhances it.

All advantages are very sensitive to business growth. In general, expansion of the business can be used to enhance a competitive advantage. This will only occur, however, if the entrepreneur is sensitive to the nature of the competitive advantages that their venture enjoys and strives to actively manage that advantage as the business grows and develops.

Growth and cost advantages

The main source of cost advantages are experience effects. Practice in delivering the outputs leads to a reduction in cost (strictly, the cost of adding a particular amount of value). Costs tend to fall in an exponential way as output increases linearly. Hence, experience cost advantages are (usually) held by the business which has achieved the greatest cumulative output. This can lead to a 'virtuous circle' (Figure 24.4). Cost leadership means that the customer can be offered a lower price. This increases demand for the firm's outputs relative to those of competitors. This leads to the firm developing a volume output lead over competitors. In turn, this volume advantage leads to enhanced cost leadership and the ability to offer customers an even lower price, and so on.

Clearly, the entrepreneur can build in cost advantages as the business grows. Such a strategy offers the potential for a consistent and sustainable advantage in the marketplace. It is, however, a strategy which requires certain conditions to be met and it is not without risk. If the strategy is to work the entrepreneur must be sure of a number of features of the market they are developing.

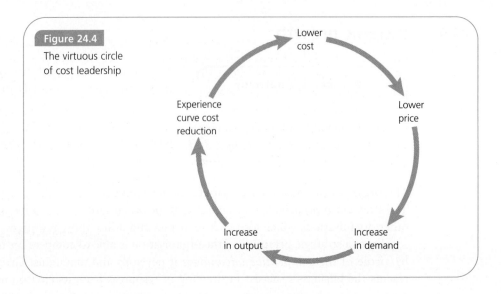

Figure 24.4

The virtuous circle
of cost leadership

Cost advantages have not already been established in the market

If cost advantages have already been established in the market, then the business
will risk being a follower rather than a leader. If the venture's costs are not *genuinely* lower than those of the leading competitor then undercutting the leader
to subsidise costs and offer the customer a lower price will demand a high level
of investment. In some instances such 'undercutting' will be construed as anti-
competitive by regulatory bodies. It is, in any case, always expensive.

In order to become a cost leader it is better if the entrepreneur is first into a
market. In effect, what this means is that the innovation on which the venture is
based is sufficiently different to constitute a 'new' market.

Potential volume outputs make entry into the market worthwhile

Experience curve cost reductions only become meaningful when the output
volumes are quite high. Consequently a cost leadership strategy is not a realistic
option for a small or even a medium-sized business serving a local market. Cost
leadership really becomes a serious option for the business which is an industry maker and which aims to deliver its outputs to a wide (which increasingly
today means *global*) market. This is not to say that price is not an important
factor for smaller businesses or that they should not manage costs, rather that
cost as the *mainstay* of competitive advantage is really the prerogative of the
large player.

A corollary of this fact is that the entire market must be ready to accept a fairly
homogeneous product. If too much specialisation is required at a local level then
the extent to which production is repetitive will be lost and hence the possibility
of cost-reducing experience will also be lost.

Sales of the product they are offering to the market are sensitive to price

Experience cost advantages are gained via volume output. The virtuous circle will only be followed if customers respond to lower prices by buying more of the price leader's offerings. This demands that the products offered are *price sensitive*, which means that the firm's products must be *substitutable* with those of competitors. Substitutability implies that the products of different suppliers are pretty much equivalent (from the buyer's perspective) and can replace one another in use. To be substitutable, products must not only be similar in a technical sense but they must not have any switching costs associated with them; that is, there should be no additional expense for the customer when moving from one supplier to another.

If switching costs are present *and* the entrepreneur is the first to get customers on board then they may use these costs as the basis of a competitive advantage. Again, this emphasises the importance of innovation in entrepreneurial success.

The experience curve will be steep enough (but not too steep!)

An experience curve has a *gradient*. This is the rate at which increasing output reduces costs, that is, the speed at which learning takes place. The experience curve needs to be steep enough for the volume advantages that the pioneering entrepreneur can gain to lead to cost advantages which have a meaningful impact on prices in the marketplace. If, however, the curve is too steep then followers will find it easier to catch up, and any advantage gained initially will be quickly eroded.

Distribution can be maintained

A price advantage offered to the customer is only useful if the customer can get hold of the product. This implies that distribution can be readily achieved. If independent agencies are involved in the distribution process (e.g. wholesalers or retailers) then there is always the danger that a follower will, in some way or other, interfere with the cost leader's ability to distribute. In effect, they will look towards distributors as the basis for developing a non-cost competitive advantage. If such a distributor 'lock-out' occurs, then the leader will lose volume and any cost advantage can be rapidly lost. Often, such actions are restricted by anti-trust legislation. However, such legislation is difficult to enforce. If the business is multinational, then distributors may be tempted to favour local suppliers. Governments that have seen a 'strategic' advantage in supporting local producers have been known to resist pressure to open their markets by accusing global cost leaders of 'dumping' (i.e. of selling below cost to establish their presence in a market). Even if such accusations are eventually disproved, volume sales may have been lost already. With a cost leadership strategy, time equals volume which means costs which equals money.

Technological innovation will not reset the experience curve

Experience is gained by repetitive utilisation of a particular operational technology to manufacture or deliver a service. If the technological basis of an industry changes then descent down a new experience curve begins. In cost terms, all bets are off! Innovation, both in the type of product offered to the customer and the means for its delivery, offers both an opportunity and a threat. It may be the means by which the entrepreneur first enters the market and gains an advantage over existing players, but, once they are established, and competitive advantage has been built on a particular technology, they are vulnerable to a new generation of innovators. This means that the entrepreneurial business, even if it is following a cost leadership strategy, must still look towards maintaining innovation.

The entrepreneur (and financial backers) have patience!

Cost leadership is not a short-term strategy. The payoffs are far from immediate. While competing on a price leadership basis, profit margins must be kept slim, i.e. just sufficient to cover overhead costs. This is the only way in which the business can be sure that it is reflecting its cost advantage with the most competitive market price. However, it will be tempting to raise prices and to increase short-term profit margins. The entrepreneur may be looking for additional returns to invest in the growth of the business. Investors may be eager to see a positive return on their investment. The business may see a price increase as a viable option. It will be in a market-leading position (certainly in volume terms). It may have established a strong relationship with customers. Competitors may have found it hard to gain a foothold in the market. However, the temptation to increase prices must still be resisted!

All these advantages are a *consequence* of keeping prices low. They are the basis on which the business can gain a future reward for maintaining tight profit margins. If the business increases its prices too early then it can create a 'cost umbrella' under which less efficient competitors may shelter. It may be just the gap a competitor needs in order to gain a toe-hold in the market. If a cost leadership strategy is to be effective then the business pursuing it must keep its nerve and keep prices as low as possible for as long as possible. Optimally, prices should be kept to a minimum until market growth has stopped. After this the market will start to lose its attractiveness to new entrants as gaining market share will tend to require the conversion of existing customers rather than drawing new ones into the market. At this point the cost-leading business can start to raise prices above costs, to increase profit margins and to harvest its investment.

Figure 24.5 shows how technological innovation and the creation of cost umbrellas both present risks for a cost leadership strategy.

Costs are actively managed

Even though costs often follow a mathematical relationship to output volume this does not mean that increasing output *automatically* drives down costs. Increasing output gives the firm's managers the *opportunity* to drive down costs but that is an opportunity they must grasp actively. The management of cost must become the focus of managerial activity. In fact, it must become the key criterion around which decisions are made.

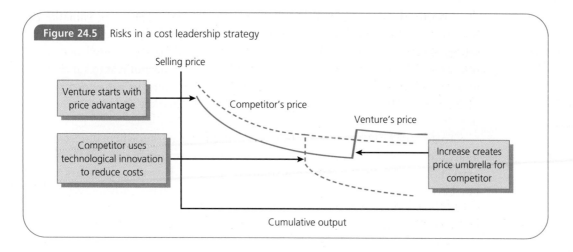

Figure 24.5 Risks in a cost leadership strategy

Cost leadership is a strategy which has an impact on, and must be supported by, all the firm's stakeholders. As noted above, customers must be responsive to price and investors must be willing to play a long game. In addition, suppliers must recognise that they must be competitive in the price at which they offer inputs to the business. Further, employees will become aware (and if not managed properly, *acutely* aware) of the fact that they themselves are 'costs' as well as partners in the creation of the business. There is a danger that this will lead them to see their interests as being counter to those of the business. A focus on managing costs must be single-minded. It must also be implemented with sensitivity.

Growth and knowledge advantages

Knowledge advantages arise from knowing something about the customer, the market or the product offered that competitors do not know, which enables the business to offer something of value to the customer. The development of a knowledge-based advantage is dependent on two factors: the *significance* of the knowledge advantage and the rate at which it will be *eroded*.

How significant is the knowledge advantage?

How *valuable* is what is known? Is the knowledge sufficient in scope and does it have significance to enough customers in order to sustain the growth of the business? If so, what level of growth can it sustain?

How will the knowledge advantage be eroded?

How long will it take competitors to *gain* the knowledge and use it themselves? Can they discover it for themselves or through others? Will the venture's activities *signal* it to them?

Clearly, these two factors work against each other. The more valuable the knowledge, the more that competitors will be encouraged to get hold of it for themselves. Knowledge is difficult to protect. A particular piece of knowledge rarely offers more than a transient advantage. If the business aims not just to survive, but to *grow*, on the back of knowledge advantages, then it must be active in a process of constant re-discovery about what it is offering the market and why the market buys it.

To do this the business needs to position itself in a market where discovery and innovation are well received and rewarded. This is certainly the case in 'high-tech' markets where technological innovation is the norm. However, the market does not have to be high-tech. More generally, knowledge-based advantages can be gained in any market where customer expectations are in flux and they are likely to respond well to new offerings.

In order to respond to this the entrepreneurial business must ensure that two activities are given priority. First, it requires that resources are put into understanding the market and its customers. In a functional sense this means *market research*. More broadly, it means that the whole organisation must be attuned to new ideas and new initiatives. It particularly demands that the organisation be responsive to the signals sent out by customers about their needs and desires. Second, it requires that the organisation be active in creating, developing and offering new products and services to the customer. Product development activity must be supported by the processes and systems within the organisation. Indeed it must be *prioritised* by them. These systems must be given centre stage as the growth and development of the organisation is managed.

Growth and relationship advantages

Relationships exist between *people*, not just organisations. During its early stages, the business may be 'fronted' directly by the entrepreneur. He or she will be directly responsible for building productive relationships with the venture's stakeholders. Indeed, tying together and securing the threads of the network into which they have entered may be the entrepreneur's key role. Customers, suppliers, employees and investors will be drawn to the venture as a result of the positive relationship they develop with the entrepreneur. The question becomes, how can the entrepreneur maintain relationship advantages as the business grows and develops? Further, how can the entrepreneur use such advantages to *drive* growth in the business?

This challenge is acute. In the first instance, the entrepreneur will be located at the centre of the web of relationships and will be in control of them all. As the organisation grows and develops then the web of relationships becomes much more complex. The entrepreneur can no longer represent the organisation to all the parties who have an interest in it. New individuals must develop the organisation's relationships on a specialist basis. For example, salespeople will make representations to customers. Procurement and purchasing specialists must work with suppliers. At some stage it may even be necessary to have finance specialists to manage the venture's relationship with its investors.

To understand how relationship advantages may be maintained and developed as the business grows, it is necessary to have a deep understanding of the ways in which the relationships the business has with its stakeholders are *different* from those of competitor organisations; why that difference is important in offering *value* to those stakeholders; and why competitors find it hard to *imitate* those relationships. In particular the entrepreneur must ask the following questions.

Why are the relationships valuable?

What aspect of the relationship creates value for the stakeholder? Does the relationship provide trust which reduces the need for monitoring costs? Does the relationship offer benefits which satisfy social needs? Does the relationship promise the potential to satisfy self-developmental needs? Are these benefits carried as part of the product (say, through *branding*) or are they supplementary to it (say, through working in *association* with the business)?

What are the expectations of the relationships?

What matters in a relationship is not actual outcomes but outcomes in relation to *expectations*. If expectations are met (or even better, *exceeded*) then satisfaction will occur. If they are not met then disappointment will result. Human relationships are complex. The expectations they generate are multi-faceted. They may be manifest at economic, social and self-developmental levels. Often these interact with each other and the effective entrepreneur must manage relationships at each level.

What practices sustain the relationships?

Relationships are acted out. The parties to the relationship play *roles*. To a greater or lesser extent, relationships are *scripted*. Selling, for example, involves a series of reasonably well-defined steps: first approach, introduction, product presentation, close, etc. Internally, employee motivation may be sustained through appraisal and reward procedures. Not all the practices that sustain relationships are explicit. Some may not even be noticed until the practice is broken! Practices, even quite trivial ones, may almost become ritualised. In this, they are one of the building blocks out of which expectations are created. Changing a routine may have an impact on a relationship at a deep level.

By way of an example, consider an entrepreneur whose business is doing quite well. The venture's backers are very happy. Their expectations have been more than met. The entrepreneur provides the backers with a financial report every three months. After a while, this becomes routine. The backers, acknowledging that the business presents them with no concerns, stop examining the report in any detail. After a while the entrepreneur recognises this and decides that the report is 'a waste of time', so the entrepreneur, without informing the backers, stops sending it.

What are the backers to think? Should they be concerned? They contact the entrepreneur who informs them that they should not worry, that the business is still doing well and that the report was stopped because it was not giving them any new information and so the communication 'was not important'. How are the backers likely to interpret the attitude of the entrepreneur towards them?

What relationship skills are required to maintain them?

Relationships must be managed and this management, like any other form of management, calls upon knowledge and skills. As discussed fully in Section 7.3, the key skill areas that are important for managing the relationships in and around the entrepreneurial venture include *communication* skills, *selling* skills, *negotiating* skills and *motivational* skills.

What behaviour standards are demanded?

Behaviour standards (which are as much about what should *not* be done as what should be) are a critical dimension of relationships. A society will, in general, define the behavioural standards expected for business practice. This is only a minimum guide. The entrepreneur may always look for competitive advantage in accepting discretionary responsibilities that go *beyond* those normally expected for a business in the sector (see Section 12.4).

Growth and structural advantages

Structural advantages arise when the business organises itself in a way which gives it more flexibility and responsiveness in the face of competitive pressures. This is often a key area of advantage for the entrepreneurial business. Lacking the cost and possibly the relationship advantages enjoyed by established businesses, the entrepreneurial venture must prosper by being more acute to the market's needs and innovating to satisfy them.

The challenge to the entrepreneurial business is to retain this responsiveness and drive for innovation as the business grows and matures. The key to this is understanding the nature of the structural advantages the business has gained and designing the development of the business's structure and organisation so that these are sustained and encouraged to flourish. This important idea will be developed further in Sections 24.5 and 24.6.

24.5 Structural growth

> **Key learning outcome**
>
> An understanding of the factors which drive the structure of the organisation as it grows.

Every organisation has a unique *structure*. An understanding of this structure is best approached from a broad perspective. It has both static and dynamic aspects. At one level it is the framework of reporting relationships (who is responsible to whom) that describes the organisation. This is how the

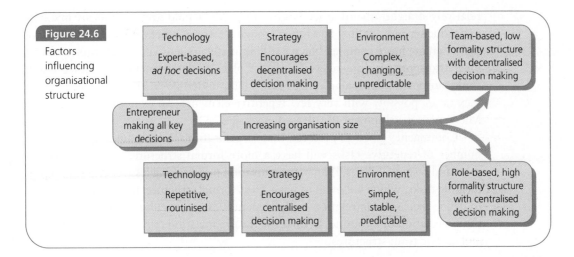

Figure 24.6

Factors influencing organisational structure

| Technology | Strategy | Environment | |
| Expert-based, *ad hoc* decisions | Encourages decentralised decision making | Complex, changing, unpredictable | Team-based, low formality structure with decentralised decision making |

Entrepreneur making all key decisions ——— Increasing organisation size

| Technology | Strategy | Environment | |
| Repetitive, routinised | Encourages centralised decision making | Simple, stable, predictable | Role-based, high formality structure with centralised decision making |

organisation is often depicted in hierarchical 'organograms'. This formal structure is however just a skeleton. The organisation gains its flesh from the way in which those reporting relationships are played out in terms of the *communications* that take place, the *roles* that must be performed and the *power structures* that define, support and confine those roles. Some of these are formal and explicit, others are informal and implicit, but the entrepreneur must learn to manage all of them.

The structure of the organisation, and the way that structure develops as the organisation grows, is both a response to the circumstances in which the organisation finds itself and a reaction to the opportunities with which it is presented. One well-explored approach to understanding how the particular situation of an organisation defines its structure is provided by *contingency theory*. In essence, contingency theory regards the structure of an organisation as dependent on five 'contingencies', or types of factor. These are the organisation's *size*, the operational *technology* it uses to create value, the *strategy* it adopts, the *environment* it is in, and the way *power* is utilised within it (Figure 24.6).

Organisation size

In general, the larger the organisation, the more complex its structure will be. A larger organisation provides more scope for tasks to be differentiated. As more information needs to be passed up to decision makers and more instructions passed back down again, there will be room for more layers of management. Once a certain size is reached, the complexity of the organisation may become so great that it is better to break it up into a series of sub-organisations (functions or departments), each reporting to a common centre.

Operational technology

In broad terms, an organisation's operational technology is simply the way it goes about performing its tasks. Some organisations are involved in repeating a series of relatively straightforward tasks. For example, McDonald's restaurants are involved in producing and retailing fast food through a large number of outlets. Others face tasks that are more complex but are still ultimately repetitive. For example, easyJet must transport air passengers from one place to another. On the other hand, some businesses, particularly 'high-tech' ones, undertake a small number of complex tasks, possibly with very few repetitive elements. An example here might be Microsoft's development of software packages.

Contingency theory predicts that organisations which undertake a large number of repetitive tasks will have a more formal structure, with well-defined roles and responsibilities, than an organisation undertaking less repetitive and predictable tasks, which will tend to have a less formal structure. Individuals will tend to define their roles in relation to the demands of a particular project, rather than the expectation of a routine. In this case the organisation may develop expert roles and *ad hoc* team structures.

Organisation strategy

The strategy adopted by a business is the way it goes about competing for its customers' attention. It is, in essence, what it offers, to whom and the reasons it gives customers to buy. Some organisations, having established their business, take up a defensive posture. They understand their products and the reasons why customers buy. They compete by being better at serving 'their' niche than anyone else and they only react to competitors when they move in on 'their' territory.

Other businesses – and entrepreneurs must be in this class – are more aggressive. They aim to grow their business by attacking entrenched competitors. They compete by offering the customer a new innovation which serves a need, or solves a problem, better than existing offerings. Some organisations may combine both these generic strategies: defending established business and using the resources gained to attack in other areas.

More specifically, the organisation's strategy is the way it goes about developing and sustaining competitive advantage, in particular *cost advantages*, *knowledge advantages*, *relationship advantages* and *structural advantages*.

There is no simple relationship between strategy and structure. The defining tension is the way in which decision making within the organisation drives the strategy. In short, if decision making can be centralised then a more regular, and formal, structure should be expected. If, on the other hand, decision making must be 'pushed down' to lower levels of the organisation then a less formal, more flexible, structure might be expected. Organisations pursuing cost leadership (for example, the Japanese engineering conglomerate Minebea) tend to centralise control in order to ensure that costs are managed. Retail organisations which depend on a strong brand presence (for example, The Body Shop) may also enact strong central control in order to ensure that the brand, and the products and services it endorses, are carefully managed.

Businesses based on knowledge advantages, especially where there is a lot of expertise involved, may avoid strong central control systems. Decision making may be localised. Actions may, however, be guided by a strong organisational culture. Team structures may be important, as may informal mentoring of less experienced employees by more experienced. Many professional organisations with an entrepreneurial background (for example, Saatchi and Saatchi) have adopted this approach.

The organisation's environment

Organisations find themselves in an environment made up of macroeconomic features, stakeholders and competitors. This environment both offers resources and challenges their availability. Opportunities offer new possibilities whereas threats present the danger that what is enjoyed now may be lost in the future. The environment is defined by a number of factors. In particular, how *complex* it is (that is, how much information must be processed in order to understand it), how *fast* it is developing or changing, and how *predictable* those changes are. As with strategy, the influence of the environment on structure impacts through the way in which decision making is shaped. A known, slow-changing, predictable environment encourages centralised decision making. A new or fast-changing and unpredictable environment encourages decision making to be passed down to those at the cutting edge of the organisation who are 'in contact' with the environment.

Power, control and organisational politics

The structure of an organisation represents a response to the contingencies of size, technology, strategy and environment. But the extent to which it represents a controlled, deliberate and rational response depends on the extent to which, and the way in which, the entrepreneur can exert control over the organisation as it grows. A powerful central entrepreneur can be a great asset to a business. He or she can provide vision and leadership and keep the organisation focused on the opportunities with which it is presented. In the absence of this, the organisation may lack direction and so lose its momentum. Individuals, and informal coalitions of individuals, can begin to see their interests as being different to those of the organisation as a whole and the organisation can become *politicised*.

On the other hand, if the power the entrepreneur enjoys is misdirected, then the organisation may be led down the wrong path. Entrepreneurial power brings responsibility. It is important that the entrepreneur uses their position and power to create an organisational environment in which individuals are free to express, and act upon, their own analysis and decision-making skills. This is particularly important for the fast-growing, innovative business pursuing an aggressive strategy in a changing, unpredictable environment where localised decision making can offer an advantage. Even if the organisation can benefit from a degree of centralisation of decision making the entrepreneur will face practical limitations in the range and number of decisions he or she can make personally. Once the organisation reaches a certain size (and it need not be that large) the entrepreneur is well advised to call upon the skills of a supporting management team. A summary of the influence of contingency factors on structure is provided in Table 24.3.

Table 24.3	A summary of the influence of contingency factors on organisational structure
Contingency	**Influence on organisational development**
Size	Organisational complexity tends to increase with size; development of internal structure occurs. Roles and responsibilities become more specialised
Technology	Structure driven by nature of organisation's tasks: are they repetitive, *ad hoc* or based on expert judgement? Repetitive tasks tend to favour routinised activities and repeated unit structure with centralised decision making *Ad hoc* and expert tasks encourage de-localised decision making, perhaps within a strong 'organisational cultural' framework
Environment	Well-understood, stable and predictable environment favours centralised decision making and formal, routinised structures Poorly understood, unstable and unpredictable environment favours decentralised decision making and empowerment at low levels in the organisational hierarchy
Strategy	Influence depends on how strategy is sustained through decision making Does strategy adopted demand strong central control or does it favour decentralised decision making?
Power	Can entrepreneur impose strong central control? By what means?

24.6 Organisational growth

> **Key learning outcome**
>
> An appreciation of how the resource requirements of the organisation can be used as a guide to its design.

The entrepreneur is faced with the task of designing and creating an organisation. A study by Chaganti *et al.* (2002) suggests that the entrepreneur, and his or her leadership style and strategy, is an important factor in shaping the dynamics of small business growth. Contingency theory provides a valuable insight into the variables that mould the organisation but it does not provide a detailed guide to shaping a particular organisation. A better approach is to consider the resource requirements of the organisation and to design its structure around them.

The 'traditional' path of development for an entrepreneurial venture is sometimes related as follows. At its inception, the business consists of just the entrepreneur and perhaps one or two others. The entrepreneur makes the decisions and undertakes the task of performing the business's activities, perhaps with a little delegation. In its early growth stages, as the business takes on more staff, the entrepreneur is freer to undertake the decision making and delegate more of the actual business-generating activity. As growth continues, the entrepreneur may develop a management team to support his or her own decision making. In time, the members of this management team may act as the nucleus for more formal departments or business functions. As this process continues, the entrepreneur's role becomes that of the chief executive and the organisation settles down to maturity.

While this presents a plausible story for the growth of a business it is, at best, retrospective. Models that define the development of an organisation in terms of definite stages should be met with some caution. An important example is Greiner's (1972) model that describes organisational growth in terms of five growth phases in which the business can expand with its resource base and structure intact, and five intermittent crisis phases during which the business must acquire new resources and radically modify its structure if it is to survive and move into the next growth phase. Failure to do so leads to decline. While such models may provide an account of what *has* happened they have little power to predict what *will* happen. Even if particular stages of development do exist, an individual business will move through different stages at different rates and may miss out some stages altogether. Such models are of limited use as a guide to decision making. It is hard to say at a particular time exactly what stage a business has reached or when it can be expected to move on to the next stage.

For the decision maker attempting to design an organisation it is more profitable to ask what governs the structures a particular business should adopt given the (unique) situation with which it is faced. One option is to consider the *resource requirements* of the organisation.

The resource requirement approach

The nature of the resources available to the entrepreneur have been considered in Chapter 10. In essence, the entrepreneurial venture needs only three things: *information* from which an innovation can be developed, *capital* (money) for investment and *people* to make the venture happen. The initial resource requirements of an organisation are shown in Figure 24.7. In practice, the venture will obtain these things through a variety of routes.

Information

In the first instance, information will be obtained via the entrepreneur's experience within a particular business sector. As the business grows, market intelligence gathering will become increasingly important. As it develops further this may be supplemented by formal market research to provide market information and a research and development programme to provide information on products and technology.

Capital

The entrepreneur may use his or her own money to initiate the business. This may be supplemented by formal and/or informal investment capital. If the business is to be sustained, however, it must attract money from customers. This will, of course,

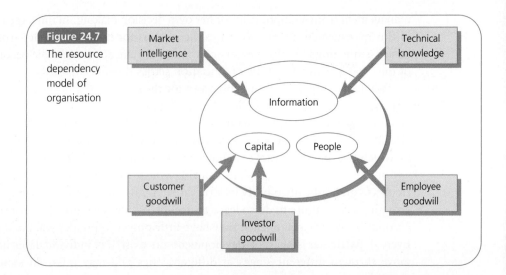

Figure 24.7

The resource dependency model of organisation

be a result of the business selling its products to them. If this is to occur then the customer's interest and *goodwill* towards the business, and what it offers, is needed. If the business is to grow at a sustainable rate then additional capital may be needed from investors. Again, their interest and goodwill towards the venture is needed.

People

In the early stages of the business the entrepreneur may invite close associates to join in the venture. However, as the business grows more formal, procedures for identifying and recruiting personnel and gaining their goodwill will be needed.

The structure adopted by a particular organisation can be thought of as a response to its requirements in relation to these three key resources. Particular functions appear within the organisation in order to manage the acquisition of these resources. The 'conventional' response for the large, mature organisation is to set up *departments* with specific responsibility for the acquisition of particular resources. Thus customer goodwill is captured by marketing and sales; investor goodwill by the finance department; market knowledge by the marketing research function (perhaps integrated into the marketing department); technical knowledge by the research and development function; and so on.

The complete organisation will include two additional functions. The operational system which actually produces the outputs of the business (i.e. production or service provision) is responsible for adding value to the inputs, and a strategic control function co-ordinates the operation of the organisation as a whole.

The resource acquisition approach

This is, however, only *one* of a range of possible responses. It represents the limitation of the organisation as it reaches maturity. It also reflects a traditional

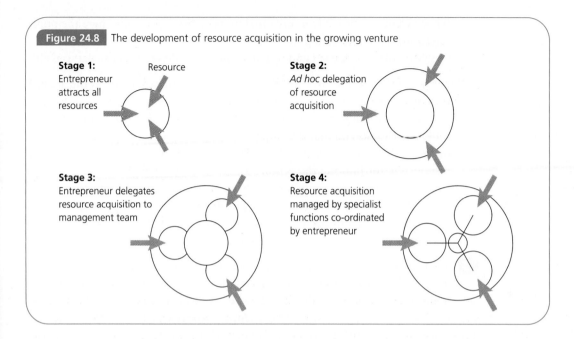

Figure 24.8 The development of resource acquisition in the growing venture

Stage 1: Entrepreneur attracts all resources

Resource

Stage 2: *Ad hoc* delegation of resource acquisition

Stage 3: Entrepreneur delegates resource acquisition to management team

Stage 4: Resource acquisition managed by specialist functions co-ordinated by entrepreneur

environment in which different types of resource are independent and quite predictable in the way they may be acquired. It is this feature which allows them to be acquired by 'specialist' managers. The evolution of the entrepreneurial organisation can thus be thought of in terms of it developing internal structures to manage the acquisition of the resources it needs to undertake its business.

In its early stages, the entrepreneur will take a great deal of responsibility for attracting the critical inputs: customer, investor and employee goodwill as well as information. In other words, he or she must be the marketing, sales, finance and development specialist rolled into one. The entrepreneur must also maintain strategic control over the business and may be responsible for undertaking operations as well. At this early stage, the entrepreneur's role is a challenging one!

As the business grows then tasks can be differentiated, and the role of the entrepreneur can become more distinct. Usually, he or she will relinquish participation in operational activities and concentrate on managing the business as a whole. As the business grows further, roles can become even more specialised. Individuals can focus their attention on obtaining critical resources. As a result, specific resource acquisition functions can start to emerge. The evolution of input acquiring functions in the development of the entrepreneurial business is shown in Figure 24.8.

This approach can be used as a guide for decision making about the structure the organisation should adopt. The key issues in relation to deciding on structure are:

1 *How large is the organisation?* How many people work for the organisation? How much latitude is there for individuals to take on specialist roles? To

what extent is it possible to use outside specialists? (Consider here the points raised in Section 20.3 in particular.

As a rule, tasks, roles and responsibilities should be specialised, if possible.

2 *What are the critical inputs?* All inputs are important. However, the acquisition of some will take priority at any one point and this will alter at different stages of development. The question is what matters *most* at this point in time: information on markets and product technology, or investment capital, or sales to customers, or people? Is the lack of any one of these *in particular* responsible for limiting the venture's potential? To what extent is it possible to dedicate available resources to the acquisition of a particular input? How might this situation change in the near future?

As a rule, attention should be focused on critical inputs – but it is important not to neglect other inputs.

3 *What is the venture's skill profile?* What skills are available in order to be dedicated? How is the venture served for people with selling, marketing, financial, negotiating and research skills, etc.? How might these be acquired (e.g. through training, new recruitment or external support)? What does this say about the venture's skill requirements for the future?

As a rule, the venture's skill profile should be built up (but an awareness of fixed costs is important). The entrepreneur must be willing to call on outside help in the short term if necessary.

4 *What is the nature of the inputs needed?* The nature of inputs the venture needs will differ depending on the environment in which it finds itself. Are they well defined? (If the business is very innovative or if it is in a business environment which is not well developed then they might not be.) Are they easily obtainable? How intense is the competition for them? On what basis does competition take place?

The key issue here is how *specialist* the task of managing the acquisition of a particular input needs to be in order to be successful. As a rule, the possibility of gaining competitive advantage by building in-house specialisation should be considered.

5 *How do different inputs interact?* Different inputs interact with each other. The acquisition of one cannot be considered in isolation since how one input is acquired affects how the others will be. Technical knowledge means little without consideration of what the market wants. The acquisition of investors' capital will be facilitated if the venture has a good knowledge of market conditions. Similarly the goodwill of employees will provide a strong platform on which to build a culture which attracts the goodwill of customers.

This means that one input-attracting function must communicate with the others. Those responsible for market research must talk to those responsible for development. The finance department must talk to those responsible for marketing. Inter-function communication is facilitated (or hindered) by organisational structure. If the acquisition of inputs can be considered largely in isolation of each other, then a structure which features dedicated special-ist functions co-ordinated centrally (perhaps supplemented by informal inter-functional communication) may be suitable. On the other hand, if detailed co-ordination of input acquisition is necessary, then a matrix or a team struc-ture may be more effective and offer a better route to developing a structural competitive advantage.

24.7 The venture as a theatre for human growth

Key learning outcome

A recognition of the importance of the human dimension in organisational growth.

Business organisations are not just systems for generating wealth. They are the stages on which human beings live their lives. Individuals use their organisational role to create images of themselves. For many people, what you *do* is who you *are*. In build-ing an organisation, an entrepreneur is not just generating employment opportunities but also creating a theatre in which people will play out the parts which are critical to their personal development. Organisations are the places where people meet and interact. The entrepreneur is offering not only economic rewards, but social and personal development ones as well.

Effective entrepreneurs will recognise this. They will understand that an indi-vidual working in the organisation is bringing a number of different expectations operating at different levels with them. Entrepreneurs should be aware of the meaning that the organisation offers to the people who are part of it and, critically, of how that meaning changes as the organisation grows.

The small, informal organisation will offer a different environment to the larger one where roles and relationships are more formal. Of course, there is a trade-off. The larger organisation offers more security and the possibility for employees to use and develop specialist skills whereas the smaller one may offer a more flexible and personal environment. The entrepreneur must recognise the balance of benefits from the perspective of the individual employee.

An entrepreneur, like any good manager, recognises that the development of the organisation is also the development of the people within it. Its growth offers them the potential for their growth. Developing and communicating vision means writing the story of how the organisation will develop, the roles that particular individuals will play in that development, and what those roles will mean for them.

In practice this means that the entrepreneur must discuss the changes that are taking place within the organisation with individuals, and use those discussions to develop an understanding of what those changes mean for the individuals. Presenting the future possibilities offered by, and removing the fear of, change is the platform on which motivation is built. Such discussions may be quite formal (for example, regular appraisals and objective setting) or informal chats with employees.

Understanding what the prospects and achievement of growth offer and the fears and apprehensions they create for the individual within the organisation is crucial since these are the platform on which the entrepreneur builds his or her leadership strategy.

Summary of key ideas

- The growth of the venture must be approached from a number of perspectives of which the key perspectives are: *financial*: growth in income, expenditure and profits; *strategic*: growth in market presence and competitive advantages; *structural*: growth in organisational form, process and structure; and *organisational*: growth in the organisation's culture and attitudes.

- Effective entrepreneurs recognise that the growth of the venture provides all of its stakeholders with an opportunity for personal growth and development.

Research themes

Patterns of growth in entrepreneurial businesses

A large body of financial data is now available on the Internet. Many businesses publish their accounts on the web and specialist databases such as FAME provide stock market information. This availability is creating the opportunity for studies into the patterns of growth achieved by fast-growing entrepreneurial businesses. Such a study could examine the shape of growth profiles using metrics such as turnover, profits and asset base. The methodology would be to examine growth in these measures against time. What patterns are evident? Is growth generally smooth and incremental, or does it tend to be erratic? What rates of growth are seen? Do fast-growing businesses tend to have downturns as well as upturns? How does change in turnover relate to change in profits and assets? Quite a number of different patterns are likely to be seen. Can these be grouped and classified in any meaningful way? There are mathematical techniques for comparing such patterns in a rigorous way, but quite a lot can be achieved with simple visual inspection. Conclude by suggesting a generic scheme for patterns of growth. The more businesses introduced into the study, the more general and valuable will be the findings. A sample of at least 100 drawn from either one particular sector or on a cross-sectional basis should be used.

Financial growth and strategic and organisational turbulence

Models of growth such as Greiner's (discussed above) suggest that fast-growing organisations experience growth as periods of incremental increase based on relatively stable organisational forms and strategic approach interspersed with periods of crisis during which significant changes in organisational form and strategic approach must be made if the organisation is to continue growing. One way of validating such a view would be to correlate a detailed history of a business with financial measures of size. Use the historical information (which might be obtained from good, detailed case studies or primary research) to define growth and crisis phases. You should be explicit and rigorous in your criteria for identifying these. Do this before examining the financial information on the business. Is there a correlation between the historical phases and size as measured financially? Does this confirm Greiner's concept? A sample of at least five businesses (either from one sector or cross-sectional) should be considered. The more organisations studied, the more robust will be the findings.

Suggestions for further reading

Birley, S. and Westhead, P. (1990) 'Growth and performance contrasts between "types" of small firm', *Strategic Management Journal*, Vol. 11, pp. 535–57.

Brocklesby, J. and Cummings, S. (1996) 'Designing a viable organisational structure', *Long Range Planning*, Vol. 29, No. 1, pp. 49–57.

Chaganti, R., Cook, R.G. and Smeltz, W.J. (2002) 'Effects of styles, strategies and systems on the growth of small businesses', *Journal of Developmental Entrepreneurship*, Vol. 7, No. 2, pp. 175–92.

Gibb, A. and Davies, L. (1991) 'In pursuit of frameworks for the development of growth models of the small business', *International Small Business Journal*, Vol. 9, No. 1, pp. 15–31.

Glancey, K. (1998) 'Determinants of growth and profitability in small entrepreneurial firms', *International Journal of Entrepreneurial Behaviour and Research*, Vol. 4, No. 2, pp. 18–27.

Greiner, L.E. (1972) 'Evolution and revolution as organisations grow', *Harvard Business Review*, July–Aug, pp. 37–46.

Mintzberg, H. (1979) *The Structuring of Organizations: A Synthesis of the Research*, Englewood Cliffs, NJ: Prentice Hall.

Scott, M. and Bruce, R. (1987) 'Five stages of growth in small business', *Long Range Planning*, Vol. 20, No. 3, pp. 45–52.

Smallbone, D., Leigh, R. and North, D. (1995) 'The characteristics and strategies of high-growth SMEs', *International Journal of Entrepreneurial Behaviour and Research*, Vol. 1, No. 3, pp. 44–62.

van de Ven, A. and Poole, M.S. (1995) 'Explaining development and change in organisations', *Academy of Management Review*, Vol. 20, No. 3, pp. 510–40.

Tapping into UK cashpoints

FT

10 September 2002

By **Mark Nicholson**

Imagine an advertising medium that could account for at least 2bn ABC1 adult hits a year and, potentially, even identify precisely the individual it is targeting on each hit. Direct hits at that, since it could deliver the ad while a potential customer is physically withdrawing cash to spend, and hand them a receipt that could carry discounts, special offers or other advertising messages.

It could even tailor ads specifically to the customer's location – so any special offers could be redeemable in a shop right next to the customer. It's called an ATM network. And described as above, it seems a wonder that no one has ever exploited the monitor screens of Britain's 35,000 cashpoint machines as an advertising medium.

In part, it's down to technology. Until recently, there hasn't been a software package available that has been able to run and manage advertising campaigns across big and diverse ATM networks.

Another impediment, though, has been the reluctance of the network owners – the banks and building societies – to countenance third-party ads.

But such resistance has changed in the past three years. Increasingly, network owners are having to reconcile an explosive growth in demand for ATMs, which now account for 75 per cent of all cash withdrawals, with the awkward fact that they are expensive to run – on average, about £20,000 to install, and costly to maintain thereafter.

It's for this reason that banks and the aggressive new breed of independent ATM network owners are beating a trail to the offices of I-Design, a small Scottish software company in Newport-on-Tay.

I-Design, an 11-year-old software company specialising in ATM monitor display design, has spent the past three years refining a software package which, because it is platform independent, should solve most of the technical issues in distributing advertising across ATM networks.

The software offers ATM operators the chance to show an eight-second video short over the screen – the duration of a standard transaction. It also allows ATMs to display advertising images between transactions, and for advertising and branding to be printed on to receipts. Eventually, given the data available on cards, each user could be identified, and the ad message tailored accordingly – all without adding a second to the overall transaction time.

It can even judge the weather. One confectionery company asked I-Design if, when the temperature rises, ATM adverts for chocolate could change to ads for ice-cream. The answer is, they can.

Moreover, as an advertising medium, it is fully accountable. Campaign managers can know exactly how many people they have reached, along with when and where.

I-Design began life designing the graphical interfaces of ATMs. But increasingly, says Ana Stewart, sales director and co-founder, ATM operators wanted applications that allowed their ATMs to carry own-brand marketing. And as the operators increasingly looked for ways of earning revenues from ATMs, this evolved into demands to develop a platform for third-party advertising.

The first company to exploit the possibility was Nationwide, the mutual building society. Last year, it ran two pilot campaigns for third-party advertisers across part of its 2,000-strong ATM network. It is now planning a further series of third-party campaigns and, by the year end, aims to use the technology to provide own-brand marketing in all its in-branch terminals, following 'really positive' user feedback from the pilots.

As network operators wake up to the potential of ATM advertising, the hope now is that advertising agencies and brand managers will bite too. With this in mind, I-Design ear-lier this year appointed Jim Faulds as chairman, bringing on board perhaps Scotland's most successful advertising entrepreneur.

The prize, says Ralph Hasselgren, I-Design's managing director, is a relatively small share of the UK ad market – perhaps worth a total of £50m a year – but a potentially huge fillip for I-Design, which currently turns over about £600,000 a year.

Source: *Financial Times*, 10 September 2002.

Case 24.2

FT

Growing pains force China's entrepreneurs to look west

4 February 2002

By **Richard McGregor**

It may be a long way from the rustbelt of China's interior to Nasdaq in New York, but for Zhou Furen there is nowhere closer to hand. He is searching for capital for the business he wants to float on the world's high-tech stock market – even though it consists of fertiliser factories.

Mr Zhou, in common with many Chinese entrepreneurs, faces a dilemma; entrepreneurs say they are forced overseas to raise capital because of discrimination against them at home. But they are ill-prepared to face the intense scrutiny of analysts and investors in foreign bourses.

Last Friday, Greencool Technology Holdings – a private Chinese refrigerants distributor which is listed in Hong Kong – revealed how difficult Chinese companies can find life in developed stock markets. It issued a writ for defamation against Joe Zhang, a UBS Warburg analyst.

The libel charges centre on comments allegedly made by Mr Zhang, one of the pre-eminent analysts of private Chinese companies, in a note to clients after a conference call with Gu Chujun, the chairman of Greencool.

The problems entrepreneurs face at home, and their battle for credibility abroad, is a worrying trend for China, as the private sector increasingly drives the economy and creates much-needed jobs.

'It's quite obvious – the government clearly has the intention to help state companies list at our expense,' Mr Zhou said in an interview at the headquarters of his Xiyang Group, near Haicheng, in Liaoning province in China's rugged north-east.

Beijing has acknowledged the private sector's rising importance by raising the political status of entrepreneurs over the past year, and giving their assets greater legal protection.

The stock market authorities also – in theory – removed the main obstacle to businessmen taking their companies to the market, with the abolition in 2000 of the quota system for initial public offerings.

Under the quota system, provinces were allowed to nominate the companies to be listed, resulting in preferential treatment for well-connected state enterprises regardless of their financial health.

Mr Zhou's Xiyang Group missed the cut in 1997, when Liaoning chose four companies to go public. With the end of the quota system a queue of 200–300 companies waiting for IPOs remains, encouraging Mr Zhou to look abroad.

'It's just about personal relationships with top leaders – many companies were much worse than us, but they still got listed,' he said. The figures bear out 51-year-old Mr Zhou's complaints. Of China's 1,250-odd listed companies, only about 50 are private. Even with the abolition of quotas, the ratio is not expected to rise substantially soon.

In Zhejiang province, bordering Shanghai, a region with a vibrant entrepreneurial economy, 100 private enterprises have restructured into shareholding entities and 73 have undergone the 12-month long 'tutorial' period that is required by market regulations. But only nine companies were listed in 2000 and two in 2001, according to the Securities Times.

Many entrepreneurs have already headed offshore to list, mostly to Hong Kong, and often with the backing of their local governments, which rely on the businesses to sustain the community. Mr Zhou, however, has his sights on Nasdaq.

A pugnacious commune leader-turned-entrepreneur, he first made his fortune manufacturing fire-resistant materials. In 1996, he moved into fertilisers. Six years later, Xiyang dominates the Chinese market, and expects,

with a recent acquisition, to be making 1.5mn tonnes annually by the end of the year. He ranks 51st in Forbes' China rich list, with a fortune of USDollars 132m.

Whether Xiyang can meet Nasdaq's IPO standards is something that Mr Zhou has left to Benchmark Global Capital, a US company specialising in finding private Chinese businesses to list overseas. 'We wooed Xiyang when we knew it was desperate for capital, but was having trouble getting listed in China,' said Wang Zhengfang, a Beijing-based manager for Benchmark.

Benchmark will still have to get Xiyang's accounts into order, a hurdle for many private businesses which have developed as personal fiefs.

Mr Zhou dominates the Xiyang Group, holding 70 per cent of its shares. In a gesture which is as much about control as politics, he also still heads the local Communist party committee.

After early enthusiasm, foreign investors are growing more wary of listed private Chinese companies – especially those dominated by strong personalities. Ms Wang acknowledges the problems of standardising Xiyang's accounts. 'If his company is not standard, that's only because he knows little about standard practices,' she said.

But Mr Zhou says he has been advised he will qualify for Nasdaq this year.

Source: *Financial Times*, 4 February 2002.

Discussion points

1. Develop three different growth options for I-Design. Compare and contrast the financial, strategic and organisational challenges each of these growth options presents.

2. What are the questions investors want answering about the financial, strategic and organisational aspects of the growth of Chinese entrepreneurial ventures?

Chapter 25

Strategies for expansion

Chapter overview

Expanding the business means increasing the amount of trade it undertakes with the intention of increasing profits. Expansion from any base can be achieved in one of four fundamental ways, by **increasing core market share**, by **launching new products**, by **entering new markets** and by **acquiring established businesses**. This chapter considers each of these generic strategies in turn and the decisions the entrepreneur must make in order to deliver them.

25.1) Increasing market share

Key learning outcome

An understanding of the decisions that need to be made when considering an expansion strategy based on increasing market share.

Expansion demands an increase in the volume of the venture's sales. These sales are made into a market. The impact of this increase in sales volume on the market depends on the dynamics of the market itself. If the market is enjoying rapid growth then the business may increase its sales even if its market share is static. On the other hand, if the market is mature and not increasing in volume, then an increase in sales implies an increase in market share. Sales growth, then, is a combination of overall market growth, and increase in the share of that market. As the American business academic Ansoff pointed out in his seminal book, *Corporate Strategy* (1965), any expansion strategy must involve a decision as to whether to

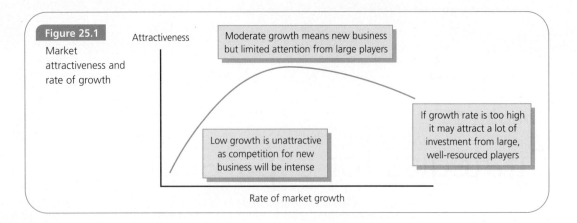

Figure 25.1

Market
attractiveness and
rate of growth

Attractiveness

Moderate growth means new business
but limited attention from large players

If growth rate is too high
it may attract a lot of
investment from large,
well-resourced players

Low growth is unattractive
as competition for new
business will be intense

Rate of market growth

base expansion on existing products or to develop new ones, and whether to rely on established market presence or to enter new markets.

The attractiveness of a market depends on its rate of growth (Figure 25.1). Studies of business performance in a number of market areas has suggested that the most attractive type of market (defined as the one which offers the best return on investment) is one of moderate growth. This is rationalised as follows. In a low-growth market, increases in business can only be obtained at the expense of competitors. This makes the fight for market share expensive. Conversely, in a higher-growth market the business can be expanded by taking the 'new' business as it becomes available. This reduces competitive pressures. Competitors may not even realise each other's presence. If the growth becomes very high, however, then the market may be seen as so attractive that the attentions of a large number of competitors may be aroused. Big players may invest heavily to gain control of the market. If this happens, then the cost of competing may increase again.

In practice, the simple formula of market growth versus share increase needs careful inspection. The dynamics of a market, and the share of a particular business within that market, are dependent on how the market is defined in the first place. A market represents the collection of goods which can be substituted for each other, but a variety of goods can be substituted in different ways. Some goods may make better substitutes than others. The situation is complicated further if the good in question serves a number of different needs.

For example, consider the jewellery that was marketed so successfully by Gerald Ratner in the 1980s. Clearly, the products were in competition with those on offer from other jewellery stores. However, jewellery is often purchased as a gift item and in this they were in competition with a whole host of other products which make interesting gifts such as books, CDs, flowers and so on. Ratner's target market was young people who bought the product to wear when they socialised with one another. With respect to this, the products were in competition with other fashion items that were bought for purposes of socialisation, particularly clothes. In a wider sense still, they were in competition with other areas in which young people could spend money in order to socialise such as meals

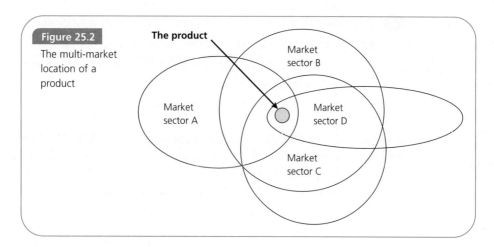

Figure 25.2

The multi-market location of a product

The product

Market sector A

Market sector B

Market sector C

Market sector D

out, attending concerts and so on. Thus a product sits in a number of markets depending on its pattern of substitution for other goods (Figure 25.2).

An entrepreneur must recognise that 'the' market in which their business operates is not a single thing at all, but a complex arena of overlapping market sectors. Whether or not a business is growing by increasing its share, or by capitalising on a growth market will depend on which sector of the market is under consideration. The business may, in fact, be doing both of these in different areas of the market at the same time.

This framework indicates the considerations the entrepreneur must have in view when developing a market share expansion strategy. These considerations have three parts:

1 *What market sectors are available into which expansion might take place?*
- What product (or products) do the venture's offerings substitute? (What will people stop using if they buy the venture's products?)
- In what ways does substitution take place? (Directly or indirectly?)
- Who supplies the substitute products?
- What benefits does the venture's product offer to the customer in each sector?

2 *What are the attractions of each sector?*
- What is the volume potential within the sector?
- What are the dynamics of market growth in each sector?
- What are the competitive pressures (for example, the strength of competitors, the investment needed to build and sustain market share)?
- How are competitors likely to react to the venture's actions? (Passively or aggressively?)
- As a result, what is the likely return on investment?

3 *What are the venture's competitive advantages in a particular sector?*
- How effectively can the offering be positioned in that sector?
- What are the venture's competitive advantages in each sector in relation to costs, market knowledge, relationships, and structural factors?
- How can competitive advantage be maintained within the sector?

In summary, even though an entrepreneurial venture sells its products into a competitive marketplace, and although increasing the size of the venture means taking competitors' business (and facing their reaction to this), the entrepreneur is free, to a degree at least, to decide which competitors they wish to confront and the way in which they wish to compete. The latitude which the entrepreneur has to do this is dependent on the potential to position the offering in different ways in different market sectors. The decision as to which sector, or indeed sectors, into which expansion will be directed is a feature of how attractive that sector is and the competitive advantages the venture enjoys within it.

25.2 Developing new products

> **Key learning outcome**
>
> An understanding of the decisions that need to be made when considering a strategy of expansion through new product development.

Most businesses sell more than one product. Many offer hundreds, if not thousands, of lines. When it is initiated, the entrepreneurial venture is likely to have only one or at most a few lines. Thus developing new products must be a critical factor in the venture's plans for expansion. New product development is not just about adding on new lines, though. No business can afford to stand still in a fast-moving marketplace. New products must be developed to replace existing ones and to keep ahead of competitors as the customer's expectations develop.

Product development covers a range of activities from minor modifications of existing products through the development of new variants and models, to the development of entirely new product concepts. Existing product development (EPD) and new product development (NPD) lie at opposite ends of a developmental spectrum.

The details of what existing and new product development mean for a particular business will depend on the nature of the products it is involved with. Clearly, advanced, technology-intensive products will require a different approach to 'simple' products based on established, well-understood technologies. Thus The Body Shop is involved constantly in developing new formulations and variants based on the ingredients that Anita Roddick collects on her world travels. The development of Windows 95 represented a major new product launch for Bill Gates and the Microsoft corporation. The satellite broadcasting channel BSkyB, which was initially set up via Rupert Murdoch's News International Corporation, demanded the initiation of a whole new industry. Whatever the nature of the product, its complexity and the resources involved in its launch, the basic 'rules' of effective product development and the decisions that are involved in developing the strategy are similar.

The key is to remember that a product is not a thing in itself but a means to an *end*. The value of a product lies in the benefits it can bring to its users. The product is just a way of delivering an innovation to the market. The entrepreneur must apply the same market-orientated insights to the development of new products as were brought to the innovation on which the business was originally founded.

New product development is not just a technical process. It is something which cuts across every facet of the business. There will be a technical element to the actual creation of the product but product development must be considered in much broader terms than the purely technical. Some of the critical decision areas include the following.

Market positioning

What problems will the product solve? Why will it solve them better than existing products do? How will it be positioned in its marketplace? Against which competitors? How will it be priced relative to competitors?

Branding

Will the product be branded? If so, will it use its own branding or draw on corporate branding? Will it use an existing brand (i.e. a brand extension) or will it represent the establishment of a new brand identity?

Communication

How will the customer get to know about the product? How can it be promoted to them? What communication routes will be used? Will the customer need to be educated about the product? Will endorsement and professional recommendation be a factor in its position? What demands will promotion make on existing sales and promotional resources?

Distribution

How will the customer get hold of the product? Who will be involved in the distribution process? What support will be needed from distributors and other partners to promote the product?

Financial and operational forecasting

What is the anticipated demand for the product? What revenues are expected? Over what period? On what assumptions are these forecasts based? What are the risks if they are wrong?

Technical research and development

What technical challenges does the product present? How does its development fit with the venture's current technical competences and skills base?

Production and operations

How will the product be manufactured (or the service delivered)? How does its production fit with existing competences? Is production capacity adequate or must new capacity be established? What are the logistical implications (for example, in terms of storage)?

Supply issues

What factors are involved in producing and delivering the new product? Is it based on components which are currently supplied? Does it demand new components from existing suppliers or does it demand that new suppliers be brought on board? If so, how will they be identified and managed?

Resource implications

Does the business currently have the financial resources to fund such a strategy of expansion? Will it create cash-flow problems? Does the business have sufficient human capacity? Are sales resources sufficient to open and serve the new market sectors?

Strategic concerns of product development

Product development demands an investment. That investment must be considered in light of risk, possible alternatives and opportunity costs in the same way as any other investment within the business. This means that the development of new products must be considered strategically. The key questions in this consideration are as follows.

- How does the new product fit with the innovation on which the business was founded? Is it a way of presenting this innovation further or is it a diversification into a new area of innovation?

- How does the new product build on the venture's existing competitive advantages?

- How does the new product contribute to making those competitive advantages sustainable?

- How does the product fit into the venture's existing portfolio of products?

- What will be the resource demands (financial, operational and human) in developing the product?

● Over what period is the product to return the investment made in it? Does it represent a short- or long-term investment?

● What will be the implications of the product for the sales of existing products? (In particular will there be any 'cannibalisation' of existing sales?)

The success of a new product development expansion strategy does not depend solely on the success of the new products themselves. It also depends on the venture's ability to identify and deliver them. An ability to respond to customer demand through the capability of producing new products quickly and effectively is an important way of developing a structural competitive advantage.

25.3 Entering new markets

> **Key learning outcome**
>
> An understanding of the decisions that need to be made when considering a strategy of expansion through entry into new markets.

When a new venture is initiated, its market scope is usually quite limited. This is only to be expected since the business's low resource base means that it is well advised to concentrate on serving defined and narrow sectors where it can gain an initial competitive advantage. Once this has been established, then the option of expanding the business by delivering the product or service on which it is based to a wider audience quickly becomes attractive.

The routes to expansion through new market entry are varied. To a great extent the options available will depend on the way in which the niche of the business is defined. The main options for new market expansion include the following possibilities.

New geographical areas

In its early stages, a business tends to serve a local geographic area. Therefore, expansion of the business into other geographical areas is an important option. Ultimately this might include expansion into the international arena through exporting, international marketing or even locating offices overseas. In fact, few businesses can now achieve any real size without taking on the international option.

New industry sectors

A new business will usually concentrate on marketing its products to a narrow range of customers. The composition of this customer base will reflect the entrepreneur's knowledge and experience in the application of their innovation. Again, this represents a sound move in terms of creating a defendable niche in the market.

It is likely, however, that the innovation will be attractive to buyers with similar needs in other industry sectors. Developing a strategy to market the product to these groups is an important option for expansion.

New groups of consumers

A new product is often targeted at quite a narrow group of consumers. If it is particularly innovative then the nature of buyers will change over time. Initially, take-up will be led by *adopters*, that is, consumers who actively seek out innovations in the product area and greet them positively. *Non-adopters* will hold back until the innovation becomes more familiar. *Resistors* will reject the product out of hand. The product will also have a positioning which will make it more attractive to some groups of consumers (defined in demographic, sociographic or psychographic terms) than others.

Expanding the appeal of the product from the founding target groups to a wider audience demands careful consideration of how the product is communicated, promoted and distributed to different consumer groups. The option is often attractive but when developing the positioning to attract new groups care must be taken to ensure that core groups are not alienated.

The strategic issues which need to be considered in relation to new market entry parallel those that arise in relation to increase of market share and new product development strategies.

Positioning and branding

How does the competitive environment differ between the original sector and the new sectors? Can the positioning that has been developed for the product continue to be utilised as it is expanded into new sectors, or must a new positioning be developed? Can any branding that has been developed continue to be used or must a new branding, or sub-branding, be developed? Can the current pricing strategy continue or must it be changed?

Communication and promotion

What message must be sent to the new sector? How does this compare to the message that is being sent currently? What medium of communication must be used? What promotional tactics might be used in conjunction with the new sector? Can the current sales and selling strategy be used or must a new one be developed?

Distribution

What distribution routes are available to reach the new sectors? Do these demand that new distributors be used? Does this demand that a new *type* of distributor be used?

Resource implications

Does the business currently have the financial resources to fund such an expansion strategy or will it create cash-flow problems? Does the business have sufficient human capacity? Are sales resources sufficient to open and serve the new market sectors?

Product development and expansion into new market sectors

A strategy of expansion by entry into new market sectors can be adopted in conjunction with new product development strategy. Indeed modification of the product to make it more attractive may be an essential element of the strategy of expansion into new markets. A balance must be struck between ensuring that the offering is right for the sector at which it is aimed on the one hand and ensuring that the business does not lose its economies of scale and create logistical complexity by having a large number of low-volume lines on the other.

(25.4) Entrepreneurial exporting

> **Key learning outcome**
>
> An understanding of the opportunities and challenges that exporting presents and the approach of entrepreneurial businesses to take advantage of the opportunities and meet the challenges.

If the entrepreneur has developed a significant innovation then the chances are there will be demand for it outside the local market into which the business first entered. If so, exporting can be a very attractive growth option for the venture. This is for a number of reasons. Exporting offers the possibility of:

● increasing demand for the firm's products or services, resulting in greater income and an improved cash-flow position;

● more efficient utilisation of the firm's resources;

● reducing fixed costs;

● faster gains of experience curve cost savings;

● reducing the venture's overall risk, especially when there are significant demand fluctuations in local markets;

● an expanded strategic presence on a global stage.

A study of US small firms by Pope (2002) indicated that small businesses are motivated to export if they have a unique product and a technological advantage over competitors. The main rationale was the potential to generate additional sales by capitalising on foreign opportunities and to achieve improved economies of scale domestically. All these things might be achieved with no, or only incremental, expansion in the business's capacity. Exporting can offer the possibility of gaining new income without the need for a significant and high-risk up-front investment. Exporting is increasingly being seen as an important platform for, and indicator of, an entrepreneurial business's success (Edmunds and Khoury, 1986; D'Souza and McDougall, 1989; Buckley *et al.*, 1990). However, being effective in an export market does make demands on the venture's existing knowledge base and its ability to acquire and manage new knowledge. In particular:

- knowledge of demand conditions in international markets;

- knowledge of customers, their needs and tastes in these markets;

- knowledge of why the offering will be attractive in these markets and why they will have an advantage over locally based and other exporting competitors;

- knowledge of the proper pricing levels in the export markets;

- knowledge of the distribution systems and partners who have access to the export market;

- knowledge of how the product or service might be promoted (either through advertising or direct selling) in the export markets.

Hart and Tzokas (1999) found that investment in preliminary market research paid dividends in terms of export performance. In addition, the venture's managers must be aware of the political, economic, social, cultural and legal situation that might have a bearing on exporting activity. This is for both strategic (assessing the risk of and prioritising the firm's exporting activity in relation to other growth opportunities) and tactical reasons (preparation by representatives of the venture before travelling out to meet with potential customers or partners). Crick (1999) examined the willingness of small businesses in the UK to invest in translating marketing and technical literature into foreign languages, and found that many did not and so missed out on the potential to gain an advantage by doing so. Leonidou and Adams-Florou (1999) review the exporting information management systems that are adopted by small businesses to acquire and use this knowledge.

Given the opportunity exporting offers, and the investment needed to exploit that opportunity, it is evident that exporting is not just an adjunct to the entrepreneurial process; it is very much central to it. Exporting presents an opportunity. But it takes drive and initiative to take advantage of that opportunity.

There have been a number of studies into the exporting activity of small and entrepreneurial businesses. The findings are far from clear-cut. Recent studies by Bonaccoursi (1992), Calof (1994) and Westhead (1995) attempt to clarify the situation. The general picture that emerges is that:

- the larger the firm, the more likely it is to be an exporter;

- the older the firm, the more likely it is to be an exporter;

- manufacturers are more likely to export than service firms;

- there is no significant effect due to owner-managing on exporting propensity.

It must be said that these effects, when observed, are weak statistically. It is dangerous to generalise about any one particular firm given its size and age. Even just considering manufacturing firms, different studies have demonstrated great variation in exporting propensity within sectors, for example, from just 4 per cent actively exporting (manufacturers in Merseyside, England (Lloyd and Mason, 1984)) to 70 per cent (high-tech manufacturers, south-east England (Oakey and Cooper, 1989)).

A number of workers have proposed models of the process through which firms learn to export (e.g. Bilkey and Tesar, 1977; Joynt and Welch, 1985). Czinkota and Johnson (1981) suggest that a number of stages are involved, including an 'unwilling' starting point, moving through 'experimenting' and finally moving on to 'experienced'. Many observers are keen to distinguish between none, sporadic and regular exporters (Samiee and Walters, 1991). Czinkota and Ursik (1991) have proposed a sales-growth matrix that can be used to classify exporting firms. De Toni and Nassimbeni (2001) examine the structural and practice differences between exporting and non-exporting business units in Italian manufacturing firms.

The reason usually given as to why manufacturers are more likely to be exporters is that it is easier to transport physical goods than it is to deliver services over a long distance. This may be so, but the Internet is changing the rules of service delivery and the future promises a lot more exporting opportunities for service firms in international markets.

A number of workers have examined the factors that encourage exporting. In a study of Australian very small enterprises (VSEs, firms with fewer than 10 employees and a turnover of less than Aus\$1 million), Philp (1998) identified the following as important:

- a preparedness to invest and risk resources;

- a positive attitude towards exporting;

- a willingness to bring in outsiders with exporting expertise;

- having a product that is innovative and can be delivered price competitively into the export market.

Cavusgil and Kirpalani (1993) identified a distinct, but sympathetic, set of factors. These included:

- managerial commitment to exporting;

- export market entry strategy;

- choice of product range to export;

- product positioning in the export market;

- adaptation of the product to suit the export market.

Naidu and Kanti Prasad (1994) emphasise the importance of learning from sporadic export activity as an encourager of more regular, and strategic, exporting for small businesses. Axinn *et al.* (1995) also emphasise the importance of a positive managerial attitude towards exporting and the opportunities it presents. Burpitt and Rondinelli (2000) found in a study of US small firms that the motivation for exporting went beyond financial returns and included the desire to learn about new markets. Crick (2002) points out that the division of firms into exporters and non-exporters is simplistic. There is an important distinction between non-exporters who have never exported – the *disinterested* – and those who have tried it but have now stopped – the *dissapointed*. Ending exporting should not be regarded as a failure. It might represent a rational and clear-sighted decision. His study of UK exporters indicated that there were significant differences in the perceptions of the two non-exporting groups as to the issues surrounding exporting and their need for support in (re)developing an export base. Networks are an important aspect of the entrepreneurial process. They provide the conduits through which resources and information flow to the venture (see Chapter 11). Holmlund and Koch (1999) found in a study of small Finnish firms that networking with overseas agents was a significant aspect of exporting activity. On the other hand, Chetty and Hamilton (1996) found that many small businesses in New Zealand had low expectation about the rewards from, and were acutely aware of the obstacles to, exporting. Clearly, such beliefs limited exporting activity.

Exporting is usually the first stage of internationalisation for an entrepreneurial venture. The costs and rewards for, and managerial perception of, internationalisation are dependent on the global stage on which business takes place. The attractiveness of exporting can change quickly as a result of changes in international politics and economics. The growing pace of trade liberalisation is particularly important. Christensen (1993) suggests that the North American Free Trade Agreement (NAFTA) will create a host of new opportunities for entrepreneurial exporters. A study of trade liberalisation in Tanzania by Grenier *et al.* (1999) shows that many manufacturing firms had taken the opportunity liberalisation presents to become active exporters. Chhibber and Majumdar (1998) found that recent economic reforms in India had encouraged exporting and that those Indian firms that had taken the opportunity to do so were rewarded with growth and profitability. On the other hand, Filatotchev *et al.* (1999) found little evidence that the economic liberalisation had encouraged exporting for firms in the transition economies of eastern Europe. Smallbone *et al.* (1999) found that there was a great deal of variation in exporting propensity between different business sectors in transition economies. These and other issues of small business internationalisation are considered in detail by Wolff and Pett (200) and by Lu and Beamish (2001).

Given its importance to success, both from the perspective of the specific entrepreneurial venture and national economies, and the rewards that can be gained from a successful exporting strategy it is not surprising that a number of agencies, both governmental and private, have emerged to support the small and entrepreneurial venture develop its exporting activity. Barrett (1990, 1992) has produced reviews of where SMEs can obtain information on help with exporting.

25.5 Acquisitions

> **Key learning outcome**
>
> An understanding of the decisions that need to be made when considering a strategy of expansion through acquisition.

Success in the marketplace generates the financial resources which the entrepreneur can use to expand the business further. This money can either come from retained profits or be additional funds offered up by investors. This capital can be used to invest in increasing the market share of existing products, to develop new products or to enter new market sectors. Such growth comes from 'within' the business and is sometimes referred to as *organic* growth. An alternative to organic growth is to acquire other businesses in their entirety and 'add' them onto the venture. This is referred to as growth by *acquisition*.

There are three sorts of acquisition. These differ in the way in which the integrated firm sits in relation to the venture in the value addition chain. The first is *vertical integration*. This happens when the venture acquires a firm which is either above or below it in the value addition chain, i.e. it acquires a business which is a *customer* or a *supplier*. The acquisition of customers is referred to as *forward integration* and that of a supplier as *backward integration*. The second type of acquisition occurs when the venture integrates a business which is at the same level of value addition as itself, i.e. a business that is, ostensibly at least, a *competitor*. The third type of acquisition occurs in the remaining cases when the integrated business is not a supplier, nor a customer nor competitor. These might be referred to as *lateral* integrations. The various types of integration are shown in Figure 25.3.

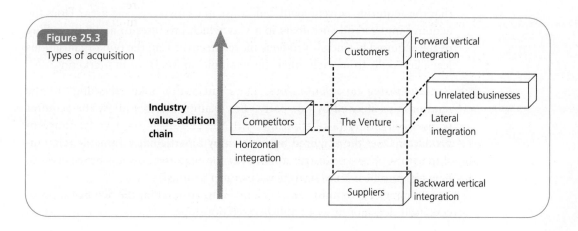

Figure 25.3
Types of acquisition

Acquisitions are an attractive option for rapid growth because the only limitations on growth rate are the availability of targets and the funds to buy them. For example, Howard Hodgeson built up his funeral directing business from 18 parlours to well over 500 over a three-year period solely by acquisition. Acquisitions do, however, represent a fundamentally different approach to growth than does organic expansion. With organic growth new resources are brought together by the entrepreneur in an innovative combination to create new value. An integrated business, on the other hand, represents resources which are *already combined*.

This means that an acquisition is not valuable in itself unless new value can be created from it. This demands that the acquiring venture must do something *different* with the business in order to make the acquisition worth while. In short, the entrepreneur must decide how he or she is going to add value through the acquisition; that is, what they can do, why that is valuable for the business's customers, and why the management of the acquired firm cannot do this on their own.

In strategic terms this means asking how acquisitions can be used to create and develop the venture's competitive advantage. There are four fundamental processes by which acquisitions can help in the development of competitive advantage:

1 *By reducing costs.* Does integration reduce overall costs? This may be achieved by eliminating some fixed or overhead costs. Alternatively, it may be gained by achieving some economy of scale in a key functional area. Production and sales are particularly important here. Existing production capacity may be used more efficiently especially if there is some overcapacity. The sales team may find it relatively easy to add new items to the portfolio they are selling. They may also find it possible to serve additional customers in their area. (However, care needs to be taken to ensure that they can still develop a good understanding of the benefits offered by the things they are selling and that they can still give each customer the time they need in order to manage the supplier–buyer relationship.)

2 *By combining and creating knowledge.* Does integration increase the value of the knowledge held by the individual organisations? For example, can the acquired firm offer information on products, operational technology or markets that the acquiring entrepreneur can utilise in its own business area? Does the acquirer understand customers in a way which promises to make the selling of the acquired business's products more effective? Can the two organisations learn key skills from each other, for example, in R&D, or in marketing?

3 *By capitalising on relationships.* Does integration take advantage of the relationships enjoyed by one party? For example, does it allow the acquirer to use their brand (a relationship with the customer) on a wider range of products? Does the acquired business enjoy a particularly valuable relationship with suppliers or distributors? Does the acquired business have access to new geographical areas or to new customer groups?

Of course, care must always be taken to ensure that the acquisition process itself does not upset established relationships.

4 *By developing organisational structure and function.* Does the integration allow the organisation as a whole to develop structural advantages? For example, does it make the processing of information on the market more effective? Does it make the business more responsive to customer needs? Does it allow the business to react more rapidly in producing new products? Does it enable the business to get its products into new areas or to new customer groups?

It is important to note that these things do not happen just because the organisation becomes larger, but because it changes the way it does things, in particular because it differentiates tasks in a more effective manner.

In summary, an acquisition is not a way of adding value in itself. Two businesses added together are not automatically more valuable than two separate businesses. In fact, the reverse is often the case. An acquisition only creates value if it allows the venture to offer the customer something new and useful and allows the new venture to develop its competitive advantage in the marketplace.

Summary of key ideas

- The entrepreneurial venture is characterised by a potential for growth. After initiating the venture, the entrepreneur must develop a strategy to *expand* it.

- The *generic* options for growth are by increasing core market share; by developing new products; by entering new markets; and by acquiring existing businesses.

- The attractiveness of the first three of these options depends on the market characteristics, particularly *growth rate*.

- The attractiveness of the acquisition option depends on the ability of the entrepreneur to genuinely add value to acquired businesses.

Research theme

Determining modes of expansion in entrepreneurial businesses

Different entrepreneurial businesses differ in their prefered mode of expansion. It might be hypothesised that the nature of the sector in which the venture is operating, the dynamics of the markets it serves, the opportunities competitors are presenting and the objectives of the entrepreneur and business would play an important part in determining this. A first stage in investigating this is to establish a strict methodology for investigating the strategic history of a business in terms of the product–market domains it occupies, its presence within these and how these evolve. A useful project would be to evaluate the potential of various information sources for doing this. This is the area known as *business historiography*. Such information sources would include managers' recollections of the business's strategic development, documentary evidence such as old catalogues and price lists, old business plans and publicly available information such as financial reports and market sector report. For a series of entrepreneurial businesses, attempt to obtain such information. How easy is it to gain the information? If obtained, how easy is it to piece together an unambiguous picture of the business's strategic history from the information? Where are the information gaps and what other sources might be used to fill them? Conclude by detailing successes and failures and make suggestions for making historiographical techniques more effective in the future.

Suggestions for further reading

Andersen, O. (1993) 'On the internationalization process of firms: a critical analysis', *Journal of International Business Studies*, Vol. 24, No. 2, pp. 209–31.

Ansoff, H.I. (1965) *Corporate Strategy*, New York: McGraw-Hill.

Axinn, N., Savitt, R., Sinkila, J.M. and Thach, S.V. (1995) 'Export intention, beliefs and behaviours in smaller industrial firms', *Journal of Business Research*, Vol. 32, No. 1, pp. 49–55.

Barrett, G.R. (1990) 'Where small and midsized companies can find export help; a number of government agencies have programmes to assist in all phases of exporting', *Journal of Accountancy*, Vol. 170, No. 3, pp. 46–50.

Barrett, G.R. (1992) 'Where small businesses can find export help', *Journal of Accountancy*, Vol. 174, No. 2, pp. 48–9.

Biggadike, R. (1979) 'The risky business of expansion', *Harvard Business Review*, May–June, pp. 103–11.

Bilkey, W.J. and Tesar, G. (1977) 'The export behavior of smaller-sized Wisconsin firms', *Journal of International Business Studies*, Vol. 8, pp. 71–8.

Bloom, P.N. and Kotler, P. (1978) 'Strategies for high market-share companies', *Harvard Business Review*, Nov–Dec, pp. 63–72.

Bonaccoursi, A. (1992) 'On the relationship between firm size and export intensity', *Journal of International Business Studies*, Vol. 23, pp. 605–35.

Bourantas, D. and Mandes, Y. (1987) 'Does market share lead to profitability?' *Long Range Planning*, Vol. 20, No. 5, pp. 102–8.

Buckley, P.J. and Casson, M. (1998) 'Analyzing foreign market entry strategies: extending the internationalization approach', *Journal of International Business Studies*, Vol. 29, No. 3, pp. 539–61.

Buckley, P.J., Pass, C.L. and Prescott, K. (1990) 'Measures of international competitiveness: a critical review', *Journal of Marketing Management*, Vol. 4, pp. 175–200.

Burpitt, W.J. and Rondinelli, D.A. (2000) 'Small firms' motivations for exporting: to earn and learn?' *Journal of Small Business Management*, October, pp. 1–14.

Calof, J.L. (1994) 'The relationship between firm size and export behaviour revisited', *Journal of International Business Studies*, Vol. 25, No. 2, pp. 367–87.

Cavusgil, S.T. and Kirpalani, V.H. (1993) 'Introducing products into export markets: success factors', *Journal of Business Research*, Vol. 27, pp. 1–15.

Chaney, P.K., Devinney, T.M. and Winer, R.S. (1991) 'The impact of new product introductions on the market value of firms', *Journal of Business*, Vol. 64, No. 4, pp. 573–610.

Chetty, S.K. and Hamilton, R.T. (1996) 'The process of exporting in owner-controlled firms', *International Small Business Journal*, Vol. 14, No. 2, pp. 12–25.

Chhibber, P.K. and Majumdar, S.K. (1998) 'Does it pay to venture abroad? Exporting behaviour and the performance of firms in Indian industry', *Managerial and Decision Economics*, Vol. 19, No. 2, pp. 121–6.

Christensen, S.L. (1993) 'Is there a role for the small business in the North American Free Trade Area?', *Business Forum*, Vol. 18, No. 1/2, pp. 44–6.

Cooper, R.G. (1994) 'New products: the factors that drive success', *International Marketing Review*, Vol. 11, No. 1, pp. 60–76.

Crick, D. (1999) 'An investigation into SMEs' use of language in their export operations', *International Journal of Entrepreneurial Behaviour and Research*, Vol. 5, No. 1, pp. 19–31.

Crick, D. (2002) 'The decision to discontinue exporting: SMEs in two UK trade sectors', *Journal of Small Business Management*, Vol. 40, No. 1, pp. 66–77.

Czinkota, M.R. and Johnson, W.J. (1981) 'Segmenting US firms for export development', *Journal of Business Research*, Vol. 9, pp. 353–65.

Czinkota, M.R. and Ursik, M. (1991) 'Classification of exporting firms according to sales and growth into a share matrix', *Journal of Business Research*, Vol. 22, No. 3, pp. 243–53.

De Toni, A. and Nassimbeni, G. (2001) 'The export propensity of small firms', *International Journal of Entrepreneurial Behaviour and Research*, Vol. 7, No. 4, pp. 132–47.

D'Souza, D.E. and McDougall, P.P. (1989) 'Third world joint venturing: a strategic option for the smaller firm', *Entrepreneurship Theory and Practice*, Vol. 14, pp. 19–33.

Edmunds, S.E. and Khoury, S.J. (1986) 'Exports: a necessary ingredient in the growth of small business firms', *Journal of Small Business Management*, Vol. 24, pp. 54–65.

Filatotchev, I., Wright, M., Buck, T. and Dyomina, N. (1999) 'Exporting and restructuring in privatised firms from Russia, Ukraine and Belarus', *World Economy*, Vol. 22, No. 7, pp. 1013–14.

Grenier, L., McKay, A. and Morrissey, O. (1999) 'Exporting, ownership and confidence in Tanzanian enterprises', *World Economy*, Vol. 22, No. 7, p. 995.

Hamermesh, R.G., Anderson, Jr, M.J. and Harris, J.E. (1978) 'Strategies for low market share businesses', *Harvard Business Review*, May–June, pp. 95–102.

Hart, S. and Tzokas, N. (1999) 'The impact of marketing research activity on SME export performance: evidence from the UK', *Journal of Small Business Management*, Vol. 37, No. 2, pp. 63–75.

Holmlund, M. and Koch, S. (1999) 'Relationships and the internationalisation of Finnish small and medium-sized companies', *International Small Business Journal*, Vol. 16, No. 4, pp. 46–63.

Joynt, P. and Welch, L. (1985) 'A strategy for small business internationalisation', *International Marketing Review*, Vol. 2, pp. 64–73.

Leonidou, L.C. and Adams-Florou, A.S. (1999) 'Types and sources of export information: insights from small business', *International Small Business Journal*, Vol. 17, No. 3, pp. 30–45.

Lloyd, P.E. and Mason, C.M. (1984) 'Spatial variations in new firm formation in the United Kingdom: comparative evidence from Merseyside, Greater Manchester and South Hampshire', *Regional Studies*, Vol. 18, pp. 207–20.

Lu, J.W. and Beamish, P.W. (2001) 'The internationalization and performance of SMEs', *Strategic Management Journal*, Vol. 22, pp. 565–86.

Naidu, G.M. and Kanti Prasad, V. (1994) 'Predictors of export strategy and performance of small- and medium-sized firms', *Journal of Business Research*, Vol. 31, No. 2/3, pp. 107–15.

Newton, J.K. (1981) 'Acquisitions: a directional policy matrix approach', *Long Range Planning*, Vol. 14, No. 6, pp. 51–7.

Oakey, R.P. and Cooper, S.Y. (1989) 'High technology industry, agglomeration and potential for peripherally sited small firms', *Regional Studies*, Vol. 22, pp. 347–60.

O'Farrell, P.N., Wood, P.A. and Zheng, J. (1998) 'Internationalisation by business service SMEs: an inter-industry analysis', *International Small Business Journal*, Vol. 16, No. 2, pp. 13–33.

Philp, N.E. (1998) 'The export propensity of the very small enterprise', *International Small Business Journal*, Vol. 16, No. 4, pp. 79–94.

Pope, R.A. (2002) 'Why small firms export: another look', *Journal of Small Business Management*, Vol. 40, No. 1, pp. 17–26.

Samiee, S. and Walters, P.G.P. (1991) 'Segmenting corporate exporting activities: sporadic versus regular exporters', *Journal of the Academy of Marketing Science*, Vol. 19, No. 2, pp. 94–104.

Schuster, C.P. and Bodkin, C.D. (1987) 'Market segmentation practises of exporting companies', *Industrial Marketing Management*, Vol. 16, No. 2, pp. 95–102.

Smallbone, D., Piasecki, B., Venessar, U., Toderov, K. and Labrianidis, L. (1999) 'Internationalisation and SME development in transition economies: an international comparison', *Journal of Small Business and Enterprise Development*, Vol. 5, No. 4, pp. 363–75.

Szymanski, D.M., Bharadwai, S.G. and Varadarajan, P.R. (1993) 'An analysis of the market share–profitability relationship', *Journal of Marketing*, Vol. 57, pp. 1–18.

Walters, P.G.P. (1991) 'Segmenting corporate exporting activities: sporadic versus regular exporters', *Journal of the Academy of Marketing Science*, Vol. 19, No. 2, pp. 93–104.

Westhead, P. (1995) 'Exporting and non-exporting firms in Great Britain', *International Journal of Entrepreneurial Behaviour and Research*, Vol. 1, No. 2, pp. 6–36.

Wolff, J.A. and Pett, T.L. (2000) 'Internationalization of small firms: an examination of export competitive patterns, firm size and export performance', *Journal of Small Business Management*, Vol. 34, No. 2, pp. 34–47.

Selected case material Case 25.1

Pulp friction for Korean entrepreneur

1 May 2002

By **Peter Marsh**

At a sprawling plant in Blankenstein in the Thuringian hills in eastern Germany, Jimmy Lee is planning to do his bit to revitalise the country's paper industry.

It is a curious mission. Mr Lee, a South Korea-born chemical engineer, is chairman and president of Mercer International, a Seattle-registered company with its head office in Zurich and virtually all its production assets in Germany.

Mr Lee is a self-confessed maverick who since taking charge of the Nasdaq-listed Mercer in the late 1980s has steered the company from its roots in property investment into a variety of other schemes including mining, insurance and trading aircraft parts.

Mercer's involvement in Germany dates to 1993, when Mr Lee spotted an investment opportunity in buying a series of paper mills in the former East Germany that had been run as part of a giant state-owned conglomerate.

Around the same time, Mercer acquired a plant in Blankenstein, again formerly owned by the East German government, for pulp production. An essential pre-requisite for paper, pulp is made from processing cellulose from trees.

After a €450m ($405m) project, finished in 1999, to improve and expand the Blankenstein plant, Mr Lee is poised to begin a still more ambitious programme: to spend another €1bn on building a new pulp plant in Stendal, near Berlin, employing similar technology to that used in the Thuringian factory.

Assuming bank financing can be agreed for the project, construction at Stendal could begin this year, with the site starting up in 2004.

Last year Mercer's revenues of $197m, on which it made a net loss of $2.5m, came primarily from its German pulp and paper interests, although it also owns a Swiss speciality paper company.

Pulp production is a highly cyclical industry, normally left to large paper-makers that integrate this process into large paper production sites. In Europe it is uncommon to find entrepreneurs wanting to get involved in such a sector where prices swing about wildly and planning is difficult.

But Mr Lee shrugs off such negative thoughts. 'Mercer is a contrarian investor,' he says.

'It's hard to make money from ventures if everyone else has the same idea (about putting money into projects).'

Within the paper industry, questions have been raised about Mercer's long-term intentions. Many expect Mercer's two pulp mills – assuming the Stendal project proceeds – to be sold off to bigger paper companies in the next few years.

That would follow on from Mercer's disposal in a similar way of most of its eastern German paper mills, from which Mr Lee says it made a modest sum of money.

Mads Asprem, a paper analyst at Merrill Lynch, says the two pulp mills that Mercer is poised to run in Germany are unlikely to be profitable in the long run, on account of the high costs of using wood that is cut from local forests as the feedstock.

He says that the company has benefited from government subsidies that Mercer says will cover roughly 30 per cent of its investments – intended to boost the former East German economy. 'The subsidies are unjustified,' says Mr Asprem.

However, Mercer defends its involvement in the German paper industry, saying that its activities are giving the sector a boost that no German-owned investor was willing to make.

Wolfram Ridder, Mercer's vice-president, says the 900,000 tonnes a year of pulp that the company's two plants should be making by the middle of this decade will reduce the need for Germany's sizeable paper industry to import 4m tonnes a year of pulp from other countries.

Mercer sells the 280,000 tonnes a year of the pulp it makes in Blankenstein (double the amount produced there when the company took it over) to 50 paper companies, mainly in Germany and Italy.

'We have proved our ability as a pulp producer and this has given us the confidence to proceed with the Stendal project,' says Mr Lee. Saying it is unlikely Mercer will want to invest in further pulp mills, Mr Lee adds it is conceivable the company could sell its assets on to other groups, though it has no plans to do so.

As for the criticism that the company has attracted from the mainstream paper industry, Mr Lee says: 'Because we are outsiders, it's inevitable we'll have a different way of doing things.'

Source: *Financial Times*, 1 May 2002.

Case 25.2

John Singleton

22 January 2002

By **Ed Charles**

Would WPP boss Sir Martin Sorrell go into business with an entrepreneur who has traded blows in a car park with the head of an ad agency, and appeared in court accused of headbutting an accountant while drunk? Well, yes he would. Twice in fact.

The entrepreneur in question is Australian advertising boss John Singleton, and this unlikely marriage of convenience dates back to a deal in 1998 that saw Ogilvy & Mather in Australia and New Zealand merge with local group John Singleton Advertising.

This was unusual because instead of O&M taking control, the Australian Stock Exchange-listed Singleton Group ended up owning two-thirds of Singleton Ogilvy & Mather, and half of media buying shop MindShare, with Walter Thompson.

In spite of Singleton's apparent dislike of accountants, the reason for the deal was all in the numbers – his group's managers make some of the fattest ad agency margins in the world. In Australia, the average agency margin is less than 14 per cent. SO&M, whose client list includes Telstra, Qantas and Lion Nathan (Tooheys beer), makes almost 34 per cent.

Singleton's group, capitalised at A$500m (£200m), expects SO&M's profits of A$31m to grow more than 10 per cent this year while competitors are languishing in a post-September 11 depression.

Small surprise then that in December Sorrell and Singleton did another deal, this time giving the Australian outfit 49 per cent of J Walter Thompson in Australia and New Zealand. WPP now owns 11 per cent of The Singleton Group, which changed its name to Singleton Thompson WPP.

Behind these two deals looms the figure of John Singleton, affectionately known as 'Singo'. Six times married, he makes even the usual array of colourful advertising figures seem grey – in April 2000 he spent A$30,000 on buying every racegoer on the course a beer after his horse, Belle Du Jour, won Sydney's prestigious Golden Slipper.

His maverick approach even extends to appearing in court. Booked for driving at 160kmh, he was let off, arguing that his Bentley was safe at that speed. He's had his own radio and TV shows, been a boxing promoter and built up a large personal fortune.

But Singleton is also well-connected, counting media billionaire Kerry Packer and former prime minister Bob Hawke among his friends, and has business interests that extend from

advertising and a stake in the travel publisher Lonely Planet to property and bloodstock.

One of the top copywriters in Australia, Singleton's style is brash even by Australian standards, but he maintains a knockabout Aussie charm. And he has combined some wild ways with a relentless approach that dates back to his early days and produced rules that still stand in his agencies: no leaving the building for lunch and definitely no booze.

SO&M maintains this policy. Staff are compensated with one of the best bars in Sydney – on the 18th floor of SO&M's building in Darling Harbour – which opens daily at 5.30pm sharp. Friday night is party night, when staff and clients rub shoulders with Australian sporting heroes brought in for the occasion. The agency does not bother going in for creative awards and shuns its competitors.

As Russell Tate, chief executive of The Singleton Group, explains: 'We don't go anywhere near the advertising industry. I regard it as the enemy.'

Increasing client sales is deep in the Singleton psyche. Every Monday morning the whole agency meets to review the sales success of their campaigns from the previous week.

Tate, who as well as running The Singleton Group, is head of SO&M, has client responsibilities and now sits on the board of JWT in Australia and New Zealand, says: 'The whole ethos of this place is – John's quote – "advertising exists to sell product". David Ogilvy said very much the same thing.' Singo has been likened to David Ogilvy by many, including his own modest self and O&M's worldwide chairman and chief executive Shelly Lazarus.

The JWT deal does differ from the O&M tie-up in some respects. At the time of the latter, John Singleton Advertising wanted to open up growth opportunities locally and there was significant rationalisation. At JWT, Tate is not operationally involved and works only with the top management.

'Ogilvy was doing pretty badly. It had very good revenue – high-quality revenue – but clearly it hadn't been run well for some time,' says Tate. By contrast, JWT, whose client list includes Ford, Unilever, and Diageo/UDV, is already performing better than many local rivals, with margins of 18 per cent.

Yet, despite its comparatively hands-off arrangement, JWT will be subject to the same Singo formula as O&M – increasing margins by cutting pitching costs, eliminating head-hunters and staff expenses, and cutting back heavily on travel, especially conference trips that have little or no impact locally.

As at O&M, Tate will also be looking to increase margins by encouraging the agency to use the marketing services companies it owns to offer clients a fully integrated service. At SO&M, reports Tate, 'we made enormous savings out of the synergies'.

Ultimately, Singo will no doubt be called upon to export his philosophy to sate Sorrell's desire for higher margins across his empire. Tate admits that logic suggests that if the JWT deal works as well as the O&M deal, Young & Rubicam will enter their orbit. As Tate says: 'We're starting to look a little like the WPP in Australia.'

Source: Financial Times, 22 January 2002, © Ed Charles.

Discussion points

1. Consider the relative advantages and disadvantages for Jimmy Lee and his venture in setting up overseas production plants rather than relying on exporting.

2. Develop a range of expansion strategies for Loudcloud. What criteria would you use to select the best strategy?

Chapter 26

Organisational growth and development

Chapter overview

This chapter is concerned with developing an understanding of how organisational growth and development present themselves as opportunities and challenges to the decision-making entrepreneur. The first section explores some of the metaphors that decision makers can draw upon to create a picture of organisational growth. Subsequent sections of the chapter deal with setting objectives for growth and then planning for and controlling it.

26.1 Conceptualising growth and organisational change

Key learning outcome

An understanding of the metaphors used to describe organisational growth.

The idea that organisations and organising are best understood through the use of metaphor was introduced in Section 11.1. The point was made that the way in which management is approached is dependent, to some extent, on the metaphor being used to provide an image of organisation by the entrepreneurial decision maker. As well as influencing the way in which organisation is perceived in a static sense, metaphors also influence the way in which organisational *growth* and *change* are seen to take place. Again, such metaphors provide a base for recognising the challenges the organisation faces and the approaches the entrepreneur might take to meet them.

Andrew van de Ven and Marshall Scott Poole (1995) have summarised the most important metaphors of organisational change. These are based on

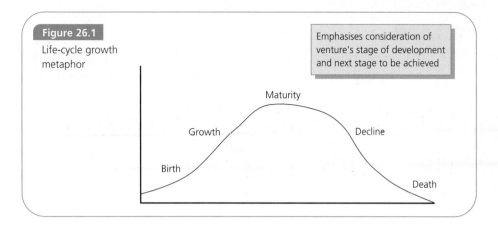

Figure 26.1

Life-cycle growth
metaphor

Emphasises consideration of
venture's stage of development
and next stage to be achieved

Maturity

Growth

Decline

Birth

Death

the notions of *life-cycle*, *evolution*, the *dialectic* and *teleology*. In addition, the
metaphors of the trialectic and chaos complement the picture.

Life-cycle

The notion of life-cycle suggests that the organisation undergoes a pattern of
growth and development much like a living organism does. Life for an organism
consists of a series of different stages: it is born, grows, matures and eventually
ages and dies (Figure 26.1). This pattern is pre-programmed and the changes that
take place are both unavoidable and irrevocable. Drawing on the experience of
living things, this metaphor accounts for the view that youthful entrepreneurial
organisations are dynamic whereas older organisations are more sedate and sluggish and that this is a fate that will eventually befall the entrepreneurial venture as
it matures itself. The metaphor does not give a definite lifespan, however; it does
not say *when* this must happen.

   This metaphor is limited in that it (falsely) suggests that organisational decline
is inevitable. It does, however, serve to warn the entrepreneur against complacency
as the venture becomes successful.

Evolution

Evolution is a theoretical scheme which explains changes over time of the morpho-
logy of biological populations. It is founded on the concepts of *competition*, *fitness*,
selection and *survival*. This scheme has been co-opted from biological science to
describe changes in populations of business firms (Figure 26.2).

   As a metaphor, evolution reminds the entrepreneur that they are operating in
a competitive environment, that they must compete for scarce resources and that
the venture must be efficient ('fit') in the tasks it undertakes. While evolution may
conjure up an image of untrammelled competition – of a nature 'red in tooth and
claw' in the words of Tennyson in his poem *In memoriam* – a more sophisticated
reading reminds us that co-operation within and between species is also a feature

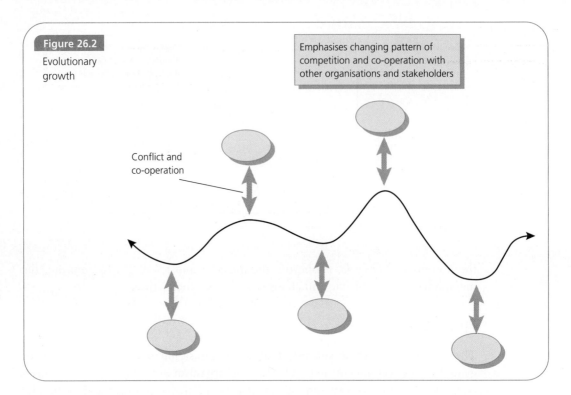

Figure 26.2

Evolutionary growth

Emphasises changing pattern of competition and co-operation with other organisations and stakeholders

Conflict and co-operation

of the natural world. This is similar to the entrepreneurial venture which not only competes, but also grows within a stakeholder network which may be supportive as well as competitive.

The dialectic

The dialectic is a concept which can be traced back to classical Greek philosophy. It has been extensively developed by thinkers such as Marx and Freud and is based on a notion of progression through conflict and resolution. A system is initially unified but, over time, distinct parts begin to distinguish themselves. These parts recognise that their interests conflict and so they begin to oppose each other. Neither part can actually win the conflict and what eventually emerges is a newly unified system in which both parts have been changed and reintegrated (Figure 26.3).

As a metaphor of organisational development, the dialectic illuminates conflict and conflict resolution at a number of levels, for example between the entrepreneurial venture and competitor firms, between different stakeholder groups within the venture such as investors and employees, and within stakeholder groups. This latter level would include, for example, political manoeuvring by managerial factions within the business.

The importance of this metaphor for the entrepreneur is not so much its emphasis on the inevitability of conflict as in the idea that value can be created by resolving that conflict. The entrepreneur brings stakeholders (whose interests may differ) together in a way in which all benefit.

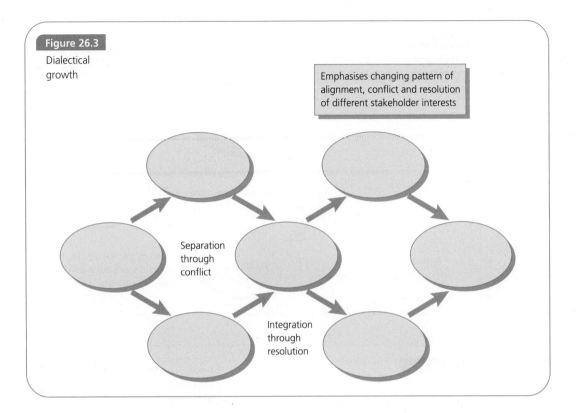

Figure 26.3

Dialectical growth

Emphasises changing pattern of alignment, conflict and resolution of different stakeholder interests

Separation through conflict

Integration through resolution

The trialectic

Jeffrey Ford and Laurie Ford (1994) have drawn upon a development of the dialectic to present a new metaphor for describing organisational growth. This is the *trialectic*. The dialectic suggests that a system separates into two conflicting parts. As its name suggests, the trialectic suggests that systems have a dynamic consisting of three parts. However, the way that these three parts attract rather than conflict with each other is emphasised. Trialectics takes as its starting point the notion that all things are in a state of flux. This flux is the fundamental 'stuff' of the universe, not the objects we see. When we recognise objects or systems we only do so as a result of our seeking out transient 'resting points' or 'material manifestations'. The three aspects that are important to the growth of an organisation are its current state or 'manifestation' and two alternative possible futures or potential manifestations. These possible future states act to attract the venture and pull it forward. In pursuing these, the organisation creates new pairs of possible future states (Figure 26.4). This process is ongoing, continuous and dynamic. Again, we only notice these states because we continually seek out the transient manifestations.

The metaphor of trialectical change calls upon some deep philosophical ideas. As a metaphor for growth in the entrepreneurial venture it does, however, emphasise the fact that change is not just an aspect of the organisation; it is fundamental to it. It also emphasises the possibility of choosing a number of different

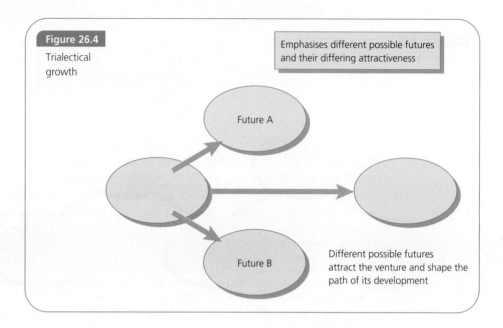

Figure 26.4

Trialectical growth

Emphasises different possible futures and their differing attractiveness

Future A

Future B

Different possible futures attract the venture and shape the path of its development

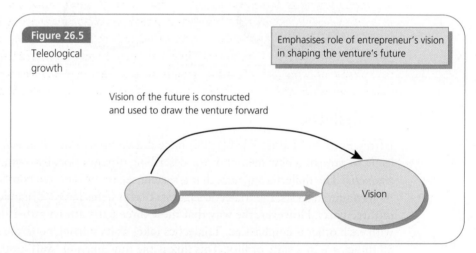

Figure 26.5

Teleological growth

Emphasises role of entrepreneur's vision in shaping the venture's future

Vision of the future is constructed and used to draw the venture forward

Vision

future states and the freedom the entrepreneur has to create his or her own entirely new world.

Teleology

Teleology suggests a process of change in which a system is progressing toward some future state or *teleos*. This future state both attracts the system or pulls it forward, and defines the shape the system takes as it progresses (Figure 26.5). More than any other metaphor, teleology introduces the notion of *purpose* to organisational change and growth. The entrepreneur can use his or her vision as the future state which pulls the organisation forward. It can be used to define goals and objectives and it is a critical element in leadership. Visionary leadership is a teleological process.

Chaos

In addition to these 'traditional' metaphors, a new perspective is becoming increasingly important in providing a context for understanding organisational change. This is based on the notions of *complexity* and *chaos*.

Complexity science has its origins in the physics of turbulent and far-from-equilibrium systems. Its insights have escaped from the boundaries of these narrow concerns and they now inform thinking on a wide range of topics including biology, economics and organisation theory. The defining feature of complexity is its rejection of simple lines of causality which characterise traditional systems thinking. In a complex system a small cause may, in time, have a very large and unpredictable effect (Figure 26.6). The beat of a butterfly's wing eventually causing a hurricane is a dramatic example. Systems theorists modelling the Earth's atmosphere discovered that a slight movement of air in one part of the world (say, from the beat of a butterfly's wing) could cause enough of a disturbance of the global atmospheric system to result in a large effect (such as a hurricane) some time later in a distant part of the world. The atmosphere is a chaotic system. A small cause leads to a large effect that cannot be predicted *ex ante*. Complex systems are not simply disorganised, however. They may show higher levels of form and order as a result of 'emergent' features which do not have a straightforward one-to-one relationship with lower levels of order. This is a perspective which has been

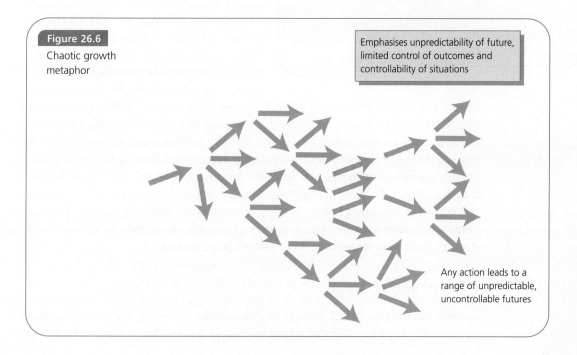

Figure 26.6

Chaotic growth metaphor

Emphasises unpredictability of future, limited control of outcomes and controllability of situations

Any action leads to a range of unpredictable, uncontrollable futures developed extensively by Ralph Stacey in his book *Strategic Management and Organisational Dynamics* (2000).

The main question which complexity theory poses to management thinking is, if organisations are chaotic systems, can they be 'managed' at all? The answer usually leads not to a rejection of management but to demands to view it in a more sophisticated light. What is rejected is the idea that management can be reduced to a simple process of moving the venture to a pre-determined end-point by a series of controlled steps.

The entrepreneurial venture is inherently unpredictable. By its very nature, it creates a future which is uncertain. Systems emerge to manage this uncertainty, for example the network of stakeholder relationships which define the venture, but they cannot eliminate it completely. The chaos metaphor reminds the entrepreneur that control and direction cannot be 'programmed' into the organisation. Events cannot be foreseen and each contingency must be responded to on its own terms. Entrepreneurial management is a *dynamic* process and it demands a 'hands on' approach. The future of the venture is not pre-determined by its present, rather it is actively shaped by the entrepreneur as new, unseen and often unseeable possibilities emerge.

As with metaphors of static organisation, entrepreneurs must learn to enrich their decision making by recognising the metaphors they are using and by drawing on as wide a variety of metaphors of organisational change as possible.

26.2 Growth as an objective for the venture

> **Key learning outcome**
>
> An appreciation of the issues associated with setting growth as an objective for the venture.

The entrepreneurial venture is characterised by its growth potential, but why might an entrepreneur wish to take advantage of that potential and grow their venture? There are a number of answers to this question. It might be the result of a desire to increase personal wealth but this is not usually the main motivation of an entrepreneur. More usually it relates to a sense of achievement. In a sense, the size of the venture is a way of 'keeping the score'. Entrepreneurs are also driven by a desire to make a difference to the world. And in general, the larger the venture they create, the bigger the difference they have made. Driving growth can also relate to the desire for personal control. The bigger the venture, the greater the domain over which the entrepreneur can express their power.

For these reasons growth is often an important objective for the venture. However, setting growth targets creates challenges in relation to the venture's strategy and resources and the risk to which it is exposed.

Growth and strategy

Growth has to be achieved. It must be delivered by obtaining a greater volume of business. Ultimately, it must be driven by increased sales. The venture must have a strategy in place to develop its sales base. As discussed in Chapter 24, such a strategy may be based on exploiting market growth, increasing market share, developing new products or entering new markets.

An expansion strategy must be consistent with the capabilities of the venture, it must draw upon and develop the venture's competitive advantages and be viable given the competitive situation it will have to face. Growth targets must be demanding but they must also be reasonable given the strategic constraints the venture faces.

Growth and resources

Growth is dependent on the venture's ability to attract new resources. The ultimate source of resources is customer money. Investment and loan capital can only be a means to the end of attracting customers.

Capital is not useful in itself. It must be converted into productive assets in terms of people and operating resources. Growth targets must take account of the resources the venture will be able to acquire. Consideration must be made not just of the ability to attract capital from customers, lenders and investors but also the ability of the venture to *use* that capital to bring in the people and specialist assets the venture depends on. If these are in short supply, then any limitations imposed on growth must be taken into account.

Growth and risk

There is a complex relationship between growth and risk. In general, the larger a firm, the less risk it is exposed to. There are two reasons for this. First, size reflects *success*. A large firm is successful which implies that it is good at what it does. Clearly, being effective in the marketplace is the best way to reduce risk. Second, the larger the firm, the more resources it will have. In particular, larger firms tend to have more 'slack' resources. These are resources that are not dedicated to specific projects and can be moved around quickly. The large business can use these resources to buffer themselves from short-term environmental shocks better than can the small firm.

However, growth carries some risk in itself. Growth implies developing new business which means venturing into the unknown. The degree of risk depends on the way in which the expansion draws upon the venture's capabilities, its knowledge of products and markets and the environment in which it competes. Using resources to fuel growth is an *investment* regardless of whether new investment capital is obtained or profits are reinvested rather than distributed back to shareholders. As an investment, growth must be judged like any other in light of the risks it presents, the returns it offers and the opportunity costs it imposes.

The growth objective for the venture must be set following consideration of these factors. It must define the growth of the venture in terms of increased sales, increased income (including new investment capital) and how these revenues will be converted to assets. Growth targets must be consistent with, and feasible from, a strategy to achieve that growth and they must be acceptable to the venture's stakeholders in terms of the risks this creates.

Not all entrepreneurs set out with high growth objectives in mind. When Anita Roddick established The Body Shop in Brighton she intended to start only a small business capable of providing an income for her and her family. However, once the potential of her innovation became evident, growth (particularly through franchising) became a strategic priority for the business.

26.3 Controlling and planning for growth

> **Key learning outcome**
>
> A recognition of the ways in which growth can be controlled by the entrepreneur.

The fact that growth presents strategic, resource and investment decision-making issues to the entrepreneur means it is a process which must be both planned for and controlled. Indeed, the objective of growth, once it has been established, should lie at the heart of and drive forward the venture's planning and control process. The idea of controlling growth is critical to entrepreneurial success. It draws together a number of themes which have been developed in this book so far.

The *desirability* of growth must be reflected in the entrepreneur's vision (see Chapter 13). This vision must act as a force which co-ordinates and focuses the whole organisation on the tasks it faces. To do this, the vision must not only illuminate the *what* of growth but also the *why*, that is, not only what is in it for the organisation but why the stakeholder will gain from it.

The *potential* for growth must be recognised in the venture's mission (see Chapter 14). This mission should be reasonable given the venture's capabilities and competitive situation but it should also stretch the organisation to make maximum use of its capabilities and exploit its competitive potential.

The *direction* of growth must be indicated by the venture's strategy (see Chapter 15). This should indicate the products the business will offer, the markets it will operate in and the competitive advantages it will develop and exploit in order to serve the customer better than competitors in those markets.

The *management* of growth demands the management of resource flows within the organisation. It means designing the organisation so that appropriate resource-acquiring functions are in place to co-ordinate resource-acquiring activities effectively. This relates to the ideas developed in Chapter 24.

In summary, the *achievement* of growth is a result of the decision-making processes that go on within the venture. The entrepreneur must control these through their power and leadership strategies. The entrepreneur's need (and desire!) to impose their will on the organisation must always be tempered by the value to be gained from letting individuals use their own insights and initiative. This is a theme to be developed further in Chapter 28.

Summary of key ideas

- Organisational growth, like organisation itself, is best understood through *metaphors* of change.

- Growth is an important objective for the venture. The growth objective must be considered in the light of the venture's *market potential*, its *strategic capabilities*, its *resources* and the *risks* it wishes to undertake.

- Growth must be both planned for and controlled by the entrepreneur, both in terms of *rate* and *direction*.

Research themes

Entrepreneurs' growth objectives

It is often assumed that all entrepreneurs wish to grow their businesses. However, as pointed out in the discussion of differential advantage theory (Section 2.1), growth may be one objective among many and may be a means of achieving other objectives rather than an objective in itself. Select a sample of entrepreneurs and survey them to ascertain their attitudes towards the growth of their ventures. Issues to be explored include whether the entrepreneur sees growth as a priority or not, to what extent growth should take precedence over other objectives (such as short-term profitability and consolidation of existing position) and what level of risk is acceptable to achieve growth. What managerial challenges does growth entail and what long-term rewards does the entrepreneur expect for delivering growth. Further, inquire into how growth might conflict with wider stakeholder concerns (including those of the entrepreneur him- or herself) and perhaps its impact on broader social responsibilities. Do all entrepreneurs hold the same attitudes towards growth? Is growth an objective in itself or is it actually a means to an end? Summarise by considering the implications for supporting entrepreneurs in achieving growth.

Entrepreneurs' metaphoric perceptions of growth

As outlined above, growth is often understood through the mirror of metaphor. The metaphors described can be translated into propositions about growth. For example, the teleological metaphor can be related as 'I know where I want to be in growing this business', the dialectic as 'growth always results in conflict', the biological as 'all businesses eventually die', and so on. Work on a series of propositions relating the metaphors in this way, creating several for each metaphor. Present these to entrepreneurs (nascent or experienced) and have them indicate their agreement or disagreement with them (use a Likert scale).

In order to discriminate between different metaphoric representations, pairs of propositions drawn from different metaphors can be presented with the subject indicating which of the pair he or she most agrees with. Additionally, have the entrepreneur detail his or her growth objectives and ambitions as well as approach and perceived issues in achieving growth for his or her venture (this study might well follow on from the one above). Do individual entrepreneurs tend towards a single metaphor, or do they draw from several? How does the dominant metaphor relate to approaches to and understanding of growth management? Conclude by making recommendations about how supporters of entrepreneurs may use an understanding of the individual entrepreneur's metaphoric underpinning to enhance communication with entrepreneurs about growth and its management.

Suggestions for further reading

Bitner, L.N. and Powell, J.D. (1987) 'Expansion planning for small retail firms', *Journal of Small Business Management*, Apr, pp. 47–54.

Ford, J.D. and Ford, L.W. (1994) 'Logics of identity, contradiction and attraction in change', *Academy of Management Review*, Vol. 19, No. 4, pp. 756–85.

Gaddis, P.O. (1997) 'Strategy under attack', *Long Range Planning*, Vol. 30, No.1, pp. 38–45.

Hunsdiek, D. (1985) 'Financing of start-up and growth of new technology based firms in West Germany', *International Small Business Journal*, Vol. 4, No. 2, pp. 10–24.

McKergow, M. (1996) 'Complexity science and management: what's in it for business?' *Long Range Planning*, Vol. 29, No. 5, pp. 721–7.

Oakley, R. (1991) 'High-technology small firms: their potential for rapid industrial growth', *International Small Business Journal*, Vol. 9, No. 4, pp. 30–42.

Stacey, R. (1996) 'Emerging strategies for a chaotic environment', *Long Range Planning*, Vol. 29, No. 2, pp. 182–9.

Stacey, R. (2000) *Strategic Management and Organisational Dynamics* (3rd edn), London: Pitman Publishing.

Tuck, P. and Hamilton, R.T. (1993) 'Intra-industry size differences in founder controlled firms', *International Small Business Journal*, Vol. 12, No. 1, pp. 12–22.

van de Ven, A.H. and Scott Poole, M. (1995) 'Explaining development and change in organizations', *Academy of Management Review*, Vol. 20, No. 3, pp. 510–40.

Lessons from a grim market

FT

20 June 2002

By **Katharine Campbell**

The moment at which you decide to go fundraising from the venture capital community would not be the time to be fretting about your work/life balance, advises Stuart Evans, chief executive of Plastic Logic.

The Cambridge-based company, which is developing a plastic electronics technology, secured £6.3m of first-round financing in April from a syndicate of venture capitalists led by Polytechnos, a Munich-based firm. Mr Evans began the process last September and says he spent two-thirds of his long working days on getting the funding.

Meanwhile, Charlie Muirhead, founder of network management software group Orchestream, recently hauled in £10.3m for telecommunications networking company Nexagent from venture capitalists Atlas Venture and Benchmark. In that case the process took about a year but it represents another funding for a company that is not yet making sales.

Do these two deals at least indicate that the venture capital market is stirring again – even if the process is highly time-consuming?

Both cases are, in different ways, unusual. But their experiences nevertheless offer useful lessons to others trying to raise venture money.

Overall, the funding picture is still grim. In the first quarter of 2002, early-stage venture funding across Europe fell by about a third compared with the final quarter of 2001, according to figures compiled by Ernst & Young and Venture One, the venture capital research company. The UK held up comparatively well within those figures but the scale of the contraction of venture funding in the UK is clear, representing a 68 per cent fall from the first quarter of 2000.

To compound matters, most of the investment activity has been follow-on rather than first-stage financings, as venture firms scramble to shore up sections of their existing portfolios. What is more, if they are investing in so-called series A financings – the first institutional round – they are opting for companies with customers.

However, Nexagent does not plan to launch a commercial service until the third quarter of this year; and Plastic Logic's funding is designed to take it to the point where it signs its first licensing agreements with customers at the end of 2003.

So what are the tricks?

First, the idea. A few venture capitalists are still prepared to take a risk for something that could be really big. '[Plastic Logic] is a truly disruptive technology,' says Simon Waddington, partner at Polytechnos, which says it is building a balanced portfolio to include one or two ventures that, while risky, are potentially huge hits. Nexagent is also a grand vision – aiming to link data networks across multiple telecoms carriers with the simplicity and reliability of the phone network.

Both deals are unusual – but then a large part of the process was convincing the venture capitalists of that potential to be a big idea.

'You need to think about fundraising as a professional relationship sales campaign. If you make more calls you will make more sales,' says Mr Evans.

You also have to be 'properly introduced' to potential investors. This was one of the areas where Plastic Logic was well placed. Amadeus Capital Partners, the venture capital firm, was a seed investor; and on Plastic Logic's board is Hermann Hauser, co-founder of Amadeus and a well known figure in the European high-tech community. So the company was at least likely to get the right sort of introduction.

This in itself is a lesson, says Michael Ledzion, chief executive of data storage company Polight Technologies, in Cambridge. 'Later fundraisings are made easier or harder depending on who your initial investors are. To the extent you have the luxury of choosing between investors, you should ask yourself if they are going to be able to get you contacts at the next level,' Mr Ledzion says.

An experienced management team with previous experience in early-stage companies is more than ever a necessity in the minds of venture capitalists today.

'I don't want to sound smug,' says 52-year-old Mr Evans, 'but the reason we did well is that it is a wonderful idea, it is really deep science – *and* we have done it before.'

Mr Evans founded and ran Cotag International, an early pioneer of electronic tagging in the mid-1980s. Plastic Logic's chief scientist, Richard Friend, Cavendish professor of physics at the University of Cambridge, co-founded Cambridge Display Technology, which uses light-emitting polymer technology for computer displays.

Mr Muirhead is also a serial entrepreneur but the fact that he is still only in his mid 20s probably counted as a slight negative, when it would have been the opposite just two years ago.

'It did help having done it before – but it only helped a bit,' says Mr Muirhead. 'It meant the VCs were very happy to have the first meeting.'

But it was Gerry Montanus of Atlas who took the lead in the end. Mr Montanus had been an investor in Orche-stream, which at one time had a market capitalisation of nearly £900m before crashing back to earth in the telecommunications collapse.

Mr Muirhead's particular achievement at Nexagent – in addition to the grand vision – had been to assemble a team of seasoned executives from Cable & Wireless and Cisco.

The company is already looking for a chief executive 'with grey hair', Mr Muirhead says.

Responsiveness is another essential quality for success in the process, says Andrea Bonafe, who worked on the Nexagent fundraising and is now chief operating officer of the newly merged Venture Capital Report/Pi Capital angel network. 'You have to keep adjusting to what the venture capitalists want – more focus, more proof of customer interest.'

Flexibility in accepting some of the terms venture capitalists are now imposing is also necessary, although there can still be scope for negotiation.

Milestones, for instance, have made a comeback: Nexagent has tranched funding in which £4m of the £10.3 total is dependent on achieving certain milestones.

'The VCs are trying to mitigate risk,' says Jason Purcell, chief executive of First Stage Capital, which helps companies raise venture money. 'The devil is in the detail. You need to make sure these milestones are measurable, achievable and consistent with the direction in which the company is going.'

Other terms of the deal are also important and advisers say companies should balance the valuation they achieve against other aspects of the agreement.

Entrepreneurs will need to become rapidly acquainted with unfamiliar provisions such as 'liquidation preferences'. A 'three-times liquidation preference', for instance, would stipulate that an investor who puts £5m into a company receives £15m back from any sale of the business before others receive a cent. A lower valuation and less onerous liquidation preferences might be considered preferable, advisers say.

One feature of the current market is that there is still plenty of competition for the deals that are considered 'hot'. Plastic Logic, for instance, had half a dozen firms doing due diligence on it.

But, in the end, there are few hot deals and the whole system is in danger of getting out of balance, says Richard Ord, chief executive of Vulcan Machines. Vulcan, a Cambridge-based microprocessor company with exciting applications for Java-based technology in mobiles and set-top boxes, is looking to raise a further £3m-£4m after winning funding from 3i in a competition in 2000.

Mr Ord has attracted interest from smaller venture capitalists but has not made headway with the larger groups. 'At some point the larger venture capitalists are going to need to support a decent number of really early-stage companies – if not directly, then through relationships with seed investors. Otherwise their own deal flow will simply not be there in two years' time.'

Source: Financial Times, 20 June 2002.

Case 26.2

Angels with their feet on the ground

FT

24 May 2002

By **Katharine Campbell**

David Giampaolo doesn't much care for the term business angel. 'Sometimes one's not very angelic,' he says. The new chief executive of Venture Capital Report, a UK private investment network that yesterday said it would merge with Pi Capital, a private investor fund manager, has grand ambitions to professionalise the private investment business in Britain.

'This is a real business,' Mr Giampaolo says. Which means that the whiff of altruism attaching to the handle 'business angel' is dangerously misleading.

A US serial entrepreneur who arrived in London in 1987 to launch a chain of fitness clubs, he has also been an active private investor – so he understands the capital-raising process from both ends. That marks him out at once from many of those in charge of networks in Britain, who have neither run businesses previously nor invested their own cash.

Private investment is a matter of scale, he believes, and the fragmented patchwork of clubs and networks that exist at the moment is unsustainable. Most are losing money, are providing only a fraction of the services to companies that they set out to, and suffer from poor deal flow, he argues.

The collapse in the technology sector has only highlighted the problem. On the one hand, the need for private investment has become more acute, as risk-averse venture capitalists raise the minimum sums they are prepared to invest to £3m ($4.4m) or more.

At the same time, the various networks are suffering a liquidity crisis, as realisations from the companies they have backed have proved few and far between. Many were set up with optimistic business models that relied on fairly rapid cash generation from the exercise of warrants or options when companies floated or found trade buyers – which has simply not happened.

Pi Capital, for instance, which represents a particularly well connected group of investors, has not seen an exit in the four years since it was set up – except the unwanted kind, namely company failures.

Despite the money lost, Pi found 'an immense amount of inbuilt loyalty' among its members, according to Simon Oliver, chairman of Pi, who becomes chairman of the combined entity. So Pi decided to continue and sought the merger with VCR. The new group – whose backers include Michael Stoddart, the former head of Electra Investment Trust and one of the founding fathers of venture capital in the UK, and Thomas Hoegh, founder of venture capitalist Arts Alliance – aims to become 'the first choice' for entrepreneurial teams raising sums of less than £2m.

Pi and VCR will retain their separate identities and methodologies. Pi, whose roughly 120 members invest on average between £80,000 and £100,000 a year each, carries out the due diligence on investments itself, and behaves more like a fund, investing as a syndicate. Club members can take part in a mentoring programme for the businesses backed and can also be involved in other ways, including taking part in the due diligence.

VCR, whose members put up an average of £30,000 a year, tends to invest in smaller chunks than Pi. Founded in 1978 by Lucius Carey, a pioneer in technology investing in Britain, it has, despite its 300 members, been fairly limited in its fundraising. It pulled in about £3m last year. This compares, for example, with the team behind AcornCapital – a network based in Cheshire, north-west England, and run by Ian Templeton, formerly head of accountancy firm BDO Stoy Hayward in Manchester – which has raised £73m in the past four years.

Mr Giampaolo is overhauling VCR's business, with a focus on improving the deal flow. He has instituted regular events where companies pitch, the most recent held last week at the Four Seasons Hotel in London.

While it screens opportunities, it leaves individual members to cut their own deals, although, under Mr Giampaolo, it will take a more proactive role in herding investors and helping them form their own syndicates.

Stephen Ross, chief executive of Springboard, the Aim-listed investment company, sees 'a real opportunity for someone to pull together what is a very fragmented market'. MeetingZone, one of his portfolio companies that is a low-cost automated conferencing services provider, presented at the Four Seasons event. It was looking for top-up funding for its latest financing round and appeared to be oversubscribed as a result.

Another participant was Helena Boas, co-founder of Bodas, a lingerie business selling over the internet and mail order as well as in stores, who is seeking £1m in expansion capital. She too reported a strong response from the 160 who attended. 'People asked very detailed, informed questions, down to the cost per square foot of decorating [the shop].' She went away with more than 30 leads.

In the private investor market, as elsewhere, the technology rout has sorted the wheat from the chaff.

'In 1999 and 2000, someone introduced a deal to angels – and if it was broadly technology, people pulled out their chequebook and wrote a cheque for £100,000,' says Ryan Prince, co-founder of iGabriel, an angel network that counts US technology guru Esther Dyson among its members. 'Now it's much more symbiotic. They really want to understand the business.'

And, despite the money lost in the stock market, wealthy investors are still very much in evidence. 'People are very nervy – and things have to be very well valued and have a real story to attract,' says Mr Templeton 'but there *is* money around.'

Source: Financial Times, 24 May 2002.

Angels growing more cautious

15 August 2002

By **Harriet Arnold**

Entrepreneurs are getting more of a grilling from potential private investors but both sides benefit from the new caution, according to David Giampaolo, chief executive of Venture Capital Report, a UK private investment network that recently merged with Pi Capital, a private investor fund manager, and which plans to extend its operations this year including further strategic alliances.

'The caution of the investors now is positive for both the investor and the entrepreneur because it involves [greater] vigilance, analysis, strategic planning and so on. The smart money is looking closely at the business proposition, the capital requirements, the board,' he says,

adding that the process is, not surprisingly, taking longer.

Mr Giampaolo puts this partly down to the fact that there are still 'too many theoretical aspects to the propositions'. Investors are, for instance, pressing management teams to justify sales projections. 'Sales cycles are longer and orders are smaller currently. There is nothing wrong with that but it affects the capital requirements,' he says, pointing to the danger of raising too little money.

Business angels also want more from investment networks and clubs, he believes, which is why the VCR and Pi partnership is seeking to make significant alliances.

Source: Financial Times, 15 August 2002.

Discussion point

Might the business angel model of investors who make a long-term, supportive intervention in an entrepreneurial firm be better than the short-term, hands-off venture capital model for supporting and encouraging new venture growth? What are the limitations and risks of the angel model as compared to the venture capital model?

Chapter 27

Leadership, power and motivation in the entrepreneurial venture

Chapter overview

Managing the human dimension of the venture is critical to entrepreneurial success. This chapter deals with the tools for managing human relationships within the venture: power, leadership and motivation and the way in which they are interconnected.

27.1 The human dimension: relating leadership, power and motivation

Key learning outcome

An appreciation of the way in which the concepts of leadership, power and motivation are inter-related.

Entrepreneurs are managers, but they are not just any sort of manager. If we were to seek the one characteristic that distinguishes entrepreneurs from their more conventional colleagues it would most likely be found *not* in their strategic or analytical insights (though these are important) but in the *human dimension*: the way in which they use leadership and power and their ability to motivate those around them. Any discussion of entrepreneurship must, therefore, develop an insight into the ways in which leadership, power and motivation may be used as managerial tools.

An economic perspective suggests that human organisations exist to process resources. The differentiation of labour within them allows that processing to be carried out more efficiently. However, once those resources are processed they must be distributed to the stakeholders who make up the organisation. That distribution is rarely on an 'equal' basis. Further, organisations are not just rational orderings of activities but are also the stages upon which their members act out the roles which define them. Hence any discussion of leadership, power and motivation must be willing to take its cues from a variety of perspectives: *functional* ones, which construe the organisation as a deterministic system, *interpretive* ones, which explore human experience within organisations, and *radical* ones, which question the way in which different individuals benefit from organisational life.

In light of this, no one definition can possibly hope to fulfil the complete potential of any of these concepts. However, it is important to give the ideas some kind of conceptual location, and basic definitions can be suggested as follows.

> Leadership might be defined as the power to *focus* and *direct* the organisation.
> Power might be defined as the ability to *influence the course of actions* within the organisation.
> Motivation might be defined as the *process of encouraging* an individual to take particular courses of action.

Leadership, power and motivation are distinct concepts but clearly any discussion of one will usually draw in the others since they are different aspects of the overall process of control over the venture. It is useful to regard them as different aspects of the approach the entrepreneur takes to controlling the direction of the venture (Figure 27.1).

Leadership, power and motivation come together in the means the entrepreneur chooses to shape and drive their venture in the *direction they wish to take it*. They are tools the entrepreneur adopts in order to turn their vision into reality, and as such, they lie at the heart of their project to create an entire new world.

It is important to recognise that entrepreneurial leadership, power and motivation cannot be confined within the formal organisation. They must extend beyond it to draw *all* the venture's stakeholders (its investors, customers and suppliers as well as its employees) together.

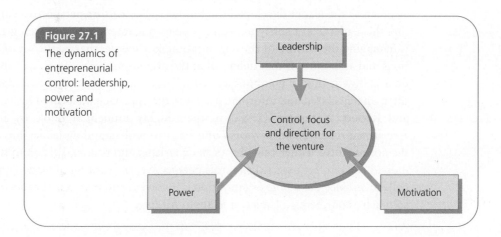

Figure 27.1

The dynamics of entrepreneurial control: leadership, power and motivation

27.2 Understanding leadership

> **Key learning outcome**
>
> An understanding of the factors which underpin entrepreneurial leadership.

Leadership is one of the most essential ingredients for entrepreneurial success yet it is conceptually elusive. We recognise leadership when we see it but it is very hard to say *what* we are recognising. The way in which the concept has been used and the framework for understanding it have evolved considerably over the time that leadership has been seen as a proper subject for investigation. The challenge is not just to understand leadership but also to provide recommendations on how leadership skills can be developed and used to enhance organisational performance.

Early approaches to leadership looked towards 'great men' to provide examples of how to behave. The main tool was the biography which detailed the life and exploits of appropriate leaders. A development of this approach was to try to distil out the personality traits which made great people 'great' and which underpinned their leadership. Both these approaches still inform a good deal of popular thinking on leadership but they are very limited because they make leadership inherent in an individual. They fail to recognise that leadership involves followers as much as leaders and that leadership takes place in a social setting.

Later modes of thinking looked towards *influence* (how leaders coax followers) and *behaviour* (what leaders actually *do* rather than who they *are*) in an attempt to minimise these limitations. An important avenue of exploration into leadership amalgamated all these approaches with an integration of behavioural, personality, situation and influence factors. This approach is known as contingency leadership theory.

A number of distinct approaches to leadership emerged in the aftermath of contingency leadership theory. The *transactional* approach emphasised the importance of the pattern of one-to-one relationships or 'dyads' the leader established with the followers. In this perspective the follower was seen to develop the leader as much as the leader developed the follower. The *culture* perspective emphasised that the leader is not solely managing one-to-one interactions or even groups, but is managing the culture of the organisation as a *whole*: that is, the set of expectations and assumptions that define what the organisation should do and should not do and how it should go about its tasks. These expectations and assumptions are often unarticulated and informal. This was the approach advocated by Tom Peters and Robert Waterman (1982) in their highly influential book *In Search of Excellence*. The *transformational* approach to understanding leadership develops the notion of the leader using his or her charisma and personal vision to transform individuals into followers. From this perspective, the process of leadership is both collective, since the *whole* organisation is involved, and dynamic. Leadership is not so much about being a leader; it is about *leading*.

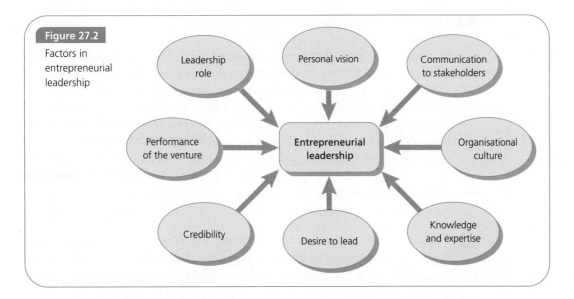

Figure 27.2

Factors in entrepreneurial leadership

Thinking about leadership is developing rapidly. In some ways a new post-transformational integration which draws from the whole tradition on leadership thinking is emerging. By distilling this integration, entrepreneurial leadership can be thought of as having eight key elements (Figure 27.2).

1 *Personal vision.* The entrepreneur's vision is the driving force behind leadership. It is vision which transforms a disparate group of stakeholders into the people who will act to move the venture forward. Vision must be rationalised and communicated. As discussed in Chapter 14, it is critical that the entrepreneur turn their vision into a 'narrative' which provides the venture's stakeholders with roles and responsibilities and defines the rewards they will get for participating in the venture.

2 *Communication with stakeholders.* The entrepreneur must relate their vision to stakeholders through a variety of communication channels and forums, for example, one-to-one talks, meetings, formal presentations, sales pitches, business plans, etc. Such communication is not simply a passing of information, it is a *call to action.* What matters to the entrepreneurial leader is not so much what people know as a result of a particular communication but what they will *do* in response to it. The content of communication is not confined to what is said. *How* things are said is just as important. In face-to-face communication non-verbal aspects such as body language can have a great influence on how things are interpreted. Leadership is built on effective communication and the style of communication can be as important as content.

3 *Organisational culture.* An organisation's culture is the web of rules which define how it goes about its tasks. These rules are often unspoken. Culture is, in a sense, 'the way things are done round here'. The culture defines what is allowed, and what is not allowed, for both internal and external relationships. An organisation's culture is created along with the organisation itself. It is the entrepreneurial leader's role to shape that culture by setting standards and defining values for the organisation. It also becomes manifest through the objectives the entrepreneur sets for the venture and the rewards and sanctions used to manage outcomes and expectations for both individuals and groups. The relationship between leadership and culture is reciprocal. Leadership creates the organisation's culture and, in return, the organisation's culture creates a space to be filled by a leader.

4 *Knowledge and expertise.* Entrepreneurs are experts. This expertise may be in some specialist technology (for example, Bill Gates' knowledge of computing) or in the particulars of an industry sector (for example, Rupert Murdoch's extensive knowledge of the newspaper business). In addition to this specialist knowledge there is the general sense of an entrepreneur being an 'expert' decision maker. Expertise provides a basis for leadership in that it offers authority for decision making.

5 *Credibility.* Credibility is critical for leadership. If credibility can be built up, then leadership (that is, attracting followers) becomes easier. Conversely, if an entrepreneur loses credibility, then leadership is likely to be made more problematic if not lost altogether. Leadership offers the possibility of shaping the venture and directing it in a particular way. Leadership will only be accepted by followers if they are confident in the ability of the entrepreneur to take the venture in a direction that will benefit them.

6 *Performance of the venture.* Credibility comes, in the main, from being seen to make decisions which lead to successful outcomes. This is often an issue of association rather than causation. Decisions, not least those made at the higher levels of the organisation, usually lead to a cascade of further decisions. Causal chains can be hard to trace, especially when a good deal of latitude for decision making is allowed to subordinates. Further, success itself cannot be reduced simply to financial performance, it needs to be considered in the light of all the stakeholders' expectations (see Chapter 12).

If credibility comes from being associated with success, it is not *necessarily* true that credibility is automatically lost as a result of the occasional failure. Failure might have occurred for the 'right' reasons (a risky option was taken and it didn't pay off even though it was well thought out, the course was well managed and all parties involved were prepared for the possibility of failure). An ability to learn quickly and effectively from failure can, in fact, be a way to build credibility. One sure way to lose credibility, however, is to attempt to distance oneself from failure and to shirk responsibility when it is clear where responsibility lies!

7 *Leadership role.* The entrepreneur will usually be the most senior manager in the venture. They will be expected to take on a leadership role merely by virtue of being an entrepreneur. Entrepreneurship itself comes, as it were, with the option of taking the position of leader.

However, care must be taken here. Though being an entrepreneur presents the *possibility* of being a leader, it does not offer it as a matter of *right*. Setting up the venture provides authority, not power (a distinction to be developed in Section 27.3). While people involved with the venture will look towards the entrepreneur for leadership, that is, they will set themselves up as followers, the entrepreneur must actively fulfil their expectations by exhibiting leadership behaviour. The entrepreneur must constantly use his or her position to reiterate the leader–follower relationship.

8 *Desire to lead.* The thing which ultimately underpins leadership is the desire to lead. No one can be an effective leader unless they *really* want to take on the role of leader. Effective entrepreneurs recognise this in themselves. They accept positively the need they have to express their desire for power. The freedom to lead and use power is one of the great motivators driving many, if not all, entrepreneurs.

27.3 The basis of power and using power

> **Key learning outcome**
>
> An appreciation of the nature and role of power within the entrepreneurial venture.

As with leadership, power is a concept which appears to be central to successful management and which has resisted being reduced to a simple conceptual formula. To many people the term has a negative connotation. Power means power 'over' people. It suggests coercion and is something which must be curtailed.

Wilson (1975) drew on evolutionary concerns to define power as 'the assertion of one member of the group over another in acquiring access to a piece of food, a mate, a place to display, a sleeping site or any other requisite to the genetic fitness of the dominant individual'. Watson (1971) referred to a 'stable personality characteristic' that was functional in the emergence of dominant individuals in a group. Ray (1981) also considered power to be a consequence of genetic (unlearned) and environmental (learned) factors.

An alternative approach (e.g. Emerson, 1962; Thompson, 1967; Hickson *et al.*, 1971; Pffeffer and Salancik, 1978; Bacharach and Lawler, 1980) has risen to dominance, especially in management studies. This is the idea that power is not centred on an individual at all. It is a result of the structural factors that define how people work together and interact with each other. House (1988) offers a good review of the development of this idea.

However, if we define power as an ability to influence the course of actions within the organisation it becomes a necessary feature of organisational life.

Power is a feature of situations in which resources are limited and outcomes are uncertain. Under these conditions actions *must* be influenced or the organisation would not be an organisation! In this respect power is an inevitability and, like the organisation itself, it can be made to work for good as well as ill. Certainly, entrepreneurs must recognise the basis for power within their organisation and learn to use it both positively and effectively. This is an approach taken by Jeffrey Pfeffer (1981) in his important study, *Power in Organizations*.

Power must be distinguished from *authority*. Authority presents a *right* to influence the course of actions due to the position the holder of that authority has within the organisation. This right is not the same as *ability*. The way in which authority translates into actual power depends on how the people who make up the organisation regard the holder's standing and the position they occupy. While one group may recognise the position, others may not do so. The entrepreneur may be given a high degree of ostensible authority by the social system in which they operate. The venture may 'belong' to them and be seen as the property of the individual entrepreneur. They will probably be seen as the chief executive, that is, the most senior decision maker. However, this in itself is no guarantee that they will actually have power over their venture. As with leadership, the entrepreneur's position *potentiates* power rather than provides it.

An important line of analysis sees power manifest itself as the control of different aspects of the venture. The relationship is reciprocal. Power gives access to control, and control provides a basis for power. Dimensions of control which are important for the development of the entrepreneur's power base are *resources*, *people*, *information*, *uncertainty*, *systems*, *symbols* and *vision*.

Control of resources

The fast-growing entrepreneurial venture is characterised by a constant influx of new resources. The decision as to how those resources will be used is one which must be addressed constantly. The entrepreneur, if not actually making those decisions, will normally be in a position to influence them greatly and to sanction those they oppose.

Control of people

The phrase 'control' of people sounds ominous and has authoritarian overtones. However, in the context of the entrepreneurial venture, the notion corresponds more to positive qualities of leadership (offering people a direction forward) and motivation (encouraging and supporting them in taking that direction) than it does to the negative aspects of coercion.

Control of information

Information informs decision making and makes it more effective. It has a critical role to play in establishing power structures. The entrepreneur is in a special position in relation to the information on which the venture is founded. In the early stages of the venture, he or she may actually be responsible for bringing in information on products, customers and finance. Later they will have control over what information is regarded as important and should be invested in. At every stage of development, it is the entrepreneur who has the unique position of viewing the venture from a strategic perspective.

Control of uncertainty

All stakeholders experience some uncertainties in relation to the entrepreneurial venture. Employees will be concerned about their remuneration and job security. Customers are often concerned about continuity of supply. Suppliers have an interest in the success of their customers, and investors are eager to ensure that their investments are sound ones. Managing this uncertainty provides a basis for power and the entrepreneur is in a unique position when it comes to managing this uncertainty. After all, it is the entrepreneur who will deliver the venture and ensure its success. As was discussed in Section 12.1 the process of managing success is as much about controlling *expectations* as it is about delivering outcomes.

Control of systems

Once the organisation grows beyond a certain size it becomes impossible for the founding entrepreneur to make all resource allocation decisions. At this point a number of systems emerge to control the process of resource allocation. These take the form of routines, procedures and operating practices. As the organisation grows the entrepreneur can, and indeed must, develop their power base by shifting their attention from controlling resource allocation itself, to controlling the systems which guide resource allocation.

Control over symbols

Symbols are very important in organisational life. Symbols may be overt, like company names, logos or brand names, or they can be more covert, like the arrangement of office space. They may take the form of stories or 'myths'. A good example is the way the Disney Corporation has co-opted the story of its founding father, Walt Disney, as a defining force for the organisation. The entrepreneur can access power within the organisation by learning to use, and claiming the right to use, the venture's symbolic forms in the right way. This can be an important factor in managerial succession for the entrepreneurial venture (see Section 29.4).

Control of vision

Vision, when properly used, is a powerful driving force for the entrepreneurial venture. However, there can only be one vision which dominates within the venture. There is no room for an alternative. Two or more visions offering different directions within the same organisation will inevitably come into conflict. An important, perhaps *the* most important, element in the power base of the entrepreneur is the ability to compose, articulate and control the elements of *the* vision that shapes and drives the venture as a whole.

Power brings responsibility. The right to exercise power brings with it the need to direct it in an appropriate way. Many entrepreneurs are seen to be motivated by power, but effective entrepreneurs are motivated not by power as an end in itself, but by using power as a tool to deliver the venture in a way which offers success to all its stakeholders. This is not only a positive use of power, it is, in the long run, the only way in which power can be sustained.

27.4 Approaches to understanding motivation

> **Key learning outcome**
>
> An appreciation of the approaches that have been made to understanding the phenomenon of motivation and its importance to successful entrepreneurship.

Motivation, the condition that makes individuals undertake, or at least desire to undertake, certain courses of action, is a subject that has received a lot of attention from psychologists over the past hundred years. Because of its impact on organisational performance, it is of great interest to management theorists and practitioners. A number of approaches to its understanding have been developed. These approaches are varied, emphasise different factors and generally supplement, though, at times, they do contradict, each other. They all offer unique insights. They differ in the impact they have had on the understanding that has been gained of managerial motivation in general and on entrepreneurial motivation in particular. A major dichotomy exists between those theories that regard motivation as an outward expression of inner drives and those that regard motivation as something directed towards achieving externally defined and rewarded goals. Some approaches attempt reconciliation between these two factors.

Historically, the most significant of the former is Freud's *psychoanalytic theory*, which regards behaviour as being driven by basic sexual and aggressive instincts. Despite its influence on psychology and psychotherapy, this theory has had relatively little impact on management thinking. This is mainly because the theory at one level attempts to explain the generalities of the human condition and, at another, account for the maladaptive behaviour of individual subjects. It has been less able to explain the adaptive behaviour of individuals and small groups in organisations. Though they are of great historical importance, Freud's ideas have come under increasing attack from more empirically minded psychologists.

Another drive-based conceptualisation of motivation is Hull's (1943) *experimental drive* theory. Hull explained motivation in terms of the drive to fulfil four basic, internalised, primarily physiological needs: *hunger*, *thirst*, *sex* and the *avoidance of pain*. In simple terms, behaviours that achieve the fulfilment of these drives are motivated. The weakness of this theory is in explaining how these generalised needs are manifest in the wide range of varied, complex and sophisticated actual behaviours exhibited by people in a social and managerial setting. From this perspective, it is difficult to say specifically why pursuing an entrepreneurial path is able to fulfil these needs better than, say, a career as a conventional manager.

The idea of human needs is a fundamental one and it has informed a number of approaches to understanding motivation. Lewin (1952) developed a theory in which motivation arose from a 'tension' in the perceived difference between actual states of being and desired states of being. According to this theory, these states cannot be resolved into components based on specific needs. Rather they are integrated wholes – psychologists call them *gestalts* – which are experienced holistically. Lewin's approach resonates with the idea of *entrepreneurial vision*; a picture of the state the entrepreneur wishes to create that acts as a driving force for them. (We have considered entrepreneurial vision earlier in Chapter 13.)

The idea of a series of needs that can be resolved into separate components was the basis for Maslow's (1943) well-known theory of need hierarchy in which physiological, security, social and self-development needs were satisfied in that order of priority. Maslow's ideas will be explored further below.

The role of 'achievement' in motivation has been studied extensively by McClelland (1961). In McClelland's view behaviour is directed towards an aspirational picture of delivering personal excellence. What constitutes this excellence may be derived from internally referenced considerations or it may be picked up from external signals. McClelland was particularly interested in achievement as a motivator for entrepreneurs. The goals that are set for people are also considered relevant in motivation theory. A number of studies suggest that individuals are motivated to achieve specific, well-defined goals. These suggest the way these goals stretch an individual, or team, are important. Goals that are too easy do not motivate. They are regarded as trivial and unimportant. Goals that are too ambitious also fail to motivate if they are seen to be unachievable. The most motivating goals are those that are demanding, but within the bounds of possibility: precisely the kind of goal a good entrepreneur sets for him- or herself.

A number of motivation theories take a cognitive approach in that they are concerned with motivation as a goal-directed phenomenon. In these explanations, behaviour that achieves an individual's goals is motivated; that which fails to deliver them is demotivated. The process is dynamic and iterative. Behaviour that delivers desired outcomes is *reinforced* – encouraged as the basis for future behaviour. Behaviour that does not deliver is discouraged. An important factor in behaviour is *expectation*, that is, the belief that a particular course of action will result in a particular outcome. The key thing is not so much that an action actually delivers, just that the actor believes it will. So, in this view, entrepreneurs become entrepreneurial because they expect it will deliver the set of financial, social and self-developmental conditions they desire. This conceptualisation of motivation is one that is readily quantified and can be expressed in mathematical form.

A particularly sophisticated development of expectancy theory is that of Vroom (1963). Vroom breaks motivation down into four components: *outcomes*, *valence*, *expectancy* and *instrumentality*. An *outcome* is the state of affairs that might be achieved as a result of some course of action. *Valence* is the desire that an actor has for a particular outcome, either in absolute terms or as a ranking of priorities from a set of outcomes from which one must be selected. *Expectancy* is the belief as to what outcomes are possible, that is, how likely it is that they might be achieved given the investment of time and effort in a particular course of action. *Instrumentality* is the perceived effectiveness of a particular course of action in achieving an outcome. Actors will, in part, choose between different courses of action based on how effective they will be in achieving what they want. Together these factors will define the *force* – the intensity – of the motivation to undertake particular actions.

Together, these approaches to understanding motivation add up to a general picture of what motivates the entrepreneur. Entrepreneurs, like everybody else, have basic economic needs that they aim to fulfil through their entrepreneurial careers. But entrepreneurial motivation goes beyond this. Entrepreneurs have a need to achieve and so gain social standing and effect personal development. They want to see their visions turned into reality. The course of action entrepreneurs adopt is based on the desire for these outcomes and a belief that certain actions will result in their delivery. Expectations are the things that link an entrepreneur's objectives to the effectiveness of the strategy they feel the venture should adopt in order to achieve them. The specific motivations of the individual entrepreneur are shaped by, and can be explained in terms of, this general framework.

27.5 Self-motivation and motivating others

> **Key learning outcome**
>
> An insight into how entrepreneurs may motivate themselves and those around them.

People work best when they are motivated to do so. The entrepreneur cannot *demand* effort from someone; they must *support* the individual and encourage them to offer their efforts.

Self-motivation

The first person whose motivation the entrepreneur must address is his or her own! It is difficult, if not impossible, to motivate others if one's own motivation is lacking. This can be a challenge. The entrepreneurial course offers great rewards but it also demands resilience. The knocks are frequent and often hard. Failure, as well as success, must be managed with a positive response. Some important elements to address in terms of self-motivation are as follows.

Why am I doing this?

Good entrepreneurs know why they have chosen to be entrepreneurs. They constantly remind themselves why they have chosen the entrepreneurial path. The model developed in Section 8.2 gives an insight into this process. The attractions of entrepreneurship can be understood in the way that the course fulfils economic, social and self-developmental needs better than alternative routes open to the entrepreneur. Self-motivation must be built on an understanding that the option taken is one which is desirable.

Learning from mistakes

Like any other manager, entrepreneurs make mistakes from time to time. Sales may not be made or investment propositions may be rejected. Personal interactions may be mismanaged. Entrepreneurs are, however, very sensitive to the mistakes they make. This is not just because the consequences of the mistakes are greater than those made by other managers (although they may be) but because entrepreneurs present themselves as experts in managing their venture and its associated uncertainty. Errors of judgement cut to the heart of this role. They can be a great blow to the entrepreneur's confidence.

Of course, mistakes are an inevitable part of any managerial career, not just the entrepreneurial one. Effective entrepreneurs try to avoid mistakes by thought and preparation before entering situations, but when mistakes do occur they are met positively. The good entrepreneur does not try to deny the mistake or pass off responsibility to others. Rather, mistakes are regarded as an opportunity to learn. This means that ego must be detached from the incident and a cold analytical eye used to view the situation to identify a way of avoiding a similar mistake in the future.

Enjoying the rewards

All too often the entrepreneur can become so involved in running the venture that they forget to enjoy its rewards. At one level, this could mean spending the money that has been made. However, this consumption can only be a narrow part of the rewards of entrepreneurship. Money is rarely a complete motivating force for the entrepreneur and, in any case, significant financial rewards may only be accrued a long way down the line. The main rewards lie in the job itself: the challenges it presents, the opportunity to develop and use new skills, the power to make changes, the satisfaction of leadership, and so on.

Learning to recognise these rewards and to savour them is a major factor in developing and sustaining self-motivation.

Motivation of others

Once self-motivation has been achieved the entrepreneur is in a strong position to start motivating others. Motivation is a behavioural phenomenon. Individuals are motivated (or demotivated) by the way people act towards them. This behaviour is an integral part of leadership. It is sensitive to personality and situation. As such, motivating behaviour is a complex process although some common patterns of

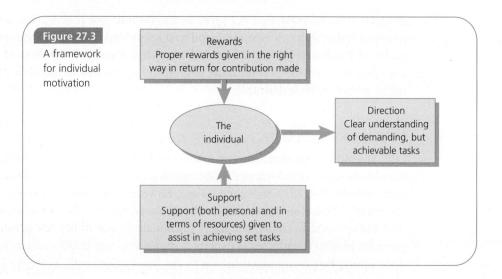

Figure 27.3
A framework
for individual
motivation

motivating behaviour can be identified. Figure 27.3 shows a framework for managing individual motivation. Its key elements are:

● *Understanding personal drives* – before someone can be motivated it is important to recognise what they want to gain from their situation. Management occurs in a social setting and the needs which individuals bring to a situation are a complex mix of financial, social and developmental ones. The effective entrepreneur lays the groundwork for motivating the people in the venture to undertake specific tasks by involving them in the vision that has been created for the venture. This is achieved by communicating the role they will play in this vision and what they will get out of it.

● *Setting goals* – people are not just motivated in an abstract sense. They are motivated to do something, i.e. motivation must lead somewhere. The entrepreneur is responsible for setting the goals that must be achieved. The degree to which these are specific objectives and the formality they take will be dependent on the situation, the entrepreneur's personal style and the cultural setting.

Whatever their form, individuals must recognise their goals and be able to locate them in relation to the goals of the organisation as a whole. Such goals should stretch the individual but also be realistic. They should demand effort but must be achievable given the personal and organisational resources the individual commands.

● *Offering support* – setting objectives is just the first step in motivating people. If people are to deliver, they require support. This can take the form of ongoing encouragement, advice, the provision of resources and influencing behind the scenes. The support offered should be commensurate with the level of the task and the demands on the person undertaking it. Effective motivation means giving people room to use their skills and insights but never letting them think that they are out on their own.

● *Using rewards* – rewards take a wide variety of forms. In character, rewards are the means that satisfy an individual's economic, social or developmental needs. In scope, the term 'reward' covers everything from a simple nod of approval from the entrepreneur to a complex deal offering a share in the financial performance of the venture. Whatever the nature of the reward an entrepreneur who knows how to motivate understands how best to use it.

First, rewards must be *appropriate* for the task undertaken. They must match the individual's expectations of what the reward should be. Second, their magnitude must be right: too small and they can lead to cynicism; too large and they can engender suspicion. Third, rewards must be used on the proper *occasions*. Rewards which are given too freely (and this includes simple things like comments of approval) become devalued. Fourth, they must be seen to be *equitable*. If the reward structure for different individuals and groups is seen to be unfair then jealousy and conflicts can result.

● *A positive approach to sanctioning* – the entrepreneur must occasionally resort to sanctioning individuals who fail to perform in an appropriate way. How this necessary task is handled is important, not just for maintaining the motivation of the individual, but for the signals it sends to the organisation as a whole. In general, a positive approach to sanctioning is to be advocated. The objective of the sanctioning must be seen to be one of helping the individual to deliver at the proper level, not just as a punishment. It should not (primarily) be about what was done wrong in the past, but about how performance can be improved in the future. This should also encourage a forum which allows the issues to be discussed while personality and ego are put to one side. Indeed, it can provide an opportunity for the entrepreneur to show his or her goodwill. All in all, sanctioning, so far as possible, should be seen as a positive experience.

Summary of key ideas

● *Leadership*, *power* and *motivation* are inter-related and interdependent tools which the entrepreneur can use to control the venture and give it direction.

● Leadership is the power to *focus* and *direct* the organisation. Entrepreneurial leadership is based on the communication of *vision*.

● Power is the ability to influence the *course of actions* within the organisation. Power is based on the control of *resources* and the *symbolic* dimensions of the organisation, particularly the vision which drives it.

● Motivation is the ability to *encourage* an individual to take a particular course of action. Motivation is based upon an understanding of drives and the ability to reward effort.

Research theme

Profiling entrepreneurial leadership styles

Entrepreneurs are highly individual and personal in their leadership styles. No two entrepreneurs lead in exactly the same way. However, the eight-point framework developed in Section 27.2 offers a potential means of profiling leadership style. Each of the factors detailed can be translated into propositions with which entrepreneurs can agree or disagree when it comes to evaluating their own leadership style or as judged by those they come into contact with. For example: knowledge and expertise might be related as 'people follow my instructions because I am an expert in the field', credibility as 'I gain authority from my past successes', or the desire to lead as 'I enjoy and seek leadership opportunities', and so on. Create a series of propositions based on each of the eight factors (at least two for each). Select a sample of entrepreneurs. Survey them with the propositions, ascertaining their agreement with them (use a Likert scale: strongly agree, agree, . . . , strongly disagree, etc.). Individuals who come into contact with the entrepreneur should also be surveyed with the aim of ascertaining their beliefs about how the propositions fit the leadership of the entrepreneur. To be more discriminating, the propositions may be presented in pairs with the entrepreneur (contact) required to select the one most agreed with. A graphical line profile of the eight factors can be generated. By way of analysis, compare the leadership profiles of different entrepreneurs. How much consistency is there? Is there a single entrepreneurial leadership style, or does it vary? How do the self-generated profiles compare with those generated by contacts? Do entrepreneur-leaders and their followers tend to agree or disagree on perceived leadership style? Make recommendations on how this methodology may be developed in the future.

Suggestions for further reading

Bacharach, S.B. and Lawler, E.J. (1980) *Power and Politics in Organizations*, San Francisco, CA: Jossey-Bass.

Boyce, M.E. (1996) 'Organisational story and storytelling: a critical review', *Journal of Organisational Change Management*, Vol. 9, No. 5, pp. 5–26.

Cropanzano, R., James, K. and Citera, M. (1992) 'A goal hierarchy model of personality, motivation and leadership', *Research in Organisational Behavior*, Vol. 15, pp. 267–322.

Emerson, R.M. (1962) 'Power-dependent relationships', *American Sociological Review*, Vol. 27, pp. 31–41.

Hamilton, R. (1987) 'Motivations and aspirations of business founders', *International Small Business Journal*, Vol. 6, No. 1, pp. 70–8.

Hickson, D.J., Hinings, C.R., Lee, C.A., Schneck, R.J. and Pennings, J.M. (1971) 'A strategic contingencies' theory of intraorganizational power', *Administrative Science Quarterly*, Vol. 30, pp. 61–71.

Hofstede, G. (1980) 'Motivation, leadership and organisation: do American theories apply abroad?' *Organisational Dynamics*, Summer, pp. 42–63.

House, R.J. (1988) 'Power and personality in complex organizations', *Research in Organizational Behaviour*, Vol. 10, pp. 305–57.

Hull, C.L. (1943) *Principles of Behaviour*, New York: Appleton-Century-Crofts.

Kuratko, D.F., Hornsby, J.S. and Naffziger, D.W. (1997) 'An examination of owner's goals in sustaining entrepreneurship', *Journal of Small Business Management*, Jan, pp. 24–33.

Lewin, A. (1952) 'Group decisions and social change', in Swanson, G.E., Newcombe, T.N. and Hartley, E.L. (eds) *Readings in Social Psychology* (rev. edn), New York: Holt.

Maslow, A.H. (1943) 'A theory of human motivation', *Psychological Review*, July, pp. 370–96.

McClelland, D.C. (1961) *The Achieving Society*, Princeton, NJ: Van Nostrand.

Peters, T. and Waterman, Jr, R.H. (1982) *In Search of Excellence*, New York: Harper & Row.

Pfeffer, J. (1981) *Power in Organizations*, Cambridge, MA: Ballinger.

Pfeffer, J. and Salancik, G.R. (1978) *The External Control of Organizations: A Resource Dependent Perspective*, New York: Harper & Row.

Ray, J.J. (1981) 'Authoritarianism, dominance and assertiveness', *Journal of Personality Assessment*, Vol. 45, No. 4, pp. 390–7.

Seters, D.A. Van (1990) 'The evolution of leadership theory', *Journal of Organisational Change Management*, Vol. 3, No. 3, pp. 29–45.

Tait, R. (1996) 'The attributes of leadership', *Leadership and Organisational Development Journal*, Vol. 17, No. 1, pp. 27–31.

Taylor, B., Gilinsky, A., Hilmi, A., Hahn, D. and Grab, U. (1990) 'Strategy and leadership in growth companies', *Long Range Planning*, Vol. 23, No. 3, pp. 66–75.

Thompson, J.D. (1967) *Organizations in Action*, New York: McGraw-Hill.

Vroom, V.H. (1963) *Leadership and Decision-making*, Pittsburgh, PA: University of Pittsburgh.

Watson, D. (1971) 'Reinforcement theory of personality and social system: dominance and position in a group power structure', *Journal of Personality and Social Psychology*, Vol. 20, pp. 180–5.

Wilson, E.O. (1975) *Sociobiology: The New Synthesis*, Cambridge, MA: Harvard University Press.

Zaleznik, A. (1977) 'Leaders and managers: are they different?' *Harvard Business Review*, May–June, pp. 67–78.

Selected case material Case 27.1

All change in the customised workplace

FT

22 October 2001

By **Hamid Bouchikhi** and **John Kimberly**

Five centuries ago, the Polish astronomer Nicolaus Copernicus realised that the Earth revolves around the Sun, not the reverse. In management, we may be in the midst of a similar revolution, in which the relationship between the company and the employee is inverted and the 'customised workplace' replaces the hierarchical, military-inspired model that has served so long.

Comparing the dominant managerial models of the past two centuries will help in understanding the concept of the customised workplace and how it differs from other management methods. This will also clarify the importance of flexibility – for the worker and the company.

Evolving models

More than tools and techniques, it is the company's flexibility and responsiveness to stakeholders that differentiates management models (see the table on the following page). The 19th century model, still alive in many

Management styles over three centuries		
	Individual's demand for flexibility	
	Low	**High**
Organisation's need for flexibility — **Low**	***19th century management*** Responsiveness neither to customers nor people Manufacturing-driven organisation	
High	***20th century management*** Responsiveness to customers Market-driven organisation	***21st century management*** Responsiveness to customers and people Customised workplace

industries and areas, does not respond to shareholders, customers and employees together. The company is often family-owned and managed as a closed system. Customers buy whatever is made available. Employees are hired and fired at will and have little voice or choice. For them, opportunity lies in finding a paternalistic capitalist who can make life less painful and the constraints of work more tolerable.

In the past 50 years, customers and shareholders have been more proactive and managers needed to become more responsive to them. As a result, market-driven strategies and flexible organisations developed. In contrast to the 19th century model, 20th century management is more open. The company actively listens to customers and shareholders and involves them in decision processes.

In the 20th century model, customers are the main drivers of the company's needs for flexibility and employees are required to adjust their work schedules, tasks, holidays, geographic assignments and jobs in light of these needs. Because they are at the receiving end, workers often complain about this kind of flexibility.

The challenge for management in this century will be to invent flexibility based on the employee. To do this, managers will have to customise the workplace to suit both customers and workers. The company will have to apply the logic of marketing, developed for customers, to relationships with workers. Much as managers had no choice about dealing with shareholders and customers, they will also have to cope with the demands of autonomous and proactive individuals whose collaboration and commitment can no longer be taken for granted. Managers will have to adapt to the sociological context of this century.

Sociological context

The challenges facing companies force us to move beyond the limits of conventional business thinking and consider the consequences of sociological trends. The foundations of management were established in the 19th century and built on a view of the worker as a reluctant individual whose efforts needed to be predefined, monitored and sanctioned. This still underpins much managerial action but is outdated.

According to British sociologist Anthony Giddens, post-traditional societies are marked by a declining role of tradition and hierarchy in governing people's attitudes and behaviour. Disenfranchised from tradition, the individual discovers a new form of autonomy and discretion in making life decisions. In this context, individuals draw on an extensive body of knowledge about social life and actively develop a sense of self-identity through strategic life planning.

People are making choices in areas where before they did not or could not. For example, they are deciding about their physical appearance, sexual life and gender, parenting and eating habits. If the 19th century witnessed the advent of the business entrepreneur, the late 20th century saw the birth of the life-entrepreneur.

Caught between micro and macro social changes, the company faces challenges to its legitimacy. It is no longer perceived as favourably as it has been and is criticised on many fronts. The proportion of people for whom a traditional career is no longer the natural path is increasing and many of those who work for established companies are drawing less and less on the company for their sense of identity. Successive waves of restructuring and downsizing, and the development of a debate on employability, are inducing individuals to dissociate their fate from their company's.

The labour market in developed countries is already affected by these trends. Companies in traditional sectors, hampered by their unprogressive image, are finding it difficult to hire people. In other industries, companies are competing for a limited pool of talent. Younger people seem to be increasingly attracted to self-employment, entrepreneurial opportunities and the professions. And the business press regularly contains reports of high-flying executives who quit comfortable jobs to start a business, work as consultants, or simply to spend more time with their families.

These trends reflect a need for people to reclaim control over their lives. As the company listens to and involves people in these decisions, in the same manner that it has internalised the needs of customers, customisation of the workplace will inevitably emerge.

Collision coming

The Hawthorne experiments of the 1930s emphasised the importance of a motivated and involved workforce in achieving organisational goals. Techniques were designed to enhance motivation and involvement. However, in spite of such efforts, surveys continue to show low employee satisfaction and little trust in management. In a Financial Times article, Robert Taylor wrote: 'At the other end of the satisfaction stakes, British workers were among the most discontented. "Despite significant attempts at corporate restructuring and re-engineering, employee attitudes towards the organisation and the efficiency of their work are among the least favourable in Europe" says the [International Survey Research] report. "Despite a strong commitment to total quality management in many companies, attitudes to the quality of work performance are more critical than in any other European country."'

Unless we think, as some senior managers may, that people are never satisfied, these data may point to a more serious problem.

Managerial innovations had a limited impact because they were driven by the company's needs. People don't come first. The record of downsizings, restructurings and lay-offs is no doubt largely responsible for the distrust of management. Aaron Bernstein in a 1998 BusinessWeek article reported the findings of another survey showing employees' trust in management had declined in the 1990s (under 50 per cent in 1997). Even more telling, 70 per cent of senior managers thought that employees trusted management. The gap suggests that the reality of the workplace may not match the promise of management discourse.

After thriving on marketing and product customisation, companies will have to transfer this mindset to their relationships with employees. Management will achieve the next Copernican revolution only when it acknowledges that its object – the individual – is no longer willing to sit passively on the receiving end of managerial policies and incentives. The life entrepreneur will no longer be the object but a subject of management. This evolution will require a genuine co-exercise of power instead of 'empowerment', with its implication that power is 'owned' by one party and delegated to the other.

The new workplace

Because it represents a radical departure from accepted principles and techniques, the customised workplace cannot be conceived without a radical shift in thinking. The main differences between management models over three centuries are summarised in the table.

In contrast with traditional management, where structures and systems are derived from a pre-defined strategy, the design of the customised workplace will seek to balance what matters for the company (its strategy) and what matters for individuals (their life strategies).

The above trends suggest that the individual will reclaim some control over fundamental aspects of work life: what to work for, content, when and where, how to accomplish the work, with whom and for whom to work, for how long to work, direction of career plan and skills needed to pursue the personal career plan.

People's needs and aspirations have historically been viewed as disturbances for management but they represent the starting point for the design of the customised workplace. Balancing companies' needs for predictability and effectiveness with diverse individual needs requires a new employment contract, one where managers and employees confront their strategic and life plans, and seek common ground.

Although the customised workplace has yet to be invented, a few organisations display some of its characteristics. For example, at Semco, the Brazilian company discussed in Ricardo Semler's book Maverick, employees are involved in deciding about siting factories and buying machinery. Further, they have substantial freedom in setting their work schedule and control the investment of a portion of the profits.

At Metanoiques, a French medium-sized company specialising in collaborative software, there are no employees. Every member owns an equal share of the company and acts as an independent entrepreneur with profit and loss responsibility. The company does not operate from a head office and people are free to organise their own schedules. Internal collaboration is carried out through extensive use of information and communication technology.

The founder of Compagnie Francaise de Defense et de Protection sold this small French insurance company to employees and agents, and dismantled the head office. He hopes to create a 'community of independent entrepreneurs' where associates are free to conduct their local business and use network-like mechanisms to co-ordinate with other members of the organisation.

Therese Rieul, founder manager of KA-L'informatique douce, a medium-sized computer and software retailer, refuses to write formal job descriptions because she believes staff should design their own jobs. She believes managers should be concerned with outcomes and leave people free to work out the best way to do a task.

The customised workplace is primarily a philosophical attitude towards people management issues. It entails a replacement of the traditional hard-nosed, macho attitude with one that is more open to people's needs and more tolerant of conflict and divergence. The customised workplace requires recognition of individuals as strategic life planners. In 20th century management, even its most enlightened versions, the company is the only strategic planning agent. Managers form a strategy and then seek the optimal organisational and incentive structure to motivate people to implement it. In the customised workplace, people can influence strategy, in a sense more consistent with their own life strategies. This evolution will not come easily given the deep-seated belief that strategy belongs in top management's territory.

Sharing information and responsibility for the company's situation with employees is another ingredient of the customised workplace. Contrary to the idea that people never make decisions that can hurt them, sharing a problem with employees can be an effective turn-around strategy. Bertrand Martin, the former chief executive of Sulzer France, joined the company at the height of a crisis. Instead of devising a plan unilaterally, he told employees that the company's fate was in their hands and challenged them to find a solution with him.

Experience shows that people will commit a great deal of time, resources and self-identity in trustful relationships. After being pushed to the background by 'scientific management', the importance of trust in business life is being rediscovered. Trust must be put at the core of the employment relationship. Its importance is particularly evident in times of hardship. Only a trusting workforce can voluntarily make sacrifices and explore with management every option to improve the organisation's condition.

However, trust must be built before hard times, and for trust to grow, reciprocity is required. People will put part of their fate in managers' hands only if managers put some of their own fate within the hands of people. Reciprocity develops only when each partner in a relationship is potentially vulnerable to the decisions of the other. Managers who seek control can never establish trust.

In the customised workplace, individuals actively plan and negotiate their employment. Managers will find this transition difficult because they have used policies designed for aggregate groups, such as blue collar workers, hourly workers or part timers. In the customised workplace, people can no longer be managed in this way. They need to be treated as individuals. The challenge for managers will be to achieve sufficient predictability with individuals whose behaviour is less subject to control.

Achieving organisational predictability in the customised workplace requires mutual commitment and accountability. The customised workplace is not viable if it is made up of employees who can change their behaviour or withdraw from the business at any time. The type of contract formerly reserved for senior executives will have to be more widely diffused. When people are bound to the company for a pre-determined time, they no longer fear being treated as disposable assets and the company can count on their full collaboration for the life of the contract.

Because it is based on participation, power sharing, trust, negotiation, reciprocity and commitment, the customised workplace will require adult, as opposed to charismatic, leadership. Because shareholders, customers and employees are equally important, the customised workplace will require a governance structure where the interests of stakeholders can confront and balance each other.

Are these ideas out of touch with the often harsh realities of the marketplace? Perhaps; but the kinds of changes described here have been developing over decades. Capitalism needed the better part of the 20th century to win the battle of the free enterprise. It will now have to win the heart and soul of the free person.

Source: *Financial Times*, 22 October 2001, © Hamid Bouchikhi and John Kimberly.

This article is adapted from a chapter by the authors in Chowdhury S. (ed.) *Management 21C: New Visions for the New Millennium*, Financial Times Management, 2000.

Hamid Bouchikhi is a professor of strategy and management at ESSEC Business School, France. John Kimberly is Henry Bower Professor at the Wharton School of the University of Pennsylvania and Novartis Professor in Healthcare Management at Insead.

Case 27.2

Entrepreneur pays price for nervous energy

FT

29 May 2002

By **Sheila McNulty** in Houston

Seventeen years ago, when Chuck Watson began building what would become Dynegy, he made a commitment to do what was in the best interests of the US energy company. That is why, Mr Watson told his 6,000 employees, he resigned yesterday as chairman and chief executive.

'Stepping down was not an easy decision,' Mr Watson said in an e-mail. 'It was the right one.'

The collapse of Enron, the US's biggest energy trader, in December had shaken the sector to its very foundations.

Investors and analysts had grown increasingly nervous about companies, such as Dynegy, that were engaged in the murky world of energy trading.

That Dynegy had withdrawn, at the last minute, from a bid for Enron had drawn it into a $10bn lawsuit.

It was not long before the rating agencies began closely reviewing Dynegy's books for a possible downgrade of its debt to below investment grade.

So when Dynegy revealed several weeks ago that the Securities and Exchange Commission was investigating one of its transactions, it marked the beginning of the end for Mr Watson.

It put Dynegy's main shareholder, ChevronTexaco, under intense pressure to stabilise its 26.5 per cent investment in Dynegy. That, in turn, led the US oil and gas company's vice-chairman, Glenn Tilton, to be appointed interim chairman of Dynegy.

'Chuck Watson is the epitome of an entrepreneur,' Mr Tilton told a conference call with analysts following Mr Watson's resignation. It

was meant as praise for the man who had built the company. But such a characterisation of Mr Watson also underscored why he had to leave Dynegy and, at only 52, 'retire from corporate life'.

The market wants stability, not entrepreneurship.

'Chuck wanted a freer hand to shape Dynegy and jump on opportunities,' said John Olson, vice-president of research at Sanders Morris Harris, a Houston-based investment banking and securities firm.

'I don't think the board was willing to go that far any more.'

ChevronTexaco insists it did not oust Mr Watson but that the board's independent directors had asked Mr Tilton to take over. Yet it clearly supported Mr Tilton taking time away from his duties at San Francisco-based ChevronTexaco to restore Dynegy's investor stability, build on the company's strong assets and solidify its trading business.

Analysts said Mr Tilton was a strong addition to Dynegy's management team, as is Dan Dienstbier, president of the Northern Natural Gas pipeline company, who will serve as interim chief executive.

Steve Bergstrom, Mr Watson's right-hand man, will continue as president and chief operating officer.

Mr Bergstrom said there would be no change in company focus but that management would meet the board in the next week to 10 days to outline its immediate plans before making them public. 'These are consistent with where Chuck and I were going all along,' he said.

Such statements – that Dynegy would remain the same, even without Mr Watson – were aimed at easing investor fears about how Mr Watson's surprise departure might affect the company and its shares. And they seemed to help, with Dynegy trading up 7.5 per cent at $10 in midday trading.

Mr Tilton said Mr Bergstrom, whom analysts have come to know and respect over the years, was a contender for the top job, should he choose to go for it. Mr Bergstrom indicated he would do so.

'We are going through a transformation in this industry that will change it forever,' Mr Bergstrom said. 'I'm going to bring this [company] out of this thing for Chuck and the whole team.'

Source: Financial Times, 29 May 2002.

Discussion points

1. What issues does the Bouchikhi and Kimberly article raise for the leadership style adopted by entrepreneurs? Does it indicate any ways in which entrepreneurs can (advantageously) distinguish their leadership from that of 'ordinary' managers?

2. What are the leadership challenges to a new leader of Dynergy after the exit of its founding entrepreneur?

Chapter 28

Consolidating the venture

Chapter overview

The entrepreneurial venture is characterised by growth, but at some stage growth slows and the venture becomes a mature organisation. This chapter is concerned with describing the process of consolidation, how the rules of success change and how some of the entrepreneurial vigour of the venture might be retained through intrapreneurship.

28.1 What consolidation means

Key learning outcome

A recognition that maturity is accompanied by significant changes in the way the venture functions at a financial, strategic, structural and organisational level.

No business can grow for ever. There must come a point at which its expansion slows. In the same way the entrepreneurial venture must *mature*. However, maturity is associated with more than a simple cessation of growth. As discussed in Chapter 24, the growth of a business is a complex and multi-faceted phenomenon. It has financial, strategic, structural and organisational dimensions. As the venture matures, the slowing of growth is associated with a number of changes in each of these aspects of the organisation. Together these changes are referred to as *consolidation*.

At the *financial* level, consolidation means that turnover (and profits) begin to plateau out. Turnover should still increase, at a rate not less than the overall expansion of the economy in which the business operates (which would imply a contraction in real terms), and it is not unreasonable to set growth objectives above this. But dramatic increases in turnover are not to be expected (unless, perhaps they are achieved through acquisitions). Growth in the assets supporting turnover will also slow to a similar level. New assets will tend to be a replacement for the depreciation of existing assets.

Consolidation means that *investment* in the growth of the business can be reduced. So it is at this point that financial backers will be looking for their returns. Shareholders will expect to receive a greater share of the profits and to see their dividends increase. Venture capitalists will look to exit and liquidate their investment.

Strategically, consolidation means that the venture has successfully defined its position in the market. The place it occupies in the industry value addition chain, the customer groups it serves and the technology it uses to serve them will be *largely* established – only largely because there is always room for development of the strategic position through organic developments and acquisition. The business's attention will shift from aggressive strategies aimed at encroaching into competitors' territory to more defensive postures aimed at preventing competitors (including new entrepreneurial ones!) from taking business away.

In *structural* terms, consolidation means that the internal configuration of the business develops some permanence. During the growth phase organisational structures and the roles and responsibilities they define will tend to shift, merge and fragment as the business's complexity increases. Consolidation allows the venture to give key roles and responsibilities a longer-term definition. These roles and responsibilities will tend to be defined around the resource needs of the organisation with structures emerging to manage the acquisition of key inputs.

Alongside structural consolidation there will also be *organisational* consolidation. Growth means that the organisation's systems, procedures and operating practices must be in a state of constant flux. Maturity allows these systems to settle down into more permanent patterns of activity. Out of the complex interaction between the entrepreneur, the venture's stakeholders and the wider social world, the organisation's culture will take a final shape.

The prospects and rewards the business offers its employees will also change as it consolidates. Risks will be lowered and job security may be higher. The positions within the organisation will be better defined and career pathways will become more predictable. Change will be at a slower pace. On the other hand, some may miss the challenge that comes from managing rapid growth, including the day-to-day changes this brings and the excitement of not knowing, exactly, what the future might bring.

28.2　Building success into consolidation

Key learning outcome

An appreciation of how the rules of success change as the venture matures

The rules of success change as the entrepreneurial venture consolidates. The business becomes less concerned with making rapid strides forward and more concerned with progressing in a measured and sure-footed way. Success is measured not so much by what might be achieved tomorrow but by what is being achieved today. This is not to say that the mature business can afford to forget about the future. Far from it. All businesses must plan for an uncertain tomorrow and invest accordingly. It is to suggest, however, that the balance of interest shifts from the possibility of long-term returns towards the reality of short-term rewards.

In Section 12.1 the success of the venture was defined in terms of the *stakeholders* with an interest in it, their *needs* and their *expectations* of what it will offer them. This framework provides an insight into how the terms of success change as the venture consolidates.

For investors, the main shift in their expectations is in relation to the risks and returns offered by the venture. After initiation, and while it is growing strongly, the entrepreneurial venture is offering the prospect of high returns for the investor at some point in the future. Returns cannot be offered immediately because any profits generated will need to be ploughed back into the business. In any case, profits are often low during growth. This is certainly the case if a cost leadership strategy is being pursued (as described in Section 22.3). The future is uncertain: profits promised in the future carry a higher risk than those on offer today. The plan for the venture must be based on assumptions. Risk enters the equation because there must be some doubt about the validity of those assumptions.

Investors accept risk if the future returns, properly discounted, are attractive enough. There will come a point, however, when they will want to see those returns. Many investors hold a *portfolio* of investments. This portfolio mixes investments which are currently net generators of money (and are therefore low risk) with those demanding money on the basis of future return (high risk). The entrepreneurial venture starts as a high-risk absorber of capital. If it is to remain in the investor's portfolio long-term it must eventually move to be a lower-risk generator of capital (Figure 28.1).

From the perspective of the investor, the success of the venture stops being measured in terms of the way it is growing its sales and assets and establishing its position in its marketplace to the short-term return it is generating on the (investor's) capital it is using. The key measures of performance become the *profit margin* and *return on capital employed*.

Stakeholders other than investors also share in the risks taken on by the entrepreneurial venture. Employees who make a contribution to the venture in its early stages are called upon to make a special effort. The demands will be high. Roles and responsibilities may be poorly defined. Job security will be relatively low. The immediate financial rewards may be less than can be obtained elsewhere. In return for this commitment employees will, in general, expect an increase in remuneration, a well-defined role and an improvement in job security as the venture consolidates.

While the financial and security rewards of the entrepreneurial venture may be more limited than those offered by the established business, working with a fast-growing and dynamic organisation brings its own rewards at the social and personal development level. Some may perceive a loss in the way the organisation can satisfy these needs, as it consolidates. To such people, the venture's

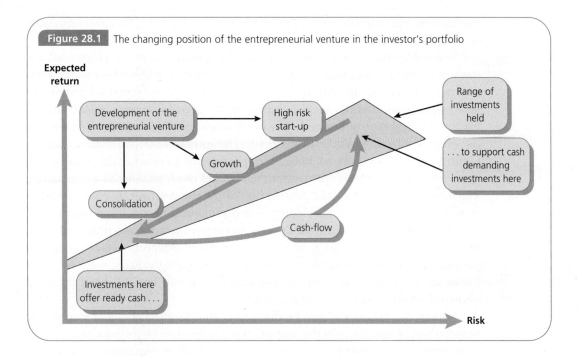

Figure 28.1 The changing position of the entrepreneurial venture in the investor's portfolio

consolidation may signal an end to the sense of personal success it promises. They may feel it is time to move on to new entrepreneurial pastures.

Suppliers and customers may also have offered a commitment to the venture in its early stages. The turnover of the business will have been quite low. Many suppliers may nonetheless, have made a commitment to supplying it with a high level of customer service even though it may have cost more in real terms than they received. Customers may have taken on the business as a supplier even though switching costs had to be faced and continuity of supply was not assured. Such suppliers and customers will see the venture as successful if it returns this early commitment by operating within the business network as a fair, effective and rewarding customer/supplier itself.

28.3) Encouraging intrapreneurship

Key learning outcome

An appreciation of the potential and limits to intrapreneurship in the consolidating organisation.

In recognising the power of the entrepreneurial organisation, it is important not to be too dismissive of what the established 'non-entrepreneurial' organisation has to offer its stakeholders. After all, an established business is only established because it has enjoyed success. The entrepreneurial organisation and the established organisation both have advantages. The entrepreneurial shows an acceptance of (even a need for) change and an ability to exploit new opportunity. The established demonstrates an ability to consolidate around success, manage risk and control resource flows.

A combination of the two, that is, an organisation which recognised the basis of its success and was able to manage it to reduce risk and yet at the same time was flexible to the shifting needs of its stakeholders, remained attuned to new market opportunities and responsive to the need for change, would suggest itself as an ideal type of business. The *intrapreneur* provides a means of achieving the established–entrepreneurial synthesis. The intrapreneur is a role defined by Gifford Pinchot (1985) in his book, *Intrapreneuring*. In essence, the intrapreneur is an entrepreneur who works within the confines of an established organisation. The intrapreneur's role would parallel that of the entrepreneur. In particular they would be responsible for developing and communicating organisational vision; identifying new opportunities for the organisation; generating innovative strategic options; creating and offering an organisation-wide perspective; facilitating and encouraging change within the organisation; challenging existing ways of doing things and breaking down bureaucratic inertia. This role has also been described as that of a 'change master' (Kanter, 1985).

Intrapreneurial activity can be directed at four levels within and outside the organisation. These differ in the impact they will have on the organisation and its surroundings, their effect on the venture's stakeholders, the resources they will require and the level of risk they entail.

- *The management of specific projects*. All businesses engage in new projects of some type. Projects such as new product development, the exploitation of a new market opportunity (perhaps international through exporting or strategic alliance), the integration of a new technology into the firm's operations or the acquiring of new funding are especially important to the maturing entrepreneurial venture that wants to keep its competitive edge. Such projects may be best managed in an entrepreneurial way that cuts across conventional organisational boundaries. They may be made the responsibility of a particular cross-disciplinary team that operates with intrapreneurial flair. Ahuja and Lampert (2001) develop a model of how intrapreneurism helps large firms achieve breakthrough inventions.

- *The setting up of new business units*. As the venture becomes larger, new and distinct business functions and units come into their own. A particular part of the business may operate best if it has a distinct character and a degree of independence. The setting up of new business units is a demanding project. Not only must the structural and external strategic issues be considered. There are also the resourcing issues (including human) and the relationship with the parent business to be taken into account. Again, an intrapreneurial team, the members of which may have a future role in the new unit, may best manage this sort of project.

- *Reinvigorating the whole organisation*. Entrepreneurship, and the success of entrepreneurial ventures, is largely based on their flexibility and responsiveness to new and unmet customer demands. Such flexibility can be lost as the business grows and its attention is drawn to internal concerns. Reintroducing the inventive spirit back into the business may be a radical process. Making the organisation entrepreneurial again is clearly an intrapreneurial project. An intrapreneur must lead such a project with entrepreneurial vision for the organisation's future, with an entrepreneurial approach to using power, leadership and motivation and an ability to overcome organisational resistance to change.

● *Reinventing the business's industry.* Entrepreneurs make a difference. The world is not the same after they have built their venture. The most successful entrepreneurs do not just enter a market: they reinvent the industry in which they operate by introducing new technology, delivering new products or operating in a new, more effective way. There is no reason why the maturing entrepreneurial venture should not hold on to this ambition. A business can win by playing to the rules well; but it can also win by changing the rules to suit itself.

   Clearly though, such a project is wide in its scope and challenging to implement. It demands an eye on the future, strategic vision, comfort with risk and an ability to lead people forward. It is at this level that intrapreneurship meets up with and becomes entrepreneurship.

   Intrapreneurism offers an exciting option for the consolidating entrepreneurial venture. It promises a way to build on success while retaining the original dynamism of the venture. It suggests a way to reduce risk while still pursuing fleeting opportunities. However, any organisational form which promises such high rewards must also present some challenges. There are limitations to intrapreneurship, a point developed by Ross (1987).

Entrepreneur's comfort

Allowing a role for the intrapreneur to develop demands that the entrepreneur actually create space for the intrapreneur to operate. That means letting go of some degree of control. The entrepreneur, having brought the organisation to where it is by exerting control, may not feel comfortable with this. In effect, allowing the intrapreneur to operate means that the entrepreneur must share a part of his or her own role at a core rather than a peripheral level. After all, as Young (1999) points out, intrapreneurial management is about breaking rules. And this means the rules the entrepreneur has created.

Decision-making control

Entrepreneurs exist to challenge orthodoxies. They seek a better way of doing things. They must be dissatisfied with the status quo. This same dissatisfaction must also motivate the intrapreneur. Unlike the entrepreneur, however, the intrapreneur must operate within some sort of organisational decision-making control. If they were not, then they wouldn't actually be working for the organisation at all! The question here is to what extent the intrapreneur can be allowed to challenge existing decision-making procedures and to what extent they must be bound by them. A balance must be created between allowing the intrapreneur freedom to make their own moves and the need to keep the business on a constant strategic path.

Internal politics

The intrapreneur must question the existing order and drive change within the organisation. For many individuals and groups within the organisation such change will present a challenge. As a result the intrapreneur is likely to meet resistance, both active and passive, to the ideas they bring along. An ability to predict and understand that resistance, and developing the leadership skills necessary to overcome it, presents a considerable challenge to the manager. Intrapreneurs are a rare breed. Tom Peters (1989) has suggested that intrapreneurs must be able to 'thrive on chaos'.

Rewards for the intrapreneur

This point really results from the latter. The intrapreneur, if he or she is to be effective, must bring along the same type, and level, of skills that entrepreneurs themselves offer. The question is, can the organisation *really* offer the intrapreneur the rewards (economic, social and developmental) they might come to expect in return for using them? In short, if someone is an effective intrapreneur how long will it be before the temptation of full-blown entrepreneurship is felt and they move off to start a venture of their own?

Clearly intrapreneurship presents itself as a spectrum which, as a style of management, acts to connect 'conventional' management with entrepreneurial management. It offers a way to bring the advantages of both types of management together. In this it is a compromise. The entrepreneur can only facilitate intrapreneurship within the business by recognising the nature of this compromise and making decisions in relation to it. The central question relates to how much latitude the venture's strategy gives individuals to make their own decisions. The question is not just strategic. An entrepreneur must decide to what extent he or she will be willing to accept dissent from the intrapreneur. Will it be received as a challenge? How does active dissent fit with the leadership strategy the entrepreneur has nurtured?

Entrepreneurs must also ask how the reward structure they have set up encourages and discourages individual decision making. What does the individual get in return for venturing on behalf of the business? What sanctions come into force if things go wrong? The entrepreneur must remember that such rewards and sanctions are not always formal and explicit. Further, the entrepreneur must recognise the level of resistance that agents driving change meet from the organisation and accept responsibility in helping the intrapreneur to overcome this. No less than any other member of the organisation, the intrapreneur needs support, encouragement and leadership.

Summary of key ideas

- As the venture matures, its rate of growth slows. This process is known as *consolidation*.

- Consolidation involves changes to the *financial*, *strategic*, *structural* and *organisational* dynamics of the venture.

- Consolidation offers the venture a chance to create a defendable competitive position in the marketplace. This offers the promise of rewarding the commitment stakeholders have shown towards the venture.

- *Intrapreneurism* is a form of management which, potentially, offers the venture a way of combining the flexibility and responsiveness of the entrepreneurial with the market power and reduced risk of the established organisation.

Research theme

Entrepreneurs' anticipation and experience of venture consolidation

Consolidation offers both opportunities and challenges to the entrepreneur. It would be interesting to compare and contrast the anticipation of these prior to consolidation and the remembered experience of then afterwards. Select two samples of entrepreneurs, one group whose venture is in an early growth stage, the other, whose ventures have reached maturity and have consolidated. This may be judged by considering the history of the ventures. With the former group, conduct interviews to ascertain their expectations of consolidation, the positive and negative experiences they expect and the managerial issues these will entail. Consider strategic, financial and human issues. Conduct similar interviews with the post-consolidation group, ascertaining the entrepreneurs' experience in terms of its positive and negatives, again in strategic, financial and human terms. What generic issues are identified by each of the two groups? A positive–negative versus type-of-issue grid may aid coding of responses. How do these compare and contrast between the two groups? Do entrepreneurs have realistic expectations about the consolidation experience? Do entrepreneurs in the growth phase even think about consolidation? In what respects are they being optimistic or pessimistic? Does any mismatch go on to encourage serial entrepreneurship? Summarise by making recommendations about how entrepreneurs may be supported in effectively managing the consolidation process.

Suggestions for further reading

Ahuja, G. and Lampert, C.M. (2001) 'Entrepreneurship in the large corporation: a longitudinal study of how established firms create breakthrough inventions', *Strategic Management Journal*, Vol. 22, pp. 521–43.

Kanter, R.M. (1985) *The Change Masters*, London: Unwin Hyman.

Mauruca, R.F. (2000) 'Entrepreneurs versus chief executives at Socaba.com', *Harvard Business Review*, July–August, pp. 30–8.

Osborne, R.L. (1991) 'The dark side of the entrepreneur', *Long Range Planning*, Vol 24, No. 3, pp. 26–31.

Osborne, R.L. (1992) 'Building an innovative organisation', *Long Range Planning*, Vol. 25, No. 6, pp. 56–62.

Peters, T. (1989) *Thriving on Chaos*, London: Macmillan.

Pinchot, III, G. (1985) *Intrapreneuring*, New York: Harper & Row.

Ross, J. (1987) 'Corporations and entrepreneurs: paradox and opportunity', *Business Horizons*, July–August, pp. 76–80.

Stopford, J.M. (1994) 'Creating corporate entrepreneurship', *Strategic Management Journal*, Vol. 15, pp. 521–36.

Vrakking, W.J. (1990) 'The innovative organization', *Long Range Planning*, Vol. 23, No. 2, pp. 94–102.

Weseley Morse, C. (1986) 'The delusion of intrapreneurship', *Long Range Planning*, Vol. 19, No. 6, pp. 92–5.

Young, A.P. (1999) 'Rule breaking and a new opportunistic managerialism', *Management Decision*, Vol. 37, No. 7, pp. 582–8.

Selected case material Case 28.1

Branson smooth, the softer-textured brand

FT

30 April 2002

By **Martin Dickson** in London

Virgin empire flotations

The makers of Branston pickle recently launched a more finely blended version of the relish, Branston Smooth, for those who prefer it without any chunky pieces. A similar process appears to be under way at Sir Richard Branson's Virgin empire. Welcome to Branson Smooth.

In an interview with Monday's FT he outlined plans to float at least eight companies from the group and step down as their chairman. Virgin's stakes in some of them might be cut from 50 per cent to nearer 30 and – depending on government corporate tax changes – he might move Virgin holding companies back to the UK from their offshore domiciles.

All this marks a distinct shift from his past attitudes. Virgin Group, the empire's former holding company, spent a brief and unhappy two years on the stock market in the 1980s before Sir Richard took it private again.

Sir Richard is known for announcing initiatives that do not necessarily materialise, but some elementary forces look like moving him in the direction outlined above. Critics of his secretive approach to business will doubtless claim his empire is in financial crisis. He insists it has a comfortable cash cushion and the leisurely flotation programme, stretching all the way to 2007–10, hardly smacks of desperation.

That said, the value Virgin appears to place on some of its businesses looks hugely inflated compared to analysts' estimates, casting doubt on the success of offerings. Still, the process at least appears to play to his strengths as a serial entrepreneur/marketer of the Virgin name and as a venture capitalist able to get large partners to invest in his initiatives – such as Singapore Airlines in Virgin Atlantic and AMP in Virgin Money.

Like any investors, they will eventually want to exit and flotation is an obvious route. Sir Richard, for his part, will need large amounts of cash to develop his new projects, the largest of which is to attack the US mobile phone market.

He also seems to have recognised that running businesses is not his strongest suit. Virgin companies have rarely made huge amounts of money. The empire has benefited most by developing businesses and generating profits by selling them on. 'My skills are more in creating and building companies,' he says. Quite so.

Cynics – and they are never far away when discussing Sir Richard – will note that this echoes remarks made this month by another of Britain's most prominent entrepreneurs, Stelios Haji-Ioannou. He was widely praised for stepping down as chairman of EasyJet, the low-cost airline he founded, to focus on developing new companies. Perhaps both men are maturing in tandem.

However, maturity carries a potential downside for Sir Richard. The strength of Virgin's brand is intimately tied up with his brilliant public relations skills in projecting an image of youthful, man-of-the-people iconoclasm. As potential flotation investors will doubtless note, the older he gets, the harder that could be to sustain.

Aberdeen

When a large stake in Aberdeen Asset Managers was placed last May by Cazenove and JP Morgan, investors rushed to take up the offering. Less than two months later, the same investors would have received a research note across their desks from Cazenove warning of 'systemic risk' in the split capital trust market, where Aberdeen has been a leading force.

This may demonstrate admirably strong Chinese walls at Tokenhouse Yard but investors cannot have been particularly pleased. The shares have fallen 47 per cent from the placing price of 500p to 237p, partly because of market falls but also in large measure to concerns over the impact of the split trust debacle.

The direct financial fallout appears to be limited. Aberdeen is temporarily waiving about £4.5m of fees on £524m of assets of eight of the most stricken split trusts it manages. But the real damage is reputational, and for a fund manager reputation is all. What had been a lucrative bandwagon for Aberdeen has turned into a nightmare.

The fund manager will be hoping for a quick end to the Financial Services Authority's inquiry into the split trust sector in the next few weeks, if only to try to put the continuing uncertainty behind it. Lawsuits remain a threat but Aberdeen's exposure may be limited by the fact that some of the split trusts were sold through professional intermediaries.

The outlook for the shares will depend greatly on the success of Aberdeen's attempt to put the split trust uncertainty behind it, given the flat outlook for both its earnings and the direction of the stock market. The stock has fallen from trading on a price/earnings multiple of more than 20 to about 12 times.

Given that Aberdeen's total split capital trust operations account for about 15 to 20 per cent of profits and the shares have halved, the reputational risk seems priced in. Add in a slight premium for the possibility of a takeover and there could be the prospect of a bounce in the share price once the split trust cloud starts to clear. Investors in the more troubled split trusts are not likely to fare so well.

Source: *Financial Times*, 30 April 2002.

Talking the talk, walking the walk

FT

4 November 2002

By **Maggie Urry**

Peter Long is tough. The chief executive of First Choice Holidays says he was born tough, brought up tough with the quality reinforced by his early business training. Years in the notoriously volatile travel industry have only served to make him, well, tougher.

What is more, he looks tough. Taller than six feet, his rugged face and bristly dark hair are only slightly softened by clear blue eyes. It is hard to warm to someone so assertive about their hardness, though people who work for him say he has a sense of humour too.

Since he joined First Choice in 1996 he has had to make some tough decisions, not least after September 11 last year when he swiftly cut 1,400 jobs, anticipating a sharp decline in business. 'It's not pleasant . . . but I've never had a difficulty making hard decisions that I know are right for the business.'

His success in turning round First Choice has won him the respect of people in the travel sector, especially since arch-rival MyTravel – which had launched a hostile bid for First Choice in 1999 – issued a string of profit warnings and is now having its accounts scrutinised by regulators. By contrast, First Choice issued an upbeat trading statement last week.

With the possibility of conflict in Iraq, and the probability of further consolidation in the travel industry – perhaps initiated by First Choice – Mr Long will be someone to watch in the coming months.

And he will need that quality he claims to have in such abundance. 'My mother's tough, my grandfather was tough, so it comes partly in the genes.'

Mr Long's father was in the Navy and his early years were spent enduring the frequent moves inflicted on service children. 'Just as you were getting settled you moved on. So that probably toughened me up.'

After school he took a business studies course. 'I always felt I would like the cut and thrust of it'. He qualified as a management accountant, and worked in the construction industry during the difficult years of the early 1970s, then honed his financial skills at BTR, since renamed Invensys.

It was BTR's heyday when Owen (now Sir Owen) Green and Norman Ireland were in charge. 'In that era there were a lot of very inefficient companies and [BTR's] style of management – grabbing hold of them by the scruff of the neck, rationalising them – worked.'

Mr Long also learnt to be unemotional about business, and is scathing about managers who are not. If Plan A does not work, it is time for Plan B. Even when he says of his current position: 'My job is to deliver dreams to our customers,' his even tone makes such a romantic notion sound prosaic.

In 1984 he joined Harry Goodman's International Leisure Group, ending up as chief executive of the tour operating division. ILG had been a highly successful cheap and cheerful tour operator and charter airline in the 1980s, but it went spectacularly bust when an ill-judged move into a scheduled airline coincided with the slump in travel during the Gulf War.

Mr Long tried to buy out the still-profitable tour operating business but was unable to. 'I came home one night feeling very miserable, very sorry for myself. I woke up the following morning thinking – there's no point sitting around sulking. There's a job to be done here, there's a business we can rebuild and we're going to have to move very quickly.'

With a partner, a Spanish hotelier, he launched Sunworld to take advantage of ILG's demise. ILG went under in March. Sunworld had 'gone on sale at Easter with our first departure on the first of May. We sold 250,000 holidays in our first year.'

As he now contemplates MyTravel's difficulties, he can recall the Sunworld lesson – that it is not necessary to buy the assets of a business if you can simply win over the customers.

Sunworld was a bold gamble. With a wife and three young children, he could have played safe and got another job as an accountant. 'I guess I was comfortable taking that risk, in that I believed we could build a business.'

But his accounting background ensured he did not go too far. 'An accountant can't become an entrepreneur, because at the end of the day I wouldn't risk everything, whereas an entrepreneur would.'

His decisiveness paid off. Within five years, Sunworld was the UK's fifth largest package holiday company. Mr Long and his partner sold it to Thomas Cook for a little less than £40m. Although he was the minority partner, he must have had enough money not to need to work again.

Mr Long is reticent on how much he did make. 'I didn't have to rush out and get another job, but I wanted to. I was looking for a new and a bigger challenge.' First Choice provided that, and within weeks of joining he had become group managing director in a boardroom shake-up.

It was his first chance to run a quoted company. When he arrived he found a car park full of Jaguars – he has no time for such 'status symbols' – and 'an organisation that felt condemned. It had been under pressure for a number of years, never making the right returns. The huge challenge was the big turn-on for me. I thought, "I can turn this business round".'

Although there were good people at the company, he says, it lacked direction. 'The pilots were saying, "What the hell is going on?" You've got to lead from the front, and you've got to have a very clear plan. You can't do that as a shrinking violet. You've got to do it by being very visible in the organisation.'

One business associate says of him: 'He has lots of leadership skills, he is a great motivator and builds good teams. He can be quite ruthless if necessary and doesn't suffer fools gladly.'

Mr Long's determination to talk to staff throughout the business is apparently appreciated, and he does not appear to be an autocrat.

'I believe in having a very strong team of people. I will give clear direction but I will also listen to people, and I will be persuaded to do something different if their arguments are more compelling than mine.'

In 1999 he had to concede an argument when First Choice failed to convince shareholders to back a merger with Kuoni, the Swiss travel group. Had it succeeded, Mr Long would have been in charge of a larger business, with the chance of eventually running the whole company.

He says the merger had 'compelling logic' but shareholders were also eyeing the hostile bid from Airtours – the former name of MyTravel. Kuoni lost interest and the Airtours bid was blocked by the EU.

Again, he refuses to be riled, saying he was not annoyed that the Kuoni deal was not done, and bowing to shareholders as owners. 'It's our job to deliver. We manage the train set, we don't own it.'

Although First Choice is unlikely to bid for MyTravel, at least in the near future, Mr Long would like to see his company involved in the consolidation he predicts in the travel industry across Europe, and then worldwide.

That, he declares, 'would be fun'.

Source: Financial Times, 4 November 2002.

Discussion points

1 What issues are evident about the strengths and limitations of entrepreneurs running a large, mature organisation?

2 Is retrenching a firm during tough times a job for an entrepreneur?

Chapter 29

The changing role of the entrepreneur in the consolidated organisation

Chapter overview

This chapter is concerned with an exploration of the way in which the entrepreneur's role changes as the organisation's rate of growth slows and it consolidates its position in the marketplace. The role of the entrepreneur is compared and contrasted to that of the chief executive. It is considered why, despite its many strengths, entrepreneurial control may not always be right for the mature venture. The chapter concludes with a consideration of the responsibility of the entrepreneur in planning for passing on control to others after they have departed the organisation.

29.1 The entrepreneur versus the chief executive

Key learning outcome

An appreciation of the differences between the roles of the entrepreneur and the chief executive officer.

The vast majority of organisations offer a role for a single, most senior manager. This position has a number of titles. In for-profit businesses it is often the *managing director* or *president*. Generically, the role is referred to as the *chief executive officer* (CEO). While all organisations have a chief executive officer of some description, not all are led by someone we would recognise as an entrepreneur.

So while the entrepreneur *may* be a chief executive officer, the chief executive officer is not *necessarily* an entrepreneur. Clearly, both roles present considerable management challenges. Both demand vision, an ability to develop strategic insights and provide leadership. That said, the two roles are distinct in a number of ways.

Internal co-ordination versus external promotion

The resource-based view of the organisation presented in Section 24.6 emphasises the role managers have in bringing in the resources that are critical to the success of the venture: capital, information, people and the goodwill of customers. The entrepreneur, especially when the venture is at an early stage and has limited management resources, will take on the responsibility for bringing in nearly all of these things. He or she will be the venture's salesperson, its finance expert, its recruitment specialist and so on.

The chief executive of even a moderately large organisation will not have direct responsibility for doing these things. He or she may not even have responsibility for *delegating* them, at least directly. What they will have responsibility for is setting up *management structures* within the organisation which will enable these tasks to be co-ordinated and carried out in a way that is effective and is responsive to the overall strategic direction chosen by the business. They may also recognise a need to manage the organisation's *culture*. The chief executive is not, primarily, responsible for acquiring resources so much as making sure that those which are acquired are used at a strategic level, in the best possible way.

In these terms, the entrepreneur provides a bridge between the small business manager and the chief executive of a large firm. In growing the venture, the entrepreneur transforms the role of acquiring resources into that of creating and maintaining structures to manage resources. The role changes from one of *external* promotion (that is, managing the venture in its wider *network*) to one of *internal* co-ordination.

Managing continuity versus driving change

As related in Section 2.1 entrepreneurs are interested in driving change. So are chief executives. In a fast-changing world organisations must change if they are to survive and prosper. The management of change is now properly recognised as one of the key responsibilities of senior management, in whatever sector their organisation is operating. Entrepreneurs and chief executives are both interested in changing their organisations in response to the opportunities presented to them.

However, there is a difference in the *degree* of change entrepreneurs wish to see and that which chief executives would normally wish to occur. Entrepreneurs are interested in *radical* change. The entrepreneur's vision is created out of a tension between 'what is' and 'what might be'. For that vision to be powerful, the difference between what is and what might be achieved must be great. Chief executives, on the other hand, are more likely to be interested in slower and more measured *incremental* change. This is understandable. After all, their organisations have proved their success, at least historically. They must be doing something right! Incremental change can build on that success: strengths are managed in, while weaknesses are managed out. Radical change threatens to throw away the strengths as well as address the weaknesses.

Management by 'right' versus management by appointment

The third feature that distinguishes entrepreneurs from chief executives is the basis on which they obtain authority to manage the business and the influence this has on the power base they develop. As noted in Section 27.3, *authority* and *power* are quite different things. Power is an ability to influence the course of actions within the organisation. Authority merely offers the potential to influence the organisation by virtue of a position within it. Authority is an *invitation* to power, not power itself.

Chief executives obtain their authority to run the business by virtue of appointment to the position. They may arrive at this position as a result of internal promotion or by being recruited into the organisation. The appointment process is governed by established organisational procedures. The views not only of internal managers but also of important investors may be sought. Once in this position, the power of the chief executive arises from the way they control resources and systems and the leadership they offer.

Entrepreneurs also gain authority from the position they occupy, their management of resources and systems, and the leadership they give to the organisation. However, an entrepreneur has an additional source of authority providing not only authority to run the business, but also a *right* to run it. While the chief executive is employed by the organisation, the organisation is perceived as 'belonging to' the entrepreneur. This perceived right can be derived from the entrepreneur's ownership of the business. However, owning the organisation they lead is not a necessary characteristic of the entrepreneur. The business is actually owned by those who invest in it. More important is the entrepreneur's historical relationship to founding the organisation and their association with *building* it up.

This difference is important not only for the way the entrepreneur actually manages the organisation but also for the way in which they are exposed as a result of its performance. While we would expect a chief executive to be ousted if the organisation he or she manages fails to perform, we can still be surprised when an entrepreneur who is seen to have created the organisation is greeted with the same fate.

Of course these three criteria do not create hard and fast categories. We are dealing with fuzzy concepts in the same way as we were when we discussed the distinction between the small business and the entrepreneurial venture in Section 4.1. Whom we regard as an entrepreneur and whom we see as 'merely' a chief executive is a matter of judgement based on a consideration of the balance between all three criteria.

As with the distinction between the small business manager and the entrepreneur, we should not rush to make a judgement as to who is, or is not, an entrepreneur. We should not look towards the individual to assess whether they are an entrepreneur or not, rather we should look at what and how they manage in terms of the balance between internal and external co-ordination, the change they seek to create and the way authority is ascribed to them, i.e. the basis of their power (Figure 29.1).

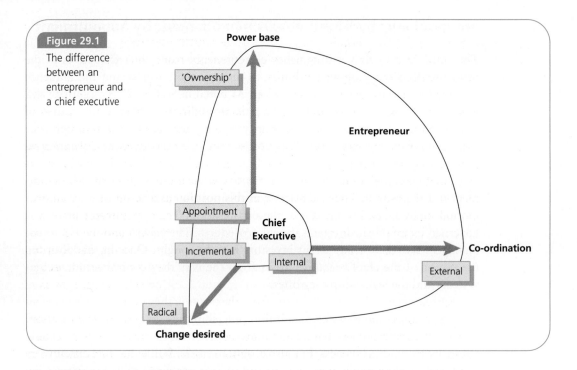

Figure 29.1

The difference between an entrepreneur and a chief executive

29.2 The dangers of entrepreneurial control in the mature organisation

Key learning outcome

An appreciation of some of the limitations of an entrepreneurial style of management in the mature venture.

Entrepreneurial management has a lot to offer. The entrepreneur's vision offers the potential for leadership. That vision and leadership can be used to give the venture direction. It provides an impetus for the changes that are necessary if a venture is to survive and prosper in a rapidly changing world. However, as a *style* of management, entrepreneurship is merely one style among many, and while entrepreneurship is a very powerful style of management it, like any other style, has its limitations.

Entrepreneurial management is concerned with the *whole* organisation. In the early stages of the venture this allows the entrepreneur to manage the organisation in an integrated way. The entrepreneur can put balanced emphasis on attracting all the resources the organisation requires: money, people, customers and knowledge. Unfortunately, this may lead the entrepreneur to underestimate the value of the management of particular functions. They may be quite dismissive of the need for a dedicated approach to marketing or finance or human resource management as the venture grows and matures (relate this back to the heuristics described in Section 15.6). This can lead the entrepreneur to underestimate the contribution that specialists can make to the venture. Having made a success of the venture themselves they can become suspicious of the need for 'experts'. As a result, the entrepreneur may find it difficult to give specialist managers sufficient room to make the decisions they need to make.

Further, entrepreneurial management is concerned with driving change. This is a key and positive aspect of the entrepreneur's approach. It is only from change that new value can be created. However, it is often the case that the entrepreneur exhibits a greater desire for change than do other stakeholders. The entrepreneur may still be seeking new ways to push the venture forward while investors and employees seek consolidation and stability. As a result there may be a conflict over the type of investments undertaken by the mature venture. A number of high-profile run-ins occurred between highly successful entrepreneurs and institutional investors at the end of the 1980s in both the USA and the UK as the financial climate became more difficult. For example, both Anita and Gordon Roddick, founders of The Body Shop and Alan Sugar, founder of Amstrad, became involved in expensive share buy-backs to increase their personal control of their enterprises.

This touches on a wider issue. All organisations develop an *inertia* or resistance to change. Entrepreneurs and the organisations they create are not immune to this. While the entrepreneurial organisation is founded on an innovation there is no guarantee that it will be innovative in its innovation! Often, the innovation sets a pattern of strategic activity which the venture attempts to repeat in another sector. The initial success may not always translate to other sectors. Alan Sugar and his Amstrad venture were phenomenally successful with a formula which presented uncomplicated, easy-to-use and low-cost hi-fi systems to the general public. However, the same formula was not repeated so successfully with business computers, a sector where the customer-buying criteria were quite different.

All in all, an entrepreneurial style of management has a great and valuable role to play in the mature organisation. However, it is essential that entrepreneurs recognise that the way they involve themselves with and apply their talents to the mature organisation differs from the way they did when the organisation was in a fast-growing state. This is a theme explored by Hamm (2002).

(29.3) The role of the founding entrepreneur in the mature organisation

> **Key learning outcome**
>
> An appreciation of the types of role the entrepreneur can undertake in the mature organisation.

The role of the entrepreneur must change as the venture develops. Growth offers founding entrepreneurs the same opportunity as it offers every other member of the organisation: the chance to develop and specialise the role they play within the organisation. Some of the more important types of specialisation are listed below (see also Figure 29.2).

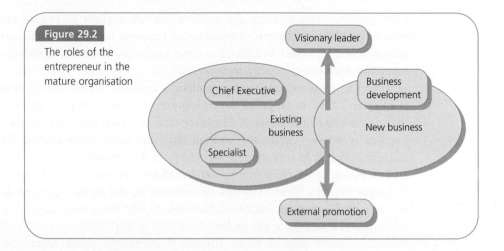

Figure 29.2

The roles of the entrepreneur in the mature organisation

Chief executive

The most obvious role for the entrepreneur to play is that of chief executive. In this the entrepreneur has a clearly defined position at the head of the organisation. He or she retains the power to make and influence key decisions about the way the business should be conducted. The chief executive role is, of course, one which the entrepreneur can drift into by virtue of always being at the head of the business. However, the points made in the previous section about the differences between the way the entrepreneur leads the growing business and the chief executive manages the mature business must be considered here in relation to the evolution of that role.

Visionary leader

As discussed in Section 11.2 the entrepreneur has a variety of means at his or her disposal when it comes to influencing the direction the organisation takes and the way it manages its resources. Entrepreneurs do not have to direct every decision personally. They can use indirect means of communicating vision, directing strategy and controlling the organisation's culture. This means that the entrepreneur can specialise the role they play along the leadership dimension. By taking on the role of a visionary leader, the entrepreneur avoids making decisions personally. Rather they create an environment which brings out the best in the organisation's people by motivating them and giving them an overall sense of direction. This is the kind of role played by the Virgin chief, Richard Branson, who while providing leadership to his organisation leaves most of the decision making to his professional managers.

Manager of business development

Entrepreneurs sometimes find it difficult to let go of the entrepreneurial approach they have developed. They do not find the chief executive role a comfortable one. Yet they can still recognise the need for a consolidatory approach to the management of the mature venture. They may resolve this dilemma by concentrating on the development of new business, a task which is well suited to an entrepreneurial style. The entrepreneur then delegates management of the established business to another manager. If the business is made up of a number of independent business units then this arrangement can be made explicit. The entrepreneur can leave the running of the business units to their managers and can concentrate on making new acquisitions, for example. On the other hand, if the business is a single coherent organisation then the arrangement may be more implicit and be based on internal delegation.

An example here might be Rupert Murdoch with his News International and BSkyB business ventures. While taking a very active interest in the established business, Murdoch is most active at the cutting edge of his growing empire.

Technical specialist

Sometimes the entrepreneur may decide to give up the chief executive position altogether and take on what, at face value, appears to be a subordinate role within the organisation. In this role they will specialise in some way, perhaps in managing product development or marketing. Though uncommon, this sometimes occurs in high-technology organisations which have been founded by technical experts. An example of this is Martin Woods, a physicist, who while based at the Cavendish Laboratories founded the successful Oxford Instruments Company, a major manufacturer of components for hospital scanners. Once the venture had passed the stage where product innovation was the most important thing, and marketing and financial management became of greater importance, Dr Woods passed on the day-to-day running of the company to marketing and finance professionals and moved back to the laboratory as the company's research and development director.

Promoter of the venture

The entrepreneurial venture must continue to attract the support of external stakeholders, not least customers and financial backers. The entrepreneur may take on the role of figurehead and work at promoting the organisation to these stakeholders. An important example of this kind of approach is that of Anita and Gordon Roddick and The Body Shop organisation. The conventional chief executive role is largely played by Gordon while Anita Roddick represents the organisation in the media, promotes it to existing and new franchise holders and seeks out new ingredient suppliers in the developing world.

Entrepreneur in an alternative venture

Entrepreneurs can, of course, decide that the consolidated organisation has little to offer them. They may decide to liquidate their holding and use the resources to start another venture. This is precisely what the serial entrepreneurs Howard Hodgeson of Hodgeson Holdings and James Dyson have done in the past.

29.4 Succession in the entrepreneurial business

> **Key learning outcome**
>
> A recognition of the importance of managing leadership succession when the entrepreneur leaves the venture.

The average life of a business is probably about the same as the working life of a manager. However, this average can be misleading. It includes a lot of businesses which only last a few years, and a few which have existed for hundreds. The successful entrepreneurial venture should be expected to last a lot longer than the career span of the founding entrepreneur. This longevity raises the issue of *succession*.

Succession creates a number of issues for the venture. Even though the business has an existence independent of the entrepreneur, the entrepreneur is more than an 'optional extra'. He or she is an integral part of the organisation. The loss of the entrepreneur represents the loss of one of its key resources. The entrepreneur must be replaced. How the entrepreneur is to be replaced, by whom, when, and in what way, represent critical decision areas for the business.

As Harris and Ogbonna (1999) make clear, founding entrepreneurs leave a *strategic* as well as a personal legacy. Reuber and Fischer (1999) develop a perspective on founder contribution that emphasises that the founder's knowledge and experience is not so much a 'stock' but a continual 'stream' that flows into the organisation.

The need for continuity . . .

All organisations need some continuity. The entrepreneur, especially if they are a motivating leader, offers a reference point about which the organisation can cohere. After the entrepreneur has gone that coherence may be lost. As a result the business risks losing focus and direction.

. . . and for change

On the other hand, all organisations must recognise the need for change in response to a rapidly changing environment. Founding entrepreneurs, while they may be effective managers of subsequent change, may also impart an inertia to the business which makes some changes difficult. Bringing a new leader presents an opportunity which, if used properly, offers the chance to effect necessary and beneficial changes in the way the business is run.

Choosing a successor

Change at the top is a contingency which may be planned for. The entrepreneur may not like to think in terms of ending their relationship with the venture but they owe it to all the other stakeholders to consider the possibility and prepare for it. A major part of this is identifying a successor. It is important here for the entrepreneur to recognise the opportunity for change. The business will have moved a long way from its foundation. The characteristics the entrepreneur originally brought to the venture may not be the same ones it needs from a chief executive now. In choosing a successor, the entrepreneur must look for someone who is right for the business, not someone who is a copy of themselves.

The entrepreneur should also look for advice in choosing a successor. The opinions of other managers and key outsiders (particularly investors) may be valuable and influential. A successor may be sought within the business or they may be brought from outside. There are a number of key questions that must be asked about any candidate for succession.

- Do they have the necessary technical knowledge of the business sector?

- Do they have the right business skills?

- Do they have the ability to manage and develop the relationships the entrepreneur has established?

- Do they have an ability to lead the business?

- How will the leadership style offered compare with that of the outgoing entrepreneur?

- Do they have the ability to take on the entrepreneur's vision and continue to communicate it?

- Do they have the ability to provide a sense of continuity?

- Yet are they also capable of offering a new perspective?

- Will they be acceptable to all the stakeholders in the venture?

A 1992 issue of the *Journal of Accountancy* (Vol. 174, No. 4, p. 24) offers a comprehensive checklist for managing family succession. Fox *et al.* (1996) consider the management of these issues.

Mentoring

The entrepreneur may be replaced as the head of the business. However, this is only a transfer of title. Being made the new chief executive only offers a promise of *authority*, that is, the potential to create change, not *power*, which is an ability to create change. (Consider the points made in Section 27.3.) Exercising power demands not only a position but also influence over the organisation's resources. This means not just tangible resources, but also the intangibles of generating vision and control of the symbolic dimensions of organisational life.

Mentoring may offer a means by which these things may be transferred. The entrepreneur selects a successor well ahead of the time when succession actually need take place and the successor is then trained to take over. This process involves the transfer of knowledge, education and support and a passing on of power. The successor is made *visible* as a successor. The organisation is made to recognise the successor as its future leader. The entrepreneur educates his or her successor not only in the details of the business, but also in terms of how it may be led and controlled. The actual transfer of power may be gradual with the successor given responsibility for distinct aspects of the business over time.

Remember the business

Choosing a successor is not easy. It demands that the entrepreneur admit to being mortal. It may also be tempting for the entrepreneur to favour a relative as successor if a relative wishes to take over! Many do not wish to (Stavrou, 1999). Morris *et al.* (1996) detail some of the challenges family successors meet on taking over the business. While the offspring of entrepreneurs often show great business acumen and leadership ability, there is no reason why they *must* do so. Entrepreneurship is learnt, not inherited! Keeping a business within the family may be appropriate (especially if it is privately owned). However, the entrepreneur has a responsibility to *all* the organisation's stakeholders. The entrepreneur should always remember the business and select a successor who is able to manage it as effectively as they themselves could.

Succession is an important issue and it is one which good entrepreneurs address openly, rationally and honestly. Successful entrepreneurs build entire new worlds. There is no reason why that new world should not continue after they have left it. The businesses they leave are testaments to the differences they have made.

Good luck in making the difference you want to!

Summary of key ideas

- The roles of the entrepreneur and the chief executive are subtly different, although they overlap in many ways. The entrepreneur is more interested in creating change, and may be more willing to take risks than the role of chief executive properly calls for. This can expose the mature venture to unnecessary risk.

- Consolidation gives entrepreneurs an opportunity to specialise their roles within their organisations.

- Effective entrepreneurs manage the process of *succession* (the handing over of power within the venture) positively and effectively when it is time for them to move on.

Research theme

Entrepreneurs' management of the succession process

Use a case study approach to explore and describe the way entrepreneurs manage their succession. Use published information supplemented by personal interviews. You may need to spend some time building up trust with the subject organisation if this type of study is to be effective. In particular, inquire into the entrepreneur's feelings about the succession, the concerns of key stakeholders such as employees and investors, the managerial issues that were identified and the approach taken to dealing with them. How far in advance was succession planned for? To what extent was mentoring used to groom a successor? Did the entrepreneur back out quickly or was the handover a more gradual process? Use the ideas developed in this chapter to guide the inquiry. What went right with the process and what went wrong? How would key players have handled things differently, if they had the chance to do them again? If more than one study is conducted, then comparisons and contrasts may be made. Are there any generalisations that might be made about how the process should be managed?

Suggestions for further reading

Fox, M., Nilakant, V. and Hamilton, R.T. (1996) 'Managing succession in family-owned businesses', *International Small Business Journal*, Vol. 15, No. 1, pp. 15–25.

Gabarro, J.J. (1985) 'When a new manager takes charge', *Harvard Business Review*, May–June, pp. 110–23.

Hamm, J. (2002) 'Why entrepreneurs don't scale', *Harvard Business Review*, December, pp. 110–15.

Harris, L.C. and Ogbonna, E. (1999) 'The strategic legacy of company founders', *Long Range Planning*, Vol. 32, No. 3, p. 333.

Kransdorff, A. (1996) 'Succession planning in a fast-changing world', *Management Decision*, Vol. 34, No. 2, pp. 30–4.

Morris, M.H., Williams, R.W. and Nell, D. (1996) 'Factors influencing family business succession', *International Journal of Entrepreneurial Behaviour and Research*, Vol. 2, No. 3, pp. 68–81.

Pearson, G.J. (1989) 'Promoting entrepreneurship in large companies', *Long Range Planning*, Vol. 22, No. 3, pp. 87–97.

Reuber, A.R. and Fischer, E. (1999) 'Understanding the consequences of founders' experience', *Journal of Small Business Management*, Vol. 37, No. 2, pp. 30–45.

Slatter, S., Ransley, R. and Woods, E. (1988) 'USM chief executives: do they fit the entrepreneurial stereotype?' *International Small Business Journal*, Vol. 6, No. 3, pp. 10–23.

Stavrou, E.T. (1999) 'Succession in family businesses: exploring the effects of demographic factors on offspring's intentions to join and take over the business', *Journal of Small Business Management*, Vol. 37, No. 3, pp. 43–61.

Wills, G. (1992) 'Enabling managerial growth and ownership succession', *Management Decision*, Vol. 30, No. 1, pp. 10–26.

The continuity conundrum

FT

8 November 2002

By **Michael Horvath**

The strengths that allow the founder of a start-up to succeed can be fatal flaws as the company grows. While continuity is desirable, it is rare for one leader to fit all phases of a developing company.

Michael Horvath is an associate professor of management at the Tuck School of Business, Dartmouth College. In 1996 he cofounded Kana Software, Inc., a software company.

Many successful ventures are personified by their founders. Think of Bill Gates and Microsoft, Richard Branson and Virgin or Michael Dell and Dell Computers. The list goes on.

While no longer start-ups, these companies were built from nothing and grew to formidable sizes with the founder at the helm. Strong leadership is necessary for start-up survival and is perhaps the most critical element to the growth of a new company. Any venture capitalist will tell you that good ideas abound but good management teams are rare.

Why is strong leadership so important for an entrepreneurial venture? The answer lies in the words of Thomas Edison: 'Genius is 1 per cent inspiration, 99 per cent perspiration.' Simply put, start-ups are built by their founders – their leaders construct them for success or, unwittingly, for failure. The strengths or deficiencies of the business are usually the result of action or inaction by its chief executives. This seems obvious – and is perhaps the norm at the companies we know and love – yet one must consider that we only study the companies and leaders we do because they are already successful.

Of course, established companies also benefit from strong leaders. But they differ from start-ups in that the leadership needs of young companies typically evolve as the company develops. Despite this, keeping the same leader throughout the growth phases is beneficial to a start-up because it helps maintain a sense of cultural continuity.

The evolution of entrepreneurial ventures can be broken into four distinct periods, each representing a different leadership challenge. Ideally, one leader would be capable of near-perfect execution in all four phases, but this is rarely the case. Thus the conundrum: changing leadership requirements coexist with the need for leadership continuity, yet are at odds with one another much of the time. It is easy for an entrepreneur to misread the tea leaves and either remain too long or exit too quickly.

Without attempting a scientific analysis on the art of entrepreneurship, I like to think about a start-up's development in terms of four leadership phases: that of visionary, followed by the building phase, the achiever and the solidifier.

The phases

In the visionary phase, the leadership challenge is to come up with an innovative product or service – usually one that solves customers' problems. To be successful, the founder must be able to convince prospective investors, employees, vendors and industry experts that his or her view of the world and business concept is novel, sound and represents a profitable business opportunity.

In the builder phase, the successful entrepreneur must assemble a team around the company plan – in essence create reality out of a mere idea. Think of a player-coach; a successful leader in this stage will share the same attributes.

The achiever phase repeatedly challenges the leader to keep promises in many areas, including financial results, employment policies or product R&D plans. In this phase, the successful leader must recognise that success equals results minus expectations. So the leader must not promise too much, as he or she often has more control over setting expectations than delivering results. Unfortunately, leaders who are strong in the visionary and builder phases may be too optimistic when setting expectations, making it difficult for them to succeed in this phase.

In the solidifier phase, the leader must convert the start-up into an established company that will be there for the long haul. This often requires disciplined management and organisational practices to control costs, improve productivity and increase margins – activities that differ from the chaotic style characterising a company's formation. It therefore represents new challenges to the leader who successfully navigated the previous phases.

Value in continuity

Though the leadership challenges posed by these four phases are markedly different, successful start-ups benefit tremendously from leadership continuity. Most of a company's points of contact – with employees, investors, key customers and vendors – are developed personally by a young company's chief executive. These relationships are disrupted if another leader steps in.

This was readily apparent when Tim Koogle stepped down from the top spot at Yahoo! in April 2001. Within a month, several of the company's executive managers also departed and the company's favour with investors soured.

Against this backdrop of changing leadership needs, the start-up chief executive still needs to get things done. In my opinion, the three most important tasks for the leader of a start-up are recruiting, R&D and organisational design. Unfortunately, founders too often think of these tasks as ones that can and should be delegated – to the head of human resources, to the head of R&D, or to consultants with nifty organisational chart software. But sticking with these activities long enough will help the founder pass through the four growth phases without losing control.

As long as a start-up leader plays an active role in all hiring decisions, he or she maintains control over the company's corporate culture and value system. Corporate culture is a tricky beast to control because culture is shaped by all employees and evolves as new employees are added to the mix. This means that those making the hiring decisions are, in effect, establishing the corporate culture through those they hire and those they turn down.

Influencing culture

Founders should be at least minimally involved in the recruitment and hiring of the first 100 employees, and they should expect all hiring decisions to be taken with the corporate culture in mind. Formalising this by writing down the values that define corporate culture helps maintain consistency in hiring. The founder can thus hand-pick the first two dozen or so employees and then trust them with future recruitment.

At Kana Software, we established the Kana Credo – a set of principles concerning team, customer, community and performance that we expected our recruits to follow. Prospective recruits were shown the Kana Credo during the interview process near the moment of final decision. If they did not understand the importance of these elements they would not be asked to join the team. Make no mistake – this is a tall order, often requiring a founder to spend more time on recruiting than on anything else. But the consequences of hiring the wrong employees are dire indeed.

The second activity of the leader is R&D – defining, building and selling a product or service. Chief executives must decide to what extent they will focus the company on selling vs building. If a start-up moves too quickly into selling, it risks failing to deliver on promises made to customers concerning its products or services. But if too much focus is placed on building, then it will fail to generate the necessary revenue for sustained growth.

To sell or to build

Contrast Apple Computer with, say, SAP or Siebel Systems. In Apple's case, Steve Jobs, the founder, was all about building the coolest, most elegant computers around. The original Apple machines were incredibly creative compared with anything on the DOS platform. But Jobs lost sight of what makes a start-up grow: sales.

Apple faltered when it refused to help independent software developers create software for its operating system, allowing the much-cloned IBM PC, with lots of software available, to gain a slight edge in market share. The importance of standardisation and user numbers in computer software – otherwise known as network externalities – soon drove a majority of the personal computer market away from Apple to the Microsoft platform and the PC.

By contrast, SAP and Siebel were built on a sales culture. Tom Siebel, one of the top salesmen from Oracle, accumulated revenues before finalising products in Siebel System's early years by cementing strong relationships with system integrators like Andersen Consulting – companies that knew how to sell very large implementations of enterprise software. At the time of Siebel System's stock market flotation in 1996, three years after the company's inception, over 60 per cent of its revenues still came through its relationship with Andersen Consulting. Similarly, SAP has a reputation for selling high-priced software but not necessarily for selling solutions that are easy to implement and maintain.

Organisational structure

A final job for the leader of a start-up is designing an organisational structure in which information can flow easily, aiding the company's growth. Start-ups grow in many directions at the same time. They add new employees, customers, vendors and investors at double- or triple-digit growth rates. In a short time, information for senior managers switches from being first-hand to being second- or third-hand. The chief executive has two basic choices: the youth/chaos style and the experience/structure style. Think of the contrast between young Yahoo! and AOL/Time Warner.

The youth/chaos style is characterised by a collaborative management team of company executives, board members and outside investors. It greatly assists the flow of information when the scale of operations is small, and information can go direct to managers from its source. Information gets lost as the enterprise grows, however, since the same number of senior managers cannot maintain contact with ever-increasing numbers of employees.

In the experience/structure style, control is centralised among senior managers. Information flows into this group through a series of gates – middle managers, customer groups, investor representatives – so decisions are rarely made at the top with primary information. This limits senior managers from drawing on their gut instinct – they are never close enough to information sources to get a good feel for events. But centralised control does stop a growing company from losing information simply because it has lost its ability to maintain its primary points of contact. The leader of a start-up must construct his or her organisational chart so that the transition from a collaborative environment to centralised control can proceed without major turmoil or sore feelings.

As leadership needs and tasks change substantially over the course of a company's growth, it is easy for founders to make one of two mistakes. First, they may fail to see that they no longer fit the leadership needs of the company and stay on too long. Or, second, they may recognise that the demands on the leader are changing, incorrectly assume that they are no longer suited to the job, and exit too soon.

Steve Jobs at Apple exemplified the first type of error. Jobs continued to build the most innovative computers and hold Apple's proprietary operating system close to his chest. Ultimately, Apple's share of the PC market plummeted to less than 10 per cent. By the time John Scully replaced Jobs as chief executive, Apple had dug itself into a hole too deep to escape. Today Apple, with Jobs at the helm again, continues to focus on building and therefore remains a source of creativity and innovation in the personal computer industry. But its platform is unlikely ever to pose a serious challenge to that of Microsoft.

Mark Gainey, my cofounder at Kana, left the chief executive spot too soon. With Kana set to go public in the summer of 1999, just three years after the company's inception, he brought in a seasoned chief executive who had been in senior management at other publicly traded companies. Mark, then 31, thought his lack of experience at the achiever and solidifier stages made him unfit to master the challenges these presented. With hindsight, Mark was at least aware of what he did not know – and was dedicated enough to the Kana Credo to find the answers. The seasoned chief executive resigned 18 months after joining, coinciding with the first of many quarters in which the company missed its financial projections.

Impartial advice

Leaders of start-up ventures who want to avoid these mistakes should make active use of their boards of directors, appointing new directors if needed. Outside board members, especially those without a financial stake to cloud their judgment, can advise the venture manager on the relevance of his or her experience and abilities to the company's needs. If board members and the chief executive schedule a twice-yearly discussion of his or her role and the leadership challenges facing the company, they will avoid at least some of the pitfalls described here.

The thrill of realising a business vision is the main source of motivation for most start-up executives; building a start-up from scratch to stand-alone success is a goal many founders dream of achieving.

While they may plan company strategy for the long run, entrepreneurial leaders too often fail to develop their own long-term leadership strategy and misinterpret the company's changing needs. Start-up leaders need continually to assess their own strengths and weaknesses against what the business requires. Once these challenges have been identified, the chief executive can then marshal the resources to meet them – and continue to lead a successful venture.

Source: *Financial Times*, 8 November 2002,
© Michael Horvath.

Case 29.2

The family that plans its future together

14 February 2002

By **Clare Gascoigne**

It is as important to have a good business family as to have a good family business, says Christopher Oughtred, chairman of William Jackson & Son. 'Sometimes the two get confused but both need to be managed quite carefully. You need a family plan before you have a business plan.' He should know – he is in the fifth generation to run the family business.

The Oughtreds found a way to combine family and business: in 1996 they drew up a family constitution, or creed (see right).

'A family can significantly improve its chances of success (in business) by planning its future together,' says Peter Leach, head of the Stoy Centre for Family Business. 'A creed is an insurance policy against conflict and the only place where you can combine non-binding, moral statements of intent with legally binding issues such as employment or exit routes.'

A family constitution bears similarities to a company mission statement and to a shareholder agreement but is wider in scope than either. What goes in depends on the family but it hangs on two main points, says Joachim Schwass, professor of family business at IMD business school in Lausanne and board member of the Family Business Network, an international organisation of family-owned companies. They are: how the family works as a family; and how it works as a business.

'Many family businesses do not know why they are "family businesses". Each generation should develop a vision of the business and capture the value system behind it. You have to work out how the family adds value to the business – and if it doesn't, have to consider selling up and investing your money elsewhere.'

This is heresy to many family businesses, which struggle in conditions that would not be tolerated were it not for the emotional pull of working in a company built by Granny. Fear of facing the possibility of selling stops many from writing a family constitution; others may be frightened of exposing hidden rivalries or skeletons in the cupboard.

'If someone in the family doesn't want to write a creed, there is always a reason and it is usually the threat of openness,' says Mr Leach. 'Families will put forward all kinds of arguments against it – we haven't got the time, or we don't need one, or it's always worked fine in the past – which are all rubbish. It's a power thing: once it is written down, you have to live with it. It ups the ante.'

Writing a constitution should not be seen as a chance for the chairman to bully everyone into agreement. Indeed, the experts say it will not work unless all the family members buy into it.

'A creed has to suit everyone in the family system, whether they are owners, work in the business or are married to a family member,' says Barbara Murray of the Centre for Family Enterprise at Glasgow Caledonian University. 'You have to engage people who have a vested interest and that includes in-laws.'

Mr Schwass sees the constitution creating an emotional tie for later generations, who do not have the passion of the first entrepreneur. He cites a German family business that had manufacturing operations across the world. 'The creed laid down that the same environmental rules applied whether the factory was in Germany or Gambia. That environmental vision bound the family.'

A constitution can also help explain a business to children. 'Introduce it to children early on, from age 12 or so,' says Andrew Godfrey, head of Grant Thornton's Prima service to family businesses. 'That way you can manage expectations. The day your eldest son leaves university is not the time to start discussing employment of family members.'

How do you go about writing a constitution? Expect it to take anything from a couple of days to a year, depending on the willingness of family members and any existing tensions. Note, though, that a constitution cannot be written to solve existing conflict. 'Doing it can highlight issues that have to be dealt with before you can write it,' says Mr Leach.

A good plan is to start the process with a weekend retreat, preferably away from home. Larger families may want to appoint an executive committee to work through the ideas and explore options, reporting back regularly.

A family member who refuses to have anything to do with writing a constitution does not necessarily put a stop to it. 'I worked with one family where the biggest shareholder would not participate – she was not on speaking terms with the rest of the family and put the phone down on me every time I called,' says Mr Leach. 'The rest of the family went ahead anyway and wrote a constitution, including a prescribed exit route.' A year later, the uncooperative shareholder decided to sell and was able to do so according to the procedure set out, without speaking to her family. 'Without the creed, she would have hung on to the shares rather than deal with her relatives,' says Mr Leach.

The family probably needs an outsider to adjudicate. 'This sounds like something consultants dream up to give themselves work, but you need a neutral person who has been trained in family dynamics and can deal with the emotional issues,' says Ms Murray. 'It is difficult to have a voice if it's your father-in-law sitting at the head of the table, chairing the family council as if it is a business meeting.'

For a small family business, this may seem like too much time, effort and money. Given the diversity of family businesses it is difficult to pin down likely costs, though it can easily run into thousands of pounds. But, says Ms Murray, 'look at what is at stake here. You are talking about your wealth, your family and their lives. Get it wrong and you may end up destroying the business and never speaking to your brother again. What kind of price can you put on that?'

Source: Financial Times, 14 February 2002,
© Clare Gascoigne.

Discussion points

1. Relate the issues raised in the Horvath article to each of the different roles an entrepreneur can play in the mature organisation described in Section 29.3.

2. Given its similarities to a mission (Chapter 14) devise a consulting approach to implementing a family constitution in a family owned business. Pay particular attention to the issue of succession.

Index